Praise for

THE JOURNEY HOME

"I have been waiting a long time for a book like this. This extraordinary story of Jewish women's efforts to repair our complicated twentieth-century world is an inspiration to us all. Now at last we know the full range of Jewish women's contributions to every sphere of American life. Antler shows that on picket lines and in synagogues, in the workplace and the home, in their politics, their writings, and their art they have made the world a better and more humane place for us all."   —Bella Abzug

"This grand pageant of Jewish female radicalism is more nourishing for the soul than a bowl of chicken soup. It will be my gift of choice the next time I'm invited to a Bat Mitzvah, Sweet Sixteen party, or Jewish wedding."
—Susan Brownmiller, author of
Against Our Will: Men, Women, and Rape

"*The Journey Home* promises to rescue American Jewish women from their marginality within Jewish-American and American history. By connecting individual life stories with broader cultural change, Antler's account offers a rich view of the collective experiences of American Jewish women in the twentieth century."
—Kathryn Kish Sklar, Distinguished Professor of History,
State University of New York at Binghamton, and author of
*Florence Kelley and the Nation's Work: The Rise of Women's
Political Culture, 1839-1900*

"Written with verve and integrity, this collective biography of twentieth-century American Jewish women vividly brings to life the complexity and diversity of the modern Jewish experience. Whether on the picket line or the breadline, the stage or behind the scenes, the galaxy of women who inhabit these pages emerge as fully realized personalities, at once buoyed and frustrated by the multiple challenges of being modern, American, female, and Jewish."   —Jenna Weissman Joselit, author of *The Wonders
of America: Re-Inventing Jewish Culture, 1880-1950*

"In teaching us about our Jewish-American foremothers, this groundbreaking work—an ambitious blend of history, biography, and consciousness-raising—teaches us about ourselves. Never again can Jews, feminists, or scholars of American studies claim ignorance of the remarkable contributions of Jewish women to our common heritage."
—Letty Cottin Pogrebin, author of *Deborah, Golda and Me: Being Female and Jewish in America*

"This well-documented history of outstanding Jewish women in America brings together biography and social history, private lives and the public issues these lives enact. This is a terrific book, especially enjoyable for its author's insights about icons of this century's popular culture as well as its high art: Sophie Tucker alongside Gertrude Stein."
—Susan Weidman Schneider, Editor-in-Chief, *Lilith, The Independent Jewish Women's Magazine,* and author of *Jewish and Female*

"Antler examines the complex struggles of Jewish women to balance their feminist and Jewish commitments. Her analyses are insightful and sensitive, and bound to touch the hearts of her readers."
—Susannah Heschel, Abba Hillel Silver Professor of Jewish Studies, Case Western Reserve University, and editor of *On Being a Jewish Feminist*

THE JOURNEY HOME

ALSO BY JOYCE ANTLER

Lucy Sprague Mitchell: The Making of a Modern Woman

*The Educated Woman and Professionalization: The Search
for a New Feminine Identity, 1890–1920*

*Year One of the Empire: A Play of American Politics War
and Protest* (with Elinor Fuchs)

EDITED BY JOYCE ANTLER

America and I: Short Stories by American-Jewish Women Writers

*The Challenge of Feminist Biography: Writing the Lives of Modern
American Women* (with Sara Alpern, Elisabeth Perry, and Ingrid Scobie)

Changing Education: Women as Radicals and Conservators
(with Sari Biklen)

Talking Back: Images of Jewish Women in American Popular Culture

THE
JOURNEY HOME

How Jewish Women Shaped
Modern America

JOYCE ANTLER

SCHOCKEN BOOKS   NEW YORK

Grateful acknowledgment is made to William L. Rukeyser for permission to publish
portions of poems by Muriel Rukeyser from *Waterlily Fire*, *Beast in View*,
The Speed of Darkness, *Breaking Open*, and the unpublished work "July 4, 1972"
from the Rukeyser Collection, Library of Congress, all rights reserved;
to Stewart M. Rosen, trustee of the Edna Ferber Literary Trust, for permission to
publish excerpts from Edna Ferber's *A Peculiar Treasure*; to Betty Friedan for
permission to cite materials from the Betty Friedan Papers at the Schlesinger Library,
Radcliffe College; and to the following institutions for permission to cite material
from their collections: the American Jewish Archives; the American Jewish Historical
Society; Boston University Library, Department of Special Collections;
Brandeis University Library, Department of Special Collections; Central Zionist
Archives; Columbia University Rare Book and Manuscript Library; Hadassah,
the Women's Zionist Organization of America, Inc.; the Library of Congress
Manuscript Division; the New York Public Library, Jewish Division and Rare Books
and Manuscript Division; Schlesinger Library, Radcliffe College; Syracuse Library,
Department of Special Collections; Tamiment Library, New York University.

Library of Congress Cataloging-in-Publication Data
Antler, Joyce.
The journey home : how Jewish women shaped modern America / Joyce Antler.
p. cm.
Previously published: New York: Free Press, c1997.
Includes bibliographical references and index.
ISBN 0-8052-1101-2 (paperback)
1. Jewish women—United States—Biography. 2. Jews—United States—Biography.
3. Jews—United States—History—20th century. I. Title.
[E184.36.W64A57 1998] 920.72'089'924073 [B]—DC21 98-4191 CIP

Random House Web Address: www.randomhouse.com

Printed in the United States of America

First Paperback Edition
2 4 6 8 9 7 5 3

For Lauren and Rachel
—badkhntes—the next generation

and
the memory of my mother

Always the journey   long   patient   many haltings
Many waitings for choice and again easy breathings
When the decision to go on is made
Along the long slopes of choice and again the world . . .

—Muriel Rukeyser, from "Journey Changes"
in *Waterlily Fire*

CONTENTS

INTRODUCTION

For decades, many American Jewish women were in exile, but now they are journeying home. This book will explain why, telling the story of a century of impressive achievement in professional, cultural, community, and political life that nonetheless also chronicles a cross-generational pattern of tension, ambivalence, struggle, and displacement.

For most Jewish women, identity has been a blend of opportunities and traditions, an intersection that could reconcile their multiple loyalties—as Jews, women, and Americans—but often only in a manner that was painful, inconsistent, and equivocal. Jewish women have lived "braided lives," as Marge Piercy titled one of her novels.[1] Sometimes these braids had many strands flying loose; at others, they held strong and firm. "To live as poet, woman, American, and Jew," the poet Muriel Rukeyser wrote in 1944, "this chalks in my position. If the four come together in one person, each strengthens the others."[2]

Yet Jewish women have frequently found it impossible to straddle the different components of their identity. These women felt like strangers in their cultures, outsiders to either the Jewish or the American world, or to both. Adrienne Rich described herself as "split at the root," pained from seeing "too long from too many disconnected angles" and fearful that she could "never bring them whole."[3] The necessity of moving from one cultural environment to another caused displacement, fragmentation, and conflict, not only for immigrant Jewish women early in the century, but for their descendants. Contemporary feminist writer Kim Chernin told her daughter: "I've been to Europe at least six times since you were born. I've been to Israel. Always looking for my 'real home.' When I first got interested in feminism, I had the feeling every time I went to a woman's event that I'd found a homeland. I've never been able to settle in."[4]

Ironically, this spiritual homelessness has existed despite Jewish women's successful assimilation and manifold achievements in American society. Their extraordinary devotion to their families has been the subject of much comic treatment, yet behind the criticism stands the reality of the Jewish mother's strength, nurturance, and competence. As activists and rebels, Jewish women like Emma Goldman, Maud Nathan, Rose Schneiderman, Bella Abzug, and Betty Friedan influenced many of the key social movements of their eras— suffrage, trade unionism, international peace, and the contemporary women's rights movement. Jewish women have worked in their communities, synagogues, and homes; their temple sisterhoods played a key role in supporting Jewish institutional life while also helping to promote necessary change. Jewish women also established local, regional, and national organizations that have been among the most active and numerous women's groups in the country. They played vital roles in the international arena, leading the rescue of Jewish refugees from Nazism, helping to spearhead the development of a Jewish homeland in the Middle East, working for peace.

Despite their numerically small representation in the American population, Jewish women have made major contributions to fiction, poetry, drama, film, and other popular arts. From the ghetto stories of Mary Antin and Anzia Yezierska to the pioneering modernism of Gertrude Stein; from the romances of Edna Ferber and Fannie Hurst to the biting realism of Tillie Olsen and Grace Paley; from the intense spirituality of Cynthia Ozick to the more secular feminism of Anne Roiphe, Jewish women novelists have probed the changing meanings of the Jewish female experience in America. The poetry of Muriel Rukeyser, Adrienne Rich, Marge Piercy, the plays of Wendy Wasserstein, the radio scripts of Fannie Brice and Gertrude Berg, and the songs and performances of Sophie Tucker demonstrate a similar linguistic and thematic inventiveness.

Jewish women's contemporary accomplishments parallel their past achievements. Today, Jewish women are among the most highly educated women in the United States. The proportion of their daughters graduating from college is twice that of non-Jewish white women. The majority of working Jewish women hold professional, semiprofessional, or managerial positions.[5] Within American political life, Jewish women have achieved unusually high appointive and elective positions. In 1993, Ruth Bader Ginsburg became the second woman, and the first Jewish woman, on the Supreme Court; two years later, Dianne Feinstein and Barbara Boxer of California became the first all-female state delegation in the United States Senate. Barbra Streisand is only the most notable of a number of Jewish women artists, performers, and producers prominent in the cultural world.

In spite of this impressive record, Jewish women have been marginalized or ignored in most surveys of American Jewish history; they inhabit chronicles of American women's history primarily as first-generation East European immigrants or as members of charitable groups. Because there have been few documented historical accounts that place their dynamic contributions in the foreground and connect immigrant lives to later generations, they have been absorbed into more universal histories of Americans, women, or Jews, or turned into caricatures like the Jewish American princess and the Jewish mother.

Jewish *matriarchs,* however, have been at the *matrix* (meaning both "womb"—or "origin"—and "public register") of historical change.[6] Placing women's life stories at the matrix of historical narrative enables us to see Jewish matriarchs not as stereotypes or invisible presences, but as actors on the world stage and in their own lives.[7]

This book recounts the stories of more than fifty American Jewish women whose lives throw the larger movements of twentieth-century history into bold relief. The individual lives revolve around major public issues: immigration, social reform, political radicalism, Zionism, the emergence of popular culture, professionalism, internationalism, Cold War culture and politics, feminism, "postfeminism." I have brought together biography and social history in a way that is admittedly selective, but that both encapsulates history and evokes the compelling, dramatic experiences of particular lives.

While these stories illuminate Jewish women's considerable influence on a century in which the United States became a dominant cultural as well as political force, they also reveal the inner turmoil and tensions that accompanied those accomplishments. Each of the high achievers in this book confronted a difficult struggle to integrate what it meant to be Jewish, American, and female. Some, like Emma Lazarus and Henrietta Szold, equated traditional Jewish values with American democratic ideals; others, like Mary Antin, shrugged off or repudiated their ethnic identity. Writers and activists like Maud Nathan worked ceaselessly for women's issues, while her sister, anti-suffragist Annie Nathan Meyer, refused to. Each grasped at acceptance and assimilation by engagement in the world; each, perhaps, was forced to throw off an essential part of herself to gain it.

In both the secular and the Jewish world, Jewish women confronted troubling inequalities. Excluded from public aspects of worship, they often resented their disenfranchisement. As Cynthia Ozick remarked, though she asserted her Jewish identity proudly in the "world at large," in the synagogue, "when the rabbi speaks the word 'Jew,' I can be sure that he is not referring to me."[8] Some staunchly identified Jewish women found the Jewish communal world even more alienating than the religious one. Others, whose parents had assimilated or who had directly suffered anti-Semitism, denied their Judaism. Whether inherited or chosen, this distancing could have positive effects. Jewish women's homelessness and sense of themselves as outsiders shaped many of the social movements that they joined and led, including women's liberation. Yet mainstream feminism did not necessarily welcome Jewish women. By the 1970s and 1980s, Jewish women increasingly felt alienated from the international women's movement because of its strident anti-Semitism. Many declared that they no longer felt that "passing" as "ordinary" non-Jewish American feminists was a viable option.

For some women, Judaism or Jewish affiliation had always been the salient feature of their lives, whether played out in the secular or the religious sphere. Others held membership in both secular American women's groups, like the League of Women Voters and local women's clubs, and such Jewish groups as Hadassah and the National Council of Jewish Women, finding no difficulty in bridging their dual loyalties. A third group, whom we might call the universalists, had no specifically Jewish affiliations. Dedicated to the common cause of humanity, they espoused an ideology of "mutuality" that held that all people, regardless of ethnicity, race, religion, gender, or class, must be accorded basic human rights.

In different periods and at different points in an individual's life, any one of these patterns could become primary. Discarding or affirming their heritage or shaping it in new directions, Jewish women altered the tradition and gave it new meanings, blending options, changing directions, sometimes reversing course. Thus the history of American Jewish women is not so much a single story as a history woven of many threads, with many distinct and divergent patterns. At times that pattern is Marge Piercy's braid; at others, the braid unravels to reveal not harmony but dissonance.

In other contexts, I have written about the notion of "feminism as life process," suggesting that women's attempts to mold their destiny and achieve autonomy may take various directions at successive stages of life.[9] I now understand that for the dozens of women whose stories are chronicled in this book, Judaism, too, was a life process. At different points in the life cycle, Jewish women—whatever their inherited traditions—have chosen to identify with particular Jewish values or institutions in which they discover meaning. Rather than being a fixed entity framing them as a group apart—coherent, unitary, singular, and unchanging—identity for them has been multiple, changeable, fluid. As anthropologist James Clifford suggests, when identity is conceived "not as a boundary to be maintained but as a nexus of relations and transactions actively engaging a subject," ethnicity becomes "more complex, less . . . teleological."[10]

Understanding identity as being neither linear nor static but loose and "linked" to different life-course and historical events illuminates the variability of notions of ethnicity and selfhood. As we shall see, rabbis' daughters as well as the daughters of fully assimilated Jews have wrestled with dilemmas of identity that took them on spiritual—and often physical—journeys astonishing in their boldness, originality, and complexity. Experiences of change and fluidity are as characteristic of the contemporary women chronicled in this book as they were of their turn-of-the century ancestors.

At some point, often after many years in spiritual or emotional exile as outsiders, it became possible for some of these women to locate a common core of Jewish values that they could adopt as their own. In spite of patriarchal domination or maternal overprotectiveness, some women's ambitions received unusual legitimation within the family, with mothers and fathers becoming fulcrums for their daughters' creativity and ambition. At a time when the American family, itself under continual assault, continues to be maligned in the popular media, the ways in which Jewish families have provided their daughters with the freedom to exercise their will actively is of unusual interest. Despite (or because of), the Jewish family's "curiously strong bond," as Edna Ferber put it, Jewish daughters have historically been given the power to choose, or the power to struggle, and it has served them well.[11] Often they also found support for the assertion of a fuller Jewish identity in mentors or colleagues; still others were startled into awareness through the experience of anti-Semitism.

But only with the development of a newly assertive Jewish feminism in all denominations of Judaism, as well as in secular culture and politics, has it been possible for many thousands of Jewish women throughout the country to join a proud Jewish identity with an equally vibrant female, and feminist, consciousness. This mutual enhancement has enabled the expression of a multiplicity of Jewish women's voices unparalleled during this century.

My own struggle to come to terms with Judaism, and my relatively recent return to heritage, reflects the journey of many women of my generation.

Both sets of my grandparents immigrated to the United States in the early 1900s, settling in the East New York section of Brooklyn. There my parents met as teenagers, when my mother's family moved in next door to my father's. Like most members of their generation, my paternal grandparents were deeply religious, observing *kashruth* (the Jewish dietary laws) and most Orthodox practices. Every day of his life my grandfather went to *daven* (pray) at the shul around the corner, where the women sat upstairs, apart from the men, in typical Orthodox fashion. My grandmother lit the Shabbat candles and maintained a kosher house with vigor and commitment.

My father, however, rejected all observance; his indifference to religion colored my own upbringing. A socialist in his youth, like many of his generation, my father became a successful professional, though he never moved from Brooklyn. He was "my son, the doctor," about whom his parents never tired of boasting. Our family never attended synagogue—even on the high holidays—and my father, especially, had little tolerance for other Jewish rituals. My mother, quiet and acquiescent, voiced no objections to my father's renunciation of tradition; her parents had been less religious than my father's. But as I grew up, I questioned my parents' attitudes, for I admired my grandfather, whose deep spirituality seemed very special to me. "I have God in my heart," my father told me. "I have no reason to show my feelings outwardly."

When my grandparents visited we hid the bacon, though we always assumed they knew about our dietary apostasy, and hung up our Christmas stockings openly.

Even as a child I regretted my family's seeming denial of its Jewishness, envying friends who seemed more connected to their heritage. I begged my parents to allow me to attend Sunday school, which they did reluctantly. But my father flatly forbade me a bat mitzvah, the celebration of the young girl's entry into Jewish womanhood. Such ceremonies he found foolish and wasteful, and my mother voiced no dissent.

It was on Barbey Street, at my grandparents' home, that my connections to Jewish life seemed most satisfying. I enjoyed the Passover seder (the prolonged Haggadah reading, the sumptuous, noisy ritual meal, the songs and gaiety of our large extended family) and other family gatherings on Jewish holidays.

But my identity as a Jew was tenuous. I suspect I chose to go to Brandeis University, when the college was still new, primarily because it was Jewish-sponsored. But when I got there I felt the school was "too Jewish." I took no Jewish-related courses and studiously avoided any association with Jewish groups. To escape my own confusion, I went abroad during my junior year and fell in love with a Gentile foreigner, whom I married shortly after graduation. My father's resistance to the marriage, which my mother echoed, puzzled me. Despite his rejection of Judaism, he felt himself to be extremely Jewish. While we never lit Sabbath candles, Friday night dinner at our home was always mandatory for the children, even after we became young adults. Thus it was in the interest of Jewish continuity that my parents opposed my choice of husband, a choice that, I now understand, flowed from my own ambivalence about family bonds. My husband and I divorced after only a few years of marriage.

At the end of his life my father became a synagogue-goer, albeit briefly, accompanied by my mother. When I remarried, this time within the religion, and had children, I, too, turned, rather stumblingly, to seek out firmer Jewish ground. But it was not until I connected with Judaism within the feminist movement—until I became a Jewish feminist—that I found a meaningful way to be a Jew.

My journey might have been accelerated had I understood the choices that women in my family had made about their own lives as American Jewish women. Several years ago, after I had spoken to a large group on the topic of American Jewish women's history, my aunt, who was in the audience, told me an anecdote about the garment workers' strike to which I had referred in my talk. In 1909, women workers in New York's garment district had courageously instigated and led a three-month strike against manufacturers to obtain better working conditions. The strike, or "uprising" as it is usually called, involved 20,000 workers at its height and is widely credited with having paved the way to the unionization of the garment industry.

"Did you know," my aunt asked, "that your grandmother [my father's mother] was arrested during that strike and sent to jail?" I shook my head incredulously. As it turned out, my grandmother had been arrested—for striking a policeman! The judge presiding at her trial admonished her for unbecoming conduct—"In America, we don't hit policemen," he told her—but let her off without further punishment. My grandmother, I am told, nodded her head demurely although she probably didn't understand his English. Nevertheless, the story goes, she smiled slyly to herself as she was led off to freedom.

My surprise at hearing this tale did not come from astonishment that my grandmother had been capable of such an act. Though tiny in stature and unlettered, my grandmother was the unchallenged matriarch of her family, a good-natured woman of boundless determination who ruled with an iron hand. Rather, my surprise came from learning that my grandmother had been a working woman, a factory operative. I knew her only as a wife, mother, and grandmother, a *baleboste* (expert homemaker) to be sure, but one who had lived a purely domestic life. In fact, my grandmother's life probably followed the pattern common among most of her garment worker colleagues. She worked in the factory until marriage, shortly before the birth of her first child in 1912.

As I had never imagined that my grandmother had a history outside the home, it never occurred to me how much the household economy, and her children's futures, stood in her debt. My grandfather, a milliner, was a seasonal worker, like many factory hands of the period. During the Depression, when he was out of work for many months at a time, the family's always precarious economic situation worsened. All during these years, with her children still young, my grandmother stayed up late at night sewing neckties, which she would deliver the next day to her contractor. My grandmother's work supplemented the family income and helped put all of her children—including two daughters—through college.

Accounts of twentieth-century history do not often include such stories. Similarly, they omit the experience of women like my maternal grandmother, a widow who supported her family by taking in boarders; my father's two sister, one of them a mother and volunteer for Jewish women's organizations, the other a mother and laboratory technician; and my mother, who ran my father's two medical offices, although she, too, never officially worked after marriage.

Only after I began this book did I also learn from my Aunt Dina, our family's storyteller, that for many generations, the members of my grandfather's family in the shtetl of Libovna, Poland, had earned their livings as *badkhonim* (entertainers and merrymakers, or bards), making up stories, poems, and songs at weddings; they received their pay, usually extremely meager, from the banquet table. Long after he had settled into Brooklyn and the millinery trade, my paternal grandfather carried on the family tradition by making up stories and poems during similar celebrations. My grandfather's stories and my grandmother's activism, whether in protest of unfair labor practices or the high price of kosher meat, make up the dual aspects of my heritage. I believe they come together in the many stories of activist women that form the basis of this narrative, and in the fact that it is now also Jewish women who are telling the stories, recreating rituals, and creating and shaping history. Because narrative and memory remain the central instruments of Jewish community and identity, I believe that Jewish women today, vitally engaged in the project of remembering, constitute the most dynamic resource for the survival and continuity of Jewish life in America. I am hopeful that the next generation will find new meanings in the stories contained in this book. I am counting on these young women to retell and rediscover for themselves the manifold aspects of American Jewish women's lives that require us to bear witness. In so doing, they will become part of the cultural chain that carries forward the varieties of Jewish experience and identity.

THE JOURNEY HOME

Prologue

ON THE EDGE OF THE
TWENTIETH CENTURY

O n the edge of the twentieth century, it seemed possible to predict a remarkable future for American Jewish women. The most promising
portent appeared in September 1893 at the World's Columbian Exposition in
Chicago. At that World's Fair, elaborately organized to celebrate the four hundredth anniversary of Columbus's discovery of America, hundreds of Jewish
women came together for the first time ever to attend a Jewish Women's Congress held at the fair's Parliament of Religions. The excitement of the event
was intense. As one journalist reported:

> Women elbowed, trod on each other's toes and did everything else they could do
> without violating the proprieties to gain the privilege of standing edgewise in a
> hall heavy with the fragrance of roses. . . . By 10 o'clock the aisles were all filled,
> ten minutes later there was an impossible jam at the doors that reached far down
> the corridor. Few men were present. They were thrust into the background into
> the remotest corners. They had no place on the program and seemed to look upon
> themselves as interlopers. But the ladies did not consider them so: they did not
> consider them at all: they had something better to think about.[1]

The idea for the Congress had originated with Hannah Greenebaum
Solomon, a well-to-do Chicago matron who was the first Jewish member of
the influential Chicago Women's Club. Members of that club, led by Berthe
Potter Palmer and Ellen Henrotin, had been planning a special Woman's
Building where women's achievements could be showcased, and had asked
Solomon to call together Jewish women to organize a contribution for the
event. Believing that the word "Jewish" should have a "purely religious con-
notation," Solomon suggested that Jewish women join a different exhibit, the
Parliament of Religions.[2] When Jewish men refused to allow women to participate in their scheduled program at the Parliament (according to one
source, the men had responded, "Yes, Mrs. Solomon, you can be hostess"),
she organized a separate Jewish Women's Congress. "The only part of the pro-

gram they wished us to fill was the chairs," she recalled in her memoirs. The anomaly of the Jewish men's response was noted in the publicity of the fair's women's committee: "In most of the religious Congresses the men's and women's committees have acted together and will hold one Congress. But the rabbis refuse to give the women adequate time, place or representation, so they were compelled to hold a separate Congress."[3]

In sparking the formation of the Jewish Women's Congress, the rabbis' refusal to give representation to Jewish women in fact provided a new opportunity for Jewish women's collective life. For four days, scores of speakers, including outstanding American Jewish women leaders like settlement pioneer Lillian Wald, educator Julia Richman, and Zionist leader Henrietta Szold (then secretary of the Jewish Publication Society), presented papers on a variety of issues, including social service, religion, the professions, the arts, and business. For all four days, participants' enthusiasm remained enormous, in stark contrast to the poor attendance and "cheerless" atmosphere characterizing the Jewish men's Congress, as one journalist noted.[4] The Congress gathered enormous momentum and resulted in the creation of the National Council of Jewish Women (NCJW), with the goal of uniting Jewish women in the work of "religion, philanthropy and education."

The significance of organizing Jewish women separately from Jewish men and Christian women should not be minimized. The issue was directly addressed by Sadie American, a Chicago reformer who had been a member of the Congress's organizing committee and who would become the new NCJW's corresponding secretary: "Are not the interests of Jewish men and women alike, and the same as those of other men and women? Why, then, if they organize at all, should they organize separately?"[5] The answer, American acknowledged, lay in the distinctive role Jewish women occupied in the Jewish home, a role that set them apart from their Christian counterparts.

American referred to the traditional functions of the *eyshet hayil*, the "woman of valor" described in *Proverbs*. Instructed to be diligent and compassionate as wife, mother, and dispenser of charity, the woman of valor found fulfillment through service to others; exempt from the obligations of religious study and participation in regularly scheduled public worship, she prayed privately.[6] Men, however, were honored with the timebound obligation of public worship; for this reason the Jew daily thanked God that he had not been born a woman. As Sadie American explained, this prayer was not said "because [the woman] was degraded far below him . . . but because she was prohibited from the observance of certain rites and he considered himself much more fortunate than she. . . ." There was recompense, according to American, who felt that in the home the Jewish woman "reigned as queen."

But she acknowledged that the division of spheres called forth by the ideal of the woman of valor had profoundly negative consequences. "Because her work has been done largely in the home," American contended, "because the man has been the medium of communication, the Jewish woman has been a little slower to feel the heart-beats of her time than other women. . . . [A]s a body Jewish woman are behind the times, they have done nothing." Her prophecy was dire: unless Jewish women awoke to their responsibilities, "inertia" would sink them "through the quicksands of apathy to death." The Jewish woman would remain "a passive agent . . . [a] child that follows the path laid out for it with no responsibility, no duty but obedience."[7]

American's warning was exaggerated. In cities across the United States, Jewish women had formed societies to aid the poor, orphan asylums, hospitals, homes for the aged, nurses' training schools, and Sabbath schools. In New York and a few other cities, they had started synagogue sisterhoods to conduct religious schooling and charitable work; some areas also boasted Daughters of Zion clubs and Hebrew Women's Benevolent Societies. But in American's view, these associations lagged behind Gentile women's reform work and relegated Jewish women to the traditional functions of nurturing, motherhood, and charity.[8] American and the organizers of the Jewish Women's Congress had a more active vision for Jewish women, challenging the notion of separate spheres even while agreeing that for Jewish women, the home must continue to be "most sacred."

What American wanted was an organization that would unite "all thinking Jewish women." From its head would spring "Minerva-like a free and fiery spirit" that would overcome their inertia and be "animating" and "actuating."[9] As free spirits, such women could engage in a new public activism that would help resolve the problems of poorer Jews, especially immigrants. If women acted, men would follow, avoiding the possibility of a permanent gender-based separation of interests. And if Jewish women organized separately from non-Jews, yet worked on behalf of the "elevation and progress of all mankind," perhaps they could reduce prejudice to a greater degree than if they joined majority groups.[10]

In many respects, the idea of a separate Jewish women's identity seemed to reverse the course in which most German Jewish women had directed their energies. Sadie American, Hannah Greenebaum Solomon, Lillian Wald, and most of the other leading speakers at the Congress were members of the German Jewish elite and, like the male members of their families, they had prided themselves on their integration into the highest circles of American life. From the early colonial period, when Jewish settlers found that America offered full economic rights, freedom of worship, and political citizenship, Jews had enjoyed an extraordinary freedom of association in their new homeland.[11] To some Jews worried about the survival of their race, the blessing of American pluralism proved a double-edged sword, since some of their brethren converted to Christianity or cast off their Judaism when they married Gentiles.

By the end of the nineteenth century, the threat was not so much intermarriage itself as the continued weakening of the fabric of Jewish religion as Jews took on the customs of Americans.

While the earliest Jewish settlers had been a small band of Sephardic Dutch Jews who had found their way to New Amsterdam after being expelled from Portugal, the Jewish population of the country had become overwhelmingly Ashkenazi by the eighteenth century. Nevertheless, congregational life continued to be organized according to Orthodox Sephardic tradition. A new stream of immigration began in the 1820s, when migrants from Germany and other countries in Central and Western Europe (including Austria, Hungary, France, England, and the Netherlands), and to some degree from Eastern Europe, left in large numbers to seek political, religious, and especially economic opportunities on American shores.[12] Within fifty years, the population of American Jewry grew from 25,000 to over ten times that number, with most immigrants and their families enjoying remarkable economic success. While some Jewish poverty remained, a high proportion of German Jewish peddlers, artisans, and small shopkeepers became members of the American middle class; some of them parlayed family stores and businesses into hugely successful commercial enterprises.

To the members of the German Jewish elite and those who aspired to it, becoming American meant behaving as Americans did. For many, maintaining the laws of *kashruth* and observing the Sabbath no longer seemed essential. Of course, many German Jews had grown more secular long before they left Europe. Now, enjoying the even greater openness of American life, some abandoned religion entirely; others adapted Judaism to American requirements. The Reform movement, which began in Germany in the mid-nineteenth century, spread rapidly in the United States, its liberalization of ritual an attractive alternative to Jews eager to stem the growing tide of nonobservance. Offering mixed rather than the separate seating of Orthodox Judaism, with the women curtained off by a *mechitza* (partition) or relegated to an upstairs balcony, Reform Judaism had particular appeal to German Jewish women. Yet, as Sadie American noted in her remarks to the Congress, only one Reform congregation in the entire country, Chicago's Temple Isaiah, allowed married women full membership in the synagogue. Just two others admitted single women or widows as voting members.[13] Nor could women participate in the central governing body of the Reform movement, the council of the Union of American Hebrew Congregations. The ordination of women as rabbis lay far off in the future.

The organization of the Jewish Women's Congress at the 1893 World's Fair, and the subsequent founding of the National Council of Jewish Women, was a clarion call from Jewish women to Jewish men that however far Reform had moved to accommodate the demands of the American lifestyle, where women were concerned even this liberalization had not moved fast enough. Jewish women wanted the "animating" purpose that they believed Christian women possessed as a group, and they would organize, they now announced, to get it. As long as they remained active only within Gentile women's associations, even including the influential Chicago Women's Club, which openly welcomed them, they would not succeed at empowering themselves as *Jewish* women.[14]

Yet the challenges facing Jewish women were formidable. The life stories of a number of late-nineteenth-century "thinking Jewish women"—the kind who might be expected to become "free and fiery spirits," in Sadie American's words—indicate the manifold difficulties that they faced.

Domestic Prisons: Fannie Brandeis Nagel

For Fannie Brandeis Nagel, elder sister of Supreme Court Justice Louis Dembitz Brandeis, the lack of an animating purpose proved tragic. The first child of Adolph and Frederika Brandeis, Nagel grew up with all the advantages that a wealthy, assimilated, upper-middle-class German Jewish family could offer its sons and daughters. Born in Louisville, Kentucky, in 1850, she was the eldest of two daughters and two sons, six years older than Louis, the youngest child; all the Brandeis children were given every educational advantage that the city and their parents could afford. Nagel spoke several languages (German, French, Italian, and Greek) and became an avid reader of the classics, mostly in the original. She was a talented musician, playing the piano (she eventually owned four) and violin. According to a biographer, Louis Brandeis in his mature years declared that Nagel had "the best mind he had ever known—a remarkable tribute from a man, who in sixty years, met so many exceptional people."[15]

In 1877, Fannie married German Jewish lawyer Charles Nagel, the son of an abolitionist physician, and moved to St. Louis. The two had an affectionate marriage, but Charles, involved in politics, was frequently absent from home. Nagel found little solace in the cultural life of St. Louis, which she found "uncivilized," and she missed her family back East, especially her adored brother Louis (Lutz, as she playfully called him), to whom she wrote regularly and lovingly, sending advice about his career, health, and romances.

Despite her love for her husband and children (a son, Alfred, was born in 1878, and a daughter, Hildegard, in 1886), Nagel was increasingly lonely and subject to what she termed "miserable depression [of] body and soul."[16] She tried to erase the "Puritan tone" that weighed down her household, bringing in more "Semitic" customs, and though she admitted that "Jewish traditions . . . echo in my heart," her husband (who later became president of the St. Louis Ethical Culture Society) was uninterested, and Nagel herself had little knowledge or experience with Judaism.[17] The Brandeis children had grown up in a nonreligious family; as adults they celebrated Christmas with gifts and a tree. Louis Brandeis's wife Alice was the sister of Nellie Goldmark, wife of Felix Adler, the charismatic leader (and rabbi's son) who founded the Ethical Culture movement; its morally based universalist humanism found a ready welcome in the Brandeis–Nagel circle.

Though Nagel tried, it was hard for her to hide her feelings, especially from Louis, to whom she admitted that she was an "utterly decrepit, miserable whining invalid."[18] The cause of her illness is unclear, though she did suffer from mental depression, recurrent bouts of malaria, and eating disorders (Louis advised family members not to force her to eat.)[19] The death of eleven-year-old Alfred from typhoid in 1889 was a brutal blow, and the family feared for her fragile health. Despite their concern, Nagel took her life the following year. No doubt the loss of Alfred had intensified the pain and purposelessness she had felt for many years during periods when, as she had written to Louis, life seemed like "prison and I know nothing more unsatisfactory."[20]

Nagel's life of upper-class comforts could not erase her intellectual and spiritual loneliness. Nor could the strong bonds she shared with her beloved older brother, husband, and children. Despite her own talents and accomplishments, Nagel felt empty; she came to dwell on her own moods. As in the case of Alice James, the sister of the brilliant William and Henry James, her melancholia and somatic ailments were rooted in her inability to find an arena for her own intellectuality.[21] Either a strong community of women or a community of faith might have offered her a lifeline, but lacking these, she succumbed to her self-definition as an invalid. Isolated by her intellect and lacking the society of friends, she lived vicariously through the successes of the men around her. But this satisfaction, coupled with the loss of her child and her illnesses, proved insufficient; even more than her body, Fanny Nagel's soul suffered.

The American Jewess: Rosa Sonneschein

Fannie Nagel may have known Rosa Sonneschein in St. Louis, but there is no record of the other in either woman's papers. Highly cultured like Nagel, and a gifted writer who organized the first literary society for Jewish women in St. Louis, Rosa Sonneschein would have had much to offer her contemporary. But Nagel may well have been scandalized, as was much of the city's elite, by Sonneschein's unconventional behavior.

Born in Hungary in 1847, Sonneschein was the daughter of one of Europe's most eminent rabbis, Hirsch-Baer Fassel.[22] Despite her intellectual bent, Rosa was expected, like all traditional Jewish daughters, to be married by age sixteen. After she turned down two prospective suitors, Rabbi Fassel insisted that the next proposal be accepted. Thus, in 1864, Rosa married

Solomon Hirsch Sonneschein, a twenty-five-year-old rabbi who had recently taken his Ph.D. at the University of Jena.

From the beginning, the marriage went poorly. Sonneschein later told her grandson David Loth that her husband was "by far the worst of the three men" who had proposed to her. Loth recounts that the "disaster of the marriage began . . . on the wedding night when the lusty young bridegroom introduced his 17-year-old bride to sex and managed to horrify her." After their marriage the couple settled in Prague, where Solomon Sonneschein held a congregational post; they moved to New York some years later because, their grandson wrote, Solomon was "already demonstrating a love of drink" and Rosa was under the illusion that Americans consumed less alcohol than Europeans.[23]

With their four children, the Sonnescheins eventually moved to St. Louis, where Solomon accepted a synagogue position. Though admired for his scholarship and eloquence, it was rumored that Sonneschein "drank, beat his wife, [and] chased other women."[24] Solomon's extravagant spending and heavily mounting debts did not help the marriage; nor did Rosa's habit of responding to every article and sermon her husband wrote by claiming that her father could have done better. Years later she admitted, "I was as bad for him as he was for me."[25] Sonneschein's unconventional public behavior did not help her husband's career: she smoked small cigars, dressed in fashionable Parisian outfits, and powdered her face. Worst of all, while her husband led Friday night services, Rosa attended the theater in the company of her congregation's most eligible bachelors.

Because of Rabbi Sonneschein's eminence within the Reform Jewish community and the rarity of divorce at the time, the couple's divorce suit created a sensation. The story ran on page one of the *New York Times,* where it was finally reported that Rabbi Sonneschein was granted a divorce on the grounds that his wife had deserted him. (She had refused to accompany him on a trip to Europe, moving instead to Chicago.) Rosa did not contest the divorce, which was finalized in January 1893, and therefore received no alimony. Two years later Sonneschein established *The American Jewess* as a forum for the new Council of Jewish Women and the incipient American Jewish women's movement; she hoped it would provide a steadier income than she could earn as a free-lance journalist. For the next four years, she edited and wrote articles and stories for this first English-language magazine dedicated to "Jewish women in particular" and to all others interested in the "pulsating" questions of national, social, and religious life.[26] The magazine also included material on Zionism; Sonneschein was one of the earliest journalists to champion a Palestinian homeland.

In her articles and editorials, Sonneschein castigated Jewish women for dwelling in a "more restricted domestic sphere than their Gentile sisters"; in the busy world of American womanhood, they were a "mere cipher." While she urged Jewish women to maintain their traditional "religious mission in the home," at the same time she believed that some of the time they spent in "kitchen religion" might well be devoted to the "science of charity."[27]

Sonneschein's message did not carry into the new century. Sold on newsstands for ten cents, *The American Jewess* at first attracted favorable press and the assistance of such successful publishers as Adolph Ochs and Joseph Pulitzer; financially it proved a modest success. But facing competition from better-financed American ladies' magazines, it did not find the wide readership Sonneschein had hoped for. She was even more disappointed at the abandonment of the journal by Jews: "Most of them are ashamed to have their neighbors and the letter carrier know that they are interested in Jewish matters," she wrote in the last issue of August 1899.[28] After the magazine's demise, the public never heard from Rosa Sonneschein again; she died in St. Louis on March 7, 1932, forgotten even by former associates.

Girl Rabbi: Ray Frank

The contradictions of American Jewish feminism in the late 1890s were embodied as well in the woman whose dramatic opening benediction had startled and excited the 1893 Jewish Women's Congress. Twenty-seven-year-old Rachel (Ray) Frank, the daughter of Bernard Frank and his wife Leah, pioneer settlers on the northwestern coast of the United States, came by her skill at religious oratory naturally: through her father, she claimed to be the great-granddaughter of the learned Rabbi Elijah ben Solomon, the legendary Vilna Gaon. After she began preaching to Jewish audiences in the early 1890s, Frank became known as "the first female rabbi in America."

Born in 1866 in San Francisco, Frank had grown up in the heart of the Sierra Nevada mountains and later on in the state of Nevada, where her father was an Indian agent. Despite the rarity of Jews in these communities, from an early age Frank was interested in everything Jewish. At the age of fifteen she was teaching in the public schools; at night, she conducted free classes for miners. After moving to Oakland (she called it "the Brooklyn of San Francisco"), Frank taught literature and elocution at a Christian college as well as classes in Biblical history at a Jewish Sunday school.[29]

Frank also began a career as a journalist. Sent by a local paper to Spokane, Washington, to interview a number of Indian chiefs prominent in earlier Indian uprisings, she was asked to address the Jews of the city during the High Holidays. Though she had never delivered a sermon, Frank agreed on condition that the Jewish population of Spokane, which had been unable to surmount denominational conflicts, establish a synagogue. The bargain was struck, and that very evening, Frank addressed an overflow crowd of a thousand men and women—Jews and Gentiles—at the Spokane Opera House, the novelty of a woman's preaching on the Day of Atonement to a mixed audience having spread through the city. Frank's pulpit debut led to offers to preach to Jewish groups up and down the Pacific coast, resulting in the establishment of several new congregations. She was an eloquent speaker who attracted huge audiences to her talks on Jewish subjects, particularly the Bible as literature; for some years she employed a professional manager to promote her. As her fame spread, so did the hyperbole that surrounded her. Called a prophetess and even a "female Messiah," Frank preferred to see herself as a "modern Deborah," defender of her people.[30]

To increase her knowledge of theology and Jewish history, Frank took courses in philosophy at the University of California. In 1892, she became the first woman to be accepted at the Hebrew Union College at Cincinnati, the Reform movement's rabbinical training college; she studied there for only one semester. In Frank's view, ordination was unnecessary for both preachers and teachers (the title she preferred).[31] She asserted that since rabbis were beholden to congregations for their salaries, they could not preach freely. She saw no reason for women to enter a "thoroughly masculine" rabbinate.[32]

Despite these arguments and her trailblazing pulpit performances, Frank was no feminist. She claimed that she did not oppose women's intellectual or vocational endeavors so much as she did the blurring of spheres; those who did not marry might adopt professions, but married women needed to perform their duties properly.[33] To women's rights advocate Charlotte Perkins Gilman, she wrote of her disagreement with the idea of an "organic alliance" of women focused on men as the problem; such thinking would cause women to "cut off the head of one serpent" only to have "two spring from the wound."[34]

Frank also opposed woman suffrage: if women had the ballot, the home would have two leaders and become contentious. She submitted that Jewish women, in particular, did not need the vote, since in their tradition women were considered men's equal. Urging them to remain "Mothers in Israel" and make their homes into "temples," she often cited the Bible to suggest the evils that would follow women's assumption of greater authority.[35]

Despite her own disclaimer and the fact that she was never ordained, Frank became widely known as the world's "only woman rabbi." The news that one congregation in Stockton, California, wanted to install her as its spiritual leader fueled the myth, as did Frank's revelation that she had been offered a rabbinical post in Chicago and "many others."[36] She did not view her own notoriety as the "girl rabbi" as contradicting her own beliefs, and neither did traditionally minded audiences. "There can be nothing more gracefully feminine than Ray Frank," ran a typical comment; despite her forceful sermons, "in her pretty gown, with her expressive dark face" and striking figure, she could never be mistaken for a "man in petticoats."[37]

Frank abided by her own admonitions. In 1901, at age thirty-five, she married Simon Litman, a professor of economics twelve years her junior.

Busy from then on with the standard activities of a Jewish faculty wife in Berkeley, California, and later in Champaign, Illinois, she lectured only occasionally to community and university audiences.[38] She died in 1948, a quiet presence in the twentieth century.

Mother of Exiles: Emma Lazarus

Another Jewish woman whose voice was not fully heard in the twentieth century was Emma Lazarus, the writer best known for her poem "The New Colossus," engraved on the Statue of Liberty. Had Lazarus been alive at the time (she died of cancer in 1887 when she was only thirty-eight), she would surely have attended the Jewish Women's Congress and no doubt been its principal speaker. As it was, her older sister Josephine and Henrietta Szold were the only two women eventually included in the Jewish men's program at the 1893 World's Fair.

Lazarus was the major American Jewish literary figure of the nineteenth century.[39] Despite her success as an "American" writer, eventually she acknowledged her position outside the cultural mainstream and claimed bonds to the Jewish people. Her story illustrates another aspect of the divided nature of American Jewish women's identity so apparent in the mixed messages of the Jewish Women's Congress leaders.

Emma Lazarus was born in 1849, the fourth of seven surviving children of Moses Lazarus, a well-to-do sugar merchant, and Esther Nathan. Moses Lazarus was a member of one of America's leading Sephardic Jewish families, tracing his ancestry to the Jewish community that had lived in Spain until Queen Isabella and King Ferdinand expelled all Jews in 1492. Proud of their heritage as descendants of the poets and philosophers of the medieval Golden Age of Hebraism in Iberia and of their ancestors' contributions to colonial America, they scorned the less educated Jewish immigrants from Germany, the Ashkenazim. By the 1840s, however, when Moses married Esther Nathan, daughter of a prominent German Jewish family, Ashkenazi Jews had joined the Sephardim among the elite of American Jewish society.[40]

Lazarus grew up in an upper-class household in New York City, summering at Providence, Rhode Island, with other wealthy German and Sephardic Jews. Tutored privately in European languages, music, and literature, she enjoyed the privileges that her family's fortune bestowed. She showed an early talent for poetry and by age seventeen had written a volume of poems, which her proud father privately printed.[41] Like two of her five sisters, Emma never married, although she wrote frequently of love.

Though derivative and sentimental, Lazarus's first volume attracted the attention of leading critics and writers. William Cullen Bryant thought the poems "better than any verses I remember to have seen written by any girl of eighteen"; William James recalled his pleasure in reading "the simpler little things" in the book.[42] Lazarus sent the poems to Ralph Waldo Emerson, whose writings stood among her chief literary inspirations. Emerson replied frankly, criticizing some poems but praising her general achievement.

Emerson continued to serve as her mentor, advising her on her reading and the craft of writing; he was her "father" and she was one of his "children," she wrote in a sonnet. Deeply hurt when he omitted her poems from his anthology of English and American verse, *Parnassus,* printed in 1874, Lazarus, then twenty-five, wrote to scold her teacher for what seemed like a deep betrayal. While Lazarus's correspondence with Emerson lasted until his death in 1882, the *Parnassus* incident revealed the fragility of her own developing position as a writer.

In her twenties, Lazarus had not evinced much of a Jewish literary consciousness, preferring to see herself as an aspiring author in the American mode. Occasional poems like "In the Jewish Synagogue at Newport," which she wrote in 1867, had secular American antecedents (in this case, Henry Wadsworth Longfellow's "The Jewish Cemetery at Newport") rather than a genuine foundation in Jewish interests. When, ten years later, Rabbi Gustav Gottheil of New York's Temple Emanu-El asked Lazarus to translate several hymns written by medieval Jewish poets of Spain and Portugal, and to write several of her own, Lazarus responded that she lacked the "fervor and enthusiasm" for such work; she had, after all, been raised in an assimilated home and had attended services only on the High Holidays. Nevertheless, she told Gottheil that she was "glad to prove . . . that my interest and sympathies were loyal to our race, although my religious convictions (if such they can be called) and the circumstances of my life have led me somewhat apart from our people."[43]

In the next four years, Lazarus published approximately two dozen translations of verses by medieval Jewish poets; the work of these poets brought Lazarus to a proud Jewish consciousness and inspired her belief in the return to Zion as the best solution for the exiled Jewish people. By 1880, Lazarus's own poetry, now focused on the destiny of her people, lost its derivative quality.

Lazarus's coming to voice as a Jewish writer coincided with the catastrophic upheavals of Eastern European Jewry. Following brutal pogroms in the early 1880s and the imposition of increasingly stringent restrictions on the Jewish populations in Russia and Poland, hundreds of thousands of refugees fled their homelands for the security and freedom of the United States. Lazarus, who had come to admire the courage of Jews in the past, was transformed by her visits to the refugee station at Castle Garden, the immigrant reception center in New York, where she saw at first hand the desperation of the new arrivals. She began to use her pen to wake up America's Jews to the immediate needs of these immigrants; in the next two years she wrote over twenty essays on the "Jewish problem" in both Jewish and secular magazines, urging American Jews to "deepen . . . and quicken . . ." their "sources of Jewish enthusiasm."[44]

In a series of "Epistles" written between 1882 and 1883, Lazarus excoriated American Jews for their indifference to the fate of East European Jewry. Rather than being too "tribal," she asserted that Jews "are not 'tribal' enough; we have not sufficient solidarity to perceive that when the life and property of a Jew in the uttermost provinces of the Caucasus are attacked, the dignity of a Jew in free America is humiliated." As she remarked in a line that would often be quoted in the twentieth century, "Until we are all free, we are none of us free."[45]

Yet Lazarus understood the reasons why American Jews maintained their distance from immigrants. Just beneath the surface freedoms that Jews experienced in the United States lurked a bitter anti-Semitism. "The word 'Jew' is in constant use," she observed, "even among so-called refined Christians, as a term of opprobrium, and is employed as a verb, to denote the meanest tricks." If wealthy Jews became too closely associated with the lower-class arrivals, their progress into the American mainstream might be retarded; the better class of Jews would always be identified with the "meanest rascal."[46] Moreover, American Jews lacked knowledge of the "common creed [and] common history" that they shared with the "poorest Jew-peddler" from abroad.[47] Only by returning to the intellectual roots of Judaism, studying Hebrew literature, history, and law, could Jews unite.

Lazarus helped to found the Hebrew Technical Institute to provide vocational training for the immigrants. But she acknowledged that the newcomers' Old World customs would necessarily impede their adjustment to the United States. A full decade before Theodor Herzl organized the modern Zionist movement, she envisaged a homeland in Palestine as a "better" solution to the problem of Jewish exile than settlement in the United States. In her poem "Rosh-Hashanah, 5643 (1882)," she portrayed Zionism and Americanism as interrelated aspects of the Jewish "nation":

> In two divided streams the exiles part,
>   One rolling homeward to its ancient source,
> One rushing sunward with fresh will, new heart.
>   By each the truth is spread, the law unfurled,
> Each separate soul contains the nation's force,
>   And both embrace the world.[48]

It was out of empathy with the exiles, whether bound "homeward" to Zion or "sunward" to America, that Lazarus had come to claim her own identity and to embrace the world as a Jewish-identified activist and writer. Just two years earlier, in her poem "Echoes," Lazarus had intimated her sense of isolation and fragility. "Late-born and woman-souled," she feared that as a woman writer she could not "cope . . . with the world's strong-armed warriors" who told of "the dangers, wounds, and triumphs of the fight." In contrast to this "modern manly passion," she described her "veiled and screened . . . woman-hood," her immersion in "solitude and song."[49]

By 1882, Lazarus's solitude had dissolved. In its place, as one critic suggests, a "fighting fraternity" with the Jewish people arose. The bond, however, was more of maternity than fraternity, as the opening of Lazarus's famous poem "The New Colossus," written the following year, indicates. In the poem, Lazarus introduces an image "not like the brazen giant of Greek fame" with "conquering limbs," but of a "mighty woman with a torch/Whose flame/Is the imprisoned lightning, and her name/Mother of Exiles." Like Deborah, the ancient savior of Israel, this rescuer was not a conquering hero but a mother who was a welcoming, albeit "mighty," presence, with "beacon-hand" and eyes that "command."[50]

As a single woman, Lazarus could speak out to Jews and act more boldly than such married "women of valor" as Rosa Sonneschein and Ray Frank Litman. Yet the pervasive influence of nineteenth-century gender mores affected her literary reputation. After Lazarus's death, her sister Josephine, a powerful intellect in her own right, minimized Emma's independence, describing her in a eulogy as a "true woman, too distinctly feminine to wish to be exceptional, or to stand alone and apart even by virtue of superiority."[51] Other critics also muffled Lazarus's distinct voice and contributed to her banishment from the literary canon.[52] Lazarus's untimely death cut off the possibility that she might sustain her authentic stance as an American Jewish woman writer and activist, just as "superior" Jewish women like Rosa Sonneschein and Ray Frank, hemmed in by the myths of "true" womanhood, could not find a secure or permanent outlet.

However bright the promise of American Jewish womanhood might have seemed to the women who gathered to hear the electrifying speeches at the Jewish Women's Congress in 1893, or to the women who joined the National Council of Jewish Women in subsequent years, none of the new movement's leaders was able to resolve the contradiction of remaking Judaism so that it empowered women as public-spirited activists while preserving the notion that their fundamental place lay in the home.

Yet the need for change—and the direction of innovation—had been signalled. In the new century, Fannie Brandeis and her sister-in-law Alice Goldmark Brandeis, Louis's wife, would be followed by daughters whose access to advanced education would enable them to establish highly fulfilling professional careers. Rosa Sonneschein's and Sadie American's call to Jewish women to liberate themselves from the yoke of patriarchal dependency and servitude by organizing separate Jewish institutions for women would be answered by a flurry of gender-based organizational activity. Ray Frank's insistence on the integrity of Jewish women's spiritual lives would be echoed in numerous proposals for expanding women's religious entitlements and their domestic responsibilities in the wider world.

Emma Lazarus's midlife conversion from full assimilation to active Judaism also proved exemplary. This volitional act, along with her attempt to awaken American Jews to their responsibilities, was the first of many attempts by Jewish women to counteract assimilation. Lazarus's work in Jewish educational and social welfare and her poetry of witness were precursors to later Jewish women's political and intellectual activism. Pointing inward to a more fully realized Jewish consciousness and a liberated female selfhood, as well as outward to a future in which Zionism and Diaspora loyalties, or a philosophy of universalism and a deeply felt ethnic pride, could coexist without conflict, Lazarus demonstrated a harmonious intregration of ideals that for many others seemed mutually exclusive.

By century's end, however, traditional notions of Jewish womanhood existed uneasily with newer possibilities. Jewish women experienced deep anxieties as they seized upon the opportunities set in motion by the events of the Chicago World's Fair and the arrival of the new immigrants. They would move in vastly different directions as they experimented, innovated, and ultimately shaped new patterns of being Americans, women, and Jews.

FROM THE GHETTO AND BEYOND
1890–1930

Chapter 1

THE PARADOX OF IMMIGRATION

Autobiographies of Alienation and Assimilation: Mary Antin and Anzia Yezierska

"I was born, I have lived, and I have been made over."[1] So did Mary Antin begin the chronicle of her experiences as an immigrant in the New World. So extraordinary were the changes that Antin underwent after she emigrated as a young girl from Russian Poland to America that she felt she had experienced the creation of a "second self" completely divorced from her earlier life.

Antin's autobiography, *The Promised Land,* published in 1912, became an immediate best-seller, catapulting its author to national fame and establishing her as the creator of one of the first great works of American Jewish literature. By the time of Antin's death in 1949, *The Promised Land* had gone through thirty-four editions, becoming one of the most popular immigrant autobiographies of all time. A classic tale of assimilation, hope, and transformation, it spoke to the imagination of diverse immigrant groups, as well as to native-born Americans who saw it as proof of the inclusiveness of the American dream.[2]

Antin's book was one of more than a dozen accounts of immigrant life in the new land written in English by Jewish women.[3] The large number of these works published by American presses is striking, considering that almost all of their authors were unknown, and that for most of them, English was a second language. What made them appealing was the universality of their theme—the encounter with America. Each author wrote about her personal struggle to respond to the hardships and opportunities of American life by creating a new, distinctly American self. Autobiography became a means for them to assess their experience as immigrants confronting a new culture and, by writing about their struggles, to impose order on events that were disruptive and confusing.[4]

It is significant that the first and most influential account of Eastern European immigrant experience was written by Antin, a woman. For Jewish

women even more than for Jewish men, America offered a revolutionary opportunity to transcend the limits of the Old World. This hope is reflected in
Antin's pioneering book and in the works of another autobiographer and fiction writer, Anzia Yezierska: in both women's stories, the cultural myth of
American freedom merges with the triumph of a woman's autonomy.

For Jewish women, however, the act of writing was at once liberating and
dangerous. Traditional Jewish culture assigned the tasks of textual study and
literary creation solely to men; women who assumed such roles challenged
traditional gender divisions and religious identities. Thus, in winning the
right to independent "American" womanhood, immigrant writers like Antin
and Yezierska had to engage in a fierce battle with their heritage, one quite
different from that experienced by immigrant men. For some female immigrants, becoming a writer would require figuratively killing their Jewish fathers or husbands and the Jewish religion itself, forces that they saw as linked
in their patriarchal domination of women's lives.

Both Antin and Yezierska describe contradictory feelings of triumph and
loss engendered by their complex identities as Jews, new Americans, and
women.[5] Their stories help us understand immigration as an inward journey
that took new immigrants as far from the biblical ideal of the woman of valor
as from the shtetls and towns of the Russian plains. Through their imagina-
tions, immigrant Jewish daughters recreated themselves as American Jewish
women, breaking with tradition and offering the public its first glimpse of the
immigrant Jewish woman as modern feminist.

New World Princess   Mary Antin was born in Polotzk, Russia, in June 1881,
three months after the assassination of Czar Alexander II triggered a series of
violent pogroms that spread to hundreds of communities throughout the
Pale of Settlement. The following year, the passage of the May Laws
prohibiting Jewish settlement in villages drove a half-million Jews from rural
areas and signalled the end of the shtetl in the Pale. The May Laws also
drastically reduced Jewish quotas at gymnasia and universities, and restricted
many Jews from holding jobs.[6] As conditions worsened, more and more
Jews fled to America. While the Jewish population of the United States
numbered only about 250,000 in 1880, by 1924, when Congress passed
legislation restricting immigration from Eastern Europe, approximately one-
third of the Jewish population of Eastern Europe had emigrated to America.
The Jewish population of the United States, merely 3 percent of world
Jewry in 1880, by then numbered four million—almost one-quarter of the
world's Jews.[7]

The journey to America required extraordinary courage and resilience. At
every step of the way, the migrants were beset by harrowing, bewildering, and
dangerous challenges. Antin described her family's passage to America in
1894 in a series of letters to an uncle who had remained in Eastern Europe;

the letters, published in book form five years later, recount frightening encounters with border patrols, travels in crowded trains through the vast expanse of Europe, and rough conditions in steerage crossing the Atlantic.

Little more than a decade later, when Antin was barely thirty, she wrote her autobiography, not because she had "accomplished anything" but because she believed her life was representative of other New World immigrants.[8] Writing also brought Antin "personal salvation," taking her on a "double voyage of discovery" that explored her inner transformations as well as "the new outer universe" of America. "All the processes of uprooting, transportation, replanting, acclimatization, and development took place in my own soul" she acknowledged, as well as in the physical world; her book would describe the literal and spiritual journey by which she had explored these dual realms.[9]

Antin opened her memoirs with a stark portrait of Russia as the "Egypt" from which Jews had made their exodus to the promised land of America. Their journey to the United States—and Antin's own transformation into a liberated, assimilated, secular woman—ironically became an act of spiritual deliverance tied to Jewish history. Suffering from the sharp divisions that separated the Pale from the rest of Russia, Jews from Gentiles, men from women, Antin spent her childhood manacled by the dual shackles of sexism and anti-Semitism. Though she rejected Judaism's "medieval" superstitions, she took pride in its "living seed"—the inward belief that "God was, had been, and ever would be."[10]

> I was fed on dreams, instructed by means of prophecies, trained to hear and see mystical things that callous senses could not perceive. I was taught to call myself a princess, in memory of my forefathers who had ruled a nation. . . . Sat upon by brutal enemies, unjustly hated, annihilated a hundred times, I yet arose and held my head high, sure that I should find my kingdom in the end. . . . God needed me and I needed Him, for we two together had a work to do, according to an ancient covenant between him and my forefathers.[11]

Long after she had renounced the practice of Judaism, she retained the spiritual attachments of her childhood.

Antin associated this childhood religion with memories of her mother's magical lullabies and stories of Biblical heroines: "I heard the names of Rebecca, Rachel and Leah as early as the names of father, mother, and nurse."[12] Yet matriarchal heroines proved insufficient guides to a religious faith that privileged patriarchy; Antin's observant mother, "bred to submission" even though she was her husband's equal business partner, took her religion on her husband's authority. Antin angrily acknowledged that the problem lay in a religious culture that celebrated maleness: the birth of sons was celebrated with ritual ceremonies and feasts; boys were sent to learn Torah in *cheder* (elementary religious school); even at table, boys were served first because "nothing was too good for them." In Antin's short story "Malinke's Atonement," the shtetl mother asks, "What are daughters worth? They're only good to sit in the house, a burden on their parents' neck, until they're married off. A son, at least, prays for the souls of his parents when they're dead; it's a deed of piety to raise sons."[13]

In this story, nine-year-old Malinke is a renegade who outrages her mother by challenging traditional customs and the notion that "girls don't need to know things out of books."[14] The reward for the purity of her own faith, the promise of an education, came to Antin herself only after her own exodus from the Old World. In Russia, despite the liberal attitudes of her own family, it had been impossible for her to receive the gift of sustained learning equivalent to that received by Jewish boys. For women,

> education really had no place. A girl was "finished" when she could read her prayers in Hebrew, following the meaning by the aid of the Yiddish translation especially prepared for women. If she could sign her name in Russian, do a little figuring, and write a letter in Yiddish to the parents of her betrothed, she was called *wohl gelehrent*—well educated.[15]

Antin knew, however, that without education, women were destined to a life without aspiration, as "empty and endless and dull" as a "treadmill horse."[16]

In America, Antin was at last able to obtain the education she had dreamed about. *The Promised Land* describes in glowing terms the opportunities available to ambitious immigrants when given access to free schools, free libraries, and citizenship unrestricted by race, religion, and ethnicity. Even in the midst of poverty, such advantages offered a route out of the ghetto and into American prosperity.

In fact, like many younger children, Antin was permitted to attend school only because her older sister, Fetchke (called Frieda in America), had gone to work in a sweatshop to help support the family. All that the future held for Frieda was an arranged marriage and domestic drudgery, yet she and her mother gave unstintingly of their labor to allow Antin the chance to attend school.

Within six months, she had completed the first five grades; one of her teachers was so impressed with her talent that only a few months after Antin enrolled, she sent an essay the girl had written (entitled "Snow") to an educational journal, which published it. Antin's literary prowess came to the attention of several board members at the Hebrew Industrial School, a training institute for immigrant boys and girls, who introduced her to Lina Hecht, a German Jewish philanthropist. With Hecht's help, a translator and publisher were found for the letters Antin had written in Yiddish describing the family's emigration. The result, *From Plotzk to Boston,* was published in 1899 when Antin was only eighteen, with an introduction by Israel Zangwill, the distinguished British Zionist (*Plotzk* being a printer's misspelling of Antin's birthplace).

Because of this astonishing success and the intervention of her German

Jewish mentors, Antin's family allowed her to enroll at Boston Latin School for Girls, a public preparatory school for Radcliffe College. Antin also became active at Hale House, the South End settlement sponsored by the literary notable Edward Everett Hale, who joined Mary's coterie of admirers.

Even more important to her was Emma Lazarus's sister Josephine, who became acquainted with Antin after reviewing *From Plotzk to Boston*. Lazarus became Antin's friend and mentor. The two women shared a spiritual sensibility: together they probed the origins of the universe, the meaning of life, questions of immortality and the soul. Taken with the younger woman's insights, Lazarus urged her to continue writing. Encouraged by such friends Antin prospered, even as her family, its fortunes continuing to decline, was forced to move from one desperate tenement to another. Unable to master English or maintain a steady income, Antin's father became bitterly disillusioned. Contemplating her mother's and sister's constant labors, Antin was reminded again of the "treadmill horse" of shtetl days; only she had escaped the hardships that afflicted the family even in the promised land.

While Antin's narrative acknowledges her family's poverty, she emphasizes her own success as the product of talent and America's "open workshop"; she writes that only a "certain class of aliens" could make use of her new country's freedoms. "I had only to be worthy and it came to me . . . my friendships, my advantages and disadvantages, my gifts, my habits, my ambitions—these were the materials out of which I built my after life. . . ."[17] Ignoring the economic forces that exploited immigrant workers, Antin never joined the protests that other immigrant women helped initiate. Instead she emphasized her own rise as an individual in the Gentile world: "Steadily as I worked to win America, America advanced to lie at my feet. . . . I was a princess waiting to be led to the throne."[18]

Focusing on her own intellectual and moral worthiness, Antin glosses over her sister's contributions to her success, stating only in passing that the true "glory" belonged to Frieda. She also minimizes the unusual connections to the philanthropists who helped her. At least one Jewish reviewer resented Antin's portrayal. "To me," wrote Harry Saltpeter in *The Menorah Journal* in 1919, "[Antin] reveals herself as a smug, parvenu snob of the East Side, the sycophantic protégée of the nice and respectable persons who patronized her, a person to whom the East Side existed as inspiration for her writing moods."[19]

Yet most reviewers focused on the apparent universality of her story rather than on the exemplary and privileged achievements of Antin as heroine. "The argument for immigration . . . is implicit in every chapter of 'The promised land,' " wrote the *New York Times* critic.[20] Few noted its ambiguities regarding questions of class relations or ethnic and religious attachments.

Like many immigrants who quickly Americanized, Antin had given up her religious customs almost immediately. For the God of her fathers, she substituted a worship of American heroes like George Washington. Later she believed that she might not have been so ready "to put away my religion" if its truths had not been cloaked in "motley rags of formalism." At the time, though, she felt "absolutely, eternally, delightfully emancipated from the yoke of indefensible superstition"; this was for her the essence of Americanism.[21]

In hindsight, however, Antin recognized the high cost of the family's liberation from tradition (even her mother—an Orthodox woman for whom religion was "interwoven with her soul"—gave up Judaic practices within half a dozen years). Without a system of American ethics to replace the family's religious orthodoxy, "chaos took the place of system; uncertainty, inconsistency undermined discipline," and the Antin family, "formerly united and happy," disintegrated.[22]

In her book, Antin wondered whether her father regretted his early, violent rejection of Judaism, and in later years, missed his heritage and community; she asks "to what, in short, his emancipation amounted."[23] Did her family's abandonment of its faith mean that, in the interest of Americanism, they had forever alienated their descendants from Judaism? Such a trajectory was double-edged: while assimilation was the most "hopeful" course for the Jews, and the most inevitable, Antin felt at the same time that "nothing more pitiful" could be written in the annals of the Jews.[24]

Readers may have passed over this cautious note because the "official" story in *The Promised Land* is one of celebration and optimism; Antin's concerns about religious decline and the debilitating effects of poverty on immigrant families appear as ambiguous subtexts.[25] The central narrative of the book describes the emergence of "I, a new being," a self "absolutely other" than the heroine whose development she recounts in the memoir—the young Russian girl ("she") who is gradually transformed into an American. But Antin's authorial voice stands outside this story of Americanization, revealing that despite her chronicle of triumphant change, Antin continued to see herself as other, an immigrant aware of the struggles of her impoverished neighborhood, a Jew worried about her family's loss of faith, a woman unsure of future possibilities for her gender.

At the beginning and end of the book, Antin acknowledges that she is split off from her authentic, historic self, and indeed, that she wants to distance herself from history overall. "The Wandering Jew in me seeks forgetfulness," she writes, although she admits that "I can never forget, for I bear the scars. But I want to forget . . . I want to be now of to-day."[26] Only by recording and reinventing her story could Antin expunge her ethnic heritage, her foreignness, her family's poverty: the enormous pain of transition. Unable to obliterate memory, it is through storytelling that Antin can abandon the past.

Antin ends her book by portraying herself as a "human creature, emerging from the dim places where the torch of history has never been." Such a person, embodying Antin's vision of herself as a contemporary intellectual woman, born in the "Middle Ages" and living in the twentieth century, was not "tied to the monumental past, any more than my feet were bound to my grandfather's house below the hill . . . the past was only my cradle, and now it cannot hold me, because I am grown too big."[27]

She concludes this reverie on a note of high romantic rhetoric, calling forth the "shining future" she saw in America. Yet this vision comes out of Antin's frank admission of how painful it is to be "consciously part of two worlds"—Russia and the United States, Christian and Jewish, her old and new selves. Rather than assimilating her past to her new identity, she constructs an American persona that can move forward only by disconnecting from the past. Invoking the image of the Ancient Mariner who told his tale in order to be rid of it, Antin tells her tale—"for once, and never hark back any more. I will write a bold Finis at the end, and shut the book with a bang!"[28]

Antin's words reveal her almost desperate wish to jettison the albatross of memory that weighed so heavily upon her and from which she was not yet free. But in her real life, as opposed to her representation of it in *The Promised Land,* it was not so easy to say "finis" to the past. For the next several decades, Antin wrestled with the problem of living her life according to her vision of herself as "an American among Americans . . . a daughter of Israel and a child of the universe," a woman of the present not tied to history.[29]

In 1901, when she was twenty, Antin had married Amadeus William Grabau, a geologist whom she had met on a field trip he was conducting for the Boston Society of Natural History. Eleven years Antin's senior, Grabau, the son of a German-born Lutheran minister, dazzled her with his research into evolution. Science now replaced the theological bent that had, since childhood, made Antin question the mysteries of the universe. But her marriage to a non-Jew displeased Antin's supporters; in a letter, she admitted that although she hadn't "changed [her] faith," all of her devoted friends fell away.[30]

The couple moved to New York, where Antin took courses at Barnard and later at Teachers College; in 1907, she gave birth to her only child, Josephine Esther, named after Antin's beloved friend Josephine Lazarus and her mother, Esther Weltman Antin. Lazarus's death in 1910 spurred Antin to begin writing her autobiography, as Lazarus had urged. She published its first installments in *The Atlantic Monthly* in 1911. The publication of *The Promised Land* the following year brought Antin immediate success. Reissues as well as fees from lectures Antin gave on such topics as "The Responsibility of American Citizenship," "The Civic Education of the Immigrant," and "the Public School as a Test of American Faith" assured her a substantial income for several years after the book's debut.

In 1914, Antin published her third and last book, *They Who Knock At Our Gates: A Complete Gospel of Immigration.*[31] At a time when the sentiment for restrictions on immigration was growing, the book was a passionate plea for the continuation of unrestricted admission to newcomers, arguing that the ethics of American democracy as well as the Ten Commandments demanded an open door policy. In calling her work a "gospel," Antin indicated that the subject of immigration was of vital concern to Christians as well as Jews; she also unwittingly revealed her drift away from Judaism.

Antin never tempered her support of assimilation, arguing that in the United States, where cultural tolerance, social equality, and freedom of choice held sway, more narrowly based ethnic and national group identities were throwbacks to an archaic age. Yet Antin's fervent Americanism did not conflict with Zionism. However much Jewish life became absorbed within American life, she insisted that the "community of sentiment," "culture," and "memories" of the Jewish people could survive as emblems of Jewish nationality. Influenced by her mentor Josephine Lazarus and her good friend Jessie Sampter, a Zionist writer, Antin urged all Jews to work for the creation of a national homeland, an idea then unpopular with most middle-class Jews.[32]

Antin had more difficulty maintaining unity in her personal life than she did among her varied public concerns. The agonies of World War I split the Grabau household, with Antin lecturing around the country on behalf of the Allies and Grabau supporting Germany. As Antin's daughter Josephine recalled, "We fought the World War right in our house in Scarsdale. Mother was for the Allies and Father was for the Germans. Mother hung the Allied flag out her study window and Father put the German flag out his study window. They fought the war upstairs and downstairs, into the attic and into the cellar. It was too much for me and I fell apart. They saw what they were doing to me and finally agreed to separate for my sake."[33]

After the Grabaus separated in 1918, William Grabau left for China, where he taught paleontology until his death. Josephine was sent to boarding school, while Antin's sister Frieda, who had managed the Grabau household after her own arranged marriage broke up, moved in with another relative. Despondent about the rising xenophobic trend in American life and the breakup of her marriage, Antin suffered from recurring physical ailments and an apparent nervous breakdown from which she never recovered. After more than a decade of depression and wandering, she wrote to a friend in 1930, "I have so little mastered the art of tranquil living that wherever go I trail storm clouds of drama around me."[34] Unable to find a home, she journeyed from one rehabilitative facility for nervous invalids to another, often following the spiritual ministrations of such gurus as Shri Meher Baba, an Eastern mystic. After a few years at the Austin Riggs Psychiatric Center, she wound up at the Gould Farm in Monterey, Massachusetts, a Christian restorative community for the mentally ill. Antin lived there periodically from 1922 until her death in 1949, becoming a fervent follower of "Brother Will" Gould and his wife Agnes, and their philosophy of Christian love.

Though Antin wrote only a few essays in the remaining quarter century of her life, she collected a vast amount of material for a proposed book on Will Gould, intending to relate his life and work to the story of Jesus and the Christian community through the ages. That she never completed the book was a source of pain and embarrassment to her, an indication of her "long ordeal of nonperformance." Near the end of her life Antin explained to Agnes Gould that her decades-long "silence and inactivity" were products of the "deep soul sickness" and "loneliness" that were much worse than all the "external illnesses" from which she suffered.[35]

Even at the Christian home, where Antin was both patient and sometime secretary, she turned "Jew on occasion," describing herself as a "Jewish member of the staff" and showing sensitivity to references to Jews.[36] For Antin, there was no inconsistency between affiliating herself with Will Gould's philosophy of Christian brotherhood and identifying herself, when necessary, as a Jew. "One current of continuity runs underneath all the abortive phases of my life," she explained while in her fifties. "From childhood on I have been obliged to drop anything I was doing to run after any man who seemed to know a little more than I did about God . . . I most want to write about: how a modern woman has sought the face of God—not the name nor the fame but the *face* of God—and what adventures came to meet her on this most ancient human path."[37] That Antin would boldly declare her ambition to encounter God's visage, which according to Hebrew Scripture was seen only by Moses, indicates the distance she had already traveled from Orthodox Judaism, creating her own defiant spirituality.

While Antin saw no incongruity in rejecting the formal practice of Judaism only to dabble throughout her life with other religious philosophies (including anthroposophy, Eastern mysticism, and Christianity) it is startlng that this apostle of Americanization, without publicly admitting the failure of her secular philosophy, came to spend her last decades in a frantic search for spiritual meaning. She revealed privately that, after her marital breakup and the onset of her nervous illness, she began to unload "the pyramid of honors, civic and literary, which had been heaped on me by the usual headlong process of rewarding a popular success. One day, I sat down and wrote a wholesale lot of letters of resignation. When I finished, I didn't belong to a single author's club or patriotic society. I was myself again, whatever that was."[38]

Antin recognized only belatedly the problems of being herself and discovering who that "self" was. The narcissism so apparent in *The Promised Land,* which had allowed her to transverse the difficult course of assimilation seemingly without incident, had less positive consequences in later life. But Antin never acknowledged that her failure to realize full selfhood and her nervous illnesses might have been caused, at least in part, by the same alienation from the roots of her heritage that she suspected in her father. Instead, she continued to celebrate America for the freedom it gave her to follow her "inborn drive" toward religious exploration without reference to Judaism. "For decades I lived cut off from Jewish life and thought, heart-free and mind-free to weave other bonds," she wrote without regret in 1941.[39] Because "American life followed a democratic pattern," Antin believed she could sharpen her kinship with "all earnest seekers after God," not only Jews, and to help to close the gap between Jew and Gentile.

By the early 1940s, however, Nazism caused Antin to reclaim her Jewish identity openly: "It is one thing to go your separate way, leaving friends and comrades behind in peace and prosperity; it is another thing to fail to remember them when the world is casting them out."[40] But Antin refused to be drawn back into Jewish particularism—what she called a "Ghetto without walls"—because of anti-Semitism. She admitted that "I can no more return to the Jewish fold that I can return to my mother's womb": such a return, for all assimilated Jews, would in fact be a "historic tragedy."

> I shall not let myself be stampeded. I have found my wider world of the spirit, and nothing can dislodge me. . . . In all those places where race lines are drawn, I shall claim the Jewish badge; but in my Father's house of many mansions I shall continue a free spirit.[41]

Antin declared, finally, that "the point where I come to life as a member of modern society, where my fullest sense of responsibility is kindled, is deep below the ache and horror of the Jewish dilemma." This point—at the seat of her most vivid sense of self—occurred when she witnessed the persecution of *"any* group"—"whether of race, creed or color," an offense that constituted a wholesale "attack on democracy." Only here, "where the spiritual foundations of America are threatened," did Antin finally "feel alive." It was the danger to Americanism, not just to Jews, that touched her deepest self.[42]

Antin spent much time during her last years at Gould Farm, often with her daughter and visited by her younger sisters.[43] Yet despite her family's loyalty and the affection of Agnes Gould and other farm residents, Antin did not know "where I belong[ed]; whether among family or the Farm's friendly 'strangers,' " she continued to complain of the "desert of loneliness."[44]

Antin's nervous illnesses never abated. Nor did the productivity of earlier times return. However much she espoused a fervent, universalist Americanism and denied the validity of ethnic or religious particularism, her cosmopolitan beliefs did not fulfill her spiritual or emotional needs. Though she considered herself a representative American, a Jew (when the identification was important), and a feminist, the blend of the three identities remained uneasy and would not support ongoing creative endeavor.

Sweatshop Cinderella   For Anzia Yezierska, a contemporary of Mary Antin's, the struggle to become an American, to realize her potential as a writer and defy the age-old destiny of Jewish women, became the central theme of an extraordinary, if abbreviated, literary career.[45] Yezierska burst onto the American literary scene in 1915 with the publication of her short story "Free Vacation House" in a literary journal; the story movingly describes the humiliating encounters of a Jewish mother from the Lower East Side tenements with benevolent but condescending charity workers.[46] In 1919, another Yezierska story, "The Fat of the Land," won the Edward J. O'Brien prize for the best short story of the year; O'Brien was so impressed that he dedicated his anthology to Yezierska. This story, and the appearance of the collection *Hungry Hearts* in 1920, followed by five more books in the next dozen years, established Yezierska as one of the nation's preeminent chroniclers of immigrant life.[47]

Yezierska became the "Cinderella of the sweatshops," as the press dubbed her, when Samuel Goldwyn purchased the rights to *Hungry Hearts* and with much fanfare brought her to Hollywood to assist in translating immigrant life to the screen. But she left after only a short while, disillusioned with the false values of the film colony and unable to work apart from the ghetto community that had given her inspiration. Having abandoned her roots, however, Yezierska found she could no longer return home. Her writing career fizzled, and she spent the next decades impoverished, lonely, and forgotten.

Born in the Russian-Polish village of Plotsk, Yezierska had come to America with her parents, three brothers, and three sisters in about 1890, when she was eight or ten years old (like many offspring of large immigrant families, she did not know the exact date of her birth); three younger siblings were born in the United States. When they arrived at Castle Garden, the Yezierskas were instantly Americanized, receiving as their surname the first name of an older brother, Meyer, who had arrived two years earlier. Anzia became Hattie Mayer, a name she would discard only upon her emergence as a published author almost three decades later.

Yezierska's older sisters went to work in sweatshops but Anzia, being too young for such labor, began public school and learned English. After school, she sold paper bags (pasted up the night before in the family kitchen) to help support the family. But Yezierska's father, a rabbi and Talmudic scholar in the old country, thought women's education a waste of time; soon she was forced to leave school to work full-time. Many of her stories would recount the mistreatment she received in sweatshop and factory jobs, even from Jewish employers, including prosperous relatives whom she served as a live-in domestic. Yezierska learned the bitter lesson that had eluded Antin: that the American dream was available only to those with unusually good fortune, especially those who could afford to receive America's vaunted free education.

According to Yezierska's daughter and biographer, Louise Levitas Henriksen, Anzia's sisters, unlike their fictional counterparts, seemed reasonably content in their marriages and did not appear to resent the differential treatment they received from their father because they were women. Henriksen notes that in their world, "women had always waited on men; it was the universal, immutable law of life."[48] In fact, the sisters never noticed the injustices that so grated on Yezierska and that she would fight, fiercely and often, in her life and fiction. The germ of Yezierska's passionate feminism, very much ahead of its times, grew out of her own fiery temperament and sensitivities rather than merely from the circumstances of her childhood or family heritage.

Against her father's wishes, Yezierska began attending night school at the Educational Alliance, hoping eventually to enter college. By withholding money from her paycheck and working in a laundry in the mornings and afternoons, she was able to finance a year at the New York City Normal School. Yezierska's father disapproved of all this; in his eyes, the only reason for an unmarried daughter to stop supporting her family was marriage. In the face of his relentless opposition, Yezierska left home and took a room at the Clara de Hirsch Home for working girls, a Jewish-sponsored philanthropy. There she came to the attention of a wealthy German Jewish patron who agreed to pay her tuition at Columbia University's Teachers College, in the department of home economics. Cooking was not what Yezierska had in mind but, starved for education, she accepted the offer. For several years she taught home economics in New York City schools, though without enthusiasm and with little success, garnering only the lowest-paid substitute teaching assignments.

With her outgoing personality, Yezierska decided that a career as an actress might be more suitable. She soon won a scholarship to the American Academy of Dramatic Arts, but after her studies ended, the theater, too, proved a dead end. Yezierska then turned to writing, hoping that she could perhaps find a way to communicate the drama of immigrant life to America's reading public. With the help of her older sister, Annie, who assisted in developing characters and plots, Yezierska wrote her first stories and sent them out for publication; all were rejected.

In 1910, Yezierska married Jacob Gordon, an attorney. Within months she realized she had made a mistake and had the marriage annulled. The following year, just as quickly, she married Gordon's friend, high school teacher Arnold Levitas, in a religious ceremony: Yezierska refused to participate in a legally binding civil one. When the couple's only child, Louise, was born in 1912, Yezierska found herself confined to a domestic routine, her writing career on hold. She was miserably unhappy.

Taking her daughter, Yezierska left for the West Coast to visit another sister, Fannie. She stayed for a year, resuming her writing. When her first story was published in 1915, her separation from her husband became permanent. Determined to make a success as a writer, she left Louise with the child's father, a situation that would also become permanent.[49] Both actions signalled a radical break with Jewish family mores: the ideal of the *eyshet hayil* would have little place in Yezierska's life.

A turning point came in 1917, when, with characteristic brashness, Yezierska called upon the eminent philosopher John Dewey, at Columbia University, to complain that Anglo-Saxon America, and Columbia, discriminated against the foreign-born. Yezierska had returned to teaching to support herself, but found that despite her degree, she could not be accredited. Suspecting discrimination, she rushed to Dewey's office, having read in the paper the day before about a speech he had made on democracy in education.

The astonished Dewey found himself immediately drawn to his unexpected visitor: auburn-haired and blue-eyed, with creamy skin and a robust figure, she seemed highly original and exotic as she harangued him about American fairness and the need to express her special vision. Yezierska had brought some writing samples and Dewey, favorably impressed, invited her to audit his graduate seminar in social and political philosophy, hoping that she might be able to contribute firsthand knowledge of immigrant life. Yezierska accepted, participating in a study of immigrant women in Philadelphia.

The personal association between these two deeply opposite types proved more important to Yezierska than any academic lessons she may have learned. For two years, they conducted a romantic liaison, apparently never consummated but nonetheless inspiring the distinguished, white-haired academic to write a sheaf of poems to Yezierska; Yezierska, for her part, fell hopelessly in love. Dewey admitted that this colorful, unpolished immigrant brought passion and intensity into his life. "You are translucent," says the Dewey-inspired character in Yezierska's novel *All I Could Never Be,* "and the world's own understanding and love shine through you. . . . You suffer from striving, but it is unnecessary. *You are already.*"[50] In many of her later stories, Yezierska would romanticize her own vivacity, contrasting immigrant emotionalism to the stiff repressiveness that Dewey purportedly acknowledged in his letters to her and that came to characterize her fictional lovers.

But she was deeply disappointed that her affection for the flesh-and-blood Yankee would go unrequited; Dewey drew back when he realized his protégée's volatility and the risk he was taking in continuing his friendship with her. Yet his private poems, which he never showed her, demonstrated how much he had been affected by their relationship. As for Yezierska, Dewey would stand forever as the love of her life. Symbolically, the liaison suggests the allure to Yezierska of an idealized Gentile lover through whom her union with America could be consummated. But because she was always the "other" in Dewey's eyes, Yezierska's hope would remain unfulfilled.

Though the failed affair left Yezierska alone and depressed, Dewey's encouragement of her writing, at a time when most of the outside world and especially her own father were denying her writing's legitimacy, served as a spur to Yezierska's ambitions. It became an "absorbing, growing thing," she wrote in her 1950 autobiographical novel, *Red Ribbon on a White Horse.* "It fed and devoured me. It blotted out nights and days. . . ."[51] The story she was working on, "The Fat of the Land," which won the 1919 short story award, was the first product of her renewed devotion. Henceforth she labored painstakingly over her craft, enlisting all of her family, even her young daughter, to help her perfect her language and style. As far as Yezierska was concerned, all of them owed whatever time and assistance they could render to her greater talent.

Yezierska's crowning literary successes came in the 1920s. Although she was then in her forties, her autobiographical heroine was usually much younger, a struggling immigrant girl in her twenties. There were other female types in her stories—the ghetto mother and the charity worker, for example—yet this young heroine predominated. Yezierska, whose stories were generally received as autobiographical and realistic rather than creative (one critic commented that she wrote by "dipping [her] pen in her heart"), had simply blotted out twenty years of her life, the years of college, teaching, marriage, and motherhood.[52] In her stories, she was the young girl fresh from the ghetto whose perseverance and talents led to her eventual conquest of America.

One critic suggested that Yezierska erased two decades of her own experience because she came to believe in her own myth; it was only as a ghetto writer that she could be accepted by the American reading public, and so she modified her life story, though unintentionally, to meet its demands.[53]

But even when she had long faded from public view, Yezierska kept writing stories with the same theme over and over again, stories about the conflict between immigrant dreams and American realities, about the pain of becoming a real American and of fighting the men—usually fathers or idealized Anglo-Saxon lovers—who denied women their independence or withheld love. In her eighties she continued to tell this tale of immigrant struggle in almost the identical words she had used a half-century earlier. She could not stop imagining this story, because she had never resolved the conflicts it expressed: in writing, she relived the traumas that were the defining marks of her identity.[54]

Yezierska's continuing conflicts about assimilation, religion, and the role of women are most artfully expressed in her full-length novel, *The Bread Givers* (1925). Subtitled "a struggle between a father of the Old World and a daughter of the New," the book recounts the efforts of the seventeen-year-old heroine, Sara Smolinsky, to break away from the domination of her father, Reb Smolinsky, a rabbinical scholar and patriarch of the family. Devoted to his Torah studies, the father sends his four daughters out to work—they are the bread givers of the title—and marries off the three eldest to men whom they do not love, in the mistaken expectation that the husbands will support him. Sara, the rebellious youngest daughter, called "blood-and-iron" by her father because her will is as strong as his own, refused to submit to his tyranny. But rejecting her father, she must also reject his religion. Sara laments the fact, for example, that

God didn't listen to women. . . . Women could get into Heaven because they were wives and daughters of men. Women had no brains for study of God's Torah, but they could be the servants of men who studied the Torah. Only if they cooked for the men, and washed for the men, and didn't nag or curse the men out of their homes; only if they let the men study the Torah in peace, then, maybe, they could push themselves into Heaven with the men, to wait on them there.[55]

Sara challenges traditional roles: "I'm smart enough to look out for myself," she tells her father as she leaves home to make her own way in the world. "In America, women don't need men to boss them."[56] Taking poorly paid, exploitative jobs in a laundry and sweatshop, she manages to attend night school and college (like the author), and eventually becomes a teacher. But to her father, Sara is not a success but a "lawless, conscienceless thing . . . a dried-up old maid. . . . Woe to America where women are let free like men," he rebukes her.[57]

The last scene of the book provides a reconciliation of sorts between father and daughter. Sara brings her fiancé, a school principal, to her father to learn Hebrew; the couple offers to take in the embittered old man even though it means they will have to keep the Orthodox customs Sara has rejected. The father is skeptical since Sara is "not a Jewess and not a gentile" and has shown "contempt for God's law." But Sara feels a shadow upon her that she cannot shake off: "It wasn't just my father," reads the final line of the book, "but the generations who made my father whose weight was still upon me.[58]

In Yezierska's life, such a reconciliation with her own father and Jewish tradition would prove impossible. After *The Bread Givers* was published, she returned to her old neighborhood to see her father. In her fictional autobiography, Yezierska narrates his excoriating lament:

"Woe to America!" he wailed. "Only in America could it happen—an ignorant thing like you—a writer! What do you know of . . . history, philosophy? What do you know of the Bible, the foundation of all knowledge?"

He stood up, an ancient patriarch condemning unrighteousness. . . . "It says in the Torah: He who separates himself from people buries himself in death. A woman alone, not a wife and not a mother, has no existence. No joy on earth, no hope of heaven. . . . You're not human!"[59]

Yezierska's father went on to castigate her success, calling it an "evil worship of Mammon" that had taken her away from Judaism. "Poverty becomes a Jew like a red ribbon on a white horse," he told her. "But you're no longer a Jew. You're a *meshumeides,* an apostate, an enemy of your own people. And even the Christians will hate you."[60]

Accusing his daughter of not being a writer, a woman, or a Jew—all the things she was—Yezierska's father's words would haunt her well after his death. Indeed, she titled her own autobiography after his frequent citation of the proverb about the red ribbon on a white horse: she knew it meant that a righteous Jew should neither seek worldly success nor mind poverty. Yezierska could never escape her father or the "ghetto" she carried with her wherever she went—"the nothingness, the fear of my nothingness."[61] Despite her success, she felt that without her father's approval, she had "no life": "When you deny your parents, you deny the ground under your feet, the sky over your head. You become an outlaw, a pariah. . . ." Such was her confession to Samuel Goldwyn over lunch in Hollywood: Yezierska told him that the story he had purchased was a "double-murder story" (in which the parents and their rebel daughter each denies the other's existence). But Yezierska could never achieve the expiation she hoped for by writing the book; apart from her family and community, she saw herself as "lost in chaos, wandering between two worlds." Because she had wanted what now seemed impossible—to bridge those worlds—she stood "empty, homeless—outside of life. Not a woman—not a writer."[62] Her father's curse had found its mark.

The portrait of the immigrant daughter who becomes Americanized, leaving behind both her ghetto heritage and Judaism, appears in many of Yezierska's short stories as well. In her aptly titled "Children of Loneliness," Cornell-educated Rachel Ravinsky, now a school teacher, rejects her parents, whom she sees as "two lumps of ignorance and superstition" leading "dumb, wasted lives." Rachel's father, like Sara Smolinsky's and the patriarch of Yezierska's family, felt his daughter was "a Jew-hater, an anti-Semite . . . a betrayer of our race who hates her own father and mother like the Russian Czar once hated a Jew." Rachel understands that Americanization has destroyed this family: "It is the battle to the knife between parents and children. It's black tragedy that boils there. . . ."[63] Yet because she is rootless and, metaphorically speaking, homeless, apart from her family and community, she questions her success: "Nothing is real but love . . . nothing so false as ambition." Like so many other immigrant offspring, she is a child of loneliness, a failed success.

In an unpublished story entitled "We Can Change Our Moses but Not Our Noses," Yezierska wrote about having obtained a bank stenographer's position by hiding the fact that she was a Jew. "But I couldn't get away with it. . . . The day I gave up my Jewish name I ceased to be myself. I ceased to exist. A person who cuts himself off from his people cuts himself off at the roots of his being; he becomes a shell, a cipher, a spiritual suicide."[64] Although Yezierska borrowed this supposedly autobiographical account from the experiences of her daughter and a nephew, Henriksen believes it underscores the deep remorse her mother felt at having rejected her heritage. In her autobiography, Yezierska admits that when she had tried to hide her Jewishness to find work in Gentile offices she felt that she was cutting off part of her self: "That was why there was no wholeness, no honesty, in anything I did. That was why I always felt so guilty and so unjustly condemned—an outsider wherever I went."[65]

Despite her acknowledgment of otherness, Yezierska proclaimed the viability of the American dream. This triumphant mode is most apparent in "America and I," a 1923 story that fictionalized her own history of disappointment with exploitative jobs and patronizing reformers. At first, the narrator of the story loses hope, feeling that the "America that I sought was nothing but a shadow—an echo—a chimera of lunatics and crazy immigrants." But reading American history, she discovers the Pilgrims and learns that like contemporary immigrants, they had to surmount difficult situations. A light came to her—"A great revelation!"

> I saw America—a big idea—a deathless hope—a world still in the making. I saw that it was the glory of America that it was not yet finished. And I, the last comer, had her share to give, small or great, to the making of America, like those Pilgrims who came in the *Mayflower.*
>
> Fired up by this revealing light, I began to build a bridge of understanding between the American-born and myself. Since their life was shut out from such as me, I began to open up my life and the lives of my people to them. And life draws life. In only writing about the Ghetto I found America.[66]

This story, which Yezierska continued to rewrite in her final years, never failed to inspire her. But in real life, she had found that the role of bridge-builder did not endure. The American public tired of her immigrant stories, not coincidentally, perhaps, because they presented unusually strong-willed, rebellious women at a time when such heroines were not in demand. After 1930, the sales of her fiction diminished, and she was to produce little new work (other than her autobiography) until her very last years. Unhappily, Yezierska could not find a community to nurture her: neither the Lower East Side nor Hollywood was comfortable, and a brief stay in Arlington, Vermont, where she hoped to make a home near writer Dorothy Canfield Fisher, proved disastrous. In rural Vermont she felt more alien than ever, more alone and Jewish than ever, and yet, because she had denied her heritage, she believed that she was not a real Jew. With sudden clarity she realized that "the battle I thought I was waging against the world had been against myself, against the Jew in me."[67] She berated herself for thinking that cultural differences would spur her to creativity; they merely left her feeling isolated and alone.

Condemned by her father's conscience as well as her own experience to be a "perpetual outsider," Yezierska would discover, again and again, that she had no home. In her daughter Louise's words, "There was no way back to the ghetto."[68]

The Face of God   Though late in life Yezierska had begun to acknowledge her Jewishness as the core of her real identity, Mary Antin continued to celebrate Americanism, exalting a universalist, "free" spirit as the central component of her personality.

Having left Judaism behind, both women found themselves groping for spiritual meaning. Antin became a proponent of transcendental experience and mysticism. Yezierska, too, dabbled in Christian Science, Theosophy, Baha'i—whatever spiritual, inspirational philosophy she could lay her hands on. Yet it was the Hebrew Bible to which she returned most often for spiritual comfort. Henriksen reports that for Yezierska, the Bible was literature, revelation, and consolation; she read it regularly, keeping a concordance handy, and quoted it often.[69]

Though Yezierska rejected the masculine religion of her father, she, too, like Antin, sought the "face of God." "She remained a believer, according to Henriksen, and on certain occasions might tell her that "God was in the room." According to her daughter, these spiritual yearnings came from Yezierska's excruciating loneliness. Apart from community, without lasting friends, she was "the loneliest person I knew, like someone who had malaria and who could not get warm, no matter how many blankets she had."[70]

Yezierska may have read Antin's account of her journey to and through America: there are many similarities between their stories. Both celebrated education as their means of escape from Old World backwardness and poverty. As younger daughters, both had been privileged to receive not only an education but the lifelong support of sisters. Both had powerful mentors in the more established American Jewish community and in the Gentile world, as well as contacts with settlement houses that helped to transform their lives. Each had experienced an unhappy marriage and had borne a daughter; neither mentioned these relationships, in any fashion, in their autobiographies. For both, creating themselves as intellectual women with the authority to write about their experiences meant negating those aspects of their identity that seemed to recall more traditional female roles.

Their greatest similarity lay in their determination to surmount the limitations of women's lives. Both had to assert their independence against traditional community values that defined women according to family responsibilities. Challenging this status necessarily meant rejecting their religion, which both women equated with patriarchy. The battle is more fiercely joined in Yezierska's work, but Antin, too, in her autobiography, came to equate her mother's piety with submissiveness and to reject it, while in several of her best short stories, she railed against the secondary place of women in Judaism.[71]

Anger at patriarchal culture, often directed at fathers, is an important hallmark of Antin's and Yezierska's work; both women give much greater attention to fathers than to mothers in their own and their characters' lives. Though mothers appear in the background in supportive ways, the daughters must break away from them because they stand for the subordination of women to religious and domestic patriarchy. In *Red Ribbon on a White Horse,* Yezierska admits that she pawned her mother's hand-woven shawl, her finest possession ("her Sabbath, her holiday"), for a quarter to pay for carfare to her agent. In getting her to the agent, who had just received an urgent call from Samuel Goldwyn, the shawl in fact got Yezierska to Hollywood. But the loss of the shawl—which all her money could not later reclaim—"shadowed" her trip to Hollywood, just as the alienation from her heritage would weigh heavily on her psyche.[72]

Among the Americans: Rose Gollup Cohen

As educated women with college training, Antin and Yezierska stood out from the common lot of Jewish immigrant daughters. The memoirs of less notable immigrant women nonetheless indicate that their stories are true to the emotional experiences of first-generation Jewish women. One of these was Rose Gollup Cohen, whose 1918 autobiography, *Out of the Shadow,* vividly recounts her family's journey from western Russia to the Lower East Side of New York. Cohen narrates a story of survival and eventual triumph despite poverty and illness: the book ends with her parents emerging from destitution to open a grocery store and her brother's winning a prize in a school essay contest. We hear nothing about Cohen's own future direction, and in fact, outside of the autobiography, there is very little material available about her life. We know, however, that Cohen married and stopped working after the birth of a daughter, yet continued her education at the Educational Alliance and Rand School. Cohen published several short stories in New York literary magazines that describe how a Jew who began "among the Russian peasants" and lived "among the Jews of Cherry Street" was now "among the Americans."[73]

The predominant motifs of *Out of the Shadow* concern Cohen's assimilation, her loss of faith, and her struggle for independence from familial control. As with Antin and Yezierska, issues of gender, religion, and Americanization are closely intertwined, suggesting that the theme was a universal one even for less prominent immigrant women writers. In Russia, Cohen had learned to read by studying the Bible—one of the only books her family owned—becoming devout in the process. In America, her questioning of religion was fueled by secular books and Christian literature, which she read over her father's intense objections. Cohen's fierce battle with her father, like Yezierska's, colors the entire book. His opposition to her American ways, his demand that she submit to him "in the old custom," set off a cycle in which "father commanded and I refused."[74] Cohen's mother's piety, like Esther Antin's, seemed more genuine and durable than her father's, but while Cohen admires her mother's "fight," it offers no protection from, and no alternative to, her husband's domination. Like Yezierska, Rose Cohen must leave her family and her tradition entirely in order to secure her freedom.

The way out for Cohen was provided by Lillian Wald and the Henry Street Settlement. Cohen had come to the United States with an aunt a year after her father's migration; her mother and younger siblings followed some time later. Moving in and out of work, her father was unable to support the family even with the help of his older children: Rose was employed in a series of jobs—as a worker in a sweatshop, as a factory worker, and then, in utter desperation, as a domestic servant. Having heard about the family's plight, Wald came to visit. "A new world opens for us" was how Cohen reported the event in her autobiography.[75] Wald helped her obtain schooling and employment, which were interrupted when Cohen became seriously ill. Wald then sent her to uptown hospitals and to country rest homes, where, out of the ghetto for the first time, Cohen came to know Gentile men and women, the "real" Americans. As a consequence of these encounters, she lost her "intense [Jewish] nationalism." Nonetheless, she was shocked when one of her Henry Street mentors, whom she had known for several years, admitted that she believed in the Jewish "blood libel" (charges of ritual murder). "I felt alone, a stranger in the house that had been a home to me," Cohen acknowledged, but she went on to accept the woman's friendship: "After all we were living in the nineteenth century."[76]

Rose Cohen's final break with tradition came when she refused the marriage her parents had arranged for her, breaking off her engagement to a prosperous suitor, a storeowner, who offered the family a chance of improving its living standard. Cohen insisted on making her own match: as Antin had written in *The Promised Land,* "A long girlhood, a free choice in marriage, and brimful womanhood are the precious rights of an American woman."[77] Cohen's choice was a man who had not only renounced his Jewishness and been baptized by missionaries, but was studying in a Christian seminary. Such a choice was a special disgrace to the family because, as an "apostate," her fiancé had deliberately renounced Judaism. This young man, modern, liberal, and well educated, found the Cohen family's vestigial Orthodoxy quaint and even "pitiful." Perhaps that is why she chose him.[78]

Cohen did not marry this suitor, her feelings for him having cooled during his years in the seminary. But this attachment to a "Christian" lover repeats the pattern of Antin and Yezierska, who also found it necessary, in struggling for their artistic and emotional freedom, to seek affirmation, in the form of an idealized love, from the "other." Rejecting the patriarchalism of their fathers and their religion, they needed validation of their new identities from men not limited by the traditional handicaps of ethnicity. Yet these men were ultimately unable to love them physically.[79]

Jewish women were the first American Jews to employ this convention, although the pattern of Jewish writers seeking validation through romantic involvements with Gentile others would become characteristic of Jewish men of later generations. Intellectual immigrant women, even more than men and native-born American women, had to live lives of exile, rejecting normative female destinies and seeking legitimation for their desire to become Americans and writers by figuratively merging with the male other.[80] Choosing such a life meant crossing gender boundaries, as critic Alvin Rosenfeld has noted. It is no coincidence, Rosenfeld believes, that it was Mary Antin—a woman writer—who invented the type of the "Intellectual as Hero," a type that in the works of later Jewish writers would replace the "more traditional type of the Hero as Pious Man." In America, he explains, "where no Temple was more revered by the immigrants than College, women were put on an equal footing with men before the fundamental Jewish piety of Learning." As a woman, Antin came to symbolize, even to invent, the "liberated, secular intellectual" divorced from traditional piety; the "feminization of intellect" in America and the "secularization of intellect" were two sides of the same coin.[81]

Rosenfeld ignores the fierce emotional struggle in which Jewish women had to engage in order to create careers for themselves as intellectuals. To receive her education, Mary Antin had to distance herself from the lives of the women in her family and neighborhood. Identifying with a male model of intellectual development, she succeeded—for a time—as a writer, but in losing her female self as well as her community she eventually lost her power to create. In 1912, shortly after the publication of *The Promised Land*, Maimie Pinzer, a Jewish former prostitute recovering from a morphine addiction, wrote a scathing portrait of her visit to Antin's Scarsdale home detailing Antin's snobbery, her disgust with "common" people, and her rejection of her immigrant past. Attired in a fine (albeit rumpled) white linen dress that matched her gleaming white "picture book house," Antin greeted Pinzer coldly and was shocked when Pinzer intimated that her daughter might understand Yiddish. "Not a word," Antin replied haughtily. Although Antin "thawed out" somewhat when discussing the village in Russia where both she and a friend of Pinzer had been born, it was still, said Pinzer, "with that same important reference to the fact that she had so many new interests, that the older ones were quite vague." ("I never saw such conceit," Pinzer concluded, "especially in a person of her intelligence.")[82] At the end of her life, in one of the last stories she would write, Yezierska, too, acknowledges that in her "obsession" to become a writer and to "have room with a door [she] could shut," she had "shut out" the past—friends, neighbors, and family. "Father, Mother, sisters, brothers became alien to me, and I became an alien to myself."[83]

Ironically, these women pioneered a new kind of literature of the self even though in their own lives they were unable to reconcile the complex components of ethnic heritage, national identity, and assertive womanhood in a manner that provided self-realization. Their later silence speaks to the difficulty of sustaining creativity in the face of literal and figurative homelessness. Each of these writers seemed not to belong anywhere; although "liberated" intellectuals, they remained on the margins both of American social and cultural life and of their own communities. "Seeking forgetfulness" and throwing off history, they were denied a path to the future; rather than leading home, their journey led to a dead end.

Male immigrant writers, of course, could suffer a similar fate. Leaving home, recalled Henry Roth, author of the extraordinary Depression era novel, *Call It Sleep*, "was a disaster. It took me out of a homogeneous environment, broke my association with Judaism . . . diluted my religiosity. It made the artist, but hell, I wouldn't pay the cost [again]."[84] Despite his isolation from community, which widened his horizons but threw him into a long-standing writer's paralysis, Roth enjoyed a rich and sustaining marriage that mitigated his despair. Antin and Yezierska, breaking gender as well as ethnic boundaries, were denied this crucial support.

The passage from home became obligatory for the generation of male Jewish writers who followed these immigrant pioneers.[85] Yet the alienation from the Jewish past that marked the works of such later writers as Norman Mailer and Philip Roth was matched by a profound disillusionment with America missing from Antin's and Yezierska's more optimistic renderings. Because as women, they had more to transcend in replacing Old World models with New World ideals, they believed profoundly, though not uncritically, in the American dream. Whatever the personal costs, they continued to propound the interlocking myths of American democracy and independent female selfhood.[86] Only in America, Antin wrote, could she have an immutable vision of herself as a "human creature . . . leaping, at last, strong and glad to the intellectual summit of the latest century."[87] And Yezierska, despite her years of wandering and spiritual homelessness, acknowledged the possibility of selfhood even apart from community: "All that I could ever be, the glimpses of truth I reached for everywhere, was as in myself."[88]

Antin's and Yezierska's Americanism reflected fundamental contradictions. The search for integration and unity—to fill the "dark abyss of separation between Jew and Gentiles," as Mary Antin put it—led them to adopt a universalist philosophy in which the "persecution or belittlement of . . . *any* group, whether of race, creed, or color," became "an attack on democracy." As immigrant writers, they endeavored to mediate—to provide a "bridge of understanding," in Yezierska's words—while not denying their own "race" heritage.[89] Yet this combination of mutuality and particularism could not be satisfactorily sustained within their own lives or their families. As Antin had feared, once tradition was lost, it became difficult to pass on. Her daughter and granddaughter also became followers of the Eastern philosopher Meher Baba; Yezierska's daughter, given no Jewish connection from either parent, fell away from Judaism as well.[90]

It was left to other immigrant daughters, less ambitious about breaking the barriers that inhibited women, to maintain the ethnic "communities of sentiment" whose importance Antin acknowledged. Even when they became rebels, they did not necessarily renounce religious custom and community. Many in the immigrant generation did not want to become Americans as rapidly or totally as did Antin and Yezierska, or were unwilling to pay the high costs exacted by assimilation.[91] Yet it was these very women, silent and anonymous, to whom Antin, Yezierska, and other first-generation immigrant writers gave voice.

What stands out, finally, in these writers' own life histories is that Judaism was a heritage they could not totally relinquish. At the end of their lives, each acknowledged that in spite of the fact that she had been cut off from Jewish bonds and remained associated with mystical, even Christian, spirituality, she could say to the Jewish people, as Antin put it, "that I am as one of them."[92] Late in their lives, each returned to Judaism in this fashion, choosing to reaffirm her Jewish identity while insisting on the congruity of Jewish belief with a wider, universalist humanism. Notwithstanding her desperate battle with her patriarchal, self-absorbed father, Yezierska absorbed from him, as her daughter Louise Henriksen avows, "the poetry of the Bible" and a tendency to look for God throughout her life.[93] Antin's religiosity was influenced by her mother's piety rather than her father's devotion, but in her case as well, a passionate, continuing search for God derived from deeply embedded Jewish values and lessons learned in childhood.

Chapter 2

"UPTOWN" WOMEN AND
SOCIAL AND SPIRITUAL REFORM

A Witness for Religion: Rebekah Kohut and Maud Nathan

In 1925, sixty-one-year-old Rebekah Bettelheim Kohut looked back at the changes that had taken place in Jewish women's lives over a quarter of a century. She told an interviewer that "the emergence of the Jewess not only as high priestess of the home but in the larger position—as high priestess of the higher life" was one of the chief developments of the era.[1] Although Jewish women had not yet emerged as spiritual leaders in synagogues, she believed they had secured a prominent place in communal work, cultural movements, and arts and letters.

Kohut's personal history as a leader of the New York Council of Jewish Women exemplified this assertion. In two well-received autobiographies, she wrote about herself as "a worker in the front ranks of American Jewish Womanhood," striving to assert her own "Jewish womanhood as well as Jewish womanhood the world over." Unlike the sagas of Antin and Yezierska, which told of family and religious disruption caused by assimilation, Kohut's tale was of a Jewess "striving for Jewish ideals and Jewish culture," a story of the "effective linking together of generations," as her friend Henrietta Szold wrote in her introduction to Kohut's memoir.[2] Like several other strongly identified Jewish women who struggled to develop independent identities as activists within traditional familial and religious contexts, Kohut successfully maintained the "community of [Jewish] sentiment" that Antin believed held the key to blending modern American with inherited Judaic ideals. At the same time, she challenged and subtly subverted the patriarchal foundations of these ideals.

Working with the National Council of Jewish Women to provide aid to immigrants, middle-class Jewish women like Kohut and consumer advocate Maud Nathan expanded the arenas for female activism. For such women, the challenge of helping the new immigrants became an extraordinary opportunity to build their own self-esteem and establish themselves as the kind of "actuating" public citizens that Sadie American had envisaged in her speech to the Jewish Women's Congress. Jewish women had been active in charity for many generations but, as several of their Gentile sisters reminded them, they had remained aloof from the worst problems of urban impoverishment. Such reprimands, along with the encouragement of Christian philanthropists and the example of earlier Jewish activists, pulled traditional Jewish wives like Kohut and Nathan away from the domestic realm and into active engagement with immigrants, and eventually into the movement for social and political reform.

Yet the rigid patriarchy of Jewish institutions and the anti-Semitism of Christian feminists reminded them that their newly designed blend of American and Jewish feminism could prove fragile. At the same time, the objects of their benevolence, the immigrant poor, often recoiled from their interventions, bitterly reproaching them for class bias and authoritarianism. Thus, the struggles of privileged Jewish women to define their mission could be as unsettling, complex, and hard fought as those of poorer and newer arrivals.

The Best History Is Biography: Mother Sarah and Deborah   Born in 1864, Rebekah Kohut was the daughter of a Hungarian rabbi, Albert Bettelheim, and his wife Henrietta, an unconventional woman who scandalized her village by becoming the first Jewish female schoolteacher. Prejudice against Jews in the trades and professions of Hungary during the 1850s and 1860s of course ran deep. "But a woman!" Kohut recalled, "It was against all tradition for a woman to be anything but subservient."[3]

In 1867, when Kohut turned three, the family emigrated to the United States following a dispute between Rabbi Bettelheim and Jewish leaders in Hungary. A few years later, Henrietta Bettelheim died after a long illness. Though she lost her mother at a young age, Kohut recalled her mother's piety and love for Judaism, and her stubborn determination to become educated, as a beacon for her own development. Once in San Francisco, where her father had accepted a rabbinical post after appointments in Philadelphia and Richmond, Virginia, Kohut, though barely a teenager, was pressed into teaching at a religious school. One day, the chairman of the board visited her classroom to find her teaching the story of Ruth, an unauthorized text. "Why are you not teaching the catechism?" he asked her. "I teach what I please," Kohut responded. She was immediately dismissed.[4]

Kohut's rebellion coincided with the awakenings of adolescence, for her a time of tremendous suffering and "spiritual growing pains." Bridling at her father's ungrateful congregation and the family's continuing struggle with poverty, Kohut began to doubt the "worthwhileness of all the sacrifices" the family had made for Judaism.

> What was the use of it all, I questioned. Why make a stand for separate Jewish ideals? Why not choose the easier way and be like all the rest? The struggle was too hard. Too bitter.[5]

In contrast to her father's unappreciative congregants and the "anguish of soul" that she felt characterized most Jews, Kohut discovered the "poise and cheerfulness" of Christians. Visiting a favorite classmate's home, she was profoundly stirred by the family's devotion to Christian ideals. "Never had I seen such a beautiful home life. . . . happiness and gentleness fairly radiated from them." Looking beyond her own religion and seeing that "others were good," she meditated on "the thorny patch which the Jew travelled." Only "if the Jew could assimilate with the Christian," she thought, would his "irksome trials . . . be eliminated, with no spiritual loss." So did this daughter of an eminent rabbi recognize herself as an "apathetic, indeed antagonistic Jewess," and come to espouse assimilation.[6]

Three Christian women—two teachers and the principal of the teachers' training school that Kohut attended before college—changed her mind. Desiring a better understanding between Christians and Jews and interested in Jewish tradition, each woman encouraged Kohut to think more positively of Judaism. Under their influence, she came to feel proud, indeed "overproud," of her "race . . . religion . . . sublimity in its martyrdom."[7] While she continued to believe in "only one God for us all," she stopped blaming Jews for the anguish of their history and took notice of the role that Christianity had played in the sorrows of the Jews. Yet she, her father, and her husband-to-be, Alexander Kohut, maintained warm lifelong relations with Christian friends, including members of the clergy. (It was two Catholic priests, friends of Rabbi Bettelheim, who persuaded him to make a trip to his homeland during a long illness. When the rabbi died at sea, the priests, who were accompanying him, read the Hebrew burial service over his body. As they opened his prayer book, Rebekah recounts, "a small American flag dropped out.")[8]

Both in Hungary and the United States, the rabbi had been caught up in the maelstrom of denominational struggle that swept over organized Jewry in the late nineteenth century. As Kohut recalled, it was then a period of "white heat in the battle between Orthodoxy and Reform. Rabbis thundered, personalities were bandied."[9] In Hungary, Bettelheim had been opposed for refusing to cling to "every last portion of ritual"; in the United States, he resisted radical reform of the synagogue service, preferring gradual change. He was a "conservative," Kohut thought, "or perhaps he might have been called a progressive."[10]

Rabbi Bettelheim's handling of his daughter's religious crisis mirrored his ability to navigate a modern course amid the shoals of Jewish denominationalism. Though Rebekah never confided her misgivings to her father, the rabbi sensed that she was "drifting from [her] bearings." Intrigued by the idea of his daughter's "picking [her] own course to safety," he nonetheless opposed too-frequent interaction with Christians, fearing that she might be tempted to give up her faith.[11] Yet he refused to probe too deeply into her searchings, giving her enough autonomy to find her own way.

Bettelheim encouraged Rebekah to pursue university training at a time when higher education for women was still in its infancy. Kohut recalled that the idea was as strange to her father's congregants "as my mother's learning had been to the little communities in Hungary," and they strongly disapproved, warning the rabbi that "it was dangerous and altogether too radical to allow one of the opposite sex to imbibe the higher knowledge."[12] The rabbi held his ground, and Kohut became one of the University of California's first women students, studying English literature and history there for two years.

Kohut's father also turned her into a suffragist. On the day she left for college, Rabbi Bettelheim called his daughter into his study. "Ah Sing will probably be a citizen by the time you have finished college," he told her, referring to the campaign to grant immigrant Asians the vote. "But you, because you are a woman, will never become one—unless you and other women fight for this right."[13] Kohut was a staunch suffragist from that moment on.

Kohut's awakening to women's rights coincided with her dawning pride in herself as a Jew. It was no accident that, prodded by Christian mentors whom she felt knew more than she did about Jewish history, she decided to catch up by studying Jewish women's lives—"the best history is biography," she averred.

> As I learned of the careers of some of the great women of Israel—of the Mendelssohn daughters, of Sarah Copia Sullam, Deborah Ascarelli, high in the councils of the Italian Court, of Rebecca Gratz, most beloved and honored woman of her time, who served as the model for Rebecca in Scott's *Ivanhoe*, of Emma Lazarus, equally beloved a century later, of Grace Aguilar and a host of others—a new pride possessed me. More cause for worship, more examples of nobility, richer race consciousness.[14]

These Jewesses who had "saved Judaism and perpetuated it as well" seemed to Kohut very much like the contemporary leaders of the women's rights movement—Lucy Stone, Susan B. Anthony, Elizabeth Cady Stanton, Julia Ward Howe, Harriet Beecher Stowe.

> I associated the work of these women with the history of the women of my own people, and found much similarity in their ideals and aspirations. Deborah became to me not a prophetess but a great political emancipator. Mother Sarah stood for the single standard of wife and mother in the home.[15]

Studying Jewish history made her aware of the Jews' perennial position as a minority—especially a "protesting minority"—and of women's special contributions in maintaining Jewish culture and identity in the past. The history of the women of Israel passed on a "burden of responsibility" to Jewish women of the present and future, which in no way conflicted with their duties as Americans interested in emancipating their sex.

As for myself, no matter how wide my interests might become, and how intensely I felt everything that affected the United States, it appeared to me that my real mission in life should be as a worker in the front ranks of American Jewish womanhood.

There were no conflicting aims in my program as I mapped it out. It was possible to be fully devoted to both religion and country, which were not in any way opposed, but rather dependent upon each other.[16]

In her certitude about the ease with which the interests of "religion and country" could be blended, Kohut reflected the beliefs of one of her role models, Emma Lazarus; in fact, Kohut accompanied Lazarus on trips to Castle Garden in the early 1880s to welcome new immigrants.

By the first years of her young womanhood, Kohut had weathered the crisis of religious identity. Her return home was predicated on her conscious self-creation as heir to a Jewish tradition that combined female authority and self-assertion with Jewish practice. After her marriage, however, she found herself struggling once more to define herself according to the ideals represented by the "great women of Israel" past and the American women's rights leaders of the present. For Kohut, as for so many Jewish women of her class, becoming a wife and mother marked the assumption of the traditional domestic responsibilities assigned to her sex. In the United States, where a cult of "true womanhood" exalted women's role as guardians of morality, religion, and culture, the separate, gendered spheres of Jewish tradition found ready sanction. It would be no easy feat for Kohut to be both Deborah, the Hebrew Bible's prophetess or "political emancipator," and Sarah, wife of Abraham, mother of Isaac, and progenitor of all to come—"the standard of wife and mother in the home."

The circumstances of Kohut's marriage made such a fusion of identities all the harder. She had fallen in love with Alexander Kohut, a newly arrived Hungarian rabbinical scholar twenty-two years her senior. A widower with eight children, the emigré rabbi was a "commanding and dramatic figure," over six feet tall and with a gentleness, magnetism, and carefree youthfulness that greatly appealed to Rebekah. Clearly there was much about Kohut that resembled her own father, a happily remarried widower with six children who, like Kohut, was a prominent figure in the theological realignments of nineteenth-century Judaism. Immediately upon his arrival, Kohut became "the storm Centre of the conflict between Orthodoxy and Reform," according to Rebekah; he helped to found the Jewish Theological Seminary in 1886, established to revitalize Judaism and enable it to respond to changing historical conditions. One of the seminary's preeminent scholars, Kohut helped to shape its still evolving doctrine of Conservative Judaism, which was to have a profound influence on American Jewish life. "I was truly my father's daughter," Rebekah remarked about their shared admiration for Alexander Kohut.[17]

But neither her father nor the rest of her family approved of her plans to marry the eminent rabbi. No one objected to the match more than Rebekah's own stepmother, who knew at first hand the pitfalls of mothering a large family of stepchildren. Having experienced poverty as a rabbi's daughter, Rebekah responded that she did not expect opulence as a rabbi's wife, and she dismissed her family's warnings about assuming too much responsibility. When a cousin questioned her decision to marry a man with eight children, she responded haughtily that it "wouldn't make any difference to me if he had eighty."[18]

Rebekah, then twenty-two, married Alexander Kohut in Baltimore on February 14, 1887, with Rabbi Benjamin Szold, a close family friend, officiating. It was a small and "none too cheery" wedding party, Rebekah recalled; except for her friend Henrietta Szold, the rabbi's daughter, only family members attended. Henrietta did her best to enliven the "dismal" ceremony by playing Mendelssohn's "Wedding March," but could not dissipate the collective gloom. As Rebekah's oldest and dearest sister considered the burdens awaiting the bride, the marriage seemed more like a "funeral ceremony" than a wedding.[19]

For a while, Kohut remained undaunted—"I go to New York to be the wife of a great man, and to become a mother to the motherless" she wrote her sister.[20] But serving as helpmeet to a great man and mothering his large brood were Herculean tasks. In addition to the Kohut children, there was another offspring: for twenty-five years, her husband had been working on a vast theological compendium, the *Aruch Completum,* to which he devoted at least ten to twelve hours a day. Kohut's children were jealous of this sibling, and so too would Rebekah feel of "secondary importance" to Alexander's lifework.

Dedicated to her husband, home, and children, Kohut found little time or inclination for the communal work she had begun before marriage. Shortly after the Kohuts' arrival in New York, she was asked to attend a neighborhood rally sponsored by the Women's Health Protective Association to protest the city's failure to enforce sanitation regulations. She accepted, and the next day, an article about the rally in the New York *Herald* cited her remarks lambasting the city fathers for the odors emanating from East Side slaughterhouses. "The wife of the new rabbi is a comely young woman," the *Herald* commented, "but she has hardly been in the city long enough to qualify as a critic of public affairs."[21] Nor was Rabbi Kohut pleased. "While rather proud that what I had said seemed worthy of quotation," he was dubious of the "wisdom of a public career for me. He felt that I had much to do at home, and was more or less jealous of any time I gave to others."[22] She eventually quit the association to give her family her undivided attention.

If Kohut was troubled by this not so voluntary reduction in her activities, she did not admit it. Yet her return to the female sphere clearly did not fit with her own alleged beliefs about women's roles: "My sisters and I had always felt that while woman's interests ought to begin at home and ought to end there, they need not necessarily confine themselves to it alone."[23]

An opportunity to expand her interests came in the midst of tragedy. In the early 1890s, Kohut lost both her older brother (the only family member to have encouraged her marriage) and her father. To ease her pain, she engaged in public activities, rejoining the Women's Health Protective Association and doing "whatever offered forgetfulness."[24] After attending meetings of the new "sisterhood of personal service" at Temple Emanu-El, the first sisterhood in the United States, she was impressed with its mission of directly aiding the Jewish poor and urged that a similar group be formed at her husband's temple, the Central Synagogue on Manhattan's East Side. "It seemed to be the work that I could do for him, and he consented," though not, we can imagine, with enthusiasm.[25] Kohut now organized what she believed to be the second Jewish women's sisterhood and became its president. Establishing the sisterhood's headquarters in the immigrant district on the Lower East Side gave Kohut and other members a new opportunity to assist the impoverished immigrants. Kohut visited them at their synagogues, helped them find work and started a day-care center and kindergarten for their children. Nearby were Lillian Wald's Henry Street Settlement, the Minnie Louis Downtown Sabbath School (which later became the Hebrew Technical School for Girls), and other services established by Jewish women. Kohut at last began to feel that she was joining the activist women of Israel who had inspired her renewal of faith.

When word of Kohut's activities spread to the organizers of the Jewish Women's Congress at the 1893 Chicago World's fair, they invited her to address the delegates. But her delight at the invitation was short-lived when her husband, then seriously ill, indicated his reluctance to let her go. After Kohut's sister left for Chicago to read the paper she had written for the occasion, Rebekah went to her room and wept. When she heard later that the momentous gathering had established a permanent Council of Jewish Women, she felt "sorrier than ever that I had not been present." Still, she convinced herself that her absence was "one of the finest sacrifices I had ever made for Alexander Kohut."[26]

Her husband died a little more than a year later, during which time Kohut never left his side. After his passing, she was faced, suddenly, with the problem of supporting the large Kohut clan. For a while she gave parlor lectures, then the vogue on Manhattan's East Side, to several hundred friends gathered in the living room of Mr. and Mrs. Jacob Schiff; she also taught confirmation classes at her synagogue. But a more reliable income was necessary. With the backing of Schiff, she started the Kohut School for Girls, a boarding and day school offering general and religious education. Kohut herself took charge of the girls' religious instruction, hoping to communicate her own "religious enthusiasm" to the pupils.[27] The new venture manifested Kohut's simultaneous passion for American secular and Jewish learning.

Five years later, she sold the school for a substantial profit. Kohut had wanted to continue her work as an educator, but when her children demanded more of her time, she decided she would "rather lose my school than my children." Even more than her marriage, she considered the loss of this vocation the "greatest personal sacrifice" she had ever been forced to make.[28] But within a few years, she found a way to fill the deep void left by her sacrifice of the school. Because of her own struggles, she understood the plight of others denied work through no fault of their own, and decided she would help fight for their greater economic security. In 1914, Kohut established the Employment Bureau of the Young Women's Hebrew Association. During World War I, she pressed for greater employment opportunities for all Americans, chairing the Re-Employment Council of the United States Employment Service and the Employment Committee of the Women's Committee for National Defense, and serving as a member of the United States Employment Service and Federal Employment Committee. Praising her volunteer administrative services, the press dubbed her a "Dollar-a-Year" patriot.[29]

In 1931, New York State Governor Franklin Roosevelt appointed Kohut to his Advisory Council on Employment; she also served as advisory commissioner of the New York State Employment Service and on the state's Joint Legislation Commission on Unemployment, the only one of its sixteen members to advocate for unemployment insurance. During the Depression, she was particularly concerned that Jews were the "first sufferers" as the gates of employment closed.[30] In November 1935, to celebrate Kohut's fifty years of public service, many of New York City's leading political and cultural figures, including Mayor Fiorello La Guardia and writer Fannie Hurst, honored her with a gala golden jubilee dinner.

Kohut's prominence in public life came in large part from the skills she learned as a member of the Council of Jewish Women. After her husband's death, she became deeply involved with the Council and served as president of its New York section from 1894 to 1898. She also worked for the Council in many other capacities over the next several decades. For Kohut and a growing number of Jewish women who chafed at, yet continued to obey, the restrictions of domestic Jewish womanhood, the Council was able to expand their personal options in a way that did not threaten traditionally gendered roles. All of its innovative social welfare programs (including an international crusade against the white slave trade and campaigns to improve hygiene, nutrition, housing, schools, and playgrounds) relied heavily on images of maternalism—"adopting" immigrant families, rescuing runaway "daughters," teaching "housewifery" and domestic skills to immigrant girls.[31] Such rhetoric helped legitimate the activist roles that women like Kohut assumed.

"Bediamonded Hands . . . Sav[ing] the Unfortunates": Belle Moskowitz, Lillian Wald, Julia Richman, Alice Mencken   According to Elisabeth Israels Perry, granddaughter and biographer of Belle Moskowitz, a Democratic Party leader who served as advisor to Alfred E. Smith (a four-term governor of New York and a presidential candidate), Moskowitz's affiliation with the New York Council of Jewish Women made possible many of her later achievements.[32] After her marriage to painter Charles Israels and the birth of her first child, Moskowitz joined the New York Council of Jewish Women, becoming the head of its philanthropy committee. In this capacity, she supervised work among hospitalized children and the religious instruction of delinquent girls, and organized the Council's police court probation work and its aid program for "wayward" teens. Her efforts led to the creation of the Council's first home for pregnant girls on Staten Island in 1905.

At a time when neither Jews nor women received top positions in charitable institutions, the Council's "all-female all-Jewish environment gave [Moskowitz] unmatched opportunities to develop leadership skills," Perry remarks. "No matter how far Belle Israels strayed from the Council, she remained indebted to it."[33] The Council also provided Moskowitz with inspirational role models, most of whom were married with several children. Perhaps most important, Perry believes, was the Council's focus on women and children, which allowed her grandmother and other activist women to resolve their doubts about working in the public arena. In Moskowitz's view, the Jewish woman tended to be more fearful than her Christian counterpart about accepting nontraditional work. She believed that "her only place [is] in the home, and that, going outside of it, she unsexes herself and gives up all opportunity as well as all thought of founding her own home. . . ." The primacy of maternalism in Council work alleviated such anxieties while providing new opportunities for Jewish women to shape social reform agendas and influence public policy.[34]

Framed by the rhetoric of class as well as gender, however, National Council of Jewish Women (NCJW) programs tended to distance Council members from the objects of their intervention and to enforce the existing hierarchy of superior "uptown" German or Central European Jews and "downtown" East European co-religionists. Rebekah Kohut's paper at the 1893 Jewish Women's Congress had addressed the distaste that "opulent" Jews felt at contact with their less fortunate brethren. Considering the Russian Jew a pariah, this privileged class exhibited a kind of "Semitic anti-Semitism," Kohut admitted. When Gentile philanthropist Josephine Shaw Lowell asked Kohut why she had never met any of the "better class Jewesses" in the poorer districts, Kohut confessed that "the dart went straight home. . . . We Jewesses are not missionaries; we do not go into the camp of the lowly and the oppressed; we await our sisters at our own doors."[35]

The NCJW overcame this reluctance by creating a dozen settlements throughout the country where privileged Jewish women came in daily contact with immigrants. Yet Council women retained the belief that their primary task was to help immigrants assimilate to the customs of American life; for most, this meant the virtues of middle-class living: order, cleanliness, discipline, routine. "Americanization is not only English and Civics, but right living and right thinking," proclaimed the New York Council.[36] "Instilling habits of cleanliness promotes ideas of economy and exactness in the recipient, awakens dormant ambitions, and instills a feeling of self-respect," Kohut explained. "With a pure soul," she insisted, "must be a clean body."[37] In their own persons, NCJW women demonstrated the high standards they championed; in Chicago, Hannah Greenebaum Solomon cut a remarkable figure in white lace—long flowing dress, lace parasol, lace hat, and white gloves—as she went from dump to dump ordering the city to clean up its garbage.[38]

Kohut felt it was important that Council members follow the standards set by Christian Americans; religion meant not only "the chanting of prayers" but "the living of our faith in our contact with our neighbor." She insisted that "we must not be clannish and narrow-minded," proclaiming:

> Down with the wall that divides us from our Christian brother! High up with the standard of Judaism in the other camp. Act in every sense of the word as *American Jews.* . . . It is a glorious privilege to be a Jew, but it is also glorious to be an American. . . .[39]

Kohut warned Jews to be "refined, chaste, quiet in our manners and dress" and also to adopt the American vernacular: "No foreign tongue, no jargon! We are Israelites, but we are Americans as well."[40] Acknowledging her class-based attitudes, which Kohut had begun to do under the influence of Josephine Shaw Lowell, ultimately proved much easier than eliminating them.

Lower-class immigrants were quick to sense, and condemn, such superior airs. The *Jewish Daily Forward,* the widely read Yiddish Socialist paper, nastily wrote of the aristocratic pretensions of Council women, "with their bediamonded hands more to show their delicate alabaster fingers with well-manicured nails than really to save the unfortunates."[41] Anzia Yezierska's contempt for Jewish charity-givers appeared in many of her stories. Long after she left the ghetto she found it difficult to overcome her "burned-in acid prejudice against any organization that suggested the thought of philanthropy."[42]

The haughty attitudes of uptown Jews, and their insistence on quickly assimilating their East European brethren, sprang in good part from the fear that Gentile Americans might identify them with the new arrivals: "We, who are the cultured and refined constitute the minority," remarked one speaker at the 1893 Congress, "but we shall be judged by the majority, the Russian Jews, the children of the ghetto."[43] Julia Richman, the first female school superintendent in New York City, considered immigrant poverty and turmoil as "full of menace to the entire Jewish community. . . ."[44] Such attitudes engendered deep hostility in the Lower East Side community she served. Eventually residents petitioned to have her transferred, protesting that she had "revil[ed] and malign[ed] the inhabitants of the East Side" and had been "systematically engaged in degrading and lowering" them in the eyes of their children.[45] Denying that she was "entirely out of sympathy" with the community, as its residents charged, Richman defended herself as a "warm Jewish patriot" who simply wanted to "help make the children good people and good citizens." Privately, however, she complained to friends about the "utter inability of creating a civic conscience" in "these people." Publicly, like Kohut, she defended her philosophy of Americanization: "We are not Jews first and Americans afterward," she told Council women, "we are American Jews."[46]

Not all uptown Jewish women appeared unsympathetic to their downtown neighbors. Lillian Wald, another middle-class German Jew, made her Henry Street Settlement House a haven for immigrant culture. While Richman railed against unlicensed immigrant pushcart peddlers, Wald supported them and allowed them to organize at Henry Street. A leader in the campaign for protective legislation for women, Wald also helped establish the reform-minded National Women's Trade Union League and became a member of the state's Factory Investigating Commission, appointed to prevent industrial abuses like those that caused the horrific Triangle Fire of 1911, in which 146 women garment workers lost their lives. Like her good friend Jane Addams, director of the Hull House settlement in Chicago, Wald was one of a small number of Progressive reformers who staunchly opposed the movement to restrict immigration, on the ground that it reflected ethnic and racial prejudice (Kohut and NCJW members concurred). "From the very start" the immigrants became "her people," commented photojournalist Jacob Riis.[47] According to Josephine Goldmark, sister-in-law of Justice Louis Brandeis and a notable social reformer in her own right, Wald was "the great interpreter of one social class to another, of the newcomer and the alien to the native-born, of people of different racial backgrounds to one another, of the under-privileged to the over-privileged"; she had achieved, in fact, Anzia Yezierska's goal of serving as bridge-builder between classes.[48] Wald's enlightened attitude toward immigrant constituencies, like that of Jane Addams, appears in many ways to have been influenced by her participation in the women-centered community of the settlement house, where social reformers lived in daily contact with their neighbors.

By the 1910s, as more daughters of East European immigrants became Council members, a more accepting and open attitude toward lower-class Jews challenged the NCJW's class bias. Alice Mencken, a Sephardic Jew who traced her ancestors back to colonial America and boasted of her membership in the Daughters of the American Revolution, was another liberalizer within the Council. President of the Shearith Israel Sisterhood, Mencken established the Neighborhood House settlement in a Lower East Side tenement. With its Talmud Torah for local youth and a synagogue, the first in a neighborhood settlement, as well as a variety of clubs and Americanizing classes, the Shearith Israel Sisterhood settlement also initiated innovative services for troubled immigrant girls. Its Probation Committee, in cooperation with the New York Council's Delinquency Committee, which Mencken chaired, worked with the city magistrate and the Women's Night Court to assist the many "wayward" Jewish girls, who were often charged with prostitution. Mencken became a leading national figure in probation, parole, and remedial services for delinquent girls, arguing that the cause of delinquency lay more in poverty and lack of opportunity than in immoral character. Although Mencken rejected the opportunity to become president of the New York Council, preferring to lead the Shearith Israel Sisterhood, she was influential in developing the chapter's social consciousness. Mencken also headed the Society of Political Study, which trained women for political office.[49]

Under the influence of these and like-minded women, the Council gradually began to appreciate immigrant "gifts," and to acknowledge the causes of poverty and family disruption that lay beyond their control. Another blow to the doctrine of Americanization came with the realization that for a growing number of immigrants, assimilation had become a route to Christian conversion. While she preached interfaith tolerance, Rebekah Kohut was shocked by the attempt of some of her closest Gentile friends, including philanthropist Grace Dodge, to convert ghetto Jews to Christianity. Sadie American became bitter over the fact that Gentile friends remained silent after the slaughter of thousands of Jews during the 1903 Kishinev pogrom. While Council leaders worked closely with Christian women in reform activities, their commitment to the NCJW reflected their belief that ultimately, Jewish women's interests were distinct from those of non-Jewish women. The prejudice of Christian Americans awakened many to the bonds they shared with Jewish immigrants.

Emancipation into Religion   For Rebekah Kohut, the recognition of a common Jewish womanhood meant that the Council's Americanization activities should be joined by programs of religious education that highlighted Jewish tradition and values. In order to educate their clients, however, Council women first had to educate themselves. Under Kohut's guidance, study groups were established in the Council's early years to teach Jewish history and examine the situation and achievements of Jewish women. These study circles functioned as a "middle-class women's yeshiva," even a substitute for entering the rabbinate.[50]

However, within twenty years, the Council had almost entirely abandoned its focus on religious education. Caught in the crossfire between Reform and Orthodox Judaism, its promise to represent all shades of Jewish opinion meant that the most controversial, and often the most significant, religious topics were avoided. When they were not—for example, when the issue of observing the so-called Sunday Sabbath bitterly divided delegates—the organization compromised its claim to represent a unified Jewish womanhood.

By the 1920s, the identity of the NCJW as a religious body had declined to such an extent that the national board was forced to remind members of its policy that "no woman may hold office nationally or officially represent the National Council of Jewish Women who has any Non-Jewish church affiliation." Dietary customs reflected religious declension: at its triennial conference in New Orleans in 1935, the Council served "baked ham aux légumes or Swiss and bacon" for Sabbath dinner.[51]

The establishment of national organizations of temple sisterhoods meant that Jewish women could find alternative gender-specific arenas in which to express common religious bonds.[52] Ironically, national sisterhood organizations were created in part because of the success of NCJW's social philanthropy, which increasingly attracted Jewish women to secular organizations. Alarmed at the decline of religious sentiment among Jewish women—including increasingly frequent open conversions to Christianity and participation in Christian Science—Mathilde Schechter established the Jewish Women's League of the United Synagogue, the Conservative Women's sisterhood, in 1918, hoping to "religionize ourselves . . . and to rebuild our Jewish homes."[53] The Reform movement's organization, the National Federation of Temple Sisterhoods, created five years earlier, was headed by Carrie Obendorfer Simon, a long-time NCJW member and officer of its Cincinnati section. Simon hoped to provide a place of "equal *privilege, prayer, activity* and *responsibility*" for Jewish women within the synagogue; in 1928, her organization ended fifteen years of affiliation with the NCJW, asserting that its religious goals were fundamentally different from the NCJW's secular purposes.[54] The Women's Branch of the Union of Orthodox Congregations of America was established in 1924.

Even as she came to play an increasingly prominent role in nonsectarian state and national social welfare organizations, Rebekah Kohut never relinquished her interest in Jewish women's organizations, nor her belief that the basis for a revitalized, unified Jewish American womanhood lay in religious tradition. With men attending synagogue in declining numbers, she acknowledged that women played an essential role in maintaining the community's religious life: "We might say she is the synagogue," Kohut observed.[55] In spite of her own dedication to immigrant welfare, she agreed with the sisterhood federations that "Social Service . . . can not be a substitute for religion." She would have agreed with them, too, that any movement for Jewish women's rights should lead to women's emancipation "not from, but into, Religion," into Judaism and the synagogue.[56]

Although less observant than Kohut, Hannah Greenebaum Solomon was another "uptown" leader who considered Judaism an important component of all her activities. When her nomination as first president of the NCJW was challenged by Orthodox women who considered her unqualified because she did not observe the Sabbath, Solomon thrilled the Reform women by proudly proclaiming, "I consecrate every day"; she was elected easily. According to her granddaughter, in fact, Solomon did live "every hour of every day as a Jewish woman," observing home rituals and holidays, and she was a serious student of Jewish history.[57]

It was the more observant Kohut who consistently opposed the patriarchalism of Jewish religious life, arguing that women needed to wield more authority in all aspects of religion. To counter the tradition that Jewish women's place was solely inside the home, she pointed out examples of Jewish women's public religious participation throughout Jewish history— Miriam, who led her people from bondage to freedom; Deborah, who typified the ideal of the righteous judge; and the many nameless women who enabled Jews to survive the persecutions of the Inquisition and their dispersion to foreign lands. Despite the rigid segregation of the sexes in prayer by the Middle Ages, Kohut maintained that Jewish women had their own public worship and led prayer meetings. Numerous heads of congregations were female and many were revered as learned women, thoroughly conversant with the Talmud and rabbinical literature and influential in advising disciples, including men.[58]

Like feminists of the later twentieth century, Kohut skillfully used history to bolster her unconventional ideas about religious change. She was ahead of her time, standing out from Council colleagues who did not support the empowerment of Jewish women in either the religious or secular realm. The Council opposed the ordination of women as rabbis, for example, just as it refused as a body to endorse suffrage.

For Kohut, Jewish women needed to guarantee full participation in both the life of their country and their religion. "The denial of woman's ability to serve the synagogue in every part of its work is cruel and dangerous," she argued, insisting that they should serve on boards of trustees, as presidents of congregations, and as "spiritual leaders" in the pulpit. Only as a woman's "inner consciousness of depth" was joined to "outward manifestations of power" could she employ the wide range of her competencies to best serve the House of Israel, and in so doing, foster the faith and identity that would allow Jews to play their part in the religious pluralism that Kohut believed was central to American democratic ideals.[59] Only in so doing would they measure up to the achievements of their Christian sisters.

Kohut's greatest organizational triumph came in May 1923 when, under her aegis, the NCJW convened the first World Council of Jewish Women in Vienna, with over two hundred delegates from seventy countries. This council then organized the permanent International Council of Jewish Women, with affiliations of more than a million Jewish women, and elected Kohut its first president. Kohut had played a leading role in establishing contacts between American and European Jewish women after World War I. Angry that the male executives of the Jewish Welfare Board and other Jewish communal agencies would not allow the Council to equip a unit of women workers to be sent to Europe during the war, Kohut had established an NCJW Committee on Reconstruction in 1920. The committee sent several units of American Jewish women to aid Jews in cities throughout Europe, and established close ties between American Jewish women leaders and European Jewish feminists. As a result, Council affiliates were established in Rotterdam, The Hague, Amsterdam, Antwerp, Riga, and other cities.

With the establishment of the International Council of Jewish Women, Kohut found a worldwide forum for her belief that women would remain susceptible to "victimization" in all spheres of Jewish life unless Judaism viewed Jewish women as equal to Jewish men. At the same time that it championed such secular feminist causes as suffrage and the campaign against forced prostitution, the International Council incorporated religious as well as social reform among its goals. It was this dual agenda, promoted by the combined strength of Jewish women all over the world, that Kohut thought would lead to Jewish women's exercise of their rightful power.[60]

Kohut had good reason to celebrate Jewish women's accomplishments. In her own life, she had triumphed over forces that would have denied her the active public role she cherished. Drawing upon a variety of influences—her mother's piety and determination, her father's support of women's rights, the encouragement of Christian mentors, and the example of biblical heroines— as well as the lessons she learned from leading Jewish women's organizations, she constructed a model of committed Jewish womanhood that drew no distinction between activism and piety. Lacking the equivalent will, role models, or opportunities, other Jewish women of her class found it difficult to equal Kohut's achievements. Nevertheless, women like Hannah Greenebaum Solomon, Julia Richman, Alice Mencken, and Belle Moskowitz were models for a new sort of Jewish feminism that blended secular reform with Jewish sorority. Another of these pioneers was Maud Nathan, a New York society matron who became a leading advocate for working women and, later, for women's suffrage. Maud's sister, Annie Nathan Meyer, would choose the opposite route, renouncing both Judaism and feminism while championing her own idiosyncratic brand of reform.

The Heart of Judaism   Just as it influenced her good friend Rebekah Kohut, Jewish religious tradition shaped the career of Maud Nathan. But while Kohut worked toward empowering Jewish women within Judaism, Nathan deliberately left what she considered to be the "narrow communal circle" of Jewish life to enter broader, nonsectarian venues of philanthropy, communal service, and feminism. She came to these arenas as a confident, proudly identified Jewish woman with a coherent set of spiritual values that she applied, explicitly, to her public activism. For Nathan, the "heart of Judaism"—the title of one of her most influential addresses—lay in its sense of "righteousness and justice, mercy and lovingkindness," a spiritual ethic that mandated the improvement of the conditions of daily life.[61]

Maud Nathan was born in New York City in 1862, the daughter of Sephardic Jews whose ancestors came to New York from England in the eighteenth century. Maud and her sister Annie were immensely proud of their heritage, considering the Sephardim "the nearest approach to royalty in the United States," as Annie put it in her autobiography.[62] Nathan began her own with an account of the Sephardim who settled America in the seventeenth century, seeking religious freedom; she pointedly emphasized that their descendants, like those of the Pilgrims, were entitled to consider themselves "one hundred per cent Americans."[63] Nathan voiced a special admiration for her great-grandfather, Gershom Mendes Seixas, a rabbi and ardent patriot who protested against taxation without representation and closed his synagogue in New York rather than fly the British flag; he became a trustee of King's College (later Columbia) and a long-term member of its board of trustees. Later in life, acknowledging their descent from this revolutionary hero, Maud and Annie applied to join the elite Daughters of the American Revolution—which counted few Jews among its members—and were accepted. Among their own contemporaries in this illustrious family were their cousins Emma, Sarah, and Josephine Lazarus and Benjamin Nathan Cardozo, who served as chief justice of the New York State Court of Appeals and became the second Jewish justice of the United States Supreme Court.

Nathan grew up in comfort in a brownstone on West 36th Street, just off Fifth Avenue in a "socially correct" neighborhood; when the family moved to a less prestigious address west of Eighth Avenue a few years later, Nathan's private-school classmates "tilted their noses." These attitudes, further encouraged by lessons at the appropriate dancing, music, and etiquette schools, imbued Nathan at an early age with the "spirit of New York's social directory"; she would retain her childhood sense of privilege throughout her life.[64]

Yet her childhood was far from idyllic. After her father's business failed, the family moved to Green Bay, Wisconsin, where Robert Nathan, formerly a member of the New York Stock Exchange, became a railroad general passenger agent. Estranged from New York society and upset by her husband's financial machinations and a series of affairs he had conducted with her close friends, Maud's mother, Annie Nathan, became increasingly anxious and was narrowly prevented from taking her own life, once with a pistol and on another occasion with an overdose of drugs. Though she tried to establish a new home in Green Bay (Robert left after a year), she died before four years had passed, and the Nathan children returned to New York.

Yet Annie Nathan, according to Maud an "ardent Jewess," had instilled a strong sense of Orthodox Judaism in her daughter. Though Maud went to synagogue, the core of the family's religion was its home-based celebration of the Sabbath and holidays like Passover, and its strict observation of *kashruth*. Nathan was sent to Sunday School with her older brother, where she learned to read Hebrew and studied Jewish history and tradition. At the time, she resented the observances that kept her from joining her friends—the strict dietary laws, the prohibition against riding or attending social functions on the Sabbath and from joining friends for Easter and Christmas celebrations. Later, she appreciated that "all this training in Jewish ritual, Jewish principles, and Jewish traditions had formed the background of my spiritual life," providing her with a sense of "group consciousness" and a "distinctive religious background" that became the basis of her lifelong code of ethics.[65]

The religious lesson Nathan learned from her mother included tolerance for the faith of others: out of respect for their New York neighbors, the young Nathans were forbidden to practice piano or play outdoors on Sundays. In Green Bay, where they were the only Jewish family, Annie Nathan encouraged the children to attend occasional Presbyterian services to broaden their interfaith understanding. They returned from Wisconsin less provincial in outlook than when they had arrived because of the opportunity they had been given to mix with others. This lesson, too, stayed with Nathan in later years.

Nathan also had the opportunity to attend a coeducational public high school. Stimulated by the presence of boys, she enjoyed debating with them and winning, vindicating her nascent belief in the "equality and perhaps even the superiority of our sex!" It was a thrill to learn the fundamentals of the U.S. Constitution, never taught in eastern young ladies' schools, since girls "would never become citizens."[66] In provincial Wisconsin, on the other hand, women already had the vote.

But although Nathan had graduated as her high school salutatorian, her education had come to an end. Her mother had refused to let her go to college, contending that a daughter needed "the constant care and devotion of her mother," even a sickly one.[67] Unlike Rebekah Kohut, whose father supported her educational ambitions, Nathan was made to follow the conventional path of a well-bred Jewish daughter. Permitted to assume only domestic duties, she took charge of the pantry, learned to cook and sew, and went twice a week to a convent to learn to embroider. Within a few years, she wed her first cousin, Frederick Nathan, a handsome, prosperous broker nearly twenty years her senior. Married in an Orthodox ceremony at the Shearith Israel Synagogue, she was pleased that her husband had a strong loyalty to his faith. In their thirty years of marriage, they remained observant, frequently traveling to Europe and visiting local synagogues, especially Sephardic ones.

At the beginning of her marriage, in the early 1880s, Maud Nathan lived the life of a typical society woman. In the mornings, after completing her housekeeping chores, she practiced her singing and did embroidery; afternoons were devoted to shopping and visiting, except for Wednesdays, when she was "at home." Evenings were filled with "soirée musicales"; tall and handsome and possessing a fine mezzo voice, Nathan loved to perform, and invitations to her musical evenings were highly prized.

Although she enjoyed her social duties, Nathan was restless and bored. Seeking to be more useful, she became a member of the board of directors of Mt. Sinai Hospital, chairman of the kindergarten subcommittee at the Hebrew Free School Association, and first president of the sisterhood at Shearith Israel Synagogue. Yet these part-time charitable endeavors, all of them associated with Jewish agencies, did not satisfy her longing for a more fulfilling existence.

A turning point came after Nathan heard social reformer Josephine Shaw Lowell talk one evening about the hardships of women prisoners; Lowell had been instrumental in motivating Kohut as well. Tremendously moved by her account, Nathan determined to assist in resolving the problem; soon she came under the older woman's wing, and in 1890 helped her establish the New York Consumers' League, an organization that hoped to use the organized power of consumers to improve the wages and working conditions of women in industry. When Lowell stepped down from the presidency of the society in 1896, Nathan assumed it. Two years earlier, Lowell had formed the Women's Municipal League with the goal of fighting civic corruption; she became its first president and Maud Nathan its vice-president.[68]

This political activity signified the opening of Nathan's own prison doors. "Women had been kept behind bars, their hands manacled, their feet tied by the ball and chain of conventionality." Now, even though they lacked political status, they were at least "summoned to go out in the open and do our share of human uplift work."[69] Nathan believed that the "latent feminism" she had felt as a child was at last coming into its own; she recalled her rebellion at the gift of her father's "old tarnished cup when my brother had been presented with a bright, shiny new one, the spirit which had resented the fact that my brother was given more pin money than I, because he was a boy, the spirit that failed to understand why girls should wait for boys to invite them to dance. . . ." These experiences became the "germ" of the "ardent feminism" that now enveloped her life.[70]

In contrast to Rebekah Kohut's husband, Frederick Nathan welcomed his wife's increasing involvement in activities outside the home. One reason, perhaps, was that such involvement helped stem the grief that they felt at the loss of their only daughter, Annette, who had died in 1895 at the age of nine. In any event, Frederick Nathan became a strong supporter of his wife's reform activities and himself played a role in working for women's suffrage. A leader of the Men's League for Equal Suffrage, he founded the International Men's Suffrage League as well. Whenever Nathan spoke on the suffrage trail, he accompanied her, usually leading the applause and cheering. "My comrade, my pal, my knight," Nathan called her husband, "[he] never failed me."[71] Frederick Nathan, however, was the only man in Maud's family to support women's suffrage. Her two brothers (and her sister Annie) opposed it, as did her cousin Judge Cardozo (who ultimately voted for the law guaranteeing women the vote, but continued to have "sore doubts").[72]

Nathan had come to suffrage through her work in the Consumers' League; lobbying for better protective legislation for working women, she saw that lawmakers ignored women's point of view because they had no political status. With many other close friends also working for suffrage—particularly Harriet Stanton Blatch, daughter of the founder of the women's right's movement, Elizabeth Cady Stanton—this "society woman in politics" became increasingly active, serving as first vice president of New York's Equal Suffrage League. Within a short time she had become one of the movement's boldest and most original tacticians. Boasting that she left "no stone unturned to get our propaganda over," she invented open-air automobile campaigns, "24-hour" simultaneous speeches from cars stationed at various locations throughout the city, "silent" speeches from motorized placards, suffrage literature wrapped around coins and thrown into crowds. "There is little use in arguing against that kind of genius," one editorial commented.[73] Because suffragists were associated with aggressive, "masculine" women—short-haired, short-skirted, and supposedly outfitted in bloomers—Nathan dressed in her finest gowns when she spoke at mass meetings or performed in the suffrage skits and burlesques in which she frequently participated.[74] After one of Nathan's speeches, President Woodrow Wilson commented to a friend that "when I hear a woman talk so well . . . it almost makes me believe in woman suffrage." Nathan assumed the credit when the president converted to the suffrage cause.[75]

While Jewish immigrant women supported suffrage in greater proportions than either native-born women or those from other ethnic communities, few women of Nathan's class showed the spirited devotion to the cause that she did. This led observers to believe, incorrectly, that Jewish women as a whole were uninvolved in suffrage.[76] Nathan's speeches emphasized that women's suffrage was vital to the American democratic tradition and, to Jewish audiences, that Jews had a special interest in universal suffrage. Extending the franchise was essential because women's sphere, the home, had already become part of the modern political world, and the woman's traditional functions—caring for the young, the feeble, the aged—meant involvement in public arenas like schools, hospitals, parks, and playgrounds and departments of health, sanitation, and police. Although Nathan did not deny the basic principle of the separation of spheres fundamental to suffrage opponents, she shrewdly deployed this civic housekeeping argument in favor of more female influence in public life. At the same time, she insisted that equality of representation and function did not imply that men and women were identical. To the contrary, she held, "men and women think differently. Men think in terms of dollars and cents while women think along the lines of conservation of human life. Just as a party of men is called a stag party so is a nation with men serving alone stag-nation."[77]

Nathan's rationale addressed issues of particular concern to the Jewish elite, most of which continued to adhere to the doctrine of separate spheres. "There is no doubt in my mind in regard to the beneficial influence of equal suffrage upon family life," she wrote in an article in the *American Jewish Chronicle.* "Perhaps because Jewish people have clung more tenaciously to Oriental customs, it may seem more difficult for them to adjust themselves to the new conditions," she admitted. But she prophesied they would continue to show their adaptability to the American environment.[78]

In a 1917 letter to New York rabbis, Nathan urged a stand on suffrage at least as courageous as that of the state's Christian ministers. Linking the ideal of suffrage to the Jewish woman of valor, she argued that Jews ought to welcome suffrage because "womanhood has occupied a unique place in Jewish life." And since Jews had such a long history of unjust political discrimination, "no one ought to be more sympathetic to the ideal of enfranchisement than Jews."[79]

Nathan had conveyed much the same message in a speech to an enthusiastic audience of over four thousand Jews at the Arch Street Theater in Philadelphia in November 1915. "Judaism has always been the keynote of liberty," she remarked on that occasion, "and I cannot conceive of one [Jewish] man voting against the amendment. . . ." Persecuted more than any other race, Jews had come to America to realize the benefits of freedom and the opportunities for self-expression; now was the time to be true to themselves by providing these same opportunities to women.[80]

Maud Nathan's vigorous support of women's suffrage, as well as her life-long interest in promoting the welfare of working women, was deeply rooted in a prophetic Judaism that highlighted the individual's obligations to the social good, to communal responsibility and justice. For Nathan, righteousness—the wellspring of all Judaic inspiration—meant the application of spiritual ideals to "social growth" as well as private morality. As parents needed to inculcate principles of right and honor in their children, so did employers, for example, need to respect employees: this meant adequate wages and hours, safe and sanitary conditions, appropriate mechanisms for grievance. "We must make our business ethics . . . correspond with Bible ethics,"

Nathan liked to say; she often quoted biblical texts to show their applicability to contemporary society.[81]

For Nathan, "mere morals" or a "code of ethics" unaccompanied by religious principles was an insufficient guide for human conduct.[82] True religion did not mainly mean attending synagogue, but included "the larger life . . . the entire character"; philanthropy, especially, was "the living out of one's religion." Bound together in a "common cause," a "bookless religion" that went even beyond the Bible, Jewish women could measure their religiosity only by assessing the quality and quantity of righteousness they brought to daily life.[83]

Confident in her own Judaism, Maud Nathan found little disjunction between her feminist and reform objectives and her Jewish concerns. "Notwithstanding my ever-widening interests," she wrote in her autobiography, "I never discarded my Jewish affiliations." When the New York Council of Jewish Women sought a new president, Nathan's name had been brought forward. Although she refused the post, she felt that the nomination recognized that she stood for "Jewish interests, Jewish thought, Jewish feeling" quite as much as "a more universal outlook." Like her ancestors, whom she always cited as "100 percent Americans," she recognized her own urge "to be part of the fabric—not merely a tiny thread weaving its way along the edge of the great pattern." Nathan believed that by choosing to work outside the circle of Jewish philanthropy, while still identifying as a Jew and representing Jewish interests, her usefulness "increased tenfold."[84]

Although Nathan boasted of her ability to work with people of all races and creeds "without any dividing sense of difference coming between us," the evidence of anti-Semitism she cites in her memoir challenges her belief in interfaith harmony. Once, for example, at a meeting of a patriotic society, Nathan rose to her feet to protest a chairman's report that was laced with anti-Semitism. "I . . . made an impassioned plea for fairness, for the kind of patriotism which is the spirit of our American Constitution; freedom of conscience, liberty to follow one's religion. . . ." The speech caused a sensation, forcing the chairman to resign.[85]

In fact, Nathan had so frequently to raise her voice against intolerance that "a spirit of rebellion against injustice" soon became characteristic. "I so often found myself in the minority," she explained. "It seemed cowardly to me not to protest whenever I considered an act of injustice was being done to me or to others. Many a time when I was considered fearless, my actions were due rather to a sense of fear—fear lest I be weak and cowardly; fear lest I be weighed and found wanting."[86]

The lesson Nathan learned from these experiences put her in the company of more radical Jewish women like Emma Goldman and Rose Pastor Stokes. As Nathan remarked: "One individual, handicapped by sex and by having been born into a minority group . . . has been able to make her protests count, because she persisted. She refused sheep-like to follow the majority."[87]

Yet there was an important difference between these rebels and Nathan and Kohut, who like her friend, battled anti-Semitism and fought for women's rights within Judaism. Not only were more radical activists much less identified as Jews than Kohut and Nathan; they also faced them across a great chasm of class.

Nathan offers an anecdote about herself and Rose Pastor Stokes, the Jewish-born socialist and eventual Communist Party leader, when both shared a platform in a New York church at a meeting on behalf of working girls. After Nathan spoke, Stokes

> launched forth in denunciation of "society women" who wore expensive jewelry, while girls were working for "starvation wages." During her remarks, she turned and I fancied her eyes had a special glare as they fixed themselves on my amethyst watch chain. I grew very self-conscious and was sure that every woman in the church was mentally appraising that amethyst chain.

Requesting permission to respond, Nathan pointedly referred to the fact that Stokes (who had married out of her class when she became the wife of millionaire James Graham Phelps Stokes) was wearing "a large exquisite handsome lace collar, fastened by a diamond pin," and noted that while jewelry makers received relatively high wages, lacemakers were both poorly paid and apt to ruin their eyesight and health. According to Nathan, her argument won the day, for the audience burst into loud applause.[88]

Nathan had tellingly questioned Stokes's insistence that, as the title of her autobiography proclaims, she "belong[ed] to the working class."[89] Yet Stokes had made an equally incisive point by suggesting that perhaps upper-class society matrons like Nathan were not the best spokespersons for poor working girls. Maud Nathan's beliefs, like those of Kohut if perhaps more subtly so, were marked by her entitlements. While she protested racial and religious discrimination, it was not on behalf of less cultivated Jewish women, however needy or deserving of material aid, but "to plead for tolerance, to protest against the bigotry, the prejudice, the injustice of socially ostracizing Jewish people of culture and refinement."[90] At the core of Nathan's proud American Jewish womanhood, no matter how closely she melded the concerns of gender, ethnicity, and nationality, she could not totally escape the "social ghetto," as she described it, of her own "cultured Jewish class."[91]

Even such empathic reformers as Lillian Wald had been unable to completely bridge the distance between themselves and the new immigrants. In Wald's case, the differences were in large part religious ones, demonstrating that the barriers of class included those of heritage as well. For Wald, it was not so much education, culture, and manners that set her East Side neighbors apart; it was their Orthodox religious customs, which she admired yet considered part of a vanishing, nonessential past.

In certain instances, the ties of status and purpose that "uptown" Jewish women shared with privileged Gentile feminists may have counted for more than those they shared with the immigrants. As Ellen Henrotin, president of the General Federation of Women's Clubs, told the first gathering of Jewish women at the Parliament of Religions, what mattered most was not one's religion but the answer to the question, "Are you clubable?"[92]

By the new century, many second-generation Jewish-American women were indeed clubable, and eminently so. So were their Sephardic sisters, who had even more permanent roots in America. These privileged women often combined membership in a Jewish sororal organization—a temple sisterhood, female Hebrew benevolent society, or local Council of Jewish Women's group—with participation in nonsectarian women's civic groups or social reform agencies. Jennie Purvin, well-known as the "Jewish Jane Addams," was a leader in the Chicago Council of Jewish Women, the Chicago Woman's Aid (an earlier Jewish women's charitable group), and at least a half dozen other nonsectarian women's clubs. NCJW founder Hannah Solomon, who with her sister was the first Jewish member of the powerful Chicago Woman's Club, always credited that organization with stimulating the formation of the Council by asking her to represent Jewish women at the 1893 Chicago World's Fair.

Most of these women were proudly conscious of their acceptance in the world of non-Jewish female philanthropy, and often boasted that they joined these groups not to hide their ethnic identity but to augment it. Solomon, Kohut, American, and Nathan were pleased at their frequent invitations to speak to non-Jewish women's groups about Judaism or Jewish interests, and they repeatedly cited their friendships with leading Christian feminists (for example, that of Solomon with Jane Addams, American and Kohut with Susan B. Anthony, and Nathan with Harriet Stanton Blatch).

Thus, while espousing Jewish religious values and claiming their identity as Jewish females, these women were highly cognizant and appreciative of their ability to live and work in the non-Jewish female and feminist world. Yet if Jewish women were among friends in the non-Jewish world, they were not always among equals. As Nathan came painfully to learn, respect for Jewish culture and religion did not come automatically, and anti-Semitism was a recurring problem, even among liberals. While they participated relatively easily in the pluralistic world of early twentieth-century feminism, Jewish women were still considered "other."

With fascism on the rise in Europe and the evidence of anti-Semitism increasing in her own country, Nathan remained vigilant to its dangers. Yet, like Kohut, she was comfortable in her ability to be part of the multiple worlds of American pluralism and international feminism, finding the broad fabric of her spiritual endeavors, as we have seen, much richer than the narrow borders of sectarianism. Like their associations, these women's identities were multiple, and they found little disjunction in representing themselves as Jewish women, as American women, and as feminists. Their feminism, however, was predicated either on contingencies—great wealth, the death of a husband or child, or unusually supportive family members—or on conscious choices—not to marry, in the case of Sadie American, Wald, and Richman—uncommon among others of their background.

Achieving such a richly textured Jewish-centered feminism was therefore unlikely in their own time. Even for Kohut, the daughter, mother, and sister of rabbis, it did not come without a painful struggle to overcome the powerful attraction of Christian models; that assimilation tempted a woman of such a staunchly Jewish background testifies to the compelling force of the desire of Jews, members of the more settled middle class as well as new immigrants, to acculturate.

Once Kohut had found her place as a committed Jew and an activist concerned with women's rights, however, she discovered that the Jewish tradition was flexible enough to withstand the challenges of activists like herself. Even less Jewish-affiliated social reformers often came to recognize the strength of the tradition because of shocking encounters with Christian anti-Semitism at home (sometimes from feminists). Such events reminded traditionalists like Nathan and Kohut that the bonds of interfaith cooperation were often more tenuous than they realized.

The great accomplishment of "uptown" Jewish women was to carve out a space for Jewish womanhood outside the traditional arena of Jewish family life. Considering the tenacity of the "woman of valor" ideal, this feat was impressive, and it was achieved, very often, in the face of outspoken hostility to changes in Jewish women's sphere. According to critics, many of them rabbis, Jewish women's abandonment of the home was a primary reason for the decline of the Jewish home itself and the growing tide of assimilation.[93] Jewish women activists denied the charge, maintaining their allegiance to the *eyshet hayil* ideal; many refrained from acknowledging the fact that they had indeed make a radical break with tradition.

Leaders like Rebekah Kohut, Hannah Solomon, and Maud Nathan who maintained both a Jewish spiritual mission and membership in a broader, universalistic program of American reform did so by overlooking the tensions between the two. Ultimately, such a stance was possible because of these women's abiding faith in America; despite occasional setbacks, they continued, like Antin and Yezierska, to affirm the promise of pluralism and the power of democratic liberalism. It was left for more radical Jewish women to expose the flaws at the heart of their optimistic vision and, in challenging America's possibilities, offer an alternative version of Jewish American womanhood.

Withholding Sisterhood: Annie Nathan Meyer   Annie Nathan Meyer, founder of Barnard College and prolific playwright, novelist, and essayist, identified with few of the reform causes that her sister Maud Nathan aggressively championed. Although they were brought up in the same home—relatives say precisely *because* they were siblings—they took opposite sides on most social issues, and particularly on the question of women's suffrage. Where Maud vigorously denounced anti-Semitism, her younger sister was less vigilant, at times sympathizing with selective admissions policies that screened out what she called the "least desirable type of Jewess" from Barnard and in other respects internalizing anti-Semitism.[94]

In her early years Annie seemed destined even more than Maud (who was older by five years) to make her mark as a feminist. In 1885, when she was eighteen, she and a group of friends organized the Seven Wise Women, a club modelled after Margaret Fuller's conversations, to study the work of women writers.[95] That same year, Meyer studied secretly for the examination for admission to the Collegiate Course for Women at Columbia. When she finally found the courage to tell her father of her intentions, he drew her to him, tremendously concerned, and announced, "You will never be married. . . . Men hate intelligent wives." Meyer declared her willingness to forgo all chances of winning a husband, because a college education seemed "even more delectable."[96] Meyer passed her qualifying examinations even though she refused to answer questions drawing on lessons that excluded women.

In 1887, when she was twenty, Annie married Dr. Alfred Meyer, a German Jewish tuberculosis specialist fifteen years her senior, and quit the Collegiate Course. She had accepted Meyer's proposal only on the condition that he would support her writing; for the duration of the marriage, which lasted more than fifty years and attracted an admiring portrait in *The New Yorker* in 1943, she would withdraw every morning to the privacy of her study to write; in the early years, a nurse attended to her young daughter, Margaret, so that Meyer could have her solitude. A prolific if not frequently published author, she produced three novels, an autobiography, several books of nonfiction, articles and short stories, and over twenty-six plays.

Though Meyer had left the Collegiate Course, she was determined to establish a separate women's college affiliated with Columbia. With the help of Melvil Dewey and writer Mary Mapes Dodge, she wrote a petition to the trustees of Columbia, urging the creation of a female college with the highest academic standards and committing herself (though she was barely twenty-one) to find independent funding for it. Fifty prominent New Yorkers signed the document; also persuasive was an article Meyer wrote for *The Nation* in 1888.[97] Meyer's husband gave the first large donation to the school, which Annie suggested be named after the late Frederick A.P. Barnard, the tenth president of Columbia University and an advocate of coeducation. In 1889, after Meyer had signed the lease for the first building (no one else had the faith to do so), the college opened its doors. Except for one gift, she raised all its operating expenses for the first few years.[98]

Although Meyer served as an active trustee of Barnard for fifty years, raising considerable sums for the college, Barnard would recognize her only as one member of the group that established the college, not as its founder; historians suggest that Jewishness was an "undesired trait" for a Barnard "founder."[99] Meyer bitterly resented the failure to acknowledge her primary role; she considered it "cruel and utterly lacking in realism" to call her "only one of a group" that founded the college.[100] Yet Meyer never addressed the role played by the "Jewish question" in this slight to her reputation. Her views on Jewish students were ambiguous: although she wanted to protect Jewish women at the school, she did not contest the view of Barnard's Dean Virginia Gildersleeve that despite their high academic achievements, "the intense ambition of the Jews for education has brought to college girls from a lower social level than that of most of the nonJewish students," and she agreed that the "Jewish problem" could be solved by screening out those with unbecoming behavior. Meyer intervened only reluctantly in admissions decisions in which so-called prejudice regarding Jewish women was involved, but she "never discovered one."[101] She helped promote the admission of black students, however, and became a mentor to Zora Neale Hurston, who was admitted to Barnard without funds, finding support for Hurston and taking an early interest in her writing talent.

Despite her involvement in women's education, Meyer considered herself primarily a writer. In 1891, she edited *Woman's Work in America,* a volume that surveyed the advancements of women in the professions, journalism, the arts, and politics. Two years later, she published a well-regarded novel, *Helen Brent, M.D.,* the story of a young physician who refuses to marry her fiancé, a prominent lawyer, because he insists that she give up her work; in the end, he recognizes his error and sanctions her career.

By the early 1900s, however, Meyer began to take a more conservative position on women's issues, especially suffrage. Her 1904 article "Woman's Assumption of Sex Superiority" took feminist reformers to task for neglecting their families; similar critiques appear in many of her works, including the 1911 play *The Dominant Sex,* in which the remorseful heroine tells her husband that "we women should be mastered, we want to be mastered—we adore our masters."[102]

Nonetheless, the vehemence with which Meyer came to denounce suffrage surprised everyone, especially her sister Maud:

> My sister, Annie Nathan Meyer, who had been instrumental in founding Barnard College, for the higher education of women, who had gone to Denver, Colorado, to attend a convention of the Association for the Advancement of Women, who had addressed the Parliament of Religions in Chicago, who was one of the first women in New York to ride a bicycle—at a time when it was considered most unwomanly to make herself so conspicuous—who, in brief, stood for everything that

claimed to be progressive, took her stand on the opposite side and joined the group of anti-suffragists![103]

Relatives insist that the apparent shift in Meyer's views was taken to spite Maud, who had become a leader of the suffrage campaign. Meyer's autobiography mentions a "jealousy" that grew "all the more bitter" after their mother died (when she was eleven and Maud sixteen) "because I knew I was Mama's favorite . . . so much nearer her in looks and in temperament." Meyer confesses that Maud "never meant near so much to me" as did her brothers.[104] In time, the sisters' quarrel over suffrage became public, with each responding to the other's position in letters to the editors of such periodicals as *The New York Times* and *The New Republic.*[105]

Whether or not Meyer underwent an intellectual and political metamorphosis primarily in response to Maud's increasing prominence remains unclear, however, for she seems to have been genuinely ambivalent about the issue of female ambition. The gist of her opposition to the vote for women was that "new duties, new careers," and especially the obligations of citizenship, would be a "disintegrating influence" on family life. Women ought to "put more thought in their husbands' soup," she complained, "and less into their careers!" Men and women were different, and the attempt to "ape" men's sphere—to describe this effort, she coined the word "spreadhenism," a counterpart of the masculine "spreadeagleism"—only revealed the depth of women's inferiority complex. Spreadhenism became a slogan for antisuffragists in their campaign to deny women's alleged moral superiority and hence their claim to the vote. As Meyer explained, she expected higher things of women "than to smoke and drink as men, to indulge their crimes." Rather, they needed to improve the lax standards, self-indulgence, and deterioration in morals that characterized their own sphere.[106]

For Meyer, no political rights were as meaningful as "the right to bear children in peace and comfort" and "the right to look after them without having to go and earn their bread and butter."[107] She excoriated suffragists for their view that wifehood and motherhood were merely "parasitic" domestic services since they did not bring women wages. By means of such views, the feminist (whom Meyer described as "the mutilator, the screaming protestor, the wilful destroyer") spread her "cult of discontent."[108] Misguided by "sex jealousy" and "sex hatred," feminists did not understand that women were "not nearly as good or men nearly as bad" as they claimed.[109] "Sex should not be confused with class," she declared, "there are no interests which concerned women that men were equally concerned in."[110]

Meyer's position on suffrage reflected an elitism rooted in difference and privilege. She sometimes made the distinction that she was not so much against the individual woman's demand for the right to vote, which she saw as an "obligation and an opportunity," as she was against the idea of votes for the majority. While she had admiration for unusual or exceptional women—those who rose to the top of their business or profession—at the voting booth it was "majorities only that count." If women voted "in bulk," they would "double the ignorant vote" and counteract the good that could be done by individual women. As Meyer once explained, she was "mathematically" rather than "sentimentally" against suffrage.[111] Nevertheless, she testified against suffrage for women even in school board elections.[112] So prominent was Meyer in her opposition to suffrage that some considered her "vice president" of the U.S. antisuffragists.[113]

Her argument also revealed a fundamentally conservative, laissez-faire approach to social problems. For Meyer, the pressing issues of urban life were not social but moral, and could be readily resolved by the renewal of traditional values. "We endeavor to raise wages instead of spreading knowledge," she complained. "We clean streets instead of our hearts, we build better houses, instead of better homes."[114] Whereas Maud Nathan called upon the collective efforts of women and men to remedy social inequities, her sister refused to recognize that anything other than individual discipline was necessary to improve civic life. "Are we not in danger of forgetting the power of the spirit, the power of ideals that can offset disadvantages?" she asked.[115]

Ironically, growing up in the same Orthodox household as Maud, Annie Nathan Meyer retained little of their common heritage. For Maud, women's political activism became a Jewish commandment; her sister, with no religious directive for social action, had no reason to support the public advocacy Maud urged. For Annie, furthermore, it was Christianity, not Judaism, that represented, at least to the popular mind, the ethic of "loving kindness," while the religion of the Hebrew Bible was merely that of an eye for an eye. "Why have we permitted it that their God seems one of Love and ours one of Vengeance?" she once asked in a public address.[116]

In this view, she echoed the thinking of her cousin, Josephine Lazarus, who identified Christianity with love and Judaism with law.[117] But Meyer went further. In some of her letters and manuscripts, she admitted that in regard to "the hordes of Jews who are without manners or business or professional standards," some anti-Semitic prejudice might be "justified." While according to most Jews "the Anti-Semite is wholly bad and unreasonable and unAmerican," Meyer felt this viewpoint disregarded "the need for better manners, for less smugness, for trying to uphold a standard of behavior that would mitigate, rather than exacerbate prejudice." Rather than "bellyach[ing] all over the place about their wrongs," minority group members should conduct themselves so that they become synonymous with "excellence of conduct." In *Opinion* magazine, Meyer expressed her view that since "the Jews of the whole world are on trial," any single Jew who put his own advantage before the "good name of his people" had committed "the sin of sins for which there can be no punishment too great."[118]

Meyer thus held Jews to an impossible double standard; not to draw attention to any deficiency, they had to behave more nobly than anyone else. Her position placed her within the closed circle of establishment Jews who valued recognition by the Christian elite more than they did ties to their "underclass" Jewish brethren. Internalizing the anti-Semitism of her times, she distinguished between so-called good and bad Jews. In Meyer's eyes, the threatening other became the worst characteristics of her Jewish self.[119]

Meyer's deep disappointment at Barnard's snubbing of her place in its history suggests that she personally suffered from membership in a group that was widely considered, in the early twentieth century, not a religious or ethnic grouping, but a "race."[120] But while Meyer was reluctant to take a public role in fighting discrimination at Barnard, she wrote dozens of letters to newspapers excoriating anti-Semitism and racism. In 1923, for example, she responded to a notorious series of articles by Burton Hendrick in the *New York Evening Post* that criticized Jews; Meyer defended them, especially citing their creativity in the arts. Surprisingly, she singled out Jewish women's achievements, criticizing Hendrick for not mentioning "even in passing . . . the Theater Guild [which] was manned (and womanned) by Jews."[121]

Only in the 1930s, with the dismaying consequences of European fascism at hand, did Annie Nathan Meyer begin to reassess her Jewish heritage more systematically. She wrote many letters to the editor attacking Hitler and Nazism (although she continued to demand godly behavior of Jews, pleading, for example, that German Jews end their days with "a noble gesture of defiance" rather than accept rescue).[122] In short stories, speeches, and essays she affirmed her own Jewish identity and insisted that a common spiritual and cultural heritage bound the Jewish people together. Finding herself poorly equipped to understand the deepest sources of Jewish spirituality, she had to turn for guidance to more learned members of her own family—including Maud. The sisters by this time had grown closer, perhaps a consequence of the passage of the suffrage amendment that had so polarized them earlier, as well as the bond they came to share when Annie, like Maud, lost her beloved daughter, also an only child. Barely three months married, twenty-eight-year-old Margaret Meyer, a 1915 Barnard graduate, had died by her own hand from a pistol shot; a "tragic accident," her grief-stricken mother called it, though friends suspected otherwise.

Meyer's attempt to recover her Judaism was difficult. For her, the "living spring" of Judaism had been long buried "under the dry leaves of ritualism": bored as a child by the "dry arguments, splitting of the finest hairs, [the] dull regimentation" of the Talmud, she had given up religion. Now, however, in her hour of need, she discovered it again as a "wonderful means of holding together a dispersed people . . . a proud spiritual history." "There is a spiritual tie between all Jews," she observed, "we are spiritual and cultural brothers even if we are not one people"; this link made it essential that Jews not "betray" each other by "sordid actions."[123]

Until her death in 1951, Meyer refused to sanction the idea of a Jewish state as a place of refuge for a beleaguered people. Although many non-Eastern European Jews had initially opposed the creation of a Zionist state, the Holocaust caused most to change their views. But Meyer held that allegiance to Zionism would weaken the position of Jews in America; furthermore, she had little personal sympathy for Zionists, whom she called "radical" and "intolerant."[124]

Meyer's idiosyncratic views on women's and Jewish issues have been attributed not only to family rivalries but to her self-created role as a gadfly who enjoyed provoking the establishment on any issue. Although few of her literary works were popular or critical successes (another disappointment she suffered in private), her constant letter writing kept her in the public eye; so many of her letters to the editor (over 350) appeared in print that they seemed a regular feature of newspapers and magazines. Meyer especially enjoyed attacking what she called the "pseudo-morality and pseudo-idealism" of liberal antiracists and feminists.[125]

But Meyer was more than an eccentric who used her pen to settle scores or garner attention. Unlike Maud Nathan, Rebekah Kohut, or Lillian Wald, who believed in the power of organized protest, Meyer preferred the court of public opinion, which she addressed through her writing. While she harbored the belief that the truth, sharply revealed, could bring about change, her ironic and often scathing letters tended to distance her from the groups with which she inconsistently identified—women, Jews, minorities—and lessened her impact. While she wrote drama, fiction, and essays as well as letters to express her beliefs, she lacked her sister's unfailing "spirit of rebellion"—the courage and willingness to confront anti-Semitism in any context, even among allies—and she lacked Maud's fundamental, though imperfect, sympathies with lower-class Americans.

Yet Meyer was proud of her contributions to black culture: her play *Black Souls,* produced in 1932 at the Hecksher Theater in New York, was considered by James Weldon Johnson to be "one of the most powerful and penetrating plays yet written on the race question." Meyer's onetime protégée, Zora Neale Hurston, wrote that "no one in America has a better grasp" of interracial issues: "Never before have I read anything by a white person dealing with 'inside' colored life that did not have a sprinkling of false notes." Meyer also donated books on black history and literature to Hunter College and submitted a plan, never implemented, to establish a Negro Cultural Library there.[126]

Meyer could identify the other as an object of concern when that other was much less closely associated with her own origins than were "lower-class" Jews at Barnard, Hitler's Jewish victims, or Zionists. As with Antin and Josephine Lazarus, the universalist cause of antiracism was usually more appealing than any particulars of anti-Semitism. Although the challenge of fascism caused Meyer to reassess her connections, her pride in her ethnicity—like that in her gender—was mixed.

Jewish women whose commitment to social justice was much greater, like Lillian Wald, could be equally detached from Judaism. Although Wald worked on behalf of the immigrant Jewish community and received much of her funding from Jewish philanthropists, she insisted that her concerns were "entirely nonsectarian." At the end of her life, she refused to be included in a book about Jewish women in America, because its title suggested "work done by women as Jews," which hers was not. For Wald, the promotion of a more definitive religious purpose at Henry Street would have meant the loss of "something fundamental" in the settlement—the common humanity shared by all creeds rather than a more particularistic faith.[127] Her philosophy was one of "mutuality": "No one class of people can be independent of each other," Wald insisted. The " 'mutuality' of society" dictated promoting "race welfare"; failure to accord one group dignity meant a "dragging down" for all, as people and groups "rise and fall together."[128] Active in many movements for human rights, Wald helped found the National Association for the Advancement of Colored People (NAACP), the Federal Children's Bureau, the Women's League for Peace and Freedom, and other groups.

Wald respected the religious traditions of immigrant life even as she recognized that, for immigrants to become fully Americanized, these had inevitably to be replaced by "newer appeals" like Zionism, social work, and women's rights. All of these expressed a "religious spirit" that she saw as appropriate New World reformulations of Judaism. Wald remained little interested in Jewish causes, and was slow to recognize the threat that fascism posed to Jewish freedom. In 1934, she wrote to a friend that Nazi anti-Semitism was a "red herring": "Would it not clarify thought for men and women to declare this propaganda to be not anti-Semitism but anti-Christianity?[129]

The relationship of "uptown" Jewish women to progressive reform in the early twentieth century thus reflected several different patterns. Rebekah Kohut and Maud Nathan took pride in their Jewish heritage and associations, and although they became leading activists in secular causes, they found few significant contradictions between their strongly held religious and ethnic ties and the wider imperatives of reform. They did not deny occasional conflict between feminism, progressivism, and Judaism, but rather claimed that Jewish values kept them centered on the true path to righteousness in the contemporary world.

Other members of the National Council of Jewish Women did not share Kohut's and Nathan's personal faith or their committed feminism. But the NCJW provided an organizational locus for a new Jewish style of scientific, female-centered philanthropy, offering members an opportunity to exercise leadership in public arenas from which, because of their gender or religious origins, they had been prohibited. The "clubable" women of the NCJW shared many ties with elite women in non-Jewish women's organizations. By the early 1900s, the overt anti-Jewish, anti–Old Testament rhetoric that had tarred the Christian-based women's movement of the late nineteenth century had largely disappeared, to be replaced by attacks on the catchall category of "immigrants," whose deficiencies were also the target of the NCJW.[130] "In all clubs of any kind, Jewish women . . . are not merely tolerated but welcomed," wrote Mary Garrett Hay, former president of the New York Federation of Women's Clubs and the New York Equal Suffrage League, in 1922.[131]

Yet Christian feminists' failure to acknowledge the importance of Jewish women's participation in the women's movement continued. Moreover, feminists and other progressives resisted taking pro-Jewish stands, failing to protest anti-Semitism at home and abroad. In the 1930s, for example, the National Consumers' League, with which Maud Nathan had been closely connected, refused to endorse a boycott of German goods, calling anti-Nazi (though not antilynching) actions "beyond its fixed scope.[132] Despite these and other differences, the NCJW participated in many secular feminist alliances; it was a member, for example, of the Women's Joint Congressional Committee, formed after the achievement of women's suffrage in 1920 to lobby for Congressional legislation on women's issues.

The relationship between Annie Nathan Meyer, feminism, progressivism, and Judaism was more tenuous, although Meyer, too, championed minority rights and, within proper bounds, women's right to self-expression. But her stubborn rebellion against her older sister, her focus on class privilege, and her internalization of destructive anti-Jewish prejudice often masked her sympathies and ultimately limited her effectiveness. Though she belatedly recognized "a spiritual tie between all Jews" and turned to her family to help her rediscover her Jewish spiritual roots, she found that it was "not easy to go back.[133] Stridently antifeminist in the early 1900s though supportive of greater opportunities for elite women, by the 1920s Meyer had moderated her tone and was cooperating with the League of Women Voters to secure women's political participation.

Such contradictions reveal the ambiguities inherent in many conservative Jewish women's beliefs; although they may, like Meyer, have been activists, pioneers, and leaders in the reform of education, politics, or society, they failed to adopt a coherent philosophy by which they could give meaning to their actions. Kohut's innovative use of spiritual and activist Jewish female role models, Nathan's melding of Bible and business ethics, and Wald's ideas of mutuality helped each woman counter troubling disjunctions between the separate poles of her identity. But Meyer's withholding of sisterhood—Jewish and feminist—portended what would be a lengthy absence of a unified, outspoken, and self-conscious feminist Judaism.

Chapter 3

RADICAL POLITICS AND LABOR ORGANIZING

A New World Upon the Earth: Emma Goldman and Rose Pastor Stokes

In 1885, Emma Goldman, then sixteen, left St. Petersburg for Hamburg, where she and an older sister set sail on the steamer *Elbe* for the promised land. The journey in steerage proved "terrifying and fascinating," for despite the hardships of the voyage, the "freedom from home" and the anticipation of what the New World would offer stimulated Goldman's imagination and set her "blood tingling." As the Statue of Liberty emerged from the mist of New York harbor, Goldman, overcome with emotion, glimpsed America's symbol of "hope, of freedom, of opportunity," certain that she too would find a secure place within America's "generous heart." Yet within moments of disembarking, the harsh, "appalling" atmosphere of Castle Garden was a disillusioning experience. The "violent shock" of that first encounter with American realities, coupled with her lingering romance with the idea of America as the promised land, set the stage for Goldman's ambivalent relationship with her adopted country.[1]

Although such disillusionment was common among immigrants, Goldman, who had been introduced to revolutionary ideas while still in Russia, quickly came to reject all American political, economic, and social structures as inimical to true freedom. Although few Jewish radical women went as far as Goldman or Rose Pastor Stokes, another notorious immigrant radical, many of their ideas were widely held by members of the socialist, anarchist, communist, and trade union movements and played a significant role in the establishment of American radicalism as a political force. Jewish women were so prominent in the labor movement, in fact, that women of other nationalities, and especially American-born workers, sometimes refused to participate in what they derisively called "Yiddish unions."[2] Even Jewish wives, who in the past might have been trade unionists or led protest actions, did not necessarily lose their political voice. Many joined tenant or consumer committees or participated in Yiddish *shuls,* children's camps, or some other aspect of the social and political network spawned by the immigrant radical movement. Occasionally they took to the streets, waging bitter strikes to protest the high costs of housing and food. Organizing picket lines, boycotts, and rallies, sometimes even agitating in synagogues, they taught their daughters the lesson that where the family was concerned, militancy was an acceptable, womanly trait.[3]

Thus, the sources of Jewish women's radicalism can at least partly be found in the traditional roles women played within the family. Some women, however, had been schooled in Eastern European revolutionary movements such as the People's Will, the revolutionary populist movement in Russia, and especially the Bund, the Jewish socialist movement that spread through Russia and Poland during the late nineteenth and early twentieth centuries. Others received their first taste of rebellion in the sweatshops and factories of the New World as they confronted the daily horrors of industrial capitalism, American style. While they were sometimes allied with Jewish reform leaders like Lillian Wald or Maud Nathan around women's suffrage, birth control, or tenement and labor issues, the radicals' commitment to "wholesale" rather than "retail" reform—that is, to the fundamental redistribution of social resources—separated them from progressive reformers.

The most militant radicals often paid a high price for their activism. In giving themselves up to their public role, they often wound up losing their private selves, their communities, and sometimes their homes and countries. "The tragedy every pioneer must experience," Emma Goldman wrote, "is not the lack of understanding—it arises from the fact that having seen new possibilities for human advancement, the pioneers can not take root in the old, and with the new still far off they become outcast roamers of the earth, restless seekers for the things they will never find."[4]

Becoming a Judith   Emma Goldman was widely considered "the most dangerous woman in the world." In the United States, she was simultaneously hated and admired during a public career spanning nearly fifty years. To some she was "synonymous with everything vile and criminal," "a snake," "unfit to live in a civilized country." To others, she was the "tender cosmic mother . . . the loyal comrade," a symbol of remarkable courage and commitment, fighting a lifelong battle for free speech and free assembly.[5]

Goldman's background did not differ greatly from those of many thousands of immigrant Jewish women who joined radical political movements in the United States.[6] Upon her arrival in the United States, Goldman went to work in a clothing factory in Rochester, New York, where she made her home with another sister. Owned by a German Jew known for his charitable works, the factory was viewed as a model institution. Yet the plant's poor physical conditions, the long hours and low pay of the workers, and the boss's "iron discipline" and "constant surveillance" aroused Goldman's deep antagonism.[7] This first taste of American capitalism convinced her that even when they had a common ethnic heritage, owners and workers could have nothing in common. By the time she left Rochester for New York City four years later, the twenty-year-old immigrant had become a confirmed revolutionary.

Yet the circumstances of her childhood, which Goldman glosses over in her own account of her life, had already disposed her to rebellion. Born in 1869 in Kovno (Kaunas), Lithuania, to an Orthodox Jewish family, Goldman's earliest years were marked by her parents' increasing marital conflict and declining economic fortunes. The marriage between Abraham and Taube Goldman, still in mourning for her first husband, had been an arranged one. In her memoirs, Goldman blames her mother's sexual coldness and her father's frustrations over his business failures for the loveless union and lack of affection of both parents for their children, all except the youngest, and favored, son. Emma's willfulness made her a special target for her father's anger, provoking frequent beatings. Only later did she understand that his rages were a bitter product of the anti-Semitism that frustrated his attempts to provide for the family.

Goldman's memories of Russia were clouded by other memories of tyranny: czarist cruelty toward peasants; teachers beating students; her uncle throwing her down the stairs; her own rape, as a teenager, by a friend in a hotel room in St. Petersburg. Such mistreatment disposed her to revolt. "I have rebelled against orthodoxy in every form. I could never bear to witness harshness. . . ."[8]

In 1881, shortly after the assassination of Czar Alexander II, the Goldmans moved to St. Petersburg, where her father hoped to earn a better living. After six months, Goldman withdrew from high school to supplement the family income, knitting shawls at home, then working in a glove factory and later at a corset shop. Yet her education was far from over. St. Petersburg was full of the revolutionary idealism of radical nihilists and populists, who met in clandestine reading circles and circulated forbidden literature. Though too young to understand the full program of these radicals, some of whom were friends of her sister Helena, Goldman imbibed their spirit. In particular, she became fascinated by the role that women played in the Russian revolutionary movement. Shifting from German classics, which her family and early teachers equated with high culture, to Russian texts, she eagerly read works by Turgenev, Goncharov, and especially Nicolai Chernyshevsky. The rebel heroine Vera Pavlovna in the latter's novel *What is To Be Done?* would become a lifelong role model: Pavlovna defied conventional expectations by organizing a sewing cooperative, run by workers, and living with her lover outside of marriage.

It might have been at this time that Goldman began to dream of "becoming a Judith," envisioning herself "in the act of cutting off Holofernes' head to avenge the wrongs of my people."[9] In her memoirs she says the dream, which was a recurrent one, came to her when she was eight, predating the Goldmans' move to St. Petersburg. But it is likely that the violent anti-Semitic pogroms that followed the czar's assassination, as well as the new regime's repressive May Laws of 1882, restricting the Jews' right of residency, occupation, and education, encouraged her identification with Jewish suffering and her incipient view of herself as an avenger. The example of Judith, the militant Jewish heroine, and of the Russian women revolutionaries whose histories beguiled her, convinced her that the only response to tyranny was overt, violent resistance.

The opportunity came soon enough. When she was fifteen, her father, fearful that Goldman's adolescent sexuality was turning her into a loose woman, attempt to marry her off. "Girls do not have to learn much!" he told her. "All a Jewish daughter needs to know is how to prepare *gefüllte* fish, cut noodles fine, and give the man plenty of children." Goldman, who wanted "to study, to know life, to travel," refused to listen.[10] When Helena decided to journey to American to join Lena, their oldest sister, who was already married and living in Rochester, Emma fought with her father to go too. "I pleaded, begged, wept," she recalled. "Finally I threatened to jump into the Neva, whereupon he yielded. . . . I left without regrets."[11]

But the squalor and "dull greyness" of life in Rochester, her first sour taste of capitalism, and an early, unhappy marriage (quickly annulled) to Jacob Kershner, a fellow Russian immigrant who turned out to be impotent, dashed Goldman's hopes almost immediately. For a brief period, she left Rochester to work in a corset factory in New Haven, where she became involved with a group of young Russian immigrant socialists and anarchists. But after a while she returned to Rochester, where her parents and younger brothers had joined her sisters. There Goldman yielded to her parents' urging (and Kershner's threatened suicide) and remarried her former husband. But she left him again after three months, this time permanently, incurring ostracism by Rochester's Jews. "I could not pass on the street without being held up to scorn," she recalled of those bitter days.[12] Disappointed and ashamed, her parents forbade her to visit them; only Helena stood by her. At the age of twenty, she came to New York, leaving behind memories of much "pain, hard work, and loneliness," as well as a vivid portrait of a tightly knit, punitive Jewish community whose mores she had come to detest.[13] In her autobiography, Goldman makes clear that her leaving signified her final departure from a family, and especially a father, who had kept her in "chains" in a home that was a "prison." Like Yezierska, she had to confront and denounce her father in order to secure her independence. She left without saying goodbye, with no regrets.[14]

Goldman arrived in New York City in August 1889, hoping to work with Johann Most, publisher of *Die Freiheit*, the militant anarchist paper. Goldman had been converted to the anarchist cause a few years earlier by the prosecution (which she believed was a persecution) of seven immigrant radicals accused of bombing Haymarket Square in Chicago. She read everything she could about the men, admiring their "heroic stand" on trial.[15] Their execution in November 1887 crystallized her views and made her into an active anarchist.

Goldman describes the moment of her conversion to anarchism as fraught with significance. When a visitor to her home commented that the Haymarket martyrs had been justly hanged, the young girl threw a pitcher of water at her, then dropped to the floor in a fit of crying. As she tells it,

> I was put to bed, and soon I fell into a deep sleep. The next morning I woke as from a long illness. . . . I had a distinct sensation that something new and wonderful had been born in my soul. A great ideal, a burning faith, a determination to dedicate myself to the memory of my martyred comrades. . . .[16]

Thus anarchism became Goldman's "Cause," replacing the religious ideology of her forebears. Goldman was converted: "I saw a new world opening before me."[17]

In New York, an anarchist acquaintance introduced her to Sach's Cafe, a popular radical coffee house where she met Alexander (Sasha) Berkman, the young immigrant anarchist whose life would be entwined with hers for the next fifty years. That same day she also met Johann Most: although he did not think much of women revolutionaries, Most took on Goldman's anarchist education. From this schooling and Goldman's natural gift of oratory came her polemical style—her tendency "to berate and lash with the language of scorn," as Margaret Sanger once put it.[18]

Goldman plunged into the life of New York's Lower East Side, working in a corset factory, then for a silk-waist factory that allowed her to take sewing home, an arrangement that gave her time for political work. She soon moved in with Berkman, who became her lover, and his cousin Fedya. She followed Fedya to Springfield, Massachusetts, where he opened a photography shop, and then to Worcester, where, joined by Berkman, they started an ice-cream parlor. The shop was well on its way to making its proprietors successful members of the petit bourgeoisie when they began planning an event that changed their lives forever. On July 23, 1892, Berkman attempted to assassinate Henry Clay Frick, chairman of the board of the Carnegie Steel Company in Homestead, Pennsylvania, where ten workers had been killed by Pinkerton guards hired to keep the Carnegie plant open after striking workers were replaced by scabs. Frick survived, but Berkman was given a twenty-two-year prison sentence. Most anarchists who had espoused the use of political violence and individual acts of protest, including Johann Most, condemned Berkman; Goldman stood virtually alone in her support. Although the authorities could not prove her complicity in the plot, her steadfast refusal to condemn Berkman's action, and their close relationship, strongly suggested that she was involved.

For Goldman as for Berkman, the end of revolutionary change justified the means. Inheritors of the Russian revolutionary tradition, they failed to understand why the violent tactics of Russian radicalism had little appeal in America, where more peaceful forms of protest were usually possible. As Goldman became more acclimated to American life, she came to regret her endorsement of violence, though she sympathized with those who committed political acts of terrorism. While she did not condone the actions of Leon Czolgosz, the anarchist who shot President McKinley in 1901, she publicly expressed her sympathy for the assassin's larger goals and the circumstances of his life. When the young man admitted that he had been inspired by hearing Goldman speak, the public linked her to the murder. Goldman had already served a one-year prison term on Blackwell's Island in New York for advising a Union Square audience of unemployed workers that it was their "sacred right" to steal bread if they were hungry.[19] In the popular mind, she had become "Red Emma," the archtypal revolutionary committed to terrorism and extralegal force.

A Dangerous Influence   Rose Pastor Stokes was almost as famous and perhaps as much feared for her radicalism as Emma Goldman. One of the most effective agitators in the working-class movement, Stokes was a fiery and eloquent speaker, who like Goldman attracted audiences of thousands. To some, she was a twentieth-century Moses, endeavoring to help people get out of their miserable class prisons. Hard-nosed journalists commented on her inspirational power; according to one, she had "the most spiritual expression I have ever seen in a living face . . . like that in the pictures of Joan of Arc and St. Cecilia."[20]

Stokes had been arrested numerous times, always defiantly, for opposing governmental policy. In March 1918, two months before Goldman was arrested for protesting the Selective Service Act, a newspaper in Kansas City, Missouri, incorrectly reported comments she had made to a women's group about America's support of the war. To clarify her position, Stokes wrote back: "No government which is for the profiteers can be also for the people, and I am for the people, while the government is for the profiteers."[21] For this, Stokes was arrested, tried, and convicted of sedition under the wartime Espionage Age and sentenced to ten years in prison. Stokes did not regret her remarks, defending her right to criticize the government's war aims even "if I have to go to jail for the rest of my life."[22] After a year, however, the U.S. Court of Appeals, finding that the judge had shown bias, ordered a new trial. Attorney General A. Mitchell Palmer asked Woodrow Wilson for guidance.

"I believe that Mrs. Stokes is one of the dangerous influences of the country," the president replied, yet he recognized that the popular mood might not support Stokes's renewed prosecution under the wartime legislation.[23] Although the government dropped the suit, Stokes was not pleased. "To go to prison for big principles will be truly a privilege," she wrote, warning that radicals should not be deceived by the seeming "straw in a 'liberal' wind" represented by the dismissal of her case.[24] In the 1920s and 1930s, she continued to be a main target of investigation in the intelligence community. In 1929, demonstrating against U.S. policy in Haiti, she was viciously clubbed by a policeman. Her death from breast cancer four years later was widely (though mistakenly) assumed to have resulted from that assault.

Whereas Emma Goldman looked to the heroines of the Russian revolution and to the Old Testament's Judith for role models, Rose Pastor Stokes had to go no further than her own mother. Hindl Weislander Pastor was a hardworking, family-oriented woman ("I slipped into the world while my mother was on her knees, scrubbing the floor," Stokes claimed).[25] Yet Hindl led a spontaneous strike in London to protest her employer's whitewashing of the shop windows to prevent workers from looking outside. After a week, the strikers triumphed, and the windows were restored to their previous condition. Thereafter, Hindl "never failed to agitate other workers, and exhort them to have courage and defy the masters . . . ."[26]

Hindl's courage did not extend to family matters. She had come from the Russian Pale to London with three-year-old Rose after her husband, off in America, had granted her request for a divorce. The marriage had been arranged by Hindl's Orthodox father, who refused to allow Hindl to marry the Polish man she loved. In London, Hindl fell in love with a Rumanian immigrant, Israel Pastor. But she felt so bound by her father's authority that she delayed marrying this other "desecrater of the Sabbath," as her father called him, until after his death.[27]

In 1890, after eight years in London, Hindl took Stokes and a new baby to join Israel Pastor in Cleveland, where he was attempting to eke out a living as a junk peddler. Not yet a teenager, Stokes immediately began work in a cigar factory to help support the family. She made cigars there and later in a "buckeye," a sweatshop operated in the owner's home, for twelve years, a period forever etched in her consciousness as emblematic of the working-class struggle for survival. She would never forget the sufferings of her fellow workers and her family. With constant "crisis and tragedy . . . stark hunger," conditions were so horrible that "we have no words in which to tell them, even to each other in secret," Stokes recalled.[28] Israel Pastor worked desperately to provide for the family but sank into a deep depression, compounded by alcoholism. Periodically and finally permanently, he abandoned the family.

Stokes's radicalizaton began in the shops. Despite an unsuccessful unionization attempt, she appreciated the girls' resiliency and relished the solidarity that existed among them ("when one of us was fired, the other would quit").[29] Yet she would never forget the lesson that women workers were more exploited than men. After a co-worker acquainted her with the works of Karl Marx, Stokes joined the Socialist Party, but she was not an active member. That same year, 1902, she became president of the newly organized Roses of Zion, the young woman's branch of B'nai Zion, Cleveland's Zionist club. At this point in her life, she was able to participate in both Jewish and Marxist causes.

Though she only had a year and a half of schooling, Stokes's talent as a writer finally rescued her from Cleveland's buckeyes. A request from the *Yiddisches Tageblatt* (the *Jewish Daily News*) for news from readers led to her first published piece, and an invitation to write a regular column. Stokes's "talks for girls," written under the pen name Zelda, became immensely popular. In 1903, she moved to New York City to join the *Tageblatt's* staff.

In her column, she addressed many concerns of the working-class girls she had grown up with, offering advice about dating and family and workplace relations. For the most part, she took a moralistic, didactic tone, in line with the expectations of her religiously Orthodox, socially conservative employer. Zelda condemned socialism, for example, telling factory girls to love their work, and she emphasized the importance of respecting one's parents, especially one's mother. In a poem entitled "No Sabbath," she mourned the decay of Sabbath observance and other religious traditions, while in "March to Zion" she paid tribute to Theodor Herzl and the Zionist pioneers. Yet even during this early period, Stokes's Jewish consciousness reflected broader concerns. Her editorial "Kishineffing It," written after the 1903 pogrom in Kishinev, asserted that Jews in the United States had to fight against racial violence as well as anti-Semitism. "Jew-baiting and Negro lynching are two blunders well worth being freed from," she wrote; "Kishineffing outside of the land of Kishineff is a greater blot upon civilization than in that 'hell's kitchen,' Russia."[30]

The transformative event of Stokes's life—which led to the demise of Zelda—came when the *Tageblatt* sent the young journalist to interview James Graham Phelps Stokes, a reformer connected with the University Settlement on New York's Lower East Side. Rose had some previous contact with New York settlements, having worked briefly as a counselor for girls at the Educational Alliance, a cultural and educational center for Jewish immigrants founded by "uptown" Jews, including Julia Richman. She had also interviewed Henry Street Settlement leader Lillian Wald about the assimilationist and possibly Christianizing effects of the settlement movement (there were none, Wald reassured her).

But nothing had prepared her for the handsome and charming man she met at the University Settlement. "What do you think of Judaizing the settlements?" Rose asked Stokes. "Just what I would think of Christianizing the settlements," he replied. "Sectarian work belongs to the churches and the synagogues. . . ."[31] And so, with this earnest exchange, began the fairy-tale romance that would fill the pages of the tabloids for months.

As the papers unceasingly pointed out in covering "New York's Most Interesting Romance," Rose Pastor and Graham Stokes came from two totally opposite worlds. Thirty-two years old, six-foot-three, highly educated, and exceedingly wealthy, Stokes was heir not only to a huge banking and mercantile fortune, but to the best traditions of upper-class civic and cultural philanthropy. The twenty-four-year-old Rose, diminutive, dreamy-eyed, and auburn-haired, had grown up in poverty and without education, a member not of the leisure but the working class. Yet the biggest difference between the two, in the public's eyes if not their own, was religion. For a prominent, wealthy, uptown Episcopalian to marry a downtown ghetto Jew was certainly unusual, as reflected in newspaper headlines that focused on Rose's religion to the exclusion of almost anything else. To Graham's family, some of the members of which tried at first to prevent the match, Rose was "the Jewess" or "the Israelitish maiden." Graham himself denied any difference between their beliefs. To his mother, he wrote that he knew of no one who had the "qualification which Jesus asked in larger measure than Rose." On another occasion, he called Rose "a Jewess as the apostles were Jews—a Christian by faith," a contention seemingly bolstered by the fact that Rose wore a cross to her wedding (in her own view, as a simple ecumenical gesture). According to a good friend, Rose was "above any religion or creed. Humanity is her religion."[32]

The symbolism of the marriage was not lost on Rose, who told her good friend Anzia Yezierska that she would "make history" by marrying Stokes: "Riches and poverty, Jew and Christian will be united. Here is an indication of the new era." The *New York Times* evidently agreed, approvingly writing that theirs was the "the greatest social romance . . . the one marriage of recent years that has come nearer than any other to demonstrating the ideal of universal brotherhood."[33] Yezierska later adapted her friend's Cinderella story in her novel *Salome of the Tenements.*

But some uptown rabbis were more worried, fearing that, if intermarriage were encouraged through such celebrated unions, "our religion will be merged into Christianity."[34] The extent to which Rose did in fact abandon Judaism after marrying Stokes remains an open question. Her biographers claim that as Mrs. Stokes she lost most ethnic identification. In the midst of the upper-class gentility of the Stokes clan and the socialist fervor that she and Graham shared, Rose's earlier Zionism, and most of her formal ties to the Jewish community, receded. Yet, although Rose's intimate daily involvement with the Jewish community did subside after her marriage, her involvement with Jewish culture and politics continued. For example, she translated the poetry of the radical Yiddish "sweatshop" poet Morris Rosenfeld; she set up promotional tours for Vladimir Resnikoff, a Russian musician who interpreted Yiddish folk songs; she wrote her own plays for the Yiddish theater, and spoke before Jewish audiences. Despite her emergence as a national celebrity and her newfound identity as a millionaire's wife, with all the accoutrements of mansions, vacation resorts, and servants, she never lost contact with old friends from Cleveland and New York, the Jewish working girls whose tribulations and triumphs had so burned into her consciousness.

It could be argued as well that Stokes's commitment to radical politics had been deeply influenced not only by the Jewish imperative of social justice but by the Jewish experience of injustice, as her Kishinev editorial suggests. A few years later, in an article in the *American Israelite*, a Reform Jewish newspaper, Stokes clarified the connection between Jewish history and radical socialism: "I believe . . . that the Jewish people, because of the ancient and historic struggle for social and economic justice, should be peculiarly fitted to recognize a special Jewish mission in the cause of the modern socialist movement."[35]

After her marriage, however, and perhaps because of it, Stokes's allegiance to the working class became the vital center of her life. She and Graham Stokes removed themselves from all charitable endeavors focused on the settlement movement, which they now ridiculed as hopelessly reformist, and became active members of the Socialist Party. Rejecting the notion of any common ground between the "Jewish worker and the Jewish exploiter," Stokes would spend the rest of her life agitating for working-class revolution.[36] She never forgot her Jewish identity, to be sure, but the old-time religion of the *Tageblatt* days was long past; she and Graham Stokes observed no formal religious practices throughout their marriage. "Whether you believe in a creed, or what you call religion, or not, there is something in Socialism that must move you. How can you love God, whom you have not seen, if you do not love your fellow man, whom you have seen?" Rose remarked.[37]

Comrades in Spirit   Goldman's views on radicalism, if not on Judaism, differed from those of Stokes. Under the tutelage of Johann Most, Goldman studied the leading anarchist and communist writers—Marx, Proudhon, Bakunin, and especially Peter Kropotkin; she was determined "to make passion bow to wisdom."[38] Goldman publicly acknowledged Kropotkin's influence—his utopian vision of a voluntary, cooperative society based on loosely federated residential communes was becoming the leading motif of the American anarchist movement—but privately, the thinking of Max Stirner and Friedrich Nietzsche, celebrating individual rebellion rather than "the mutual aid" cooperativism of Kropotkin, stirred her.[39]

Out of these sources and her own experiences she fashioned an anarchist philosophy—the Great Idea, she called it—that became the guiding force of her life. Goldman biographer Alice Wexler argues that her anarchism was based more on an oppositional motif—a "spirit of revolt," in Goldman's words—than on the idea of a visionary utopia.[40] Goldman found authority repugnant in all forms, vehemently opposing the state, capitalism, religion, and patriarchal repression. Her sympathies certainly lay with the poor and working classes, yet she was less inclined than Stokes and other immigrant radicals to place her faith in the tools of the labor movement—strikes and trade unions—than in individually based cultural change. Revolution would come through a change in consciousness but, in a phrase that echoed Annie Nathan Meyer's elitism, "only through the zeal, courage, the noncompromising determination of intelligent minorities, and not through the mass."[41] Ridiculing the efforts of labor leaders and socialists to organize mass support for their goals, Goldman urged individuals and small autonomous groups (radical schools, theaters, libraries, and cooperatives) to take direct action. She also mistrusted elections, which she called tools of the state. At the same time she rejected the Marxist notion of a proletarian revolution, believing that a workers' state would inevitably be as authoritarian as its capitalist predecessor.

Goldman's faith in the role of the revolutionary individual as opposed to the collectivity separated her not only from most Jewish socialists, but from the Jewish-based anarchist movement. In contrast to that movement's European cooperative voluntarism, Goldman posited the libertarianism of such American thinkers as Henry David Thoreau, Ralph Waldo Emerson, and Walt Whitman. The longer she stayed in America, the more her radicalism became rooted in the values of American individualism; at the same time, she became increasingly concerned with sexual repression. By the turn of the century, her call for sexual freedom was attracting a new group of primarily American-born intellectuals and feminists, distancing her even more from the Jewish immigrant movements that had nourished her first forays into radicalism.

In 1893, during a ten-month prison stay at Blackwell's Island after her conviction for inciting unemployed men to riot, Goldman worked with the prison physician, gaining nursing experience and sympathy for the medical problems of women, especially unwanted pregnancy. In her view, prison "proved the best school," helping her to understand human suffering and redemption and serving as a "crucible" that tested her own faith in herself.[42] She emerged more confident in her ability to stand alone apart from the men who had previously guided her political education.

After her release, she supported herself as a private nurse, working for wealthy patients who did not know her real identity. The young revolutionary would often bring home packages of food and sweets hidden in her coat.

"Here's a bomb, for you, here's a grenade," she would call out as she distributed among her fellow radicals the treasures taken from her uptown clients. That these clients would have been horrified to learn that their caring nurse, "Emma Smith," was the notorious Red Emma delighted Goldman enormously.[43]

To further her medical training, Goldman studied midwifery and massage at Vienna's general hospital, the Allgemeines Krankenhaus, from 1895 to 1896. While in Vienna, she heard Freud speak, and was deeply impressed. She recalled that, at the time, Freud was being reviled "as a Jew and irresponsible innovator," but Goldman found his denunciation of "civilized morality" exactly to her liking. In September 1909, she attended Freud's lectures at Clark University, admiring him as a "giant among pygmies," almost a proletarian, as he stood among the "stiff and important" American professors.[44]

What Goldman liked most about Freud was his message "that the intellectual inferiority of so many women is due to the inhibition of thought imposed upon them for the purpose of sexual repression."[45] It was a message she embedded in her own radical program, insisting that the denial of sexual freedom, not political or economic equality, lay at the core of women's problems. "If [women] got the ballot," she once said, "they would be whipped by the Government the same as their husbands."[46] Feminists erred by imitating the male political and professional world instead of dismantling it, and by ignoring the plight of working women. Above all, they failed to attack the evil of marriage, which for Goldman was incompatible with the true flowering of love. "Freedom in love and freedom in motherhood"—which to Emma meant love outside of marriage and the right to birth control—had, since her months on Blackwell's Island, become an essential part of the anarchist program.[47]

Goldman fell in love many times. After Berkman, she was involved with Ed Brady for seven years; then came a ten-year affair with Ben Reitman, the "hobo" physician who was the love of her life, followed by several other affairs well into her seventh and eighth decades. For all her diatribes against marriage and domesticity, Emma Goldman spent much of her life alone and lonely, never regretting her decision to forgo a permanent relationship, but despairing that she had not found a man who could "love the woman in me and yet who would also be able to share my work." Unwilling to give Reitman "a home" or to live with him and have his children, Goldman eventually lost him to a more conventional woman willing to undergo matrimony. She suffered deeply from the loss, yet admitted years later to another lover that "the struggle to maintain my own individuality and freedom was always more important to me than the wildest love affair."[48]

In the period before World War I, Emma Goldman's support for women's independence, and her championship of the still dangerous cause of birth control, made her a heroine to the bohemians of Greenwich Village and other sexual modernists. From 1906 to 1918, Goldman enjoyed growing prestige as the publisher and editor (with Alexander Berkman) of *Mother Earth*, a monthly journal focused on radical social and economic issues and avant-garde discussions of modern drama, poetry, and the arts. With a paid circulation ranging from 3,500 to 10,000 at its peak—a very respectable audience for a "little" magazine—*Mother Earth* played a significant role in attracting the attention of American intellectuals to anarchist notions of libertarianism.[49]

In this prewar decade, a more broad-based group of Americans (even "Pilgrim Fathers" and "*Mayflower* descendants," Goldman noted) flocked to her speeches.[50] Aided by the managerial skills of Ben Reitman, who became her promoter, Goldman had little trouble filling lecture halls of three thousand or more. Yet many Jewish anarchist and socialist friends derided such mainstream success, claiming that the focus on middle-class Americans diverted energy and attention away from the more crucial goal of agitating the working class.

This argument highlighted the philosophical and strategic differences between Goldman and her allies. Insisting on the importance of building a nationwide, English-speaking anarchist movement, Goldman pointed out that the "respectable classes" were now the real pioneers of anarchism; their "spiritual hunger and unrest," not the material poverty of the working class, had become powerful incentives to American radicalism. Anarchism "builds not on classes, but on men and women," Goldman asserted, criticizing the "timid" Lower East Side radicals who, unlike herself, isolated themselves from "Americans." At least the American comrades "do not sell their Anarchism in real estate, or in playing dominos in restaurants," she remarked sarcastically. She had nothing but contempt for the immigrant anarchist "alrightniks," those who had become prosperous and whose activism was awash in nostalgia for earlier days. In contrast, the American-born radicals "live Anarchism and thereby they are having a moral influence, of greater [and] more lasting value, than 10 years publication of a F[reie] Ar[beiter] S[timme]."[51] Such criticism indicated the depth of Goldman's rupture with her own immigrant past; after her release from Blackwell's Island, she came to believe that "real social changes could be accomplished only by the natives"; because "their enlightenment was . . . much more vital," she redirected herself to "propaganda in English, among the American people." Traveling through America, she aimed to "come close to the pulse of American life."[52] It was a course that alienated many of her immigrant allies.

While Goldman moved to broaden the anarchist movement, Stokes became a mainstay of the Intercollegiate Socialist Society, which her husband headed from 1907 to 1917. During these years, she lectured to college audiences and the general public up and down the East Coast and throughout the

Midwest. Even when listeners did not agree with her views, they were enthusiastic. "We have had no one in Chapel Hill during . . . the last 16 years who has left so fine an impression," wrote a correspondent from the University of North Carolina. From South Carolina came an equally upbeat report: although "socialism has fairly oozed out of every sentence," wrote a university official, Mrs. Stokes was the "talk of the town and folks were discussing socialism who, before she came, did not know whether it was a new disease like Infantile Paralysis, or some new breakfast food. She was a most excellent missionary . . . the whole city was charmed."[53]

Stokes did not limit her work to platform appearances. She was deeply involved in leading a restaurant and hotel workers' strike in 1912, which she saw as a key effort of the "working class to free itself from slavery."[54] Always interested in the plight of working women, and their potential power, Stokes ordered the city's chambermaids out on a sympathy strike, probably the first of its kind in the nation. And she attempted to include the city's women hotel workers—chambermaids, laundresses, and scrubwomen—in all union efforts.

Stokes eschewed violence as a general principle but, as she told thousands of striking hotel workers, she was not above sabotage. "If you put the grease from sewerage in butter and sell it, that's called good business," she told her listeners. "But if you put kerosene oil in a custard pie, that's sabotage." Vinegar instead of water, hair combings for raisins, salt in the sugar bowls, and sour milk in cream jugs were other hints she supplied to the cheering waiters.[55]

Following a 1913 strike of workers in the shirtwaist and dressmaking industry, exhaustion and increasingly poor health curtailed Stokes's active labor organizing. Yet she continued her lecture tours for the Socialist Party, advocating for women's suffrage and birth control and working enthusiastically for the Wage Earners Suffrage League. Stokes also belonged to Heterodoxy, a semisecret feminist club whose membership roster included some of the leading women intellectuals and activists of the period: feminist writer Charlotte Perkins Gilman, the Irish "rebel girl" Elizabeth Gurley Flynn, suffrage leaders Rheta Childe Dorr, Inez Haynes Irwin, and Henrietta Rodman. During World War I, some club members demanded that Stokes and Flynn resign because of their antiwar stance; other members supported the pacifists, and in the end, Gilman and Dorr left Heterodoxy.[56]

Despite her association with these women and their issues, Stokes refused to call herself a feminist; she sympathized with the women's movement only because she felt it could promote the political emancipation of working women. Class, rather than gender or ethnicity, remained for Stokes the marker of personal identity and the measure of social change. Contemplating writing her autobiography, she commented that she was much less concerned that it appeal to "liberal women" or intellectuals than to the working class. "My life," she insisted, "is chiefly a lesson to workers."[57]

Here is where Stokes differed from Goldman, although Alexander Berkman called her "our comrade in spirit."[58] Despite similarities of background, style, and sympathies, the bottom line was that Stokes became a member of the Socialist Party (and, even worse, of the Communist Party), while Goldman was an anarchist. Although the two groups had often worked together in the early years of immigrant radicalism, by the interwar period the movements had grown apart. Goldman, furthermore, stood at the most individualistic pole of anarchism, where it diverged farthest from socialism. For her part, Stokes rejected anarchism's "each-man-for-himself-and-the-devil-take-the hindmost philosophy," refusing to recognize the individual as powerful apart from a broader, collective effort.[59]

Yet occasionally Stokes and Goldman found themselves side by side. Outraged at Goldman's arrest for distributing birth control literature, Stokes protested by distributing the same literature herself, "to do just what Emma Goldman did." She told reporters, "I am merely honoring the law by breaking it."[60] Stokes was also present in May 1916, when Goldman, having completed her three-week prison sentence, greeted a tumultuous crowd of three thousand supporters at Carnegie Hall. When Stokes offered to hand out birth control information on a slip of paper to anyone who wanted it, she was mobbed by the surging crowd. Max Eastman, the *New Masses* editor who chaired the gathering, could not stop the onslaught, but finally Graham Stokes was able to escort his wife away to safety. The *New York Times* reported that the gathering had been "a demonstration to welcome Emma Goldman but Mrs. Stokes ran away with the meeting."[61]

Stokes agitated for the working class not only by orating and organizing, but also through her literary and artistic skills, producing poems, stories, paintings, and plays, a number of which were produced at avant-garde and socialist theaters. Most of her pieces, like *Shall the Parents Decide?*, a play about birth control, or *The Woman Who Wouldn't*, about an unwed mother who becomes a union activist, advocated the principles that fueled Stokes's political work; in some respects, they anticipated the proletarian fiction and drama of the 1930s. Like many of those works, and much of Goldman's creative writing, Stokes's writings often suffered from an overabundance of propaganda, although they garnered generally favorable reviews.

Of course, Rose Stokes had long since left behind the class of her origins to join what she referred to as the idle class. Some associates felt that Stokes fell too readily under her husband's sway and the "masculine leadership" of his friends. Stokes disagreed. "I accepted their leadership not from the point of view of their masculinity," she protested, but from their "superior opportunities." It was not a question of Victorianism, but of "the worker deferring to the intellectual."[62]

Over the course of their marriage, Stokes had emerged as a strong and vital leader in her own right. By 1912, Graham's enthusiasm for socialism had begun to wane, although it was not until World War I that he left the Socialist Party, unhappy with the movement's antiwar stand. Though Stokes had considered herself a pacifist and joined the Women's Peace Party, she too left the party. But when she learned of the success of the Bolshevik revolution and of Russia's withdrawal from the war, her Americanism rapidly evaporated. Stokes returned to the Socialist Party a few months after she left it; Graham's departure was permanent.

Moving to the party's extreme left wing, Stokes finally quit the socialists in September 1919 to help found the Communist Party, which was soon outlawed by the government as a subversive organization. Stokes was arrested several times when authorities raided its clandestine meetings; during this period she adopted the pseudonym Sasha.[63] Despite the surveillance, Stokes went to Russia to attend the Fourth Congress of the Communist International, where she helped to write a report on the "Negro Question." She also wrote for *Pravda* and the *Daily Worker*, ran for Manhattan borough president on the Communist ticket, and joined the United Council of Working Class Women—a Communist Party affiliate with many Jewish members—to work for better conditions for working-class families.[64]

All of these activities infuriated Graham Stokes, now moving inexorably to the political right. For years they lived as "friendly enemies," sharing little more than their house. A divorce decree became final in 1925; two years later Rose married Isaac Romaine (also known as V. J. Jerome), a Russian Jewish immigrant language teacher and Communist Party theoretician.

In the last years of her life, suffering from breast cancer, Stokes received experimental radiology at a clinic in Frankfurt am Main. There, in the early 1930s, before most people realized the threat posed by Nazism, she was shocked by Hitler's rise: "Hitler is the most dangerous man in the world," she wrote to a friend. In February 1933, a month after he became chancellor, Hitler came to speak at a hall around the corner from her residence. Commenting on "the rich respectable neighborhood" in which she found herself and her desire to protest Hitler's policies, she told her friend, "If I were not so ill they'd probably throw me out of the country. I agitate everybody!"[65] Four months later, before she had a chance to agitate against Hitler, Stokes died in Frankfurt.

Goldman spent her last decades in exile. Despite her scorn for radical "alrightniks," she did not realize the extent of her own Americanization until she was banished from the United States in 1919, the victim of postwar hysteria that made membership in an anarchist organization a deportable offense. Two years earlier, Goldman and Alexander Berkman had been arrested and sentenced to prison for their role in opposing wartime conscription. On May 18, 1917, at 8:00 P.M., just two hours before President Woodrow Wilson was scheduled to sign the Selective Service Act into law, the two stood before a tense and angry crowd of eight thousand assembled at the Harlem River Casino to protest the draft. Bystanders marvelled at Goldman's mastery of crowd psychology and her ability to avert violence between the heavily armed police and soldiers and the thousands of draft opponents who had come to hear the speakers. One onlooker recalled that "the way in which Emma Goldman and Alexander Berkman faced the war fury of 1917 was the most stirring manifestation of sheer physical courage that I have ever seen. They did not seem to know the meaning of fear, either of them, and Emma Goldman's oratory during this period was of the kind that lifted audiences from their seats, either in passionate support or in passionate hostility."[66]

Neither did Goldman fear her arrest, on charges that she had explicitly condoned the use of violence at that meeting (which she denied), or the trial that supporters felt was rigged. According to John Reed, Goldman's trial was "the blackest month for free men our generation has known."[67] As expected, Goldman and Berkman were found guilty and sentenced to two years' imprisonment, followed by possible deportation. Goldman was defiant: "Two years imprisonment for having made an uncompromising stand for one's Ideal. Why that is a small price."[68]

Goldman again used her time in prison to educate herself about the needs of women. In the Missouri State Penitentiary in Jefferson City, she experienced her first prolonged contact with poor black women, on whose behalf she often intervened with prison officials. According to the radical activist Kate O'Hare, who was jailed with Goldman, the other women didn't know if anarchy was "a breakfast food or a corn cure, but Emma DID things for them."[69] During her twenty months there, she viewed herself as an anguished "Slav-Jewish soul" that "exhausts itself in a vain attempt to bring solace to every tortured spirit."[70]

When she was released, Goldman faced an even more serious hurdle. Wartime legislation had made it a crime for unnaturalized immigrants to belong to any organization advocating revolution or sabotage; the punishment was deportation. Many hundreds of immigrant radicals, including Goldman and Berkman, were targeted; neither had ever applied for citizenship, but now Goldman tried to claim it through her father and her husband. The first entitlement was denied because Goldman had been more than twenty-one years old when her father became a citizen; in 1908, with Goldman the prey, the government had quietly denaturalized Kershner, then presumed dead, without notifying Goldman of the proceedings. (Oscar Straus, Secretary of Commerce and Labor, confided to the attorney general that to involve Goldman "would too obviously indicate that the ultimate design . . . is not to vindicate the naturalization law, but to reach an individual . . . .")[71]

Goldman spoke eloquently in her own defense before J. Edgar Hoover, the newly named head of the Justice Department's antiradical division, and immigrant officials. "[I]f . . . this is purely an inquiry into my social and political opinions, then I protest still more vigorously against these proceedings, as utterly tyrannical and diametrically opposed to the fundamental guarantees of a true democracy."[72] But the die was cast. The hearings on Goldman's case came in the midst of the postwar Red Scare and the raids authorized by Attorney General A. Mitchell Palmer on the headquarters of radical organizations. The raids netted thousands of aliens who had committed no crime except their foreign birth and membership in anarchist or other radical groups. Lacking the protection of U.S. citizenship, they faced deportation without formal trial or indictment. In December 1919, the U.S.S. *Buford,* nicknamed the Soviet Ark, embarked for Finland and Russia with a cargo of 294 deported radicals. Emma Goldman and Sasha Berkman were among them.

Goldman did not appeal the verdict. Since Berkman's long imprisonment following the Frick assassination attempt, she had always felt that he had paid a greater price than she for their shared convictions; now they would face exile together. Awaiting deportation in a cell on Ellis Island, she wrote to friends that she was "proud to have been chosen by the enemies of truth and justice. Their mad rush in getting us out of the country is the greatest proof to me that I have served the cause of humanity . . ." Yet, bound for the Soviet Union, she admitted that she found herself thinking of the "work I want to do for American much more than for Russia. Is it because I am forced out of here that I long passionately to do much for this country?"[73]

Tearfully whispering "Goodbye, America" as the *Buford* sailed out of New York harbor in the predawn winter's morning, Goldman nevertheless looked forward to finding sanctuary in Russia, where the workers' revolution had triumphed. Yet her encounter with this workers' paradise was a bitter disappointment. Lonesome and forlorn, unable to find a way to contribute her talents to the revolution, and soon deeply disillusioned by what she perceived to be the authoritarian cast of bolshevism, Goldman became deeply depressed. To her niece, she wrote that she felt like a "stranger in a strange land"; she was experiencing the "deepest spiritual conflict" of her life. And she admitted to a radical friend that "our people simply do not realize what it means to be cast out from the whole world, the feeling of being absolutely adrift, it is the worst I have ever experienced, and I have known some hardships in my time."[74]

After two years in the Soviet Union (she wrote an influential account of her experiences there, entitled *My Disillusionment in Russia*), Goldman settled in Germany. Despite a warm welcome by German radicals, she found German culture and politics stultifying. By 1924, she had left for England, which she saw as "somehow not quite so far away from A[merica]."[75] But Goldman was deeply disappointed by England's Jewish radicals, who she believed had become "alrightniks," and by the placidity of everyone else. "[I]f I had to spend the rest of my life talking to the British middle class, I should prefer to go to a Nunnery," she wrote to Berkman. "It is awful."[76]

In 1925, following a common anarchist practice, she arranged a marriage of convenience (to James Colton, a Welsh anarchist and former coal miner) to obtain British citizenship and a passport. Thereupon she traveled to Canada, hoping to find a niche in Toronto or Montreal, which boasted active radical immigrant communities attached to the Workmen's Circle. Lecturing on modern drama, art, and politics, she was greeted enthusiastically; fifteen months later, however, she concluded that Canada was "petty" and "visionless": "The Jews, the older ones, have become alrightniks, and there are no young."[77]

Goldman returned to Europe, burying all hope of "establishing myself in C.[anada] near enough to A.[merica] . . ."[78] With the help of such friends as heiress Peggy Guggenheim, she was able to buy a small villa in the hills above Saint Tropez in France. There she spent a few years writing her autobiography, but upon its completion became a wanderer once more, giving lectures in Germany, Sweden, Holland, and England—"Like a fish out of water," as she wrote to a friend, "throwing myself around in sheer desperation."[79] In 1934, the U.S. government finally authorized a three-month visit; she arrived to a hero's welcome, speaking to Jewish unions, Workmen's Circle branches, and other friendly groups all across the Depression-ridden country. The visit lifted her spirits—"Disgraceful, I know, for a revolutionist and internationalist to be so rooted in one country," she wrote to her friend Roger Baldwin— but her return to exile left her more desperately lonely than before.[80]

Alexander Berkman had found solace in exile by taking a young German anarchist lover as his permanent companion. Goldman felt herself bereft in comparison, bemoaning the "tragedy of the emancipated woman, myself included . . . getting on in age without anything worth while to make life warm and beautiful, without a purpose."[81] There was the occasional lover, but none of long standing. Berkman offered scant consolation, for while he welcomed Goldman's visits, the palpable jealousy between Goldman and Berkman's new lover spoiled their reunions. Despondent over a worsening prostate condition, Berkman committed suicide in 1936; despite their differences, the loss of her friend and comrade of more than forty-seven years plunged Goldman into deep despair.

The isolation of her final years, however, was relieved by the Spanish Civil War. Coming to aid anarchist-syndicalist comrades fighting Franco's fascist regime, Goldman visited Spain three times and helped raise money for the Spanish Libertarian movement, which welcomed her as a "spiritual mother."[82] But Goldman was slow to recognize the real menace of fascism and to put herself in the service of anti-Hitlerism; Wexler notes that she was more detached about the war against the Jews than she was about the war with Spain.[83] Though Goldman opposed Hitler, the conflict between her Jewish roots and her commitment to the universalist anarchist movement prevented her from aligning herself early on with the Allied cause. The impetus to fight Hitler "must come from within Germany and by the German people themselves," she held. "War . . . will only create a new form of madness in the world."[84] In 1934, the *St. Louis Star* quoted Goldman as saying that "Jews should be proud to have been singled out for persecution by the Nazis. The Jew contributed so much to the magnificent culture which the Nazis hate that they, in their determination to return to the past and throw that culture aside, ended by hating the Jews."[85] Five years later she protested that the Jews "have never lifted a finger to prevent the advent of Hitler in Germany or have shown the least resistance in any country."[86] Though Goldman argued for Jews' right of asylum in Palestine and elsewhere, she did not support the idea of a Jewish state, which she felt would replicate the evils of all state governments.

In her first years of exile in the early 1920s, Goldman had been shocked by the revelations of Ukrainian anti-Semitism, including the rape of Jewish women. That experience made her understand the depth of the anti-Semitism that remained in Russia, where she and her family had encountered it forty-five years before. Yet, although Goldman identified with Jewish suffering, her solidarity with her ethnic roots remained ephemeral, overridden by what she felt were the more urgent needs of class. Anarchism, furthermore, rejected all religions. Calling for the "emancipation of the human race from all God-heads, be they Judaic, Christian, Mohammedan, Buddhistic, Brahministic, or what not," Goldman envisioned a nonreligious, "reawakened and illumined consciousness" that would instill "a new world upon the earth."[87] This apostle of "antireligion" enjoyed preaching her atheistic sermons even to church audiences, reveling in her persona as "Satan." At one year's Red Revels, she dressed as a nun and danced to the "Anarchist's Slide."[88]

Yet she never criticized Judaism quite as harshly as she did Christianity: Jews were "the mainstay," she argued, "of every revolutionary endeavor." In most cities, she gave two lectures, one English, one "Jewish."[89] Her oratory often contained biblical references; her radical style, and her urgent concern with social justice, was itself rooted in prophetic tradition. After all, her earliest vision of herself had been as a Judith, fighting to avenge her people. Though she came to define peoplehood in a less ethnic and particularist sense than she had in childhood, she never relinquished the ideal that led her to bear witness against what she considered the evils of her time. A rabbi who knew her said she was "the most religious person I know," no doubt meaning that she dedicated her life to the pursuit of holiness.[90] Another comrade, the ex-wife of Goldman's former lover, Ben Reitman, put it more colloquially: "She had many faults, but she was a mensch."[91]

Goldman died in Toronto on May 14, 1940, at the age of seventy. Now that she was merely a dead "undesirable alien," the United States allowed her to be buried in Chicago's Waldheim Cemetery, near the graves of the Haymarket martyrs she revered. No longer dangerous, Emma Goldman, in death, had at last come home.

Bread and More Roses: Rose Pesotta and Rose Schneiderman

A less isolating pattern of radical activism marks the career of Rose Pesotta, who, although thirty years Goldman's junior, was her close friend and supporter through many hard-fought battles. A trade unionist as well as a lifelong anarchist, Pesotta, like Goldman, was ambivalent about her Jewish identity. The younger woman's ties to Judaism remained closer to the surface, however. After World War II, in the last years of her life, her Jewishness emerged as a key element in her activism.

Like Emma Goldman, Pesotta had been radicalized as a young girl in Russia, joining the revolutionary underground when she was in her early teens. She too came to admire the deeds of the women of the revolution, whom she felt were more courageous than the men. And, like Goldman, Pesotta fled Russia when she was just past sixteen to escape an arranged marriage, also threatening suicide. In 1913, she too joined an older sister already in the United States.

There the similarities end, however, for Pesotta stayed on as a needleworker in the garment factory where she found employment, becoming a union organizer in Local 25.[92] Pesotta was the first woman to join the executive board of the local; under her leadership, it established the first workers' education department in the country. In 1934, Pesotta became vice president of the International Ladies Garment Workers Union (ILGWU), the first woman to hold that position, but she continued to take on tough organizing jobs in places like Puerto Rico, Seattle, Los Angeles, and Chicago. Outside the garment industry, Pesotta helped lead the CIO's massive industrial organizing drives in the auto industry. She was attacked by antiunion thugs during the autoworkers' strike in Flint, Michigan; the beating led to a serious hearing impairment that required her to wear a hearing aid and use a microphone for the rest of her life. Attacks during strikes in other cities resulted in more beatings and other serious injuries. Pesotta was also arrested on several occasions; although she was held for deportation at one point, she was released when she proved that she was a naturalized citizen. Pesotta's fiancé, however, an immigrant Russian Jew, was deported on the *Buford* along with Goldman and Berkman; Pesotta never saw him again. Pesotta also participated in a common-law marriage and several unhappy affairs, including a lengthy liaison with labor organizer Powers Hapgood, who was married; most of these relationships left her feeling guilty and unsatisfied. Like Goldman, she believed in the primary importance of woman's untrammeled spirit, but the independence allowed by her times brought her more pain and loneliness than exhilaration.

Pesotta remained part of the anarchist movement all her life, sharing Goldman's deep hope of creating a libertarian society based on voluntary associations. Yet unlike Goldman, Pesotta believed that the success of the movement depended on awakening workers at their places of employment. Thus, she devoted her day-to-day activities to the physically exhausting and often dangerous work of organizing, while simultaneously negotiating the shoals of union bureaucracy, a world that did not welcome women. Jews as a group did not enjoy her special attention; when asked by an interviewer to explain her creed, Pesotta responded by citing an American patriot, Thomas Paine: "The world is my country and to do good is my religion."[93]

By the end of her life, however, discouraged by worker apathy, Pesotta began to wonder whether "40 years of propaganda and enlightenment" had meant anything at all. She shared her apprehensions with Goldman, whom she credited with showing her the meaning of courage. "Did not our dead comrades Peter Kropotkin and his associates overstate the goodwill and cooperation of the poor and downtrodden?" she complained to Goldman. "Wasn't it a little superficial to maintain that all the good qualities rest with the wage earners, and everything evil is part of the employing class?" She confessed that, as one who had toiled among the working class directly, "not simply lecturing or writing about them," she had become deeply discouraged.[94]

Goldman, still abroad, reassured her friend, remarking that during her three-month sojourn in the United States in 1934 she had noticed a "tremendous awakening" in literature, drama, and social life generally. Ideas for which she "had been driven from pillar to post have now entered the lives of millions as a matter or course," she observed. Because "intellectual and cultural advancement proceed the economic and not, as Marx would have it, the reverse," Goldman was encouraged that America was beginning a true revolutionary upheaval.[95] She advised her friend to continue on as a "rebel and fighter" and never to "settle down," which was "merely another name for stagnation." The frantic life of an organizer would always be preferable to the "humdrum existence of most people."[96]

Pesotta saw herself, indeed, as an "eternal rebel."[97] Following the attack on Pearl Harbor, she left the ILGWU for B'nai B'rith's Anti-Defamation League (ADL), convinced that because of the fascist threat, working to combat anti-Semitism and racism was now more important than union organizing. She traveled throughout the country for the ADL, speaking out against bigotry. At the end of the war, after a trip to Norway to participate in a Workers Education Institute, she visited Poland and was shocked at the devastation the Nazi occupation had wrought. Her visit to the Maidenek concentration camp near Lublin, and her meetings with four hundred emaciated Jewish survivors, moved her enormously. She wrote a detailed report of the misery she encountered and helped plan for the resettlement of European refugees in the United States. After the establishment of the state of Israel, she became the Midwest regional director of the American Trade Council for the Histadrut, the Israeli labor federation. She returned once again to dressmaking in the last decades of her life, but continued to devote herself to labor Zionism.

Having lived through the world war, as Goldman and Stokes did not, this lifelong anarchist ironically came to celebrate the rise of Israel as a nation-state and devote her energies to its survival. Like other radical activists, Pesotta had not identified as a Jew throughout most of her life; her assimilated lifestyle caused friction with her Orthodox mother, with whom she shared a household for many years. Yet family members believed that Rose was "outwardly an atheist, but actually a closet Jew."[98] The shock of the Holocaust caused Pesotta to reclaim her Jewishness. "Doing good" continued to be her creed, but in the twilight of her life, her focus would be Jews, Israel, and anti-Semitism, as well as American workers.

For Pesotta's ILGWU colleagues Pauline Newman and Rose Schneiderman, however, ties of class and gender meant more than those of ethnicity. Schneiderman organized the first female local of the Jewish Socialist United Cloth Hat and Cap Makers' Union in 1903. She became a leader of the ILGWU, playing a key role in the 1909 garment workers' strike. Schneiderman's greatest efforts went into the New York Women's Trade Union League (WTUL); she became its president in 1918 and served in that position for over thirty years, leading the WTUL's many campaigns for protective legislation. Through this work, she encountered Frances Perkins and Eleanor Roosevelt, who became close friends and allies. Schneiderman's association with these women, and with Franklin Delano Roosevelt, is credited with expanding the influence of trade unionism, and particularly that of women workers, in the New Deal. Through Perkins and Eleanor Roosevelt, Schneiderman was appointed labor advisor of the National Recovery Administration (its only woman member), a position she considered the "most exhilarating and inspiring" of her life.[99]

Unlike Schneiderman, Pauline Newman never left the trade union movement. But although she remained with the ILGWU for seventy years, she too found an alternative "family" at the Women's Trade Union League, which she considered more nurturing than the gruff, male-dominated ILGWU, and certainly more interested in the women's issues she cared about. Though Newman and Schneiderman remained socialists, their sphere of influence increasingly focused on the State House in Albany and the nation's capital as they looked to legislation and administrative initiatives to improve the economic status of women and workers. This emphasis distanced them from many of their Jewish colleagues in the industrial labor movement.[100]

In their personal as well as work lives, Schneiderman and Newman moved beyond the ties of their class. Newman formed a lifetime partnership with Frieda Miller, a former Bryn Mawr College professor of economics appointed head of the Women's Bureau by Franklin Roosevelt, jointly raising the daughter Miller adopted. Schneiderman, who was more in the public eye, never felt free to live openly with Maud Swartz, her intimate companion for a quarter of a century. Neither Miller nor Swartz was Jewish, nor were the many women friends who formed the core of Newman and Schneiderman's policy network.

Schneiderman's association with Eleanor Roosevelt facilitated the rescue of one of her relatives from the Nazi threat in the 1930s. Yet neither she nor Newman centered their political work on Jewish interests. Newman went to Germany after the war on a fact-finding visit for the U.S. Army. She reported that the best hope for eliminating anti-Semitism in that country was "women and . . . the trade union movement." In a visit to Israel some years later, it was the Histadrut, and especially its women's divisions, that excited Newman's greatest interest.[101]

One reason that Schneiderman and Newman moved away from the Jewish world of their youth lay in the continuing rebuffs they received from male labor leaders, mostly Jewish. Neglectful of working women's interests and hostile to female labor leadership, union officials made it difficult for female unionists to become equal partners in the struggle for better conditions for the working class. Fannia Cohn, the first woman on the ILGWU executive board, noted that "[w]orking women who aspire to leadership find . . . that hardly one place out of thousands in the labor movement is available to them." Cohn's battles with male leaders who resented her "old-fashioned feminist ideas" drove her to the brink of nervous breakdown on several occasions and twice to physical collapse. To a friend she admitted, "It was not the work that broke me down but rather the atmosphere that surrounded me."[102] Even an unusually resilient woman like Rose Pesotta (who was elected vice president of the ILGWU three times) became dispirited at the often lonely battle she was fighting on behalf of women's issues within the union movement.

Despite their problems within the ILGWU, Cohn and Pesotta did not become part of the interclass networks that sustained Schneiderman and Newman. Disapproving of these alliances, Cohn never trusted those former colleagues, who seemed to have become closer to upper-class Christian women than to Jewish workers.

These often painful splits indicate the difficulties that radical Jewish women activists experienced in finding a comfortable home in the early and mid-twentieth century. Neither the trade union movement, hostile to women's issues and women's leadership, nor interclass women's unions and networks, unconcerned about Jewish issues, represented their full interests. Nor did the radical movements of anarchism, socialism, and communism accommodate Jewish women's multiple identities.

Yet these radical leaders sought as best as they could to agitate for programs and agendas that reflected their values. Over the course of a lifetime, the priority given to class, gender, and ethnicity sometimes shifted, as did positions on violent versus nonviolent protest or political versus cultural revolution. To invent themselves as American immigrant radicals concerned about the quality of female life, these women had to create new personal lifestyles as well as political roles. These included intimate female friendships and lesbian co-parenting; serial heterosexual monogamy, including common-law marriages and extramarital affairs; and marital and child-rearing partnerships. Such relationships offended many traditionalists; they were the source of another set of tensions, which each woman worked out with more or less success in the course of her life.

Yet considering the radicals' impoverished immigrant childhoods and their unusual personal lifestyles, the status and power that several of them attained was remarkable. It was a journey of many thousands of spiritual as well as physical miles from Rose Schneiderman's birthplace in Russian Poland to the White House, where, welcomed by her friends the Roosevelts, she sometimes slept in Lincoln's bed. The journeys of Rose Pastor Stokes and Emma Goldman were no less impressive. One indication of these women's influence was the fear and trembling they brought to the highest federal officials, including presidents, who acquiesced in their arrests and occasional expulsions.

Though Goldman and her associates cited Jefferson, Paine, Thoreau, and Emerson to defend their activities as consummately American, according to the government they had gone too far. In the decades of her painful political exile, Goldman found herself longing for America. But despite support from immigrant radicals and her sympathy for Jewish suffering, Goldman created her own exile from the Jewish people, holding herself outside the community of Jews whose response to Hitler she disparaged.

Many radical activists shared her ambivalent relation to her Jewish roots. Although late in their lives some of them became deeply concerned about world Jewry in the face of mounting fascist violence, the interests of Jews as a group rarely took precedence over class-based, universalist concerns. This was one reason why the most militant activists often separated themselves from those female reformers whom they regarded as class enemies rather than ethnic allies.

Nonetheless, militant Jewish women often found themselves on the same side of economic and social issues as reformers. Organizing, agitating, lobbying, legislating, and leading, they protested the harsh conditions of industrial capitalism and the bleak lives of women workers and consumers. Whether the goal was better conditions and protection for the working class or the right to suffrage or birth control, the voices of radical Jewish women could be heard, making demands, organizing protests, leading rallies. Their agitation changed the quality of life for hundreds of thousands of their countrywomen.

Chapter 4

THE DREAM OF A JEWISH HOMELAND

The Zion in Your Hearts: Henrietta Szold and Jessie Sampter

In 1897, at the meetings of the first Zionist conference in Basel, a delegate was asked if he knew of any American Zionists. He responded that there were only two: Rabbi Stephen Wise, New York's eminent Reform leader, and Henrietta Szold of Baltimore. "And they are both mad," he added.[1]

The remark was accurate in one respect. At a time when the Jewish establishment ridiculed the idea of a Jewish homeland, Szold championed it. But she was, in fact, anything but mad.

A superb organizer, administrator, and leader, Szold was a rationalist in the extreme, a woman who devoted her entire life to the call of duty. Szold had been educated by her father, a distinguished Baltimore rabbi, for a life of Jewish scholarship. In 1881, when she was just twenty-one, she became interested in the plight of Russian Jewish immigrants arriving at the Port of Baltimore. Within a few years, she started a night school, reportedly the first in America, for the new arrivals. Converted by them to the notion of establishing a Jewish homeland in Palestine, Szold became a charter member of the Baltimore Zionist Society, one of the first Zionist organizations in America.[2]

However, it was not this organization but Hadassah, the Women's Zionist Organization, which Szold established in 1912, that catapulted her to national and international renown. Szold became for most Americans—particularly women—the living symbol of the Zionist dream. Capitalizing on Szold's image and the mission she imparted to Hadassah, the organization grew by leaps and bounds, numbering over 100,000 members at the time of Szold's death. Two decades later, with a membership three and a half times that number, it had become the largest voluntary women's organization in the world. Szold herself spent the greater part of twenty-five years in Palestine, although she thought of herself as an American temporarily pursuing Zionist projects there.[3]

Driven by the organization's needs and the demands of Zionism, however,

Szold felt deprived of the opportunity to express her private self.[4] She envied friends like Jessie Sampter, an American Zionist writer who had moved to Palestine to report on the Zionist undertaking and write poetry and novels. But Sampter suffered a series of excruciating emotional crises before she found her way to a kibbutz that met her own spiritual needs.

Goldie Mabovich Meyerson, much better known as Golda Meir, pursued a different route to Zionism, declaring herself for the Poale (Labor) Zionists and settling in Palestine after little more than a decade in the United States, to which her family had immigrated from the Ukraine. She served as general secretary of the Working Women's Council (Moetzet Hapoalat) and as its liaison to a new women's Zionist organization in the United States, Pioneer Women. But her increasing involvement in Zionist political activity exasperated her family and weighed heavily on Meir's conscience as a young wife and mother.

All three of these women's lives reflect an ongoing conflict between personal and public duty as they struggled to express their values, visions, and commitments as twentieth-century Jewish women. Their journeys reveal a spiritual quest as well as a determination to resolve concrete problems associated with the Zionist experiment in Palestine. In undertaking them, they created institutions that enhanced Jewish identity for thousands of women and helped to establish the political and social underpinnings for the Jewish homeland to come.

The Healing of the Daughter of My People Born in 1860, the same year as Charlotte Perkins Gilman and Jane Addams, Henrietta Szold was the first of five surviving daughters of Rabbi Benjamin and Sophie Schaar Szold.[5] After immigrating to the United States from Hungary, Rabbi Szold became the respected leader of Oheb Shalom, a German Jewish congregation in Baltimore. Henrietta, her father's favorite, became his confidante, companion, and disciple. Because of a severe arthritic condition in his right hand, the rabbi could write only with difficulty; Henrietta helped him with his scholarly efforts, receiving a full Hebrew education that was highly unusual for girls of the era. Though her sisters did not share this privileged training, Rabbi Szold encouraged each to develop clear opinions and always to speak her mind: such a "completely democratic" household nurtured strong-minded women, though the sisters' ideological preferences took separate courses. While Henrietta would become a passionate Zionist, Rachel matured into a fervid suffragist, Bertha into a lifelong socialist, and Adele into a communist.[6]

Late in her life, though, Szold acknowledged that her main intellectual makeup came from not her father but her mother. During Henrietta's childhood, her mother had not only busied herself with the family's domestic routines and the social responsibilities of a rabbi's wife but had also assisted at an old people's home. Henrietta was similarly "practical [with a] strong sense of duty." In this fundamental aspect of her nature, she felt she was "exactly" like her mother, although her father's influence shaped her mode of thinking. He contributed not so much the content of her Jewishness or a love of learning but the notion of a "central idea": "Adopt some central idea," he told her, "never depart from it, . . . relate everything to that central idea." This became the determining influence of her life and guided her association with Zionism.[7]

Szold's religious inheritance, like her mature style of leadership and activism, came from both her father and mother. In her own piety, she combined the intellectuality of her father—his emphasis on the need to bring the fundamentals of Jewish law not only to learning but to every aspect of contemporary life—with the warmth and graciousness of her mother's Sabbath candle lighting and holiday rituals.

At her mother's insistence and to the dismay of congregants, Szold transferred from Oheb Shalom's congregational school to public school, where she displayed a confident Jewishness. The only Jew in a class of fifty girls, she refused to recite the daily Lord's Prayer. Experiencing little anti-Semitism, she did brilliantly as a scholar and gave the valedictorian address at her high school graduation. After high school, she taught at the Misses Adams's English and French School for Girls and at the congregational school she had left as a child, giving instruction in Hebrew. Later, she taught at the night school for immigrant Jews as well, also participating actively in the Botany Club for Women and the Women's Literary Club of Baltimore.

Henrietta's intellectuality, her religious and Jewish commitment, and her penchant for teaching, which she considered an avocation rather than a career, found ready outlets in Baltimore society. Yet she deeply regretted her lack of a college education; few first-rank colleges, and none in Baltimore, admitted women. In fact, an 1883 unsigned article by Szold that appeared in the journal *Education,* calling for the endowment of a college for women in the city, attracted the attention of M. Carey Thomas (another Baltimorean), who had received a bachelor's degree from Cornell and then travelled to Zurich for a Ph.D. The two women became friends on the basis of their shared interest in women's right to a higher education.

Unlike Thomas, Szold did not leave Baltimore to fulfill her intellectual aspirations; her father, who relied on her to translate and edit his scholarly work, needed her too much, as she felt her mother and younger sisters did as well. But she did do some writing as Baltimore correspondent for the *Jewish Messenger* (her byline was Sulamith), eventually commenting not only on community events and Jewish life but on national and international affairs. When a critic from out West wrote that Sulamith did not have the authority to state her opinion on political and intellectual topics, because she was merely a "pot and pan scourer," the eighteen-year-old columnist responded by defending her own authority and the "peculiar privilege" of women's domesticity. The *Messenger*'s publisher, nervous over the controversy, urged Szold to write on less controversial topics, suggesting a handbook for girls on moral and religious topics. Sulamith refused.[8]

When Szold was twenty-one, her father took her to Europe to visit relatives. One of her keenest memories of the trip was of the Alt-Neu Shul in Prague, the oldest synagogue in Europe, where she observed how women congregants were physically separated from services. At a small window that opened into the hidden women's gallery, a woman acting as minister to the others relayed what was going on in the men's synagogue below. This is what she could do with the rest of her life, Szold thought, act as a minister and teacher to women who lacked the strong Jewish education she had received from her father. Hadn't Miriam, Moses' sister, led the women with song and prayer into the promised land?[9]

A few years after the European trip, Szold began to volunteer her services at the newly founded Jewish Publication Society, an organization dedicated to the promotion of Jewish literature. In 1893, and with a heavy heart, she left Baltimore and her family for Philadelphia, to become secretary of the Society. Szold's work there was undertaken to further the scholarly interests she shared with her father; it did little to advance the education of Jewish women specifically. Translating books on Jewish history and religion and writing over a dozen articles of her own, Szold served as editorial secretary of the Society for twenty-three years. According to Zionist leader Louis Lipsky,

> she was all there was of the Society exclusive of its canvassers and directors. She gathered all the work in her lap—whatever there was of the making of books, the editing or translating of its manuscripts, the proofreading of the galleys and the pages, the compiling of indexes and appendices . . . the motherly care of rejected and accepted manuscripts.[10]

Although Szold played a pioneering role in creating a Jewish literary culture in the United States, later in life she admitted that the Jewish Publication Society had been "too academic," "pedantic" and "afraid of life." Because it did not use "all its possibilities"—specifically, perhaps, by failing to reach the vast majority of women who had little Jewish education—Szold felt that it had fallen short.[11]

But it was some years before Szold would question the idea of domesticity as normative for women. To her sister Rachel she wrote in 1891 that "the Russian business [working with immigrants] so absorbs my thoughts that I have gone back to my early girlish longing to be a man. I am sure if I were one I could mature plans of great benefit to them."[12] But in a reply to a questionnaire on "Women in the Synagogue" that appeared in a Jewish newspaper some years later, she indicated that women's place was the home:

> I believe that woman can best serve the interests of the synagogue by devoting her-
> self to her home; by filling any administrative position for which her executive
> ability is admittedly greater than that of any available man—"Where there are no
> men, be thou a man" is addressed to both sexes—and by occupying the pulpit
> only when her knowledge of the law, history and literature of Judaism is master-
> ful, and her natural gift so extraordinary as to forbid hesitation. . . . Religion
> being sexless, no necessity exists for Jewish women's organizations, whose
> interference in religious affairs I should therefore deprecate.[13]

While making an exception for "masterful" women, Szold saw no special "necessity" for a public religious role for Jewish women as a group. Although she
continued to lead a scholarly life as an "exceptional" woman for some time,
she eventually began to develop a less traditional vision of Jewish women's options. "Women, Jewish women among them, have conquered a place in public life where it was not accorded to them," she wrote in an article in 1903.
"That place they will occupy, let the reactionary say what he will." Citing Jane
Addams, who believed that Jewish women were peculiarly well prepared to
fill a place in the larger life, Szold argued that Jewish women had been
"trained to broad conceptions by the celebration of historical festivals in the
home."[14] Her emerging public voice thus articulated a compromise between
the concept of separate spheres common to both Jewish religious tradition
and American Victorian culture, and women's increasing appropriation of the
"larger life" of public service.

After her father's death in 1902, Szold applied to the Jewish Theological
Seminary in New York to acquire the knowledge she hoped would assist her
in publishing his uncompleted manuscripts. Because of her sex, Szold's application for admission was controversial, and she was accepted only after assur-
ing the trustees that she would not pursue a rabbinic diploma. In New York,
Szold also continued with the Jewish Publication Society, putting in fifteen-
hour days to complete the *American Jewish Yearbook.*

Szold enjoyed her courses and relished her friendships with professors, especially Solomon Schechter, the director of the seminary, and his wife
Mathilde. However, she refused to attend the formal dinners held for students, no doubt considering her private relationships with members of the
seminary more acceptable than public socializing between the sexes. She also
hesitated to take a Talmud class given by one of the seminary's most impressive scholars, Louis Ginzberg, who had once told her that women were not fit
to study "Mother Torah." Szold joined the class after Ginzberg invited her to
enroll, but he refrained from discussing what she called "awkward passage[s]"
in the Talmud regarding marriage, divorce, and sexual relations.[15]

Szold was not a delicate youngster at the time; in her mid forties, she already had a well-deserved reputation as a scholar. A few years earlier, a Jewish
weekly had commented about a speech she gave before the National Coun-

cil of Jewish Women that it was "almost too profound for an American woman."[16] Yet Szold remained hesitant about asserting her womanhood too boldly. At the seminary, she began to translate and edit Ginzberg's writings, just as she had done for her father. It was not long before she fell in love. Ginzberg, thirteen years her junior, welcomed her friendship, but it is doubtful that his feelings were ever more than intellectual and comradely. The two spent many hours together, and Szold translated and edited several volumes of his masterful work, *The Legend of the Jews*. Later, friends told Szold that Ginzberg had "exploited [her] intellectually"; in her diary she agreed that she had been his "intellectual mistress."[17] When Schechter asked Szold to write an English prayerbook for women she refused, preferring to assist Ginzberg, yet she complained to Ginzberg that not one *tefilla* (prayer) "fit my modern case—not one to raise up the spirit of the so-called emancipated women."[18]

Though Ginzberg had not committed himself to Szold romantically, to her mind, and according to close friends who saw them together, the two were a couple. "We entered into the web and woof of each other's lives equally," Szold wrote in her diary. With his "eyes and manner," he had "tacitly promised" her his love; "he knew [what] I expected from him."[19] Thus, she was devastated when Ginzberg returned from a trip to Germany in the summer of 1908 to announce his engagement to Adele Katzenstein, a vivacious twenty-two-year-old whom he had first seen in the women's gallery of a Berlin synagogue. "He engaged himself to the girl that appealed to his lower nature," Szold told herself, "his material nature—for they say emphatically that so low a motive as money greed played its part."[20] Eli Ginzberg, the first child of that union, believed that in selecting Adele as his bride, Louis sought to please his own father, an Old World rabbi who was unhappy about Louis's bachelorhood and had died the summer before. The old man had not considered Szold an appropriate match. "That the apple of [his] eye should be running around with this older bluestocking," Eli Ginzberg observed, "was part of an uncouth and dangerous American environment."[21]

For months, Szold remained "wretched and despondent" at her "failure to live a full woman's life." Each day brought new suffering. "I cry out against fate! I feel so deep a capacity in me for happiness . . . and I must seal myself up," she confided to her diary. Compared to women's "real vocation," professional work seemed "artificial" and "secondary": "I wish I dared shout it out to every young girl not to run away for a moment from her natural destination. . . . I mean exclusive love and loving."[22] So desperate was her sorrow that friends and family feared a mental collapse or even suicide.

Yet Szold's life during this time was also marked by increasingly close associations with women. Her mother, who had moved to New York and was keeping house for the two of them, was a constant support, helping Szold adapt to her grueling schedule. Szold also began making important female friends, especially Alice Selisberg, thirteen years her junior, the daughter of a

well-to-do German Jewish family and one of Barnard College's first graduates. Though their families were acquainted, Selisberg and Szold did not become friends until the fall of 1908, shortly after Ginzberg's return from
Germany. Over the next few months, Alice played an important role in helping Henrietta through the "shock" of her life.[23] By the summer of 1909, one
month before Henrietta set sail with her mother for a much-needed six-
month vacation to Europe and Palestine, Alice had become a precious confidante and intellectual companion—in Szold's words, an "equal friend."[24]

By 1909, Szold had also become associated with a group of women—some
of them daughters or wives of her seminary colleagues—engaged in the study
of Zionism, one of several such groups in the city. According to Lotta Levensohn, one of the founders of Hadassah, it was Judah Magnes who suggested
that Szold be asked to join this study group. Levensohn was "so dumb-
founded at the idea of asking so renowned a scholar and editor to study Zionism with young girls far inferior to her in knowledge" that Magnes had to
extend the invitation. Szold agreed to join, but as a "working" not an "honorary" member. Although she refused to be president, "wherever she sat and
led the discussion," Levensohn recalled, "there was the head of the table."[25]
Under Szold's guidance, the organization developed a program of study that
included Zionism, Jewish current events, and Jewish history. At the time,
Zionist men considered the group to be merely "organizers of Strawberry festivals."[26] Szold herself felt that the study groups, and the entire Zionist movement, lacked direction. Nonetheless, the organization provided a vehicle for
realizing her ambition to educate women in the Jewish tradition.

An opportunity arose after her first visit to Palestine in 1909. The trip
changed Szold's life, causing the painful rejection by Ginzberg to recede.
More importantly, the trip affirmed her connection to Zionism in an immediate, urgent fashion. Contrary to her friends' expectation that the primitive
living conditions and political rivalries of Palestine would undermine her
commitment to the Jewish homeland, Szold returned "more than ever convinced that our only salvation lies that way," as she wrote to Alice Selisberg.[27]
Especially significant was Szold's visit to the Girls School in Jaffa, where she
and her mother saw "a most horrible sight—children playing with sand, with
a wreath of flies around their eyes." Horrified, Szold's mother suggested that
"this is what your group ought to do. What is the use of reading papers . . . ?
You should do practical work in Palestine. . . ."[28]

The trip to Palestine constituted Szold's second epiphany, not cancelling
out but redirecting the vision in the Prague synagogue. Supported by her
friendships with Zionist women, Szold transformed American women's Zionist activity into a practical program of philanthropy that not only aided the
desperate plight of women and children in Palestine but provided educational
and spiritual nurturance to American women in the Diaspora. Though Szold
took on consecutive positions of leadership within Palestine's male governing

elites, her association with the women's world of American Zionism supported her political efforts and sustained her spirituality.

After her return from Palestine, Szold and six other women issued a call to build a large organization of women to propagate Zionism in America and establish health and welfare services for women and children in Palestine. On February 24, 1912, thirty-eight women met in the vestry rooms of Temple Emanu-El. They took the name Hadassah, absorbing the original study group of that name. Israel Friedlaender supplied the motto: "the Healing of the Daughter of My People" (*aruchat bat-ami*).[29] It was Szold's idea that the group should devote itself to the practical purposes of healing that her trip to Palestine had revealed as so essential. Although several options were discussed—the establishment of a day nursery, maternity hospital, or vocational training; employing girls in lace-making or the pearl industry; supervising midwives—the idea of nursing immediately took hold. After funding was secured from Nathan and Lena Straus, Szold asked Lillian Wald, founder of the Henry Street Visiting Nurses Service on New York's Lower East Side, to recommend Jewish nurses willing to go to the slums of Palestine. Wald was skeptical—"You don't think you will find Jewish girls who would do that sort of work?" she asked—but an advertisement turned up many applicants.[30] Rose Kaplan of New York and Rachel Landy of Cleveland became Hadassah's first nurses in Palestine. There, according to a contemporary report, they "rented a simple home, placed the sign, 'Hadassah Chapter, Daughters of Zion' above the door, and invited the needy to come for free advice and help."[31] Notwithstanding early suspicions that the nurses were Christian missionaries, their unstinting efforts in maternal and infant care and the school health services they provided soon won them the gratitude and trust of the populace.

Hadassah's nursing project was largely based on the American settlement model of a community of residents living among the poor and working to prevent the social as well as physical causes of illness. As one Hadassah official put it, the goal was "not so much to bring relief to individual cases of illness as to organize a thorough system of district-nursing throughout the towns and colonies of Palestine, beginning with Jerusalem."[32] Szold emphasized that the nurses "must be community nurses, able to minister to all wants of the community": pre- and postnatal care, school health, tuberculosis work, infant welfare, and preventive education.[33] She no doubt had in mind the model pioneered by Lillian Wald, and she urged Hadassah nurses to spend time observing Wald's visiting nursing program before they left for Palestine. She was also influenced by the Hull House community model established by Jane Addams, who visited the nurses' settlement in Jerusalem shortly after it began operations in 1913.[34] Yet Szold never imagined a permanent body of nursing residents from the United States or a health system administered by Americans. From the very beginning, she emphasized that while Hadassah might create a Nurses Training School and develop community health services, responsibility for training and implementation should be transferred as soon as possible to the people of Palestine. Like Addams and Wald, who had come to recognize the value of connecting women residents with larger systems of government, Szold thought in terms of a broader political canvas.

As Hadassah's nurses began their pioneering health work in Palestine, Daughters of Zion chapters were organized in other cities, each affiliated with the Federation of American Zionists and the World Zionist Organization.[35] By the time the first Daughters of Zion annual convention was held, eight such chapters—in New York, Baltimore, Chicago, Cleveland, Newark, Boston, Philadelphia, and St. Paul—had been formed; Szold was elected president. At its second annual convention in Rochester in 1914, the Daughters of Zion adopted Hadassah as the generic name for the organization, because the word had already come to signify "trained nurse" throughout Palestine and was widely respected.[36]

Szold and the founders of Hadassah believed that their association could provide for women a special home that did not exist for them in general Zionist organizations. Arguing that it made sense to organize a separate women's Zionist society because the very basis of Zionism was the group, they believed that in providing an arena for practical service and a "natural social grouping of friends," Hadassah would appeal to both middle-class and immigrant women occupied with traditional domestic concerns who sought broader outlets.[37] Anticipating that Zionist men might oppose the new organization, Hadassah leaders argued that a women's Zionist group would not prevent Jewish women from working "side by side" with men: "We have not taken anything from the men's organization. Adam's lost rib leaves no gap, and in its place there was found a full grown woman and helpmate."[38]

While Hadassah would focus on the practical "healing of the daughter of my people" in Palestine, Szold always emphasized that its members would find "spiritual healing for themselves" in America through Zionism. For Szold, Zionism meant the establishment of a Jewish homeland where Jews could "govern themselves in a Jewish way." It was the only "positive, constructive movement among Jews," vital not only to Palestine but to the Diaspora, since it countered assimilation, which Szold felt had "annihilat[ed] the Jews." As she told friends, "We need Zionism as much as those Jews do who need a physical home." It was not a question of Reform or Orthodox, but of Judaism or non-Judaism. Zionism was "the only anchor in sight."[39] In Palestine, through the routines of daily living, the Zionist dream, based in Jewish law and faith, could become reality. Judaism would be "changed back from creed to a way to life"; Zionism was "Jewish messianism in a practical form. It is Jewish hope, aspiration, dream, prayer made practical."[40]

Before she left for Palestine, Szold explained to Jessie Sampter that it was the opportunity to change Jewish law—the basis of all Jewish values—that made Zionism so important:

Most of [Jewish] laws seem to me good, wise and beautiful. But some do not. Shall I break those? For me the answer lies in Zionism, in Palestine. We are a democratic people that has kept its identity for two thousand years through the preservation of its laws; but in recent centuries our developing law has stood still; it needs revisions. I cannot revise it. For an individual to revise the law is anarchy. Nor can a small group revise it. The whole people must revise it. . . . this I believe must happen in Palestine, when we shall have a nation there. . . .[41]

While the "right road to Zion" was thus necessarily the road east to Palestine, Szold believe that Zionism was also an internal, organic, spiritual turning—the "restored Zion in your hearts," as she told her Hadassah followers.[42] At the same time that Jewish women promoted righteous, healthful living in the new Zion of Palestine, Hadassah's dream would be fulfilled as American Jewish womanhood kindled a rebirth of Judaic values at home. Szold had earlier taken issue with the assertion that the National Council of Jewish Women was a "religious organization," a declaration that she believed had been made for the "propaganda purposes" of Jewish revival.[43] Yet while Szold believed that religion was a "personal, individual matter, not subject to organization," she did not doubt that true spirituality could be a by-product of Zionist women's practical idealism. As she reminded Hadassah: "We are an organization of Jewish women who believe in the 'healing of the daughter of the people,' in the healing of the soul of the Jewish people as well as its body."[44]

The identification of practical with spiritual healing that lay at the core of Szold's vision became central to Hadassah's program. "It is a mistake to think that the practical and ideal conflict," Hadassah asserted in its early mission statements. In Hadassah's formulations, women's characteristic "imagination and insight," the creation of a broad "national vision and the big national way of doing things," were given practical scope through Zionist work: through Zionism, Hadassah proclaimed, the "principles of womanliness [were] translated into public service."[45] Thus, Szold's theme of practical idealism became the rallying cry of Hadassah's gender-based Zionism. Though Szold had once considered religion "sexless" and a Jewish women's organization superfluous, her "prophetic vision" of the necessity of women's work in Palestine gave women a public role, and a public Jewish identity, in Zionism.[46]

Szold took heart in Hadassah's unusually broad appeal; its early success reflected the spiritual need of American women that Zionism could satisfy. "Isn't it curious how the Hadassah idea has taken hold of women?" she wrote to Alice Selisberg. "It is necessary to invent, actually invent, a specific Hadassah task to satisfy them. What we are doing is . . . makeshift—it doesn't meet their heart hunger. . . . "[47] According to Selisberg, Szold herself had become the symbol of spiritual purpose that guided Hadassah's astonishing growth. She observed that in the beginning, the National Council of Jewish Women had much greater prestige:

The Council of Jewish Women had a popular philosophy of American Jewish life. It was Americanized. It made fewer demands upon its members, and made no concessions to Yiddish speaking women. Miss Szold, on the other hand, from the outset, was insistent upon drawing together the women who were not Americanized and those others who were far removed in time from their immigrant forebears. We were not permitted to have more than one chapter in a city, and that chapter had to include rich and poor, Americanized socially elite and foreign born. . . .[48]

All one had to do to become a member of Hadassah was to become a "conscious Zionist," subscribing to the notion that Palestine ought to be declared the legal Jewish homeland. But it was not the theory of Zionism that brought American Jewish women—rich and poor, American-born and immigrant, housewives and the college-educated—flocking to Hadassah. It was, said Selisberg, "what every cause needs:—a living example."[49]

Despite the admiration Jewish women felt for Szold, she was not accorded her due from male leaders. In 1910, the Federation of American Zionists pleaded with Szold to untangle the financial chaos into which the organization had fallen, and Szold reluctantly complied, even though it meant staying up until the early hours of the morning after her work for the Jewish Publication Society was done. After the Federation became the Zionist Organization of America (ZOA) and incorporated Hadassah as a constituent group, Szold was the only woman chosen to head one of its departments. Yet, according to Jessie Sampter, the Zionist men "withheld their appreciation of her personality, never gave her the place she deserved in their councils." Sampter complained, "Had only the Zionist men appreciated her as we women did! She stood above them all in organizing ability, judgment, leadership. Her democratic organization of Hadassah, which now had thousands of members and covered a network of cities, was afterward made the model of American Zionist organization."[50] But Zionist men did not take the women's organization seriously. They "always made fun of Hadassah," Szold recalled.[51] "For all that Hadassah was called the Woman's Zionist Organization of America," there was "no warm feeling" for the women in the general organization. Instead there was "constant criticism because it was not political enough, or . . . it was too political—either it didn't think or it thought too independently." One male associate recalled that Szold was "very bitter . . . very openly" about her treatment by Zionist men.[52]

Nevertheless, Szold remained faithful to the cause of the Zionist organization. Judah Magnes believed that even when she disapproved of the ZOA's policies and leadership, she "slaved for it the harder," convinced that she could help it find the "right way." Her conscience must have been that of an "ascetic" or a "flagellant," Magnes observed."[53]

Szold's accommodations, which may at the time have seemed like unnecessary compromise, in fact reveal a goal-oriented vision of Hadassah as the central American women's Zionist organization, pursuing its independent fund-raising and practical philanthropy. Though she never ruled out a strategy of integration with male Zionists on common issues and sanctioned the rule that Hadassah, as a ZOA constituent agency, would pay a portion of its dues to that organization, she continually urged Hadassah to conduct its own affairs. At the same time, she insisted that Hadassah women could play a vital role in framing central Zionist policies: "Let no one tell you that it is womanly not to exercise the right, not to fulfill th[at] duty. . . ."[54]

My People, My Congregation   The idea of Zionism as a social movement especially for women brought Jessie Sampter to Hadassah, and eventually to Palestine. Sampter travelled a long, painful road to her Jewish identity. Hers was not the proud, easy absorption in religion that was Szold's inheritance; she sampled Ethical Culture, atheism, Unitarianism, and socialism before arriving at Zionism as a spiritual home.

Sampter grew up in the large house that her grandfather, clothing manufacturer Michael Sampter, had built on Fifth Avenue in Harlem. The family had come to America at the insistence of Rachel Sampter, Michael's wife, an ardent pacifist who refused to let her sons serve in the German army; in the new country, Rachel sat up nights sewing buttons on the pants that her husband made in his small tailor shop. The family attributed the success of this growing establishment to Rachel's business acumen; they all called her "the Boss."[55]

The Sampter grandparents lived with Jessie and her parents and sister, along with an uncle, his wife and four children, and assorted maids and governesses, in the splendid mansion. Sampter was crushed when they had to leave the "Old House" after the failure of her grandfather's business. She had already suffered the early death of her "strong, dominating, irresistible and vital" father from tuberculosis; now, with the breakup of her extended family, she felt that "we had no home. Having lost my childhood's dear places, I felt at home nowhere."[56]

Sampter's father, a friend and disciple of Felix Adler, the founder of the Ethical Culture movement, had brought up Jessie and her sister Elvie in the family tradition of "positivist atheism." Sampter described her family as "German-Jewish, third generation American upper middle class, well-to-do, completely assimilated, highly cultured bourgeois and individualistic." It was a family "where *trefe* (not kosher, unclean) meat was eaten as often as three times a day, where Christmas trees and Easter eggs obliterated all traces of *Hanukkah* and *Passover*, whose prophet was not Moses but Darwin," Sampter wrote. "My maternal grandfather ate on *Yom Kippur* and my paternal grandmother made fun of people who kept *kosher*."[57] In this "godless house," she came to know about the existence of God through the servants; perhaps unknown to her family, she prayed to their God (Jesus Christ) nightly.

When she was seven, some visiting children asked Sampter if she was Jewish. When she seemed bewildered, they insisted that she was. This impressed her exactly as if they had told her she was a "rag-picker, a gypsy or an idiot," since she didn't know the word.[58] But she hotly denied that she was a Jew; although she had heard the German word *Juedish* used by her family's servants with respect, the children seemed to use "Jew" as an epithet of scorn.

This incident was formative of Sampter's identity. She wrote about it in a novel, "In the Beginning," in her autobiography, "The Speaking Heart," both unpublished, and in a piece she wrote for an American magazine at the end of her life, entitled "A Confession." In the novel, she wrote that one of the children said she couldn't be Jewish because "Jews have kinky black hair and black eyes like niggers, and a hook nose," and she instantly surmised that to be Jewish was to be inferior. "And yet from that moment I was Jewish," she recalled in the autobiography. "I suffered because I could not go back and reclaim myself with those children. I was something that had been scorned, and I must vindicate it to the ends of the earth."[59]

However, Sampter had no positive identity as a Jew. Her family, which celebrated Christmas as a "folk festival," could not tell her what Judaism meant. As she grew older, she learned primarily about its negative connotations. She knew that the fashionable hotels the family frequented during the summers had separate quarters for Jews and Christians, whom her sister Elvie referred to as "Americans." Though she too was "an American and a warm patriot," Sampter took her sister's distinction for granted. During a European trip at the height of the Dreyfus scandal, the family found itself caught in the midst of a crowd shouting, *"Dreyfus, à bas les Juifs,"* and ran to take refuge in a doorway. But Sampter insisted that in Europe she never felt the prejudice against Jews that she felt in America.[60]

The path to a more positive sense of Jewishness was provided by a series of friendships, beginning in late adolescence, that were themselves in part the consequence of a second terrible blow. At thirteen, a sudden illness, probably infantile paralysis, pushed Sampter to the point of death. Although she recovered, the muscles of her upper back, left upper arm, and both thumbs had been destroyed. Her head tilted to one side, and she could not lift her arms at all.

Sampter felt "awkward, deformed," ashamed when children asked why her hands always trembled. In time, she regained some control of the muscles, but her hands were permanently weakened, and she had to wear a heavy, painful brace. Fearing for her strength, her mother took her out of the Horace Mann School, where she had been an excellent student. Even worse was the removal of her beloved violin. Sampter had been a talented student, even a prodigy. For her, music was spiritual: playing the violin, she "rose to heaven . . . I knew God." After her mother took it away, "the case seemed like a little coffin with my child in it."[61] For years she couldn't see a violin without wanting to weep.

These early tragedies brought her to despair. There could be no God, she believed, in a world that was so "meaningless and fatherless." Eventually, however, she turned from music to writing. Whenever she felt melancholy and alone, she wrote and her physical and emotional pain subsided. Sampter sent her poems to the *St. Nicholas Magazine,* a literary magazine for children and young adults edited by the distinguished writer Albert Bigelow Paine. The magazine published them all and awarded Sampter several prizes; Paine even came to meet the fifteen-year old who had written such mature poetry.[62]

As was true for the youthful Mary Antin, Sampter's literary skills won her ready access to influential mentors. One of these was Israel Zangwill, the English author and editor who had written the introduction to Antin's first book. At a reception for Zangwill in New York, the eighteen-year-old Sampter met Antin, who was then slightly older. Antin had read and admired Sampter's published poems, and Sampter knew Antin's work. "It was friendship at first sight," Sampter recalled. When Antin left for her home in Boston, the two corresponded, revealing themselves in frank and remarkably serious letters.

"I am reading James Psychology," Sampter wrote to Antin, "[and] a history of Germany. The history I cannot abide; it deals only with wars and dates and kings; those are matters that do not interest me and that I cannot remember. History does not tell the real things." She much preferred psychology, which she felt could help her find the solution to the "riddle of life." There was but one object in reading, she felt—"to find the solution, the meaning of life, perhaps one word."[63] When Antin married and moved to New York, they met frequently to talk about the problems of the universe and their own lives.

One of the topics they discussed most often was Jewry. Astonished that Sampter had never met any immigrants, Antin told her all about the Russian Jews. They were the "real Jews," she said. And the slums, where she had lived, were a "most wonderful place"; "if you have never been poor," she told Sampter, "you don't know what life is worth." "I was sure of it," Sampter remembered. And she "sat at Mary's feet and learned."[64]

Antin took Sampter to meet Josephine Lazarus, who had become her own spiritual guide. Sampter found Lazarus "stately, motherly, a bit awe-inspiring," and an intimate friendship eventually developed."[65] "Miss Lazarus was a seeker for God," Sampter remembered. "She saw in me a fellowseeker, a child with a vision, or at least with eyes strained for vision."[66] Lazarus gave Sampter a reading list—Maeterlinck, Edward Carpenter, Walt Whitman, and especially the Bible. She was "moved, exalted" to read the books of Moses, straight through, and then the prophets and psalms. "This was my Jewish heritage," she realized, the meaning for which she had been searching since childhood. Because of these forebears she had "certain capacities, tendencies, obligations"; under Lazarus's prodding, she began to study Hebrew.

Lazarus had become "a kind of intellectual mother," nursing her in "things of the spirit." Her own mother, to whom she was very close, became almost jealous, but Sampter told her that "we need more than one kind of mother." In the midst of Sampter's great hope, and then despair, over a man she loved who eventually married a younger woman, Lazarus's support sustained her. Sampter wondered why Lazarus herself had never married: "She most have loved; there was in her such a fullness of experience." After Lazarus's death, the older woman's spirit continued to guide her. "What would Miss Lazarus have said? I asked that question in regulating my life. I sought her judgment . . . We had so often ventured together on the great search."[67]

Years later Sampter reflected on the irony of her coming to consciousness as a Jew by dint of her friendships with Mary Antin and Josephine Lazarus.

> Miss Lazarus was a Zionist; at that time, Zionism was no more than a word to me, and she did not explain; but she kept Christmas as we did, and she observed Sunday, and most of her friends were Gentile, whereas most of mine were Jews. . . . Yet she treasured the Jewish spirit, she lived with the Bible, and she and Mary, both half merged in the Gentile world, were the two human links with my people, the Jewish people from which I had been cut off.[68]

After Lazarus's death, still searching for God and her identity, Sampter joined the Unitarian Church. Earlier, she had tried services at the Ethical Culture Society, and at Reform and Orthodox synagogues, but found them all lacking. At Ethical Culture, people "talked around God as if they were afraid to mention him." At the Orthodox services, "everybody prayed at once, you couldn't hear yourself." She reserved her harshest words for Reform, which she came to see as an "unconscious hypocrisy, an attempt to warm up to safe lukewarmness the religion that had gone cold." At their services, "nobody seemed to care about anything except to show they hadn't quite stopped being Jewish."[69]

Now Unitarianism seemed "too smug" and too Christian: Sampter wanted robust social ethics, not "polished surfaces." Besides, even though the minister, Merle St. Croix Wright, told her she could be both Jewish and Unitarian, she felt like an outsider when he spoke of the Jews as "they." She knew she had a different history: "This people was not my people."[70]

Wright introduced her to Hyman Segal, a young Russian immigrant who wrote poems about the Jewish people. Sampter found the poetry transforming: it gave her a "vision of life" and of the Jewish people. Suddenly she realized that her congregation need not be a church or synagogue, but could be in the "tenements, in the crowded pale of Russia and Poland, in the little agricultural villages of Palestine."[71] She credited her first stirring as a Zionist to Segal's influence. A fierce nationalist, he had no tolerance for the assimilationist customs of Sampter's upbringing. Appalled at the Christmas tree she described as "Germanic" and the Sistine Madonna that hung in her sitting room, he warned her that the Jewish people were in "a state of siege." Such symbols of a living Christianity meant the surrender of Jewish faith.[72]

Sampter's encounter with Zionism, through Segal and later his friend Henrietta Szold, changed the course of her life. She had been contemplating enrolling in a Ph.D. program in psychology at Clark University. Its dynamic president, G. Stanley Hall, author of a landmark two-volume study of adolescence that Mary Antin had brought to Sampter's attention, had been impressed by Sampter's second book, *The Seekers,* published in 1910. (She had published *The Great Adventurer* a year earlier, when she was twenty-five.) The chronicle of a series of philosophic and spiritual discussions that Sampter had held with the "Seekers Club," seven young men and women, aged fifteen to eighteen, over a period of two years in her home, *The Seekers* was an extended conversation about the search for moral meaning in a world without religion; all the members of the club (with the exception of one Christian Scientist) had nonreligious Ethical Culture backgrounds, like her own. Josiah Royce, professor of philosophy at Harvard, was impressed enough to write an introduction to the book.

G. Stanley Hall had offered to give Sampter credit for these published writings; she could move on to graduate work without any prior college training. But Zionism superseded the lure of graduate study and a scholarly career. A turning point had been reached and Sampter decided to devote herself to "my people, my congregation." "At that moment I passed over from one kind of life to another. My God had spoken."[73]

Sampter left the home she shared with her mother to move into a settlement house in Harlem, then a neighborhood attracting many East European immigrant Jews; there she worked with a young girls' club. Most important to her own development was the discussion group she conducted with adolescent students, in which they reflected on contemporary issues and their relationship to Jewish life. One of the participants recalled the questions that burned in their minds:

[Our Jewish consciousness] was a proud heritage we felt, but what connection did it have with reality, with today? Could it have any? What relationships did it bear to the movements which challenged us? What connection did it have with efforts afoot aimed at fairer economic standards? We believed in woman suffrage which then was still to be achieved. What could our Jewish heritage say on the role of women? . . . What did our Jewish heritage say on th[e] problem [of militarism]? In other words, how did our Jewishness fit into the whole problem of social justice, of the struggle for human equality and peace among nations?[74]

At about the time she moved to the settlement, Sampter began to keep kosher. Her Ethical Culturist sister, Elvie, interpreted this as a rebellion against the family, one that marked a return to an "antiquated superstition." Though the sisters remained close, Sampter avoided sharing her deepest beliefs about Zionism. "My life with her, cheerful and friendly as it was, became a cramped and partial life. . . . for the sake of peace I suppressed my individuality [to] all but its irrepressible minimum."[75] Other family members made jokes at her expense, thinking her "mildly insane, or at least peculiar." "Why take up with such a plebeian and cheap movement of East Side Jews? It would be more respectable to become a Christian Scientist."[76]

In Sampter's unpublished novel "In the Beginning," the protagonist, Evelyn, calls her family anti-Semitic for its hostility to the folkways of lower-class Jews. To her, keeping kosher was

> the symbol of an initiation, like the insignia of a secret brotherhood, that set her apart and gave her freedom and dignity. Every law whose yoke she accepted willingly seemed to add to her freedom: she herself had chosen . . . to enter that brotherhood. Her Judaism was no longer a stigma, a meaningless accident of birth from which she could escape . . . it had become a distinction, the essence of her selfhood, what she was, what she wanted to me, not merely what she happened to be.

About her family Evelyn told herself: "They want to be like Americans—well, they are like Americans. But I don't want to be like anybody else. I am truly American—free."[77]

Yet Sampter could not easily reconcile her steps toward Judaism with the assimilated Americanism of her own background. Segal and his circle of émigré Zionists placed Sampter in the "novitiate stage as a Jew," not yet "one of us." But she retorted that "I am one of us," considering their attitude merely "arrogant."[78] At the same time, she found the intellectual condescension of the upper-class settlement workers distasteful; their "benevolent patronage" insulted their indigent clients and mocked the spirit of democracy that she believed she had located in Zionism. Not only did the settlement seem anti-Zionist, but often anti-Jewish.[79]

Soon the breach had widened so far that she had no option but to leave. Although she continued her work with the girls' club, she moved into the nearby Young Women's Hebrew Association. But there, too, the ladies of the board looked upon the working girls in residence as objects of charity. Sampter tried to act as a buffer, reporting the girls' resentment. Sometimes she went further: "If your husbands who have factories and shops paid these girls enough, they would not need to receive favors from you," she told the women. It was a pleasure to shock the "fat, rich ladies," since they had to be polite to her. Though Sampter hated "class consciousness, no matter in what class," her comments on the disorderly table manners and uncleanliness of the girls at the Y suggest that she had not yet fully overcome in herself the attitudes that offended her among the board members.[80]

At about this time, Sampter lost the man she loved, a Zionist whom she thought loved her in return, to one of her own club girls. Evidently, he admired her mind but had never thought of her romantically. Her suffering, like Henrietta Szold's, was protracted and intense. Nightly she asked herself, "Can an unmarried woman remain normal? Why was I denied my essential right, doomed to a hunger that [I] could not kill?"[81]

Henrietta Szold had been rescued from the emotional suffering of a similar predicament by her vision of a mission for women in Palestine. Now Szold's vision became Sampter's. Not only did it fill the void in her life created by unrequited love, it also gave a specific grounding, a home, to her continuing search for Jewish meaning.

On Hyman Segal's suggestion, Sampter went to visit Szold. Sampter described their first meeting in her autobiography:

> She received me graciously. She was beautiful, stately, tall, with brown hair grayed over, and calm eyes. She must have been nearly 50 then, but she seemed much younger. She carried herself erect as she came to greet me, grasped my hand warmly, led me into her small and tastefully furnished library, and sat erect on a straight backed chair. Her motions were slow and vigorous, harmonious as her straight body that was neither thin nor stout. At once her humanity appeared, her warm receptiveness, and with it, like a kid glove over the caressing hand of a friend, her dignity and aloofness that held you at arm's length even as it drew you close.
>
> "I have heard of you before," she said, "I have read your writings. If you wish to serve the Zionist cause, great opportunity will be yours."
>
> I told her that I needed to learn, that I came steeped in depths of ignorance, that I knew nothing of Jewish life and tradition, almost nothing of Jewish history. I had read the Bible in English. Of Hebrew I knew little more than the alphabet. . . .
>
> When I left her my sense of ignorance had only deepened. She, learned in Jewish matters, a scholar, daughter of a famous rabbi, possessed the rare combination of general and Jewish culture. But if I was stricken with a sense of my own unfitness, I had also a new hope. She would be my guide; she had implied as much, and to know her was to desire her friendship."[82]

Szold was a different kind of tutor than Segal. For Szold, Zionism was not only a political but a spiritual ideal, shaped by deep religious convictions. Visiting the home Szold shared with her mother, Sampter was moved by the "grace of ceremonious living"—flowers and candles, the Hebrew blessings, grace after meal, the Sabbath songs. For Sampter, the door was now open to a Judaism replete with religious and ritual meaning. "My heart went out, seeking the God of my people. In thousands of homes those white candles burned tonight. I joined an invisible congregation."[83] Her growing friendship with Szold marked the beginning of her religious observance; she now joined Szold and her mother at the Conservative synagogue they attended.[84]

Inspired by her friend, Sampter resumed her study of Hebrew. She also took up Szold's invitation to work for the Zionist cause, becoming a member of the Zionist Organization of America. When Szold became chair of the organization's Education Committee, Sampter assisted her in the post. Most importantly, Szold drew Sampter into Hadassah, giving her the responsibility to develop programs and materials. Szold also urged her to take up public speaking, insisting that it was too degrading to have to go begging for speakers among Zionist men. Embarrassed by her physical deformities, Sampter at first shrank from the task, but soon became one of Hadassah's most popular speakers.[85]

At Szold's suggestion, Sampter also embarked on a project that would culminate in her most distinctive contribution to Hadassah. Without losing touch with her settlement house club, she began experimenting with a new discussion group for girls focused on questions of Zionism. The meetings of the group became the basis for the School for Zionism that Sampter started under Hadassah's auspices in 1914, and for her course in Zionism. Revised several times, her course became a key educational tool of the American Zionist movement.[86]

Sampter considered Szold the heart and soul of Zionism and came to feel "a reverent love that made her more and more necessary. . . ." Yet she knew she wanted too much from Szold; "I yearned for mother-understanding, for an emotional mothering, which withal her affection, she silently, and perhaps unconsciously refused me."[87] There was a rift between the two during the war, when both women, fervent pacifists, condemned the ZOA for joining the Allies and making war propaganda. Sampter bowed to ZOA pressure not to join antigovernment organizations (although she kept her membership in the Socialist Party, which she had joined a few years earlier, and the Women's Peace Party, she resigned from the pacifist People's Council); Szold, refusing to buckle, criticized Sampter.

For Sampter, the issue caused enormous pain. "How square myself with myself? How reconcile my Americanism, my pacifism, my Zionism?" At this moment, she felt that it was not her Americanism and Zionism that clashed; on the contrary, they were "in league." But her wartime pacifism threatened that alliance; for a moment her retreat from it threatened Szold's respect for her as well. Sampter disagreed with Szold's view that she had compromised her principles. In fact, Sampter had gone before the ZOA executive committee to oppose its taking part in the war effort. Stating her case, she "felt like a little girl arguing with a room full of school masters. All were against me;

those great and mighty men; one was rude, even insulting, another protective, courteous and fair. What could I do? I voted my solitary negative vote."[88]

Sampter believed that Szold, because of her influence, had the luxury of greater flexibility. The ZOA knew that the "whole women's movement lay in her hands; she was almost worshipped by her own little group of workers, beloved by thousands of women." Even if the men failed to honor her as they should, they recognized the danger of losing her, and her following.[89]

Sampter felt that Szold never forgave her, but she continued to express disagreement with her on occasional issues. The two remained close associates, though Sampter felt that "something intimate, something personal" that she wanted from Szold was not forthcoming.[90] Despite this disappointment, working under Szold at Hadassah's "big sisterhood" continued to give Sampter almost "undivided joy."[91]

In spite of Sampter's poor health (the war years brought intestinal attacks and a much weakened state, and the doctor warned her never to work "more than a few hours a day"), the ZOA (with Szold's blessing) agreed to send Sampter to Palestine to chronicle the work of the American Zionist Medical Unit. As Sampter prepared to leave, she experienced a terrible "vision." For days and nights, she wrestled with questions about her Jewish identity, with cosmic and prophetic questions about the Jews, Palestine, the promise of the Messiah. Several times she fell into a trance; at others, she felt the spirit of God enter her. ("I could speak to God alone. Never again to anyone else. I was alone in the world with God . . . I was a prophet.") Fearing that she belonged in "a madhouse instead of Palestine," she hired a nurse to sleep with her. Finally, after a period of "horror and struggle and exaltation, madness making ghastly grimaces, laughing at my despair," the vision subsided. During its course, she had "poured out her heart before God" and written many of her most intense and beautiful poems; she called them psalms.[92]

Sampter had probably suffered a nervous breakdown; she took it as prophecy. At the core of her agony was the question of her turn toward Zionism and the impending trip to Palestine. During the long nights of terror and anguish, she had asked her departed mother whether she approved of the trip and her adoption of Jewish tradition. Evidently, the proposed separation from her family, and from America, was more than her conscious mind could bear.

When a psychiatrist consulted by her sister advised that Sampter make the trip only for a year, the demons that had tormented her loosened their grip. Now she shopped with Elvie for a "trousseau," since she planned to be "married to Palestine." On parting, Sampter gave Elvie her will, accompanied by a letter that revealed why she had so feared her departure. "I write in the full consciousness that my not returning to America is among the likelihoods, either because I may not outlive the year of probation, or because at the end of that year I shall have found in Palestine that spiritual fulfillment, that 'at-homeness' and that opportunity for full-hearted service which I expect to find there. . . . I have never had the home-feeling anywhere since I was twelve years old; perhaps I never shall. I seem always to be standing on tiptoe at the edge of another, a different world. Perhaps Palestine, like the world of my childhood, will be nearer that world."[93]

With these words, Sampter left for Palestine to do service for the program that Szold had begun. "If I am to be one with my people," she wrote, "I must go back to the roots of my people, and be sprouted forth again. I cannot praise one thing, teach one thing, and practise another. . . . I cannot act a lie in the privacy of my own room."[94] One of the first Americans to settle in Palestine, she would be joined within a year by Szold herself.

Jewish Ground Under Our Feet   In 1919, Jessie Sampter and Alice Selisberg launched a campaign to get Szold appointed the first woman member of the Zionist Commission, then administering Jewish affairs in the Yishuv, the Jewish settlement in Palestine. Szold anticipated that the Commission would not consider seating a woman, particularly in view of the volatility of the women's suffrage question among Orthodox leaders.[95] Her intuition proved correct. Although women of all national groups supported Szold as "the only woman to be considered for such a post," the appointment was not forthcoming.[96]

The following year, however, when the American Zionist Medical Unit (AZMU) that Hadassah had organized became bogged down in seemingly intractable political and administrative difficulties, Szold was asked to go to Palestine to set things in order. As always, she answered the summons to duty.

Alice Selisberg, the first head of the AZMU, warned Szold that she was taking on an impossible mission: Zionist men never failed to tell her what a great mistake it was "that a woman was in charge"; she feared Szold would fare no better. Szold soon found herself in the midst of incredible "ferment, disagreements and misunderstandings," all the worse since everyone had been awaiting her arrival as a "prophet and a soothsayer." Jessie Sampter, who had arrived the year before, saw Szold try to cope with her role as "the butt for hundreds of complaints and reproaches."[97]

Szold poured out her rage about the dishonesty, self-seeking, and sloppy methods of the Zionist venture to Sampter.[98] To the rest of Palestine, however, she seemed a model of patience, duty, and service. It wasn't long before her management and political skills won her what, according to Sampter, few in Palestine ever attained: "the undivided respect, admiration, and affection of a hypercritical community." Her sixtieth birthday was celebrated with great fanfare by much of Jerusalem's Jewish community; Szold herself danced through the night.

On her first trip to Palestine, Szold commented in a travel diary that "the women are too patient; they sit and rock from early morning until late at night. If they had only risen up in arms and demanded better sanitation and better conditions. That is what should be aroused in them by the women from the West."[99] She was also concerned that Jewish women not lag behind Christian and even Moslem women in terms of legal rights. According to Jewish law, divorce may be enacted only by husbands; wives, furthermore, may not be guardians of their children or inherit property. Szold worked with various women's groups in the Yishuv to provide prenatal and educational services for women and promote greater religious and political equality.[100]

Once she had resolved the medical unit's problems, Szold wanted to return home to her family. But Zionist leaders, particularly Justice Louis Brandeis, thought she should remain abroad. "It does not matter what she does in Palestine," he remarked, "so long as she is there." Her sister Adele commented bitterly: "Why always Henrietta Szold, with her delicate susceptibilities? Why not Judge Brandeis, whose political career must have inured him to a thing or two?"[101]

Lonely and mired down in administrative work, Szold envied Jessie Sampter's seeming contentment. To Sampter's sister, worried about her adjustment in the pioneer country, Szold wrote that Jessie had found "exactly her setting" and seemed so full of "ideas, practical projects and fancies" that "her pen cannot keep pace with her brain."[102] One of Sampter's projects concerned Yemenite working girls, for whom she started evening classes to help them become self-supporting. With Sophia Berger, a young American Hadassah member who shared a household with Szold, she organized a Girl Scout troop for Yemenite orphans. Sampter was also active in the Histadrut, the Zionist labor federation, and in the women's association that Szold had helped to initiate.

Yet despite her outward contentment, Sampter's first years in Palestine were no easier than Szold's. In 1921, she admitted to her sister that although no one knew it, she had "suffered almost intolerably, both physically and mentally," in the two years she had been there.[103] To her dismay, she found that Zionists from Eastern Europe were extremely critical of Americans, whom they considered exploitative and manipulative. Even with the close friend with whom she had begun to share an apartment, Russian émigré Leah Berlin, it was always "we Russians" and "you Americans." Finding Americans reviled in Palestine, Sampter increasingly identified as an American, yet the spread of anti-Semitism in the United States made it hard to do so. Sampter continued to espouse Zionism as an international movement, but she hated what she saw as the Russians' lack of discipline and efficiency, and she despaired at the possibility that national habits might never mix.[104] The violence between Jews and Arabs that erupted in the spring of 1921 also disillusioned her; as a pacifist, she could bear to see Arabs killed no more than Jews.[105]

Another disappointment was the spiritual void she discovered in Palestine.

In America, Sampter's journey to find a meaningful Judaism had ended in the Conservative religious synagogue to which Szold had introduced her. In Palestine, she found that only the "antiquated," those "railed off from life," visited synagogues; the modern, progressive Jews from Europe worshipped only with their intellects, eschewing religion as a throwback to reactionary times. Furthermore, women were relegated to "undignified seclusion," railed off from the congregation. The irony was that Sampter, who had come into the Jewish fold seeking a congregation because "faith is social," could not worship in Jerusalem with her own people. The congregation she hoped to find in the Zionist masses she lost again in the Jewish land.[106]

To try to regain her faith, Sampter joined a small prayer circle that met at Szold's home. But for Sampter the services did not work; Szold's conception of Jewish law, which had inspired her in America, no longer seemed useful. She found the Torah readings and the discussions that followed dry and meaningless; they became a "reproach of the spirit" for her. Sampter became convinced that the group had first to find the roots of faith within themselves, "that we ought to unite for action before we united for prayer."[107]

Recurrent physical illness—bronchitis, pneumonia, and intestinal attacks (for which she was prescribed a daily dose of five eggs, one stick of butter, and a pound of meat)—drained Sampter physically and emotionally. Convinced that words, her only means of wielding influence, had no meaning in a land that idealized manual labor, her depression deepened. "Disillusion is the proper word to use for my feeling towards my work here," she wrote in her journal. "Towards my own part, not the venture. . . . I am worn out and thwarted beyond all hope."[108] As she descended further into despair, thoughts of suicide, recorded in her journal, preoccupied her. At one point she found herself half consciously winding her dress around her throat as if to strangle herself. She feared being alone.

But she acted to try to heal herself. As in the past, writing restored her. Along with the poems, stories, and essays that she regularly wrote for American Zionist journals about life in Palestine, she began an autobiographical novel and a memoir, "The Speaking Heart," which recounted her agonizing search for spiritual meaning. Recording her innermost struggles seemed to help.[109]

With her friend Leah Berlin she also began to read Freud. Psychoanalytic thought offered such a "liberating truthfulness" that she eagerly began an analysis with Edith Eder, a psychoanalyst from England then in Jerusalem.[110] When Eder left Palestine, Sampter suffered a major setback. Eder suggested she go to Europe, perhaps to see Freud himself, but Sampter chose to "be fixed up" in the United States. To her sister she wrote that despite her mental depression and longing to be with her family, she was terrified at the idea of not being able to return to Palestine—"my heart is bound up with this land."[111] Nevertheless, almost two years to the day after she arrived in Palestine she returned to America, unsure how long she would stay.

In the United States, Sampter located a psychoanalyst who continued the analysis she had begun with Eder. Under his guidance over the course of a year, she made steady progress in coping with her illnesses. To Szold she wrote of her preparations to return, but the response was not reassuring. While she agreed that Zionists of every country should settle in Palestine, Szold (probably out of "pure self-indulgence") wanted to return to America, which she still called home:

> I am inwardly tired. The friction, the conflict, the struggles, go on unceasingly in Hadassah and against Hadassah from the outside. Everything one does—everything I do—is misinterpreted. Selfish motives, self-aggrandizement, are attributed to every act. The struggle goes on and on, and I feel that I am no longer living, not to mention thinking. . . .[112]

Szold returned to the United States in 1923, accepting another term as president of Hadassah in order to heal the rift in the organization that had developed during her absence. But working for the organization at home lacked the excitement of living in Zion. It was "drudgery without a redeeming feature."[113] To Sampter, who had already returned to Palestine, she wrote:

> My life is made up of so many, many routine, confused details that there is no pattern to it. Occasionally there arises from the swirling mass of 'categorical imperatives' that keep me submerged spiritually, a momentary, blue electric shaft, in the light of which I see my plans for myself made oh! so many years ago. The plans were for something so different from that which has come about, and they were so much finer than this incessant wrestling with projects, organizational details, and defensive tactics.[114]

To Szold, Sampter's life seemed so much more fulfilling. Returning to Jerusalem in 1922, Sampter built a small house in the village of Rehoboth, where she felt she could live closer to nature and to the people. Leah Berlin and her mother, who had come from Russia, shared the domicile. Rounding out the household was Tamar, an orphaned Yemenite toddler whom Sampter adopted. Although Szold feared that Sampter was not strong enough to care for a child, she realized that Tamar and Sampter's continuing activities on behalf of Yemenite girls brought her friend peace of mind.

> [Y]our personal domestic trials and joys, your house and garden and daughter, your broad sympathies and outlook—was the Jewish homeland established for you? Has it given anyone else so much as you were prepared to get out of it?[115]

Szold wondered if she would have "the courage of fleeing to a Rehoboth, if I found mine." She felt that she and Sampter were fundamentally different.

Whereas Sampter had a creative impulse, the highest manifestation of the human spirit, her own "highest ideal is to know how to appreciate others."[116] Szold once told an interviewer that her "primary thing" was a sense of duty; "all my work was done in obedience to impulse[s] from the outside."[117] She would just as soon embroider an initial on a handkerchief or wash dishes, if that was her duty: "I have a desire to do what must be done effectively."[118]

Despite her conviction that she was merely a dogged, meticulous worker, Szold was in fact a "superbly aesthetic" creature, with a lifelong love of art, dance, and music as well as nature. She prided herself on her strength and fitness, spending the early hours of every morning doing gymnastics and grooming her long, silken hair. To her longtime secretary Emma Ehrlich, Szold's concern with her appearance was not vanity but a simple response to the fact that a public woman had to mind her appearance; for Szold, beauty of self and surroundings were synonymous. Ehrlich commented:

> For her, beauty begins with order, and it is her aesthetic sense which makes her so systematic. Everything around her is perfectly arranged; she can put her hand on any of her belongings in the dark. The same system and order which are an integral part of her public work are also part of her personal program, each item having its assigned time and place. The careful ordering of her life in mechanical things, she thinks, saves her time, keeps her in good condition, and leaves her mind free for the important problems of the day.[119]

Szold's sister Bertha believed that more than any of her other virtues, it was Szold's spirituality—the "steady blue flame, the holy eternal light" within her—that cast a spell on all who came into contact with her.[120] Emma Ehrlich recalled that on entering Szold's room, many had the sensation of "entering a cathedral," a "holy place." They sensed that the frail, delicate woman possessed within her the "strength of armies"; many experienced moments of "revelation" in her presence. According to Ehrlich, Szold's "spirit" pervaded even the inanimate things around her.[121]

Yet Szold resented the constant political and administrative tasks forced upon her. To Sampter, she complained that she had not been able "to disentangle myself from the web in which Zionist work has enmeshed me. Struggle as I may, I cannot free myself; my soul is a stranger to me."[122] Sampter recognized that the problem stemmed from Szold's committed Zionism, which drew her from the sisters she loved. "She cannot be satisfied away from her family, and she cannot be satisfied to live anywhere but here." She wondered if her friend would ever again live a "satisfied life."[123]

Szold returned to Palestine in 1927 when the World Zionist Organization elected her to the three-member Executive with the portfolio of health and education, a position she held until 1930. Szold was chosen as a compromise candidate; she had the respect of all sides and seemed nonpartisan. But she did not rejoice in her selection, or see it as a victory for women. "Where are the dozens of strong, experienced, trained men who should have been ready to jump in the breach?" she wrote to a friend. "The reason I am in the Executive is due to the fact that no one else could be pulled in. Others had interests, or a profession, or a wife and children. I had only sisters. . . ."[124]

Her return to Palestine was not a happy one. "My heart has turned to stone within me," she wrote to Sampter. "I am not equal to carrying the burden that has been put upon me." Nor did she think it fair that she had to postpone her plans once again.

> I was screamed at that my Zionist duty lay this way or that. . . . I planned for a return to domestic life. I longed to release my library from the bondage of seven years in a storage house; I dreamed of living in a flat, not a large one, but at least larger than the three trunks I have been living in for seven years, larger than the steamer cabins that have been my chief habitation for four years. And see what happened at Basle! [the Zionist Congress she was "forced" into attending] The most disconcerting feature is that, at this critical juncture, the great Zionist movement had none other to turn to but a worn out, tired old woman of 67.

Not only was she sure that Zionism had robbed her of her "last chance to live," she feared that the sacrifice would be unavailing.[125] She was full of "terror" for what lay ahead.[126]

Szold's appointment to the Zionist Executive had coincided with another sharp conflict between Zionist forces led by Justice Louis Brandeis and those allied with Chaim Weizmann, the European Zionist leader. Differences between the two factions had caused in a deep rift at the Cleveland Convention in 1921, and the new battles, in which Hadassah was implicated, profoundly disheartened Szold. From abroad, she expressed her misery:

> I understand the structure of an Ibsen drama through my experiences of the last few months. Everything, everything in my personal relations, in my Zionist relations, has been just as hard as I feared it would be. I cannot remember any period in my life so disharmonious. The worst of all disharmonies is that I can't get away from self-pity.[127]

Again she complained of narrow horizons and vision. "More than ever my life is devoid of spiritual content and cultivation," she wrote to Sampter. "It is made up of details without end, many depressing details, of much despair and not a little personal heartache. I don't see how I can survive two such years. . . ."[128]

Yet survive she did. For three years Szold did yeoman's service, then finally yielded to her yearning to go home to her sisters. She had begun to make a new life in the United States when the Vaad Leumi, the National Assembly of Palestine Jewry, summoned her back to organize and direct a Social Service Department in Palestine. As usual, conscience compelled her to accept. But she did not assume the post with confidence. "It still strikes me as 'funny' that

I should have gotten into social service," she wrote to friends. "What a patch work—medicine about which I know nothing, education, the technique and philosophy and modern conception of which lie way beyond my orbit, and now social service which is absolutely terra incognita to me. . . . I ought to be ashamed of myself. . . ."[129]

Despite her misgivings, Szold succeeded in establishing a modern, centralized system of services directed toward the needs of women, children, and families.[130] When she assumed office in 1932, there were no organized social services for destitute families, new immigrants, or children with special needs. In the face of considerable opposition and without adequate resources, Szold succeeded in establishing the Central Social Services Bureau, a remarkably progressive system of services including family welfare, immigrant aid, vocational schooling, child care services, and rehabilitation for juvenile delinquents.

Szold credited the practical work of women in implementing these programs. Yet because "social service is the concern of men as well as of women," she urged women to win support for the social legislation needed to sustain their efforts: "To the women who have been the creators I commend the task of becoming preachers and prophets."[131] Szold knew then what contemporary feminists have recognized only belatedly: programs to support women, children, and families would not succeed unless embraced by all, including men.

In 1933, as Szold began her work in Central Social Services, Jessie Sampter alarmed her relatives in America by leaving Rehoboth to join the kibbutz Givat Brenner two miles to the south. Sampter had come to believe that her private home and inherited income were inconsistent with Zionism's social goals. Determined to live her ideals, she sold her home and gave the proceeds and her capital to the kibbutz, where she built an experimental rest home for Jewish workers.

Despite the physical and sometimes political difficulties of kibbutz living, Sampter thrived in the communal setting. Here at last she saw the realization of the utopian principles of Labor Zionism: the kibbutz was a "mass experiment in living Socialism," which allowed her to "come home" spiritually as well as socially."[132] In the shared work and responsibilities of the collective, she rediscovered the congregation that had eluded her elsewhere in Palestine. Without prayers or other rituals, abandoning even the word "God," she came to an "inner realization, the experience of eternity. . . . Judaism, frozen so long by exile, hate and oppression" now became "completely fluid."[133]

That the experience of full equality for women was a fundamental component of this renewed faith is revealed in two unpublished manuscripts, one on the details of life on the kibbutz, where women were on an "equal footing" in all matters, and the other her novel, "In the Beginning." The novel ends with the American Zionist heroine, Evelyn (now called Hava) forming a common-law marriage with Nahman, an idealistic Russian émigré on the kibbutz; when she discovers she is pregnant, she admits that she hopes it will be a boy, since she shared every Jewish mother's hope of bearing the Messiah. In the last line of the book, Nahman asks: "And why shouldn't a girl be the Messiah?"[134]

In the last days of her life, Jessie Sampter continued to explore the new forms of Judaism sprouting in the fertile soil of Palestine. Like Szold, she believed that Judaism requires "Jewish ground under our feet and Jewish enterprise . . . a past and a future, history and prophecy, memory and direction in the eternal present." Yet while she constructed her own utopia in Palestine, she allowed that the Jewish struggle should be broader: Jews needed to "turn their eyes toward Zion," but they also had to help bring about the reign of democratic socialism in the United States and the world. Ending the "exploitation of one section of the population by another section, by one nation of another," was an international mission mandated by the values of prophetic Judaism. Furthermore, by becoming active as a "Socialist, a Zionist, an American and a Jew," the individual would counteract anti-Semitism, or would be "far too busy and too strong to feel it." She advised Americans that "the Jewish front is so wide, somewhere you will fit in." By studying Hebrew, ancient literature, and the Jewish holidays and folkways, by grounding themselves in the consciousness and values of the past, Americans and all Jews could recover their history and shape the present.[135]

This utopian belief allowed Sampter to hope for a better future at a time when the international scene, clouded by Nazism, was bleaker than it had been in years. In 1936, two years before her death, Sampter could write: "A new light is coming into the world, as it has always come in moments of darkness and must come as inevitably as the sun rises. . . . A new synthesis of our hate of war and love of our land, of our social reconstruction and our individual deepening, of radios and music, machines and art, time and eternity, man and God. . . . This is the burning bush." Just as "Moses, the thoughtful, turned aside to inquire into its cause," so would the Zionist experiment, bolstered by a revised world Jewish consciousness, usher in "new thought, new forms," changing constantly, guiding the future.[136]

At the same time that Sampter joined Givat Brenner, Szold assumed the task that would lead to the triumphant culmination of her life of Zionist service: Youth Aliyah. The idea of sending German Jewish youth to Palestine had come from Recha Freier of Berlin. At first, Szold resisted the idea, believing that the large-scale transfer of children was not feasible. But learning at firsthand of the dire situation in Germany after a visit to that country in 1933, she agreed to assume responsibility for the project and became director of a new Youth Aliyah Bureau.

Within a year, she had built an effective organization that addressed the last detail of the transfers and the training of newly arrived youth in communal settlements. From 1933 through the end of the 1940s, 50,000 homeless children arrived in Palestine as wards of the Youth Aliyah program; many were the only surviving members of their families.

Youth Aliyah occupied Szold totally. Despite her age and declining health, she met every shipload of arriving youngsters in Haifa; she visited all the kibbutzim where the children stayed, her legendary patience never exhausted. She prided herself on keeping in personal contact with her wards and their instructors.[137] Throughout Palestine, she became known as the Mother of Youth Aliyah. On her eightieth birthday, in 1940, the Yishuv celebrated for a week, and the birthday itself was declared a national holiday for Youth Aliyah children. Later, when Recha Freier immigrated to Palestine, tension between the two women and their partisans arose over who was in fact the "mother" of this humanitarian project. Most observers agreed that the idea had certainly been Freier's, but that the complex program could not have been implemented in such dangerous circumstances, and involved such large numbers of children, without Szold's administrative and political skills.

The rancor between Szold and Freier was not the main cause of dissatisfaction in Szold's last decade. After the deaths of Jessie Sampter in 1938 ("a part of myself went down with her," Szold wrote to Sampter's sister, "that part of myself which was of the best") and Alice Selisberg three years later, her continued separation from her sisters weighed heavily. Her sister Rachel's death was a major blow, and Szold felt guilty that she had not spent more time with her. Now she worried about Bertha and especially Adele, who was in fragile health. Going home to them was her deepest personal wish.

When Youth Aliyah made her return impossible, Szold convinced her sisters to visit her in Palestine. They came in 1939, their first visit to the land that had claimed Henrietta, but returned after a few months. Adele died shortly thereafter, having contracted amoebic dysentery in Palestine; Szold, blaming herself, was devastated.[138]

She lived on for another five years, passing away in her eighty-fifth year, on February 13, 1945. Her devoted secretary, Emma Ehrlich, charged that the respiratory illness that killed Szold had been brought on by another bitter controversy—the necessity of deciding whether the "Teheran children," hundreds of Polish refugees who had been orphaned or separated from their parents after three and a half years of wandering, would receive placement in religious or in nonreligious settings. Szold rejected the formulaic solution of dividing the children equally between both, and insisted on personally interviewing each child before deciding upon the type of education he or she would receive. "My misfortune is my ability to see both sides even of the fundamental religious question," Szold admitted.[139] Such evenhandedness aroused the ire of Palestine's chief rabbi, who organized the Orthodox Jewish world against Szold. The matter proceeded painfully and publicly, with ninety-three appeals from religious bodies and telegrams and cables from around the world. To Szold, it was a "long-drawn-out agony" seething with "devastating propaganda."[140]

Szold's sense of duty, fairness, and justice had served Palestine well. In America, Hadassah had also benefited enormously, becoming the largest Zionist organization, and the largest women's organization, in the country, in large part because of Szold. While she had left the organization to take responsibility for one branch of Zionist work after another, Szold had continued to exert moral and intellectual leadership of the American Zionist women's movement. The unromantic attention to detail and duty for which she castigated herself so severely seemed to others a model of cooperative service. At times, Szold acknowledged that her own acceptance of duty, however onerous, reflected the fundamental necessity of feminine idealism. In greeting the Women's International Zionist Organization in Palestine in 1935, she acknowledged the "greatest of all lessons" that she, as a Jewish woman, wanted to pass on other Jewish women: "the subordination of the individual will and desire to the common need."[141] Zionist women, like Zionist men, were never able to achieve the level of selflessness that Szold personified in her own career, but many came to Palestine to work on projects she had initiated.

Through her practical philanthropy, Szold fulfilled her vision at the Prague synagogue of leading Jewish women to a deeper spirituality. According to its leaders, the Hadassah woman was one "who lives the Jewish life in its entirety. . . . Together with creating a land, she recreates herself. She is the *chalutza* [pioneer] of her own soul. . . ." Whether or not Hadassah members visited Palestine was immaterial, since the group's vital spirit had been infused into the country through Henrietta Szold; "through her presence in Palestine [she] will carry its life to us and ours to it."[142]

Szold's contribution to Hadassah members was as utilitarian as it was spiritual. Her belief that every woman could contribute something of value, whether as volunteer or professional, housewife or public servant, fostered a spirit of creativity, self-development, and teamwork. Under her guidance, Zionist women became public speakers, fiscal experts, administrators, technicians, writers, and presiding officers. Although Szold was reluctant to accept her singular role, under her direction Hadassah's initial aim—"the healing of the daughter of my people"—was successfully carried out and extended to the healing of children. Szold herself was the living embodiment of the link between Palestine and the United States, between women's spiritual healing and their practical accomplishments. No other Jewish women's group was ever so completely identified with its founder as Hadassah was (and remains to this day) with Henrietta Szold.

Szold accepted her role as Hadassah icon with great reluctance. She hated the "mawkish" publicity, "myth-worship," and elaborate birthday celebrations that Hadassah staged for its own "propaganda purposes." The result was that she had to answer "an avalanche of letters" and put up with all kinds of "sentimental lubrication" poured on by American tourists.[143]

Nonetheless, her accomplishments, even the tremendous gratification she received from Youth Aliyah, the most rewarding of her Zionist service, did not substitute for her lack of personal fulfillment. According to Ehrlich, Szold paid a high price for her years of grinding, ceaseless work. Outside of the small pleasures of her daily routine, "she had no home, no family, no personal life." Her weekly letters to her sisters connected her to her family, but she despaired constantly of their separation and longed to make a home near them. Her loneliness grew more poignant after the deaths of Sampter, Selisberg, and two of her beloved sisters. While Emma Ehrlich, much her junior, provided comfort, she was more an adoring disciple than the frank comrade her older friends had been.

In her sister Bertha's view, Szold always suffered "from a sense of being orphaned, of moving among aliens," never able to recreate the warmth and security of her childhood home.[144] But after all, Szold had chosen to serve Zionism and Hadassah. Serving the public interest, denying her private self, became the motif of her life. As she wrote to Adele, "Palestine to me connotes wretchedness of spirit and the deepest despair I have ever known; and you know, I went deep enough down the two years before I left America. . . . But sadness or joy I know [Palestine] means duty."[145] For Szold the call of service to the Jewish people—not on a local or a national basis, but as a whole— spoke loudest. To such a call the response was clear, even if it meant stilling her own womanly voice.

On Szold's desk at the time of her death lay two yellowed clippings that indicate the continuing power of that call and the sacrifice she made in answering it.[146] One was a copy of Emma Lazarus's "New Colossus," the welcoming poem now engraved on the Statue of Liberty. The second was a cartoon from the *Evening Sun* of March 30, 1936, showing a woman struggling with mountains of letters. The attached clipping tells the story: it is about Selma Lagerlöf, who won the Nobel Prize for Literature in 1909 and election to the Swedish Academy five years later. This notable woman was sent such a "*deluge of birthday mail* [italics Szold's]" that a "*special railway car*" was needed to deliver it, and her secretaries were "*busy* for many months" answering congratulatory messages.

So Szold's Zionist work, and the notoriety it brought her, had deluged her life. Yet the standard of public service that she set at so high a personal cost inspired other American Jewish women to contribute to Jewish continuity. Even if she did not recognize her own achievement, Szold created a powerful vision of Jewish womanhood that would outlast her most concrete administrative accomplishments. Although she denied that she possessed originality, this vision was in many ways her most creative, as well as her most practical, achievement.

Pioneer Woman: Golda Meir

Szold's achievement had its counterpart in the public work of another American Zionist woman, Golda [Mabovich] Meir. Unlike Sampter and Szold, Meir was born not to privilege but to a childhood of pogroms and poverty. Meir's family left the town of Pinsk, within the Russian Pale, in 1906, to sail for America. When she was barely six years old, Meir already knew about anti-Semitism. In the aftermath of the bloody massacre at Kishinev in 1903, she had fasted, along with the adults, to mourn the murder of Jews. Her family had begged her to end the fast, but the willful child refused. "There's a *dybbuk* in her," her mother lamented.[147] Some thought her stubbornness came from *Bobe* Golda, the great-grandmother for whom she was named. Until the day she died at age ninety-four, *Bobe* had used salt, not sugar, in her tea to better "take the taste of the *Galuth* [exile] into the other world."[148]

Meir's hard early years in Kiev, where she was born in 1898, and in Pinsk, where, through her adored older sister Sheyna, she encountered young anti-Czarist radicals, shaped her fervent belief that Jewish survival required a permanent national homeland. Meir's mother, frantic that Sheyna's revolutionary activities would land her in jail, insisted that the family leave Russia. They settled in Milwaukee, where Meir's father, a skilled carpenter, was frequently unemployed, while her mother ran a grocery store connected to their apartment. Never prosperous, the store "became the bane of my life," Meir recalled, almost ruining her childhood. Sheyna, already a socialist, refused to help out: "I did not come to America to turn into a shopkeeper, a social parasite."[149] That task fell to eight-year-old Golda, who had to spend long hours at the grocery counter before and after school.

Angry at her parents' refusal to let her continue her education, Sheyna left Milwaukee for Denver's Jewish sanitarium, where she hoped to find a cure for the tuberculosis she had contracted. Soon Golda's parents insisted that she also stop school: "Men don't like smart girls," her father told her. "It doesn't pay to be too clever."[150] In addition, her mother wanted to marry her off to a Mr. Goodstein, a relatively well-off neighbor more than twice her age. When Sheyna and her new husband, a comrade from Pinsk, invited Meir to join them in Denver, she did not hesitate. She ran away.

By the time she returned to Milwaukee two years later to pursue a teacher's course, Meir had become a confirmed Zionist. Sheyna's apartment served as a way station for Jewish radicals in Denver, and there Golda quickly learned about anarchism, socialism, and, most appealing of all, socialist Zionism (Poale Zion). Despite her youth, she "understood and responded fully to the idea of a national home for the Jews—one place on the face of the earth where

Jews could be free and independent." She wrote: "I was much more interested in the kind of Jewish national home the Zionists wanted to create in Palestine than I was in the political scene in Denver. . . ."[151]

Yet it had not taken Meir long to become fully a part of her adopted country. In her autobiography, she recalls a moment, just a few months after the family's arrival in the United States, during the Labor Day parade in Milwaukee. Her younger sister became frightened at the sight of the mounted police leading the parade, crying, "It's the Cossacks! The Cossacks are coming!"; for Meir, however, the parade "symbolized American freedom. Police on horseback were actually escorting the marchers, instead of dispersing them and trampling them underfoot, as they were doing in Russia, and I felt the impact of a new way of life."[152] When she was eleven, Meir organized an American Young Sisters Society to raise money for textbooks. A Milwaukee newspaper some years later ran a photograph of a Zionist pageant with a woman identified as Golda dressed as the Statue of Liberty.

Yet Meir became fascinated by the stories of Palestinian pioneers—particularly those of the poet Rachel Bluwstein—that she heard in Sheyna's living room. By the time she returned to Milwaukee, her family was more prosperous, willing to let her continue her education, and deeply involved in Jewish communal life. Many Zionists passed through the city, including Nachman Syrkin, whose daughter Marie later became Meir's close friend. Meir's imagination was fired by the Palestinians she met, including Yitzhak Ben-Zvi and David Ben-Gurion, both of whom came to Milwaukee to recruit soldiers for the Jewish Legion. Ben-Zvi often came to her parents' home, where he sang Yiddish folk songs and answered their questions about Palestine. Meir was entranced.

> Slowly, Zionism was beginning to fill my mind and my life. I believed absolutely as a Jew I belonged in Palestine . . . to help attain the goals of social and economic equality.[153]

At the age of seventeen, she took what she considered to be "the first step on the road to Palestine" and officially joined the Poale Zion Party. Two years later, she convinced Morris Meyerson, a young Lithuanian Jew—a gentle lover of literature, art, and music—with whom she had fallen in love (although he was not a Zionist) to accompany her to Palestine. On December 24, 1917, the two married in Milwaukee. They had planned a civil ceremony, "no guests and no fuss. We were socialists, tolerant of tradition, but in no way bound by ritual."[154] But after Meir's mother informed her that a civil ceremony "would kill her," Meir relented, and the ceremony was performed by an eminent Jewish scholar, Rabbi Scheinfeld.

Meir spent the first few years of her married life travelling for the Poale Zion. She attributed the start of her political career to serving as a delegate to the first convention of the American Jewish Congress in 1918. But Sheyna began to worry that her sister's commitment to public issues was overshadowing her private life. "As far as personal happiness is concerned, grasp it, Goldie, and hold it tight," she advised.[155]

But the die was already cast. Meir had committed herself to Zionism. With Sheyna (now married), her two sons, and a close friend from Milwaukee, Golda and Morris sailed from America to Palestine on May 23, 1921, exactly three weeks to the day after Arab riots against the Jews broke out in Palestine. "I took a great deal with me from America to Palestine, more perhaps than I can express," Meir recalled. Especially important were "an understanding of the meaning of freedom, an awareness of the opportunities offered to the individual in a true democracy and a permanent nostalgia for the great beauty of the American countryside." After fifteen years in her adopted country, she left, loving America and "always glad to come back. . . ."[156]

In Palestine, however, Meir found that the East European *halutzim* scorned her American background. Twice the Meyersons' application to join the kibbutz of their choosing, Merhavia, was refused because its members doubted the young American woman's capacity for hard work. On the third try, the Meyersons were accepted. But the kibbutz members found Meir's "American" contributions to kibbutz life (tablecloths, wildflower centerpieces, ironed sackcloth clothes) "bourgeois." Meir nonetheless felt completely "at home" on the kibbutz and enjoyed all collective tasks, no matter how menial or backbreaking. Soon the kibbutz members recognized her dedication and skills, including political ones, and accepted her as a true *halutza*.[157] After a year, the kibbutz elected her as its delegate to the newly formed council of the Labor Zionist party, the Histadrut.

Her husband, however, never adjusted to communal life and resented Meir's attention to the group. Recognizing the conflict between "my duty and my innermost desires," Meir sorrowfully gave up the kibbutz and went with her husband to Jerusalem to resume a private domestic life.[158] After the birth of two children in 1924 and 1926, she found herself miserable and depressed, bitterly resenting her isolation from the collective life of Zionism. When she finally accepted an offer to become secretary of the Working Women's Council (Moetzet Hapoalot), she did so with the recognition that her already strained marriage would collapse. She remained on good terms with her husband, whom she divorced after some years, but Morris was deeply critical of Meir's growing absorption in political affairs at the expense of her family, as were Sheyna, her parents (who joined the family in Palestine in 1926), and her own children. "She is a public person, not a home-body," Sheyna complained in 1928. "Should we rejoice in this? She forgets about *tate-mame* [father-mother] and herself."[159]

During these years, Meir lived with an "overwhelming" guilt about her frequent absences from her children. To be a working mother, she admitted in an unsigned article about pioneer Zionist women in the 1920s, was to experience unparalleled "inner struggles," "despair," and "anguish."[160] In 1930, on her way to London for an international labor conference, she wrote to Sheyna that her "social activities are not an accidental thing; they are an absolute necessity for me. I am hurt when Morris and others say that this is all superficial, that I am trying to be modern. . . . Believe me, I know I will not bring the Messiah, but I think that we must miss no opportunity to explain what we want and what we are to influential people."[161]

In 1925, four years after Meir sailed to Palestine, seven American women, all of them married to activists in the Poale Zion, formed the organization Pioneer Women, which brought Meir back to the United States within a few years. The occasion for its establishment had been a call from Rachel Yanait Ben-Zvi, wife of the man who would become the second president of Israel, for $500 to dig a well at an agricultural settlement outside Jerusalem. The women raised the money, and although that particular well was never dug, it "watered the ground for Pioneer Women [which] grew out of American soil," as one of the founders remarked.[162] Within a year, there were clubs in Washington, Detroit, Scranton, Passaic, Stamford, Chicago, Toronto, Winnipeg, and New York; another dozen cities organized clubs the following year, raising substantial amounts of money to aid settlements in Palestine and provide social welfare services for women.[163]

Although Pioneer Women responded to the "call of the well," its founding also addressed the internal needs of American Zionist women. Committed in theory to equal rights, in practice the Labor Zionist Party seemed unenthusiastic about giving women responsibility; often women did little more than prepare food and watch children at party meetings. Some Labor Zionist women had formed a "ladies auxiliary" to the group's cultural arm, the Farband, which helped run *folk shulen* (people's schools) and aided the Kupat Holim (the sick fund of the Histadrut). The auxiliaries acted as a support group to the main organization, working primarily in female-oriented activities, but they possessed little power of their own.

In contrast, Pioneer Women aimed to become an independent, ideologically committed, socialist Zionist organization that would undertake actions in its own right. "Palestine created us," one early member recalled. It gave American women "the opportunity to find employment for our energies that were lying fallow for lack of inducement. . . . The more we do for them, the more we really do for ourselves."[164] According to Sara Feder, one of the group's leaders and a childhood friend of Meir's from Milwaukee, Pioneer women allowed American working-class women Zionists to find "their place and an opportunity for self-expression."[165] Although they did not call themselves feminists, they understood that the Jewish woman needed to fight masculine privilege in order to come into her own: "She must wage war against man in order to uproot herself from the dingy corner into which history and nature have set her. . . ."[166]

Most of these women believed that Hadassah had become too middle-class and Americanized. In 1929, the national secretary of Pioneer Women told Hadassah that it aimed to reach a different constituency than the older organization: "poverty-stricken Jewry, the Jewish working women, the Jewish Socialist women."[167] Emphasizing Yiddishkeit and working-class consciousness, Pioneer Women rejected what they felt was Hadassah's top-down, "uptown," charity approach in favor of mutual aid and cooperation with women in Palestine. As the American arm of the Palestinian Working Women's Council, Pioneer Women supported such Council goals as building cooperative agricultural settlements, day-care centers, and homes for unmarried women.

At the same time, Pioneer Women came to reject the belief of socialists and communists that Jewish well-being lay in the universal triumph of the proletariat rather than in a permanent Jewish homeland. Rose Wachs, a trade unionist who joined the American Communist Party shortly after its founding in 1919, moved with her husband to the Soviet Union in 1927. When she returned to the United States five years later, after becoming disillusioned by Russian anti-Semitism, she joined Pioneer Women. "[I]t hit me like a ton of bricks" she recalled. "Our problem is not the capitalistic system; it's a world problem . . . the Jews had no place in the world, under any system. . . . And being Left inclined, I wasn't going to join the General Zionists. So I joined Pioneer Women."[168]

Palestinian emissaries, or *shlichot,* from the Working Women's Council played a critical role in establishing a link between the *halutza* in Palestine and the American Pioneer Women. The *shlichot* were "really the soul of the organization," one American remembered. "Around them there was such a holy feeling! They were the ones who gave it content, who gave it wings, who gave it imagination . . . they spoke about their struggles in the fields, about the very beginnings of Israel, how they bring up their children, how the children helped plant."[169] The first *shlicha* was Rachel Ben-Zvi, who came to America in 1927. Golda Meyerson followed two years later and returned in 1932, remaining for two years as *shlicha* and editor of the journal *Pioneer Woman.* As secretary of the Working Women's Council, she had been given the assignment of organizing new chapters and broadening the base of Pioneer Women into a national organization. She also had to raise funds, which she hoped to do by stirring American women to become more active in Zionism.[170]

Meir did her job well. Though the United States was experiencing the worst years of the Depression, she travelled everywhere, telling "the latest anecdotes of halutzic life, the many humorous stories, the bits of gossip . . . [she] taught . . . the latest songs and dances, and danced the hora with us until the wee hours of the morning."[171] To her listeners, Meir created a vivid and romantic portrait of the pioneering Zionist experiment. As one St. Louis woman recalled, "Goldie brought us a waft of fragrant orange blossoms, sprouting vegetables, budding trees, well-cared for cows and chickens, stubborn territory conquered, dangerous natural elements vanquished, all the result of work, work, work. . . ."[172] In a heavily beaded silk dress "styled like old Russia, her hair in braids wound round her head, smoking incessantly," she cut an unusual figure. At least one male ZOA worker saw Meir as a colorful *femme fatale.*[173]

Meir's message of the importance of supporting Labor Zionism's economic and social program was deeply political, not sentimental. Moreover, unlike Szold and other Hadassah leaders, she claimed that the greatest contribution Americans could offer to Zionism was to make *aliyah* (immigrate) to Palestine. Anything less was not true Zionism.[174] Meir insisted that the Zionist project had to be approached without compromise. When she heard that a small midwestern Pioneer Women's club had raised money by playing cards, she was appalled. "For Palestine, you play cards?" she fumed. "If you want to play cards, you can play as long as you like, but not in our name!"[175]

At the time of Meir's visit, Pioneer Women was under pressure to expand its base of Yiddish-speaking members to incorporate younger English-speakers. Daughters of immigrants, these women were better educated, more Americanized, and often less class-conscious than the older generation. While some founding members opposed their incorporation into the organization, Meir successfully campaigned to open up Pioneer Women to younger members. In her youth, she had been on the opposite side of this issue, protesting the Poale Zion's attempt to establish English-only clubs. Now, however, she understood that a more inclusive organization could only help the Yishuv. Setting out on an eight-month tour of the United States, she inspired many new clubs, both English and Yiddish, and signalled Pioneer Women's transformation into a broader and more popular, if less ideological, organization. By the end of the 1930s, its membership had doubled, reaching 10,000.

While Hadassah vastly outnumbered Pioneer Women, the latter also represented a viable means for American women to find self-expression and spiritual satisfaction by identifying themselves with the Zionist cause, particularly the struggles of women in Palestine. As American Jewish women moved further away from their immigrant roots, the connection to the pioneering women of Palestine gave them a means of expressing their own Jewishness. Even as they became more Americanized, their affiliation with Labor Zionism served to counter the process of assimilation. It was especially as women, however, that American Jewish women, linked to the work of building up Palestine, found a new voice and purpose. "The halutza has . . . shown us what emancipation of woman is," remarked Sophie Udin, one of Pioneer Women's founders.[176]

When Meir returned to Palestine in 1934, she did not continue her work for Moetzet Hapoalot. Instead, she joined the executive committee of the Histadrut, from which position she would rise to labor secretary, foreign minister, and eventually prime minister of the State of Israel. To Meir, the greatest challenge was to work not in a separate women's organization, but alongside the top political leaders of the country, who happened to be men. Even while travelling for Pioneer Women, she had often been asked by Americans, "Why do you talk about the Histadrut in general instead of the work of the women?"[177] Meir's biographer, Marie Syrkin, points out that her friend was not a natural feminist. "She did not make a cult of women's rights but took feminine equality for granted. From the outset she was a leader who was a woman rather than a woman leader."[178] Although Meir may have been more conservative than many other women in the Palestine labor movement, her skills in negotiating her way through the male hierarchy of the Histadrut and, later, the Mapai (Israel Workers) Party, were unparalleled.[179]

Meir's involvement in Pioneer Women—like that of Szold and Sampter in Hadassah—helped create a structure that enabled generations of American women to identify with the Zionist cause. For the many members of women's Zionist organizations in America, home became, as Sampter once remarked, "my people, my congregation." In the interwar period, as the membership of the Zionist Organization of America declined, that of Hadassah and Pioneer Women mounted rapidly, a testimony to the dynamic involvement of its women.

WIDER WORLDS
1930–1960

Chapter 5

JEWISH WOMEN IN POPULAR CULTURE

Red-Hot Mamas, Iron Women, and Sob Sisters: Sophie Tucker, Fanny Brice, Edna Ferber, and Fannie Hurst

"There is a curiously strong bond in Jewish families," Edna Ferber wrote in her autobiography. "They cling together. Jewish parents are possessive, Jewish sons and daughters are filial to the point of sentimentality." The story of her own life she called "the story of an American Jewish family in the past half-century, and as such . . . really a story about America. . . ."[1] The desire to pull away from her possessive family was also central to Fannie Hurst's and Sophie Tucker's personal narratives. These women's autobiographies—and much of Ferber's and Hurst's fiction, though this ostensibly did not have "Jewish" characters or plots—are tales of the hard-fought struggle for autonomy waged between Jewish daughters and their parents, particularly their mothers.

Daughters of assimilated midwestern German Jewish families in Ferber's and Hurst's cases, and of an Eastern European immigrant family in Tucker's, these women, like popular entertainer Fanny Brice, became outspoken champions of the American Dream, reflecting in their own careers the opportunities of ethnic women to become members of the cultural elite. Only a few years younger than Mary Antin and Anzia Yezierska, Tucker, Brice, Ferber, and Hurst seemed to come from another generation. Through their writings and performances, they bridged the modern world in ways that Antin and Yezierska, first-generation immigrants focused on ghetto subjects, could not. In embracing mass culture for their own, these artists helped their fellow Jews acculturate to urban America by demonstrating how Jewish women could live as forward-looking, unconventional, innovative moderns, as "Americans" unfettered by ethnic constraints. Yet these women's romance with America would be tempered by an allegiance to their ancestral past. The road out of the ghetto, they would find, was not necessarily one-way.[2]

Tucker, Ferber, and Hurst were among the many American Jews who played a vital role in developing the new forms of mass culture—the so-called secular temples of twentieth-century Jewry—that flourished in the teens, twenties, and thirties. During these years, Jews continued their progress into the American mainstream despite a rising tide of anti-Semitism and the crisis of the Depression. Though they gathered in Jewish neighborhoods and joined ethnically based professional, business, and voluntary associations, large numbers of Jews nonetheless abandoned what to many traditionalists constituted the only meaningful core of Jewish identity: religious faith.[3] Yiddish theater, vaudeville, and radio became a new kind of Jewish popular religion as this "lost" generation of American Jews journeyed forth to find their places in a less separatist, more inclusive pluralistic society.

Meanwhile, an ocean away from the sources of this new culture, Gertrude Stein was holding forth in her Paris salon, the center of a pioneering adventure in literary and artistic modernism.

So Big and Ugly   Throughout half a century in show business, Sophie Tucker (born Sonya Abuza) was a wanderer; she called herself a "gypsy of the footlights."[4] From café supper clubs to vaudeville, burlesque, musical revues, nightclubs, and concert stages, she toured the United States and Europe. This gypsy of the theater was actually born on the road—her seventeen-year-old mother gave birth to her somewhere on the "long rutted track" out of Russia across Poland, on her way to the Baltic and then to America, to join Tucker's father, who had run away from the Russian military service. Tucker arrived in the United States in 1884 when she was three months old.

After settling in Boston, where they spent eight years, Tucker's parents, Charlie and Jennie Abuza, moved to Hartford and opened Abuza's Home Restaurant. Thanks to Tucker's mother, whose home-cooked meals attracted hungry locals plus travelling show people from the Yiddish theater and vaudeville stage, the restaurant did well. Jennie Abuza dominated the family despite her husband's traditional role as head of the Orthodox household. Laboring constantly over a hot stove and scheming to make ends meet, Jennie helped the family survive. Charlie Abuza, the cashier, managed to squander the restaurant's profits by playing pinochle and poker with an unsavory bunch of "bums and pimps," as Tucker recalled them, every night.[5] Tucker loved her gentle father, but it was her mother she admired.

Tucker contributed to the family business by drumming up customers and entertaining them with her singing. Although Jennie Abuza appreciated the tips Tucker brought in, she called her daughter *zovarecha* (whirlwind) because she rushed through her household chores to get out of the house. Tucker was already being lured by Hartford's amateur theaters and vaudeville shows; some of Abuza's customers, like Yiddish stars Jacob Adler and Boris Tomashevsky, noticed Tucker's talent and tried to convince her parents to let her join one of the Jewish companies. But neither they nor Tucker, already accumulating experience in amateur shows, was interested; Tucker recognized that Yiddish theater was losing its appeal to the more popular "American" theater. Yet she was beginning to think in earnest about a show business career: "Suppose you could earn a living by singing and making people laugh," she asked herself, "wouldn't that be better than spending your life drudging in a kitchen?"[6]

Her mother no doubt wished better for Tucker than her own life of domestic toil—she even bought her a piano with her savings but sold it after Tucker, complaining that her stubby fingers could not play scales and arpeggios, refused to practice—yet her advice was traditional. "After you are through school," she told Tucker, "then you must look around for a good, steady young man and get married. . . . Don't have anything to do with traveling men, or with show people. There are too many grifters and grafters among them. They have no real homes; no sense of responsibility." They were like the gypsies who used to wander through Russia, "thieving and making trouble."[7]

In no time at all, Tucker did find a man to marry, a handsome neighbor, Louis Tuck, a beer-wagon trucker, who made the awkward overweight girl feel like a desirable belle of the ball. A week after her high school graduation, they eloped, although Jennie insisted on an Orthodox wedding when the couple returned. Tucker became pregnant almost immediately; when her son, Bert, was born, the Tucks moved in with the Abuzas, and she found herself back in the restaurant kitchen, chopping vegetables and washing dishes.

Tuck left her when she insisted he work harder to support the family; Sophie then ran off to New York to try her luck as a singer, leaving the baby with her parents. Although in her autobiography she doesn't dwell on her emotions at leaving home, she does describe the condemnation she experienced and her pangs of guilt. When she returned for her first visit after two years away, her mother's hair had turned white and her son barely recognized her; he called Tucker's sister "Mama." Tucker learned that though her family had forgiven her, the neighbors had not. "They said only a bad woman would do such a thing. I must be a bad woman—a whore, in the unvarnished language of the Scriptures." Her sister and son were ridiculed because Tucker "wore paint on her face"; because she had gone on the stage and left her child, she was considered "no good." Tucker vowed not to return to Hartford until she had become a star, and remained away for more than five years.[8]

Her autobiography, *Some of These Days,* does not dwell on these hurts, focusing instead on her rise in show business. At every turn, she stresses the need for independence, preparation, and determination. At age seventeen, Sophie changed her name to Tucker, which seemed more melodious, and began her career by talking her way into appearances at Greenwich Village restaurants. Wherever she went, she cultivated friendships with producers, stagehands, waiters, and customers, which she knew could be useful to her. Before long she was playing in trendy rathskellers, earning $100 to $150 a week—substantial sums in 1906, and ones that allowed her to avoid prostitution, a trap into which many young performers on their own descended. She assuaged her conscience by wiring much of her pay to Hartford.

As Tucker tells her life story, luck plays as large a role as strategy. Her first triumph was as a blackface performer, for example, but it was only "by accident" that she donned the disguise. When the manager of the amateur night at a Harlem theater spotted her preparing to go on, he shouted to a assistant: "This one's so big and ugly the crowd out front will razz her. Better get some cork and black her up." Although she protested, within weeks Tucker was booked on the small-time vaudeville circuit; for the next six years, from 1906 to 1912, she was the World-Renowned Coon Shouter, Sophie Tucker, the Ginger Girl, the Refined Coon Singer, and Sophie Tucker, Manipulator of Coon Melodies. For Tucker, one of the first female entertainers to use blackface, the mask worked as well as it did for Eddie Cantor and Al Jolson, who were Jewish, and for Bert Williams, a West Indian. Audiences accepted her southern accent ("as thick and smooth as molasses," she described it) and her appearance; after a while, she began to use "high yellow" rather than jet black. "When I would pull off one of my gloves and show that I was white there'd be a sort of surprised gasp, then a howl of laughter." So she began interpolating Yiddish words, "just to give the audience a kick," she joked, but perhaps to declare as well who she really was.[9]

If Tucker resented the blackface, it was because it prevented her from appearing as herself, like the prettier girls; blackface denied her femaleness, not her ethnicity (in fact, with her hearty deep voice, critics used to refer to her as a "male impersonator"). She had little to say about the racial stereotyping endemic in the costumes, gestures, and lyrics that were part of her act. The style was ubiquitous in vaudeville, inherited from the popular minstrel shows of the nineteenth century, although by the turn of the century newer forms of burlesque had begun to replace it. For ethnic entertainers eager to show that they were "real" Americans, "coon" singing had guaranteed benefits. With African Americans the butt of their humor, immigrant vaudevillians demonstrated that, however "foreign" their own cultures might be viewed, blacks (with their supposed emotionalism and crude physicality) were even more inferior. Yet as some scholars suggest, blackface also embodied a plaintive note expressing the pain of rootlessness so deeply a part of the immigrant experience.[10]

Although blackface molded Tucker's performance style, enhancing the physicality of her performance and introducing her to the modern syncopated style of music that would facilitate her later embrace of jazz, she chafed at its restrictions and denial of her femininity. Yet she was afraid to go on stage without it. The opportunity to discard blackface arose when a Brooklyn theater manager, pretending that her trunk was lost, sent her on without it. Then another "accident" occurred that would redirect Tucker's career. Dressed one night in a tightly laced black princess gown (like a "baloney in mourning,"

Tucker recalled), with a long train of red chiffon ruffles, she slipped during her bows and caught her heel in the ruffles of her dress: "Down I went on my fanny like a ton of bricks."[11] The applause was deafening; even the cast shrieked with laughter. Tucker the comedienne was born.

Another transition in Tucker's career came when she began to incorporate "double entendre" songs into her routine. Years before, a songwriter had told her that because she was "big and gawky, and entirely lacking in 'allure,' " she could sing sexy material that, if used by attractive performers, would seem salacious and offensive. Soon her routine was set—first a "lively" rag, then a ballad, a comedy song, a novelty number, and finally the "hot" or sexy song, which would leave the audience "laughing their heads off." ("She sings the words we used to write on the sidewalks," Eddie Cantor once commented.)[12]

Tucker insisted that her songs, however off-color, were "all moral"; they had to do with sex, not vice. But the secret of her success was that they were all in the first person, poking fun at her own sexual mishaps. As she learned when she fell on her backside, audiences found personal distress funny; they laughed, but with the knowledge that they too could suffer from romantic misfortune. By hinting at her own sexual experimentation and revealing the details of her romantic life (after Louis Tuck there were two more husbands), she liberated her audience's imagination.

So Tucker—the overweight immigrant girl from Hartford—became the doyenne of the innuendo song, famous for her wiggles and shakes and for songs with titles like "Nobody Loves a Fat Girl But How a Fat Girl Can Love," "That Lovin' Soul Kiss," "Everybody Shimmies Now," "Vamp, Vamp, Vamp," and "Who Paid the Rent for Mrs. Rip Van Winkle when Rip Van Winkle Was Away?" Once she was hauled into court in Portland, Oregon, for obscene gestures—she had run her fingers suggestively down her body—but the case was dismissed. Other shows were cancelled because "sizzling" songs were on the playbill.[13]

Just as she had fashioned every new departure in her career, Tucker used her size and unattractiveness to construct a "red-hot" persona that defied cultural expectations. At a time when vaudeville and burlesque were becoming increasingly subdued as they reached out to a broader family audience, Tucker managed to elude censorship; her "ugliness" was a new mask, one that gave her the freedom to transgress. Using humor and self-mockery, she sang her "hot" torch songs about women's sexual passions and romantic agonies: all women, even "big, ugly" ones, needed sex and love; it was men's failures in bed and in marriage that denied women their due. Inattentive as lovers, unreliable as husbands, the men she sang about were not very different from the *shlemiels* and *paskudniks* her mother used to warn her against.[14] In this way, at least, Tucker was her mother's daughter.

Tucker's routines may have been comic and ribald (some would have said vulgar), yet they reveal her as an early champion of woman's liberation. Ex-

Anna Rosen Kessler, the author's grandmother, arrested during the garment
workers' uprising in 1909. *(Joyce Antler)*

(Right) Demure-looking Pauline Newman, on the
left, and Clara Lemlich, on the right, organized
strikes among shirtwaist makers across the Lower
East Side. In November 1909, Lemlich issued the
call for a general strike of the garment industry
that changed the course of union organizing and
American labor history. *(Schlesinger Library, Radcliffe
College)*

Anarchist leader Emma Goldman, often called "the most dangerous woman in the world,"
thought Jews were the mainstay of every revolutionary endeavor. A popular speaker, here she
addresses a crowd in Union Square, New York, in 1916 on birth control. *(Bettmann Archive)*

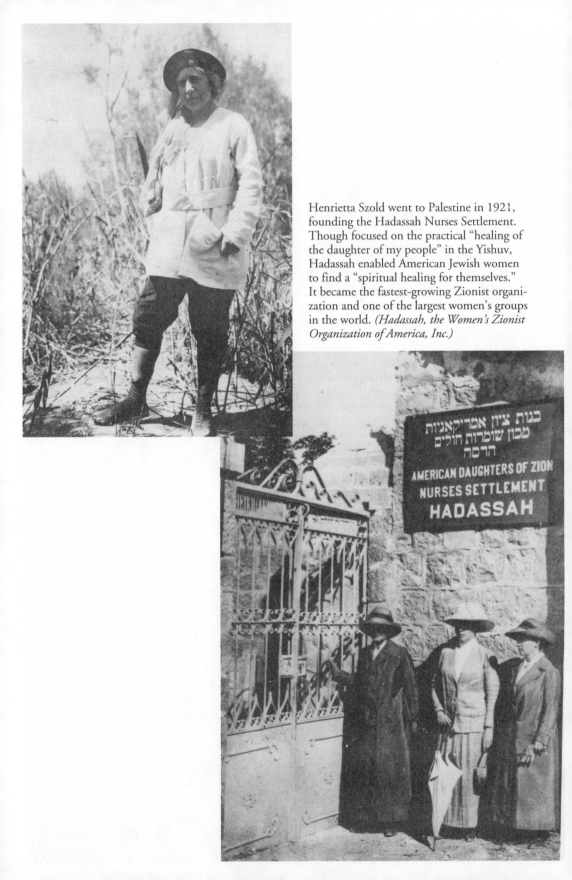

Henrietta Szold went to Palestine in 1921, founding the Hadassah Nurses Settlement. Though focused on the practical "healing of the daughter of my people" in the Yishuv, Hadassah enabled American Jewish women to find a "spiritual healing for themselves." It became the fastest-growing Zionist organization and one of the largest women's groups in the world. *(Hadassah, the Women's Zionist Organization of America, Inc.)*

בנות ציון אמריקאניות
מכון שומרות חולים
הדסה
AMERICAN DAUGHTERS OF ZION
NURSES SETTLEMENT
HADASSAH

While she continued to call the United States "home," Szold remained in Palestine for the better part of three decades, serving in the Jewish Agency Executive and directing Youth Aliyah, which rescued thousands of European youth from the Nazis and settled them on kibbutzim in Palestine. Here, in the early 1940s, she dances with Youth Aliyah children. *(Hadassah, the Women's Zionist Organization of America, Inc.)*

As reported in a contemporary newspaper, the woman dressed as the Statue of Liberty in this 1919 Labor Zionist pageant in Milwaukee is Golda Mabovitch Meyerson (Golda Meir). Two years later, she sailed to Palestine with her husband and joined a kibbutz. She returned to the United States in the late 1920s and again for two years in the early 1930s to establish a link between Palestinian women and the American Labor Zionist women's group, Pioneer Women. *(State Historical Society of Wisconsin Archives)*

The Wanderer finds Liberty in America

In addition to her sultry songs, "Red-Hot Mama" Sophie Tucker was famous throughout the U.S. and Europe for her moving rendition of "My Yiddishe Mama" sung in English and Yiddish. Inspired by her immigrant mother, Tucker served as president of the vaudeville workers' union and raised several million dollars for Jewish causes. *(American Jewish Archives, Cincinnati Campus, Hebrew Union College)*

(Left) Molly Picon was one of the biggest stars of Yiddish theater, the secular temple of American Jewry in the early part of the century. Here she appears in *Some Girl* (Oy Is This a Maydel) at the Second Avenue Theater, New York, 1927–28. *(American Jewish Historical Society, Waltham, Massachusetts)*

(Right) As Molly Goldberg in the popular radio and TV series *The Goldbergs*, Gertrude Berg was widely seen as the prototypical Jewish mother from the late 1920s to the early 1950s. Like her fictional character, Berg was dedicated to interfaith harmony, but was more political and, as the writer of the show as well as its star, much less domestic. *(Syracuse University Library, Department of Special Collections)*

(Left) "Sob sister" Fannie Hurst, known in her era as the highest paid writer in the world, wrote of the struggles of working women and often about Jews and immigrants. Her feelings toward her heritage were mixed. The daughter of bourgeois midwestern German Jews who looked down on their less privileged coreligionists, she kept her marriage to an Eastern European immigrant musician secret for several years. (Brandeis University Special Collections)

(Right) Edna Ferber, author of Giant, Show Boat, and the Pulitzer prize–winning novel So Big, attributed her success to having been born a Jew. "Being a Jew makes it tougher to get on," she commented, "and I like that." (Wisconsin Center for Film and Theater Research)

Expatriate, modernist writer Gertrude Stein held court in her Paris salon "like a great Jewish Buddha." Here she is seen at a villa outside Florence in 1905. Stein admired Jews' "clan feeling" and their high "ethical and spiritual nature." It is widely believed that she survived World War II with her lover, Alice B. Toklas (another California German Jew), because of her relationship with the Vichy regime. (Beinecke Rare Book and Manuscript Library, Yale University)

Bel Kaufman, a "subway scholar" who graduated from tuition-free Hunter College in 1934 and went on to teach for 25 years, immortalized the experience of New York City schoolteachers (more than half of whom were Jewish women) in her best-selling novel *Up the Down Staircase*. She is shown *(above left)* with her grandfather, the Yiddish author Sholem Aleichem, and *(below)* with Mayor John Lindsay and Sandy Dennis on the set of the film made from her novel. *(Courtesy of Bel Kaufman)*

A Family Court Justice for almost 40 years and a juvenile justice pioneer, Justine Wise Polier was known as "Joan of Arc" for her fiery speeches as a labor activist before she reached the bench. Polier inherited her ethical standards from her father, Rabbi Stephen Wise, and her mother, philanthropist and artist Louise Waterman Wise, whose self-portrait fills the background. *(Schlesinger Library, Radcliffe College)*

(Left) In the aftermath of the Holocaust, the Emma Lazarus Federation of Jewish Women's Clubs, a progressive, working-class, immigrant-based group, devoted its energies to promoting Jewish culture and fighting anti-Semitism and racism. Members are shown at the 1963 March on Washington. *(American Jewish Archives, Cincinnati Campus, Hebrew Union College, Jewish Institute of Religion)*

(Right) Jewish women played a leading role in establishing the second wave of feminism in the 1960s. Betty Friedan, author of the landmark *The Feminine Mystique*, felt that her "passion against injustice" sprang from her experiences of anti-Semitism in Peoria, Illinois. Here Friedan is shown at the Capitol in 1967 campaigning for women's rights. *(Photographed by Joan Roth)*

(Below) Three-term Congresswoman, peace activist, and feminist leader Bella Abzug did her first campaigning for a Labor Zionist youth group in the Bronx; she believes her early Zionism made her a political activist and kept her a rebel. At the First National Women's Conference in Houston, 1977, with First Ladies Lady Bird Johnson and Rosalynn Carter looking on, she passes the Olympic Torch. *(Photographed by Joan Roth)*

Under the influence of the feminist movement, Jewish women have enthusiastically taken up the study of religious texts and created new rituals, prayers, and ceremonies. Here feminists gather at a Passover celebration in New York in 1991, marking the seventeenth year of their women's seder. In white, in the center is E.M. Broner. To her right are Letty Cottin Pogrebin and Judith Plaskow. To her left, counterclockwise, are Adrienne Cooper, Edith Isaac Rose, Merle Hoffman, Liz Abzug, and Bea Kreloff. *(Photographed by Joan Roth)*

At the First International Jewish Women's Conference in Jerusalem in 1988, Orthodox feminist activists Norma Baumel Joseph from Canada and Rivka Haut from the United States carry the Torah to the *Kotel* (the Western Wall) to conduct a prayer service. In the face of opposition from ultra-Orthodox men, Israeli women, supported by an international group, established the Women of the Wall, and continued their campaign for the right to conduct public prayer services at the site. Also shown are Susan Alter, Shulamit Magnus, and Phyllis Chesler. *(Photographed by Joan Roth)*

posing the inevitable pathos of love and romance, she insisted upon women's right to sexual fulfillment and portrayed them as strong, indomitable, and independent. "Make Him Say Please," "You Can't Deep Freeze a Red-Hot Mama," "I'm Living Alone and I Like It," and "I Ain't Takin' Orders From No One" were among the songs that brought her message to receptive audiences, especially after 1916, when she began playing evening supper clubs rather than family-oriented vaudeville, which eschewed risqué lyrics.[15]

But it was not only as a self-styled raunchy blues singer—a "Red-Hot [American] Mama"—that Sophie Tucker reached the height of stardom. At the start of World War I, with her eye, as always, on marketability, she surmised that the American public might respond especially well to songs with emotional appeal. For this reason, she introduced the ballad "M-O-T-H-E-R, the Word that Means the World To Me" into her act. She did not introduce her most famous song, "My Yiddishe Mama," into her repertoire, however, until 1925, a few months after her mother's death.

Jennie Abuza's influence over Tucker had continued even after Tucker became a star. "No matter how set up I was with myself, the minute I set foot in Ma's house I had to fall in line with the rules of an old-fashioned, religious household," she recalled. "I had to stop being the headliner and the boss, and remember I was just a daughter. . . ." After Tucker became famous, her mother's friends made peace with her apostasy in leaving home, but they too treated her like a little girl. "You yell just as loud in the theater as you did in the restaurant," one of them told her. Tucker admired the pluck of these Yiddish-speaking women, all of whom were involved in fund-raising, under Jennie's leadership, for such causes as the Jewish Home for the Aged. Tucker called Jennie the original *pushke* lady (saver for charities) because she was always collecting pennies and distributing clothes and food to the needy. "When Mama said 'Give!' you gave—or else!" Tucker recalled. In later years, Jennie gave away all the allowance Tucker sent her, usually ending up broke herself. Jennie and her friends became models of female strength and generosity; they made it impossible, Tucker acknowledged, for her to get a "swelled head."[16]

Tucker's visits never lasted long. Instead, she showered her mother with gifts, including a pair of diamond earrings that Jennie traded on the streetcar for a pair of bigger blue stones that turned out to be glass. She brought Jennie to New York to see her show, treating her to the best restaurants, although Jennie refused to eat because the food wasn't kosher. One time, the waiter brought twelve sterling-silver teapots for Tucker's party. Jennie thought they wouldn't miss one, and slipped a teapot into her coat pocket. Sophie played a joke by asking the manager of the restaurant to call her mother and tell her she would be arrested for theft. Remembering the Cossacks, Jennie was terrified.[17]

But there is no question that Tucker saw her mother as a forceful, courageous figure. She starts her autobiography, in fact, by describing her mother's guts, her *dreistige*.[18] But although Tucker's respect for Jennie was deep, it was mixed with not a little guilt and perhaps some resentment. Jennie died when Tucker was crossing the Atlantic, returning from an engagement in London where she had become a superstar; Tucker was grateful that, as she lay dying, Jennie had asked that the funeral be delayed till Tucker arrived. Tucker realized that in suspending her Orthodox beliefs (which called for immediate burial), her "darling yiddishe mama" was demonstrating "how much she loved me and how well she understood my love for her."[19] But that she could not say goodbye because she was off like the show business "gypsies" her mother had hated may have left a "stinging mark." Jennie's will divided her possessions among Tucker's brother and sister and a neighbor. But "to my daughter, Sophie, who gave me everything," she gave "nothing because she don't need anything."[20] Was this another "slap," a reminder of Tucker's disobedience as a daughter? Or a recognition of Tucker's show business success?

Tucker suffered a nervous breakdown after Jennie died and was unable to work for months. On stage at a benefit for the Jewish Theatrical Guild at the Manhattan Opera House, she stood "paralyzed." Tucker stayed in bed for weeks, her self-confidence gone. "I had a feeling I was done for as a performer," she remembered.[21] Not long after that, Lou Pollack and Jack Yellen, her longtime songwriter and accompanist, wrote "My Yiddishe Mama" for her. She sang it first at the Palace Theater in New York in 1925, and after that everywhere there were Jews. She sang it in English and, for Jewish audiences, in Yiddish as well, and its effect was cathartic. Combining "Victorian sentiment with Tin Pan Alley," as one observer noted, the appeal of the song was universal. Mainstream American audiences appreciated its sentimenal motherhood motif; in Yiddish the song commented even more specifically on the bittersweet experience of assimilation.[22]

"Yiddishe Mama" was a nostalgic celebration of the ghetto mother's nurturing warmth and love, her generosity and forgiveness. Its poignancy came from coupling this emotion-laden tribute with the recognition that the child, however grateful to her mother, still had to leave home, to be caught forever between the pull of loneliness and the necessity of independence. The Yiddishe mama, as Tucker sang her, existed in a world where parents controlled their children's destiny and offered love with discipline; but it was a world of the past that was vanishing even when Tucker herself was growing up. A plaintive, mournful song written in a minor key, it perfectly expressed the predicament of second-generation Jews. Unlike Al Jolson's buoyant "Mammy" and other tributes to mother love by musical comedy performers, it was a song of grief. The other side of the steely determination and breezy humor reflected in Tucker's autobiography, "My Yiddishe Mama" mourned the family closeness that immigrant children lost as they set off on their own paths.

Just as Tucker's "red-hot" number, "Some of These Days," served as her theme song in the United States, "My Yiddishe Mama"—her "Jewish song"—became her signature song in Europe, where it became an anthem for Jews and a target for anti-Semitism. After Hitler came to power, her recordings of the song were ordered smashed and their sale banned throughout the Reich. The song remained a regular part of Tucker's performances through the 1960s, when she was still giving command performances in London and drawing enthusiastic crowds to New York's famed nightclub, the Latin Quarter. But the more removed the song grew from the realities of immigrant life, the more sentimental, old-fashioned, and purely nostalgic it became. Not so with Tucker's "hot" songs. Tucker retained her sexual brazenness throughout her long career, enchanting audiences with exuberant, bawdy performances that ridiculed conventional gender roles and championed sexual liberation. Enticed by the singer's frank and sultry lyrics, which seemed to promise a freer world for both women and men, a generation of young Americans grew up listening to her records, often in secret. The last of the "red-hot mamas," Tucker died in 1966; although not a "nice Jewish girl" by the standards of her mother's generation, she was one of America's earliest and most influential "popular culture" feminists.

To the Mikvah   Tucker's Jewish influences carried over to her offstage role as labor leader, social activist, and philanthropist. Although her work as union leader is little known today, and is mentioned only briefly in Tucker's autobiography, in the 1930s her labor activism was very much in the public eye.

In 1938, Tucker was elected president of the 15,000-member American Federation of Actors (AFA), a union of vaudevillians, circus actors, night club entertainers, and stagehands chartered two years earlier as a constituent union of the Associated Actors and Artists of America (colloquially known as the 4As.).[23] The first female president of the AFA, Tucker had experienced the crowded, unsanitary backstage facilities that vaudevillians and variety artists endured, as well as cheap and uncomfortable rooming houses, low pay, and lack of security. She supported their organizing apart from "legitimate" theatrical actors, even though variety artists were considered poor prospects as union members because they travelled so frequently. Notwithstanding the fact that early in her career, Tucker had dismissed her own band—the Five Kings of Syncopation—when they asked for a raise, she became committed to the labor movement in later years. In representing vaudevillians, many of whom were immigrants, blacks, ethnics, and women, almost all from working-class origins, Tucker laid claim to the heritage of union activism in which so many Jewish women participated.

Under her command, the AFA called several successful strike actions. In 1939, a bitter conflict between the AFA and its parent body, the powerful 4As, tested the quality of Tucker's leadership. When the 4As accused Ralph Whitehead, executive secretary of Tucker's union, of illegally using funds collected at benefit performances for administrative purposes, Tucker denied the charges. Hundreds of telegrams for and against the AFA flooded her office, including one from her old friend Eddie Cantor, who urged her to resign.

At a midnight meeting at New York's Hotel Edison on June 19 attended by 1,200 vaudeville actors, showgirls, and World's Fair and circus performers, Tucker refuted the charges against the AFA. Among those on stage with her were Rudy Vallee, Morton Downey, Milton Berle, and Bill Robinson, the black tap dancer known as Bojangles. But a shoving match between Tucker supporters and opponents broke out, resulting in a "virtual riot" of "flying fists, broken chinaware, [and] upturned chairs," as the *New York Times* described the melee in the next day's paper. Tucker begged the squabbling actors to desist, but abruptly dismissed the meeting when the free-for-all continued. Union officials and their exhausted but still-fighting leader beat a hasty retreat through the hotel pantry, leaving eight radio-car patrolmen to restore order.[24]

The charges against the union deeply wounded Tucker. As she told the Edison crowd in justifying the union's record, she had not been a "dummy . . . rubber stamp . . . president," but had taken an active role in all its affairs. Under her leadership, the AFA became the fastest growing of all the entertainers' unions and had obtained numerous benefits for workers. She believed that the charges against the union stemmed from these successes. Jealous and fearful of its strength, production companies and their allies attacked the AFA's management, and by inference, Tucker felt, her integrity.[25]

In September, the 4As found the AFA guilty of misusing relief funds; Tucker refused to enter a defense on the grounds that the parent body did not have the power to hold a trial over charges it had itself levied. But the 4As rescinded the AFA's charter and organized a new union, the American Guild of Variety Artists, with Eddie Cantor as temporary president. Threatening to blackball AFA actors working in venues where it held exclusive contracts— legitimate theater, film, radio, television, and grand opera—the 4As drew many members away from the discredited AFA.

Tucker refused to submit. Instead, she obtained a new charter from the powerful Stagehands' Union—the International Alliance of Theatrical State Employees and Moving Picture Operators, or IATSE. The dispute spilled over to the legitimate stage, where Tucker was appearing with Mary Martin in the Cole Porter musical, *Leave It to Me.* She was suspended from the Screen Actors' Guild, the American Federation of Radio Artists, and Actors' Equity. A strike of the entire theater industry seemed imminent.

Although Tucker received numerous telegrams in support of her stance, others blamed her for this unprecedented war in the theater. She received explicit anti-Semitic hate mail. "Who else but a Jew would do what she is skeming [*sic*] to do—putting herself at the head of a Union?" wrote one correspondent.[26] From her estate in Connecticut, Edna Ferber challenged Tucker to reverse course. "Sophie, in this matter . . . I think you are as wrong

as Hitler . . . I mean the method and the effect of the method are akin to his."
Not surprisingly, Ferber, a Pulitzer Prize novelist and one of the most popular
playwrights of the Broadway theater, sided with the "legitimate" actors:

> Actors are actors. I love and admire them. Stage-hands are stage-hands. I am for
> every fairness toward Labor. But there is no more reason why the Stage-Hands'
> Union should rule the actors' profession than that the Printers' Union (for exam-
> ple) should rule the writers of the United States. . . .[27]

Ferber advised Tucker to "sacrifice [her] vanity," but Tucker hung firm. This
dispute—between the upper-middle-class, German Jewish Ferber and the
lower-class Eastern European immigrant Tucker—recalled many previous
battles between "uptown" and "downtown" Jews. Though they were both
professional theater women who had made it in show business on their own
merits, their different upbringings placed them on opposite sides of this hotly
fought issue.

In the end, the anticipated theater strike did not materialize. The AFA's alliance with the Stagehands' Union ended after the leaders of IATSE came under investigation for racketeering. Without any recourse the AFA met its
demise, and so too did Tucker's career as labor leader.[28]

In the last few pages of her autobiography, Tucker reveals that it was her
troubles with the AFA that led friends to suggest that she present her version
of the episode in the context of the story of her life. Yet the autobiography de-
votes very little space to these events.[29] Rather than defend her integrity,
Tucker preferred to illustrate it through a candid depiction of her background
and rise in show business.

Tucker was pleased at the book's success and devoted its profits to her
favorite charities. She credits her mother with the idea of fund-raising at
nightclubs: "People who are spending so much money for parties could certainly give a little 'tzoka' [sic]," she told Tucker one night after a performance.[30] This comment led Tucker to offer for sale autographed copies of her
book and records after performances; she estimated that she collected many
thousands of dollars in this fashion. Her favorite cause was improving the
lives of mothers and children—she established a free maternity clinic at a
Jewish-sponsored hospital in Denver, a Sophie Tucker youth center at a summer camp in New Jersey, and several Sophie Tucker playgrounds for children
in Israel. Tucker acknowledged that the old-time Yiddishe mama's devotion
to her children was her own philanthropic guide: "Nothing mattered [to her]
but the *kinder*. . . . They were her whole life just as children are the whole life
of Judaism itself." While centered on Jewish children, she believed the Jewish
mother's love extended to "all childhood," as did Tucker's philanthropy.[31]

In later years, the State of Israel attracted Tucker's greatest interest, deepening her engagement with Judaism. She travelled throughout the world,

raising (she claimed) nearly four million dollars for Israel. "To me the mention of Israel is like the clang of a fire bell to a fireman," she once said.[32]

Although Tucker had abandoned the religious elements of Judaism, she retained some rituals, like saying *kaddish* (the prayer for the dead) for her parents and attending High Holiday services at the so-called actors' shul in the New York theater district. But she still thought of herself as one of the "lost generation" of Jews who had grown up "in the streets, among hostile neighbors, untutored in the faith of our ancestors, ignorant of the Holy Torah."[33] She intuitively understood a phenomenon about which many American sociologists had begun to comment: while her own generation, the children of immigrants, had abandoned religion in the rush to Americanize, the next generation was exhibiting a renewed interest in Judaism. Tucker marveled over this "Renaissance, the rebirth of Judaism," in which young Americans educated in modern religious schools were now "teaching their mothers the blessing of the Sabbath candles and their fathers the *kiddush* [the Sabbath prayer]."[34] She attributed the new popularity of Judaism to the influence of Israel. Having herself been so often to Israel, she vowed to start doing a lot of the things that "my Mother used to do and that I've neglected. I may even start going to the *mikvah* [the ritual bath for women]!"[35]

Of course, Tucker did no such thing. Her life had taken a different turn than that of her Orthodox mother and she could not go backward. Though it had meant a long apprenticeship in "beer halls, dives, burlesque and vaudeville . . . tank towns . . . flea-bag hotels [and] greasy joints," Tucker was proud that her show business "fantasy" had come true.[36] In pursuit of her dream, she had not only abandoned religious practice but given up her own family life—including the rearing of her only son. Yet although Tucker strayed from her roots, Jennie Abuza's model of familial authority, her strength and nurturance, and her concern for the wider community were never erased from Tucker's consciousness. She saw her mother's ideals at work in the women of her generation who served "their synagogues, their sisterhoods, their community centers, their settlement houses" as well as their homes. These women, she said, were "the true aristocracy of Jewish womanhood," and she envied them. "You represent what I have missed in life," she confessed in a speech to a Jewish women's group, "you are what I wish I might have been."[37]

So Sophie Tucker recognized her bond with Jennie Abuza's commitment to *tzedakah* (righteous acts) and with Jewish women who served their communities. It was in their image that she became "just a Yiddisha Momme [*sic*], begging, pleading and weeping, like Mother Rachel for her children," when she set out to raise money for Israel, her children's and women's causes, and her other philanthropies, including Brandeis University, where a chair in theater is named after her.[38] Traversing the globe on behalf of her philanthropies, this "life-long wanderer of the gypsy trails of show business" became widely known as the "Queen of Schnorrers" [beggars][39] a name that made her proud.

From her days in vaudeville and burlesque to her nightclub and stage performances and her recording career, Tucker established new standards of openness, portraying women's sexuality and desire in path-breaking ways; while a number of black blues singers and ethnic women performers went as far, few had Tucker's staying power and mass popularity. Of course, in creating the persona of the sexually assertive and independent woman, Tucker had necessarily to break with the image of the nice Jewish girl. She did not substitute an alternative persona that was explicitly Jewish—the Yiddishe mama, although an important component of her popular success, was merely a nostalgic rendition of a bygone ideal. Yet neither did Tucker attempt to mask, or ignore, her Jewish background in cultivating a wider audience.

Throughout, Tucker incorporated what she called a sense of Jewish justice, extending especially to Jews and to women and children but also encompassing, in its broad concerns, all of humanity. Her compassion was combined with a competence, tough-mindedness, and tenacity that recalled to her own mind the heritage of Jennie Abuza and the Jewish ladies of her childhood. "I ran away from [the ghetto in Hartford]," Tucker told old friends at a fund-raising speech in that city toward the end of her life. "But I've been running back to it [and] to Mama" ever since.[40]

Funny Women   While Sophie Tucker was exploring contested sexual territory in her songs and comedy, two other popular Jewish female performers of the era—Molly Picon and Fanny Brice—became mainstream hits by adopting the opposite persona of the child-woman. In the 1930s, when comic-book-type child figures were popularized by such stars as Mary Pickford, Jackie Coogan, and Shirley Temple, Picon played over a dozen comic-strip waifs, including Kid-Mother, the Circus Waif, and the Jolly Orphan. Brice began doing Baby Snooks on the Ziegfield stage in 1936; she then played the mischievous toddler for fourteen years on radio.[41] The broad physical humor of Brice's characterizations differed from the ingenuousness of Picon's child roles; Brice at one point suggested that she could more easily avoid the censors as Baby Snooks than in her adult roles. However much Baby Snooks spoofed legitimate child stars and presented occasionally risqué material, the character nevertheless fit the stereotype of the carefree, innocent child-woman. These images were poles apart from Tucker's red-hot mamas.

The trajectory from Brice's first hit character, the Yiddish-accented Sadie Salome introduced in 1909, to the unaccented Baby Snooks twenty-five years later tells us much about the changing appeal of ethnic characters in show business. At the very start of her career, Brice had gone to Irving Berlin, then a young, up-and-coming Tin Pan Alley songwriter, for new material. Berlin complied with "Sadie Salome, Go Home!" a spoof of the current show business cult of exotic dancing. Berlin's lyric tells the story of Sadie Cohen, a nice Jewish girl who leaves home and her sweetheart, Mose, in pursuit of stardom. She finds it as an actress doing a Salome striptease; Mose, in the song's refrain, suggests the moral: "Oy, Oy," he cries, "how can a nice Jewish girl disgrace her family?"[42] Brice made the song her own by treating it as broad physical farce and assuming a strong Yiddish accent that she claimed in her memoirs to have "learned" especially for the part; her Hungarian mother and French father did not teach their children "Jewish." Combining this accent with facial expressions and what Brice called "oblique, grotesque gestures," she parodied popular conceptions of stage dancing.[43]

Brice's Yiddish accent became a trademark of her routine in burlesque and musical comedy over many years, employed in such hit numbers as "I'm an Indian," in which Brice played the American Indian/Jewish girl Rosie Rosenstein. She expanded her repertoire of comic characters, considering herself a "cartoonist" who worked within the medium of performance to bring characters to life. Among her most memorable portraits were an evangelist and a neophyte nudist, both Yiddish-accented; a Jewish girl, Sascha, who becomes a sultan's wife; and "Mrs. Cohen at the Beach," a "consummate *yente*" who nags her children.[44] Even though contemporary critics referred to her comic style as "Jewish," Brice biographer Barbara Grossman believes that with the exception of Mrs. Cohen, Brice's routines, like her accent, were only "superficially Jewish"; she used a dialect-inflected accent and Jewish personas as a comic device, almost like blackface (which she wore but once), to suggest— and then dash—behavioral expectations. Thus her comedy was based on parody and incongruity rather than realism.[45]

Brice's performances garnered such an enthusiastic audience response that critic Gilbert Seldes called Brice one of the greatest entertainers of the day, second only to Al Jolson. Seldes believed Brice had an even "more delicate mind and a richer humor" than Jolson; she was a "great farceur" with an unparalleled ability to evoke a dramatic situation—and then, through gentle but hilarious parody, to critique it.[46] Yet there was a serious side to Brice's comedy. In numbers like "Second-Hand Rose," "My Man," and "Oy, How I Hate that Fellow Nathan," she mocked men's unreliability, and herself, in the same way that Tucker did. Brice portrayed women as less assertive, more needy and vulnerable; her humor, while quick-witted and satirical, was less shocking and biting than Tucker's.[47] Both women nevertheless poked fun at the social conventions of modern life and brought women's voices to vaudeville, burlesque, nightclubs, and other public spaces. Audiences related to their witty put-downs of men and marriage, and to their expressions of disappointment and unhappiness, because they knew these portrayals sprang from the entertainers' own lives. What Brice told her biographer about her use of Jewish themes was equally true of the gender issues both she and Tucker raised in their performances:

> In anything Jewish I ever did, I wasn't standing apart, making fun of the race. I *was* the race, and what happened to me on the stage is what could happen to them. They identified with me, and then it was all right to get a laugh, because they were laughing at me as well as themselves.[48]

Despite Brice's popular appeal, she longed to reach a broader public; she felt that being identified as "too New York" and "too Jewish" was limiting her career.[49] Early on she had changed her family name from Borach to Brice, claiming she wanted to stop the teasing that the original name provoked. In the 1920s she went much further, altering her "Jewish" appearance as well. The story of Brice's nose job made headlines in the *New York Times* in August 1923, sharing space with President Harding's death and the ascension of Calvin Coolidge. Brice, by then a huge star of musical comedy, claimed she wanted the rhinoplasty in order to make her appearance more suitable for serious dramatic roles; "everything about me has stopped growing except my nose," she joked.[50] Barbara Grossman suggests that Brice believed the surgery would make her look less Jewish, although she would not admit this publicly.

While Brice may have "cut off her nose to spite her race," as Dorothy Parker quipped, the hoped-for parts did not materialize.[51] Broadway critics agreed with producer Flo Ziegfeld that having the nose job was as foolish as "the clown who wants to play Hamlet."[52] Audiences preferred Brice's "comic awkwardness" (and her old nose) to her new, more serious image. Nor did the nose job help Brice's domestic relations. Four years after the surgery, Brice filed for a divorce from Nicky Arnstein, charging that her changed appearance had alienated her husband's affections; the more beautiful she became, the greater was his inferiority complex: "I was not the same Fannie he used to know."[53]

Seen in this light, Brice's adoption of the Baby Snooks persona was another in the series of measures she took to develop a more American audience. She played the infant alternately on NBC and CBS radio from 1938 until her death in 1951. Inaugurating the character at a time when Shirley Temple reigned supreme as the leading American box office star, Brice tapped into the nation's desire for innocence. While Snooks was "as bad . . . as Temple was good," Brice's mimicking of childish speech and her roguish escapades charmed audiences.[54] In the guise of a little girl—without the gestures, mannerisms, and Yiddish accent of her stage burlesques—Brice found on radio the nationwide following she coveted. One more invention that used exaggeration and incongruity to the point of absurdity, Snooks grew less risqué and more wholesome over time. Yet critics believed that the character prompted listeners to think more deeply about themselves and the human condition.[55]

It is doubtful that Brice's Yiddish parodies would have survived the transition to radio as well as Baby Snooks. Nonetheless, according to Grossman, Brice remained an "ethnic outsider," craving acceptance by the dominant culture and seeking to adopt its vision of acceptability: hence her nose job, self-mockery, and distancing from her past.[56] As an outsider laughing at herself, perhaps Brice believed she could pass as an insider. In her desire to appeal to mainstream society she mirrored the attitudes of the Hollywood moguls whose repudiation of their background was "utter and absolute."[57] The irony is that, like these powerful men, her rejection of Jewishness defined her as fully as if she had embraced it.

Wanderers and Wonderers in Search of Themselves   Tucker's and Brice's immigrant backgrounds distinguished them from Edna Ferber and Fannie Hurst. Yet despite their different origins, Ferber and Hurst, like Tucker, both resisted and modelled themselves—and the leading characters in their work—after powerful Jewish mothers. Though they were secularists who celebrated American individualism, the pull of their heritage remained strong.

Ferber and Hurst were two of twentieth-century America's most popular authors. Both women were well-established celebrities who occupied enviable positions within New York literary circles—Ferber as member of the famed Algonquin Roundtable, Hurst as president of the Authors Guild and perennial spokesperson for writers' causes. Both began publishing their fiction in the early 1910s and remained productive, best-selling writers for several decades. The early Hurst was considered "among the great American writers of short stories," and some of her later fiction received high praise, although critics generally considered her work uneven, faulting it for an overabundance of sentimentality and formulaic plots. Because of her melodramatic endings and the bathos of her prose, she was dubbed the greatest "sob sister" writer of her era. Ferber's early work likewise pleased critics, and her novel *So Big* won the Pulitzer Prize in 1925. Over time, however, she too came to be seen as a sentimental writer of variable literary merit. Yet in a front-page obituary, the *New York Times* acknowledged that Ferber was among "the best-read novelists in the nation," declaring that while "not profound," her books had a "sound sociological basis" and had become "minor classics."[58]

For both writers, it had been a long journey from their origins. Daughters of tightly knit midwestern German Jewish families, each left home, though not with Sophie Tucker's finality, to dedicate herself to her craft. In constant motion thereafter, Ferber led a "curious wandering life," considering herself an archetypal "Wandering Jew."[59] Novelist Louis Bromfield believed her to be one of the most restless people he knew—"always in search of something fascinating beyond the horizon." Perhaps because Ferber travelled so frequently, the notion of home became extremely important to her. The second volume of her 1963 autobiography, *A Kind of Magic,* focuses in large part on the planning and construction of her country estate, Treasure Hill, in Connecticut. Yet this elaborately wrought home ultimately failed to satisfy, and Ferber sold it. The autobiography ends with an image not of stasis but of restlessness: a description of Ferber's cross-country motor tour, an almost desperate trip to capture the reality of the land. "But romance has the last word, San Francisco!" Ferber concludes the book, an appropriate epitaph to a life full of wandering, spiritually as well as physically, through America and the world.

Less peripatetic than Ferber, Fannie Hurst nonetheless found herself "almost commuting" between her family home in St. Louis, Missouri, and Manhattan, where she made her own home. Her mother, whom she could not escape even in New York, had chosen Hurst's first residences from afar. On her own, Hurst selected an area of Greenwich Village that the *New York Times* later urged be given the status of a cultural landmark because both Eugene O'Neill and Fannie Hurst had lived there.[60] But it was a later residence, a seventeen-room triplex in an artists' and writers' building on West 67th Street off Central Park West, that attracted most attention. Hurst decorated it in medieval style, which one visitor described as "faintly reminiscent in proportions to Grand Central Station," full of Spanish, Italian, and ecclesiastical antiques and *objets d'art* that she had collected in Europe. Ferber commented acidly that "her living room is a vast and lovely thing, if you like a room that looks like a Roman Catholic museum."[61]

Hurst subtitled her autobiography, *Anatomy of Me,* "a wonderer . . . in search of herself." She described herself as an inward-looking "traveler" who found that the "mind and spirit" she sought to explore were in "unceasing processes of change: smoke, flame, eruption."[62] Ferber wrote her autobiography to discover "where and how I lost my bearings and missed the way." But as she attempted to confront her experiences on paper, the pattern of her life, which had once seemed "plain as a blueprint," also changed and dissolved.[63] The shifting nature of these women's identities, along with their reluctance to confront troubling demons, make their explorations of themselves tentative and partial. Like immigrant authors Mary Antin and Anzia Yezierska, Ferber and Hurst had to confront complex issues of gender, ethnic, and national identity throughout their lives.[64]

The centrality to their writing of family relationships, particularly mother-daughter bonds, reveals how closely the creation of a modern American self was entwined with the process of leaving both filial and ethnic identity behind. Their literary task was to render in narrative form the struggles of women like themselves who sought a place in the world while acknowledging the constraints that pulled them back.

An American Jewish Family   Ferber and Hurst were both born in small mid-western towns—Ferber in Kalamazoo, Michigan, and Hurst in Hamilton, Ohio—but gravitated to larger cities: Hurst to St. Louis, where she grew up; Ferber to Chicago. Each had one sister—Edna Ferber an older sibling named Fanny, and Fannie Hurst a younger sister named Edna. Both were born in 1885 (although Hurst later took 1889, the year of her four-year-old sister Edna's death from diphtheria, as her birthdate) and died in 1968.[65]

Beyond these superficial similarities, both women also present their mothers as lively, tempestuous, authoritative, and domineering; the fathers are quieter, weaker. Jacob Charles Ferber was a Hungarian émigré; Ferber's mother, Julia Neumann, was descended from an established family of merchants and bankers. Julia's father had come to the United States in the 1840s to escape political persecution. The Neumanns settled on Chicago's North Side in a vibrant, intellectual, imaginative household in which Julia grew up a "high-spirited harum-scarum girl; fun-loving, original, self-willed so far as one can be in a family ruled by a matriarch like . . . her mother." The tragedy of her life was succumbing to "parental pressure and conservative middle-class upbringing": Julia gave up the Gentile she had fallen in love with and accepted Jacob Ferber, who seemed like a good "catch" because of his business investments. "In her careless way," Ferber writes, "[Julia] thought that between engagement and wedding something or other would happen to stop the whole thing. But nothing did. And to her helpless amazement she found herself standing there in a plum silk gown being married to the wrong man."[66]

As it turned out, Jacob truly was the wrong man, his "singularly bad judgment" the cause of the family's always precarious financial situation.[67] It was left to Julia to hold the family together, especially during the course of Jacob's steadily deteriorating eyesight and blindness, and then after his death. In contrast to the ineffectual Jacob, Julia Ferber was "vital," a "born leader" who suffered nobly through her unhappy home life. But her life was for Edna a model not to be followed: "Marriage seemed to me to be less than a desirable state of being. Perhaps it was then that I decided I would have none of it."[68]

The marriage of Fannie Hurst's parents was apparently equally loveless. The families of both parents had emigrated to the United States from Bavaria in the 1860s; Hurst's mother grew up in an industrial town west of Cincinnati, her father in Memphis, Tennessee, where he became a travelling salesman. Eventually he started his own business—the Standard Heel and Counter Company, which dealt in shoe bellies. Despite occasional hard times, Fannie considered her family "bourgeois through and through," yet her mother was plagued by a dread of poverty that Fannie considered excessive.[69]

Page after page of Hurst's autobiography, *Anatomy of Me,* is filled with descriptions of Rose Koppel Hurst's uncontrollable temper. Variously described as "volatile," "unpredictable," and subject to "storms," "rages," and "volcanic eruptions," Rose was a "hurricane" that would "explode in sound and fury."[70] The chilling opening page of the book tells all:

> From the hour that I gave Mama my first stare from her bed of my birth, I must have braced my new spine against being overpowered by the rush of her personality.
>
> When Mama walked into a room filled with ladies, she doused them like so many candles blown out on a birthday cake.
>
> Yet, on the other hand, no sooner had I left the warm cover of her body than we committed the anachronism of becoming one again.
>
> Despite the fact that we had neither temperamental nor intellectual compatibility, I loved her in a deep uncomplicated way that was never to waver throughout storm and stress.
>
> And storm and stress it was. Mama's temper, fiery as lightning, terrible as thunder, was a matter of periodic blitz in our home, my own kitten of a temper, like Papa's, managing to keep its claws in.
>
> In a way, however, Papa and I were a pair of terrible meeks, huddling and waiting for the storm to pass like a pair of wayfarers, our mute surrender to her fury serving only to increase the gale which could rage out of a trifling or fancied hurt, and a clear sky.[71]

Hurst's ambivalence about this overpowering mother is palpable here and throughout the book, her "uncomplicated" unwavering love for the fiery Rose alternating with fear, fury, and guilt at her own ingratitude and inconstancy.[72] Even after the narrative brings Hurst to fame and fortune, she is still tilting at the ghost of Rose's rages yet swearing her fealty. "I loved her over and above the tortures she inflicted and her strange talent for killing the things she loved," she writes. At another point she says: "It is true I hated some of the first twenty years of my life. The going was lonely most of the time. But I loved Mama all of the time."[73]

But an anecdote Hurst recounts immediately afterwards casts doubt on this claim:

> A chance acquaintance in an English railway carriage, a member of the peerage, once said to me in four unadorned words: I hate my mother. It was the first time I had heard such blasphemy uttered. Surely God would strike him dead. But God did not take action, and the lovely countryside through which we were riding kept smiling.[74]

Though Hurst could not bring herself to utter such blasphemy, it is clear that her mother's "lavish," "violent maternalism" took its toll on Hurst and her father, the pair of "meeks." Indeed, Hurst called herself a "scared little cat," just like the kitten Rose Koppel literally frightens to death in one of Hurst's stories about her.[75]

Sam Hurst was a man cut from the same cloth as Jacob Ferber. Hurst admired him for the "nobility built into his handsomeness," his gentleness, his "kindness and courtesy." But not only did he fail to protect her from her mother's eruptions; he offered Hurst little physical or emotional affection. "I think I loved him," Hurst confesses. "Yet we remained such strangers! I lived in his home, yet I was locked out of it by his great reserves."[76] Hurst's sobriety was well-respected in St. Louis. "A prince of a man, but henpecked," commented neighbors. "How in the world did Sam Hurst and Rose Koppel ever get together?" Hurst could explain their union only with the flip remark that "opposites attract."[77] Like Ferber, she found little to imitate in her parents' relations.

Ferber's portrait of Julia Ferber may be more flattering than Hurst's of Rose Koppel, but according to her biographer and grandniece Julia Goldsmith Gilbert, Ferber too had an exhausting, deeply ambivalent love-hate relationship with her mother. After Jacob Ferber's death, Julia Ferber sold the family general store in Appleton, Wisconsin, and moved her daughters back to her beloved Chicago. When Ferber left home to seek her fortune as a writer, however, Julia was not far behind. She joined Ferber in New York and then in Connecticut; according to Gilbert, the two lived "in tandem," sharing not only a home, but vacations and friends. Occasionally, Ferber admitted to family members how difficult it was. "I am fonder of [mother] than any of her family is," she wrote to her sister Fan. "It is true that she is difficult and nerve-racking, and that living together as we have for twenty years life had often seemed too impossible for me . . . If we had seen less of each other we would both have been happier in many ways."[78]

Perhaps even more telling was the violence Ferber committed on the figure of Molly Brandeis, the mother of her autobiographical stand-in in *Fanny Herself* (1917). This, her second and only specifically Jewish novel, tells the story of a midwestern Jewish family that greatly resembles the Ferbers. Molly Brandeis appears in the book very much as Julia Ferber did in real life: attractive, witty, hard-working, high-spirited. But Ferber kills off this admirable mother midway through the book. "I killed Molly Brandeis because she was walking off with the story under the heroine's very eyes," Ferber admitted. As an author, Ferber regretted her character's fate because "when Molly Brandeis died the story died with her. She was too sustaining and vital to dismiss."[79] Yet as Julia Gilbert explains, "Ferber, the daughter, had purposely allowed it to happen."[80]

As in fiction, so it was in life. Ferber often found her mother taking over, as in an admiring essay Louis Bromfield wrote for the *Saturday Review* about Ferber. "It is impossible to write of Edna Ferber without writing as well of her mother," Bromfield chirped. "Ageless, indefatigable, handsome, entertaining, and the best company in the world . . . Much that appears in her daughter's books and plays and stories has been learned from her."[81]

According to Julia Gilbert, who was named after Julia Ferber, there was "something nasty and liverish" about her namesake.[82] Ferber's sister Fan felt that their mother was jealous of Ferber's success even though Edna was her favorite child. She was "eccentric, provocative, destructive," agreed playwright Marc Connelly, a family friend. In her memoirs, however, Edna avoids mentioning any conflict and treats her mother with admiration bordering on sentimentality.

> The truth was . . . that Julia Ferber as a human being was so dimensional, sustaining, courageous and vital that my years of close companionship with her never were dull; irritating at times, and even infuriating, but dull—never! She had and has a gigantic capacity for enjoying life and for communicating that enjoyment to those about her; a humorous gay shrewd woman with an amazing sense of values. Astringent as a grapefruit, her insight into human frailties often makes her judgments seem harsh. She belongs definitely to that race of iron women which seems to be facing extinction in today's America . . . Hardy, indomitable, of the earth and its fullness. We shall not see their like again.[83]

There is no question that Ferber admired her mother's triumph over adversity and her "iron" spirit. However difficult it may have been to break away from her, Ferber credited Julia with sparking her own interest in books and writing by her own insatiable curiosity and voracious reading. In this respect, she provided Ferber with a role model unavailable to Fannie Hurst, who constantly bemoaned her mother's anti-intellectualism. (Hurst's father, not her mother, encouraged Hurst's reading with the constant refrain, "Knowledge is power." Her mother thought books a needless and perhaps destructive detour on the route to matrimony.)

Ferber resembled her mother in personality as well as interests. According to Gilbert, she retained an "aura of despotism" throughout her life that made all people, with the exception of Julia Ferber, defer to her.[84] Eddie Cantor named her among "the most forceful women I've ever met . . . capable of filling any man's job." According to Bennet Cerf, "Edna asked for no quarter— and she certainly didn't give any. [In her home, she] was an absolute monarch who made Catherine the Great look like Little Orphan Annie." Katharine Hepburn, a close friend, summed it up: "We were dangerous women." Ferber was always honest, but she could be violent. "She called me a dithering idiot many times," Hepburn said.[85]

The "indomitable" qualities of Ferber and her mother are present in many of the female characters in Ferber's thirteen novels, eight plays, and many volumes of short stories. The wildly popular Emma McChesney, the travelling saleswoman of Ferber's first three collections of stories; Selina, the idealistic, truck-farming mother of *So Big;* the dauntless mother in *Show Boat* (1926); the pioneer heroines of *Cimarron* (1930) and *Saratoga Trunk* (1941); and the determined Leslie, who domesticates her bully of a Texas husband in *Giant*

(1952), all are strong, determined women pursuing the paths they have chosen. According to critic Carolyn Heilbrun, Ferber's female characters are the essence of her originality, all the more striking since they appeared at a time when very few strong women figured in the "relentlessly masculine world of American fiction."[86]

Hurst, too, made her mark with portraits of struggling women making their way in the world. Whether they are shopgirls (*Mannequin,* 1926, and *Anywoman,* 1950), actresses (*Star-Dust,* 1921), domestic workers (*Lummox,* 1923), or entrepreneurs (*Imitation of Life,* 1933), Hurst's heroines are plucky and determined. Despite the tribulations they must endure, they display courage and integrity. Whatever the literary failures of her novels, Hurst's greatest achievement, like Ferber's, lay in her presentation of a host of strong women experimenting with nontraditional roles.

The characters in these novels drew on the strengths of Ferber's and Hurst's powerful mothers but also on their own hard-fought struggles against them.[87] Hurst admitted that it took a "capacity for ruthlessness" to leave a home so concentrated on her. The "fierceness" of this concentration, in turn, magnified her "compulsion" to leave; only later did she understand that "despite the beating of my wings my filial instinct was deep and uncomplicated. At heart I was a conforming girl-child."[88] Rose Koppel Hurst manipulated Fannie's conformity, and her guilt, not only through her rages but with hardly more subtle verbal tactics. For example, when Hurst left for New York, her mother told her: "The house [is] dead without you. . . . I don't know how I am living through this. What does it matter, for the few years I have left?" And again, after Hurst's first story was accepted for publication: "Papa does not say much anymore about your return, but just the same you are helping make him into an old man. . . . If anything happens to him, that will be the end of me."[89]

Sam Hurst nonetheless lived on for several years, and Hurst continued to travel frequently between New York and Missouri. By this time she had become an established author and did not consider returning to St. Louis permanently. Yet her guilt lingered, reappearing throughout the autobiography and especially in these poignant lines, reminiscent of Sophie Tucker's hymn to her own "Yiddishe mama":

> Mama, Mama, my regrets for all the pain I caused you crowd in on me in these after-years. Your virtues transcended your faults. Papa knew that and bent his neck to your storms. I had neither his sweet humility nor fortitude . . . If only—I could live it over again.[90]

Leaving home was no easier for Edna Ferber. After she completed high school in Appleton, Wisconsin, she decided to enroll in the Northwestern University School of Elocution in Evanston, Illinois. But the plan provoked a "family whirlwind": "We, a family of four, were bound together in ties even closer than those of the average Jewish family. The blind man leaned on me, and I felt a great protective pity for him as he stumbled so clumsily through life. My mother was working like a man. My sister . . . talented in her own way, was too tied to the house and its duties. I tried to stand out against it all, but I was still too young and too tenderhearted and too weak."[91]

Faced with family opposition and her own guilty conscience, Ferber relented. In a "white-hot rage," she went down to the office of the Appleton *Daily Crescent,* and based on her school experience, won a job as a reporter.[92] After more than a year on the paper, she received an offer to work for the prestigious Milwaukee *Journal.* Again, Ferber was tormented by indecision. "Until now we had clung together, we four Ferbers. I am certain I never should have written if I had not gone. I was wrung by an agony of pity as I looked at my father's face."[93]

Unlike Hurst's or Yezierska's fathers, Jacob Ferber gave his blessing to his daughter's ambition, and she left for Milwaukee, where for three and a half years she served the *Journal* as its "Girl Reporter." In fact Ferber worked "like a man" on an exhausting beat that covered "the courthouse, the city hall, the prison, the *Journal* office, the theater, the city's streets and outlying districts, people's emotions and drama."[94] One day, the strain, perhaps worsened by her guilt at leaving home, proved too much, and Ferber collapsed; biographer Goldsmith believes she had a nervous breakdown. Julia came to take her home for what was supposed to be a short rest, but Ferber never returned to Milwaukee or to newspaper reporting. From then on, she would do most of her creative writing (her mother called it "Edna's typewriting") in a domicile shared with Julia.[95]

Yet if Ferber was pulled away from a life in journalism by her mother's possessiveness, Julia was equally responsible for Ferber's emergence as a creative writer. Recuperating at home after her collapse, Ferber wrote the novel *Dawn O'Hara.* But lacking confidence, she threw it in the trash, from which Julia retrieved it, insisting that she find a publisher. The novel was published in 1911, and Ferber credited her mother with launching her literary career.[96] More fundamentally, her relationship with her mother, and her ambivalent appreciation of her mother's strengths, provided material for many of her works. However difficult the bonds between the two, the relationship nurtured her creativity and supported her unorthodox career.

Following her father's death some months after her return from Milwaukee, Ferber began the wandering life that for the next thirteen years took her from one hotel or furnished apartment to another, almost always accompanied by Julia, in Chicago, New York, Vienna, Munich, Paris, Florence, London, Berlin, California. Whether or not Ferber won her struggle for individuation is unclear; in the fiction that depicts mother-daughter relationships, she shows remarkable compassion for the mother's plight even while insisting on the daughter's right to independence. In *The Girls* (1921), mothers who dominate their daughters and live their own unfulfilled lives through them are portrayed not as monsters but as deprived women who are unconscious of their failings. And although Ferber kills off the mother in *Fanny Herself*, Fanny follows on her mother's path by launching her own business. She eventually gives it up to follow an artistic career, guided by her mother's ideals and values.[97]

Fannie Hurst's portrayal of mother-daughter bonds is more negative. The mothers of Lilly Becker in *Star-Dust* and of Bea Pullman in *Imitation of Life* urge their daughters into inappropriate and unsatisfying marriages that fail. Although the daughters ultimately achieve independence and success, it is at the cost of satisfying their emotional and sexual needs. In the view of critic Janet Burstein, the "infuriating imbalance of powerful would-be mother and needy, rejecting child" lies at the core of Hurst's unhappy portrayals of romantic love.[98] Hurst punishes not only her fictional daughters for leaving home, but also the mothers who demand their loyalty; mothers either die young or go mad, or both. The saintly Delilah's death in *Imitation of Life*, followed by her daughter's voluntary sterilization, is perhaps Hurst's most powerful portrayal of the alienation of mothers and daughters. Unable to resolve these tensions in her own life, she saddled her fictional creations with the deprivations, betrayals, and confusions that were a part of her own "anatomy."

The Paradox of Romance   In spite of such conflicts, "intense family loves" are the major emotional force in Hurst's fiction, not the "romantic heterosexual ties" that drove most American novels at the time.[99] Nevertheless, the romance plot is central to Hurst's work. In her short stories, she often portrays struggling young working women who secure their own futures by quitting their jobs for marriage. The major choice they face is whether to marry the "right" man, who respects women, or the "wrong" one, who does not. However formulaic the destiny of these women, by showing their tough-mindedness, as well as the social and economic necessities that drive them to work and the alienation at work that drives them to marriage, Hurst offers a sympathetic and rather complex portrait of the working woman of the period.[100]

Hurst's treatment of women and work is even more complex in her eighteen novels, in which her heroines (like Hurst herself) are older, more financially successful, and more independent than in the short stories she wrote for the youthful readers of women's magazines.[101] Yet in many of her most popular novels—including *Star-Dust*, *Back Street*, and *Imitation of Life*—the price society exacts for the fulfillment of these women's economic ambitions is their romantic failure; invariably their transgressions against convention cost them the possibility of living happily ever after.[102] Hurst's heroines cannot challenge female destiny (that is, domesticity) without paying a penalty. If they had followed the route Hurst took in her own life, they would, like her, have had to pay a high psychological cost; there was a terrible predictability at that time to the lives of women who were talented and ambitious. Critics in our own time, who are beginning to reappraise Hurst's legacy, acknowledge that her fiction provided one of the few forums in which female readers could imaginatively try out new possibilities of love and work, family and career, even though traditional boundaries were never unequivocally crossed.[103] Hurst penetrated beneath the surface of issues that few other writers of her period even acknowledged—sexual harassment, unhealthy working conditions, age discrimination, unequal pay and benefits.[104]

Like Hurst, Ferber was one of the earliest twentieth-century writers to consistently address the issues of class and gender for working women. Although she, too, has been labelled a formulaic writer, Ferber produced a series of important novels that portray women's drive for independence and self-realization with compassion and understanding. Without fundamentally challenging marriage and domesticity as normative female roles, her best novels offer new ways of looking at female desires. Her sympathetic portrayal of the toll that hard labor takes on women's lives resembles Hurst's; she, too, romanticizes the dignity of labor compared to the greed and corruption of easy wealth and suggests that true virtue, in women's lives, means seeing beyond male swagger to appraise the core values beneath. Ferber's feminism is not always at the surface; in *Giant*, for example, the heroine, Leslie Layton, is relegated to a completely domestic role when she marries Texas rancher Bick Benedict. Yet while Leslie has little to say about politics and business, she succeeds in domesticating her husband, altering his brute, aggressive masculinity so that he becomes more tolerant of difference (not only gender but racial difference as well, for the Benedicts' son Jordy marries a Mexican woman and has a half-breed child whom Bick must defend). Blending masculine and feminine qualities, the new Bick, like his wife, becomes a model for a more expressive, more humane American. One critic wrote about the screen version of *Giant*, "Woman's world has been equated with the aggregate of pluralist values: tolerance, compromise, flexibility, civility . . . with nothing less than culture itself."[105]

Ferber's Emma McChesney embodies a similarly paradoxical fate; this independent-minded divorcée, owner of her own business, eventually marries her business partner, whom she once refused, and quits work. Unhappy as a housewife, she returns to the business, but it is clear that she will not play the dominant role she once had; marriage, albeit to a worthy mate, has changed the balance of her roles.

Ferber's heroines, like those of her contemporary, Yezierska, fight for the right to be self-determining and independent, yet eventually even they become reconciled with the culture's dominant prescription for women: domesticity. The harmony that Yezierska's Sara Smolinsky discovers at the end of *The Bread Givers* was no closer to the truth of that writer's life than the conventional romantic destinies of Hurst's and Ferber's strong-willed heroines were to theirs. The genius of these latter writers, though, was to allow their audiences a glimpse of an American future that, while not breaking with tradition, suggested more equal opportunities for women and all those aspiring to the middle class than they had at the time. Yezierska's work was ultimately limited by her didacticism and failure to surmount the immigrant saga. Ferber and Hurst were no less moralistic; in spite of much fully realized fiction, the technical quality of much of their work was limited. That they commanded their readers' passionate loyalty for many decades was a consequence less of their literary skill than of the popularity and uniqueness of their vision. Each opened a window on an emerging America in which the aspirations of women, and of minorities, were beginning to grow and also, increasingly, to be realized.

In their works, they denied the inevitable conflict that such aspirations might bring: in *Cimarron,* another transgressive intermarriage—that of the son of an old Yankee family to a Native American—is presented, like the marriage of Jordy and Juana in *Giant,* as simply an alternate version of the American way. The dark side of multiracial America is glimpsed in Hurst's *Imitation of Life,* when the light-skinned Peola denies her black mother and attempts to pass as white, even sterilizing herself to marry a white man and avoid giving birth to a black offspring; it is also apparent in Ferber's *Showboat,* in which miscegenation between a white man and a black woman light enough to be taken for white also results in tragedy.[106] But racism, like anti-Semitism, is an issue that neither author was prepared to address directly or consistently. Ultimately, they paint a benevolent picture of a multiethnic America in which women, if not the equals of men, are at least impressive, imposing, determined figures. Eschewing conflict for harmony, their pluralistic version of America's destiny was entirely in keeping with mainstream popular sentiment in the interwar years. In exile in Paris and England, many American writers of their generation had already appraised the American dream and found it flawed; Ferber and Hurst, celebrating the virtues of hard work and the fortitude of the "common people," produced a transitional American novel that would become out-of-date almost as soon as it was written.

Yet their romance with America would always be tempered by the social critiques they insisted lay at the heart of their work, even if readers did not always notice.[107] Beneath the romanticization of the working people in their stories lay a subtle critique of the alienating forces of capitalism. Although these writers were no Marxists, their fiction is steeped in class consciousness.

According to one observer commenting on Ferber's oeuvre, the ability to glorify America while criticizing it was a product of the writer's "double consciousness." Like Hurst, Ferber was both an "insider, and partly because of her Jewish heritage, a quintessential outsider," making her work more ironic and double-voiced than was recognized at the time.[108] To understand their depictions of America, which allowed Americans to see themselves in fundamentally new ways, we must first understand how these women saw themselves as Jews.

The Jew Among Nations   At one point in *Anatomy of Me,* Hurst notes that she would not have previously admitted "to what degree race heritage, which in the name of assimilation I chose to ignore, was the explanation for many of my attitudes." She continues: "It was to take me almost half a lifetime of the Biblical three score and ten to evaluate properly the richness of that heritage." Later she acknowledges that she was "not proud of my mental processes or lack of them concerning the long body-and-soul flagellation of another race—my own."[109]

Equivocal about her family, and especially her mother, it is not surprising that Hurst was also deeply ambivalent as a Jew. Her family's failure to identify positively with the Jewish people or Jewish customs left her bereft of any connection to her heritage. As a child, she had no knowledge if "being Jewish [was] one's religion" and had to ask her mother if you could be of "the Jewish race and be Lutheran or a Catholic the way you can be American and also be a Lutheran or a Catholic?"[110] The question prompted her father to consider joining a temple to promote Hurst's Jewish education, but her mother refused to be "stuck in the back pew so I can see my rich relatives up front." Rose also noted her husband's failure to speak up when business partners talked about "damn Jew[s]" in his presence; even if Sam encouraged Hurst to be proud of her Jewishness, they agreed that it made little sense to stir the waters.[111]

The incident emphasized all that Hurst was to learn from her parents about Judaism: an invidious awareness of class distinction from within and prejudice from without. In her family's lexicon, Gentiles who demonstrated anti-Semitic attitudes had *richus* (race prejudice), but Jews from Eastern Europe were "kikes."[112] *Richus* filled Hurst with "dread and humiliation," but kike, a word that "hopped about like a toad" in her German Jewish community, was perhaps even worse, since it indicated a rigid "caste system," a "race divided against itself."[113]

When Hurst's boyfriends in high school turned out to come from the wrong groups, her parents were horrified. "Your daughter has been raised like a heathen, and now we are reaping the results," her father protested to Rose when Hurst began keeping company with a non-Jewish salesman for a St. Louis lumber company. "We simply can't afford to mingle with the rich Jews of this town," her mother responded. "What is the child to do?" Neither was pleased when Hurst attracted the attention of a serious young university student of East European Jewish extraction. "I have nothing against them," Sam told Hurst at his wife's urging, "but it's high time a girl like you began to mingle more with our people."[114] Growing up with such attitudes, Hurst became a Jew who was "not proud but furtive"; when a magazine editor in St. Louis asked her what "stock" she came from, her mind "locked against what I knew I should or must reply. 'We are American,' " she answered, ashamed of her evasion. She recognized the loss in her autobiography, noting that in "our middle-western world of assimilated German Jews . . . race consciousness had been slow to awaken and then only languidly."[115]

Although relatively few of Hurst's novels or short stories include recognizably Jewish characters, often her portrayals of immigrants, some of whom are marked as Jews, include negative stereotypes such as crude speech, unruly emotions, or unreasonably possessive family relationships. Undoubtedly these portraits embody the unresolved tensions revealed in her memoirs. Hurst's stories with German Jewish characters almost always reflect a more successful version of the process of assimilation. The collection *Just Around the Corner* (1914) shows these families already out of the ghetto, struggling for gentility and mainstream business success. The stories in *Humoresque* (1919) depict families at a higher stage of acculturation and economic success.[116] In "Seven Candles" (1923), however, probably the first published story by a Jewish author to address the problem of intermarriage, and in her novel *Family!* (1960), Hurst offers positive examples of Jewish tradition carried across the generations by Jewish women and suggests that the loss of Jewish continuity through intermarriage poses a grave threat. Although these stories do not end optimistically, they reflect a more fully realized resolution of Hurst's situation as an assimilated American Jewish woman than her earlier fiction.[117]

Like Fannie Hurst, Edna Ferber wrote as an American, not as a Jew. But while she shared Hurst's assimilated, middle-class, midwestern German Jewish background, her connection to her Jewishness was much more positive than Hurst's and occupies a more central place in her self-examination. Ferber once commented that, given the choice of saving only one of her thirty published volumes, she would select her autobiography, *A Peculiar Treasure,* which she had referred to as the "story of an American Jewish family . . . a story about America."[118]

Despite the fact that she had grown up in an anti-Semitic community and her family was not religious, Ferber always felt "inordinately proud of being a Jew," a feeling that intensified as she grew older.

> I have felt that to be a Jew was, in some ways at least, to be especially privileged. Two thousand years of persecution have made the Jew quick to sympathy, quick-witted (he'd better be), tolerant, humanly understanding. The highest compliment we can pay a Christian is to say of him that he has a Jewish heart.
>
> All this makes life that much more interesting. It also makes life harder, but I am perverse enough to like a hard life. . . . I like overcoming things. Maybe a psychiatrist could tell me why, and it might not prove flattering. Being a Jew makes it tougher to get on, and I like that.[119]

Ferber's toughness was tested in the coal-mining town of Ottumwa, Iowa, where her father, in an ill-considered move, had taken the family to open a general store. But the town was virulently anti-Semitic; during the seven years she spent there, from 1890 to 1897, Ferber claimed she never went on the street "without being subject to some form of defilement." Even worse was that she had to witness her parents' victimization by town anti-Semites. Her parents had filed a lawsuit against an employee accused of theft; although there were witnesses, no one came forward during the trial to testify against "one of their own kind." Not only did the Ferbers lose their suit and have to pay thousands of dollars to the "slandered" party, but Jacob Ferber was physically attacked by the accused man's family.[120]

To such experiences Ferber attributed "anything in me that is hostile toward the world." At the same time, because she developed a "fierce resolution" to overturn the feelings of "ghastly inferiority" that these persecutions wrought, she recognized that the years she spent in Ottumwa were even more valuable, "astringent" and "strengthening," than her later successes. That Ferber did not resent her Jewishness despite these encounters with anti-Semitism she attributes to her warm admiration for her mother's family and her own parents, an ingredient missing in Hurst's experience.[121]

Like Hurst, Ferber considered the Jews to be a race, rather than a religion. Centuries of persecution had led Jews to resemble one another "in countenance, in habits, in feeling"; the long years of ill treatment had shaped a "Jewish eye" or "mask" that was "melancholy" and "tragic." At the same time, Jews had developed "great adaptability, nervous energy, ambition to succeed and a desire to be liked," qualities that served them well.[122] Ferber has only positive comments to make about Jewish intellect, style, even the Jewish palate. Like her mother, however, no part of her lifestyle could be considered particularly Jewish: "Ours were not Jewish ways," she admits.[123] The family celebrated Christmas; even as an adult, she acknowledged Passover "thoughtlessly," eating matzoh but not commemorating the meaning of the Exodus. In her later years, Julia Ferber became an avid Christian Scientist, and Edna often called for her at church. Although Edna held no formal religious beliefs (only that "God is Good" and "Good is God"), she admitted that she most admired Jewish monotheism.[124]

Had her Ottumwa experience been Ferber's only formative experience with Christian America, it is doubtful that she would have maintained both pride in her Jewish identity and faith in American pluralism. But the bitter years in Iowa were followed by a superlatively happy adolescence in Appleton, Wisconsin, a community where "creed, color, race" mattered little, and where the town's forty Jewish families were well integrated into the community; in fact, the mayor of the town was Jewish. Unlike Ottumwa, Appleton had a Reform synagogue, where Ferber studied Jewish history, sang in the choir, and participated in services; whatever Jewish education she managed to obtain during the course of her life came from these experiences.

To Ferber, Appleton represented the "American small town at its best." Free to practice Judaism if she pleased, she nonetheless mixed easily with non-Jews in all manner of community activities, including dating. The only snobbery she perceived in the town came from the German Jewish elite, who looked down on Russian- and Polish-born Jews.

Ferber's contrasting experiences in Ottumwa and Appleton shaped her identity as a Jew and her ideas about racial and religious persecution.[125] Attributing Ottumwa's bigotry to the resentments of its economically deprived citizens, she likewise saw Appleton's tolerance of diversity as a consequence of its prosperity. Anti-Semitism thus became "a criminal weapon used against society by the unsuccessful, the bigoted, the depraved, the ignorant, the neurotic, the failures. It thrives on terror, hunger, unemployment, hate, resentment. It is mob psychology displayed at its lowest and most unreasoning."[126] At the same time, she believed that anti-Semitism stiffened the Jewish backbone, cemented group consciousness, and fostered Jewish achievements. The more Jews were tolerated, in fact, the less motivated they seemed to be, a paradox she had noted during her years in Appleton where Jewish youth, because they had not experienced racial or religious oppression, were only mediocre in sports and studies. Without discrimination, the Jews would lose their identity: thus she proclaimed in 1938, in *A Peculiar Treasure,* that Hitler had done more "to strengthen, to unite, to solidify and to spiritualize the Jews of the world than any other man since Moses."[127] In a private note she dedicated her book, "in loathing and contempt," to "Adolph Hitler who has made of me a better Jew and a more understanding and tolerant human being, as he has of millions of other Jews. . . ."[128]

A Peculiar Treasure was Ferber's public declaration of her Jewishness. At a time of increasing anti-Semitism at home and of mounting Nazi terrorism abroad, she felt it imperative to openly proclaim her identity. The book abounds with anecdotes of anti-Semitic incidents and her readiness to confront the perpetrators. She was furious that Doubleday, her publisher, considered the book "special"—"not for wide appeal"—because of its Jewish content, and did little to advertise or promote it.[129]

In her life, as in this book, Ferber apparently saw no conflict between her Jewishness and her Americanness. When asked by a New York reporter to what she attributed her success, she responded without hesitation "because I was born a Jew."[130] Yet she also described herself as "an American, a writer, and a Jew," seeming to place her national and professional identities ahead of her Jewish consciousness.[131] Indeed, Ferber's entire body of work suggests her deep-seated identification with America as a land of democratic opportunity and excitement; except for *Fanny Herself,* none of her novels deals centrally with Jews. Most of her major fiction examines American ideals within a specific regional context: *So Big* is the story of an Illinois truck-farming widow; *Show Boat* is about blighted romance on a Mississippi riverboat; *Cimarron* concerns the Oklahoma land rush; *American Beauty* explores Polish immigrant life in Connecticut; *Come and Get It* is the story of Wisconsin lumberjacks; *Giant* is a saga about the oil industry in Texas; and *Ice Palace* is an historical novel about Alaska. As Ferber explained: "The American scene (hackneyed phrase) stirred me more than any other writing material. . . . Here in America, I thought, there was lightness, buoyance, and an electric quality in the air. . . . Here was a new fresh country. Why not write in American?"[132] Even though it sometimes exploited its best resources, America remained for her a "magic continent, a peculiar treasure, stuffed with riches."[133]

The notion of a "peculiar treasure" comes from a passage in Exodus that appears as the frontispiece of the book:

> Now, therefore, if ye will obey my voice indeed, and keep my covenant, then ye shall be a peculiar treasure unto me above all people; for all the earth is mine; and ye shall be unto me a kingdom of priests and an holy nation.

Thus Ferber acknowledges the central event that established the Jewish people—entry into the covenant at Sinai—as also belonging, at least metaphorically, to the American experience. For Ferber, the founding myth of Judaism and the myth of America are one: she can utilize the Jewish metaphor because it collapses so readily into her idea of an American national covenant.[134] Ferber's equation of Americanness and Jewishness is explicit:

> America—rather, the United States—seems to me to be the Jew among the nations. It is resourceful, adaptable, maligned, envied, feared, imposed upon. It is warmhearted, overfriendly; quick-witted, lavish, colorful; given to extravagant speech and gestures; its people are travelers and wanderers by nature, moving, shifting, restless; swarming in Fords, in ocean liners; craving entertainment; volatile. The *schnuckle* among the nations of the world.[135]

In this passionate celebration of America as a "quivering electric continent," Ferber resembles no American writer more than Walt Whitman, the great poet of American democracy. But her simultaneous embrace of America and Jewish peoplehood recalls another forebear, Emma Lazarus, who like Ferber insisted that there need be no contradiction between patriotic Americanism and committed Judaism. Lazarus had been a Zionist, supporting the notion of a Jewish state as a secure homeland for the world's victimized Jews; she did not include American Jews in this category and never considered any other home for them than the United States. Ferber shared these views. Her first visit to Palestine in 1930 left her full of admiration for its young pioneers. She returned after Israel received statehood, but found its people arrogant, ill-mannered, chauvinistic. Israel seemed to have become a "Jewish Texas; without oil wells."[136]

What infuriated Ferber most was the idea, promoted by Prime Minister David Ben-Gurion (who she had met on a cruise years before), that Diaspora Jews, especially Americans, should make *aliyah* to Israel because their own brand of Jewishness was inauthentic. Such a virulent, nationalistic Zionism violated her own sense of America's pluralistic democracy.[137] To the displeasure of many American Jews, she spoke out against Zionism in the second volume of her autobiography.

For the most part, however, there was little conflict between the various components of Ferber's identity as an "American, a writer, and a Jew." As a writer who wrote exclusively about America, she did include Jewish characters in several of her works. And only in rare instances (as in the case of Sol Levy, an immigrant Jew who settles in a small Oklahoma home in the novel *Cimarron*) are they discriminated against for being Jews. As Ferber saw it, Jews were part of the pluralistic fabric of American life. While Fannie Brandeis in *Fannie Herself* and Rachel Wiletsky in the short story "The Girl Who Went Right" believe that they can best succeed in business by denying their Jewishness, both realize the nobility of their heritage and proudly reclaim it by the stories' end.[138]

Her strongest characters, who are always women, share qualities that Ferber also appropriates for Jews.

> The woman for centuries was held in subjection because she was female; the Jew because of his religious belief in one God only, rejecting the Jew Jesus as a divinity. Hounded and bedeviled and persecuted, granted few rights and fewer privileges, they learned—the rejected Female and the rejected Jew—perforce to see through the back of their heads as well as through the front of their heads.[139]

In their otherness, then, women and Jews discovered the fortitude and drive that made them into pioneering "American" types. Ferber explicitly identified her mother, Julia—the prototype of many of her heroines—with the American race of "iron women" who settled the American continent, not with the European immigrant women of Jewish heritage. In this, her most enduring legacy, Ferber seamlessly joined her American, female, and Jewish identities in a romantic vision of possibility, one that acknowledges that, however much they are part of the land, women—and Jews—are different. Stronger, more resilient, more wary, they remain the other.

The Highest-Paid Writer in the World   Like Edna Ferber, Fannie Hurst was fascinated by America's cultural pluralism, the "quivering excitement" of its polyglot population. Her equivalent of Ferber's multicultural, multiregional canvas was the island of Manhattan, where she set most of her stories. Like Ferber's, these were full of rugged pioneer types, mostly women, often in conflict with their families as they made their own way in the world. Frequently, Hurst highlighted issues of discrimination and exploitation, focusing on the masses, not elites.[140] Her empathy, and her ability to convey the dramas of her struggling characters in highly emotional terms, made her famous as a "sob-sister" writer. She prided herself on having come so far from the smugness of her family background and "conservative, cautious, backbone-of-the-nation-ish" St. Louis.[141]

Hurst was widely viewed as a real-life version of her own strong, hard-working, plucky heroines. A typical description suggests the powerful impression she made on onlookers:

> Tremendous of frame, magnificent of proportion, ponderous of flesh, large of face and feature, clear of eye, heavy of hair, large of hand and foot, deep of voice, all these qualities are welded together by a personality strong, assertive, and convincing.[142]

In addition to her imposing physique, Hurst's reputation as a self-made, self-willed individual contributed to her image of toughness. The myth of Hurst as a female Horatio Alger who had made it by virtue of her own perseverance greatly contributed to her popular success. Just as Ferber was considered "a little Jewish girl" who had achieved the American dream—a "Jewish Cinderella"—so too was Hurst's apparent triumph over her ethnicity a component of her celebrity.[143]

How very much an example of the American ethic of individualism Hurst had become is indicated by the following commentary:

> Our American artists have been made of the same hardy stuff as our other pioneers. Our authors have carved the wilderness—sought the outposts—dreamed great splendid dreams and fought them through to victory. . . . Cooper—Irving—Poe—Whitman—Twain—Fannie Hurst, our Empress of Fiction. . . .[144]

While some of the myth of Hurst's rugged individualism was true—she suffered thirty-five rejections from the *Saturday Evening Post,* but she persevered and eventually sold her first story—she was surely no ghetto girl. Hurst had been nicely supported by her parents during her years of pounding the New York pavements; although she returned some of their checks she lived comfortably and had money enough for a tour of Europe. Nor was this émigré from cosmopolitan St. Louis (population of more than half a million) a "poor little country girl" making her way alone in the metropolis—another part of the Fannie Hurst legend. Also exaggerated were accounts of Hurst's slice-of-life apprenticeships—as a waitress, factory worker, nurse, salesgirl—to gather material for her stories (she spent only a few days each, not months or years, in such positions).[145]

The fantastic reports of Hurst's earnings also fed the myth of an American success story. Only a short time after selling her first story for $100 she was earning $1,200 per story and then $5,000. By 1915 she was considered one of the three highest-paid short story writers in America; by 1920, it was widely reported—to Hurst's annoyance—that she was the highest-paid writer in the world.[146] The label stuck and persists to this day, although there is no proof that she reached, and remained, at that pinnacle.

What was accurate about the Hurst legend was the author's capacity for hard work and her public reiteration of the theme that success in writing demanded total dedication. Hurst's well-publicized routine began before sunrise; after an hour-and-a-half walk with her dogs in Central Park, she settled down to a stint of five to seven hours at her typewriter. Like Hurst, Ferber was frequently interviewed about the grinding work of writing. Ferber's goal was 10,000 words a day (approximately forty double-spaced typed pages), and she too never varied her schedule. Both women prided themselves on their professional work and were highly visible in the literary world, Ferber as a member of the legendary circle of writers (including H. L. Mencken, Alexander Woollcott, Heywood Broun, and Dorothy Parker) that met regularly for lunch and witticisms at the Algonquin Hotel, and Hurst as frequent spokesperson for literary causes and onetime president of the Authors Guild. ("Since you are meeting so many writers," Hurst's always solicitous mother asked her, "how is it you never mention being at that hotel with the Indian name where they are all supposed to eat? Why don't you eat there?")[147]

Even though Fannie Hurst was considered less versatile than Ferber, she was so much in the public eye that she seemed to represent a "human pseudo-event."[148] Her stories were constantly being anthologized and serialized; most were best-sellers. Beginning with the highly successful silent film *Humoresque* in 1920, twenty-eight were made into movies (including multiple versions of *Imitation of Life* and the well-regarded *Back Street*). As a result of this success, Hurst's penchant for speaking out on social issues, and her reputation, almost everything she did attracted attention, which produced such phenomena as the Fannie Hurst dress, the Fannie Hurst picture, and Fannie Hurst tips on accessories.[149]

But nothing attracted more attention or was more revelatory of the "real" Fannie Hurst than the Fannie Hurst marriage. In 1915, Hurst had secretly married Jacques Danielson, a Russian-born Jewish pianist and composer whose father had been sculptor to the czar. Only her parents and a few relatives and close friends knew of the marriage, until it was disclosed by a journalist who accidentally discovered the marriage records. When the news leaked out, another shocking fact was revealed: not only had Fannie kept her name and career after her marriage, but the couple maintained separate apartments, seeing each other for breakfast two or three times a week, as the mood struck, and at other arranged times. Hurst and Danielson, with whom she claimed to be ecstatically in love, maintained this unconventional but happy relationship for thirty-seven years, until Danielson's death. Although she eschewed the phrase "trial marriage," many "two-breakfast-a-week," or so-called futurist, marriages thereafter became known as Fannie Hurst unions.

Hurst insisted that keeping a sense of privacy and freedom in the marriage was much more significant than the "double ménage" idea.[150] Although they enjoyed each other's companionship, she and Danielson kept their work, and often their friends, separate; compatibilities, Hurst claimed, were more central than interests. Hurst had fallen in love with Danielson upon meeting him at a hotel years earlier; at her urging, the two kept in touch via letter and post-cards for several years, then saw each other frequently after both moved to New York. But Hurst wondered whether marriage would "clip my wings"; she also had to contend with her parents' strong objections to the match because Danielson, although a world-class musician from an educated family, was an East European Jew and thus not of their "class." For years, Hurst "teetered in a state of indecision," wanting to follow her passions yet hesitating because of the "voice of the tribe" within her, wanting "Jack and marriage and . . . to be free." When Danielson grew weary of her dodges, she decided to take the plunge, but insisted on keeping the union secret for a year. After decades of "almost perfect marriage," her parents continued to believe she had not "done well" and remained chilly to her husband, who was by all accounts a polite and gentle man, distinguished for his musical artistry.[151]

Like Edna Ferber and Sophie Tucker, Hurst had always considered her-self plump, unattractive, and unappealing to the opposite sex. Only after many years in the public eye did she overcome her weight problem by means of a well-publicized routine of strict diet and exercise. Later pho-tographs show a slender woman, frequently dressed in black, with jet black hair pulled sleekly back, luminous and intelligent dark eyes, a broad mouth, and a chin and jaw suggesting determination and strength. Reporters fre-quently commented on the distinctive jewelry that complemented her out-fits, like her bracelet and gold ring set with a gargantuan Indian emerald. Everyone commented on her trademark accessory: a single calla lily that she wore on her lapel. One story had it that it was the first flower Jacques Danielson ever sent to her, although Hurst noted that the lily was "a sym-bol of serenity, a touch of peace in a violent storm"—and thus, a represen-tation of what she had needed to endure her mother's "magnificent temper."[152] The calla lily graced the cover and frontispiece of Hurst's auto-biography as well.

Short, overweight, and by her own description "ugly," Ferber, too, did not imagine herself to be a woman much desired by men. At one point, when the procedure was still very new, she took herself off to Europe and had her nose fixed; apparently she liked the results. But Ferber's wit and vivacity, and her tendency to act as if she were the leading character in a play of her own in-vention, kept her constantly at the center of attention. (If Ferber were to have mythical parents, Louis Bromfield wrote, he would choose "Sarah Bernhardt as her mother and the Prophet Jeremiah as her father.")[153] Nonetheless, Fer-ber turned down at least one proposal, and like Hurst, was never tempted by a traditional union, desiring her independence even more than the love of a man. Julia Ferber, who herself clung to Edna, pushed away the eligible men at any event they attended; none were good enough for her daughter.

The similarity between Hurst's and Ferber's personal stories, backgrounds, and self-presentations (both had wanted careers in the theater and considered themselves actresses *manquées*), in addition to their unusual appeal to a mass audience and emphasis on self-respecting, strong women, led to frequent comparisons. But according to Julia Gilbert, Ferber considered Hurst her "nemesis"; her "nails grew at the mention of [Hurst's] work." Reportedly, Ferber once remarked that "when Miss Hurst's work is compared to mine I became incensed. When my work is compared to hers, she becomes ecstatic."[154] On at least one occasion, however, Ferber attended one of Hurst's dinner parties and pronounced it "pretty darned terrible. . . . Nothing well cooked, nothing hot (except the champagne)."[155] Ferber herself had a reputation for throwing the finest parties, with the best food in town. For her part, Hurst insisted she preferred the "surging swarms" of New York's ordinary people to the "processed epigrams" of Ferber's "glib, smiting-word-at-any-price set" at the Algonquin.[156]

During their lifetimes, Ferber probably did enjoy greater acclaim. However, she could not avoid the taint of commercialism that surrounded her work; despite her Pulitzer Prize, critics debated her artistic merit. As to Hurst, while some critics applauded her dramatic use of characters and plot situations, others found them contrived, melodramatic, sentimental, and complained of the poor quality of her prose. Yet Hurst continued to sell books, and lots of them. As one *Newsweek* critic admitted in 1944:

> It happens every two years. There is a burst of advance publicity, booksellers frantically make out orders, there is an expectant hush, and then one day it appears: the new novel by Fannie Hurst. Invariably it sets into motion the same reactions. Book critics moan and try to outdo one another in writing clever, derisive reviews. The public buys it like mad.[157]

Both Ferber and Hurst agreed that the woman question was the most important issue of the day; Hurst not only wrote about it but lectured extensively on women's issues and served on dozens of committees concerned with women's welfare. Her novel *Lummox,* about the exploitation of a domestic servant, attracted the attention of Eleanor Roosevelt, wife of the then governor of New York, who had organized around the issue of women's domestic employment. Hurst and Eleanor became close lifelong friends; Hurst spent the long evening of FDR's first presidential election at the right hand of the president, "surrounded by about 10 men" in his family quarters. Later Hurst enjoyed frequent weekends at the White House, where she was assigned by Eleanor to the Abraham Lincoln suite.[158] She was active in the Women's Division of the Democratic Party, the Women's International League for Peace and Freedom, the National Woman's Party, Planned Parenthood, the Committee on Women in World Affairs, the National Organizations of Women for Equality in Education, and other women's groups. She was also (with Rose Pastor Stokes) a member of Heterodoxy.

Hurst couldn't refuse a request for help. She chaired the Committee on

Workmen's Compensation and the National Housing Committee; was a member of the national advisory board of the Works Progress Administration and of the New York Urban League and the Citywide Citizens Committee on Harlem; and participated in many other social, political, and philanthropic causes. For twenty-five years, she was a tireless supporter of Lillian Wald's Henry Street Settlement.

Hurst championed Jewish causes as well. She worked for the relief of Jews in Eastern Europe in the 1920s, helped raise funds for European refugees from Nazism, and was an active promoter of the State of Israel . A member of Hadassah, she frequently spoke before Jewish community organizations, synagogues, and national federations, including the National Council of Jewish Women, the Women's Division of the United Jewish Campaign, and other Jewish women's groups.[159] Even more than was true of Sophie Tucker or Edna Ferber, Hurst's attention to this panoply of organizational work in women's rights, civil rights, social welfare, and Jewish issues indicates the pluralism of her allegiances.

To Hurst as well as Ferber, however, Jews were less important as literary subjects than they were to Eastern European immigrant writers like Anzia Yezierska, Abraham Cahan, or Henry Roth. If their characters had any religion, it was that of "American person."[160] While Ferber and Hurst denied any conflict between their identities as Jews and Americans, their depiction of immigrant, ethnic, and racial characters and their themes of "passing" and racial otherness—as in Hurst's *Imitation of Life* and Ferber's *Show Boat*—suggest an experience of doubleness. As has been said of Ferber, these writers' "off-center ethnicity, gender, and regionality" gave them a unique vision that was prophetic not only of the despoliation of the American continent, but of the options of American womanhood, in years to come.[161] They are, in this sense, representative American women writers of the first half of the twentieth century.

Like their Jewishness, however, these writers' feminism was neither automatic nor unambivalent. While in their novels and short stories they urged women to fight the idea that, as Ferber wrote, "this is a man's world," they criticized women's failings and portrayed marriage as an inevitable, though not necessarily satisfactory, destiny.[162] Yet in their images of women, Ferber and Hurst—like Sophie Tucker—captured the tradition of strong Jewish women, which was reflected in their own lives and those of their mothers. Though the blending of the two worlds would not prove seamless, the simultaneous promulgation of sob sister and iron woman imagery, of red-hot and Yiddishe mamas, indicates the expressive continuity between generations. Being Jewish and being American were not necessarily in conflict; despite tensions, they became part of a unified and progressive cultural framework.

This imagery, together with the model of their own lives, allowed their audiences to imagine new roles and codes of behavior despite the social constraints of the times; perhaps this was their finest achievement. "If men ever discovered how tough women actually are, they would be scared to death," Ferber wrote in *A Kind of Magic*.[163] Like Jews, women had been hardened by centuries of subjection; as Americans, they had been given the opportunity, if they would only use it, to "rule the world."[164]

The Most Famous Jew in the World: Gertrude Stein

Across the ocean, another American Jewish woman writer was expanding the horizons of the imagination. In 1903, Gertrude Stein had gone to Paris to join her brother Leo. Within a decade, she had by all accounts become the "titular head of the *avant garde*."[165] With Leo, she was one of the earliest collectors of Picasso, Matisse, Cézanne, and other modern artists, many of whom vied to have their paintings hung in the Stein apartment. By the 1920s, after Leo had broken with Gertrude and left Paris, she served as mentor to such up-and-coming writers as Ernest Hemingway and Scott Fitzgerald. In her house at 27 rue de Fleurus with its famous atelier, she held court like a "great Jewish Buddha."[166]

This pioneering expatriate did more than preside over an informal salon of artists and writers. In her own writing, she conducted an extraordinary experiment in modernism, disrupting conventional grammar, subject matter, plot, character, context, and genre with narratives that were focused, in her words, on the "continuous present," the "immediate existing," or the "including everything."[167] Considered more modern than any other writer of her era, including Eliot and Joyce, Stein claimed to have initiated the "twentieth century way" in literature; she professed indifference to the fact that many considered her work unreadable.

Stein found the lifestyles of the early twentieth century as confining as its literature. Stein's forty-year lesbian marriage to Alice B. Toklas, also a German Jew from California, broke new ground, even among her bohemian circle. Bold, energetic, and shrewd, she was, said writer Katherine Anne Porter:

> of the company of Amazons which nineteenth-century America produced among its many prodigies: not-men, not-women, answerable to no function in either sex, whose careers were carried on, and how successfully, in whatever field they chose. . . . [They] played out . . . their self-assumed, self-created roles in such masterly freedom as only a few early medieval queens had equaled.[168]

There was much about Stein's grandiosity that resembled Edna Ferber and Fannie Hurst, who had also invented themselves as literary celebrities. A little more than a decade older than Ferber and Hurst, Stein was born in Baltimore in 1874 to Daniel Stein, a businessman, and Amelia Keyser Stein, both of German Jewish descent. After Daniel Stein quarreled with several of the brothers with whom he owned a clothing establishment, the family moved to

Allegheny, Pennsylvania. When Gertrude was only a few months old, Stein took his family to Austria; his wife and five children (Gertrude was the youngest) stayed on, soon settling in Paris, while Daniel returned to America. Eventually the family moved to Oakland, California, where Gertrude spent most of her childhood. Her mother, quiet and undemanding, died of cancer in 1888, when Gertrude was fourteen, and her father, mercurial and domineering, passed away three years later. The eldest son, Michael, took responsibility for raising his siblings, but Gertrude was closest to Leo, two years older, with whom she shared, from the very beginning, a passionate interest in reading.

When Leo went off to Harvard, Gertrude followed him. In 1893, when she was nineteen, she enrolled as a special student at the Harvard Annex, soon to become Radcliffe. Taking philosophy courses with George Santayana and William James, she was especially and (as it turned out) indelibly influenced by the latter's new theories of the stream of consciousness. Stein graduated magna cum laude in 1898, having fully enjoyed her college career and Cambridge, where she found that being a Jew was "the least burden . . . of any spot on earth."[169] Intending to become a psychologist, she entered medical school at Johns Hopkins University in Baltimore, but there encountered both sexism and anti-Semitism; a classmate recalled that one of her teachers, the eminent gynecologist John Whitridge Williams, commented on Stein's sloppy methods and "marked Hebrew looks."[170] Stein's enthusiasm waned and she left Hopkins without regret in her fourth year, joining Leo in Europe. Although always an enthusiastic American, she remained in exile, except for a brief lecture tour of the States in 1934, after the publication of her first great popular success, *The Autobiography of Alice B. Toklas,* and the triumphant performance of her opera, *Four Saints in Three Acts* (set to music by Virgil Thomson and performed in Hartford and New York with an all-Negro cast).[171]

Stein wrote neither about Jews nor as a Jew. Though one of her most important works, the 1,000-page *Making of Americans,* may be said to chronicle a family that is a thinly disguised version of her own, the book's real concern is to redefine time and history by focusing on the passing of generations and the ways in which people's "bottom nature" reinscribes family patterns. According to one critic, *The Making of Americans* is like the Old Testament in that generations follow one another without really succeeding one another.[172]

For Stein, the all-important "moment of consciousness" in which people locate themselves was a very "American thing." A democrat who, like Ferber and Hurst, exulted in the possibilities of pluralism, she brought her belief in social equality to the realm of consciousness rather than material life. In her influential first work, *Three Lives* (1909), about three women who are servants or daughters of the working class, consciousness is a product not of status or class but of emotion and language. Novelist Richard Wright, commenting on the portrait of the African American Melanctha in the book, noted that reading it was one of the most important events in his career.[173]

While some scholars see Stein's resistance to fixed categories and unilinear thinking as evidence of a lack of a sense of her own Jewishness, others believe that her identity as a Jew lies precisely in her "language practice": If language is seen as representing the instability that informs the Jewish notion of home, Maria Damon suggests, Stein succeeds in secularizing Jews' religious obligation to push language to its limits. In her books, she creates "makeshift homelands" with language that is "not stable, but portable, mobile, motile."[174]

Although Stein considered herself a "modern," not a religious Jew, she admired the poetry of the Hebrew Bible and the Jews' "strong . . . hereditary clan feeling"; in college she wrote that Jews had an "inborn . . . ethical and a spiritual nature"—they were a "Chosen People chosen for high purposes."[175] Later she claimed that "all men of genius" had Jewish blood; she even developed a theory that Abraham Lincoln's parents had a "Jewish strain."[176] By the 1920s, Stein was making a point of identifying herself—and Alice B. Toklas—as Jews, granting an interview in 1928 to the *New York Jewish Tribune,* which had run a story about her as a Jewish writer. When her nephew visited Europe, she boasted that she was the "most famous Jew in the world."[177]

Like Hurst and Ferber, Stein bristled at evidence of anti-Semitism in the literary as well as political world. She was particularly bothered by Hemingway's *The Sun Also Rises,* for both its homophobia and its anti-Semitism. (In a letter to Ezra Pound, Hemingway had referred to her as one of the "safe-playing kikes.")[178]

Once Stein told journalist Hutchins Hapgood "how impossible it was for a Jewish woman to marry a Gentile." Hapgood recalled the statement as "one of the most striking examples . . . of the deep-seated feeling of the Jews about their race."[179] In view of Stein's remark, it is perhaps not surprising that she fell in love with Alice B. Toklas. Toklas, a musician and aspiring writer, was a member of a close circle of Jewish women friends from California travelling or residing in Europe. Like the clannish families they came from, these women stuck together, supporting each other's talents and interests.

Stein's identification as a Jew became more problematic during the Nazi years. A supporter of the collaborationist Vichy regime, Stein wrote a four-page "Introduction to the Speeches of Maréchal Pétain," likening the Vichy puppet leader to a heroic George Washington.[180] But Stein's Random House editor Bennett Cerf, to whom she sent her essay in an effort to find a U.S. publisher for Pétain, pronounced her piece "disgusting" and refused to publish it. In spite of their notoriety as Jews and lesbians, Stein and Toklas, protected by friends of the Vichy regime, survived the war in their home in the French countryside.

"To be a good Jew" during wartime may in fact have been "just to survive," says Maria Damon, who insists that Stein was never "ashamed or conflicted

about her status as a Jew." Other Stein scholars point out that Stein's veneration of Pétain was based on a naive belief that he was a mediator who kept
France out of war and that the alternative might have been worse.[181] But a
darker interpretation has been suggested by Wanda Van Dusen, who discovered Stein's "Introduction." However vulnerable she might have been as a
Jewish American lesbian, Van Dusen writes, in "dissimulating both Jewishness and the anti-Semitic character of the Vichy regime," Stein depoliticized
and aesthetized the war.[182] Her strategy raises ethical issues that apply to other
modernist writers whose veneration of "genius and power" led them to champion "conservative—even fascist impulses . . ."[183]

Given her vulnerability to arrest and deportation, Stein's "Introduction"
on Pétain should not be taken as the last word about her sense of herself as a
Jew. Her apparent pride in her Jewish heritage and frequent assertion of Jewish particularity suggest a strong, continuing identity. Nevertheless, Stein's actions in the 1940s are troubling. On her death bed in 1946, she spoke the
now-famous lines: "What is the answer?" When there was no response, she
asked: "In that case, what is the question?"[184] One of the questions that sur-
vives her concerns the complex nature of her Jewishness and its relation to her
sense of herself as woman, lesbian, and American expatriate.

Chapter 6

PIONEERS IN THE PROFESSIONS

Subway Scholars and Seven Sisters Graduates: A New Generation of Activists

By the 1920s, though women had made significant inroads into professional as well as cultural life, few had entered elite professions such as medicine and law. Those who did encountered widespread sexual discrimination. Within the law, few advanced to prominence, and the presence of women in the judiciary remained rare. When, at age thirty-two, Justine Wise Tulin (later Polier), daughter of the eminent Reform rabbi Stephen Wise, became a municipal judge in New York, her appointment attracted considerable attention. The story goes that when the first object of her judicial skills emerged from the courtroom and was asked how it went, he replied, "Well, the judge wasn't there but his wife treated me just fine."[1]

Like other American women who came of age in the early decades of the twentieth century, Jewish women faced severe prejudice in the professions. Yet the opportunities available to them distinguished their options from those of their mothers. Jewish women made the most of them, as their manifold achievements testify. Just as the immigrant daughters who rose to the top of new forms of mass entertainment left their mark on American popular culture, so did this first generation of Jewish professional women shape public life.

By the second decade of the twentieth century, Jewish women had made rapid gains within the nation's educational system. They attended colleges, universities, and professional schools in numbers disproportionate to their representation in the population; many helped pioneer new careers for women in such areas as law, social work, and civil service. Even larger numbers became teachers, particularly in urban centers like New York City. By the early 1930s, Jewish women constituted almost half of all city teachers.[2]

Jewish women made these advances in a single generation. Fannie Brandeis Nagel, sister of the Supreme Court Justice, had been unable to find an outlet for her intellectual interests and lived a life of despair and inactivity. Brandeis's wife Alice had also suffered from chronic illness and depression.[3] But

Brandeis's own two daughters, born in the last decade of the nineteenth century, graduated from prestigious Seven Sisters colleges and went on to distinguished professional careers. Susan Brandeis Gilbert, who studied at Bryn Mawr, became a lawyer; her sister Elizabeth Brandeis Raushenbush, a Radcliffe graduate, earned a Ph.D. in economics and became an authority in labor law, teaching at the University of Wisconsin for forty years.[4]

The daughters, sisters, and close relatives of other distinguished American Jewish leaders—most of them from the German Jewish elite—also fared well. Justine Polier attended Bryn Mawr and Radcliffe before graduating from Barnard College in 1924, and she received her LL.D. from Yale Law School, where she edited the *Law Journal.* An authority in juvenile justice and child welfare, Polier had a distinguished career as judge in the Family Court in New York. Judge Julian Mack's daughter, Ruth, a Radcliffe classmate of Elizabeth Brandeis, received a medical degree from Tufts and studied in Vienna with Sigmund Freud, becoming his associate at the Vienna Psychoanalytic Institute. Estelle Frankfurter, sister of Supreme Court Justice Felix Frankfurter, was also a member of Radcliffe's class of 1918. After graduate work at Bryn Mawr and the London School of Economics, Frankfurter worked for the National Labor Board and in various civil service positions in the field of manpower and labor relations. Hetty Goldman, niece of Felix Adler, the founder of the Ethical Culture movement, received her B.A. at Bryn Mawr and her M.A. and Ph.D. at Radcliffe; a celebrated archeologist specializing in the Baltic area, Goldman was the first woman appointed to a distinguished professorship at the Institute of Advanced Study at Princeton.[5]

But it was not only the daughters of prominent, upper-class German and Central European Jews who took advantage of expanding educational opportunities for women. Second-generation East European daughters, too, were well represented in public colleges and universities, especially New York's Hunter College. Like most American women graduates, the majority of Hunter alumnae became teachers.

In the years after the attainment of suffrage in 1920, when the women's movement entered its "decades of doldrums," professional Jewish women like Justine Wise Polier, international attorney Fanny Holtzmann, and schoolteacher Bel Kaufman pioneered new directions for female endeavor. Notable for their public service orientation, their concern with the welfare of women and children, and their attention to questions of religious and racial discrimination, these women were distinguished both from their Jewish male peers and from the non-Jewish women with whom they often worked.

Teacherly Love: Bel Kaufman

The experience of New York City schoolteachers in the mid-twentieth century was immortalized in the best-selling novel *Up the Down Staircase,* by Bel

Kaufman, the daughter of East European immigrants and granddaughter of Yiddish novelist Sholem Aleichem.

Kaufman, who had emigrated from Odessa with her family in 1923 when she was twelve, quickly learned English and, like Mary Antin, used the public libraries voraciously. In 1930, she entered Hunter College, commuting daily to its concrete campus like other "subway scholars." Despite their high academic achievements, to college officials these women seemed unrefined in both manners and appearance. According to Hunter's president George Shuster, the "foreign" students were "raucous, gawky, and afflicted with acne, halitosis, and deplorable hair-dos."[6] To correct their social ineptitude, the school mandated courses in grooming, hygiene, and health, in which they were informed, among other advice, that bagels were nutritionally unsound.[7]

The generation of students who attended Hunter College between 1920 and 1940 called themselves "the lost generation," as Lucy Dawidowicz, editor of Hunter's literary magazine in the early 1930s, recalled. According to historian Katherina Grunfeld, these women had been socialized to succeed at the same time that they were "ostracized by American society and academia due to their (half-rejected) ethnic roots."[8] In a story (appropriately titled "The Lost Generation") that appeared in the *Hunter College Echo* in 1931, one student wrote, "You struggle, you work; you come just so far, and then a blank wall opposes you." The deserving young woman in the story has been denied the scholarship she needs for graduate school because, "after all, my name's Rubin. And my father hems neckties for a living."[9] Ashamed of their backgrounds yet feeling guilty for harboring these feelings, Jewish women at Hunter considered the college a symbol of their own otherness: Hunter students were known as "girls," a professor told Kate Simon, whereas "women" attended the elite Seven Sisters schools.[10]

Yet these women made the most of their educations. Many went on to distinguished careers: Simon became a much published writer, Dawidowicz a scholar of Jewish history, and Rosalyn Yalow, who had to take night courses at City College to complete her physics major, a scientist and Nobel Prize winner.[11] Bel Kaufman gravitated to courses in English and French. Inspired by the high standards of her teachers, whom she credited for her own love of literature, she graduated magna cum laude in 1934, a member of Phi Beta Kappa.[12] After college she went on to Columbia University for a master's in English, specializing in eighteenth-century British literature.

But it was a course in education at Hunter that set the direction of her career; when she found herself in front of a class of eager youngsters as a student teacher, she felt she had discovered her metier. Still, she might have gone into journalism if her mother had not insisted, like so many other Depression era immigrant mothers, that "even if you marry, you must have a profession," and teaching was the most secure.[13]

To receive a New York City teaching license, however, Kaufman had to submit to a rigorous written examination (which she passed with flying colors) and undergo an even more grueling oral interview. "The candidate was judged on her appearance, neatness, 'breeding,' energy and alertness," historian Ruth Markowitz notes. "Her voice was supposed to be audible, pleasant, and well modulated, without being nasal, high pitched, monotonous, strident or noisy. . . ." She was required to speak articulately and grammatically, without any vulgarisms or foreignisms. Mispronunciations not only could be imitated by pupils, the examiners held, but indicated significant and ultrimately disqualifying cultural defects.[14]

Although candidates with defective "foreign" speech were likely to be screened out early on by teacher training programs, even well-spoken Jewish immigrant girls frequently failed the oral exam. Kaufman remembers waiting outside the Board of Examiners' hearing room, in a cold sweat, as one after another of the candidates staggered out, often in tears. "Watch out for dentalization," they warned the waiting applicants. "Watch out for the sibilant S." "Watch out for lateral emission."[15]

"I thought if you taught in college all you had to do was give them a reading list," Kaufman, then a graduate teaching assistant, remembered. "But the examiners fixed me with their collective eye, asked if I were born in this country, [and] then had me pronounce some very difficult sentences." Although she took numerous speech courses, she failed the test three times. Kaufman still remembers the sentence that got her through on the fourth try—"He still insists he sees the ghosts"—"I hissed it to their satisfaction."[16]

To pass, however, candidates also had to interpret a piece of literature. Kaufman received negative grades on her reading of Edna St. Vincent Millay's "Euclid Alone," and failed the test again. This time she fought back, sending the Board of Examiners affidavits from her professors testifying to her literary skills, as well as a letter from Edna St. Vincent Millay herself, to whom she had sent a copy of her analysis of the poem. Millay wrote to the examiners that Kaufman's interpretation was extraordinarily perceptive. Yet, in an incident that Kaufman later fictionalized in *Up the Down Staircase,* the examiners voted her down once again. The following year, perhaps because they had had enough of her, Kaufman passed the orals and received her teaching license.

This kind of bias on the part of the examiners was all too frequent where Jewish applicants were concerned; concentrating on the pronunciation of East European Jews, the oral exam did not screen out all so-called New York accents, such as the easily identifiable Irish brogue. Although not overtly anti-Semitic, the oral exam tended to eliminate many qualified Jewish candidates. Furthermore, the interview often included questions about applicants' political attitudes. Kaufman recalls that many of her Hunter classmates worked actively for social justice and peace, participating in numerous antiwar and antifascist protests. The disqualification of candidates involved in such activism also effectively discriminated against Jews.

Kaufman began teaching in the mid-1930s; her career lasted some twenty-five years and took her to fourteen different public high schools in all parts of New York City. Although she taught for many years at the High School of the Performing Arts, her formative years in the profession were spent in less selective neighborhood schools where she had to deal with sullen, unmotivated adolescents. Her attempt to make a difference in the lives of these students, coupled with her often hilarious encounters with local and downtown school bureaucracies, became the life experience that shaped *Up the Down Staircase.*[17]

Published in 1964, *Staircase* was a national best-seller. With over six million copies in print, the book has by now gone through forty-seven editions and been translated into sixteen languages. *Time* magazine called it "easily the most popular novel about U.S. public schools in history."[18] It was made into a hit movie in 1967.

A compendium of classroom dialogue as well as memos, letters, and notes from student work, teachers' mailboxes, blackboards, and wastebaskets, the book recounts the struggles of a neophyte urban teacher. From the student who fails to turn in his homework "because the dog peed on it," to the anonymous pupil who signs his work "Me," Kaufman engages her readers' sympathy with the portraits of lost, unmotivated teens, committed if frustrated teachers, and a rigid, irrelevant bureaucracy. "Please admit bearer to class," runs the principal's note from which the book gets its title. "Detained by me for going Up the Down stairway and subsequent insolence."[19]

Kaufman had begun writing fiction during college. In 1941, she sold her first story to *Esquire,* which at the time published only male authors; to get around this, she lopped the final "le" off her given name, thinking that Bel sounded more masculine. But she wrote only sporadically during her teaching career, and had long felt inferior to the members of the literary clan into which she was born: besides her grandfather, her mother Lyalya was a prolific author of more than two thousand short stories, many of them published in the *Jewish Daily Forward.*

With the success of *Staircase,* however, Kaufman felt she could claim her family heritage. She finds similarities between her writing and her grandfather's—a sympathy for ordinary citizens, interest in social reform, a tone of wit and irony. Like her grandfather, she considers her writing a kind of Jewish humor, which she describes as "laughter with tears, turning the table on tragedy and snubbing disaster."[20] Now in her mid-eighties, Kaufman continues to travel throughout the world to speak about Sholem Aleichem's legacy. A living link to the Russian Jewish past, she has been involved in cultural exchanges with the former USSR; one of her goals is to make Jewish culture more visible in Russian cities and provinces. In 1992, Jews flocked to the Great Hall of the Moscow Conservatory to hear Kaufman narrate, in flawless Russian, a Jewish oratorio about the Holocaust. She is interested in Russian women as well, and is a founding member of the Alliance of American and Russian Women, established in 1991.[21]

Kaufman's sympathetic portrait of the teacher in *Staircase,* and her continuing interest in educational and social reform, reflect the career histories of many teachers in New York City. More than most others, Jewish women schoolteachers were activists within the school system and outside. In 1925, though they constituted less than 25 percent of New York City teachers, they represented 50 percent of the executive board of the teachers' union; twice as many Jewish women as Jewish men attended union meetings.[22] Anti-Semitism, however, remained a powerful threat to their activism. During the 1930s, when New York City teachers were under attack for purported radicalism, Jews felt especially threatened. Linking anti-Semitism to antiradicalism, the demagogue Father Charles Coughlin gave wide exposure to the notion that Jewish "Reds" were in charge of the New York City schools; in one notorious article, he variously labeled the officers and prominent members of the Teachers' Union as "Jew," "Jewess," "Gentile," or "Undetermined."[23] Many Jewish teachers were harassed during the 1930s, and even more in the unbridled McCarthyism of the postwar era. Whether they belonged to the Communist Party or not, Jewish teachers felt themselves to be suspects; to them it was no coincidence that almost all of those accused of being party members, and fully all of those dismissed during the McCarthy purges, were Jewish.[24]

As Jewish women secured a place for themselves within the New York public school system, they found it impossible to hide their ethnic heritage under the protective cover of professionalism. "We grew up on stories of the pogroms in the old country," one teacher emphasized, "and it always surrounded us here in America. It was a fact of life."[25] Some attacked it head-on in the classroom, teaching about tolerance; others turned the other cheek, thinking that anti-Semitism would disappear when its perpetrators were taught how "illogic[al] and un-American" such prejudice was. Yet according to the teachers' informal code of conduct, to be silent in the face of a direct ethnic or racial slur was a serious failure of character. While most were able to achieve a level of occupational security unavailable to first-generation mothers, in their readiness to confront bigotry and fight against the conditions that oppressed their students, they demonstrated a commitment to Jewish values that linked them to those who came before.

Prophetic Justice and Celebrity Zionism: Justine Wise Polier and Fanny Holtzmann

While the majority of educated Jewish women who entered professional life chose teaching, a high percentage became lawyers. In 1920, a study of 106 prominent educational institutions throughout the country found that out of the total number of Jewish women at the nation's colleges and professional schools, the proportion studying law (14 percent) was nearly identical to that of Jewish male students. In comparison, only 1.7 percent of non-Jewish women were studying law.[26] According to one historian, the legal profession at that time represented "institutionalized masculinity" at its most extreme. The close connection between law, business, and politics, together with the assumption that practicing law meant "doing [in] your neighbor, and doing him first," tended to discourage women, who were told by such eminent practitioners as Clarence Darrow that they were "too kind" and "not cold blooded" enough for the law.[27] In the face of continuing hostility, few women who entered law school graduated, and no more than one-third to one-half of women lawyers actually practiced; in 1920, women constituted little more than 1 percent of the nation's attorneys.[28] In light of this, and the additional fact of anti-Semitism, the large proportion of Jewish women who entered into and continued to practice law, particularly in New York City, was "very noticeable," as Susan Brandeis commented in an address on women and the law in 1929. Despite the fact that her father was a member of the U.S. Supreme Court, Brandeis herself had been denied a position in a large law firm in New York solely on the basis of her sex. Having also been refused entry to Harvard Law School because she was a woman, she became active in the fight to open the school to other women.[29]

Evidence suggests that a compelling factor in Jewish women's choice of the law was the belief that they could be useful to others.[30] Justine Wise Polier came to the law hoping to alleviate the worst evils of industrial capitalism; she stayed on to work for better conditions for women and children. Jennie Loitman Barron organized and became first president of the Women's Suffrage Association of Boston University; as a municipal court judge like Polier, she too became a powerful advocate for the rights of women and children.[31] And Susan Brandeis, who had been an active suffragist before beginning her legal career in 1921, was deeply involved in labor law, tenants' claims, and legal aid for female offenders. With so many issues requiring their involvement, she proclaimed that "the call to women to enter this new field is irresistible."[32]

Often Jewish fathers, particularly those who were themselves middle- or upper-class professionals, guided their daughters' entry into the law, providing moral and financial support and, in some cases, a place in the family business. The crucial contribution of fathers and other male relatives consisted not only in practical support, but in their validation of professional ambition and advanced learning for women, which Jewish men had long claimed only for themselves. Jewish women professionals also called upon female role models from their tradition.

Whatever the advice of parents or mentors, the journeys of these women were their own. In 1917, when Susan was attending law school at the University of Chicago, Louis Brandeis, recently appointed to the Supreme Court, worried that his daughter's political views could endanger her future and embarrass him. Although he acknowledged to his wife that "[Susan] really does not belong to our world," Brandeis refused to interfere with his daughter's choices.[33] His trust proved not to be misplaced; within a few years after graduation, this unkempt radical pacifist had become the first female special assistant to the U.S. Attorney in New York. In 1925, she became the first woman to argue a case before the Supreme Court.[34]

Children of Destiny   Justine Wise Polier was the daughter of Rabbi Wise and Louise Waterman Wise, a painter of considerable renown and founder and director of the Free Synagogue's Child Adoption Committee. Later known as Louise Wise Services, the agency worked with hard-to-place children. During her many years with the organization, Louise personally selected the children to rescue and the families with whom they were placed.[35]

Louise Wise's interest in child welfare and her feisty, stubborn determination were an inheritance that became part of Justine Polier's professional armor. Her mother's bravery and willfulness were legendary. When Stephen Wise refused the offer to become rabbi at Manhattan's Temple Emanu-El because the board would not guarantee him freedom of the pulpit, it was Louise, "standing behind the curtains shaking her head against his yielding," who bolstered his resolve.[36] In 1932, Louise Wise inaugurated the Women's Division of the American Jewish Congress, hoping to unite Jewish women in furtherance of the goals of the Congress, specifically against fascism. While Stephen Wise rallied Americans at Madison Square Garden to protest Hitler's boycott of Jewish goods, Louise led her own well-publicized boycott against Nazi-sympathizing businessmen. On a visit to Palestine in the 1930s, Louise had been asked by the vice consul if there was anything he could do for her. "Have the roads paved for all these people," she responded. The official complied.[37]

As much as she was influenced by her mother's willfulness and humanitarian concerns, Justine worshipped her father even more: even as an adult, her attitude toward him combined admiration, reverence, and love.[38] Unitarian minister John Haynes Holmes, recalling an incident that reflects the sexism of the era as much as Justine's attitude toward her parents, has described how the Wise children once rushed out to greet him when he came to visit. Jim Waterman Wise, then six years old, asked the visitor if he was there to see his father or mother. Four-year-old Justine immediately piped up: "Daddy, you silly! He's the only one around here who's important."[39]

The Wises were indulgent, permissive parents who brought their children up in an atmosphere of openness and liberty, but they impressed upon their offspring from an early age the importance of ethical conduct and tolerance as well as respect for their own heritage. Justine often recounted the story of a notable Christian minister who told her father that he couldn't be expected to sit down with a distinguished expatriate black artist whom the Wises had invited to dinner. "Oh, I'm so sorry," Stephen Wise replied. "May I take you downstairs and help you get your coat?" For Justine, the incident highlighted the qualities she most respected in her father—"the strength, the courtesy, and the absolute unyielding on matters of principle."[40]

From both her father and her mother, whom she considered "always a rebel," Justine Wise inherited her tenacity and grace. When she was appointed justice of the Domestic Relations Court in New York City—the first woman in the state to hold such a high post—Stephen Wise exulted that the appointment was "better than any prophecy—even your parents'." But he was not surprised, he told his daughter, because she was a "child of destiny."[41]

Fanny Holtzmann came from a family of Jewish Republicans who were active in party politics and closely associated with Theodore Roosevelt. While their politics distinguished them from the Wises and most Jews of their Brooklyn neighborhood, the Holtzmanns shared with the Wises a deep commitment to Jewish values. After studying for the rabbinate in Eastern Europe, Fanny's father, Henry Holtzmann, had come to the United States from Galicia in 1888 with his young wife, Theresa. According to Fanny, they emigrated to promote the Zionist idea in the United States; her father, convinced of the need for a Jewish homeland in Palestine, had corresponded with Herzl and determined on an American mission. Settling first on the Lower East Side and then in Brownsville, an immigrant section of Brooklyn, Holtzmann taught citizenship classes at the Hebrew Educational Society and ran a tutoring school. Later he turned to real estate and was instrumental in settling Jews in Brownsville. Profiting from prosperous times, the family later moved to Eastern Parkway, which Fanny called the Jewish "Gold Coast"—a kind of "Brooklyn Champs-Elysées"—populated by a rising class of Jewish merchants and professionals.[42]

Despite his growing involvement in Republican politics, Holtzmann did not stray from the Zionist cause, serving as president of the Brooklyn Zionist Society and correspondent for Herzl's Viennese newspaper *Die Welt*.[43] Holtzmann's passion for Zionism was shared by his wife, a friend of Henrietta Szold and a member of one of the first Hadassah groups; both Holtzmanns frequently addressed Jews on the idea of a Jewish homeland. Though Henry was more scholarly, Theresa was more dynamic; she could make a speech at the drop of a hat. Holtzmann heard so much about Zionism growing up that she became "fed up with it"; later in life she would claim the cause as her own.[44]

Holtzmann's vision of the law was deeply influenced by Jewish concepts of righteous action that she learned from her father and from her maternal grandfather, Hirsch Bornfeld, a Hasidic rabbi from Galicia whom Fanny called Zaida. In the eyes of the eight other Holtzmann children, Zaida, with his long, white beard and rigid observance of *kashruth*, was eccentric and old-fashioned.[45] But Fanny and Zaida formed an immediate alliance—she combed his beard and made his food; he took care of her intellectual and spiritual development.

Although he was over seventy when he came to the United States, Zaida became an active community leader, establishing yeshivas and officiating at many neighborhood religious ceremonies. Like his son-in-law, he became an avid Republican. Politics, however, did not always mix with religion; when Zaida refused to allow socialists or Democrats, whom he considered akin to anarchists, to read the Torah in his shul, the congregants deposed him, leading the rabbi to found another synagogue.[46] But the community appreciated his regular appearances in municipal court to plead the case of immigrants evicted from their homes. To Fanny, who attended all of Zaida's court arguments, he explained that these appearances helped him to fulfill the Talmudic command to perform *mitzvot* (meritorious acts) without concern for personal gain.[47] At home, Zaida ran his own *bet din* (rabbinical court). Sitting at his long kitchen table, he would pass judgment on the disputes of neighbors, mainly small businessmen. From these sessions at home and in court, Holtzmann learned an important lesson that she would put to use in her own career: that the law should be used to "harmonize differences—not aggravate them."[48]

Although Holtzmann dropped out of high school (by "mutual agreement" with her teachers), she began to entertain the idea of going to law school. Her grandfather's municipal court appearances and *bet din,* and her father's involvement with his students' citizenship papers and contracts, had given her an unusual exposure to the law. In addition, her oldest brother Jack, a newly minted lawyer who had begun attracting attention for his courtroom victories, allowed her to do errands for him. But her brother merely scoffed when Holtzmann—a woman and a "family disgrace" because of her academic failures—announced her intention to enter the practice of law herself; the more Jack ridiculed the idea, the more determined Holtzmann became.[49] However, Zaida and Holtzmann's mother supported the girl's ambition. Theresa brought in a female attorney who offered concrete advice: learn dictation, get a day job, and study for the Regents examinations at night to earn the credit needed for law school. Holtzmann followed her suggestions, and eighteen months later was admitted to Fordham Law School. Working by day at Keppler and Hochman, a law firm located in the same building where her classes were held, she attended law school at night, the only woman in her class. She graduated in 1922, at the age of twenty-two, and passed the bar the following year.

Joan of Arc   Justine Wise Polier's decision to go to law school was not inspired by the example of family practitioners but came at the direct suggestion of her father, who saw a legal career as the best way for Justine to pursue her passionate interest in the rights of workers. Polier had begun her college career at Bryn Mawr, where she was admitted after a grueling interview with President M. Carey Thomas about her family background and life goals.[50] (Thomas, a notable anti-Semite, was determined to keep "undesirables" out of Bryn Mawr.)[51]

Although Polier was admitted, she left Bryn Mawr after two years, seeking more advanced courses in economics. She transferred to Radcliffe, where students were permitted to take graduate courses from Harvard professors. Yet Polier was dissatisfied with these courses because they failed to connect students with the poor people on whom they often focused. So she moved out of the "blue-stockinged world" of Radcliffe and into the Elizabeth Peabody House, a settlement in Boston. During the day she attended classes at Radcliffe and taught foreign residents English; at night she worked at a local factory to gain still more firsthand experience. When, after the fact, she wired her parents that she had moved, Stephen Wise came immediately to Boston. Although he was concerned to find Polier living next door to the Charles Street jail, he believed she should be able to do what she wanted. Polier remained at the settlement until she finished the year at Radcliffe.

Then, "fed up on dried-up old maids studying problems of people about whom they knew nothing," Polier left Radcliffe for Barnard, where she spent her last year.[52] Though an economics major, she took philosophy courses with John Dewey and education psychology with William Kilpatrick at Teachers College. With the approval of her advisor, William Ogburn, she arranged to obtain course credit for working on a New York State Labor Department investigation of the industrial accidents of women workers. Surveying the women's loss of earning power following their injuries and the inadequacy of workmen's compensation coverage, she became deeply interested in problems of economic insurance and the labor movement.

Polier's first published articles—for *The New Student* at Barnard and *The World Tomorrow* after graduation—expressed her belief that young people had to "claim responsibility" in solving the social problems of their time, rather than seeking their own material gain. She advised direct work in industrial communities, alongside poor people and immigrants, to gain the firsthand knowledge necessary for developing labor policies and legislation. She cited the English Fabian movement as a model of such involvement.[53]

Taking her own advice, Polier and four friends (including the granddaughter of the Bishop of Maryland, married to an Sephardic Jew, and Sy Whitney, descendant of Yale's Eli Whitney) sought work in the textile factories of Passaic and Paterson, New Jersey. She found the conditions there "abominable"; what incensed her most was the employment of mothers on night shifts, "while their husbands slept"; exhausted, they would then put in another full day caring for their households and children. In spite of the heavy toll on women, employers took the "plumpest" ones they could find and sent them to testify at the State House on behalf of night work. Just as appalling were the "Gestapo" tactics employers used to keep workers from organizing—spying on them in their homes and workplaces and "blacklisting" those who caused trouble.[54]

Believing that revealing her true identity as the daughter of Stephen Wise (whose prolabor positions were well known) would have prevented her from being hired, Polier had told the Passaic bosses that her father did "clerical work" and her mother "housekeeping." After two months as a quiller on the evening shift at the Passaic Cotton Mills, she applied for work at the Wool Council of Passaic and was given a card entitling her to apply directly at any woolen mill in the city. At one interview, the personnel director, impressed with Polier's "high school education," determined to make her a forelady and explained that, because she would then be moved from department to department, they would pay her in advance. Polier was called in to accept her first check; when she signed a receipt as "Justine Waterman," the supervisor turned upon her, saying, "We know who you are, you are Rabbi Wise's daughter," whereupon he announced his intention to arrest her for taking money under false pretenses.[55] Polier explained that she had merely wanted to live and work with women in the mills so that she might better understand their problems. Although the owners retreated from the threat of arrest, Polier and her friends were fired and blacklisted from working at Passaic's mills and factories.

Polier then spent a summer at the International Labor Office in Geneva, Switzerland, examining labor relations from a comparative perspective. Her studies led her to write an article, "World Peace and Industrial Peace," for a British publication, *The Jewish Woman,* in which she emphasized that economic security was vital to international peace and urged her government to eschew the isolationist path on which it seemed headed.[56]

At summer's end she met her parents in London. While her father respected her "good intentions," he wondered what she could do without specific skills. "Why didn't I get myself to law school and learn something about people's rights?" Polier recalled him asking, presenting her with several folio volumes of Blackstone's *Commentaries.* Although she had no intention of practicing law, Polier agreed with her father that a law degree could help her pursue her goal of furthering social equality and the labor movement. She asked family friend Felix Frankfurter to recommend a law school that accepted women. Frankfurter could come up with only two—Yale and the University of Chicago. Polier applied to Yale; accepted immediately, she began the following fall.[57]

While there were only five women students out of 125 at the law school, Polier found the atmosphere cordial to women's learning. She was elected to Coif, the honorary legal society, and became an editor of the *Yale Law Journal.* When, after becoming president of Kappa Beta Phi, an honorary society for women, she learned that its charter limited membership to Caucasian women, she asked the national body to revise the policy. When her request was rejected, she dissociated the local chapter—the "prize" of the organization—from the national body. The next year, a black woman student joined the Yale club.[58]

Midway through her second year at Yale, in January 1926, 4,500 workers at the Passaic mills went out on strike. Much to the displeasure of Yale's respectable crowd, including the president of the university, Polier became deeply involved, and spent the next few months commuting back and forth between New Haven and Passaic. Though some of her father's wealthier congregants resigned from his temple because of her activities, Wise was fully supportive and himself became deeply immersed in the strike. Of his meeting with mill owners he wrote to Polier, "It did more to take me over into radicalism than any experience of a lifetime."[59] Wise urged his daughter to "speak out and speak up" regarding the workers' cause. On March 2, she addressed a mass rally of workers, denouncing the employers' "feudal tyranny," their "octopus-like espionage system," and the toll that the abysmal conditions took on workers, especially women and children. She urged the workers to persist in the strike even though owners might denounce it as "Communist."[60]

Polier's fiery words were well covered in the metropolitan press. The *New York Journal* wrote that Justine Wise had assumed "the role of a Joan of Arc of the Mills," leading Passaic's workers on a crusade for justice. The *Daily News* carried an account with a full-page photo and caption stating that the "rabbi's daughter was threatened with arrest" because of her role in the strike. The *New York Evening Post* ran an interview in which Polier spoke of her double life as a strike leader and law student, explaining that she hoped to use her legal training to promote the cause of industrial workers.[61]

There would be other rallies and other speeches, warmly endorsed by Stephen and Louise Wise, who wrote letters of love and encouragement. Her friend Susan Brandeis wrote how impressed she was at the mill owners' complaints that it was "not only flappers who are making trouble but the strong minded young women who butt in where they are not wanted." Brandeis was amused by how employers found it "disgraceful" that Polier had taken her father's money for an education that she was now using to promote direct social action against her father's wishes, or so they said. The Brandeis and Wise daughters might both have responded that in fact their fathers had encouraged them in these activities.[62]

The strike continued for almost a year before it was settled, with workers winning the right to bargain collectively and a promise from employers that they would be rehired.[63] Polier's mettle had been tested, and she emerged as full of oratorical eloquence and passion, and as committed to social justice and the cause of industrial democracy, as her father. Polier's activism did not please the traditionalists at Yale, but she was much admired by one of her professors, Lee Tulin, who was just a few years older than she. The two fell in love and married shortly after Justine's graduation. Their son, Stephen, was born a month before the bar examination, which she passed easily. There was one difficult moment, however, when Polier was called before the character committee of the bar association and asked if she believed it was ethical to have used the name Justine Waterman—her own first and middle names—when applying for work in Passaic. Polier explained her reasons. The examiner then asked her if, having taken legal ethics, she still felt she had made an ethical choice. Polier replied that she had been excused from the course because Robert Hutchins, dean of the law school (and later president of the University of Chicago) felt that she had no need of it.

Hutchins now advised Polier to present testimonies about her "moral character" from influential individuals. "Who do you know?" he asked. Polier mentioned Chief Justice Taft, who visited the Wises at their summer home, and "Judge Cardozo," who had been her legal guardian during her parents' trip to the Middle East.[64] Then she called her father, and with Wise's intercession, Taft and Cardozo wrote to explain why Polier would be a gift to the bar. And so Polier was admitted, "not on merits of my morals, but who my father knew." Although she recognized the injustice of her privileged circumstances, Polier also knew that the character committee had often discriminated against applicants because of politics and anti-Semitism. "If a poor Jewish boy hadn't paid the florist bill for his girl, that was a reason for not admitting him for a year." Gender in this instance had been less an issue than ethnicity and activism; when women were "nice good people who hadn't caused any trouble," they easily passed the character examination.[65]

At the time Polier began her legal career, few women lawyers were being hired; those who found employment generally did office rather than court work, performing routine jobs such as bill collection, title searches, and other tasks that one female attorney labeled as the "dishwashing" of the law.[66] In spite of her good record in law school, Polier was told that "there wasn't a single law firm in New York which would employ me unless I was willing to sit in a back room and draw wills and trusts but not see clients."[67] Polier opted for a government job and was hired as referee for the Workmen's Compensation Division of the New York State Department of Labor, where she remained for almost five years.

Discovering that the referee system was riddled with politics and favoritism toward bosses, she began an all-out effort to change the rules so that workers could choose their own physicians, subject to checkups by state doctors.[68] This work led to her appointment as head of a Commonwealth Fund research survey on national labor laws; she then became secretary and counsel to the Mayor's Committee on Unemployment Relief, producing a report that the *New Republic* labeled the "best report on the problem of relief for the unemployed ever issued in the United States."[69]

Because Polier was now employed in New York, her husband obtained an appointment at Columbia, where he became the youngest professor on record. But tragedy struck when Lee, who had developed leukemia right after the birth of Stephen, died just before the boy's fourth birthday in 1932. Although devastated, Justine carried on, continuing her job and raising Stephen with the help of a group of friends.[70] Whatever her responsibilities, she made it a point to take him to school in the morning and to have dinner together every night. As for her other commitments—such as campaigning for the Republican-Fusion reform ticket in New York—she worked at night while Stephen slept.[71]

When the victorious Fusion candidate, Fiorello La Guardia, took over as mayor of New York City in 1934, he appointed Polier Assistant Corporation Counsel, heading the Workmen's Compensation Division. In this post, she was able to implement many of the reforms she had recommended in her earlier policy studies. Within a year, she had completely reformed the office, ridding it of political favoritism, and drafted the city's first statute ensuring fair treatment of workers in the adjudication of compensation disputes.

The following year, La Guardia asked Polier if she would like to be a judge in the Domestic Relations Court. Having been told that judges in that court were rubber stamps for probation officers, she hesitated, even though the appointment would make her the first woman in the city to occupy such a high-level judicial post. More importantly, her interests lay in the trade union movement; despite her mother's lifelong interest and her father's earlier involvement in child welfare, she had never been absorbed in such matters. "If I were to be a judge," she told La Guardia, "I'd rather be a magistrate."[72] Magistrates handled labor cases, and at the time, injunctions against trade unions were routinely being issued; here was where she could be of most use. La Guardia persuaded her to observe the court; after seeing a case in which the children of an unwed couple were to be removed from their custody, she agreed to take the job for a few years, until she had thoroughly studied abuses in the court system and been able to develop recommendations for reform.

In July 1935, Mayor La Guardia appointed Polier judge of the Domestic Relations Court for a ten-year term at a salary of $10,000—an increase of $6,500 over her previous city position. At thirty-two years of age, she became the youngest municipal justice in the country and one of only a few women holding the post. "As case after case came up," she recalled, "I saw the vast chasms between our rhetoric of freedom, equality and charity, and what we were doing to, or not doing for poor people, especially children."[73] She stayed for thirty-eight years.

At the time when she began her service, female judges were a great novelty. That the judge liked "pretty things . . . just like any other woman" was evidently surprising enough that reporters continued to comment upon it well into the second decade of her term of office. Tall, slender, and graceful, with expressive grey eyes and a shock of wavy black hair often compared to her father's white mop, this "vivaciously attractive," "feminine" justice reassured the dubious.[74]

While an advocate of women's rights, Polier eschewed identifying herself as a "woman judge," one who might be expected to perform in a "female" manner or to insist on equity in the representation of women in the courtroom. "I can't say that a woman is better equipped to judge the wrongs of children than a man," she admitted. "I'm not a very good feminist." In her view, merit rather than gender ought to be the sole criterion for appointment to the bench.[75] Less interested in the concerns of individual professional women than in the possibilities of women in the mass—especially poor and minority women—she linked the abstract notion of women's rights to the concrete mission of obtaining economic as well as legal security for women and children. For this reason, she urged the formation of a "real labor party" to provide "security and freedom," as well as the implementation of a coordinated program of social insurance to help the unemployed and the poor—"I don't care whether you call it socialism, communism, or what," she remarked in a *New York Times* interview a few months after her appointment.[76]

Although she voted the Socialist ticket for president in 1932, supporting Norman Thomas, and had taken a three-month trip to the Soviet Union in 1934 (which would cause her political difficulties later), Polier was neither a socialist nor a communist. Locally she stood for the Republican-Fusion reform ticket, and later supported most Democratic candidates. More interested in principles than politics, her sympathy for the underprivileged usually aligned her with groups endorsing reform; she thought of herself as a "hard-working, old dray horse," not an uncompromising "crusader."[77]

During Polier's judicial career, she spoke out as forcefully as she had when leading strikes in Passaic. In her first appointment to the temporary post of district court judge, she became embroiled in a dispute with Mayor La Guardia and General Hugh Johnson, administrator of the Work Projects Administration (WPA), over the latter's condemnation of city relief officials and his "work or jail" order, intended to encourage the unemployed, whom he called "loafers," to seek work; La Guardia supported Johnson's initiative. Polier sent a stinging letter of protest to Johnson, then called a press conference in which she said that "it's time someone told the truth." La Guardia demanded that she withdraw the statement but she refused; he then ordered her—"as Mayor of New York"—to withdraw the statement, warning her that if she did not comply, he would not reappoint her to a full term on the court. "I said that was up to him," Polier recalled, "but I could not do what he was asking. This was a matter of conscience." When her term expired, La Guardia did not reappoint her. Again Polier was saved by her contacts: as it happened, Felix Frankfurter was visiting La Guardia at the time; La Guardia fumed to him about Polier's insolence—"I have got to have discipline in the judiciary," he told his friend—but acceded to Frankfurter's request that he speak with Polier personally. At her interview with the mayor, Polier recalled that he said her problem was that, "like my father, I said whatever I wanted to and didn't care about the consequences." Polier agreed, noting that Stephen Wise stood behind her. In the end, La Guardia relented and Polier was reappointed.[78]

Throughout her career, Polier never hesitated to speak out on nonlegal as well as general judicial issues. Many attributed her failure to win the post of presiding judge of the Domestic Relations Court of New York in 1959 to Mayor Robert F. Wagner's ire at Polier's criticism of his treatment of a black family court colleague. Child care professionals and civic leaders waged a vigorous campaign on her behalf, urging the mayor not to let the fact "that she is a woman, that she is Jewish, that she is a militant progressive who has spoken out without fear" stand in the way of considering her for the post. Despite her acknowledged qualifications, the mayor appointed a less qualified candidate.[79] Religion helped to decide the case against her: Catholic agencies opposed Polier, seeing her as a threat to their dominance in the courts, while Protestant groups were split on whether to support her on her merits or hold out for a Protestant appointee. She was warmly endorsed, however, by Jewish organizations and black groups, who admired her handling of cases in which race was an issue.[80]

Though deeply disappointed, Polier continued in her battle to reform the court.[81] At the time she became a judge, juvenile and domestic courts were largely "poor people's courts" with heavy caseloads, overworked and underpaid staffs, inadequate facilities, and little funding; because of these disadvantages, delinquent and neglected children were served "leftovers from the table of justice."[82] Most judges focused on punishment and retribution rather than the treatment of delinquents, which they considered "coddling"; judges routinely removed "neglected" children from family homes solely because of poverty. Polier was instrumental in promoting a preventive and rehabilitative approach to delinquency and family dysfunction that called on the social and behavioral sciences to aid judges in treating offenders and those in need of supervision. Urging that courts learn about the social, economic, and educational situation of individual cases before passing judgment, she led the New York Family Court in the development of mental health and clinical services, school liaison departments, and assistance with economic security. Her court became a national model of open communication between the legal system, the behavioral sciences, and the human services delivery system.

Polier also assumed vigorous public leadership on the issue of church and state. From the 1930s through the early 1970s, judges regularly imposed religious obligations on children and parents and determined placements solely by religion; whether or not the family showed religious devotion was considered a test of morality in the home. Probation officers were similarly appointed on the basis of religion, and religious practice routinely became a condition of probation. Agency representatives acted like policemen on behalf of sectarian agencies, reporting parents and children for nonconformist behavior, and judges themselves often appeared to be tyrannized by sectarian demands for religious correctness.[83]

Polier's own "baptism by religious fire" came in the 1936 *Vardinakis* case, when she had to decide the fate of four neglected children of a Roman Catholic mother married to a Muslim father by a Protestant minister; one teenage son, baptized in the Catholic faith, wanted to live with a paternal uncle and become a Muslim. A thirteen-year-old daughter, initiated in the Muslim faith, wanted to be a Catholic. When Polier held that infant baptism did not make a child the property of any church and placed the children according to their wishes, she was roundly criticized by the Cardinal of New York and by an anti-Semitic Catholic newspaper, *The Brooklyn Tablet,* which ran the headline, "Daughter of Rabbi Wise Gives Child of Christ to the Black Bearded Prophet of Mohammed."[84]

In this influential decision and other cases, Polier argued for the principle of separation of state and church as the soundest basis for enforcing justice; she helped to popularize the notion of "the best interest of the child" as a substitute for religiously determined outcomes. Although her attack on such religious tests brought her up against powerful political figures allied with sectarian agencies and the presiding judge of her own court, she kept up the battle.

Polier also waged a powerful campaign against institutionalized racial discrimination in the courts and other public and voluntary agencies. When she began her first term, facilities and services for minorities were greatly inferior to those for whites—in 1939, only four voluntary agencies in New York accepted black children for placement in segregated and inferior institutions—and judges often discriminated openly. After Polier described to Mayor La Guardia the shocking plight of black children, he called on the Episcopal Bishop of New York and, with the help of the Protestant Episcopal Mission Society, established a summer camp for black children and the Wiltwyck School for Boys. Polier chaired its board and secured the involvement of her friend Eleanor Roosevelt. The school, which was the first agency in the Northeast to accept neglected and delinquent black boys without regard to religion, became an important part of Roosevelt's life.[85]

With her second husband, Shad Polier (a constitutional lawyer active in the NAACP Educational Defense Fund whom she married in 1936), Justine wrote New York State's first antidiscrimination law, designed to prohibit the pattern of discrimination she had worked to end in public agencies. Her most controversial decision—*In the matter of Skipwith* (1958)—was in the area of race. Dismissing charges of neglect against black parents who refused to send their children to inferior, segregated schools, she helped establish the right of citizens to demand equal education for their children without fear of reprisal.

At the time of her retirement in 1973, she was involved in another controversial case, *Wilder v. Sugarman* (1971–1978), involving an African American adolescent girl in need of placement. Angry at the failure of city and voluntary agencies to take the girl, she encouraged Legal Aid to bring an action against all involved city, state, and voluntary agencies, including Louise Wise Services, of which she was then chairman of the board.

Polier was an activist judge who believed that the law must be used as an agent of social change. Possessed of her father's natural eloquence and dramatic force, she was a sought-after speaker on the subject of children's rights. She was a fluid and effective writer as well, producing a series of books about her experiences in the court and her prescriptions for reform.[86] She also made her views known through regular letters to the editor and personal interviews, criticizing judges for their "arrogance and self-righteousness"; juvenile, divorce, and custody laws as "museum piece[s] for antiquarians"; the public schools for their "rigid curriculums, and demands for conformity"; and private child care agencies for their "Oliver Twist treatment."[87]

In the 1940s, Polier had been the guiding force behind the formation of the Citizens' Committee for Children of New York, a powerful advocacy group. A meeting at her house in 1960 set in motion a sustained effort for welfare reform; she also helped inspire the mobilization of lawyers on behalf of the poor.[88] When she lost a battle, she simply devised another strategy, continuing the fight. David Bazelon, chief judge of the Court of Appeals, called her the fighting judge; to other associates she was a "gentle warrior," her low-key manner undergirded by a "steely determination." Like her father, she "*never* compromised her position regardless of issue or circumstance."[89] As one visitor to her court noted:

> There was nothing soft or charitable about Judge Polier. She means business—but she *knows* her business and she is a planner . . . direct[ing] all cases to some kind of action. . . . Judge Polier is professional in everything she says or does. She is full of honest sympathy and interest, is alert for other more subtle factors than those discussed, but most important of all, she has tremendous social vision, and one sense[s] the purposive quality of her work.[90]

"If I were a good judge," Polier explained, "it was because I felt I might have committed every crime or offense charged against the children brought before me. That I had not was largely a matter of luck, privilege, and always feeling loved."[91]

Greta Garbo of the Law   Fanny Holtzmann's career took an entirely different direction. Her association with Keppler and Hochman, the firm she worked for as a law student at Fordham, turned out to be serendipitous. On her own, she undertook to collect a number of unpaid bills for one of the firm's clients, *The Morning Telegraph*; in the course of this work she came in contact with the British actor and writer Edmund Goulding, helping him to manage his complex financial and legal matters. Goulding sang the praises of the second-year law student to Broadway notables and introduced her to the writers who lunched at the Algonquin Roundtable—Alexander Woollcott, Dorothy Parker, and Robert Benchley. Though still a law student, Holtzmann seemed to Goulding "the greatest lawyer in the world—man or woman," combining an imaginative mind with the interpersonal skills of a psychiatrist and intimate friend. It was "not only my business coups," Holtzmann recalled, "but what he portrayed as my saintliness. I was different, according to Goulding: incorruptible, untouchable."[92] It was not long before the Roundtable members and other of Goulding's theatrical acquaintances (including Gertrude Lawrence, Noel Coward, and Coward's producer, Charles B. Cochran) sought the services of the fledgling lawyer.

Holtzmann's success came despite the formidable obstacles of her sex and ethnicity. When, just after she completed law school, Goulding offered to pay her an annual retainer of $15,000 (a substantial sum for the time), brother Jack told Holtzmann that she should join his firm, since it wouldn't look right for Goulding to be represented by "a little girl." When the state Court of Appeals denied her application for immediate admission to the bar, the family suspected an anonymous letter written to the court's Character Committee, complaining of the fact that she was a "little Jew-girl." To Holtzmann's relief, the taint of scandal caused the cautious Jack, concerned about the effect of anti-Semitism on his own career, to withdraw his offer.[93] Taking matters into her own hands, Holtzmann argued her case before the Appeals Court, which reversed its decision. The head of the court, Benjamin Cardozo, was so impressed that he became Holtzmann's backer when she took the unprecedented step of applying for an office in the Bar Building in New York. Cardozo became a lifelong mentor, her "guardian angel."[94] At the time, the Bar Association had no women members and few Jews (her brother Jack, partner to a New York City congressman, did not belong). Appearing before the association's Character Committee, Holtzmann argued her case eloquently:

> Gentlemen, women have the vote. Further progress is inevitable. Our common concern should be to attract the best types of women to the law, to set honorable standards. Why admit a woman to the practice of law if you're going to ban her from the Bar Building? A tolerant approach will reflect greater dignity on all of us.[95]

Holtzmann won her argument and moved into the building that would house her offices for the next five decades; Cardozo was also a tenant and she visited him frequently, listening to his views on many subjects, particularly Jewish history, philosophy, and the law. Cardozo's views on the law seemed to have "the weight of Mosaic pronouncements" for the young woman. "In his piety and dignity," she recalled, "he was a throwback to the rabbinical sages of antiquity."[96] Along with Zaida's ideas about *mitzvot*, Cardozo's credo—use the law to remedy wrongs, even when precedent and statute seem contrary, and "above all, stick to your own beliefs, your private values—no matter what people say"—became her ethical guide. Years after Cardozo had become a Supreme Court justice, Holtzmann mused, "If there was any man in the world I would like to have married it was Cardozo."[97]

Within a few years, Fanny's career had more than fulfilled its promising start. Adding such clients as George Bernard Shaw, Rudyard Kipling, John Galsworthy, John Gilbert, Fred Astaire, and Ina Claire, she shuttled between London, the West Coast, and New York, her comings and goings a matter of press attention. A big boost came from Edward Marshall, an English journalist who frequently put out stories about Holtzmann through his news syndicate. Not only her legal skills but the fact that she reminded him of his dead daughter, who "resembled her Jewish mother," endeared Fanny to this newest male mentor.[98] By 1932, a rising Hollywood film star had cause to wonder "how famous one must become to be able to qualify as one of Fanny Holtzmann's clients."[99]

It was the sensational *Rasputin* trial of 1934, however, that catapulted Fanny Holtzmann to international fame. Holtzmann's client was Princess Irina Alexandrovna Youssoupova, wife of Russian nobleman Felix Youssoupoff, who in 1916 had killed Rasputin, the "mad" monk who had exercised a sinister influence over the prerevolutionary Romanov court. The princess alleged that MGM's film, *Rasputin, the Mad Monk* (released in America as *Rasputin and the Empress*), implied that she had been intimate with the monk; now living in England, where the picture was about to open, Irina wanted Fanny to sue MGM. Although few thought Holtzmann had the slightest chance of success against the corporate giant, which claimed its representations were clearly fictional, she agreed to take the case after receiving assurances that the princess and her husband had played no part in any anti-Semitic actions of the Romanov family. To everybody's surprise but Holtzmann's, she won the case, along with $125,000 in damages for the princess and the possibility of an additional financial settlement. The greatest sensation of the trial was when Prince Youssoupoff took the stand to tell how he had poisoned, shot, clubbed, and drowned Rasputin in Petrograd; Holtzmann herself became a *cause célèbre* when the barrister defending MGM portrayed her as an American intruder forcing the case down the throats of the reluctant Youssoupoffs. With the Court of Appeals also deciding against the appellants, the trial became a landmark case on defamation, cited in legal texts; never before had victory in a libel case been achieved through a deliberate confession of murder. Holtzmann was adopted en masse by British royalty and the British press. The *Daily Sketch* reported that she was the wealthiest woman lawyer in the world; the Paris *Herald Tribune* told of a victory party at her London apartment where "more than one hundred members of the English aristocracy and the Hollywood screen world mingled." One of the guests was another immigrant daughter, Sophie Tucker, who like Holtzmann had become a celebrity in Britain.[100]

Those who knew her well recognized that Holtzmann's achievements were a consequence of her fierce determination. Despite the impression she gave of "wistful helplessness," playwright Moss Hart said, Holtzmann was as helpless "as the Bethlehem Steel Company and as delicate as 'Jack the Ripper.' "[101] Her bold and inventive tactics, her ability to put her contacts to work in a seemingly unending pyramid of influence ("I've never met a stranger," she once observed), and her talents at negotiating made her, according to Louis Bittayer, a "female Solomon." To others she was a "Greta Garbo of the law," the "most unpredictable, brilliantly accomplished woman lawyer in American history."[102]

Prophetic Judaism   Although she did not attend synagogue or share her father's personal faith in God, Justine Polier considered herself a religious person. To Polier, religion meant "righteous action in the tradition of the prophets" rather than prayer. She considered justice more important than mercy. While transgressions before God could be atoned for through religious ritual, she explained, wrongdoing could only be forgiven when the injustice was rectified. Polier liked to quote the rabbinic dictum that "the most important thing is study which leads to action."[103]

She feared, however, that in the rush to the gilded ghettos of suburbs or city, Jews had abandoned this prophetic heritage. In speeches to Jewish groups, she cautioned against "false assimilation" and "the running away from one's self," urging her audiences to take up the "battle for human freedom—whether it is or is not good for the survival of the Jewish people."[104]

"Seeing clearly" and "speaking truly . . . without fear"—two attributes of the Hebrew prophets and, she believed, of her father—were the guiding goals of Polier's own life. Active in campaigns against anti-Semitism and for support of Israel, she was passionate in her advocacy of civil rights for African Americans. In the 1960s and 1970s, when Jewish agencies began to question policies of affirmative action that benefited minorities at the apparent cost of Jewish advancement, she implored Jews not to let the criterion of individual merit become an excuse for forgetting "the more basic moral teachings of Judaism"—commitment to justice and humanity.[105] "Justine's understanding of racial issues transcended anything that I had encountered before from one who was not born black," commented one African American colleague.[106]

Like her father she became known as a voice of conscience, playing a leading role within the American Jewish Congress, the organization formed in 1917 by Wise, Justice Brandeis, and other Jewish liberals as an alternative to the more patrician American Jewish Committee. During the 1920s and

1930s, it framed a new agenda, combining campaigns against anti-Semitism with programs to enhance civil rights for all Americans. Polier served as vice-president of the national organization, president of the Women's Division, and a member of almost all the Congress's commissions dealing with social action, democracy, legislation, civil rights, education, and welfare.

With her husband, who drafted many of the Congress's major legislative initiatives in the area of civil liberties, Polier set the organization on a steady course that melded a passionate commitment to Jewish life with an equally passionate concern for the rights of minorities. It was a course that both her parents had pioneered, and she took her place as the leader of the next generation struggling to reconcile Jewish heritage with Americanism. In 1978, when Polier believed that the Congress's leadership had compromised its integrity through political maneuvering, she resigned as honorary vice-president and asked that her name be removed from its letterhead and publications. Despite the breach, she continued as a foot soldier in the Congress's basic programs.[107]

For Polier, there could be no retreat from the prophetic imperative. This ideal guided her work on the bench, her advocacy for children's rights and social justice, and her leadership in the American Jewish community. She believed that each generation of Jews had to rewin its freedom, making choices and acting in accordance with conscience, relying "on the moral imperative of the spirit" rather than the external compulsions of the world.

It was not accidental that Polier cited Emma Lazarus as a role model, for Lazarus too had reconciled Americanism, Judaism, and Zionism—another passionate interest of Polier's—with women's issues, and had spoken out when others were cautious. Nor was it coincidental that among the Jewish women she most admired were two other rabbis' daughters, Henrietta Szold and Rebekah Kohut, who like herself had inherited their fathers' learning and piety, but whose feminist leanings had propelled their concerns with Jewish ideals into new arenas.

According to her daughter, Polier was a Don Quixote, always tilting at windmills. In fact, in the hallway of her home was a framed lithograph of a favorite Daumier painting of Don Quixote, a gift from family members that seemed to embody Polier's own determination and passion. "Passionate concern may lead to errors of judgment," Polier once said, "but the lack of passion in the face of human wrong leads to spiritual bankruptcy."[108]

Although Fanny Holtzmann did not become active in Jewish organizations, according to her biographer and nephew, Edward Berkman, she "gloried in *mitzvot*," consciously using her influence to promote "the good deeds prescribed by the Talmudic sages" and Jewish causes.[109] Chief among these was the rescue of children from fascist regimes in Europe and, after the war, helping to negotiate a favorable vote at the newly established United Nations on the question of Israeli statehood.

Because the British held her in high esteem, she was able to obtain British visas for hundreds of European Jews seeking to escape the Nazis; she was aided in this work by Joe and Jack Kennedy, then in their early twenties, the sons of the anti-Semitic United States Ambassador to Britain, Joseph P. Kennedy. Holtzmann also used her contacts, including Justice Felix Frankfurter, to try to persuade President Roosevelt that extraordinary efforts were required to rescue Jews from the Nazis; Fanny's idea was for the United States to settle half a million refugees in a sparsely populated area either in southern California or the Nevada desert. Discouraged by Roosevelt's lack of commitment to rescuing Jews after a personal meeting, she gathered support from leading Republicans. The scheme, which she incorporated as the Association for the Resettlement of Oppressed Peoples, eventually came to naught, but Holtzmann continued her mission of helping refugees and families on an individual basis. She also played a leading role in bringing dozens of children from an Actors' Orphanage in Britain to the United States, and worked with Jewish leaders in an unsuccessful campaign (in which Justine Wise Polier also participated) to secure the passage of the Wagner-Rogers bill to admit 10,000 refugee children to the United States.

Her crowning achievement was her work on behalf of Israeli statehood. Asked by Ambassador V. K. Wellington Koo of China (whom she had represented in other matters) to be his special counsel at the founding session of the United Nations in San Francisco in 1945, Holtzmann accepted at the urging of her mother.[110] Still a passionate Zionist, Theresa Holtzmann had foreseen that Koo, a widely admired senior diplomat who had been at the League of Nations, would be deeply involved in the Palestine question. An expert on trusteeships, Koo was besieged by lobbyists; Holtzmann relieved him of some of this burden, meeting with Stephen Wise and Rabbi Abba Hillel Silver, who were representing American Jewry, and setting up secret meetings between American Zionists and the British, with whom her ties remained excellent. Holtzmann's participation averted several confrontations and allowed proponents of Israeli statehood time to make their case. When the issue came to the United Nations in New York, she continued to set up secret meetings in her apartment between Arthur Creech Jones, the British colonial secretary, and Rabbi Abba Hillel Silver, the American Zionist. ("I felt like Mata Hari Holtzmann," she recalled.)[111] Her influence extended to the Chinese, probably the single most important vote at the U.N. With its large Muslim population, China had been expected to vote against the creation of an Israeli state. According to Berkman, Ambassador Koo, because he owed Holtzmann a debt from San Francisco, cabled Chiang Kai-shek, asking permission to abstain, which was granted. China's abstention led the way; when six Latin American countries followed suit, the vote on behalf of statehood was ensured. Though she received no public recognition for her contribution, Holtzmann's strategic position gave her a pivotal influence on the course of Jewish and world events.[112]

Holtzmann's negotiations in this matter and her involvement in Jewish refugee questions reveal that, despite her celebrity practice, her Jewish identity remained strong. Yet she claimed that she had few, if any, Jewish clients. Jews didn't need her services, she quipped, since every Jewish family raised its own lawyers; in her own family, not only Holtzmann, but two younger sisters (another was a teacher) and three brothers became attorneys: "I gave birth to a bar association," her mother used to say.[113] Her younger brother, David, eventually practiced with her, and her sister Stella joined the practice for a time as well.

Holtzmann believed that being a Jew was not a "handicap"; in fact, she had earned her international reputation "as a Jewess. Always a Jew, you know, that smart Jewish lawyer." Never a "smart American girl" but "that smart Jewish girl." The "Jewish" was an "extra compliment," she claimed.[114] Holtzmann's powerful clientele and her worldwide network of influence suggest that her practice did not suffer from anti-Semitism despite such labeling. Late in her life, Holtzmann acknowledged that she had never socialized with clients because she considered their social status far above her own. Despite her fame and power, inside she remained the Jewish girl from Brooklyn, different and other.

Never forgetting that she was "an outsider in a man's profession"—a woman as well as a Jew—Holtzmann tried "to dress as inconspicuously as possible, not to be strident . . . to tone down my femininity and not to try to be masculine."[115] She did not associate herself with women's causes and expressed feminist feelings infrequently, like the time she wrote to her parents of her outrage that women had to be seated separately from men in the Orthodox shul she visited in Poland in the early 1930s.

While Holtzmann downplayed the importance of gender barriers in the law, she acknowledged that her success scared away "the right kind of mate." Her sister Stella managed to combine legal practice with marriage and children, but this goal proved unobtainable for Holtzmann. Yet Holtzmann pronounced herself satisfied with the family life she did have; after her siblings married, she continued to live with her parents, whom she "worshipped," in an apartment on East 64th Street in Manhattan.[116]

Holtzmann's parents passed on the notion that "the American flag was what one worships. . . . God gave us America." While Fanny became a faithful Republican, it was not party politics or religious ritual that held her deepest loyalty, but "my American heritage, my birth as an American."[117] She had been taught this lesson mostly by her father, the former rabbinical scholar who had become a completely assimilated Jew. Practicing the Jewish faith in America, he told his daughter, was not "what you mumble" or "what you eat," but "how you think and how you help your fellow man." When in the 1930s Holtzmann returned to her father's birthplace in Austrian Poland, the elder Holtzmann was annoyed. "I've spent a lifetime trying to forget them," he confessed to Holtzmann, warning her not to be sentimental about her roots. Holtzmann needed to do what he told his immigrant students, to "shake off all memory."[118]

To Holtzmann, however, forgetting was impossible. Like her father, she lived an assimilated life; indeed, she greatly surpassed her parents in integration into middle-class, professional culture. Yet unlike some of the "lost generation" of immigrant children, her bonds to culture and heritage remained vibrant. When, in her late forties, she took up painting, she found herself possessed by a "dybbuk," which made her draw "from an inner memory." Among her most admired works was a series of portraits of immigrant women on the stoops of the Lower East Side ghetto where her family had once lived.[119]

Although Holtzmann had abandoned the Jewish rituals she had shared with her beloved Zaida, at her bedside she kept a well-worn Book of Psalms, crammed full of personal notes. Like Yezierska, another assimilated immigrant daughter with a bedside Bible, Holtzmann helped pioneer a new path for Jewish women. Yet each took with her an older part of her culture.

In Holtzmann's professional life, the teachings of Zaida and her parents remained formative. While she did not associate herself with a specifically Jewish imperative for social justice, Holtzmann nonetheless drew on the Jewish values she imbibed from her family to guide her work. As her most important mentor, Cardozo also provided crucial professional support and reinforced the tradition of righteous action. As she matured into a creative, unconventional lawyer, she became, according to her nephew, a "preeminently Jewish" attorney, known for her compassion and fairness.[120] But empathy may not have been a common trait among Jewish attorneys at the time. According to historian Jerold Auerbach, "Within elite circles, one looks almost in vain beyond the examples of Louis D. Brandeis for any model of professional responsibility that elevated the social good above a client's needs." Assimilation into the profession was usually accomplished "at the expense of independent moral vision and any sustained commitment to social justice."[121]

Like Holtzmann, Justine Wise Polier saw no inherent conflict between Judaism and the wider goals of Americanism. Nor did she see any contradiction in advocating for women's liberation and for human rights. In a commencement address she gave at Bryn Mawr College in 1973, the year she retired from the bench, she highlighted the work of Angelina Grimké, a Southern woman of wealth, who with her sister, Sarah, had pioneered women's battle against slavery; out of their struggle for the freedom of others the first movement for the liberation of women had been born. Polier voiced her hope that the newly forming contemporary women's movement would not be separated from the struggle to advance the freedom of all Americans denied equal opportunity. In later years, she would criticize the feminist movement for being "too middle-class and professionally minded,"[122] not addressing the needs of minorities. While Polier was not a leader of the feminist movement, as lawyer, judge, and citizen activist she became a role model for the next generation of Jewish women lawyers. Polier died in 1987, seven years after Fanny Holtzmann.

The one professional field in which Jewish women could not overcome the obstacles that confronted them was the rabbinate. When in the 1920s, Martha Neumark, daughter of David Neumark of the faculty of Hebrew Union College in Cincinnati, determined to become a rabbi, even the support of her father and the endorsement of Stephen Wise could not open doors. After studying at Hebrew Union College for several years and being approved by its faculty for the rabbinate, the Central Conference of American Rabbis refused to ordain her. Disappointed, Neumark went on to a varied career in social work, education, and Jewish journalism, combining part-time work with marriage and childrearing.[123]

Neumark could only cheer when, in 1972, fifty years after she determined to enter the rabbinate, the Reform movement ordained Sally Priesand as its first female rabbi. But she had been there, too, to congratulate Justine Wise Polier in the early 1930s, when she became the first woman to become a municipal judge in New York. Neumark realized that the success of even a few Jewish women in public life would accelerate the possibility for all women to achieve their goals. Providing new models of service and achievement, these first female Jewish professionals helped redefine possibilities for American womanhood in the expanding twentieth century.

Chapter 7

ENTERING THE THEATRES
OF THE WORLD

Fighting Fascism, Building a State: Rose Jacobs and Cecilia Razovsky

"In facing history we look at each other," wrote poet Muriel Rukeyser, "and in facing our entire personal life, we look at each other."[1] In the 1930s and 1940s, American Jews were brought face to face with history—and themselves—in the starkest way possible. Confronted with the terror of Nazism in Europe and a sharp rise in anti-Semitism in the United States, the Jewish community turned away in fear, unable to respond to the threat facing European Jews in a unified manner. Many historians argue that, given fundamental disagreements about the extent of both the Nazi danger and Jewish communal power, no other response was possible, especially in light of prevailing isolationist sentiment and an increasingly virulent xenophobia. But others indict Jews for their passivity.[2]

Although the controversy about the nature of the Jewish response ignores the role of women, in important ways Jewish women did not turn away from the challenges of history, but faced them, as Rukeyser wrote, by looking "at each other." This mutual gaze characterized Jewish women's civic and political contributions during this period; it became the essence of an expansive, revitalized Jewish female ethic of activism that led Jewish women, again in Rukeyser's words, into the "theatres of the world."[3]

Involved in the fight against immigration restriction, the rescue of refugees from Nazism, and the ongoing struggle to create a Jewish national homeland, Jewish women's civic activism during this period challenges standard notions about American Jews' response to the Holocaust and women's political participation. Their intense involvement in operations to rescue European Jewry and to establish a democratic Jewish state in Palestine reveals an expansion, not a contraction, of Jewish women's political activity in the mid-twentieth century.

During this period, Jewish women became part of a vanguard that challenged the boundaries between public and private, the state and civil society,

203

and male and female spheres. In Hadassah and the National Council of Jewish Women, a new generation of leaders, mainly married middle-class women, took power. Modifying organizational strategies developed by their predecessors, Council leaders, under the direction of Cecilia Razovsky, spearheaded a comprehensive migration program and projects for the rescue and resettlement of refugees. In the Middle East, Rose Jacobs, the most important Hadassah leader after Henrietta Szold, used a combination of older and newer strategies to adapt to the exigencies of the Zionist struggle in the interwar years.

While Jacobs and Razovsky represented elite women in top leadership positions, their activities filtered down to thousands of ordinary Jewish women in local chapters who debated the grave events taking place across the sea and acted on their decisions. At a time when women's political and voluntary activities had ostensibly declined after the apparent collapse of the women's rights movement, Jewish women played a critical role in sustaining the progressive goals that had shaped their organizations while responding to new crises with flexibility and boldness. In addition to the contributions of Jewish women's groups, poets and journalists like Rukeyser and Ruth Gruber invented a politics and a poetry of witness in direct response to these international challenges.

Diaper Zionists and Miss America   One of the first members of Hadassah when it was created in 1912, Rose Gell Jacobs played an instrumental role in the development of the organization over the next thirty years. She served as acting president in the early twenties, during Szold's sojourn in Palestine; she was president in her own right from 1930 to '32 and from 1934 to '37. At the conclusion of her term, she was elected to the Executive of the Jewish Agency, the representative body of the Jewish people that had assumed responsibility for Jewish immigration and settlement in Palestine. Recognizing the "importance of according Zionist women a place on the Agency executive," she accepted.[4]

Jacobs had long supported women's rights. Active in the suffrage campaign and eager to stimulate women's interest in the political process, she had joined the newly formed League of Women Voters in the 1920s and become vice-president of her district. She was also an active member of the Women's League for Peace and Freedom and the Women's Division of the League of Nations, and worked with the American Civil Liberties Union. Overall, her concern was "not in alleviation, not in fleeting help," but in the fundamentals for bringing about change. Her deepest leanings were toward the "Socialist pattern," meaning not the political party but policies dictated by the "Jewish concept of social justice."

While she considered questions of women's rights and social justice fundamental, Jacobs dedicated her life to promoting Jewish interests, specifically

Zionism. She believed that while non-Jews could fulfill the goals of most liberal and progressive movements, Jewish needs had to be met by Jews. But she held that to be effective in Jewish causes, Jews had to have "broad human interests and sympathies"; her lifelong involvement in women's rights, civil rights, and the peace movement demonstrated her commitment to the principles of mutuality.

For Jacobs, Zionism and Hadassah were the central activities of a committed international life. Jacobs became involved in Zionism shortly after 1910, when she was twenty-one, after meeting Henrietta Szold. Szold had just returned from her transforming visit to Palestine, and came to talk about her experience to the young women studying ethics with Alice Selisberg. Jacobs was mesmerized by Szold's description of the settlement in Palestine and its significance for the Jewish people. She began to read avidly about the movement and to attend lectures given by such spokesmen as Judah Magnes and Stephen Wise. Her Zionist thinking was also guided by Louis Brandeis, whom she met through her brother; Brandeis would become a long-term counselor and friend.

In 1914, after six years of teaching in the New York City public schools, she married Edward Jacobs, a businessman from Atlanta whom she met through their common interest in Zionism. Married within a year, they honeymooned in Palestine: Zionism continued to serve as the cornerstone of their long and mutually supportive relationship. At the time she became involved in Hadassah, Jacobs had been planning to take the examination for assistant principal; a career in the public schools offered a good income, tenure, and retirement benefits. When her husband's business failed in later years (which she admitted only to Szold), she recalled without regret her abandonment of that professional path. Voluntarism—and Hadassah—had become so deeply a part of her being that the idea of accepting remuneration for her work was unthinkable even then.

For Jacobs, Hadassah was not an "extra" but a "daily part of the greater . . . program of living." It demanded

> intense activities, long hours not only during the day but into the night, every day, year after year . . . absences from home and . . . long trips and separations for visits to Palestine and other countries where there were Jews.[5]

Although Jacobs acknowledged that mothers who volunteer outside the home became more "alert, fresh, and interesting," she nonetheless worried that in committing herself to Zionist work, she was being unfair to her children. She had to wean them young, travelled even when they were ill, and made other personal sacrifices. In 1921, when her youngest child, Joshua, was still an infant, Jacobs received a visit from Szold about the possibility of her assuming the presidency of Hadassah. But finding Jacobs bathing the child, Szold did not have the heart to raise the subject, because in her view, child-rearing took precedence over everything else. With few exceptions, she insisted that Hadassah's married women not compromise their family responsibilities.

Jacobs's husband reassured her that "far from being unfair to our children, my activities in the larger field were helpful to our children and to himself." Though her participation in Hadassah did not require her husband's "urging, persuasion, or full consent," Jacobs doubted that without his support she could have assumed her absorbing responsibilities without destroying "the very unity of my being." When Jacobs once told Joshua that she was going to quit Hadassah to teach him to read, he responded, "No, don't do that. The Jewish people need you." Both children became involved in Jewish volunteer work as adults, although Hadassah did not become "the exclusive business of living" for Ruth as it had been for her mother.[6]

How well Jacobs succeeded in her multiple endeavors is best summed up by her good friend and teacher, Alice Selisberg:

> How you, dear Rose, despite your divided vocations—wife, mother, daughter, sister on the one hand, and heavily burdened public servant on the other, can still have heart and time for constant and devoted attention to friends, I do not know.[7]
>
> There is no one else in my range of friendship who is like you in always having time, no matter how busy she is. You never seemed weighed down or troubled by the things waiting to be done, you always are serenely ready to take on one more task. You are not flurried, you don't lose poise. . . . I marvel at this, for I am thrown out of gear under pressure and become depressed; and even Henrietta— even when I first knew her, always seemed rebellious against herself because of the volume of tasks that packed every minute of her inordinately long days.[8]

At a time when most Hadassah leaders were single women with the time to devote to their responsibilities in the office and on the road, Jacobs was the exception. Over time, however, the balance shifted, and most volunteers were married; for many of these women, as for Jacobs, voluntarism was a full-time, absorbing avocation, undertaken despite the difficulties of balancing the demands of service with those of family, and as much a "career" as paid work might have been. Jacobs believed that the husbands of the "presidents and officials of hundreds of chapters" throughout the land were as enriched by their wives' Zionist involvement as her husband and family had been by hers. At one point, when she was next in line for the presidency of Hadassah, Jacobs admitted that her Hadassah work had become too demanding. Unable to slow down, she felt that withdrawing from leadership would be the best course. Having always wanted to return to academic work, she enrolled at Fordham Law School. But after completing her first year in 1926, Hadassah asked her to travel to Palestine to resolve a pressing issue regarding its medical unit. "Henrietta Szold said she would not go unless I went along," Jacobs recalled.[9] Her love of Zionism, and Szold's urging, proved too strong and she relented, although it meant abandoning law school. Her "career" would remain entwined with Hadassah.

Jacobs's Jewish identity had always been strong. Her maternal grandparents, who played an important role in her upbringing, had emigrated from Lithuania to the Lower East Side. Her grandfather, a peddler who specialized in linens, eventually bought property and built a prosperous dry goods business. Her grandmother, purportedly descended from the Vilna Gaon, was devoted to her family and Jewish charities, helping to establish homes for the elderly and collecting money to bring over and care for relatives and friends from the old country.

Despite her grandparents' "passionate Americanism," Rose perceived them as being "concerned with Jewish values as well as the Americanizing process." They held fast to Jewish practices and raised their children to value the importance of public service and Jewish concerns. Their example was followed by Jacobs's parents. Her father owned a dry goods store, and like his father-in-law, made profitable real estate investments. Her mother, though she had received little education herself, stressed it continually for her five children, all of whom received higher education or professional training. (Jacobs graduated from the New York Training School for Teachers and later took graduate courses at Teachers College and field training at Marietta Tree's Organic School in Greenwich, Connecticut.)[10]

According to Jacobs, both her husband's and her own family typified a large group of immigrant Jews who had risen to the middle class without abandoning their heritage. After she married, Jacobs maintained a traditional Jewish home, although Judaism became more of a cultural than a religious faith, intimately connected to Zionism. While she kept the Sabbath rituals, after Friday dinner she held an open house where Zionists gathered. In 1922, the Jacobses joined the new Society for the Advancement of Judaism, appreciating Mordecai Kaplan's attempts to promote Jewish cultural aspirations and to bring Judaism more into line with modern thinking. Especially important to Rose was the fact that "women were given recognition" in his Reconstructionist services and were called to the Torah. Shortly after Kaplan's daughter, Judith, received the first Bat Mitzvah in 1922, Jacob's daughter, Ruth, celebrated hers.

The combination of inherited family values, her husband's encouragement, and the influence of Henrietta Szold and Alice Selisberg positioned Jacobs for the significant role she played in building Hadassah in its formative years. During the early years of her marriage, when the Jacobses lived in the South (a "wilderness," she observed, from a Jewish, and especially a Zionist point of view), Jacobs organized Hadassah chapters in Columbus, Georgia, and Chattanooga, Tennessee. When the family moved to New York in 1918, she became a member of Hadassah's Executive Committee. Her astute political instincts frequently rescued Hadassah from the swamp of Zionist politics.

Against the advice of Henrietta Szold, who had less stomach for fighting divisive issues, she played a crucial role in saving Hadassah from a proposed ZOA reorganization that would have compromised its autonomy.

Relations with male Zionists were problematic. Hadassah leaders were referred to as "diaper Zionists," and Jacobs herself was called "Miss America" because of her frequent defense of the United States. According to Jacobs, "men who have been fighting Hadassah and clamoring to put Hadassah out" never realized how ridiculous they would look without Hadassah; they would be reduced to a little *chevra* (gang) with a small membership.[11]

Jacobs believed that Louis Lipsky, the ZOA president who had led the Weizmann faction in its 1921 victory against the Brandeis group, wished to destroy Hadassah. During the 1920s, Jacobs helped to avert several crises engineered by Lipsky. By 1928, for example, Hadassah had grown to such numbers and resources compared to the declining base of the ZOA that its newly elected president, Irma Lindheim, a Brandeis adherent, was demanding a larger voice. She also insisted that Hadassah be represented in Zionist congresses by its own delegates in proportion to its membership, instead of by ZOA men. At Hadassah's 1928 convention in Pittsburgh, Lipsky, opposing Lindheim, "harangued" delegates with an emotional appeal that threatened to split the organization. Jacobs recalled the moment as "one of the most dramatic and decisive incidents in Hadassah's life and my own":

> Miss Selisberg who was presiding seemed to flounder for a way to meet the situation. I rushed to the platform and demanded an executive session. There was pandemonium but I stood my ground, shouted and gesticulated until order was restored and an executive session ordered. Mr. Lipsky was compelled to leave and the day was saved.[12]

During this period, Jacobs also helped to overcome Chaim Weizmann's opposition to Hadassah's involvement in the joint planning of a hospital with the American Jewish Physicians Committee. Jacobs informed Weizmann that unless he withdrew his opposition, Hadassah would organize an independent committee and proceed with the plan. Mutually acceptable terms were eventually reached after negotiations with Hebrew University, Hadassah, and the Physicians Committee; Hadassah Hospital was completed in 1937 and remains one of Hadassah's crowning achievements.[13]

Hadassah faced difficulties not only with male Zionists but with other Jewish women's groups. Jacobs and Szold had pioneered Hadassah's relationship with the Jewish women's group in Palestine, the Histadrut Nashim Ivriot, which it helped establish. Unliked WIZO (the Women's International Zionist Organization), which started a Palestine chapter, Hadassah preferred to help build an autonomous women's organization responsible for providing social services. "What we tried to do was to help [create] a woman's organization that would be the organic result of living in the country," Jacobs said.

Though the organizations occasionally joined in common projects, WIZO was consistently at odds with Hadassah's approach.[14]

Jacobs also attempted to enlist the National Council of Jewish Women, the other major American Jewish women's group, in support of Jews in Palestine. In 1932, she appealed to the NCJW to present a plan for a Palestinian project at the Council's upcoming Triennial Conference in Detroit.[15] However, the NCJW refused to allow the matter to come before delegates. Some members who also belonged to Hadassah resigned in disgust; according to one Detroit member, the idea of a Palestine mission might have earned such a sympathetic response from delegates that other NCJW programs would have been jeopardized.[16] Szold was amazed that the Council had held out so long against "Zionist onslaughts against its fortresses."[17] To Jacobs, NCJW's reluctance to move on the Palestine issue led to a decline in numbers and was the reason why Jewish women's groups could not develop a unified program.

Jacobs herself had been involved in all of Hadassah's work in Palestine during its first two decades: operating its medical unit and developing a nationwide system of rural health services; establishing the Nurses Training School; developing an infant welfare program; initiating a network of playgrounds; administering the school lunch program; creating a social services system comprising orphan care, family casework, and coordinated child care.

Under Szold's and Jacobs's leadership, the guiding concept was that communities and inhabitants would take over increasing responsibility for administration and material support, eventually executing all programs. When the final stage came, Hadassah would withdraw and arrange a lump-sum gift for the initial period. Helping to design and guide this program of "devolution," Jacobs recognized that the development of the Yishuv into a more assertive, self-propelled community required a proactive relationship with the Diaspora. By 1935, she knew a turning point had been reached. With the Yishuv controlling more of its own health, welfare, and educational needs, Hadassah, if it were to remain a vital force, needed a new focus.[18] Unless it remained closely allied with developments in the Yishuv, it risked becoming one of many fund-raising groups rather than an effective agency of Zionist activity. Accordingly, Hadassah sought other venues. With Szold then directing social services for the Palestine governing agency, Jacobs played the key role in determining Hadassah's future.

In the summer of 1935, the board sent Jacobs on a mission to Palestine to survey possible future endeavors. Over two months, consulting with Szold at every point, she examined a variety of projects—nutrition, school lunches, the National Fund, tuberculosis work, vocational education, and the settling of refugee children. The field gradually narrowed down to the two latter areas.

In 1934, Jacobs accompanied Szold to a meeting in Germany to discuss the prospects for Youth Aliyah. In her memoirs, she offers a vivid portrait of the contrast between Szold and Bertha Pappenheim, the German Jewish feminist leader also in attendance. Szold, dressed in casual clothes, her hair all windblown, was "progressive, forward-looking, not daunted at all" by the difficulties of rescuing and resettling German youth. Pappenheim, the same age as Szold, swept in like "la grande dame." Staid and proper, like a "martinet" in appearance and demeanor, her mind was "also straitlaced when it came to Jewish affairs." An anti-Zionist who had no sympathy with Youth Aliyah, Pappenheim told Szold and Jacobs that Jews leaving Germany were like "rats deserting a sinking ship."[19]

Szold, however, was determined to carry out the mission. The following year, when Jacobs surveyed Youth Aliyah in Palestine, six hundred children had already arrived in the country, and four hundred more were on their way. The children were sent to kibbutzim, where Szold had set up a revolutionary educational system designed, in her words, "to inure young Jews of urban tradition and centuries-long removal from the plough and the saw, to the labor which lies at the foundation of the social structure."[20] Also imperative was immersion in the Hebrew language, Jewish history, Jewish lore and tradition, the Bible, and general academic subjects. All of it worked, Jacobs learned, because of Szold's deep personal involvement and the system of group living she had established. Although Szold hoped that Jacobs would recommend Youth Aliyah to Hadassah as its new mission, she did not hint at her own wishes.

She didn't have to. Deeply excited by the rescue operation, Jacobs believed that Youth Aliyah would "link Hadassah with the problems of world Jewry, making a triangular connection—America—Europe—Palestine." The appeal—the rescue of youth—was irresistible; moreover, it fit the mission that Hadassah had announced twenty-three years earlier: concrete, practical work in Palestine relating to women and children, and the spread of Zionism in America. Through Youth Aliyah, Hadassah's mission—the "healing of the daughter of my people"—remained a personal, hands-on mission, crucial to the lives of children and the creation of a Jewish homeland.

Jacobs went to Lucerne with Szold to attend the biennial congress of the World Zionist Organization; there she drew up a tentative contract whereby Hadassah would be the recognized agency for collecting Youth Aliyah funds in the United States. Hadassah would undertake to raise $30,000 yearly for the next two years to transport and maintain one hundred Youth Aliyah wards in Palestine; all other agencies in the United States were to clear their collections through Hadassah.

When Jacobs returned to the United States, however, strong opposition came from the ZOA, which feared that its own collections might be hurt if Hadassah became the exclusive channel for child rescue. Yet its attempts to divert Hadassah from approving Jacobs's report proved abortive; the recommendation to sponsor Youth Aliyah was enthusiastically accepted at Hadassah's convention in Cleveland at the end of 1935.

The adoption of the program further stimulated Hadassah's growth. Within one year, from a membership base of approximately 35,000, Hadassah added ninety-five chapters and saw its membership climb to 60,000. In the next two years, it raised over $126,000, more than double its commitment. Within a few years, Hadassah pledged to collect a quarter of a million dollars annually for Youth Aliyah. By 1954, the twentieth anniversary of the program, Hadassah had collected $23 million. So completely was it identified with the project that many members did not realize that Hadassah was merely the agency for collecting funds for Youth Aliyah and had no separate voice in its management.[21] By the time of the founding of the State of Israel, Hadassah's commitment to the program had enabled the absorption of 50,000 children, including 20,000 orphans rescued from concentration camps. Still in operation, Youth Aliyah has succeeded in bringing to Israel, educating, and rehabilitating more than 300,000 children from eighty countries.[22]

Always Resistance to Women in Political Affairs   Jacobs's Zionist objective involved not merely the regeneration of Jewish culture and religion in Palestine but the resolution of conflict with Palestine's Arab population. Jacobs shared Henrietta Szold's passionate hope that Arab-Jewish relations could be improved.

Jacobs's most important contribution to the cause of peace was Hadassah's Arab-Jewish Relations Committee. To reach a compromise with the Arabs, Jacobs believed it was vital to understand their culture. At the time, the notion that the Arabs were a people with an "old tradition . . . way of life, a Koran, a history" was not a popular one. Beginning in 1933, at Jacobs's urging, Hadassah formed a committee to study questions of Arab-Jewish relations. Yet opposition within the executive board prevented real progress. Most Zionist leaders questioned the value of research on Arabs. At the Jewish Agency in Jerusalem, only a minor official kept tabs on Arab politics; Jacobs felt his reports were little more than "gossip." Chaim Weizmann, however, did not agree: "If Mrs. Jacobs thinks that study will solve the problem, she is mistaken." Ben-Gurion was more blunt, publicly stating that he thought it "ridiculous" that "persons without authority" undertake such studies. Although he later regretted his dismissiveness, Jacobs refused to accept his apology. "As a leader of a cause which I regard as holy," she told him, "I expect you to conduct yourself in a manner befitting your office. That you did not do and I believe I am justified in resenting it." On another occasion she told him, "You are a nasty man."[23]

Jacobs increasingly believed that a wedge in the political maneuvering common in male Zionist politics might be provided by Hadassah, especially around questions of Arab-Jewish relations. In 1938, she wrote to Alice Selisberg that Hadassah remained the "jewel in the whole [Zionist] organization," but she was concerned that its "left-leaning" members might be driven out.

In order to prevent the triumph of demagoguery, American Zionist women had to act decisively, not through "regular organization methods" but in a "quick revolutionary way." "Does this sound like Emma Goldman?" she asked Selisberg.[24]

As usual, encouragement came from Louis Brandeis. For many years, Brandeis had advised Jacobs as to policy, politics, and financial and labor matters; Jacobs considered him a veritable "architect" of Hadassah.[25] During the Depression, when Jacobs, as president, was concerned that Hadassah meet its commitments, the justice scrutinized Hadassah's budget, giving Jacobs steady encouragement. He was pleased with the strategy of devolution, and heartily endorsed new directions, from the alliance with Hebrew University to construct a hospital to Youth Aliyah. Brandeis noted that in all his experience with professional or social organizations, Hadassah was unique in its methods and work, in its spirit of devotion, in its selflessness to the cause it served.[26] Always "he expressed confidence in women," Jacobs recalled. "[H]e saw no reason why the contribution made by women on the voluntary base in welfare work should make any difference in evaluation."[27] After Jacobs returned from Palestine in 1940, Brandeis offered to provide her with a substantial sum to return to Palestine for three years to work on improving Arab-Jewish relations. She was considering the offer at the time of Brandeis's death in 1941.

Jacobs headed Hadassah's Committee for the Study of Arab-Jewish relations from 1936 through 1943. Under her leadership, the committee collected materials that led to the publication of several volumes on Arab culture. The study stimulated further analyses by the Esco Foundation, in which Jacobs participated, and the establishment of the Middle East Research Council. Nonetheless, within Hadassah, opposition to the work of her committee increased until Jacobs felt it was no longer worth endangering her physical and mental health. In 1943, the work of Jacobs's committee was taken over by the Emergency Committee for General Zionist Affairs headed by Abba Hillel Silver; soon afterwards it became the research department of the Zionist Council. Even more than the demise of the effort she had personally led, Jacobs regretted the failure of Ben-Gurion and his colleagues to make an "honest effort" to negotiate with the Arabs. In Jacobs's view, Ben-Gurion's belief that "everything depends on us, and only us" was dreadfully wrong.

Jacobs was unhappy with the Biltmore Resolution engineered by Ben-Gurion and adopted at the ZOA convention at New York's Biltmore Hotel in May 1942. Calling for the "fulfillment of the original purpose of the Balfour Declaration and Mandate," which recognized the historical connection of the Jewish people with Palestine and the creation of a Jewish commonwealth, the resolution signified for Jacobs the abandonment of any effort at rapprochement with the Arabs. She spoke out against the resolution in an address, arguing that a planned program of cooperation with the Arabs was a prerequisite to any sound Zionist policy. Hadassah, however, gave unqualified support to the commonwealth idea and Jacobs's remarks were not favorably received.

When the Ihud (or "Union") was established the following year, based on the idea that "a union between the Jewish and Arab people" was essential for the upbuilding of Palestine, Jacobs strongly championed the group's focus on peace through mutual understanding and education. Headed by Judah Magnes, the president of Hebrew University who was also leading Hadassah's wartime Emergency Committee at Jacobs's request, Ihud counted Henrietta Szold and Martin Buber among its five commission members. Ihud's supporters were "Western" as opposed to Eastern European Jews, generally expressing, according to Jacobs, "an upper-middle class, liberalist approach." They were a "prestige" group, whether because of wealth, social standing, or intellectual achievement.[28] Although Ihud was committed to the Zionist principle of the right of Jewish return and the establishment of an autonomous Jewish state in Palestine, it favored a "binational order," recognizing the Palestinian Arabs' right to a "national autonomous life." Affirming a commitment to the "nondomination" of one people over another, Ihud supported a federation with neighboring nations.[29]

In a letter to Hadassah, Szold explained that Ihud was not a political body but one that hoped to stimulate discussion about the rights of both Jews and Arabs in Palestine. Affiliating with Ihud was one of Szold's most controversial actions, and Hadassah's resistance to it embittered the remaining years of her life. The ZOA adopted a resolution condemning the binational program; Hadassah repudiated Ihud at a heated convention that Jacobs believed reached a "new low" in "Tammany methods" and "machine built power politics." "A delegation of men came to influence Hadassah and the women were lobbying and stirring up sentiment . . ." she reported to Szold.

> I defended you and your associates as responsible Zionists who had a right to your views and charged the Convention with not being informed on the matters up for action. I was voted down—but I still feel victorious because I did what I believe was right and fair and decent and honest.[30]

Many in Hadassah agitated against retaining Judah Magnes as head of Hadassah's Emergency Committee because of his views on the Arab-Jewish question.

Jacobs was so disheartened by Hadassah's treatment of her "dissident" views that participating in the work of the National Board and chairing the Arab-Jewish Relations Committee because increasingly distasteful to her. To Szold she explained: "I could not accept the methods and standards which were so at variance with what was Hadassah. Instead of lifting the Zionist Organization to the higher level, Hadassah fell in line with the ways of the men's organization, building a Lipsky machine and adopting Ben-Gurion as the standard-bearer." Singled out as a "symbol of resistance," Jacobs was increasingly subject to "personal rancor and malicious ugliness."[31] Refusing to accept this "tendency for totalitarianism" and "sabotage ... and resistance" to her ideas, she resigned as chairman of the Committee on the Study of Arab-Jewish Relations.

Jacobs reassured friends who worried about her break from the organization with which she had been associated for more than three decades. No matter, she told them.

> I have independence, and am able to carry myself by my own guides to action. What has happened is that I am a pioneer ploughing the way and seeking the path for those who will come after me. There is always resistance to women in political affairs in general, and especially so in Jewish political life.

This resistance had ultimately corrupted the women's Zionist organization itself, Jacobs felt. When its members could no longer "look at" or hear each other, when "personal rancor" replaced the gaze of friendship, the ethic of friendship, cooperation, and mutual connection that had distinguished the group was lost. She felt she had no choice but to leave. "I never regretted that I assumed the burden," she told friends, "nor that I laid it down when I did."[32]

Achieving the Personal Touch   In the interwar period, Jewish women's gaze turned not only to Palestine, where they were involved in successive efforts to build and strengthen the Jewish community, but to Europe. For decades, the NCJW had been the leading agency involved in the work of immigrant aid, offering direct assistance to newcomers in all manner of services. With the passage of laws that drastically reduced immigration from eastern and southern Europe in 1921 and 1924, the NCJW's Department of Immigrant Aid, headed by Cecilia Razovsky, became an even larger player in the international arena, working on thorny problems of international migration and family disunity. In domestic matters, Razovsky and the NCJW remained leading advocates of immigrant interests, working both to counter the nation's increasingly virulent antialien sentiments and to "Americanize" the immigrants. For Razovsky and the NCJW, however, Americanization was not a coercive attempt to impose a single "melting pot" standard on the newcomers. Respectful of the immigrants' cultural heritage, they worked to preserve immigrant customs while "harmonizing" them with modern American ways. In the debate between "100% Americanizers" and cultural pluralists, theirs was the middle way.

Razovsky's experience as secretary of the Department of Immigrant Aid positioned her to play a leading role in the unfolding refugee crisis of the 1930s. In the eyes of most observers, she was the decisive figure in the establishment and development of the National Coordinating Council in 1934, and of its successor organization five years later, the National Refugee Service. Indeed, Razovsky largely set the course of the refugee aid movement before and during World War II, and was personally responsible for assisting thousands of victims of Nazi persecution. In the face of a hostile public and a government fearful of seeming too concerned about aliens—especially Jews—she negotiated a course that allowed private rescue agencies to play a significant international role. Razovsky's vision was largely responsible as well for the policy of "integration" that helped new refugees adjust to community life in the postwar period. In the continuum of her work from the 1920s through the 1940s, she was guided by a philosophy of personalism that she helped instill throughout hundreds of local NCJW sections and in the thousands of volunteers who worked on behalf of immigrant aid and the rescue of refugees from Nazism.

Cecilia Razovsky was the native-born child of immigrant parents who had settled in St. Louis, Missouri, in the 1880s. Growing up among immigrants, Razovsky was always interested in their culture; she delighted in reading stories about them and considered authors like Abraham Cahan and Anzia Yezierska her "heroes and heroines."[33] Because the family was poor, Razovsky worked in a variety of jobs after school and during vacations all through her adolescent years: sewing buttons on overalls in a factory, working as a salesgirl in a department store, pasting labels on cards in a wholesale clothing company, washing towels in a bathhouse, waitressing. After graduating from high school in 1903, she took a job as a stenographer for the local *St. Louis Star,* the first of several clerical positions she held in the next seven years. In addition to her paid job, she volunteered as a teacher and leader of clubs and classes for the Jewish Educational Alliance, giving lessons in English and history to foreigners; she also taught evening classes in civics and literature and Sunday classes for children in biblical literature and Hebrew. When the St. Louis Board of Education took over programs of adult education for foreigners, Razovsky taught classes in English, citizenship, and business subjects in the evening public schools. Any free time she had was spent on her own evening and summer courses—Spanish, German, Latin, and English literature; sociology and case work; drama, economics, psychology, short story writing, labor relations, law, and social work.

While continuing her volunteer work as a teacher of immigrants, in 1911 Razovsky found paid employment as an attendance and probation officer for the St. Louis Board of Education, handling cases of predelinquent children, including those involved in the "street trades"; she also worked for a time under Jane Addams at the Hull House settlement in Chicago. In 1917, Razovsky became an inspector for the Child Labor Division of the U.S. Children's Bureau in Washington, working to enforce the child labor law. In this job she inspected cotton mills, glass and tobacco factories, and other industrial plants throughout the South and North, working under the direction of

Julia Lathrop and Grace Abbott, Progressive reformers who had been closely associated with Jane Addams at Hull House. During World War I, Razovsky prepared a study of the effects of war on child labor and school attendance in the United States, the first such study of its kind.

After a Supreme Court decision in 1918 declared that the federal law regulating child labor was unconstitutional, the Children's Bureau discontinued its Child Labor Division. Razovsky then went to work for the National Council of Jewish Women. With her extensive experience as a teacher of immigrants, her work in the field of child labor and social reform, and her academic background in labor economics, Razovsky came to the NCJW with unusual expertise and a personal connection to the lives of immigrants. Unlike most first-generation Council leaders, she was separated by no barrier of class or national origin from the foreign-born newcomers who were the agency's clients.

A year after Razovsky arrived at the NCJW, President Harding signed into law an emergency immigration bill temporarily restricting immigration from Eastern and Southern Europe; fashioned in haste and without communication with foreign consuls or shipping companies, the new law stranded thousands of immigrants who did not understand the new quota system. In 1924, swept in by an overwhelming tide of anti-immigrant sentiment, a permanent restriction bill was passed by which immigrant quotas were determined according to the census of 1890 (when the Jewish population was smaller by several million). The effect was drastic: with the combined quota from Poland, Russia, Romania, and the Baltic countries reduced by 90 percent, Jewish immigration slowed to a crawl. In the seven years between 1924 and 1931, only 73,000 Jews came to the United States, compared to 656,000 during a similar period earlier in the century.[34]

In the face of such reduced numbers, the NCJW redirected its attention to helping immigrants already in the United States, working to unite separated families and lobbying for legislative change. Razovsky believed the organization's tasks had grown more difficult. Not only did NCJW volunteers have to work in a climate of increased antiforeign feeling, but they had to confront the newcomers' own antagonism to Americans, a reaction to the hostility they had been shown. In *The Immigrant,* the NCJW bulletin Razovsky edited, she argued that the only way to counter the new immigrants' suspicions was to be "real neighbors and real friends." Razovsky and NCJW officials asked their volunteers to become an "aristocracy of the kind heart and sympathetic spirit," reaching out to the immigrant girl so that she would know "there is some one who is her friend, ready to help her at every time."[35]

"Achieving the personal touch" in relation to the newcomers meant helping them to preserve their cultural heritage. "We cannot and should not force detachment from the old world cultural associations of these men and women," Razovsky insisted. In her view, the "ancient Jewish spirit of integrity" still vibrant in immigrant communities might provide the broader society with a "sense of spiritual values," the "unifying principle" so desperately lacking in modern secular America.[36] In response to writer Willa Cather, who in a *New York Times* interview in 1925 had derided social workers' "poking into personal affairs," trying to turn immigrants into "stupid replicas of snug American types . . . Americanizing everything and everybody," NCJW president Florine Lasker observed that intervention meant not social control but friendship, helping immigrants to solve the problems of modern industrial life and providing crucial emotional support.[37] As Razovsky explained on another occasion, the NCJW's function was to "harmoniz[e] existing differences between racial groups" and act as "Clearing Bureaus for racial understanding and interpretation." In such a mediating role, the Council could prevent the extreme of a "polygot boarding house" or "crazy quilt of nationalities": its aim was "a single unified (not uniform) whole," based on "mutual sympathy and understanding . . . toleration and respect."[38]

These goals were tested throughout the 1920s as a consequence of the laws of 1921 and 1924 and a series of antiforeign amendments in 1929 that further restricted citizenship opportunities. The Cable Act, passed in 1922, also challenged the NCJW's philosophy of mutuality. Presented to President Harding for signing by Maud Wood Park, who had led the clubwomen movement's lobbying effort on behalf of the bill, the Cable Act declared that foreign-born women could no longer become citizens by marriage to naturalized or American-born men, but had to take out citizenship papers in their own right. While American feminists rejoiced at this acknowledgment that every woman was an independent human being, Razovsky's appreciation of the victory was more guarded. NCJW leaders pointed out that foreign-born women were much less likely than foreign-born men to acquire American customs and manners or to attend English and citizenship classes to prepare for the citizenship exam. They suspected that the law would burden immigrants in other ways, separating them from their husbands and children through deportation and barring them from receiving mothers' pensions, public employment, health benefits, and other services.[39]

Theresa Malkiel, an immigrant socialist leader who had become chairwoman of the Women's Citizenship Committee, shared Razovsky's concern about the effect of the Cable Act on foreign-born women. In Malkiel's view, the immigrant working woman—still a "beast of burden in her home"—desperately needed the benefits of citizenship to improve her condition. While Jewish labor leaders like Rose Schneiderman favored the Act, more radical activists like Malkiel found themselves in agreement with the NCJW that it deprived immigrant women of civil and political privileges they had previously possessed.[40]

The concerns of Malkiel and the NCJW were apparently justified, since the number of women applying for naturalization papers declined after the

passage of the Cable Act. In addition, the problem of desertion, already serious among Jewish immigrants, grew worse. Since the immigration of married
women to the United States was now restricted to the quotas of their native
countries, naturalized male immigrants often remarried, granting their original wives a *get*—a rabbinical divorce—and assuming that the new marriages
were now legal.[41] Other anomalies included American-born children separated from noncitizen mothers, and a drastic increase in "women without a
country"—European-born women who lost their native nationality because
they had married American citizens, yet did not acquire American citizenship
through their husbands.[42]

Family disruptions caused by the Cable Act and the restrictive immigration acts of the 1920s created many such hardships. In September 1923, as
one of the NCJW's delegates to the first World Congress of Jewish Women
and chair of its session on migration, Razovsky implored representatives from
twenty-three countries to respond to the crisis of transnational migration by
providing more refugee havens, greater direct assistance to migrants and de-
portees, and better coordination of services and information between countries.[43] She then visited Cuba to determine whether that country might
become a haven for homeless Jewish immigrants; her report to the NCJW
helped obtain funding to establish a model refugee program in Havana.[44]
The favorable publicity generated by this project led to an invitation to the
NCJW to join with six national organizations in issuing a call for a conference on the crisis facing Jewish refugees; chaired by Stephen Wise and Louis
Marshall, the conference resulted in the decision to form an Emergency
Committee on Jewish Refugees.

The onset of the Depression and the rise of Nazism in the 1930s turned
the refugee situation into an international crisis. With over a decade of experience as head of the NCJW's Department of Immigrant Aid, Razovsky was
well equipped to deal with all the major elements of that crisis: international
negotiation, domestic lobbying, direct personal aid to immigrants and
"stranded" family members. In 1934, she became "the moving spirit" in the
creation of the National Coordinating Committee (NCC), designed to max-
imize the influence of its eighteen constituent social agencies and coordinate
their work with government and the general public.[45] In view of the divisions
among Jewish leaders concerning the appropriate strategies for opposing
American as well as world anti-Semitism, the common front reflected in the
NCC's work was a rare instance of unity during these years.

As executive secretary of the NCC, Razovsky, more than anyone else, was
responsible for the crucial work of the agency's first years. She had drawn up the
document that set forth the course of action to be followed in years to come
by the NCC and its successor agency, the National Refugee Service (NRS).
The functions she outlined included selecting and distributing refugees; communicating with local American organizations; disseminating information

about entrance requirements and property transference; meeting refugees upon their arrival; and coordinating services regarding settlement, adjustment, employment, housing, legal aid, medical care, and vocational training. When Razovsky began her work at the NCC, she was assisted by only a stenographer and a clerk; expenditures for the first six months amounted to little more than $3,000. But soon the NCC had developed into the second largest voluntary social agency in the United States, with over eight hundred employees and a budget of millions of dollars.[46] Through Razovsky's participation, the NCJW, which had "loaned" her to the NCC, retained a significant influence over the direction of refugee work and the development of Jewish social service in the 1930s.[47]

Aiding German refugees turned out to be a vastly different, and in some ways even more difficult, task than helping earlier arrivals from Eastern Europe. During the Depression, when alien groups were scapegoated for the country's economic ills, German Jews faced widespread opprobrium. Whispering campaigns about businesses firing employees and hiring refugees, or about special privileges granted refugees by the government, were common. Even Jews feared that "there were too many [Jews] coming in, that this will cause trouble for the Jews here." At an NCJW Institute in 1936, Razovsky described the attitude many Jews held about the refugees—"that they are not grateful enough," that they were "arrogant, impolite, look[ing] down on Eastern European Jews." She asked NCJW volunteers to be sympathetic toward the new arrivals and to challenge anyone who seemed to misinterpret their behavior. "Put yourself in place of them," she implored them, and remember that while the older refugee "was at the bottom of the ladder going up," the new refugees "were on top of the ladder . . . on their way down"; they required as much emotional support and personal attention as had earlier immigrant groups.[48]

Because of the mounting refugee crisis, helping agencies found it essential to speed up the process by which immigrants became involved in community life, a process that most organizations, with the exception of the NCJW, had seen as automatic and self-directed. Pioneered by the NCJW, the NCC, the NRS, and the United Service for New Americans (formed in 1946 after the NRS merged with the NCJW's Service to the Foreign-Born), the new program, called "integration," was a deliberate attempt to make refugees feel "at home" in America through intensive community involvement.[49]

Razovsky and the leadership of the NCJW played a key role in promoting the concept of integration and stimulating national interest in the well-being of the refugees. According to Lyman White, their efforts led not only to the refugees' relatively smooth adjustment to the United States, but to the strengthening of Jewish community life throughout the country; the work of the refugee agencies became "the greatest joint undertaking" on which the Jewish community had yet embarked.[50]

The success of the integration effort largely resulted from the strategy of organizing local committees of volunteers in hundreds of communities. Previously, social agencies and family welfare organizations, staffed by professional social workers, had conducted much of such work with the assistance of NCJW volunteers. As the numbers of refugees increased, it became necessary to expand the volunteer base and also to increase the authority of the NCJW's professional social workers. According to NCJW directors, this new arena provided a "training ground" for women social workers increasingly squeezed out of positions of prominence by men.[51] Throughout the country, refugee aid committees worked as lay groups that included both volunteers and professionals, promoting strong ties between community volunteers and Jewish agencies.[52] To reduce "social distances" between the refugees and other Americans, the NCJW also established "interracial" groups with such agencies as the YWCA, the National Conference of Christians and Jews, and the Business and Professional Women's Clubs.

Despite these successes, there were many disappointments, and none was greater than the United States' refusal to relax its stringent requirements for granting asylum to refugees, and its failure to admit the maximum number of refugees allowed even under its own limited quotas. Razovsky was present in Havana in the spring of 1939 when, despite her best efforts and those of others involved in the rescue movement, the Cuban government cancelled the visas it had previously granted to the 930 Jewish refugees aboard the S.S. *St. Louis*. In flight from the Nazis, the ship then sailed from port to port in a futile search for asylum. Most of the passengers were eventually distributed among Belgium, France, Great Britain, and the Netherlands; many were later deported back to Germany and killed.[53] To Razovsky, who had made numerous trips to Cuba and helped establish its Jewish colony, the loss was devastating.

She was more fortunate the following fall, when the S.S. *Quanza,* also bearing a cargo of refugees fleeing the Nazis, was denied landing rights in Vera Cruz, Mexico. Knowing they would be doomed if forced to return to Europe, the passengers telegraphed an appeal to the NRS; when the ship arrived at Norfolk, Virginia, for refueling, Razovsky (then director of the Migration Department of the NRS) was there with Evelyn Hersey, executive director of the American Committee for Christian Refugees. The scene they witnessed was terrifying, with women screaming from the deck, "begging piteously that they and their children be given a chance to live again in the sunshine of a free land."[54]

Although the State Department initially refused to waive its visa regulations, which required that visas be issued by an American consul in another country, it finally agreed to admit those who qualified as "political refugees," children under the age of sixteen who could be placed in the charge of the U.S. Committee for the Care of Refugee Children, and those with valid visas to Central or South American countries. A Board of Special Inquiry was set up to consider each case, and with Razovsky and Hersey guaranteeing that their agencies would take financial responsibility for the refugees and ensure that those with valid visas left the United States as soon as possible, the majority of passengers, three-quarters of them Jewish, received asylum.[55]

That same year, Razovsky became a participant in the establishment of a refugee haven in the Dominican Republic, the only one of a plethora of refugee resettlement schemes involving the United States that was actually implemented. At the Evian Conference on the refugee crisis in 1938, General Rafael Trujillo of the Dominican Republic proposed opening up 26,000 acres in Sosua, on the coast of Santo Domingo near Puerto Plata, the principal port in the northern part of the island, to refugees. Trujillo had bought the land from the United Fruit Company and kept it as his private estate; desiring skilled workers, farmers, and "better European stock," he offered to take up to 100,000 refugees as colonists, provided they be carefully selected. Despite Trujillo's dubious motives and with the government's reluctant approval, the Dominican Republic Settlement Association (DORSA), headed by James Rosenberg, chairman of the American Jewish Joint Distribution Committee's (AJJDC) resettlement agency, was established to develop financing and manage the project.

Because of its experience in aiding refugees and arranging temporary asylum, the National Refugee Service assisted DORSA in planning and implementing the scheme, which became operational in late April of 1940. Razovsky played a crucial behind-the-scenes role in establishing the refuge; two weeks before the opening of the colony, she resolved a major impasse regarding financial guarantees for the refugees.[56] Italy's entry into the war, however, now cut off the transportation route for most of the refugees selected for resettlement at Sosua and further bureaucratic difficulties prevented expansion of the project. Despite high hopes, little more than five hundred out of the nearly 30,000 projected settlers ever reached the Dominican Republic.[57] But Razovsky and the NRS provided vital support to the colony, enabling this sole example of a U.S. "mass" rescue outside its borders to survive.

Early in 1943, following a change in board leadership, Razovsky resigned from the NRS, unable to accept the reduced status and responsibilities that followed an internal reorganization.[58] Coincidentally, her departure from the refugee organization that owed so much to her guidance took place at the same time that Rose Jacobs left Hadassah following a relationship of more than three decades with the organization that she had helped to build. Razovsky's organizational skills and commitment to working with volunteers as well as professionals had produced a series of effective organizations—first the National Coordinating Council and then the National Refugee Service—but friction between the cooperating agencies could not be avoided. Too often, largely male-run refugee assistance groups tried to dominate programs established by Razovsky and the NCJW; they continued to view NCJW's role in the coalitions as "trainer and provider of volunteers" to the paid staff of other organizations, a view with which the NCJW vociferously disagreed. Disagreements between the NCJW and NRS festered for several years, the "suspicion . . . and bitterness" growing before an agreement was reached that specified each agency's functions. The NCJW continued to forestall attempts to supplant its immigrant aid programs.[59]

Razovsky's departure from the NRS did not end her work with refugees. In 1944, she was appointed specialist in the Displaced Persons Division of the United Nations Relief and Rehabilitation Administration (UNRRA). In this capacity, she was loaned to the European headquarters of the American Jewish Joint Distribution Committee (JDC). Following the surrender of Germany in 1945, she organized the Central Location Index in Paris, helping thousands of concentration camp survivors to locate relatives throughout the world; she also organized a personal service division, which gave emergency relief to refugees and repatriates.

Razovsky assisted the JDC's rescue of the few thousand Jewish children who survived Buchenwald, Dachau, and other camps. With an UNRRA unit, she helped bring convoys of children out of Germany to havens in Switzerland and France. As director of immigrant operations in Germany and Austria, Razovsky also assisted in the implementation of President Truman's directive of December 22, 1945, which authorized the admission of displaced persons to U.S. zones in Germany and Austria. She visited every consular district where camps were located, obtaining firsthand knowledge of the abilities and character of the thousands awaiting resettlement, and training JDC workers in the necessary procedures. In 1946, she worked with the Citizens Committee on Displaced Persons, functioning as liaison with national organizations to secure Congressional legislation to admit the refugees. The following year, she went to Brazil, Argentina, and other Latin American countries on behalf of the JDC to help refugees emigrating from Europe. On her return to the United States, she joined her husband, Morris Davidson, a physician in the Veterans Administration, in Jackson, Mississippi. There and in Austin, Texas, where the couple lived later on, they participated in the developing civil rights struggle.[60]

In the late 1950s, Razovsky was sent by United HIAS Service to assist in the resettlement of Hungarian and Egyptian Jewish refugees in Brazil, Chile, Ecuador, Peru, and Colombia. Her last trip to the region was in 1963, when she visited cities throughout Latin America, giving lectures and conducting courses on social service work. She took the opportunity to examine the status of women in each of the countries she visited and hoped to publish a study analyzing her research, but she died in 1968 before the project was completed.

After a lifetime in immigrant aid, mostly in association with the National

Council of Jewish Women, it is not surprising that Razovsky turned her attention in her last years to women's roles. Earlier, her association with Jane Addams and the Children's Bureau reformers had given her a deep appreciation of women's influence in delivering social services and creating public policy, and she used that sensibility to shape and direct the NCJW's Department of Immigrant Aid and the successive immigrant and rescue organizations with which she worked. During the European catastrophe of the 1930s, her interest in the special plight of female immigrants, which she had explored throughout the 1920s and the early years of the Depression, was superseded by the exigencies of refugee rescue. Razovsky played a vital role in shaping the nation's refugee assistance program in the 1930s and 1940s, helping to negotiate the few successful instances of American involvement in mass resettlement, as well as a Jewish communal approach to the refugee crisis. Spending countless hours addressing volunteers throughout the country, she helped create public interest and support for refugee aid at a time when prejudice against the foreign-born remained widespread. Her philosophy of personalism and her insistence that immigrants' cultural heritage must be respected and preserved endeared her to the many thousands of new Americans with whom she worked.

Razovsky's ideas about the sanctity of immigrant culture were influenced to some degree by her association with progressive settlement reformers like Addams, but also by her own firsthand experience as the child of immigrants. While she supported the women's movement, her point of view diverged from mainline feminist positions. In the case of the Cable Act, for example, her role as representative of immigrant women's interests put her at odds with leading feminists. Yet throughout her life, she was deeply influenced by a woman-centered vision of service that linked her to the larger feminist movement.

Although Razovsky married, she worked full-time as a paid professional; in her speeches and writings and especially in the public nature of her work, she demonstrated to other married women in the middle decades of the twentieth century that homemaking, however important in their lives, need not and ought not claim their complete attention. "We owe it to ourselves and to our families to take an active part in the civic and communal affairs of the city in which we live," she told a meeting of the NCJW's committee on Americanization during the early years of her employment with that organization. But such a local focus should not be the extent of women's participation in public affairs. "As intelligent voters we must try to understand state and national issues," she insisted. "Above all, we must help create an intelligent public opinion as how best to promote international understanding." For the women of the world, no question was as vital as the "achievement and maintenance of permanent peace."[61]

In 1929, Razovsky had been appointed by Jane Addams to represent her at the League of Nations' International Conference on Migration; she attended several women's international peace conferences in the 1930s as well.[62] For Razovsky, who in her quiet way became one of America's preeminent actors in the arena of refugee service—rescuing Jewish victims from the ravages of war and the horrors of Hitler's Final Solution—peace would always be the ultimate and guiding objective. As a woman and as a Jew, she devoted her life in service to this ideal.

Writers, War, and Witness: Ruth Gruber and Muriel Rukeyser

On an individual basis, writers like Ruth Gruber and Muriel Rukeyser also bore witness to the political crises of the 1930s and 1940s. Rukeyser, who began as a journalist writing about southern racism and the Spanish Civil War, emerged as the leading exponent of a new poetry of witness that demanded honest and open testimony to the cruelty of all forms of oppression, personal and social. Though it seemed anomalous at the time, Rukeyser's committed art—linking the self to the world and poetry to politics—would have enormous influence on a later generation of Jewish women poets, especially Adrienne Rich, Denise Levertov, and Grace Paley.[63] Gruber, who began as a poet and developed into a journalist covering international affairs, documented the extraordinary stories of the one thousand Nazi refugees given temporary haven at Fort Ontario, New York, the only large refugee group to be granted asylum inside the United States during the war; her reports, which grew out of her personal relations with the refugees, helped change government policy. Both Gruber and Rukeyser insisted on the essential unity between personal experience, artistic concerns, and social and international problems. Rebellious, articulate, and committed, they were feminists who went against the grain of a conventional, domestic era. At moments fraught with personal and political significance throughout their lives, each identified with, and relied upon, Jewish tradition.

Born in 1911, Gruber was the daughter of East European immigrants who ran a liquor store in the "shtetl" of Williamsburg, Brooklyn. As such, her childhood was vastly different from Rukeyser's; Rukeyser was two years younger and considered her second-generation parents to be immigrants "from America." Muriel's father, Lawrence Rukeyser, a concrete salesman from Wisconsin who became partner in a sand-and-gravel company, and her mother, a former bookkeeper from Yonkers, enjoyed a comfortable lifestyle on the Upper West Side of Manhattan. Sent to the Ethical Culture School and then to Fieldston, Rukeyser grew up without "a trace of Jewish culture," not knowing what a Jew or Christian was. For Gruber, in contrast, "Jewishness was my home, and God sitting up in the sky, was my friend"; she grew up thinking that everyone in her neighborhood, and indeed the "whole world," was Jewish.[64]

Rukeyser's Jewish awakening coincided with her early adolescent rebellion.

For some years previous, her mother had turned from visiting museums to going to temple; for Rukeyser, the "religion of reassurance" that her mother discovered in the Reform synagogue had little meaning. Yet in temple, she read the Bible, and there discovered a personal connection: "Its clash and poetry and nakedness, its fiery vision of conflict resolved only in God, were true to me. . . ." While she repudiated organized religion, which she found "torpid and conservative," and wrestled with Judaism's ethics, still formless in her own life, the third aspect of religion—the "poetry and fire" of the Bible—was already becoming for her "a deepening source of power."[65]

In her twenties and thirties, as she sought to express her developing social conscience in her own writing, she would join the ethics together with the passion of the Jewish tradition in a poetry remarkable for its powerful, oracular voice.[66] Rukeyser's poetic stance was influenced by her growing involvement in world affairs. After two years at Vassar College, she had gone south to cover the trial of the Scottsboro Boys for Vassar's leftist *Student Review.* Like the Sacco and Vanzetti trial five years earlier, the conviction of nine young black men who had allegedly raped two white girls on a freight train in Scottsboro became a *cause célèbre* for American radicals; for Rukeyser, the death sentence meted out to apparently innocent men (and later overturned by the Supreme Court) symbolized the victimization of the weak by the powerful, and confirmed the racism inherent in American justice, made all the more real after her own arrest in Alabama for talking to black reporters.[67]

Because of the failure of her father's business during the Depression, Rukeyser did not return to Vassar; though she had been expected "to grow up and become a golfer, a suburban matron" after college, she now turned to full-time writing as a journalist, editor, and poet.[68] In 1935, when she was twenty-one, her first book, *Theory of Flight,* was published to critical acclaim in the Yale Series of Younger Poets; that year she also began work as associate editor of the magazine *New Theatre.* The following year, she traveled to West Virginia to investigate the deaths of hundreds of miners from silicon poisoning, a consequence of the mine owners' deliberate disregard for the workers' health. Her pathbreaking poetic narrative account of the tragedy, the *Book of the Dead,* which combined documentary evidence—including interviews with miners, Congressional hearings, and stock market printouts—with her own multivoiced, multisectioned poetry preceded James Agee and Walker Evans's classic indictment of poverty in Alabama, *Let Us Now Praise Famous Men,* by three years.[69]

But nothing was more significant to Rukeyser's development of a theory and practice of poetic witness than her experience during the Spanish Civil War. Rukeyser went to Spain in 1936 by accident, substituting for an editor of the British magazine *Life and Letters Today,* who had been assigned to cover the Anti-Fascist Olympics in Barcelona. On the day she and the Olympic teams landed, intense fighting broke out, and after five days, all nonessential foreigners were evacuated. "Now you have your responsibility," they were told. "Go home; tell your peoples what you have seen."[70] Exiled from the battle that had moved her profoundly, Rukeyser knew that she had work to do; the rebels' battle for freedom made an enduring impression that would inspire her poetry and her personal life. In Spain, Rukeyser also lost the German athlete she loved, killed while fighting with the loyalist forces. For decades she sought to express the personal and political meanings of warfare through her poetry. In a 1945 essay, she acknowledged that "war has been in my writing since I began."[71]

While Rukeyser was beginning her studies at Vassar, Ruth Gruber was completing undergraduate work at New York University in Manhattan, her "escape route" from the orthodoxies of Brooklyn. Gruber, too, began writing poetry, soon filling thick notebooks with anguished poems of "how I was squeezed like a sponge and would die if I didn't escape." Selecting German as a major, perhaps so that she could "driv[e] Yiddish out of [her] head," she received a graduate fellowship at the University of Wisconsin. Despite the troubling presence of anti-Semitism on the part of both students and faculty there, she completed a master's degree, then accepted a fellowship at the University of Cologne. Arriving in Germany in the fall of 1931, she witnessed the rise of Hitler and the spreading poison of anti-Semitism among the populace. As she attempted to write her dissertation on Virginia Woolf, Hitler's hysterical voice blared on the radio. In the streets, she saw the Nazi "thugs in brown shirts march . . . insolently, stopping pedestrians, halting traffic, screaming their curses: 'Death to the Jews—Weimar Republic. *Jude Verrecke* (Croak the Jews).' "[72]

By the following August, Gruber had defended her dissertation on Woolf's will to write as a woman—an unusual gender-based analysis for the time—and received her doctorate *mit sehr gut* (the German equivalent of magna cum laude). After the *Frankfurter Zeitung* ran an article trumpeting the fact that Gruber, at twenty, was the "youngest Ph.D. in the University of Cologne and the youngest Ph.D. in Germany," the *New York Times* picked up the story and ran its own feature, celebrating her achievement as the youngest Ph.D. in the "whole world."[73] She arrived home a celebrity, but in the midst of the Depression could not find a university position anywhere in the country. She turned instead to journalism, and was soon publishing articles for the *Times* and the *New York Herald Tribune*. In 1935, a travelling fellowship from the New Jersey Women's Clubs took her back to Germany as well as to England, France, the Netherlands, and the Soviet Union to write a comparative report on the condition of women under fascism, communism, and democracy.

Her experiences abroad would inform her future work. The first correspondent to penetrate the Soviet Arctic, she wired back to the *Tribune* a series of articles that highlighted women's pioneering role in Arctic exploration and later wrote a book about her experiences in the Arctic and the Gulag.[74] In

Britain, she obtained an interview with her literary idol, Virginia Woolf, to discuss the situation of women in Western democracies, but the meeting was brief and disappointing. Many years later, reading an account of the visit in Woolf's diaries, Gruber was shocked at the upper-class snobbery and apparent anti-Semitism of Woolf's mistaken and derogatory references to her as a "Gerwoman" and "German Jewess." Despite Gruber's admiration for Woolf's feminism, she could not excuse her prejudice, which was all the more surprising since Woolf was married to a Jew. "I had gone with her 'To the Lighthouse,' " she observed. "Now I was back."[75]

What she learned in Germany was more alarming; women had lost whatever gains they had made under the Weimar Republic and the Nazi menace had grown. Even Ruth's former lover, a poet, had joined the Party. When she went to visit the headquarters of the Jewish community in Berlin, a concerned leader, fearful for Gruber's safety, insisted that she leave the country immediately. She was given a mission very much like the one Rukeyser would receive when she was forced to leave Spain: "Go home to America and *scream,*" she was told. "Scream about what's happening here."[76]

Neither Rukeyser nor Gruber forgot her mandate to bear witness to the terrors of fascism. Gruber's opportunity came in 1944 when, as special assistant to Secretary of the Interior Harold Ickes, she was asked to accompany the group of one thousand refugees who President Roosevelt had announced would be brought over from Italy to be housed in a "temporary haven" at Fort Ontario, a former Army camp in Oswego, New York. Flying on a secret mission as a simulated "general" and accompanied by dozens of military officials, she arrived to greet the refugees on board the *Henry Gibbons* dressed all in white, "like an angel," as one of the waiting refugees recalled.[77] Gaining their trust despite her role as a government representative, Gruber abandoned journalistic objectivity and, trying "to feel as they felt, through every cell in my body," became a friend and counselor.[78] As their stories poured forth, she learned that every one of the nearly nine hundred Jewish passengers was alive as the result of a miracle. But she began to see something far more profound:

> That every Jew in the world was alive through a miracle. That since Egypt's Pharaoh, persecutors had tried to do to Jews what Hitler was now trying to do in Europe. Before Hitler, I was an innocent, convinced that some day there would be no more nationalism, no more racism, no more anti-Semitism. Hitler had taught me I was wrong. I became a "Hitler Jew" with three thousand years of history.[79]

In spite of the Jewish identity she had assumed automatically as a child and the experiences of anti-Semitism that helped alert her to the Jews' precarious status in Europe and the United States, Gruber had not yet made a deliberate commitment to any Jewish group, communal or religious, or to any social or political movement involving Jewish interests. Now, however, she experienced a "revelation":

I realized that even if we were born Jews, there was a moment in our lives when we *became* Jews. On this ship, I was becoming a Jew. . . . From this voyage on, I knew my life would forever be inextricably interlocked with Jews. . . .[80]

After the ship landed, she stayed on to help the refugees at Oswego, where the group was housed behind barbed wire and, except for children sent to local schools, prohibited from leaving the camp. Gruber played an essential role in ameliorating critical problems—labor disputes, conflicts among nationality groupings, depression, ill health, and idleness. She also persuaded the NCJW and NRS to underwrite classes for adults, with the result that over five hundred were able to study English and a variety of vocational subjects.

In a feature article, the *Jewish Daily Forward* highlighted Gruber's role "as guardian angel" at the camp. "They came to her," Gruber's mother boasted, "like she was a rebbe."[81] Gruber had long been a "maverick" to her parents, whose "highest ideal" for her was "to be a secretary or a schoolteacher." Gruber wrote: "In their Old World yearnings, I was a stranger who had invented myself." At Oswego, however, "for the first time, I was doing something they could understand. I was helping Jews."[82]

Gruber became a spokesperson for the refugees, documenting their stories and presenting them to government officials; in a report to Ickes, she called upon the government to reverse FDR's promise that the refugees would be returned to their countries of origin at war's end. She fought for the right of the refugees (her "family") to remain, and she fought against their growing demoralization. "Our Ruth is really like Moses," one refugee declared at a public meeting at the camp:

> Moses helped the Jews through the wilderness for forty years. But he couldn't see the Promised Land. Our Mother Ruth led us to Oswego—and sometimes it seems we have been there thirty, if not forty years. But that's where her role changes. She goes back and forth, but her children can't see the Promised Land.[83]

In late December 1945, President Truman finally issued a directive on the refugee problem that allowed the Oswego refugees to reenter the United States as displaced persons after first receiving visas in Canada; it was an unusual arrangement that the NCJW and NRS had helped to negotiate through a corporate affidavit from the agencies and the Jewish community guaranteeing the financial independence of the refugees.[84] As their representative and friend, Gruber had taken the refugees' stories to Congress, to the highest administration officials, and to the American public, helping to reverse a seemingly unshakable policy. While she still felt guilty, castigating herself and her friends for not doing enough ("Why didn't we scream?" she asked), she would remain connected to the Oswego refugees and, through her personal contacts, document their successful integration into American society.[85] Her shipboard commitment to Jewish causes was also expressed in a series of seven books she wrote on the state of Israel—including *Raquela,* a prize-winning study of women's lives in that country—and in a growing affiliation with the American and Israeli women's organization, Pioneer Women (now called Na'amat). Bearing witness to the struggles of the Jewish people, she could be satisfied that she had fulfilled the goal she set for herself in the mid-1930s when she returned from her second trip abroad:

> To write with my heart. To think and speak with my heart. To be adventurous, to be an activist, to be a rebel, to be compassionate, and most of all, to be a *mensch*— a decent human being.[86]

In the 1940s and 1950s, Rukeyser continued to write poetry that grew out of the resolve she had made in Alabama, West Virginia, and Spain to fight oppression with the truth of her words. At a time when some artists were retreating from politics in the face of the trauma of World War II and the disappointments of Marxism, her spirited poetry of social consciousness seemed increasingly out of sync. Continuing to regard poetry as a "fight" with which she could battle the evils of her time, Rukeyser attracted the scorn of the literary establishment, then steeped in the ironic detachment and ambiguity of the New Critics.[87]

The reaction to her 1942 poem "Wake Island" was typical. Rukeyser, who was then working in the poster division of the Office of War Information, intended it as a "public" poem: it was published as a pamphlet and sold for 50 cents. Described on the cover as "the first poem of major importance written about the war," it took as its subject the defense of Wake Island by a small garrison of Marines; in the poem she associated the Marines' stance with antifascist struggles throughout the world, fulfilling the mission she had been given on the boat leaving Spain.[88] Critics attacked the poem unmercifully; the *Partisan Review* printed an unsigned piece on Rukeyser entitled, "The Grandeur and Misery of a Poster Girl." Not only was the title "baldly sexist," as Rukeyser's biographer Louise Kertesz points out, but "it would be difficult to find a comment with more malice and distortion on any modern writer in a major publication. . . ." The piece, "replete with innuendoes, personal abuse, and sexism," attacked Rukeyser for her belief that the meaning of the war should be exhibited in popular art and for her attention to the role that women, including "Vassar girls," could play as alert public citizens.[89] In a subsequent issue the magazine published eloquent defenses of Rukeyser by such critics as F. O. Matthiessen. But in a final statement on the matter, *Partisan Review* editors Philip Rahv, William Phillips, and Delmore Schwartz savaged "Wake Island" and Rukeyser's *William Gibbs* as examples of "a neo-American inspirational literature" that sprang from "intellectual demoralization."[90] Even female critics like Louise Bogan derided "Wake Island's" "rhetorical hollowness" and Rukeyser generally for her alleged lack of "female lyricism." Rukeyser's poetry, says Kertesz, was "too bold . . . too sweeping and assertive" for her times, especially for a woman.[91]

As she developed her theory and practice of poetic witness in the 1940s, however, it was women and poets to whom Rukeyser assigned a visionary role. "Women and poets see the truth arrive," she wrote in her 1944 poem "Letter to the Front":

> All the strong agonized men
> Wear the hard clothes of war,
> Try to remember what they are fighting for.
> But in dark weeping helpless moments of peace
> Women and poets believe and resist forever. . . .

A later section of the poem places Jews in the category of those who, like women and poets, receive the "gift" of the human spirit, the power of prophecy and resistance:

> To be a Jew in the twentieth century
> Is to be offered a gift. If you refuse,
> Wishing to be invisible, you choose
> Death of the spirit, the stone insanity.

The gift, though a "torment," was the guarantee,

> For every human freedom, suffering to be free
> Daring to live for the impossible."[92]

Defining the meaning of resistance and the triumph of the Jewish spirit in the face of Hitler's Final Solution, Rukeyser's eloquent poem is now included in the Reform Jewish prayerbook.

Throughout her career, Rukeyser would continue to write "war poems" that bore the mark of the torments of the Spanish Civil War and World War II. After the 1950s, when she bared her personal life as a single mother and disappointed lover, the poems more than ever revealed the significance she attached to her identity as a woman; her faith in the artist as seer, and especially in the artist as activist, would also ripen over time. In *A Turning Wind,* she celebrated the life of Anne Burlak, the communist labor organizer whose "words live" despite the agonized lives of the workers for whom she spoke. In "Käthe Kollwitz," her poem about the German artist, women's power to speak and bear witness assumes mythic proportions:

> What would happen if one woman told the truth about her life?
> The world would split open.[93]

The figure of the woman and artist as hero-seer is combined with that of the Jew in "Searching/Not Searching." "What kind of woman goes searching and searching [for truth]?" she asks. Her answer is a woman who is a poet, like Miriam:

> I alone stand here
> ankle-deep
> and I sing, I sing,
> until the lands
> sing to each other."[94]

In her poem "Akiba," Rukeyser explicitly identifies with the Jewish hero Akiba, who she notes is "identified with the Song of Songs and with the insurrection against Hadrian's Rome, led in A.D. 132 by Bar Cochba [*sic*]." The story in her mother's family "is that we are descended from Akiba—unverifiable, but a great gift to a child."[95] Here her connections to her Jewish heritage become vital to the enterprise of witness. In the last section of the poem, entitled "The Witness," she asks readers (whom she calls "witnesses") to take her poems into their lives, as she has taken the legend of Akiba into her own, and break the destructive habit of silence. The world could be transformed, she insists, by connecting to others, by speech and the witness of poetry.

Following her identification with Akiba as Jewish revolutionary poet, Rukeyser's poetry, and her life, became more explicitly concerned with political speech itself. In the 1960s and 1970s, she wrote poetry in opposition to the Vietnam War and protested with her person. In 1972, she was arrested with members of Redress, a movement of Concerned Clergy and Laymen, for acts of civil disobedience in Washington. Her defense was what she called the "Nuremberg Obligation":

> The wars say it to us—all of Europe, all of Vietnam—and
> Nuremberg: never wait to speak against these horrors.
> To act against these horrors
> Do not let them be abstract and distant.
> They look at you with human eyes. . . .[96]

"To remember the death of the Jews," all people had "to bear witness, to protest" so that "the horrors—and the abstraction"—of war became personal. Before the feminist movement adopted "the personal is political" as its slogan, Rukeyser seemed to say that "if we look long enough and hard enough . . . we will begin to see the connections that bind us together, and when we recognize those connections, we will begin to change the world."[97]

Rukeyser's life and career brought together the immediacy of protest as witness, the urge to stand accountable and speak the truth about social and political crimes, especially as Jews, women, and artists. Though derided in her own time, she pioneered a type of "witness poetry" that is quite popular today. Writing about her credo for a roundtable of Jewish writers in 1944, she explained that her themes "and the use I have made of them have depended on my life as a poet, as a woman, as an American, and as a Jew." While she could not isolate "what part of that is Jewish," she had tried to integrate the four aspects, and "to solve my work and my personality in terms of all four. . . ." Rukeyser concluded with a statement integrating the multiple aspects of her identity: "To live as poet, woman, American and Jew—this chalks in my position. If the four come together in one person, each strengthens the other."[98]

Having, like Ruth Gruber, deliberately chosen her connection to Judaism, Rukeyser, again like Gruber, lived her life as a compassionate "activist . . . rebel . . . and . . . *mensch.*" In their insistence that women had the power to change the world through the force of their shared feelings, open communications, and personal witness against violence and war, both women joined such leaders of the Jewish women's movement as Rose Jacobs and Cecilia Razovsky in demonstrating that the theatre of the world was in fact women's place.

Chapter 8

IMAGINING JEWISH MOTHERS

Cold War Comedies and Tragedies: Gertrude Berg and Ethel Rosenberg

For most Americans, and not least for American Jews, the postwar period represented a paradoxical time in political as well as popular culture. Recovering from the Depression and World War II, Jews continued their move into the mainstream of American life, enjoying unprecedented economic prosperity and a great increase in opportunities for education, the professions, and business.[1]

Yet troubling signs rippled the smooth surface of Jewish acculturation. Despite its decline, anti-Semitism remained a significant factor in American life, with almost sixty known anti-Semitic organizations operating in 1950.[2] Also ominous was the association of American Jews in the public mind with the menace of communism, an association fostered by the trial and conviction of Ethel and Julius Rosenberg. Although the trial did not trigger the kind of virulent anti-Semitic tirades that many Jewish leaders had feared, the anxiety it caused among Jews suggested that they were perhaps not as at home in America as they had believed.

The polar experiences of American Jews in the 1950s—their spectacular arrival in the American mainstream coupled with lingering fears of anti-Semitism and doubts about Jewish acculturation—are represented by two famous Jewish women of the time: the cherubic, smiling Molly Goldberg, the radio and TV sitcom heroine of the long-running series "The Goldbergs," and the taut, drawn, unsmiling Ethel Greenglass Rosenberg herself.

Although a fictional character, Molly Goldberg was played with such verisimilitude by Gertrude Berg—in fact an American-born, middle-class Jew—that the public easily confused the mythical Molly with her real-life impersonator. Berg, who also created the character, lived a very different life from that of Molly Goldberg. Yet Molly/Gertrude was powerful in popular culture precisely because she ostensibly represented reality. Molly's character, tied to Gertrude Berg, not only mobilized the cultural power of a "real" person but, in some sense, became a real person.[3] In much the same way that Molly Goldberg enjoyed a reality independent of Gertrude Berg, so did the media representations of Ethel Greenglass Rosenberg came to dominate public perceptions of the real Ethel. Yet the flesh-and-blood Rosenberg differed as much from the media's Ethel as Gertrude did from Molly.

Second-generation daughters of East European immigrant families, Gertrude Berg and Ethel Rosenberg exemplify the changing aspirations, and the changing representations, of Jewish women in the 1950s. Both women defied convention: Gertrude, by building a media career and directing and producing a long-running hit series, all the while managing her own household and family life; Ethel, by combining a staunch commitment to radical ideology with a conscientious, even obsessive, motherhood. For a generation or more, however, the cultural construction of "Molly" and "Ethel" has left little room for imagining the full historical matrix in which Gertrude and Ethel lived their lives. The potent alliance between media and politics that characterized the Red Scare years obliterated all but the masks of Molly and Ethel.[4]

Molly and Ethel were not the only representations of Jewish women in the politicized culture of the 1950s. Another archetypal middle-class Jewish woman of the decade was "Shirley," a type made famous by Herman Wouk in his 1955 novel, *Marjorie Morningstar.* Selling millions of copies and made into a successful movie starring the popular actress Natalie Wood, the book depicted the transformation of a young, ambitious, "emancipated" Jewish girl into a conventional suburban matron, a Shirley. Rebellious as a youth, Marjorie/Shirley matured into "the respectable girl, the mother of the next generation, all tricked out to appear gay and girlish and carefree but with a terrible threatening dullness jutting through"; later Marjorie/Shirley became a "regular synagogue goer, active in the Jewish organizations of the town," a model, in fact, of the many thousands of Jewish women who belonged to temple sisterhoods, Hadassah, the National Council of Jewish Women, and similar organizations.[5] While Wouk treats Shirley sympathetically, Mrs. Patimkin, the Shirley-like Jewish mother in Philip Roth's 1959 novella, *Goodbye Columbus,* is portrayed as vain, empty-headed, materialistic.[6] Her daughter, Brenda, demonstrating the worst qualities of 1950s suburban Jewish affluence, joined Marjorie Morningstar as one in a series of indelible images of a new kind of Jewish heroine—assimilated, smoothly confident, flirtatious, beautiful, spoiled. Together with Ethel and Molly, these fictional representations would provide enduring images of Jewish American womanhood—mothers and daughters, protectors and princesses—that would wield more power and influence than their creators could ever have expected.

Yet these images do not do justice to the varied experiences of Jewish women in postwar America. The activism demonstrated by such groups as the National Council of Jewish Women and the Emma Lazarus Federation of

Jewish Women's Clubs (a left-wing group created after the Holocaust by a group of largely Yiddish-speaking women of the immigrant generation) belies the homogeneity of the period and demonstrates that "Molly," "Ethel," and "Shirley" were cultural constructs after all.

So Basically True a Character   "The Rise of the Goldbergs" was one of the most popular serials in radio's golden era, running from 1929 through 1946, and then from 1949 to 1950. After 1931, the show aired nightly, for some years carried by both the CBS and NBC networks. In 1946, the show (known as "The Goldbergs") made the transition to television, running through 1955. It was revived in the early 1960s as "Mrs. G," a new series about Molly at college. Along the way there were also a comic strip, a syndicated column ("Mamatalks"), a published version of the show's early scripts, a cookbook, a hit Broadway play (*Me and Molly*), two films, and Berg's autobiography, *Molly and Me.* So identified was Gertrude Berg with Molly Goldberg that she signed autographs in the character's name. Yet it was Berg, the consummate professional, who wrote as well as starred in the show's five thousand-plus radio scripts as well as the later television programs.

During the second quarter of the twentieth century, Molly Goldberg became the quintessential representation of the American Jewish mother in popular culture. "Kind-hearted," "humane," "gentle," "gracious," "sympathetic," and "tender"—these were the words typically used in advertisements for the show—Molly Goldberg, like her creator Gertrude Berg, was nonetheless a woman of force and dominance; her co-stars considered Berg a Napoleon on the set. Berg's genius was to wed the iron qualities of traditional East European Jewish women with a charm and humor that counteracted the threat of their power. During the Depression, when a negative stereotype of the Jewish mother as materialistic and pushy began to appear in the works of Clifford Odets and other Jewish male writers, Berg's Molly had a more positive appeal.[7]

Molly's compassion and the comic elements in her character diverted attention from other, potentially troublesome traits. At best meddlesome and at worst nagging and controlling, Molly got her way in almost every show, but always for the purpose of helping others. Molly's speech, full of malapropisms, reflected her status as an immigrant whose eagerness to adopt American usages was greater than her knowledge: "Come sit on the table, dinner is ready . . . You'll swallow a cup, darling? . . . Throw an eye into the ice-box and give me an accounting. . . ."[8] Molly's generosity and the quaintness of her language—including the famous opening line of the show, "Yoo hoo Mrs. Bloom," which she yelled out the window to her tenement neighbor—endeared her to audiences.

No matter how exaggerated, caricatured, or sentimental the show's characters, to audiences they seemed believable and realistic. Writing in 1951, novelist Charles Angoff praised the show for its realistic representation of "virtually the whole panorama of middle-class Jewish-American life":

> There are the neighbors who borrow from and lend to one another, and who offer advice, whether asked or not . . . there are the sisters and cousins and aunts, with all their jealousies and bickerings and generosities and meddlings . . . the young folk who sometimes think they have "outgrown" their parents but who find that for comfort and counsel there are no substitutes for these same parents . . . the widowed cousin or aunt with an only daughter who is still unmarried . . . the widower uncle who is obsessively proud of his son the doctor or the lawyer or the accountant, but in whose house he cannot live happily . . . the miserly relatives who are not at all aware of their miserliness; . . . the teen-age daughter, blossoming out into young womanhood, and who sorely needs grown-up advice, which she rejects as soon as it is given . . . the perpetually complaining mother-in-law; . . . and there is Molly herself, whose heart bleeds for every unmarried girl and starving butcher and lonely grocer, and who is as quick as the proverbial lightning in concocting ideas to get the "right" girl and the "right" man together, to straighten out family squabbles, to help out a reformed thief, to get her own son to invite her to a college affair—in short, Molly the Mixer and the Fixer.

Together these characters presented "neurotic tensions, despair, ecstasy, conniving, kindliness, back-biting . . . the normal life of Bronx and Brooklyn and Manhattan and Chicago and Boston and Philadelphia and San Francisco Jews." Angoff concluded: "I have never heard anyone who knows Jewish life say that 'The Goldbergs' are not true to life. Molly Goldberg, indeed, is so basically true a character that I sometimes think she may become an enduring name in the national literature. She is the prototype of the Jewish mother during the past twenty-five years."[9]

A good part of the praise for "The Goldbergs" was due to its uplifting message about American family life and moral values. Berg once described the show to a reporter, using Molly's lines: "Jake wants the children to have everything money can buy, and I want them to have everything money can't buy."[10] This philosophical difference formed the core of the show's dramatic conflict, and despite the Goldbergs' upward mobility, it was always resolved in Molly's favor. Listeners found the message of "The Goldbergs" inspirational: ministers composed sermons around the program, and at least one Orthodox rabbi instructed congregants not to turn their radios off on Friday afternoon, so that they could listen to Molly on Shabbos evening "without breaking the law."[11] During wartime, especially, the show received accolades as "a force for decency and the democratic way of life."[12]

Three points stand out regarding the Molly Goldberg character. First, Molly as a Jewish mother was an odd but lovable, generous woman who solved all the problems of her family, neighborhood, and community through her skillful "mixing-in." She was a voluble, talkative busybody, a *balaboste,* but one with a loving heart who could always be trusted to do the right thing.

The second point is that in spite of her ethnicity, which was always prominent (even when the use of dialect subsided), Molly and her children espoused assimilationist values. Over the decades, the audience saw the family leave their Bronx neighborhood, move to the suburbs, and send the children off to college. In this respect, "The Goldbergs" was an accurate representation of the Jewish middle-class's entry into the American mainstream. Despite the family's economic transformation, Molly herself changed very little. Even in the mid-1950s, she looked and sounded like a newly arrived immigrant; in this respect, Molly remained in a television time warp.[13]

The third point is that as the Goldbergs became America's surrogate family, Molly became everybody's mother, a woman who, *because* of her ethnicity (that is, her difference), represented the American ideal of brotherly love and interreligious cooperation. This point was borne out in the huge amount of fan mail Berg received and in the accolades from non-Jewish as well as Jewish organizations.

In order to achieve such wide acceptance in both mainstream and Jewish audiences, Berg made a conscious decision, as she told one reporter, not to bring in

> anything that will bother people . . . unions, politics, fundraising, Zionism, socialism, intergroup relations, I don't stress them. After all, aren't such things second to daily living? The Goldbergs are not defensive about their Jewishness, or especially aware of it. I keep things average. I don't want to lose friends.[14]

Like other situation comedies of the 1950s, "The Goldbergs" portrayed the family as a sea of domestic tranquillity—a "suburban middle landscape," according to one critic—isolated from problems in the larger society. Sitcoms were "Cold War comedies of reassurance," in which politics, "by its telling absence . . . was a contaminating force to be kept beyond the threshold of the private household."[15] In shows like "Leave It to Beaver," "Father Knows Best," "The Adventures of Ozzie and Harriet," "The Donna Reed Show," "I Remember Mama," and "Make Room for Daddy/The Danny Thomas Show," television reinforced values of family togetherness—responsibility, maturity, adjustment, and "enlightened permissiveness."[16] In most of these comedies, it was not the maternal figure but the benevolent patriarch who navigated his family through the shoals of neighborhood life. Yet Molly Goldberg's affable, homespun wisdom, like that of the Norwegian mother in "I Remember Mama" (played by Peggy Wood), was no less authoritative than that of her male counterparts. As women in command of a vast repository of folk wisdom, Berg and Wood steered their families through the special challenges of modern American life, while demonstrating for the television audience that conflict could be easily managed and contained if "normal" family values were upheld.

But this is not the whole story. Gertrude Berg could eliminate controversy from her show, but not from her life. Philip Loeb, who played Molly's husband, Jake, on radio in the late 1940s and took the character to TV in 1949, was a victim of the blacklist in 1950. After a debate with her sponsors (who eventually pulled out), Gertrude Berg succumbed and fired Loeb in 1952; he committed suicide three years later. Comedian Milton Berle reveals in his memoirs that in 1950, when Berg was "fighting the witch-hunters" who had "enough juice to hurt [her] in every way," his sponsors and NBC would not permit Berg to appear on his show, even though she had her own. According to scholar Donald Weber, it is possible that Berg, a member of an actors' group that included many well-known left-wing artists such as Paul Robeson, was herself the target of a blacklist.[17]

The portrait of Molly Goldberg as the ideal Jewish mother of the 1950s may thus have clashed with the reality of Gertrude Berg's own politics; it certainly contrasted with the fact of her career. Married and the mother of two children, Berg had grown up writing skits to amuse the guests at her parents' summer hotel in the Catskills. Even after marriage and motherhood, she was determined to pursue her career as a writer, but the short stories she submitted to popular magazines all came back with rejection slips. Then came her breakthrough in a trial run of "Goldberg" scripts, written for radio. Almost immediately, Berg became a highly successful media entrepreneur. She was no Molly Goldberg, stay-at-home housewife, though she prided herself on her "normal" family life.

Berg's decision to eschew politics and what she described as "defensive" Jewishness reflected a common strategy of leading Jewish organizations of the period. In the late 1940s and the 1950s, these groups embarked on new ventures designed to counteract the forces of bigotry and enhance interreligious and interethnic harmony. Rather than responding exclusively to direct threats to American Jewry, they took action on a panoply of social and cultural concerns, including opposition to McCarthyism and the promotion of civil rights and the ideals of the welfare state.[18] "The Goldbergs," with its exhortation to celebrate human brotherhood and its conscious disregard of difference, mirrored these objectives.

The example of compassionate concern that Molly Goldberg demonstrated to her Christian friends and neighbors was embodied in the postwar program of the National Council of Jewish Women. In 1947, the NCJW introduced a new initiative on "intercultural relations." The initiative, entitled "cultural democracy," exposed the flaws in the idea of the melting pot and championed the free expression of cultural differences. "Something good is lost when people are melted down to a uniform consistency," the NCJW asserted; it was the "diversity of [many] cultures which make the American society strong."[19] According to the NCJW, the prophetic imperative to brotherhood and other Judaic teachings made "the universal concern for all people" a guide for American Jews. But the Council insisted that it was an American as well as a Jewish obligation to eradicate intolerance. "Jews have always participated fully in American life as Jews and as Americans who feel the obligations implicit in Americanism," the NCJW stated.[20]

To counteract prejudice, Council leaders told chapters to begin with their own. In order to feel accepted by dominant social groups, Jews sometimes had a tendency to adopt their biases. Wrote the NCJW:

> When we achieve a minimum of acceptance within the community, we often tend to take on the prejudice and discrimination of the community, not necessarily against our own group, but against racial and minority groups who have incurred the displeasure of the dominant groups. Our guilt is the greater because we fail to realize that in showing prejudice against any minority group we endanger all, including our own. When and if society turns against its minorities, it turns against them all, the Negro, the Catholic, and the Jew.[21]

Recognizing prejudice was, however, not sufficient to eradicate it. Council leaders argued that it was crucial to be " 'good neighbors,' understanding and respecting our fellow citizens of different racial and religious backgrounds." For this purpose, chapters were instructed to work with other local groups on such issues as eliminating stereotypes and stimulating public interest in building better intercultural understanding.[22] But it was equally important to develop a positive program of action, seeking "economic and social justice" for all people regardless of their race, religion, or national origin.[23] For this reason, the NCJW extended the project on interfaith harmony beyond such local issues as schools, housing, and citizenship to include broad questions of public policy, social legislation, and even international affairs, all of which it considered integral to intercultural work. During the 1950s, the NCJW promoted these objectives through public education and lobbying on behalf of such causes as immigration reform and civil rights.[24]

In 1952, the NCJW launched a related project, the Freedom Campaign, designed to educate the public to the importance of civil liberties and to encourage people in "speaking up for what they believe is right" while "respecting the beliefs of others." Declaring its staunch opposition to communism, the NCJW also declared war on Senator McCarthy and the House Un-American Activities Committee's "campaign of vilification" against "everyone who has ever held an original idea or participated in the activities of a minority group."[25] Over the next year, it enlisted numerous organizations in joint initiatives on the local and national levels to secure "freedom" against the forces of reaction. The Council formed a special alliance with the Young Women's Christian Association (YWCA) in this campaign.[26]

The common ground of racial and religious tolerance that guided NCJW's postwar intercultural effort was specifically acknowledged in 1961, when the council and the YWCA came together again to commemorate the fiftieth anniversary of both organizations' initial commitment to seek public policy protection for working women and children. At a public ceremony addressed by Eleanor Roosevelt, the two groups presented awards to several outstanding women, including Rose Schneiderman, the organizer and president of the New York Women's Trade Union, and Mary Anderson, the first director of the Women's Bureau.[27] The groups also issued a ten-point "Code of Personal Commitment," stressing opposition to prejudice, protection of individual liberties, and efforts toward world peace. "I will cultivate objectivity of thought/ And will consider new and different points of view," the statement read. "I will recognize my common kinship with all/and remember that whatever happens to anyone happens to me."[28]

Despite the NCJW's freedom campaign and its dedication to protecting the rights of political dissidents and racial, religious, and ethnic minorities, the Council, like Gertrude Berg herself, had little to say about the Rosenberg case or Ethel Rosenberg as a Jewish woman.

Not a Good Mother After All   Like Gertrude Berg, Ethel Rosenberg aspired to an artistic career, although it was as a singer and actress, rather than a writer, that she hoped to make her mark.[29] An excellent student at Seward Park High School on Manhattan's Lower East Side, Ethel planned to attend college and took college preparatory courses. Graduating in 1931 at the height of the Depression, however, she felt lucky to obtain a clerical job with the National New York Shipping and Packing Company. The Clark House Players, an amateur theater group sponsored by a settlement house around the corner from her home, was the object of most of her enthusiasm over the next few years; she also took acting classes at the Henry Street Settlement and attended lectures by members of several experimental theater companies. At nineteen, Ethel was accepted into the prestigious Schola Cantorum, becoming the choir's youngest member; the group occasionally sang at the Metropolitan Opera House. The following year, singing an operatic solo at a benefit for the International Seamen's Union, Ethel met Julius Rosenberg, who claimed she had the most beautiful voice he had ever heard. They were married three years later.

Ethel pursued her singing and acting interests only sporadically after her marriage. Her independent involvement in political action also declined. Before meeting Julius, she had helped to organize the Ladies Apparel Shipping Clerks Union at her company, serving as the only woman on a four-person strike committee that called a citywide action in which over 10,000 workers participated. Fired for her role in this strike, Ethel brought a complaint before the newly formed National Labor Relations Board; the case was later decided in her favor. By this time, she had found employment as a stenographer with

Bell Textile Company. She left this job after Julius found work with the United States Signal Corps, turning her attention to volunteer activities. Among the groups she joined were the women's auxiliary of her husband's union—the Federation of Architects, Engineers, Chemists and Technicians (FAECT)—and, after the start of World War II, the Lower East Side Defense Council.

After the births of her sons—Michael in 1943 and Robert four years later—Rosenberg became increasingly absorbed in family matters. According to one neighbor, she was "literally a mother 24 hours out of 24."[30] But motherhood did not come as easily to Ethel as it did to Molly Goldberg and Gertrude Berg. Beset by physical ailments resulting from chronic scoliosis and the emotional strain of dealing with young children, she grew increasingly concerned about her parenting skills. Setting limits for her children—responding to them with both the generosity and the authority that she felt good parenting entailed—was especially problematic; the importance of these qualities was continually being emphasized in the pages of *Parents Magazine,* which Rosenberg read religiously, and in the vastly popular performances of Gertrude Berg. Seeking guidance, Rosenberg took a course on child psychology at the New School for Social Research and enlisted the help of a social worker at the Jewish Board of Guardians; soon afterward, she began to see a private psychiatrist. Though she deeply loved and respected Julius, he could not alleviate her anxieties about raising their sons. Despite their political radicalism, both accepted the gender role division that allotted breadwinning responsibilities to the husband and child rearing to the wife. "The good mother is the key to proper child rearing," Rosenberg wrote to her lawyer, Manny Bloch, after she had been arrested and imprisoned along with Julius on charges of conspiracy to commit espionage.[31]

In view of Rosenberg's faith in communism, her resorting to psychoanalysis and social work may seem surprising. But Rosenberg's worries as a mother apparently overshadowed any doubts she may have had about succumbing to such capitalist opiates. In the emphasis she placed on child rearing, Rosenberg was in fact not far removed from Molly Goldberg. Whether she read Gertrude Berg's advice column in the 1930s, or listened to any of the Goldberg shows on radio or TV, is unknown, but her idea of what characterized the "good" mother certainly overlapped with Berg's portrayal of Molly as understanding, tolerant, generous—everything Rosenberg's own mother, Tessie Greenglass, was not.

Tessie Greenglass was an unhappy, troubled woman, disappointed in her husband's lack of ambition and inability to move the family out of poverty. Unlike the Goldbergs or the Bergs, the Greenglasses never realized their dream of American success; Tessie's frustrations with this failure were apparently visited on her only daughter. Favoring her three sons, especially the youngest, David, she treated Rosenberg with disrespect bordering on cruelty;

certainly Rosenberg was abused emotionally (and sometimes physically, since Tessie used corporal punishment on all the children). Despite (or because of) Rosenberg's excellence at school and her good-girl demeanor at home, she was also the butt of her brothers' jealousy; she was very much the scapegoat of the entire family.[32]

When, years later, David Greenglass accused Ethel and Julius of masterminding the spy ring in which he was allegedly involved at Los Alamos, Rosenberg was not surprised that her mother accepted her brother's story rather than her own. But the extent of her mother's lack of support for her, and for her children, hurt Rosenberg enormously. When Tessie first visited Rosenberg in prison it was only to scream at her for harming David and to call her a "dirty Communist."[33] After Rosenberg was transferred to solitary confinement at Sing Sing, Tessie did not visit her at all for two years; when she finally did it was only to urge her daughter to confess. Rosenberg responded angrily, but admitted to her lawyer that she would "still give anything in the world for one kind word from her." Tessie returned two months before Rosenberg's execution to insist again that she affirm her brother's account and admit her guilt. According to the prison official who was present, Rosenberg, enraged, called her mother a "witch" and "yelled and raved to such an extent that she was cautioned by the guard that the interview would be terminated unless she quieted down."[34] That was the last time Rosenberg saw Tessie.

No doubt Rosenberg's troubled relationship with her mother accounted in good part for her concerns about her own parenting. But her anxieties about her performance as a mother and her children's emotional well-being were also the product of cultural messages that she, like others with her background and aspirations, absorbed from the surrounding culture. Under the growing influence of child guidance specialists and behavioral psychologists, parenting in the late 1940s and early 1950s became more than ever a matter of expert counseling and knowledge rather than innate capability. During these years, the notion of motherhood as "pathology" was a staple in both the popular and scientific press, with all manner of experts holding mothers accountable for withdrawn, destructive, disturbed, and "deviant" children.[35] If Ethel Rosenberg blamed herself for child-rearing problems—however normal—she was merely reflecting the accepted wisdom. Rosenberg's faith in professional child guidance in fact illuminates why Molly Goldberg was so popular a figure in the postwar period. In representing an earlier time, when parents dominated their children's lives and truly "knew best," sitcoms like "The Goldbergs" provided nostalgic reassurance to a generation increasingly troubled about the viability of a harmonious family life in the context of a pluralistic society. Rosenberg's concern about her own family, and her employment of therapy for herself and counseling for the children, suggests how deeply a part of her generation she was.

In spite of her intense concerns about her children, Ethel Rosenberg's behavior during her trial convinced the jurors and the American public that she was guilty—not because of the evidence, but because she lacked "maternal feeling." That Rosenberg was arrested and tried as a "lever" to force her husband to talk is now well documented. Based wholly on the testimony of her brother David Greenglass and his wife, Ruth, the case was "not too strong against Mrs. Rosenberg," as one prosecutor acknowledged privately. Such doubts continued after Ethel's conviction and remain today, even though Julius's guilt now appears certain. "Was your wife cognizant of your activities?" prosecutors asked Julius Rosenberg in a questionnaire submitted to him at the Sing-Sing Death House.[36] Given the paucity of evidence regarding her participation in the conspiracy, Ethel Rosenberg's appearance at the trial became all-important.

To the public, Rosenberg's failure to break down under the pressure of her arrest and trial appeared to confirm that she cared more about ideology than about her offspring, and was therefore guilty. Her denial of guilt, along with her repeated reliance on the Fifth Amendment, created the impression, according to one legal scholar, of a "cold, well-composed woman lacking 'normal' feminine characteristics."[37] Because of her failure to lose her composure on the witness stand (both her husband his co-defendant, Morton Sobell, appeared much more uneasy), Rosenberg seemed enigmatic, "unnatural." To the jury foreman she was a "steely, stoney, tight-lipped woman. She was the mastermind. Julius would have spoken if she would have permitted him. He was more human. She was more disciplined."[38] According to another juror, she was certainly guilty—of being a bad mother: "I had two daughters at the time, and it bothered me how they would subject their children to such a thing. I just couldn't understand it."[39]

After the Rosenbergs were convicted and sentenced to death, the image of Ethel as an "unnatural" woman and mother blocked appeals for clemency. FBI director J. Edgar Hoover used the fact of Rosenberg's failure to talk with her own mother for two years as evidence of her evil nature; when Douglas Dillon, then ambassador to France, protested the severity of her sentence compared to those of convicted British spies Klaus Fuchs and Allan Nunn May, Hoover reported that when Tessie Greenglass urged Rosenberg to confess to spare her children, Rosenberg had rebuked her with the words, "Don't mention the children. Children are born every day of the week."[40] Although he had previously opposed the execution of Ethel as well as Julius on the grounds that it would leave two young children orphaned, Hoover changed his mind after receiving the FBI's report that "Ethel was not a good mother after all."[41] President Eisenhower used similar gender-based reasoning in his denial of clemency: "In this instance, it is the woman who is the strong and recalcitrant character, the man who is the weak one." He believed that as the unquestioned "leader in the spy ring," Ethel Rosenberg had renounced all rights to special treatment as a woman and mother of two young children.[42] She was the first American woman to be executed for the crime of conspiracy to commit espionage.

No greater contrast could exist than that between the Molly Goldberg ideal of the 1950s—friendly, garrulous, kindhearted, family-oriented, non-controversial, and nonpolitical—and the public image of Ethel Rosenberg: silent and mysterious, conspiratorial and political, dominating and evil. Blindly loyal to her husband at the cost of abandoning her own children, she seemed, above all—and perhaps most dangerously—a neglectful, uncaring mother.[43] Many Americans who loved Molly Goldberg were deeply shocked by Ethel Rosenberg.

This portrait of Ethel Rosenberg, elaborated in the media, was especially troubling to Jews.[44] In contrast to the Goldbergs, with their seamless adjustment to American society, the Rosenbergs appeared as an alien couple linked to a foreign power; their rejection of mainstream American values, such as those espoused by the Goldbergs and other TV sitcom families, spoke to the dark underside of the American dream and enhanced the presumption of guilt. Moreover, in contrast to the wholesome Goldberg family ("Allow me to ask whether in Jewish families nothing ever goes wrong," one viewer wrote to ask. "Is it always 'Papa darling' and 'Mama darling'? . . . no wrangling, no quibbling?") the Rosenberg family was fatally divided between brothers and sister, mother and daughter.[45] In the early 1950s, when such a family was not yet labeled "dysfunctional," the Rosenbergs seemed not only abnormal but un-American. For Jews who prided themselves on the closeness of their family ties, the portrait was a devastating reminder—and one that all of America could witness at first hand—that, for all their supposed warmth and closeness, they could not escape the centrifugal forces that were pulling modern family life apart.

That the Molly Goldberg ideal coincided with the aspirations of the real Ethel Rosenberg was no more ironic than the fact that Ethel—a woman excessively concerned about mothering—was portrayed by government officials and the media as a cold, uncaring "monster" of a mother. Ethel's convincing stoicism in the face of her most enormous loss—that of her children—may have been her finest performance.

Creating a Jewish Women's History: Clara Lemlich Shavelson and the Emmas

One of the few Jewish organizations to challenge the government's case against Ethel Rosenberg was the Emma Lazarus Federation of Jewish Women's Clubs, which had grown out of the response by largely left-wing working-class women to the Holocaust.[46] Established in 1944 as an offshoot of the Jewish People's Fraternal Order of the International Workers Order, the

"Emmas," as they called themselves, took as their model the poet Emma Lazarus, whom they viewed as a Jewish-identified champion of human rights and a feminist. One of the founders of the group was Clara Lemlich Shavelson, a consumer advocate and Communist Party organizer who in her youth had sparked the momentous garment workers' strike of 1909–1910 by spontaneously calling for a general walkout.[47] A vigorous defender of Ethel Rosenberg, Shavelson embodied the multiple and shifting identities of Federation members: although they supported the universalist goals of working-class radicalism, they increasingly identified themselves as Jewish partisans and especially, self-consciously, as Jewish women.

Clara Lemlich Shavelson was born in 1886 in the town of Gorodok in the Ukraine, the daughter of an Orthodox Jewish scholar who ran a grocery store. The Lemlichs left their home in 1903, fleeing the Kishinev pogrom. After a few months in England, the family arrived in the United States; two weeks later, Clara found a job in the garment shops. In 1906, she became one of the founding members of Waistmakers Local 25, affiliated with the fledgling ILGWU, then largely an organization of male cloakmakers. Clara took part in a succession of bitter strikes, and was once beaten up on the picket line. She was already a seasoned strike veteran when the waistmakers gathered at Cooper Union in November 1909.

After the waistmakers' strike, Clara served as a delegate to union conventions, a member of the executive boards of Local 25 and the Women's Trade Union League, an outspoken socialist, and a tireless organizer of women workers. As a working-class proponent of women's suffrage, she spoke frequently on the importance of the vote and its relation to the labor movement.

In 1913, Lemlich married Joseph Shavelson, a printer and union activist. The couple had three children, a son and two daughters. Struggling to make ends meet on Joseph's $17-a-week salary, they shared a home with his sister and her family on DeKalb Avenue in Brownsville, Brooklyn, then a Jewish immigrant community with an activist tradition; Clara Shavelson returned to work in a tie shop on the ground floor of her sister's building when her oldest child was two. She also resumed her organizing activities, becoming a familiar figure on neighborhood street corners. Shavelson's goal was to mobilize housewives around consumer and housing issues that affected the quality of working-class life. In 1917, she participated in a series of citywide riots and a boycott against the purveyors of kosher meat to protest its high price. In 1919, she helped organize tenants in a rent strike to protest high housing costs; that same year, she became a charter member of the U.S. Communist Party. In 1926, she helped found the United Council of Working Class Housewives, a consumer-based group organized to supplement the party's industrial organizing.

In the early 1930s, the Shavelsons moved to the working-class community of Brighton Beach, where Clara established the area's first Unemployment

Council and organized hunger marches, rent and food strikes, and kitchens for the jobless. She also participated in a neighborhood tenant council named after Emma Lazarus. In 1935, the United Council of Working Women became the Progressive Women's Council. Though the Council never intended to become exclusively Jewish, most members were Jewish immigrants; like Shavelson, many had been involved in the garment union before marriage. During the Depression, the Council organized housewives to bring down food and housing costs; a 1935 meat boycott organized by Shavelson and Rose Nelson Raynes brought Shavelson to Washington to confront Secretary of Agriculture Henry Wallace, and spread to dozens of cities.[48]

Shavelson ran unsuccessfully for State Assembly on the Communist Party ticket in the early 1930s; she was the only female candidate. It was one of the rare times, her daughter recalled, that her mother purchased a new dress.[49] In 1944, with her husband's health declining, Shavelson returned to the garment industry as a hand-finisher in a cloak shop on 38th Street, joining Local 9. She remained there for almost a decade.

Shavelson was an activist in the fight against fascism as well. In 1934, she attended the first International Women's Congress Against War and Fascism in Paris, travelling afterward to the Soviet Union. Upon her return, she lectured on the Soviet Union to the Progressive Women's Council, which she served as educational director. She became a familiar figure on Brighton Beach street corners, rallying workers against Hitler.

By World War II, the Progressive Women's Council, of which Shavelson was then president, had merged with the women's clubs of the Jewish People's Fraternal Order (JPFO) of the International Workers Order (IWO), a fraternal benefit insurance company formed after a split in the Workmen's Circle (the Arbeiter Ring) between the centrist "Forward Socialist" and the left-wing "progressive" radicals, who were friendly to the Soviet Union; nearly eight thousand of the latter left the Circle in early 1930 to form the IWO as a new "proletarian" fraternal organization.[50] After 1936, with the encouragement of the Communist Party (now in its Popular Front phase), the IWO launched a massive recruitment effort among immigrant workers. The Party's support of ethnic awareness and pride, coupled with its active campaign against domestic anti-Semitism, made it attractive to Jews; by 1939, they constituted almost 40 percent of Party membership.[51]

Although not a political or labor organization, the IWO played an active role in assisting the CIO's organizing drives, campaigning for unemployment insurance and for aid to the Republicans in Spain. With its health and insurance benefits and sponsorship of ethnic language schools, summer camps, theater, dance, and other cultural programs, it became the fastest growing fraternal order in the country. By the end of World War II, the IWO counted almost 200,000 members in fifteen nationality societies, white and black; the JPFO, with 50,000 members, was the largest. Even though the majority of rank-and-file members did not belong to the Communist Party (in contrast to the principal IWO leaders, who did), they looked favorably upon the Party's progressive attitudes regarding ethnic minorities and blacks.[52]

Clara Shavelson became New York City secretary of the IWO's Women's Division; during the war she organized its knitting circles, first aid clubs, aluminum campaigns, and bond rallies. In March 1944, the IWO-JPFO spawned an Emma Lazarus Division: that year, the IWO published *Emma Lazarus: Selections from Her Poetry and Prose,* edited by Morris U. Schappes, the first collection of Lazarus's work in fifty years.[53] Schappes highlighted Lazarus's dual consciousness as a Jew and an American, a focus that the Women's Division adopted. Advertising itself as the "home of progressive Jewish women," the Division attracted a membership of left-wing, often Yiddish-speaking women, many of the immigrant generation. Over the next five decades, while also campaigning against the proliferation of nuclear weapons, Clara Lemlich Shavelson devoted much of her energy to the Emmas.[54]

In its broad strokes, Shavelson's biography does not differ greatly from those of other women who were instrumental in founding and leading the Emma Lazarus Division (later, Federation). June Croll Gordon, a founder and longtime executive director of the group, was born in Odessa in 1901; after emigrating to Canada and then to the United States, she began to work in New York City's needle trades at the age of twelve. Gordon became an active trade unionist, leading strikes in the textile and millinery unions. By 1935, she had become secretary of the Anti-Nazi Federation, helping to rouse public opinion against the Nazis' territorialist ambitions. Rose Raynes, who became the Federation's executive director after Gordon's death, came to the United States from Russia when she was ten. Soon employed in garment and millinery shops, Raynes also became active in the textile and millinery unions. Like Shavelson, Raynes and Gordon were Communist Party members and officers of the United Council of Working Women and the Progressive Women's Council. All three became targets of McCarthyism. An unsuccessful attempt was made to deport Gordon; Shavelson had her passport revoked. All were called before the House Un-American Activities Committee and subjected to FBI harassment.[55]

The Emma Lazarus Division of the JPFO was established by these three women and others with similar backgrounds to combat anti-Semitism and racism, to provide relief to wartime victims, and to nurture positive Jewish identification through a broad program in support of Jewish education and women's rights. Its founders believed that because of the Holocaust, thousands of women had become "newly aware of themselves as Jewish women," but they urgently needed "history, self-knowledge as Jews, and cultural products" that could sustain the fight against fascism. "Since the attack by Hitler against the Jewish people," Rose Raynes recalled, "we felt that [anti-Semitism] was not only an issue for Europe but for the U.S. as well. We felt that a progressive Jewish woman's organization was the order of the day."[56] Beginning in 1945, the Division offered fellowships for works of fiction and history on Jewish themes, the first of its many efforts to heighten Jewish identity as a weapon against bigotry. It also supported a home for French war orphans and a day nursery in Israel, and championed a broad range of women's issues: full employment for men and women; equal pay for equal work; maternity, unemployment, retirement, health, and housing benefits; day nurseries and after-school care; and the inclusion of greater numbers of women in government.

In 1951, the Division became the autonomous Emma Lazarus Federation of Jewish Women's Clubs (ELF), an independent organization. Although links to the progressive left remained, the shift from division to federation marked an important transformation in the group's focus. The change in status had been influenced by attacks against the Communist Party and the IWO. In 1951, the New York State attorney general initiated proceedings against the IWO as a subversive institution formed and directed under Communist Party auspices. Although the IWO denied that it used members' funds to support the Communist Party, New York State, aided by J. Edgar Hoover and the FBI successfully prosecuted the order and forced it to liquidate in 1954. The JPFO, deprived of the financial advantages of a fraternal benefit society and much reduced in size, reorganized as the Jewish Cultural Clubs and Societies, retaining several thousand members interested in cultural programs in Yiddish and English.[57] While Communist Party leaders played a play in reorganizing IWO constituencies, the Emma Lazarus Division had in any case been moving toward a more independent, woman-centered stance since the 1940s. Cold War necessities further advanced the drift toward autonomy.[58]

During the politically charged fifties, the ELF did not relinquish its radical commitments, although some leaders broke with the Communist Party. Waging a vigorous fight against McCarthyism, Federation leaders were especially alarmed by the Rosenberg trial. Although she never met her, Shavelson spent two years working on Rosenberg's defense committee, recognizing in the accused woman's labor activism and ethnic associations a replica of her own background. As individuals and, in some cases, as chapters, many ELF members rallied to the Rosenbergs' support. Many felt that the Rosenbergs were being prosecuted for their pro-communist political views, not because they had committed acts of conspiracy or espionage; they were particularly supportive of Ethel, sympathizing with her plight as a mother and as a concerned Jewish radical. Ethel's silence on the witness stand and her "cold-hearted" demeanor appeared to them not as evidence of evasiveness but as a principled demonstration of dissent. Many agreed with her decision to deny any communist association, which in the midst of the Red Scare would only have been taken as proof of treason or conspiracy. In any event, they considered Ethel Rosenberg to be not a liar, a spy, or even a misguided wife defending her husband, but a patriot in the battle for social justice, one who had claimed her right as an American to defy authority and speak out on behalf of her convictions. In one of the ELF's publications, they likened her to the women protesters who had established America's noble tradition of dissent: Anne Hutchinson, the colonial midwife who challenged the governor of Massachusetts; the mill girls of Lowell, who protested worsening factory conditions; and Jewish women garment workers, who led the battle for fair treatment of laborers in the early twentieth century. After the executions, the Rosenberg sons were adopted by Ann Meeropol, herself a member of the ELF, and her husband.[59]

Throughout the 1950s, the Federation emphasized the progressive voice of labor as a hallmark of democracy, and called for coexistence with the Soviet Union. While Khrushchev's startling revelations in 1956 of the Stalinist terror and subsequent information about the country's virulent anti-Semitism left ELF members "shocked" and "grieved," publicly its leaders continued to hope that the USSR would return to its earlier tolerance of ethnic minorities. On at least one occasion, a branch delegate protested that the executive board did not condemn anti-Semitism within the USSR as vigorously as it opposed domestic bigotry; the group remained split between those who wanted to break all ties with the USSR and those who continued to support communism.[60]

Yet the Division's unity around the issue of cultural work overshadowed political differences. By the time the group called its first Constitutional Convention in 1951 to inaugurate the Federation, the Emmas had decided that in the wake of Nazism, nothing was more important than integrating Jewish heritage into contemporary life. The terrors of McCarthyism, which stigmatized many Jewish radicals as "un-American" communists, also contributed to the Emmas' desire to claim their Jewish identity by promoting a progressive, secular Jewish heritage. "Our purpose was to add to the fabric of American culture and democracy by advancing all that is most humane and forward looking in Jewish culture,"[61] remarked Federation president Leah Nelson at its third convention in 1959. If Jews were to survive as a people and contribute to world problems in morally responsible ways, they could not be isolated from the social mainstream.

The Federation's emphasis on creating a "culturally enlightened American Jewry" coincided with the increasing acceptance of cultural pluralism in postwar life. Even as Jews moved ever more forcefully into the American mainstream, many seemed eager to identify with their heritage. A so-called Jewish revival—reflected in the construction of synagogues and Jewish social centers, the enrollment of a new generation of youth in Jewish educational programs, and the inauguration of months in honor of Jewish books, music, and history—revealed the eagerness of many Jews to find their roots, as well as the increasing acceptability of such expressions of "Americanized" ethnicity.[62]

Yet the ELF believed this Jewish revival lacked depth and vision. Arguing that knowledge of Jewish tradition should extend beyond holidays and artifacts to an understanding of vital Jewish contributions to American history and democracy, they sought to publicize the neglected history of American Jewish women in order to create a framework for identifying in a positive way with Jewish culture and for understanding and acting on present problems. This did not mean assimilation, the Emmas believed, but its opposite: a reaffirmation of the long history of Jewish participation in American democracy *as Jews* and a recommitment to Jews' moral values and "humanistic culture."[63] Both the focus on women and the link between women's history and activism distinguished the ELF's goals from those of the Jewish Clubs and Societies (the reorganized JPFO group), whose main emphasis was the support of Yiddish culture and of a progressive Jewish culture in English.[64]

In the early 1950s, the ELF focused on two Jewish women whose achievements they believed represented two different, though compatible, directions in American Jewish feminism. The first subject, Emma Lazarus, the group's inspiration, had concentrated her attention on Jewish themes within a universalistic setting. The other, Ernestine Rose, a social reformer, abolitionist, and suffragist, had focused on important social problems of the day, although not specifically Jewish ones. Although they had been radicals in their own day, both women stood within America's democratic tradition; thus, the Emmas selected models who helped ensure their own legitimacy as political and cultural dissenters.

Although Lazarus's consciousness as a Jew and a woman was not generally recognized in the 1950s, ELF members believed that she was an inspiration for both Jewish culture and women's rights. The Federation portrayed Lazarus as a woman who had spoken out forcefully and consistently against anti-Semitism and assimilation, and as a Jew who had been concerned not only with what she called a narrow, "tribal" Judaism but with oppressed peoples the world over. "Until we are all free, we are none of us free," was the Lazarus line most often quoted by the ELF to demonstrate her concern for all humanity.[65] To the ELF, this "universal scope," coupled with Lazarus's support for Jewish culture and women's freedom, made her an admirable symbol of secular, humanistic values.

Every year the Emmas celebrated Lazarus's birthday with a trip to Liberty Island. They succeeded in having the mayors of New York and Miami declare an Emma Lazarus Day; they also arranged a commemorative stamp and republished Lazarus's poetry and prose. The true meaning of Lazarus for the Federation, however, lay less in these ceremonies than in the standard of action, authority, and leadership that Lazarus had set as a woman, a Jew, and an American. By establishing Lazarus as a historical model, the Emmas hoped to give "leadership to women in Jewish communities in our time in the same spirit as Emma Lazarus did in hers."[66]

The Federation also commissioned a biography of Ernestine Rose, by Yuri Suhl.[67] To the Emmas, Rose was as much a model of activism as Lazarus, who spoke with her pen. They cited the fact that Susan Anthony had named Rose, along with Mary Wollstonecraft and Frances Wright, the most important leader of the women's movement, praising her activism on behalf of women's property rights, suffrage, and peace.

Though none received the attention given to Lazarus and Rose, other American Jewish women were remembered by the Federation in its cultural work. It documented the experience of Jewish women outside the United States as well, paying tribute to those who took part in the Warsaw Ghetto uprising and fought for freedom as partisans. To Federation members, the courageous stand of the "mothers" of the Warsaw Ghetto merged with those of women trailblazers in the United States.[68] The ELF also cited women's heroism in the fight for Israeli independence.

Like Gertrude Berg, who masterfully built the image of Molly Goldberg into a popular cultural icon, the immigrant leaders of the ELF understood cultural symbols. In its purposeful creation of cultural heroines—especially Emma Lazarus—the ELF offered Jewish women symbols in which they could locate their hopes for a radical, oppositional political movement that was at the same time deeply imbued with the American values of civil liberty and social justice. Unlike Molly Goldberg, however, Emma Lazarus, Ernestine Rose, and other "dissenters" were overtly and proudly political.

The ELF joined this program of promoting Jewish identity through the creation and dissemination of Jewish women's history with simultaneous campaigns, in coalition with women of other religions and races, aimed at the elimination of discrimination. The connection between women's rights and civil rights was of special concern. The ELF prepared many study guides on Sojourner Truth, Ida B. Wells, and Harriet Tubman, and paid tribute to other black women leaders of the abolitionist, women's rights, and contemporary civil rights movements. It also reprinted an important but little known pamphlet, "Women in the Life and Time of Abraham Lincoln," which recorded the proceedings of a conference held by the National Women's Loyal League. Formed at a mass rally called by women's rights leaders on May 14, 1863, at Cooper Union in New York City, the League assembled over one thousand northern white women abolitionists, who pledged to rally women to obtain one million signatures on a petition endorsing the Thirteenth Amendment. The pamphlet about the League's work contained an introduction by Daisy Bates, leader of the desegregation struggle at Central High School in Little Rock, Arkansas. Bates was also the principal speaker at a celebration held at

Cooper Union by the New York Clubs of the Emma Lazarus Federation in December 1963 to commemorate the hundredth anniversary of the National League's founding. On that occasion, thirteen hundred people joined the Emmas to celebrate the unity of white and black women in the common struggle for civil rights.

With the legacy of Emma Lazarus, Ernestine Rose, and the National Women's Loyal League pointing the way, the Federation dedicated many of its efforts over the next decades to work on behalf of civil rights. The "Negro question is our question," as one club member put it in 1955. The Emmas acknowledged that while anti-Semitism and racism sprang from common roots, oppression of blacks was not only significantly greater than that of Jews, but was often fueled by Jews' own racism. They urged Jews to support equality for blacks by eliminating any white supremacist attitudes they might unwittingly hold and voiced special concern for Negro women, who suffered "triple oppression, as women, as women-workers, and as Negroes."

In 1951, the Federation joined in a common statement of principle with the Sojourners for Truth and Justice, a black women's civil rights group. The Emmas made a regular financial contribution to the Sojourners, and the groups met annually at a joint luncheon.[69] By the mid-1950s, the Emmas were sending truckloads of food and clothing to Mississippi and joining boycotts and sit-ins. In their own communities, the Emmas fought segregation in housing and schools, lobbying legislators, presenting petitions, holding forums. At annual Mother's Day celebrations, they typically honored a black woman active in civil rights. In some regions, black women's associations honored the Emma Lazarus clubs at their meetings and collected contributions for the Emma Lazarus nursery in Israel.[70]

The Federation was as vigilant about fighting anti-Semitism as it was about racism. Its targets included neo-Nazi movements in the United States and all over the world. The Federation also protested the ominous spread of anti-Semitism among the general population; it noted that Jews were too often discriminated against at public resorts, in schools and colleges, and in the workplace.[71] The Emmas called for actions to protest pernicious stereotyping as well as discriminatory quota systems. And they persistently argued that those groups most guilty of anti-Semitic bigotry also posed the greatest danger to the rights of all minorities.

The blind spot in the Federation's campaign against anti-Semitism remained the Soviet Union. The absence of a committed campaign against Soviet anti-Semitism was a consequence of the continuing political attachment of a significant number of Federation members to the Communist Party; others within the leadership had become critical of or broken with the Party. This split prevented the group from taking a vigorous stand against Soviet brutality and against Soviet harassment of Jews.[72]

The Federation worked continuously to bring women's history to a wide public so that the lessons of the past would help shape the present. In 1956, it inaugurated a year of celebration for the thirty-fifth anniversary of women's suffrage, focusing on women's history.[73] The Federation identified a host of economic and social problems that affected the lives of women, particularly working women. Far in advance of its times, a 1955 ELF discussion guide, for example, focused on the lack of equal pay for equal work; the "double" wage discrimination faced by black women; occupational segregation; unequal job security and promotional opportunities; lack of female representation in trade unions and management; and the problems of working mothers (day nurseries and after-school care). Issues of educational access and the representation of women in politics, government, and the professions were also highlighted. The ELF believed it could play an important role by publicizing the needs of working women and implementing programs developed by union members. The Federation also hoped to create a greater consciousness of black women's special problems.

Like the National Council of Jewish Women, the Emma Lazarus Federation thus found much common ground with non-Jewish women during the highly politicized 1950s. Whereas the NCJW focused on establishing intercultural programs and policy initiatives with Christian women, primarily in the areas of interfaith cooperation and social justice, the ELF concentrated on opposition to racial discrimination. Both groups were interested in attacking the roots of prejudice, but it was the ELF—largely working-class and more left-wing—that consistently campaigned for the eradication of anti-Semitism as a specific objective for American Jewish women.

The NCJW's interfaith programs, in fact, were almost entirely free of self-conscious, identifiably Jewish markers; it was in the name of universalism, not Judaism or the more secular interests of Jewish peoplehood, that it undertook cultural and social programs designed to reinvigorate the democratic ideals of American pluralism. The Council made few references to the heritage, achievements, or responsibilities of Jewish women as a group; nor, for that matter, did it acknowledge the special interests of all women. Throughout the 1950s, the NCJW opposed the Equal Rights Amendment and the notion of equality for women in the abstract as unnecessary and divisive.[74] It paid far less attention to women's or Jewish issues than to a general agenda of social action, education, and informed citizen participation.[75]

The ELF, however, was strongly identified with specifically Jewish and women's issues. During the 1950s, when the reigning Cold War ideology exerted a chilling effect on both radical activism and cultural innovation, the ELF established the rudiments of a new history of Jewish women in which even the fearsome Ethel Rosenberg could be claimed as part of the fabric of Jewish women's historical activism. Years later, at its twentieth-century anniversary convention, the Emma Lazarus Federation reconsidered its organizational roots. "Why are we calling ourselves a Jewish women's organization?"

one delegate asked. "Since we are progressive with our ideology and program to benefit all people, why the separation? Why emphasize our Jewishness?" Another wondered: "Why a woman's organization? Why the Hadassah, the Pioneer Women, the Council of Jewish Women, the Women's Division of the American Jewish Congress . . . the Emma Lazarus Federation?"

In response, the ELF's president reaffirmed the importance both of "unity as Jews, unity in variety" and of the "special approach" needed to solve women's problems because of pervasive assumptions about "male superiority": "We are a part of American life generally, and of the Jewish community in particular," she reaffirmed, as well as a member of the "family" of women's organizations.[76] Such a vision had led the ELF to create linkages with groups whose purposes complemented its own, yet it did not hesitate to criticize allies when they fell short of the mark—peace and women's groups for failing to represent working-class interests; minority organizations for anti-Semitism; "progressive" male Jewish clubs for ignoring the contributions of Jewish women. The common ground that the ELF sought with these groups did not diminish its members' clearly defined identity—or rather, their multiple, overlapping identities—as Jews, as women, as members of the working class, as radical activists, and as Americans sensitive to the horrors of race prejudice.

Thus, the two organizations, the NCJW and the ELF, were models for different kinds of interethnic cooperation. Like Gertrude Berg's benign, exemplary Molly Goldberg, the Council took the high ground in its campaign for human decency and tolerance, hoping to serve as a catalyst for "cultural democracy" and racial and religious inclusiveness. The San Francisco Section of the NCJW in fact honored Berg with a special award for promoting "better understanding and friendship between groups." In accepting the honor, Berg noted the similarities between the NCJW's intercultural programs and her show's themes: "We like to feel that each week when we invite everybody into the Goldberg apartment in the Bronx that we are helping organizations like the National Council."[77] The problem with this approach was the question of whether it was possible to accomplish the objectives of intercultural harmony without, in the words of Gertrude Berg, "bringing in anything that will bother people." In contrast, the Emma Lazarus Federation, with its different class base and long association with the radical movement, seemed to relish its ability to provoke and agitate. The Gertrude Berg ideal of "keeping things average" was not theirs.

The irony, perhaps, was that the outspoken ELF found common ground with such middle-class, conforming groups as the NCJW. To secure Jewish culture and a better world for all, the ELF argued, it was necessary to know history, to restore Jewish and female identity, and, where possible, to create alliances with women of different ethnic or political backgrounds. Yet, as the Emmas had learned from their own recent history, common fronts were notoriously short-lived. If cultural democracy was to stand a chance, each component of the fabric of intercultural life had to retain its shape and identity. By the time Molly Goldberg had bought a tract house, moved to the suburbs, and abandoned her Yiddishisms, the show had nearly run its course. "The Goldbergs" did not last much beyond the end of the 1950s. Challenged by the racial and ethnic turmoil of the 1960s, the NCJW's postwar program of intercultural tolerance, similarly noncontroversial and not particularly Jewish or feminist, would not stay alive much longer.

Nonetheless, the activities of the NCJW and the ELF reveal that, despite the pervasive ideology of domestic "containment," Jewish women were far from quiescent in the complacent 1950s. Their vigorous participation in these groups (along with their work for Hadassah, Pioneer Women, temple sisterhoods, and such secular organizations as Women Strike for Peace and Women's International League for Peace and Freedom) indicates that they were active as interpreters of their own lives and on the local, national, and international scenes. In the face of the political repression and cultural conformity that marked the Cold War era, Jewish women lived lives of intense, though varied, commitments. Many, no doubt, were "Shirleys"—obedient, bourgeois matrons—yet at the same time were engaged in their own satisfying forms of Judaism and domesticity. Others remained immigrant matriarchs in the rabble-rousing tradition of Clara Lemlich Shavelson, rather than that of Gertrude Berg's even-tempered though manipulative Molly. Their daughters may have been Jewish "princesses," idle, brash, self-centered, and focused on private, material pleasures, but they too, no doubt, had more complex identities, grappling with the conservatism of the era and the constraints they encountered in unpredictable ways.

PROBING THE TRADITION:
FEMINISM AND JUDAISM
1960–1996

Chapter 9

FEMINIST LIBERATIONS

First Mothers: Betty Friedan and Bella Abzug

On August 26, 1970, on the fiftieth anniversary of the passage of the amendment entitling women to the vote, 50,000 women marched down Fifth Avenue to demand equal rights and a political voice of their own. This Women's Strike for Equality, the first nationwide women's action since the suffrage victory, had been organized by Betty Friedan, the writer whose exposé of the so-called feminine mystique had sparked a new wave of feminist activism. The size of the march considerably altered depictions of the resurgent women's rights movement. No longer could the media portray the movement as a fringe action, for it was clear that it was attracting a large and significantly mainstream following.[1]

At the defining moment of the march, as Friedan came forward to address a vast, cheering throng in Bryant Park behind New York's Public Library, she found herself speaking—and revising—the ancient Hebrew prayer that Orthodox Jewish men recited every morning. "Down through the generations in history," Friedan declared, "my ancestors prayed, 'I thank Thee, Lord, I was not created a woman,' and from this day forward I trust that women all over the world will be able to say, 'I thank Thee, Lord, I *was* created a woman.' "[2]

Unable to remember ever having heard the prayer before, Friedan was startled by her own words. But the joining together of her feminism and her Jewishness at this historic moment was not as strange as it seemed. Friedan confessed to having always had "very strong feelings" about her Jewish identity; it is not so surprising that this Orthodox prayer, emblematic of gender differences in Jewish religious roles, now emerged from the recesses of her memory. For Friedan, it had become necessary to confront "the anti-woman aspects of the Jewish tradition in order to accept both feminism and Judaism." She had the sense that "having broken through the feminine mystique to affirm my authentic full identity as a person, as a woman, brought me to confront my Jewish identity."[3] Because feminism insisted on making

259

the personal political, her exploration would inevitably become a public one, as her oratory in Bryant Park confirmed. Assisted by a growing Jewish feminist movement, Friedan and other women's rights pioneers would slowly find their way home to a more viable Jewish identity in the 1970s and 1980s. The increasing virulence of anti-Semitism within the international feminist movement intensified their struggle and challenged many other Jewish-born American feminists to join the quest for a positive, usable, feminist Jewish identity.

Like Friedan, many of the leaders and theorists of the 1960s feminist movement had been Jews, albeit largely secular, unidentified ones. Bella Abzug, Phyllis Chesler, Letty Cottin Pogrebin, and Vivian Gornick—as well as the half-Jewish Gloria Steinem[4]—all played prominent roles in spearheading women's rights in the 1960s and early 1970s. Shulamith Firestone, Robin Morgan, Meredith Tax, Andrea Dworkin, and Naomi Weisstein were among the Jewish women active in the more radical wing of feminism—women's liberation.

Several reasons have been suggested for the prominence of Jewish women within not only the leadership but the rank and file of feminism. Friedan suggests that contemporary feminism originated in the United States because there were such large numbers of highly educated women who were expected to concentrate their energies upon the narrow sphere of the home. She speculates that the disparity between talent, ambition, and role identity was especially severe for Jewish women, who were probably the most highly educated of all American women, yet whose self-definition was based almost entirely on the family. According to writer Anne Roiphe, the "women's movement was fueled by Jewish energies" because Jewish women felt "pain and anguish" at the way they had been portrayed in the media and by Jewish men. When their anger ignited, it "exploded" into the women's movement.[5]

The feminist movement did not spring full-blown from Friedan's pen. For decades, Jewish women were among the activists who led the campaigns for civil rights, nuclear disarmament, and peace. Such work provided women with a sense of personal power as well as experience in mass demonstrations and community organization. Just as women's participation in abolitionism had created demands for greater autonomy for women a century earlier, so had a "protofeminist" consciousness arisen from within the civil rights movement of the 1950s and early 1960s.[6] After a decade of militant antiwar struggles, activists like Bella Abzug, leader of Women Strike for Peace, had come to connect war with violence against women and to identify war as a feminist issue.[7] These women's organizational know-how and skillful coalition building became essential tools in the development of feminism as a mass movement.

While leaders like Friedan and Abzug, who were then in their early forties, stimulated like-minded women to wage war on patriarchy, a group of younger women, mostly in their twenties, joined the civil rights and student movements; as the Vietnam War escalated, they became active in the protest against it. By 1967, many had become outraged at their treatment by male radicals whose belief in freedom and equality apparently only applied to men. After their attempts to introduce women's issues into the movement were met with ridicule, these women began to organize groups of their own, identifying their cause as women's liberation. "The personal is political" became their slogan and consciousness-raising their primary tool.

Jewish women played prominent roles in many of these early women's liberation groups. In time, some came to recognize the place of their Jewish roots in the struggle for women's equality; for others, however, the gap between feminist goals and Judaism's subordination of women remained wide.

Not One of "Them"   In *The Feminine Mystique,* Betty Friedan explodes the myth of domestic contentment, which she argues had infantilized women, burying them alive in their suburban homes as if in a "concentration camp." Like the victims of the Holocaust, she suggests, they too had undergone "progressive dehumanization" and could not fight back.[8] Friedan's appropriation of Holocaust imagery did not attract much attention or criticism, nor did Friedan seem especially troubled that she had broken an implicit taboo by comparing ordinary, albeit disturbing, social ills to the moral enormities of the Jewish catastrophe.

Friedan used the language of the Holocaust not merely as a metaphor, or as a tactic to shock readers, but because she had already made the connection between the oppression of women and that of Jews. Her family history provides evidence that they had long been joined in her own experience.

Born Bettye Goldstein in Peoria, Illinois, in 1921, she was the oldest of the three children of Harry Goldstein, then forty, and his wife, Miriam Horwitz Goldstein, eighteen years younger; a sister came a year and a half later and a brother five years later. Harry Goldstein had immigrated with his family from a village near Kiev when he was still a boy; leaving the rest of the family in St. Louis, where they settled, at age thirteen Harry went on to Peoria, peddling collar buttons on street corners. Eventually he owned the finest jewelry store in the community—a "Tiffany of the Midwest" according to Betty—and put his youngest brother through Harvard Law School.[9] Goldstein became a leader of Peoria's business elite and a prominent member of its Jewish community.

Despite this success, to his wife, Goldstein was a failure because he could not provide social acceptability or, especially during the Depression, sufficient material comforts. Friedan believes that her mother's scorn for her father sprang not only from these alleged deficiencies but from Miriam's dissatisfaction with her own role as a housewife and mother.

Miriam Horwitz Goldstein was the only daughter of a prominent Illinois physician and his wife. The family delighted in the apocryphal story that Miriam's father, an immigrant from Hungary, had gone through high school and college in one year; he graduated in the first class of Washington University Medical School and eventually became health commissioner of Peoria. Despite her father's status, Miriam grew up "fairly isolated as a Jew," resentful of the community's snubs. After attending the local college, she became society page editor of the Peoria newspaper, a job she loved. But, as was customary at the time, Miriam gave up her work when she married. She never recovered from the loss. Thereafter, "nothing my father did, nothing he bought her, nothing we did ever seemed to satisfy her," Betty notes.[10] Beautiful and self-possessed, Miriam nonetheless lacked fulfillment and lived vicariously through her children, especially the bright and able Betty. "She could hardly wait until I got to junior high," Friedan notes, "to put the idea into my head to try out for the school newspaper, to start a literary magazine in high school. She could hardly wait for me to go to the college she had no chance to go to, to edit the newspaper there."[11]

Her mother's unhappiness caused her not only to live through her children, but to snipe at her husband. "It was obvious she belittled, cut down my father because she had no place to channel her terrific energies," Betty recalled.[12] Things got especially bad during the Depression when Mr. Goldstein's jewelry business suffered enormous losses. Miriam did not cope well with the downturn in the family's fortunes. Betty recalled her "hiding the bills she charged, secretly trying her hand at gambling . . . and losing more, until she had to confess." The combination of her mother's greediness and her father's ferocious temper caused "terrible battles that shook our house at night."[13]

Friedan blamed Miriam for "dominating the family," for being "hypocritical" and selfish. "Discontented, running the Sunday School one year, Hadassah the next, the Community Chest, talking about 'writing,' though she wouldn't or didn't do it, taking up . . . fads," Miriam was a terrible role model. "When I still used to say prayers, even as a child, after the 'Now I lay me down to sleep' and the Sh'ma Yisrael—I would pray for a 'boy to like me best' and a '*work* of my own to do' when I grew up. I did not want to be discontented like my mother was. . . ."[14] Years later, when asked what had motivated her to write *The Feminine Mystique*, Friedan responded that it had been "a combination of circumstances" in her own life, along with the "massive crisis of identity already brewing in my mother's generation." But the first specific cause she names is her "mother, and her discontent, which I never understood."[15]

Friedan was not unaware of the specifically Jewish dimension to her mother's discontent. Despite Harry Goldstein's prominence in Peoria, the Goldsteins were never accepted socially. People who associated with her father in business would not associate with him elsewhere, and Friedan recalls that the family was not allowed into the Peoria country club, to which all the children's friends belonged.[16]

This discrimination hit her mother hardest. But Miriam blamed her husband rather than the community for the family's isolation and ostracism, faulting Harry Goldstein's immigrant background, accent, lack of education. Recalling these years, Betty acknowledged that her mother, like many Jews in smaller cities who distanced themselves as far as possible from other Jews and Judaism, had in fact become an "anti-Semitic Jew." These were people who "changed their names and did something to their noses, tried not to talk with their hands . . . and denied the very richness, the warmth, the specialness, the good taste of their own background as Jews."[17] Although Friedan told herself that her family "was somehow better, finer, more sensitive, smarter" than their neighbors, she too could not avoid internalizing some of Peoria's anti-Semitic prejudices. She grew up feeling "marginal," with the sense of being an "outsider," apart, special, "not like the others." She emphasized her Americanness. Once, in fact, she won an essay contest on "Why I Am Proud to Be an American." As a prize, she "recited the Declaration of Independence on July 4th at the fairgrounds, and Congressman Everett Dirksen patted my head."[18] Though she attended Sunday school and enjoyed family seders, she became disconnected from the religious elements of Judaism. A month before her confirmation, she announced to her rabbi that she no longer believed in God. The rabbi told her to keep it to herself until the ceremony was over. "Actress that I am," Friedan recalled years later, "I gave the flower offering, raising my eyes to the heavens."[19]

It was at about this time that the first "real trauma" of her life erupted. Although previously she had been popular, now Friedan—the only Jewish girl at school—was the only one not invited to join a sorority. "Terribly alone," "self-conscious and miserable," she felt herself a "social outcast" throughout her remaining high school years and "plumbed the depth of misery."[20] She blamed the rejection squarely on being Jewish—on not being "one of 'them.'" Her father agreed, explaining that "the people friendly to him in business would not speak to him after sundown."[21] In Peoria, Jews and Gentiles did not mix. These painful experiences strengthened her social conscience. "Ever since I was a little girl," Friedan muses, "I remember my father telling me that I had a passion for justice. But I think it was really a passion against injustice which originated from my feelings of the injustice of anti-Semitism."[22]

When Friedan was seventeen, she vowed to herself that "they may not *like* me but they're going to look up to me. . . ."[23] She made good on that vow at Smith College, becoming editor of the newspaper, starting a literary magazine, and graduating summa cum laude. Yet even at Smith, Friedan encountered anti-Semitism and the phenomenon of the anti-Semitic Jew. In her freshman year, just before the outbreak of World War II, she lived in a house with four wealthy Jewish girls from Cincinnati; when the president of the college initiated a petition urging President Roosevelt to relax the immigration quotas for refugees from Nazism, offering to admit some college-aged girls among them to Smith, many of Friedan's housemates argued against the proposal. But Friedan was most shocked by the fact that the four Cincinnati girls refused to sign the petition—"they were the type that spoke in whispery voices . . . because they did not want to be known as Jews."[24]

In a short story she later wrote entitled "The Scapegoat," Friedan dramatized the plight of Shirley, not Wouk's ambitious, sexy "princess" who matures into a bourgeois housewife, but an all-too-Jewish college girl who has a nervous breakdown when she is rejected by fellow Jews to curry favor with their Gentile housemates. Friedan's professor commented that although the theme was somewhat familiar, the "factor of race prejudice, and the less usual device of having it written by a Jewish girl," were "probably to the good."[25] After graduating Friedan came home to speak at Peoria's Reform Synagogue on "Affirming One's Jewishness." The talk—which acknowledged the problem of turning anti-Semitism "against oneself instead of affirming one's own identity"—was "strong meat" for the community, but it helped her come to terms with the anti-Semitism that she believed had been the "dominant menace" of her childhood.[26]

While Friedan continued to associate Peoria with anti-Semitism, by the time she left college—where she had dazzled friends and teachers with her brilliance and experienced a virtual transformation of personality, her awkward shyness disappearing—Friedan had ceased to imagine that her Jewishness was a detriment to achievement. Nonetheless, the experience of childhood "marginality" could not be erased: even at Smith she periodically felt "awkward," painfully isolated, and ugly. A lifelong battle with asthma began; the condition was so severe that in her sophomore year she burst one lung. Beneath the surface of her image as "big woman on campus" lay unadorned panic.[27]

When Friedan left Smith, she dropped the "e" from her first name, perhaps to show that she was no longer the girl from Peoria.[28] Yet at the University of California at Berkeley, where she began postgraduate work in psychology in 1942, her panic grew worse. Although she was a top student, her brilliance frightened away potential suitors. Blaming her achievements for keeping her from love, she quit her studies and moved to New York's Greenwich Village to take up newspaper work. When, after a while, she found herself suffering from terrible writing blocks, she began psychoanalysis. The treatment, which allowed her to vent her anger against her mother, helped alleviate her writing anxieties.[29]

In 1947, Betty married Carl Friedan, a returning G.I. interested in theater. For a while, she appeared extremely happy. In fact, however, she had begun to repeat her mother's pattern, looking down upon a husband who was less educated than she and retreating from her own work. As Friedan recalled, " 'Career woman' in the fifties became a pejorative, denoting a ball-busting man-eating harpy, a miserable neurotic witch from whom man and child should flee for very life."[30] There would be three children, several suburban homes, and work as a journalist, but the marriage soured and Friedan's self-esteem plummeted. Although after college she had been "very political, very involved, consciously radical . . . concerned about the Negroes, and the working class, and World War III and the Un-American Activities Committee and McCarthy and loyalty oaths" (but, she insisted, "not about women, for heaven's sake!") now "Doctor Spock . . . took the place of politics."[31] "With all my high-powered education and brilliant promise," Friedan admitted,

> I too embraced and lived that feminine mystique. Determined that I would find that feminine fulfillment which had eluded my mother, I first gave up psychology fellowships and then even newspaper reporting jobs. I lived the life of the suburban housewife that was everyone's dream at that time.[32]

Friedan recalled that her awakening came after a year spent analyzing alumnae questionnaires about the experiences of her Smith College classmates fifteen years after graduation. When magazine editors turned down the article that resulted, Friedan determined to write a book. Completed five years later, *The Feminine Mystique* sold 3,000,000 copies.[33]

Recently, historian Daniel Horowitz has questioned the self-presentation that Friedan offers in *The Feminine Mystique* and later narratives. He argues that while Friedan undoubtedly experienced psychological conflicts in trying to combine her writing with her family roles, she was never an apolitical suburban housewife; her involvement in the labor movement exposed her to ideas about sex discrimination and shaped her later feminism. From her political activities at Smith, to a three-year stint after college as staff writer for a left-wing news service, to a job from 1946 to 1952 as reporter on the *UE News*, the paper of the United Electrical, Radio and Machine Workers of America—the most radical and probably "the largest communist-led institution of any kind" in the United States—Friedan had become well politicized.[34] By the time she wrote *Mystique,* she may have given up her left-wing beliefs. Or, Horowitz suggests, fearful of McCarthyism and wanting to enhance the book's impact, she may have shied away from admitting the influence of her radical associations.

Whether or not the notion of continuity between 1960s feminism and earlier labor radicalism should take precedence over Friedan's sense of a sudden conversion to feminism, the relevance of her Peoria years to her feminist beliefs remains clear. "Longing to be one of 'them'," and sensing the frustrations of her mother's life, she did not, however, identify the problems she encountered then as relevant either to Jews as a group or to women. "In Peoria," she admits, "I had no sense that women lacked power."

> In my family and in others too, it sometimes seemed as if women had all the power . . . they certainly ran *our* lives, and they could make life hell for our fathers. It took a new consciousness to realize that women . . . had to dominate the family for lack of economic and political power in the outside world.[35]

Although the unhappy housewives Friedan portrays in *The Feminine Mystique* have no specific ethnicity, there is an almost exact convergence between the portrait of Miriam Goldstein that appears in Friedan's memoirs and the women of her 1963 book. Moreover, these housewives resemble many of the Jewish mothers in the 1950s and 1960s fiction of Herman Wouk and Philip Roth—*Marjorie Morningstar, Goodbye Columbus,* and *Portnoy's Complaint*—books that defined the Jewish American Princess and Jewish American Mother in the popular mind. Like Miriam Goldstein, the Mesdames Morgenstern, Patimkin, and Portnoy are members of the new Jewish suburban middle class; pushy and materialistic, they dominate their families, living through their children and belittling their weak and ineffectual husbands. Though they might belong to Hadassah and other Jewish or community charities, neither these volunteer activities nor their families provide adequate scope for their innermost desires. The failure to realize their potential is destructive to all around them. Based on these characters, Wouk and Roth would have agreed with Friedan's comment in *The Feminine Mystique* that "there is something dangerous about being a housewife."[36]

But whereas Wouk and Roth indict Jewish women for the crass materialism and smothering excesses that they see as symptomatic of the Jewish middle class's rise to postwar prosperity, Friedan is more able to empathize with the plight of women like her mother. Whatever the timing or mix of sources involved in the development of her feminist consciousness, Friedan's breakthrough was to acknowledge that the feminine "mystique" was not an individual—and not a Jewish—problem. She recognized her mother's "impotent rage" as a "typical female disorder" perpetuated by Freudian psychoanalysts, functionalist sociologists, advertisers, business leaders, educators, and child development experts.[37]

The Feminine Mystique, and Friedan's subsequent establishment of the National Organization of Women, assured her a leading role in the women's rights movement and eventually facilitated her return to Judaism. Having rejected religion early in life and identified with an "agnostic, atheistic, scientific, humanist" tradition, she had no feeling for the spiritual "mystery of being Jewish." Friedan's sons were given "aesthetic bar mitzvahs" appropriate to Rockland County, where most Jews were Unitarians; her daughter did not receive confirmation or a bat mitzvah. Feminism, however, by leading her to explore her gendered identity, started her on a journey to reevaluate her religious heritage. After the 1970 suffrage anniversary march at which she publicly connected the reform of patriarchal Judaism to feminist goals, Friedan took her first trip to Israel as part of an attempt to "get in touch with my Jewish roots." She was shocked, however, to find herself attacked by the Israeli press as a radical "women's libber" and generally treated as a "leper"; Golda Meir, then prime minister, refused to see her, a particularly disappointing affront since Friedan had met with the pope and many world leaders.[38] But Friedan made contact with a few women eager to confront the gender inequalities in Israel; along with other prominent American feminists, she worked with them over the next years helping to start a women's rights movement in Israel.

At home, Friedan began to explore her relationship with the American Jewish community, becoming cochair of the American Jewish Congress's National Commission on Women's Equality. Unhappily, she found that organized leaders seemed as disturbed by feminism as the Israelis. Even though Jewish women had been prominent in the women's rights movement, Jewish leaders seemed more profoundly threatened by feminism than non-Jews.[39]

Friedan's journey back to Judaism continued with her participation in a Jewish study group where she explored the "mystery of being Jewish." As a newly self-aware Jewish feminist, she remains concerned about the myriad issues facing Jewish women, including the perpetuation of "obscene" travesties of the Jewish mother. Friedan wants to "take back" the denigrating images of possessive, manipulating Jewish mothers spooning out chicken soup to control their children's lives and show Jewish women as strong, energetic, and nurturant, as they have been throughout history. "I hereby affirm my own right as a Jewish American feminist to make chicken soup," she declares, "even though I sometimes take it out of a can."[40] Thus, in later life she has joined the modern aspirations of feminism with the popular emblems of her Jewish heritage, understanding that the myth of a controlling, aggressive *Jewish* mother had been as dangerous to the self-esteem of Jewish women (including her own) as the earlier "feminine mystique" was to all women.

Born Yelling   While Friedan's embrace of Judaism took place in late adulthood, Bella Abzug has been a deeply identified Jew throughout her life. Although she rejected various aspects of traditional Judaism, her connections to her heritage have been positive and have shaped the trajectory of her professional and political life. The core of her social philosophy is derived from the prophetic teachings of Torah. Joining the power of these teachings with the vigor of feminist ideals, she embodied and modelled a secular Jewish feminism that spanned the half-century from her own college student activism to the forward-looking global women's movement she leads today.

Bella Abzug was born "yelling," as her family used to say more than a little prophetically, to Emanuel and Esther Savitsky, Russian Jewish immigrants, in 1920. Claiming to have been a feminist since "the day I was born," Abzug notes that the year of her birth was auspicious, since it marked the passage of the women's suffrage amendment after a campaign of more than half a century. But if she was "born a rebel," Abzug attributes this attribute to "family heritage," not astrology.[41] Her father, who hated war with a passion, had left czarist Russia in 1905 to protest the outbreak of the Russo-Japanese War; Abzug recalls him telling her how depressed he felt when World War I broke out a decade later. After President Wilson proposed his Fourteen Points peace settlement to Congress, Savitsky made his own "one point peace plank" outside his butcher shop on Ninth Avenue in Manhattan, renaming it "The Live and Let Live Meat Market." However deeply felt his pacifism, which Abzug would come to share, she acknowledges that such a platform was hardly a formula for commercial success.

Eventually her father's butcher shop failed, and Manny Savitsky took what work he could find as a bookkeeper and insurance salesman. His real love, however, was music, and the Savitsky apartment in the South Bronx—then a pleasant, almost rural neighborhood—was filled with the sounds of his rich tenor voice singing Yiddish and Russian folk songs. On Friday night, after the lighting of the Shabbat candles, the Savitsky home became a virtual concert hall, with Manny singing, Helene (Abzug's older sister and a talented pianist) accompanying him on the piano, and Bella playing the violin. (After Abzug became a notable political figure, her mother told an interviewer, "I knew Bella would be a success because she always did her homework and practiced her violin.")[42]

The Savitskys kept kosher and went to synagogue regularly, especially Abzug's maternal grandfather, Wolf Tanklefsky, who with his wife and bachelor son lived with the Savitskys. When she wasn't in school, Abzug would go with her grandfather to shul, where he prayed three times a day. With his flowing white beard and his piety, this grandfather seemed to Abzug "indistinguishable" from God. By the age of seven or eight she had learned to recite complicated Hebrew prayers "like . . . a wizard," and her grandfather would prop her on a table to show her off to his cronies. While this gave Abzug the kind of reinforcement that girls did not usually receive for learning Hebrew, her experience of being in synagogue was mixed. After her recitations, she would be sent to sit in the balcony with the women, who had no real role in the service and were hidden from the men's view. When she asked why, she was simply told that "that's the way it is." "I couldn't accept that," Abzug remembered, and the injustice smarted.[43] Yet coupled with this disappointment was the positive sense of Torah that Abzug absorbed from her grandfather, especially the visions of the prophets. Very early in life these teachings and "the way in which [her] family lived" taught her a lesson that would guide her moral development: "To be a Jew is to care—not only about ourselves, but about others."[44]

However, when she was forbidden at the age thirteen to say kaddish after the death of her father, even though there were no sons or brothers to recite the traditional prayer of mourning, Abzug was confronted anew with Judaism's unequal treatment of women. Such prohibitions had been deeply painful to generations of Jewish women, including Henrietta Szold, and had driven some away from Judaism. Abzug was different. Even at that tender age, her reaction demonstrated the defiance that would be a hallmark of her lifelong activism: "I went to the synagogue and I did it, though I wasn't supposed to. I learned that I could speak out and no one would stop me."[45] For the next year, she went to the synagogue before school and said the prayer for her father, as tradition required of male heirs. In retrospect, she recalls this determination "as one of the early blows for the liberation of Jewish women."[46] It would be another four decades, however, with the onset of the Jewish feminist movement, before a sustained attempt would be made to give Jewish women equal access to religious privileges. Abzug played a visible role in that effort, although on a personal level she had always endeavored to integrate Jewish values with feminist principles.

Abzug's Jewish identity became the inspiration for her political activism as well as her early feminist ideals. When she was twelve, Abzug joined Hashomer Hatzair, a secular Labor Zionist youth group. She was drawn to it, she recalled, because of its "moral fervor, social idealism and pioneering militancy"; Zionism, in fact, seemed the perfect activist expression of the prophetic teachings she had imbibed from her grandfather. From then on, all she thought about was "working on a kibbutz, helping to build a national Jewish home. . . ."[47] Abzug became part of a group of youths, all clad in brown uniforms and ties, who collected pennies for the Jewish National Fund by shaking cans in the subway. Her innovation was to take the cans through the subway cars and when the train stopped, make a speech to passengers. This first foray into political campaigning and public speaking led Abzug to see herself as a leader of her peers and a "rebel" working on behalf of Jewish ideals.

Her idealism continued throughout her adolescence, now nurtured by her mother. After Manny Savitsky's death, Abzug, who had gone on to study Hebrew at a supplementary religious high school and at the Jewish Theological Seminary, got a job teaching Hebrew and Jewish history at a Bronx Jewish center. Esther Savitsky—always a "good manager" in Abzug's eyes—became the family's main breadwinner, working as a department store saleswoman and cashier. Throughout these difficult years, Esther's fierce determination became a model for Abzug. Like Tucker, Hurst, and Ferber, she recognized a dual heritage that reversed traditional gender roles: while her father was "extraordinarily sweet-tempered" and generous, her mother demonstrated a strength and competence that Abzug could imitate and make her own.[48]

By the time Abzug entered Walton High, an all-girls public school, in 1934, the Depression was in full force. Deeply affected by the suffering she saw around her and by Franklin Roosevelt's message of social uplift, she began to think of a legal career defending poor people and alleviating public misery; a similar vision of the law as a tool for the promotion of social justice had motivated Jewish women lawyers like Susan Brandeis Gilbert and Justine Wise Polier, who came from wealthier, middle-class families. Although relatives found Abzug's desire to become a lawyer (rather than marry one) inappropriate, especially for a Jewish girl, Abzug's mother, who had abandoned her own goal of becoming a teacher to work in a family business, supported her daughter's ambition.

In the fall of 1938, Abzug enrolled in the tuition-free Hunter College. An outstanding student, she was elected president of her class several times and president of the entire student body of four thousand women. It was a time when "everybody had a different point of view. We used to fight each other in class—the Communists, the Socialists, the Catholic radicals, and me, a Zionist. The teacher was just the referee." Abzug led numerous protests and demonstrations. "I transferred much of the intensity I had learned in Hashomer Hatzair to the political campaign to save democratic Spain from the Fascists" and fight Hitler, she recalls. The "war in Spain, the need for collective action to oppose the threat of Nazism and the persecution of the Jews, were the searing issues of the day."[49]

With America at war when Abzug graduated from Hunter in 1942, she began working for a defense contractor, but decided that she could make a greater contribution to the war effort through the law. Turned down by Harvard Law School, which accepted no female students, she entered Columbia University on a scholarship, one of nine women out of a class of eighty-five; the relatively large proportion of women reflected the fact that so many eligible men were away at war. Abzug worked hard to prove that her scholarship, and the faith in women's abilities that it implied, was justified; she became an editor of the *Columbia Law Review,* an achievement reflecting her top academic standing. Still, her professors may have questioned her commitment when in 1944, midway through law school, she married Martin Abzug, a young businessman and aspiring novelist she had met on a trip to visit relatives in Florida. They would have been relieved to know that Martin, a gentle and witty young man, madly in love with Bella, typed the drafts of Abzug's law papers. After the birth of their two daughters and throughout her career, he supported her professional and community interests with enthusiasm. (After his death in 1985, Bella Abzug established the Martin Abzug Memorial Award, offered annually by the National Women's Political Caucus in recognition of men who have been supportive of their wives' ambitions.)

While many of her classmates went on to Wall Street law firms or government after graduation, Abzug, her idealism still intact, joined a law office specializing in labor union cases. Within two years, she opened her own office to handle tenants' rights and civil liberties cases; her clients included Jewish schoolteachers, actors, and others accused of "Un-American" activities.

Abzug's cause célèbre was Willie McGee, a black Mississippian condemned to death for raping a white woman. McGee and the alleged victim had been involved in a three-year affair, but a forced confession had been drawn from him. Feelings against McGee among white Mississippians were so intense that Martin Abzug feared his wife might become a target for white supremacists when she travelled to Jackson to plead for a stay of execution. Although she was pregnant with their second daughter, Abzug could not be stopped. She spent the night sitting up in the bus station when no hotel in Jackson would house her.

Arguing in court that McGee had been a victim of a conspiracy to violate his civil rights because of racial prejudice, Abzug was eloquent, but she failed to win the delay, as she had done on two previous occasions. McGee was executed the next day. The bitter defeat only hardened Abzug's resolve to commit herself even more to the struggle for racial equality.

Abzug spent much of the 1950s concentrating on civil rights while continuing her work in labor law and the fight against McCarthyism. By the 1960s, after the United States and the USSR renewed nuclear testing, she shifted her focus to the peace effort. The resumption of nuclear testing caused "an explosion in my mind," Abzug recollected.[50] Concerned about the prospect of nuclear annihilation and the fate of her children's generation, she joined with women all over the country in spontaneous protests against the tests, and helped to found Women Strike for Peace.

Women Strike for Peace held demonstrations at the U.N., the White House, and at hundreds of local sites throughout the country. As the group's political action and legislative director, Abzug frequently travelled to Washington to lobby legislators against continuing the arms race. However much they derided the so-called mothers' lobby, they often saw Abzug and her determined supporters striding toward them.[51]

In 1965, the Abzugs moved from Westchester County to Greenwich Village. Abzug began to organize peace action committees in the city, and led efforts to build coalitions between the peace movement, liberal Democrats and Republicans, newly established women's groups, black and other minorities, and young people. An early opponent of the Vietnam War, she was a founder of the Coalition for a Democratic Alternative, and with Allard Lowenstein helped to organize the Dump Johnson movement. Her growing visibility led to her being increasingly named, both by her friends in the peace movement and by Reform Democrat politicians, as a possible candidate for Congress from her liberal Manhattan district. With the defeat of the antiwar plank at the Democratic Convention in Chicago in 1968 and the election of Richard Nixon as president, the urgency of taking a pro-peace, pro-people platform to Washington overwhelmed any doubts Abzug had about politics as a suitable arena for her long-held goals of social justice. Supported by a veritable army of women from the peace movement, she decided to challenge the party machine and run for Congress: "By temperament and conviction, I'm an activist and I deeply believe that people . . . will act in their own best interests." Her platform would be to "take foreign policy away from the militarists and restor[e] it to the people and their elected representatives."[52]

Abzug was endorsed by the New Democratic Coalition, peace and youth groups, and most trade unions (with the notable exception of the United Federation of Teachers, which opposed her support for community control of New York's public schools). In 1969, she scored an upset primary victory over the Democratic incumbent from Manhattan's 19th Congressional District. In the general election, she faced Republican Barry Farber, a popular radio talk-show host, and campaigned with the peppy slogan, "A Woman's Place Is in the House—the House of Representatives." New York had never seen anything like the outspoken lady radical with her trademark floppy hats. At campaign stops, Bella often played the mandolin and sang, while Martin campaigned for her door-to-door saying, "Vote for my wife, she's the greatest!" Many celebrities flocked to her campaign, including Barbra Streisand, who threw a fund-raising party for her. The media had a field day. "Bella Abzug is a miracle," wrote one reporter. "She couldn't happen anywhere else in the world. She is crazy, brash, foul-mouthed, funny, sometimes violent and always sharp." "A left-wing Martha Raye," agreed another. To one journalist, she was "pure New York . . . the soul of the people," even if she did look like a "belligerent matzoh ball." But none doubted Abzug's force, or her threat to the Washington establishment. "If Spiro Agnew had a nightmare," commented one prescient observer, "it would be Bella Abzug."[53]

Abzug won the 1970 election by a margin of 10,000 votes, the first woman elected to Congress on a women's rights/peace platform. After her first term, her district was gerrymandered, and she had to challenge the popular liberal Congressman William Fitz Ryan to continue representing the 19th District. Again Abzug was victorious; in her third election to the House in 1974, she was returned by an overwhelming margin of her constituents.

Abzug's service in Congress was the culmination of twenty-five years of professional and civic activism. She used her position to further long-held views about pacifism, women's rights, and the rights of poor people, minorities, and ethnic groups. As a congresswoman, she moderated neither her tone nor the intensity of her convictions, speaking her mind without too much concern about offending vested interests or her own constituents. On her departure from the House, the *Boston Globe* wrote that Abzug "has done as much as anyone for women's liberation, and, for the liberation of everybody who's unconventional. In a profession full of telegenic evaders of questions, she's an unabashed character, and she speaks her mind." She was no doubt the "least traditional woman in politics anywhere."[54]

Yet Abzug's accomplishments were the result of more than forthright speech. Wielding power as chair of the House Subcommittee on Government Information and Individual Rights, she helped write and pass the Freedom of Information and Privacy Acts and the "Government in the Sunshine" Law, which opened up government agencies to public scrutiny; Abzug also conducted inquiries into covert and illegal activities of the CIA, FBI, and other government agencies, and was the first to call for President Nixon's impeachment during the Watergate scandal. She served as an effective member of other committees, her informed positions on the issues and long experience in coalition building enabling her to get much ground-breaking legislation through the House. In her three terms in Congress, she garnered a reputation as "vocal, controversial, and persistent," and was, according to Speaker Thomas O'Neill, the "hardest-working member" of the House and one of its most skillful power players. In Abzug's own words, she was the "strongest person in Congress." ("I get it from my mother," she explained.) A *U.S. News & World Report* survey named her the "third most influential" member of the House.[55]

Abzug's tenure in the House coincided with the intensification of the Soviet campaign of harassment against Jews, including the execution of the so-called Kishinev Jews in 1971 for the crime of trying to emigrate to Israel. She became deeply involved in the campaign to win the right of Soviet Jews to emigrate, sponsoring legislation to issue visas for Soviet Jews and to provide aid to Israel for their resettlement. She also sponsored bills aimed at denying most-favored-nation status and other commercial advantages to nations that refused their citizens the right to emigrate or to freely practice their religion. In April 1976, the House unanimously passed the Abzug Resolution, marking the first time it explicitly called upon the USSR to permit free emigration, and declaring its support for a massive public demonstration against the oppression of Soviet Jews.[56] In her testimony to Congress on Soviet Jewry's right to emigrate, Abzug drew on her identity as the "only Jewish Congresswoman in the House" and her "lifetime of involvement in the fight for human rights for all people." Describing herself as a longtime student and teacher of Hebrew, she spoke poignantly of the right of Soviet Jews to practice and preserve their language and culture undisturbed. Abzug also claimed moral authority on the issue by virtue of having been a "life-long advocate" of cooperation between the Soviet Union and the United States in the cause of world peace.[57]

Abzug's first term in office also marked the 1973 Yom Kippur surprise attack against Israel and an escalation of Arab terrorism. Abzug cosponsored resolutions expressing shock and horror at the Tel Aviv airport massacres and became a staunch Congressional advocate of increased economic and military aid to Israel. Some of her peace allies blanched at her cosponsorship of a bill to supply F-4 Phantom jets to Israel, but Abzug stood her ground. Her support for arms for Israel placed her in direct opposition to those pacifists and radical feminists who had become stridently anti-Israel after the 1967 war; with the status of victim now conferred on the Palestinians, a good number of leftists, including Jewish-born feminists, systematically denigrated Israel. Abzug's support for military aid to Israel was a political necessity, since she represented a largely Jewish district. But the passion with which she led the cause in Congress was a product of her longstanding Zionist leanings, now in conflict with her antiwar sentiments. Upon discovering that the New York section of Women's Inernational League for Peace and Freedom listed her as sponsor of a petition to end arms support for Israel, she resigned from the group.[58]

This was not the only time Abzug was caught in the crossfire between left-wing peace groups that questioned the sale of arms to Israel and Jewish groups that demanded a sustained military buildup as the cornerstone of American assistance. Abzug took a balanced position, insisting that Israel be provided with the necessary resources to guarantee her right to survive, but she stressed the importance of diplomatic efforts to improve long-term relations with Arab neighbors and of downsizing the overall military budget.[59] At election time, however, some opponents were quick to label her not only not a "pro-Israel Jew, but possibly anti-Semitic" for having noted that arms for Israel should not be seen as the total solution to the Middle East crisis. When Jewish constituents cautioned her not to criticize foreign or domestic policies supported by American presidents (including Nixon, then in the midst of the impeachment crisis of 1972) "for fear it might hurt the U.S. relationship with Israel," she refused to stifle her opinions. Nevertheless, during her six years in Congress, Abzug was a consistent supporter of Israel and opponent of terrorism. She also introduced legislation opposing the Arab boycott of Israel. She voted for every aid measure to Israel, visiting the country several times on Congressional business, and was a strong Congressional voice against anti-Semitism in the United States.[60]

Another painful clash of interests came in Mexico City in 1975 over the issue of feminist anti-Zionism, at the first of three United Nations International Women's Decade Conferences. When Third World delegates began to attack Israeli representatives as "racists," all Jewish women attending the conference felt at risk; for Letty Cottin Pogrebin, this was the "click" that initiated her life as a "*Jewish*-feminist."[61] Abzug, serving as Congressional adviser to the U.S. delegation, swiftly and vigorously responded to the attacks but could not prevent the Conference from including a "Zionism is racism" plank in its final Declaration. Abzug urged Americans to vote against the Declaration because of its "totally unacceptable statement that Zionism must be eliminated along with colonialism and apartheid," and the entire delegation,

Jews and non-Jews, complied.[62] When critics at home later charged that she had "excused" the Conference's anti-Zionist resolution by declaring that the women delegates had been manipulated for political purposes by the anti-Israel bloc, and further, that "the Declaration did not constitute the major work of the Conference," Abzug responded angrily, citing her successful effort to organize Congresswomen and many other women leaders, Jews and non-Jews, to lobby the U.N. General Assembly to reject the Declaration of Mexico. Abzug deeply regretted the failure to win this fight, not only because of the blatant anti-Semitism reflected in the resolution, but because she believed it helped "set the stage" for the adoption of the "outrageous" General Assembly resolution the following year declaring that "Zionism is racism."[63]

Yet she held her ground that the International Women's Conference had nonetheless achieved positive results in stimulating efforts to improve the status of women throughout the world. Abzug had opened her own remarks at the conference with a quote from Muriel Rukeyser: "I am in the world / To change the world. . . . If one woman told the truth about her life, the world would split open." Recalling these words, Abzug had announced that the vision of the international women's movement was also to "change the world" by speaking the "truth about the lives of women."[64] That the world's feminists had not spoken the truth concerning Zionism was a painful disappointment to this Hashomer Hatzair alumna, but she believed that it did not cancel out other hopeful results.

When the second U.N. Women's Conference met in Copenhagen five years later, Abzug's hopes were high that there would be no repetition of the blatant anti-Zionism that had tainted the Mexico meeting. But as Letty Cottin Pogrebin writes, "Copenhagen was even worse," with "Jewish women of every nationality . . . isolated, excoriated, and tyrannized." As Barbara Leslie, of the International Council of Jewish Women, recalled, "Everywhere we went we were scared to death."

> Each evening the official American delegation briefed us on the conference proceedings. One night an American black woman rose to accuse our delegation of deferring to the Jews. She said she couldn't understand what was wrong with saying Zionism is racism. Women of all races applauded her statement. Then former congresswoman Bella Abzug stood up. "I'll tell you what Zionism is," she said. "It is a liberation movement for a people who have been persecuted all their lives and throughout human history."[65]

In the face of the paralysis of other Jewish delegates, Abzug's stirring words constituted the single rebuttal of the anti-Jewish assaults.

Abzug had wanted to believe that neither anti-Zionism nor anti-Semitism was a significant factor in the American feminist movement.[66] But she was taken aback when she saw the treatment American Jewish women received from their conationals and learned how many feminists, including Americans, believed that "Gloria Steinem, Betty Friedan, and Bella Abzug all being Jewish gives the American women's movement a bad name." "Could it be that anti-Semitism was the dirty little secret of the U.S. sisterhood?" Letty Cottin Pogrebin found herself asking.[67]

Rather than ignoring this possibility, Abzug has defended and explained Jewish and Israeli interests to Third World, leftist, and other critics, and organized support for Israel among peace and women's groups. But despite her strong Jewish consciousness, she continues to align herself, first and foremost, with the feminist movement. Since leaving the House of Representatives in 1976 to run unsuccessfully for the Senate (in a four-way race, she lost by a fraction of a percentage point to Daniel Patrick Moynihan), she has worked steadily on behalf of women's rights. In 1977, President Carter appointed Abzug cochair of the newly established National Advisory Committee for Women. Several months later, he fired her—according to Abzug, as a "scapegoat" for the committee's actions. When the White House counsel called her a liar, adding that the next thing she would say was that she was fired "because she was a Jew," more than half of the outraged committee's members resigned in protest. In 1980, Abzug established a new organization, WOMEN USA, cofounded with Congresswomen Patsy Mink and Maxine Waters, her longtime colleague Mim Kelber, and Brownie Ledbetter, to mobilize women as lobbyists on behalf of economic, environmental, and political issues and to aid their development as an independent political force.[68]

Putting women at the forefront of political change has always been a priority for Abzug. But her approach to promoting women's political power has been different from that of Betty Friedan, with whom Abzug jointly conceived and founded the National Women's Political Caucus. While Friedan felt the NWPC should support any female candidate, Abzug insisted that the objective was to assist any candidate—male or female—whose positions fostered shared goals of social justice. In her view, the true women's candidate was one who had a mandate to establish national programs to end war, racism, and poverty, the goal that had driven her own activism for many decades.

The difference between Friedan and Abzug over NWPC strategy was only one of several divergences between these leading Jewish feminists. Friedan accused Abzug of "invading her turf" and Gloria Steinem of "ripping off the movement for private profit" and "female chauvinism"; women's movement activists suggested that the charge stemmed from Friedan's growing sense of exclusion from the inner circles of feminist leadership. Abzug credited Friedan for her role in inaugurating second-wave feminism, but she believed that the peace movement, the labor movement, and the civil rights and youth movements also had provided an important impetus for growing demands for women's rights in the 1960s.[69]

The two women also clashed over the relationship of feminism to lesbian-

ism and family issues. While Abzug introduced the first Congressional legislation to guarantee civil rights to gays and lesbians in 1975, Friedan was attacking lesbians as a dire threat to the women's movement. Theoretically,
Abzug should have had little quarrel with the notion of a "second-stage" feminism emphasizing shared family responsibilities as the common ground between women and men—after all, Abzug and her husband Martin had for
several decades modelled a cooperative, feminist, family lifestyle. In fact,
however, she saw Friedan's late feminism as grounded more than ever in the
dynamics of middle-class privilege. Abzug had already moved on to a more
elastic feminism that highlighted the needs of single mothers and poor and
minority women around the world.

For years before sitting down to write her feminist critique in the early
1960s, Friedan, like Abzug, had protested the injustices endured by blacks
and workers; while she has never forgotten these early allegiances, they have
shifted from the forefront to the background of her commitments. Abzug,
however, has integrated her social critique of racism, militarism, poverty, and
violence within her feminist perspective. Now dedicated to the global empowerment of women as an economic force that could lift the world's poorest citizens out of despair and degradation while transforming the destructive
effects of current environmental policies, in 1990 she founded WEDO (the
Women's Environment and Development Organization), an internationally
based lobbying group that grew out of WOMEN USA and her earlier struggles for human rights. Through WEDO, which she now serves as president,
Abzug organized the World's Women's Congress for a Healthy Planet and a
series of women's caucuses at international conferences which have had a major influence on U.N. policies regarding the environment, economic justice,
and reproductive and human rights; WEDO also created the Women's Action Agenda 21, a blueprint for incorporating women's perspectives into local, national, and international decision-making into the next century. Under
Abzug's leadership, WEDO held the first public hearings in the United States
on environmental links to breast cancer and launched an international campaign to take action to prevent cancer—especially breast cancer—caused by
environmental factors.

The differences between Abzug's and Friedan's approaches owe much to
differences of temperament and background. Friedan's feminism, which grew
out of her own unhappiness and the indelible memories of her mother's despair as well as her own research findings, has remained rooted in the drive for
the full realization of women's talents. Abzug, however, never experienced
wasted years of suburban isolation and malaise. Born "yelling," her self-
esteem nurtured by a grandfather who looked like God and who praised her
precocity and a mother who thought she could do no wrong ("I can't understand it," her mother used to say. "Bella's been against the war in Vietnam so
long and it's still going on"), Abzug followed a linear path of leadership di-

rected to the fulfillment of the idealistic goals of her youth. For this steadiness of vision, she credits her days in the Zionist youth movement and her dreams of pioneering in a Jewish homeland. "It was a dream worth every minute of the dreaming," she admits, even though she never settled on a kibbutz, "because it made me a Zionist, it made me a political activist, it kept me a rebel."[70]

Friedan, who grew up on the margins of Peoria society, self-conscious about her intelligence, her looks, and her Jewishness, never received the gift of such unblemished security or early immersion in a formative social movement. Whereas Abzug's confident Jewishness was a product of her religious and Zionist inheritance, Friedan has had to go looking in her later years for a meaningful route to Judaism. But the critical vision she derived from the precarious doubleness of her identity as a Jewish youth in anti-Semitic Peoria, academically successful though socially scorned, was crucial, as we have seen, in lifting the veils that kept many women in roles that were shadowy and insubstantial. Her breakthrough *Mystique* changed the lives of many thousands of women just as the activism of Bella Abzug pointed the way for suburban middle-class housewives, as well as women from other classes and regions, to take up arms against the social and political evils of the day.

As Jewish feminists became increasingly aware of the need to apply the insights and strategies of the secular women's movement to change Judaism itself, Friedan and Abzug, who had done so much to shape that movement, lent their support. Friedan yoked Judaism to feminism at the 1970 women's march down Fifth Avenue, and later chaired the American Jewish Congress's National Commission on Women's Equality. Abzug appeared before the First National Conference on the Role of Women in Jewish Life in 1973, one of the starting points for the American Jewish feminist movement, to speak on Jewish women in politics; she recollects it as the most enjoyable speaking engagement of her entire life.[71] Fifteen years later, she addressed the First International Jewish Feminist Conference in Jerusalem with a moving speech on Jewish women's historical achievements, and served as a spokesperson for a feminist demonstration against a proposed change in the liberal Law of Return. She was one of the early participants in the Jerusalem Link, an informal group of Jewish and Arab women which met in Israel, the United States, and Belgium to promote peace.[72] In 1995, Abzug gave the keynote address at a conference at Brandeis University, "From Beijing to Tikkun Olam," as Jewish feminists cautiously prepared for the International Women's Congress in China.

For Abzug, whose first feminist awakening came in her grandfather's shul, the flowering of Jewish feminism has been an occasion for unabashed joy. One of the most stirring moments of her life came when she arranged for Rabbi Sally Priesand, the first ordained female rabbi in the United States, to deliver the opening prayer at the House of Representatives. "She was the first Jewish woman to do so. She was the first *woman* to do so," Abzug recalls. "At that moment, I felt that two movements for social progress had merged and come of age. And I really felt at home in Washington."[73]

The Next Great Moment in History Is Theirs: Robin Morgan, Meredith Tax, Paula Doress, Phyllis Chesler, Letty Cottin Pogrebin

While the initial impulses of second-wave feminism derived from the frustrations and activism of women like Friedan and Abzug, wives and mothers who married and had their children in the 1940s and early 1950s, a younger generation born just before and during World War II ignited the spark of women's liberation that caught fire among women in their twenties and fanned the flames of a new radical women's movement. "The next great moment in history is theirs," predicted journalist Vivian Gornick in a 1969 article about the origins and rapid proliferation of radical feminism.[74] Like the older feminists, this cohort may have admired their mothers and absorbed many of their strengths, yet they adamantly rejected their domestic lifestyles.

Most women's liberationists were highly educated women who had been active in the civil rights, student, and antiwar movements. A little more than a decade after Bella Abzug journeyed to Mississippi to defend Willie McGee, a group of northern Jewish women activists went South to participate in antiracist work led by SNCC (the Student Nonviolent Coordinating Committee) and other black groups; they included such activists as Florence Howe, who would later found the Feminist Press, Susan Brownmiller, who would write *Against Our Will,* a ground-breaking analysis of rape as a feminist issue, and Rita Schwerner, who had accompanied her husband, Michael Schwerner, to Mississippi during the 1964 Freedom Summer, where he was murdered. While most of these women were not Jewish-identified, they acknowledged that a sense of otherness as Jews, along with an inheritance of progressive familial values, had stimulated their involvement in the civil rights movement.[75] Their experience as allies of African Americans had in turn encouraged them to raise questions about their identities as women. Incensed at their second-class treatment by male radicals, they began to organize women's groups in tandem with other disgruntled student and antiwar activists.

One of the most dynamic voices of the new movement was Robin Morgan, a poet and former child actress (she played Dagmar in the television series "I Remember Mama").[76] In 1967, as a self-described "refugee" from the "serious, ceaseless, degrading and pervasive sexism" of the male-dominated left, Morgan became a founding member of one of the earliest and most influential women's consciousness-raising groups, the New York Radical Feminists.[77] The following year she founded the Women's International Terrorist Conspiracy from Hell, or WITCH, and helped organize the 1968 WITCH demonstration at the Miss America pageant. In 1970, she engineered the takeover of the New Left magazine *Rat,* publishing a woman's issue in retaliation for the male staff's "sex and porn special." Her essay, "Good-Bye to All That," challenging male chauvinism within the New Left and calling for a women's revolution, became "the shot heard round the left"; with other radical women, she published *Rat* as a feminist periodical for two years.[78] Her 1970 collection, *Sisterhood is Powerful: An Anthology of Writings from the Women's Liberation Movement,* containing selections from over seventy individual women and organizations, was proclaimed the radical feminist Bible. Morgan had considerable mainstream influence as well; she became a contributing editor of *Ms.* magazine when it was established in 1972, writing frequently for this popular voice of the women's movement and helping to formulate feminist actions. When *Ms.* was reorganized in 1990 as an independent monthly that accepted no advertising, Morgan became its editor.

Morgan denigrated the impact of the reform agenda created by NOW and like-minded feminist organizations: "I have visions of women bleeding to death in the gutters while Betty Friedan has tea in the White House," she wrote in 1971.[79] During the 1970s and 1980s, the writings of Morgan and her colleagues reflected growing strains in the women's movement, not only between the older reform feminists and women's liberationists, but increasingly between lesbian and heterosexual feminists and white women and women of color. Yet Morgan continued to celebrate the power of women's voices, affirming the existence of a transcendent, universal female self and a "metaphysical" feminism. In 1985, following an international feminist institute, she edited *Sisterhood Is Global: The International Women's Movement Anthology,* chronicling the status of women around the globe and calling for action to end patriarchal oppression worldwide.

Morgan went to the Middle East in the late 1980s to interview Palestinian women in refugee camps. She included their stories in her book *The Demon Lover: On the Sexuality of Terrorism* (1989). Like many leftists who grew critical of Israel after the 1967 war, Morgan condemned Israeli occupation of the West Bank and Gaza Strip and has shown little sympathy for Israel's security concerns. Describing herself as "apostately Jewish," she does not present herself as a Jew in the women's movement or identify with Jewish organizations.[80]

A closer integration between radical feminism and Jewish identity was made by Meredith Tax, a founder of another early feminist collective, Boston's Bread and Roses. Tax chose Brandeis over Harvard in 1960 to get a "more positive sense of being Jewish" than she had known in the small Wisconsin town where she grew up. The main outlines of Tax's background—an anti-Semitic environment and a mother who was a self-hating Jew—are not much different from Friedan's. Like Friedan's mother, Tax's left a job on a newspaper after marriage and bequeathed her own fierce love of language to her daughter. But she also passed on to Tax her painfully acquired knowledge that family life was "a trap, full of bitterness, not joy. . . . it was a woman's fate, all there was." Broken by her unhappy destiny, she refused to acknowledge Tax's intelligence, using "ridicule, scorn, and rage" to belittle her powers, perhaps out of fear that she could not control this smart and rebellious daughter.[81] When Tax left home, it was with the unstated but unalterable conviction that she would never duplicate her mother's life of unfulfilled domesticity.[82]

After graduating from Brandeis, Tax went off to Oxford to do graduate work in literature but gave up her studies when she became active in the antinuclear and antiwar movements. In 1968, believing that the Vietnam War could only be stopped in the United States, she returned home. She taught briefly at Brandeis and was a part of a Marxist collective in Somerville; by 1969, female members of the group, like New Left women elsewhere, had become alienated from the male-dominated leadership. Following a women's liberation conference at Emerson College that year (the first national gathering of radical feminists), Tax and some Boston-area colleagues decided to organize a socialist-feminist collective that they called Bread and Roses. The name came from a women's labor song from the Lawrence mill strike of 1912: "Hearts starve as well as bodies/Give us bread but give us roses." Tax, women's historians Linda Gordon and Grey Osterud, sociologist Wini Breines, and the other founding members of the collective drew consciously from the past in hopes of uniting antiwar, antiracist activities with a feminist consciousness to create a "permanent social transformation."[83]

The goal of Bread and Roses was to build a "radical, mass autonomous women's liberation movement" that would attack the multiple roots of female oppression. In writings published in Boston's underground newspaper and in "Woman and Her Mind," a four-part essay published in the 1970 collection *Notes from the Second Year* (and reprinted as a pamphlet by the New England Free Press), Tax described the theory of women's liberation; the piece became one of the founding documents of the women's liberation movement and sold over 150,000 copies by mail. In the essay, Tax explained that although women needed "to build a revolutionary movement out of personal need," there could be no "individual solutions to women's oppression."[84]

> A woman comes to believe that personal truth, the truth of the nuances of individual behavior, is ultimate . . . But this concentration of the personal is another way society makes her unfit to run her mind. . . . Once people have gotten past the realization that they are neurotic as individuals, they are able to realize that their problem is not an individual one, but one they share with the rest of their community. At this point, the realm of psychology becomes the proper sphere of political analysis. . . .[85]

This was not necessarily a Jewish insight, but Tax and some of the other Jewish members of Bread and Roses found that the self-denigration in which they had habitually engaged because they were smart, inquisitive, sometimes exotic, and often undeniably Jewish-looking perfectly fit the paradigm of internal oppression—what Tax labeled "female schizophrenia."[86]

After the Bread and Roses collective disbanded, its members moving on to other feminist pursuits, Tax, newly married, left Boston for Chicago and then New York, where she would eventually undertake some of the earliest research on Jewish feminist history. Fascinated by the similarities between feminism and class consciousness, she began to examine historical parallels between female radicals and union activity. The result was a history of radical women in the late nineteenth century, *The Rising of the Women* (1980). Tax's search for historical models led her to write two novels about Jewish women radicals—*Rivington Street* (1982), a historical romance about several generations of women radicals in East Europe and the Lower East Side, and its sequel, *Union Square* (1988). Tax was the first of the women's liberationists to identify with the radical tradition of American Jewish women and to turn to popular fiction as a means of communicating this history to a mass audience. In later years, Tax organized and led women's committees of American PEN and International PEN; with Grace Paley and others, she recently formed a human rights organization, Women's WORLD (Women's World Organization for Rights, Literature and Development) to fight gender-based censorship; she sees her belief in the "holiness of the word" as "very Jewish." Tax is now working on what she describes as a biblical novel—she is reimagining the Garden of Eden from women's perspective and putting the women into the story of Moses and the covenant at Sinai.[87]

Jewish women in the early radical feminist movement were also involved in another group that emerged from Bread and Roses, the Boston Women's Health Book Collective. It pioneered the national and eventually international women's health movement and compiled the popular self-help manual *Our Bodies, Ourselves* (1976), and later *Ourselves and Our Children* (1978). Nine of the twelve founding members of the collective were Jewish. According to Paula Doress, one of the founders of the group and co-author of *Ourselves Growing Older* (1987), written in conjunction with the Boston Women's Health Book Collective, the ethical ideals of Judaism consciously informed her work in the women's movement generally and in the health book collective particularly. Doress grew up in an observant working-class family in Boston, attending the orthodox Maimonides School in Brookline through junior high. After public high school and college, she became active in civil rights and peace coalitions. With the advent of black power in the civil rights movement, Doress felt there was no place for whites to go but back to their own communities. She became involved in the early women's movement through consciousness-raising, and attended several meetings of Bread and Roses, eventually helping to found the Women's Health Book Collective. Today Doress (now Doress-Worters) remains a member of that collective, which over the years has celebrated Passover and other Jewish holidays, inviting non-Jewish as well as Jewish friends to celebrate their communal struggle for peace and freedom. Today she is involved in B'nai Or, a Jewish renewal group, and is writing a fictional biography of Ernestine Rose, the nineteenth-century Jewish feminist. "In the civil rights and feminist movements, we identified as universalists," she remarks. "We were afraid of seeing ourselves as too driven by our particularities; it wouldn't have been proper to call ourselves radical Jews. But that is exactly what we were."[88]

For some Jewish women, it was the presence of anti-Semitism on the left that shocked them into an acknowledgment of their roots. Phyllis Chesler, a feminist leader and theoretician who was born into what she describes as a "relatively Orthodox" family in Borough Park, Brooklyn, but who "forgot" about being Jewish when she learned there was no use for a woman's "passion for [Jewish] learning," suddenly remembered her Jewishness "within the bosom of the feminist movement," where she found she was treated as a "*Jewish* feminist, and not as a feminist-in-the-abstract." What she learned was that

> non-Jewish men treated me the way white men treat black women—as more "sensual," earthy, sexually accessible; as Rebecca of *Ivanhoe*. I experienced the same treatment from feminists, when I was singled out by some comrades as somehow fleshier, earthier, sexier, pushier, more verbal: "Jewish."[89]

Chesler's response was to start wearing extremely large Jewish stars when she spoke to feminist and "radical-left-socialist" audiences and to publicly identify herself as a Zionist.

Letty Cottin Pogrebin, author of *Deborah, Golda and Me: Being Female and Jewish in America* and a Middle East peace activist, had a similar experience. Though she too had been born into a religiously committed family and was educated in Hebrew schools, she came to associate Judaism with her father, a Jewish Federation and synagogue leader, and became disgusted at the misogyny of both, withdrawing from any active association with her Jewishness at age fifteen, when she was not permitted to count in a minyan saying kaddish for her own mother. She chose to go to college at Brandeis, although she thought little about its meaning as a Jewish-identified school. After college, she entered the publishing world and in the early 1970s became one of the five founding editors of *Ms.* Although half the founders were Jewish, ethnicity and religion were irrelevant to the magazine's mission or to the women's sense of themselves: "Being a Jew was irrelevant to anything I was doing professionally or socially . . . ," Pogrebin recalled. "It didn't matter one way or the other."[90] In fact, neither did it appear to matter at home. Although Pogrebin was bat mitzvah herself, neither her twin daughters nor her son became bat or bar mitzvah. At an "identity workshop" at a women's conference in the early 1970s, Pogrebin was asked to stand beneath the sign that best described her:

HUMAN, WOMAN, MOTHER, WIFE, WORKER, WHITE, BLACK, AMERICAN, CHRISTIAN, JEW, etc. Without hesitation, she placed herself beneath the sign marked WOMAN.[91]

Pogrebin's awakening as a *Jewish* feminist came in the face of the blatant anti-Zionism exhibited at the International Women's Conference in Mexico in 1980. Two years later, after interviewing scores of women all over the United States, she wrote a startling eleven-page article on anti-Semitism in the women's movement for *Ms.* Citing "anti-Semitism and sexism" as forms of "twin oppression" of women, the article described the prevalence of anti-Semitism on the political right as well as the radical left, within the black community, and among Christian feminists who blamed Jewish monotheism for the extinction of goddess cults and the death of Jesus. She also identified "the three I's" that characterized women's experience of anti-Semitism: invisibility, insult, and internalized oppression.[92] The article created enormous controversy among feminists who objected to Pogrebin's characterizations. But Pogrebin was most disturbed at the many letters she received from Jews confessing to "collaboration or silent complicity in the face of personal experience with anti-Semitism."[93]

The experiences of anti-Semitism at the International Conferences in Mexico and Copenhagen revealed other fissures in the women's movement. The American delegation included not only political feminists but representatives from Jewish women's organizations; these women behaved like "nice Jewish girls," unable to confront the anti-Zionism and anti-Semitism that surfaced at the meetings. But even more troubling to some feminists was that although these delegates represented hundreds of thousands of American Jewish women, they were reluctant to support reproductive freedom, abortion rights, and other components of the feminist agenda for fear of offending more traditional members.[94]

Both the silence in the face of anti-Zionist and anti-Semitic rhetoric and the political divisions between Jewish delegates at Mexico and Copenhagen revealed that Jewish feminists had much organizing to do. "We cannot be asked to fragment ourselves," Letty Cottin Pogrebin told a meeting of Jewish women preparing to attend another international conference years later. "We are women. And we are Jews. We are feminists. And we are Zionists. And we just take all parts of ourselves with us . . . wherever there is work to be done in the struggle for freedom, justice and dignity."[95]

In the next decades, Jewish feminism would coalesce as a religious, political, and intellectual force, uniting secular and religious women in a growing movement that would transform the American Jewish community and tradition as well as the lives of Jewish women.

Chapter 10

COMING OUT AS JEWISH WOMEN

The Feminist Assault on the Academy and Religion:
Gerda Lerner and Rabbi Sally Priesand

In 1978, fifteen years after the publication of *The Feminine Mystique*, a young activist named Jane Litman addressed a conference of Jewish women in San Francisco. Litman told the women "that the insights we have gathered through feminism must be applied to every portion of our lives, including our religion. We cannot allow ourselves as Jewish women to be treated in ways we would not allow ourselves to be treated as women." The question was how to bring the emotions and commitments of feminism into a patriarchal religion that had marginalized women. As Litman recalled:

> When, at the synagogue which I attended in my teens, the rabbi would say as he took the Torah from the Ark, "This is the covenant which declares the fatherhood of God and the brotherhood of man," I was never too excited, but everytime I say to myself—the sisterhood of women—a chill runs down my spine.[1]

In her view, the solution lay in reclaiming Jewish women's history, thus providing new role models, sources, and materials for a reinterpretation of tradition. During the last twenty-five years, as increasing numbers of women have entered the Reform, Conservative, and Reconstructionist rabbinates, and as women's prayer groups have gained increasing acceptance in all denominations, including the Orthodox, a new, more egalitarian Judaism incorporating women's voices and experiences has begun to flourish.

Jewish women played leading roles in establishing the feminist intellectual revolution that shaped these religious changes. Challenging the patriarchal organization of knowledge that excluded women's experiences, scholars like historian Gerda Lerner demanded that "women be included in whatever topic is under discussion . . . woman are the majority of humankind and have been essential to the making of history."[2] While feminists in academia did not usually write as Jews, their ideas often were influenced by their Jewish backgrounds. Like Friedan, Abzug, and the women's liberationists, many were motivated by the heritage of family and the religious ideals of *tsedakah* and social justice. As they searched for new models with which to empower women in the world, the legacy of powerful Jewish mothers and their own experiences of anti-Semitism and marginality, especially as Jewish women, also proved formative.

Feminism has also affected Jewish attitudes toward sexuality and family life. Greater openness has prompted increasing numbers of lesbian Jews to come out and to create new forms of Jewish community and spirituality. Refusing to remain invisible either as Jews or as lesbians, these women have begun to forcefully acknowledge their compound identities. Their proud stance as feminists who are Jews has complemented heterosexual feminists' reclamation of their Jewish heritage.

Passage to Women's History   In 1966, the dynamic, outspoken Gerda Lerner (born Gerda Kronstein in 1920, the same auspicious year for feminists as Abzug) had just completed her Ph.D. in American history with a thesis on the Grimke sisters of South Carolina. Lerner, a refugee who had fled to the United States from Nazi Vienna, was among the first to bring a consciously feminist lens to the study of history, producing a series of essays and books that had enormous influence in conceptualizing the field. Among her most important works are the documentary anthology *Black Women in White America* (1972), a collection of her own essays, *The Majority Finds Its Past* (1979), and the path-breaking *Creation of Patriarchy* (1987) and *Creation of Feminist Consciousness* (1993). In 1984, Lerner established a Ph.D. program in women's history at the University of Wisconsin at Madison, the first of its kind.

Before coming to the study of history, Lerner had been a fiction writer and screenwriter, often in partnership with her husband Carl Lerner, the highly acclaimed editor of such film classics as *Red River, Twelve Angry Men, On the Bowery,* and *The Fugitive Kind.* Carl Lerner had made his directorial debut with the film *Black Like Me,* co-scripted with Gerda, the story of a white man who darkened his skin and travelled as a black man in the South. In the late 1940s and early 1950s, Gerda Lerner was active in the Congress of American Women, a progressive grassroots women's group interested in economic and consumer issues; she also participated in several Emma Lazarus Federation events. Throughout the 1950s, she worked in support of the United Nations and peace; in the early 1960s, she successfully blocked the construction of the Ravenswood nuclear power plant in Long Island City. During these years she actively supported civil rights for African Americans.[3]

After completing several novels, Lerner began a biographical novel about the Grimke sisters, enrolling in courses at the New School to expand her knowledge of American history. Soon she decided to write the biography as history rather than fiction and to take the courses for credit; as an undergraduate at the New School she taught a course in women's history, one of the first in the country. In 1963, at age forty-three, Lerner earned her B.A. from the New School. Three years later she graduated from Columbia University with an M.A. and Ph.D. in U.S. history. Despite the opposition of her mentors, she gravitated to the study of white women involved in the abolitionist movement. The Grimke biography became her dissertation and first historical book.

Until very recently, however, Lerner had not connected her heritage as a Jewish refugee, and specifically her identity as a Jewish woman, to her work in women's history. When asked how being Jewish had influenced her work in women's history, she answered first that she had "never given it a moment's thought."[4] But the question prompted her to reflect on a connection she had hidden even from herself; soon she would acknowledge, quite simply, that "I am a historian because of my Jewish experience," and specifically that she was a historian of women and marginalized groups because she had so long been defined, and defined herself, as an "outsider."[5] While Lerner's dual experience as a pioneer of women's history and as a refugee is unique, her joining of feminist impulses to her background as a Jewish woman who viewed herself as other is not. Many American-born Jewish scholars, among them Carol Gilligan, Evelyn Fox Keller, Elaine Showalter, Joan Wallach Scott, Nancy Cott, and Linda Kerber applied the outsider perspective to their disciplines to reveal the male bias in what had always been considered "neutral" facts, research techniques, analytic methods, and "established" knowledge. These and other Jewish women scholars played a significant role in pioneering women's studies in the academy.

Growing up in a comfortable, well-to-do, assimilated family that considered itself "liberal, progressive," and proudly Austrian, Lerner was well aware, by the time she left Vienna in 1938, of the difficulty of being Jewish and female in a country and tradition that respected neither. While her family did not keep kosher or attend synagogue, except for the High Holidays, Lerner was sent to a Sabbath school to learn Hebrew and prepare for her bat mitzvah. Like Bella Abzug, however, she was distressed that women could not participate fully in services and were isolated in balcony pews. Shortly before the event, she announced that she had decided not to participate in the ceremony since she no longer believed in God. Thus did her first feminist action "come out of . . . experiences as a Jewish woman."[6] She stayed away from the synagogue for over fifty years.

Like Betty Friedan, who rebelled (although less forcefully) at the time of her coming of age, Lerner's disillusionment with Judaism was supplemented by the message she received at home: that being Jewish meant "not pride, but embarrassment; not collectivity, but exclusion." Told by her parents not to "act Jewish"—that is, not to speak with her hands, raise her voice, or be noisy, lively, or inquisitive—she grew up feeling, like Friedan, that "being Jewish set one apart," made her different, "not normal."[7] Like her parents, she considered herself "an Austrian first, a Jew second."[8]

Then came the Nazis. In 1938, a few weeks after her father, a pharmacist and businessman, had fled the country after being warned of his imminent arrest, a dozen storm troopers raided the family's apartment, demanding to know her father's whereabouts. They terrorized the family for hours, tearing up furniture and forcing the family to search every book in the house for supposedly hidden money. Outraged, Lerner, then eighteen, threw a handful of books on the floor at the troopers' feet and said she had had enough. They left shortly afterward, and Lerner experienced her second feminist epiphany: by resisting authority even in desperate situations, you can reclaim your dignity. In many difficult situations later in life, she would draw upon her memory of this girlhood defiance.[9]

But her respite was short-lived; soon after, Lerner and her mother were taken to jail as hostages for her father. Lerner, who had been active in the student opposition, distributing literature and caring for victims of fascism, believed at the time that she had been targeted for her politics. Separated from her mother, she was held for six weeks in a dirty, foul-smelling, single-person cell so crowded with prisoners that they felt like "slaves in the hold of a slave ship." There she was forced to listen to the sounds of prisoners crying out as they were beaten. Because she was Jewish, she was given half the minute rations given to other prisoners; like the others, she was given sedatives. To keep her mind functioning, Lerner organized a school in the cell, teaching English, literature, and history. Later, she observed that being jailed under those conditions had been the most important experience of her life: "I had to make the choice of how I was going to die. Once you've faced that, it's there for the rest of your life. It gives you a kind of basic courage."[10]

Lerner and her mother were released from jail after her father signed over his property and business to the Nazis; for six harrowing months, under immediate deportation orders, they struggled to get permits to leave the country. One week before Kristallnacht, Lerner, her sister, and mother obtained the legal papers needed to join her father in Liechtenstein, where he had established a business four years earlier. In the spring of 1939, Lerner left Europe, the only one of her family to secure a visa to the United States. Her parting from her mother was troubled. When her mother, a talented but frustrated visual artist, died some years later, after years spent in exile, she bequeathed to Lerner her unfinished emotional as well as artistic work: the challenge of "how to become a woman capable of love, a reliable mother and yet a person. How to focus and gather one's strength and discipline one's talent." Lerner understood that "in another time and place she would have been a liberated woman. In her time and place, she was flawed, unhappy and often destructive . . . but she did show me what was possible."[11]

Lerner remembers her passage to America "as six days of weeping, seasickness and fear. No matter what I tried to say and act, deep inside I was mourning. It was a tearing out, a violent uprooting, a voyage of death."[12] Though her parents survived the war, she never saw her mother again. She lost other close relatives in the Holocaust, including her mother's sister, Margit, a physician, who died at Auschwitz.[13]

After arriving in the United States, Lerner worked as a waitress, salesgirl, office clerk, and X-ray technician. All the time, however, she was writing poetry and fiction.[14] Within a few years of her arrival, she published two short stories in American magazines, one a first-person account of the horrors of Nazi occupation and the other an astute analysis of the psychology of Nazi brutality. The stories provide a glimpse of two interrelated elements that would become the basis of Lerner's theories about gender and patriarchy four decades later.

"The Prisoners," published in 1941, is the story of four girls crowded into a Nazi jail cell, where they endure the torments of inadequate food and sleep, regular beatings, and an uncertain fate.[15] The protagonist, Anna, had been arrested after being caught guiding Jewish youth and student resistance leaders to the Czechoslovakian border; despite being tortured, she refuses to provide the names of others who aided the escape. Hoping to inspire her cellmates' will to resist, she tells her story before she goes off, calmly, to meet her death. But she returns, badly bruised, having been sentenced instead to three years in a concentration camp. "I'm so happy," she murmurs, "that means a chance to come back—and fight them." The story ends with her raising her hand in a pledge to live.

The themes of this early fiction—Anna's resistance, the passing on of her story, the support, solidarity, and strength of the women—came to dominate Lerner's view of women in history. Rather than the oppression and victimization that some historians highlighted in the early years of the women's movement, Lerner preferred to see women as actors in their own lives, resisting the social and physical tyrannies that imprisoned them.

In "The Russian Campaign" (1943), Lerner presents the reverse side of the story of women's resistance to Nazi power. In a tense camp on the Russian front, German soldiers have suffered a series of defeats, their numbers thinning until there are only five men left in the unit. When one of them, a former philosophy student named Hauser, confesses his fear of death to his comrades, he is ridiculed as a "sissy" and "old woman." That evening, Hauser and another soldier, Kurt, capture a local guerrilla in farmer's clothes. In a scuffle that results from Kurt's fear that he will be "cheated out of his triumph" and prevented from torturing the prisoner, it is revealed that the captive—who meets Kurt's gaze with "proud eyes"—is female. In an instant, the soldiers are upon her, and she is brutally raped. Hauser, delighted that the seemingly tough, virile Kurt has fainted during the attack, proves his own manhood by slashing the woman; Hauser wears "the proud smile of invincibility on his ugly face" as another soldier shoots the woman to stop her moaning.[16]

The inspiration for this story had been a report of Nazi atrocities in the USSR and Lerner's own acquaintance with Nazis in Austria, including former friends, who provided the models for her fictional German patrol. Her purpose was to explore the background and thinking of ordinary people who undergo "incredible changes" and are eventually able to commit atrocities. Although focusing on the specifics of Nazi brutality, the story uncovers the fears and doubts—especially regarding masculinity—that underlie many kinds of oppression and tyranny, including the destruction of the Jews and the rape of women.

The insights that Lerner gained as a young girl would be sharpened years later in her sustained analysis of the role of gender in history. In *The Creation of Patriarchy,* she provides a comprehensive historical account of the institutionalization of patriarchal oppression over two millennia; in *The Creation of Feminist Consciousness,* she chronicles the start of women's fight against patriarchy. Although she lacked the tools of feminist analysis that would develop as a product of the women's movement, her 1940s stories reveal both aspects of her later understanding of gender—women's strength and resistance and their victimization by masculine violence and oppression.

In 1955, Lerner published a well-received novel, *No Farewell,* about Vienna on the brink of Nazi occupation, but she abandoned Europe and fascism as subjects when she turned to history some years later. Her choice of the United States as a specialty was in many respects a reflection of her continuing effort to assimilate. As a refugee, she had arrived in the United States a stateless person, with her outsider status permanently fixed. Becoming a "good American," as she desperately desired, meant erasing her foreign characteristics; it is therefore not surprising that when she decided to prepare for an academic career she chose American, not European, history. She explains: "I still wanted, as I had in Austria, to be a 'normal' person." Nonetheless, she chose women's history, a deviant, in fact a nonexistent, field. Her otherness was obvious from the moment she entered graduate school—"too old (over forty), a foreign-born woman, a Jew, insisting on specializing in a field of history [her] professors considered 'exotic' and weird."[17]

In the last few years, Lerner has recognized that her choice both of history and of women's history was influenced by her multiple experiences as a Jew, a Jewish woman, and a refugee. The "enormity of the loss of a people, of communities, of one's own past"—a loss that she feels every time she visits Vienna (six times in the past fifty years)—has given her only one "lifeline," that of "memory, personal and historical." "After the Holocaust," she muses, "history for me was no longer something outside, which I needed to comprehend and use to illuminate my own life and times. Those of us who survived carried a charge to keep memory alive in order to resist the total destruction of our people. History had become an obligation."[18] Thus she believes that her "Jewish background and . . . experience with Nazi fascism disposed [her] toward thinking historically," while her "experience of being defined as an outsider by others and accepting that definition for [her]self had predisposed [her] toward an understanding of 'outgroups.' "[19] She chose race as her subspecialty within women's history because it was a major issue in U.S. history, and because African Americans, not Jews, were the "targeted out-group" in the United States.

Lerner's experiences under Nazism, and her fear that nationalistic solutions could only lead to war and conflict, also turned her toward Marxism. However, after concluding that Marxist theory could not adequately account for problems of race and gender, she eventually returned to a more direct acknowledgment of her Jewish identity. A few years ago a swastika was painted on a poster near her office door and she received anti-Semitic death threats. "Back to square one," she writes. "The Jew remains 'the Other.' " But, she insists, "I am a Jewish woman, I am an immigrant, and I will no longer permit others to define me. . . ."[20]

As a Jewish refugee, Lerner faced distinct challenges in finding a place within the American academy; in the case of native-born Jewish women within women's studies, relatively few applied their analytic skills to Jewish issues. Nonetheless, their Jewishness was often an ingredient in their attraction to feminism. Literary critic Carolyn Heilbrun has commented about growing up in an assimilated family that disregarded its Jewish heritage: "However unobservant that identification was, however fiercely I had denied the adamant anti-Semitism around me as I grew up—still having been a Jew had made me an outsider. It had permitted me to be a feminist."[21]

Although feminist scholars have generally been more concerned with issues of class, race, and ethnicity, or multiculturalism and pluralism, than with specifically Jewish questions, increasingly they are speaking as Jews at professional associations, feminist gatherings, and Jewish forums. They are also writing more regularly on Jewish subjects, and are now devoting themselves to the effort to include Jewish ethnicity and religion in the academic discourse on multiculturalism. Within Jewish studies, too, feminist scholars have organized a women's caucus that has grown increasingly more influential in the field.[22] In the 1990s, after too long a silence, Jewish feminist academicians are coming out and asserting their heritage.

A movement to integrate Jewish women's perspectives into Jewish religious life, a direct by-product of the women's movement, is also well under way.

From Isolation to Sisterhood: The Origins of Jewish Feminism   In March 1972, a new women's study group, Ezrat Nashim (literally, "help for women," or the women's section of the synagogue), invaded the Rabbinical Assembly meeting at the Concord Hotel in Kiamesha, New York, to demand a hearing for their "Call for Change." This was a general statement of dissatisfaction with the Conservative movement's treatment of women and a list of demands, from inclusion of women in the *minyan* (prayer quorum), synagogue services, and rabbinical and cantorial schools to reform of divorce procedures and the male-dominated power structure of Jewish religious and communal life.[23] Composed of a dozen women in their early twenties who had grown up attending the schools, camps, and synagogues of the Conservative movement, Ezrat Nashim became the spark plug of the Jewish feminist movement. Like the women's liberationists of the New Left, its members had been galvanized into action by feminist consciousness-raising groups and political action projects, as well as by anger at the sexism of colleagues in the Jewish student movement. The small group set in motion an unalterable process that would gather momentum as the decade progressed.

In February 1973, with the help of Ezrat Nashim members, the first National Jewish Women's Conference took place in New York City. Attended by some five hundred women, the conference was addressed by Congresswomen Bella Abzug and Elizabeth Holtzman and other prominent Jewish women. But the essence of the conference was workshops addressing all aspects of Jewish female identity: family roles and socialization, religious life, education, politics, and stereotyping. Much as American women had been shocked into awareness by Friedan's exposé a decade before, participants at this conference were transformed by collective acknowledgment of what until then had seemed a private misery. Suddenly, with the stirring of "long-buried emotions" in the hundreds of women gathered together, "we all knew ourselves to be oppressed within our Jewishness," recalled one delegate.[24]

The conference also proved to be a turning point for Blu Greenberg, who gave the opening address. An Orthodox Jew married to a rabbi, Greenberg had been awakened to feminist issues a decade earlier by *The Feminine Mystique*. "Once I had tasted of the fruit of the tree of knowledge, there was no going back," she recalled of her encounter with Friedan's text. She began to examine the gendered separation of religious functions that had previously made little impression upon her but that now, under "the white light of equality," was revealed as part of a troubling pattern of exclusion. Yet she remained tentative and haphazard in her analysis, insisting that she was not a "women's libber" and fearful of being associated with the stridency of the "radical fringe," the women she called "orthodox" feminists.[25]

At the Jewish Women's Conference, however, Greenberg discovered hundreds of feminists who were not hostile to Judaism, many of whom, in fact, had come to Judaism through feminism. Suddenly she understood that "you could still be a mild-mannered yeshiva girl and a card-carrying feminist and not feel out of whack all the time." The real "shocker," however, was when she was asked after the Torah reading to perform the *hagba'ah* (the lifting up of the Torah before it is returned to the ark). Although reluctant, Greenberg could not refuse, and with her "defenses down," she found herself for the first time in her life holding a Torah scroll. This "exhilarating moment," and her discovery of a like-minded community of Jewish feminists, convinced her to delve more deeply into the intersections between Orthodox Judaism and feminism. In 1981, she published her path-breaking volume, *On Women and Judaism: A View from Tradition,* which outlined a Jewish feminist agenda for Orthodox women in the synagogue, the community, and family life.[26]

Even the lives of those not present were altered by the first Jewish Women's Conference. Amy Eilberg, a freshman at Brandeis University, heard from friends that Rachel Adler (the author of an article on women and Jewish law that had greatly influenced the women of Ezrat Nashim) had *davened* (prayed) at the conference with *tallit* (prayer shawl) and *tefillin* (phylacteries) (forbidden to women, according to Jewish law); at that moment, Eilberg decided that she too would take on these obligations, and she began to think of the rabbinate as a career. Eilberg became the first woman rabbi ordained by the Conservative movement twelve years later.[27]

A second Jewish feminist conference held in 1974 triggered the formation of the Jewish Feminist Organization, a loose coalition of women committed to the dual agenda of developing women's full potential through equal participation in all aspects of Jewish culture—communal, religious, educational, and political—while promoting the survival and enhancement of Jewish life.[28] Though the organization would last for only a few years, it played a significant role in moving Jewish women "out of isolation into sisterhood," as its statement of purpose proclaimed, bringing together secular leftists and committed religious Jews.

While the thrust of the Jewish feminist movement lay in creating change within the Jewish community, in a simultaneous series of developments, Jewish women began to identify, and eventually to confront, anti-Semitism within the feminist movement. In the early 1970s, even before the glaring anti-Zionism of the U.N. International Conference in Mexico sent a shock wave through Jewish feminists, Judith Plaskow, then a graduate student in Yale's theology department, began to suspect that feminists in the field of religious studies might harbor anti-Judaic perspectives. In 1973, Plaskow was spending a year at the Women's Studies Program of the Harvard Divinity School, then as now a pioneering institute for the study of women, religion, and culture. But when the Yom Kippur war broke out and Israel's survival was threatened, Plaskow felt "literally ripped in half." She acknowledged to herself that, "although I identify as a woman, I *am* a Jew, and they are Christians."[29] In a series of articles over the next decade, Plaskow identified anti-Semitism as the "unacknowledged racism" of the feminist movement: Jewish feminists had to listen to anti-Semitic jokes at women's meetings; their concerns were trivialized and treated as "Jewish paranoia"; they were silenced through the use of stereotypes—she's just a "Princess/Jewish intellectual/rich Jew/pushy Jew/cunning Jew, etc."[30] While Plaskow admired the intellectual fervor of Christian feminists, whom she felt were about "ten years ahead" of Jewish women in confronting religious sexism, she worried that they were blaming Jews for "inventing patriarchy"; the vehicle for this latest form of anti-Semitism was the new "myth" that Jesus had tried to restore egalitarian-ism but was "foiled by the persistence of Jewish attitudes." Plaskow's concern in 1980 was that Christian feminism might become an "excuse" for oppress-ing her as a Jew and another weapon in a renewed "Christian anti-Judaic arsenal."[31]

While Plaskow was charting anti-Semitism within academic feminism, American Jewish women returned from the International Women's Confer-ence in Copenhagen in 1980 in shock from the vicious anti-Semitic attacks of delegates allied with the PLO. Their enduring bitterness was the product not simply of the anti-Semitism itself, but of the other delegates' indifference to it. In Copenhagen, as one delegate said, "I saw my grandmother's wig askew and her legs in the air and Cossacks riding off. And nobody noticed and nobody cared." Neither did Jewish women find a receptive audience when they returned to the United States. What they had to say was consid-ered "exaggerated," "not worth hearing," "not feminist," or "the product of paranoia."[32] In reaction to these attitudes, Jewish women formed a new group, Feminists Against Anti-Semitism, which defined itself as explicitly feminist and Zionist. That group put anti-Semitism on the agenda of a 1981 Women's Studies Association Conference for the first time. Three years later, spearheaded by Judith Arcana, Rabbi Sue Elwell, and Evelyn Torton Beck, Jewish women formed a permanent Jewish Women's Caucus within the Women's Studies Association. The group's platform stated that "Jews exist as a cultural/religious minority within contemporary American society," but de-spite their many successes, they are still "mocked, despised, feared and scape-goated" by the Christian majority, including women of other racial and ethnic groups. For this reason, it was critical to integrate the experience of Jewish women "as Jews" into feminist associations.[33]

Jewish feminists also organized to work for change on the community level. In 1984, the American Jewish Congress focused its annual U.S.–Israel dialogue in Jerusalem on the topic of "Woman as Jew, Jew as Woman." For three days, American feminists joined Israeli academic and professional women in wide-ranging discussions about Jewish women's religious, politi-cal, and social status. "Never before in the twenty years of these annual dia-logues had there been so electric an atmosphere," recalls Israeli scholar Alice Shalvi.[34] Immediately following the conference, they established a new women's lobby, the Israel Women's Network (with Shalvi as chairwoman), to enhance women's status in Israel and promote greater equality between the sexes. The network was thus the direct outcome of interaction between

American and Israeli feminists, and it remains the leading women's rights group in Israel.

In addition to being a "landmark in the development of Israeli feminist activity," according to Shalvi, the 1984 conference also had important effects in the United States, where under the auspices of the American Jewish Congress, the National Commission on Women's Equality was created (with Betty Friedan and Leona Chanin as co-chairs). Four years later, the Israel Women's Network and the American Jewish Congress Commission jointly sponsored the First International Jewish Feminist Conference in Jerusalem. Believing that the conference could be a watershed in Jewish history, a group of delegates—led by American feminist Rivka Haut, an Orthodox activist—decided to hold a prayer service at the *kotel* (the Western Wall) as a model of Jewish cooperation; participants included Blu Greenberg; Norma Baumel Joseph, an Orthodox feminist leader from Canada; Francine Klagsbrun, a Conservative Jewish writer; and Shulamit Magnus, then teaching at the Reconstructionist Rabbinical College in Philadelphia.[35]

To accommodate Orthodox participants, the women did not constitute themselves a *minyan* or recite prayers for which a *minyan* was necessary. Nonetheless, their public reading of the Torah at the *kotel* infuriated a group of ultra-Orthodox men, who cursed and physically assaulted the women and forced them to disband the service at this time. Yet they established a new group, Women at the Wall, holding regular services at the *kotel* in accordance with Orthodox rabbis' guidelines for women's prayer groups. Because violence against the women continued, the group petitioned the Israeli High Court for the right of public worship at the *kotel*. After many delays, in 1994 the Court asked the government to develop a plan for satisfying the needs of all parties; that plan has not yet been developed.[36]

Through such organizations as the International Women of the Wall, which supports the efforts of the Israeli Women of the Wall, and Woman's Voice, a Jewish women's group in the United States that works with the Israel Women's Network, the interaction between Israeli and North American feminists has flourished. Israeli feminists are encouraged by the warm response they receive from American Jewish women, many of whom in supporting Israeli women's issues have been enabled to discover their own Jewish feminist voices. It has been through feminism, says Alice Shalvi, that Jewish women in Israel and the United States have developed a powerful and inspiring common cause.[37]

However important has been the work of women's lobbies in promoting the interests of Jewish feminists, perhaps the major arena for reform has been the rabbinate itself. Since 1972, when Sally Priesand became a Reform rabbi, more than 300 women have been ordained as rabbis within the Reform, Conservative, and Reconstructionist movements. These women are not only serving as role models to the younger generation of Jewish women but are building a new kind of clergy with ideas about authority, community, and perhaps even God that depart in significant ways from those of traditional Judaism.

Priesand did not come to the rabbinate as a feminist with a women's rights agenda; she simply wanted to be a rabbi. Yet it is not incidental that the thesis she wrote for her rabbinical degree was a design for a course on the "Historic and Changing Role of the Jewish Woman"; like Ray Frank, Rebekah Kohut, and Henrietta Szold, Priesand turned to history to find encouragement for her innovations. Her thesis offers a sweeping, if cursory, assessment of Biblical, rabbinical, and modern ideas about Jewish women and their changing roles throughout history, addressing itself to both the myths and stereotypes and the actual status and achievements of historical women. Considering that the study was undertaken before the advent of any serious academic work in Jewish women's history, Priesand's achievement is substantial and remarkably prescient of the direction of future scholarship.[38]

Priesand had known that she wanted to be a rabbi by age sixteen. While not religiously observant, her parents' Jewish identity ran deep; her mother served as president of the synagogue sisterhood in their Conservative synagogue in Cleveland, Ohio, and her father was president of a B'nai B'rith lodge. Despite the fact that no woman had ever entered the rabbinate, her parents encouraged her dream, and her "very deep belief in Judaism and . . . firm conviction that [she] might have something to offer" propelled her forward. Priesand believes that it was simply her good fortune to have applied to the Hebrew Union College-Institute of Religion at the very moment when that body decided to lift its ban on women as rabbinical students.[39] Her admission came fifty years after Martha Neumark's rejection.

Priesand's experience at Hebrew Union College was mixed. Many considered her ambition a "passing fancy" and assumed she had just come "to find a husband"; some of her professors, she suspected, would not have been disappointed had she failed. Sensing that she stood "for all women, and that the world was watching" her, Priesand struggled "to do better" than her classmates so that women's abilities would not be called into question.[40] Yet despite her successful record, many congregations refused to consider her as a student rabbi; even after she was ordained, she found it difficult to get job interviews. Eventually, Priesand took a post as assistant rabbi at the Stephen Wise Free Synagogue in New York, the temple founded by Wise early in the century to ensure his freedom of the pulpit. That the first woman rabbi found her first post at a temple that symbolized freedom of conscience seemed auspicious. Working with Bella Abzug, then in the House of Representatives, to secure passage of the Equal Rights Amendment and reproductive rights for women, Priesand felt that the congregation stood strongly behind the clergy's participation in controversial contemporary issues.

Most of Priesand's duties at the synagogue involved routine rabbinical functions such as leading worship services, preaching, teaching and counseling, supervising the youth program, and officiating at life cycle events. Though she immediately became a role model for young girls and younger women, women over fifty had more difficulty accepting her; the greatest resistance was to her officiation at funerals. Overall, however, Priesand believes that her presence at the temple "became a lesson in consciousness raising and gave women the courage they need to demand complete and full participation in synagogue life."[41]

After eight years, Priesand left the Free Synagogue to become rabbi of Temple Beth El in Elizabeth, New Jersey, serving also as chaplain at Manhattan's Lenox Hill Hospital. In 1981, she came to Monmouth Reform Temple in Tinton Falls, New Jersey, a congregation of about 250 families. While at first she felt it was her "obligation" to become rabbi of a large congregation, moving up the "category system" of Reform Judaism, Priesand has since come to believe that "success doesn't necessarily mean bigger"; today, she draws attention to her congregation's "sense of family" and the possibility of her making a greater impact on individuals in a smaller synagogue.[42]

Since becoming a rabbi, Priesand's idea of God has changed as well. "When I was in rabbinical school," she recalls, "I believed in an all-powerful God, but the older I get, the more I believe in a limited God, a God who loves and cares, who weeps with us, but who can't change things. I hope the message I give to my congregants is that we need strength to accept where we find ourselves." Her spiritual philosophy is one of "empowerment"; rather than lead them, she wants to "help other Jews become responsible for their own Judaism." Her ideal is to be part of a "creative partnership" with the members of her congregation. "I feel successful when we—the congregation and I—are Jewish together."[43]

Rabbi Sandy Eisenberg Sasso, the first woman ordained by the Reconstructionist movement, believes that Priesand's point of view is representative. "Women's center of focus is on people rather than principles," she asserts, echoing the point of view of such feminist thinkers as Carol Gilligan and Jean Baker Miller. Rather than a "hierarchical model where one's goal is . . . to be alone at the top," women have developed "a network model where the goal is to connect with others, to be together at the center."[44] Many women rabbis have altered the traditional top-down relationship among clergy, staff, and congregation, creating new structures and teaching skills to empower congregants. With women now constituting more than 50 percent of the graduating classes of rabbinical schools in the Reform, Reconstruction, and Conservative movements, this "feminization" of rabbinical styles may change ideas of leadership. According to some observers, the influence of women on the profession can already be seen in the increasing tendency of male as well as female rabbis to prefer midsize over large congregations.[45]

But others worry that female rabbis' seeming preference for smaller, more intimate congregations may not be only a matter of choice. Reform Rabbi Laura Geller, who was the first woman to head an "A" (thousand-member) congregation, believes that few women apply for such posts because, with no senior women rabbis to serve as role models, they are unable to imagine themselves wielding power in the fashion of senior male clergy. Geller cites reports showing that women rabbis also face "endemic discrimination" in compensation, as well as sexual harassment and violations of sexual boundaries.[46]

How to overcome the barriers limiting the advance of women as a class and to resolve other issues of discrimination is only one challenge for the future. Even more significant to Geller is the question of transformation. "The ordination of women was just the beginning of our journey," she observes. "What would Jewish institutions look like if they were shaped in response to the values that seem to be shared by so many women—balance, intimacy, empowerment? . . . What will Jewish communities be like when rabbis stop being surrogate Jews and instead enable their communities to take responsibility for their Jewish lives? What will Jewish institutions be like when we make room for the many different kinds of Jews we know there are . . . ?"[47]

Arthur Green, former dean and president of the Reconstructionist Rabbinical College, provides one answer to these questions. He suggests that because women are interested in empowering their congregations, they are increasingly replacing the model of the rabbi as a learned teacher and articulate spokesman of tradition with that of the rabbi as a helping professional and spiritual example.[48] In addition to developing such models within the synagogue, increasing numbers of women (such as Amy Eilberg, the first ordained Conservative woman rabbi) are leaving the pulpit to serve as chaplains in hospitals and hospices. Eilberg, who directs a hospice that she organized in connection with a Jewish healing center in the Bay Area, notes that there is a particularly good fit between pastoral care giving and the primacy of relationships in women's lives. In fact, female rabbis have generally been the leaders of the Jewish healing movement.[49]

Within Orthodox Judaism, women have taken a different kind of journey. Although it represents only about 10 percent of all American Jews, Orthodox Judaism has in recent years attracted increasing numbers of adult women, usually in their twenties and thirties, who were not raised in Orthodox homes. These *ba'alot teshuvah* (women who return) are often professional women who support equality in the workplace but prefer the traditional laws and mores offered by traditional Orthodox life. Unlike the feminist orthodoxy of Blu Greenberg, who has tried to redefine women's status in prayer and ritual so as to include them in religious obligations previously carried out by men, most *ba'alot teshuvah* do not wish for religious restructuring, believing that traditional orthodoxy offers women theological equality.[50]

"These are the women, the daughters, for whom our mothers marched and demonstrated," writes Andrea Gurwitt, a journalist puzzled about their return to traditional Judaism. "Why would women like these opt for a rigid way of life steeped in patriarchy, a life their grandmothers abandoned?" Her assessment, confirmed by several studies, is that the *ba'alot teshuvah* believe that separate but equal is true "liberation." In the Orthodox synagogue and home, "a woman can be respected for all aspects of herself," particularly her feminine qualities.[51]

Observers have found that what also draws previously unaffiliated women to Orthodox Judaism is the multigenerational give-and-take and the tightly knit community of the religious world. "What I loved about Orthodox Judaism is the sense that I was simply part of a three-thousand-year old continuum that happened to skip a couple of generations," comments one newly Orthodox woman. "You can look at my parents' or grandparents' nonobservance as a little bloop out of three thousand years. . . ."[52] As an alternative to the rootlessness and flux of modern secular life, orthodoxy offers order, stability, a sense of permanence, and a connection to the values, traditions, and rituals of the past.

While they do not often call themselves feminists, many *ba'alot teshuvah* do exhibit gender consciousness and an appreciation of the value of women's culture; they also share the ideals of self-determination and freedom of choice that have brought non-Orthodox Jewish feminists back to Judaism.

No Longer "Split at the Root": Adrienne Rich and Rabbi Sharon Kleinbaum   In the last twenty-five years, changes in the landscape of Judaism have been paralleled by a transformation of ideals and practices regarding Jewish family life. The increased options that characterize contemporary Jewish women's religious lives are mirrored in the growth of alternative lifestyles regarding sexual, gender, and family norms. Jewish women today tend to be more represented in the work force and more highly educated than non-Jewish women; they also tend to marry less (one third of Jewish women remain single) and to have smaller families.[53] While some traditionalists are not happy with these changes, and blame the women's movement for them, a more balanced assessment suggests that these demographic shifts are part of a much broader social transformation regarding work, family structures, and values affecting all Americans.

One of the most controversial phenomena attributed to feminist influences concerns the "coming out" of gays and lesbians as active members of the Jewish community. The creation of a Jewish gay and lesbian identity in the past twenty years has been a product not only of the feminist movement and gay and lesbian liberation, but of Jewish renewal itself.[54] Acknowledging the high price they paid either by keeping their sexual identity invisible within the Jewish community, or by completely exiling themselves from Judaism, Jewish lesbians began to confront their double marginality and to insist on their right to participate as full members of the Jewish community. As Evelyn

Torton Beck wrote in her introduction to the 1982 lesbian anthology, *Nice Jewish Girls,* "I was pained but not surprised to feel invisible as a lesbian among Jews. I was terribly disappointed and confused to feel invisible as a Jew among lesbians. . . ." How was it possible to be "all of who we are? What does it mean for us to identify as Jewish lesbians? In what ways have we internalized our Jewishness?"[55]

In a candid essay in Beck's volume, poet Adrienne Rich attempted to come to grips with her ambivalence as a Jewish lesbian and with the "mundane anti-Semitisms" of her entire life; the daughter of a Christian mother and Jewish father, Rich reveals the damaging self-hatred of Jewish women who learned to "pass." Growing up in a white Christian community in the South, Rich was baptized and confirmed in the Episcopal Church and taught "to speak quietly in public, to dress without ostentation, to repress all vividness or spontaneity, to assimilate with a world which might see us as too flamboyant"—too Jewish. "If you did not effectively deny family and community," Rich writes, "there would always be a cousin claiming kinship with you, who was the wrong kind of Jew."[56] That Rich thought of herself as Jewish notwithstanding the fact that she had a non-Jewish mother (and therefore, according to Jewish law, was not Jewish) and had been baptized into the Christian faith is one sign of the fluidity of affiliation in contemporary America; growing up, Rich felt that she had a blurred identity, but that she was more Jewish than half-Jewish, and something other than Christian.

Rich went off to college at Radcliffe, where she did indeed meet and marry the wrong man—a Brooklyn-born, though Harvard-educated, Jew from an Orthodox Eastern European background; her parents refused to come to the wedding. Though Rich was accepted by her husband's family, her identity as a Jewish woman became tied to her role as "an entirely physical being, producer and nourisher of children," and she was unable to separate "what was Jewish from what was simply motherhood, or female destiny." When she left the marriage years later, becoming involved in the civil rights movement and then in women's liberation and the first stirrings of the lesbian "movement-within-a-movement," she was not yet able to acknowledge or liberate the Jewish side of herself. With feminism claiming universality and Judaism seeming to be "yet another strand of patriarchy," Rich "pushed aside for one last time thinking further about myself as a Jewish woman." But she was far from content. "Sometimes I feel I have seen too long from too many disconnected angles," she confessed, "white, Jewish, anti-Semite, racist, anti-racist, once-married, lesbian, middle-class, feminist, exmatriate Southerner." What she felt more than anything was "split at the root," unable to make her identity whole.[57]

The hope with which Rich ends the essay, that in the future "every aspect of [her] identity" would be engaged and interconnected, was fulfilled in the flowering of Jewish lesbianism in the 1980s and in her own writing. Supported by other Jewish lesbians and the larger feminist movement, Rich has written poems and prose about Jewish subjects and is also a founding editor of the influential Jewish feminist journal *Bridges*.[58]

For many Jewish lesbian women, the way to a sense of wholeness has been affiliation with a gay synagogue, the first of which were Los Angeles's Beth Chayim Chadashim and New York's Beth Simchat Torah, both founded in 1973.[59] In the early years, gay synagogues were often dominated by men; for this reason, and because gay synagogues frequently retained traditional patriarchal practices and language, Jewish women did not feel welcome there. In the last dozen years, though, gay synagogues have developed more egalitarian practices; at the same time, some elements of the Jewish religious mainstream, particularly Reconstructionist and Reform, have become more accepting of homosexuals. Yet Jewish homosexuality remains controversial. A decade after she confessed to regretting statements she had made criticizing lesbian feminism as harmful to the women's movement, Betty Friedan expressed concern about "sexual issues" that could be harmful to Judaism. "Jews have always known that a strong family is important for both Jewish and human survival," she warned.[60] While Jewish lesbian voices have been prominent in the feminist and gay and lesbian rights movements, the integration of these voices into the Jewish community at large is far from ensured.

The tension between Jewish gays and lesbians and more socially conservative Jews surfaced in 1993, when representatives from Congregation Beth Simchat Torah, New York's well-established gay and lesbian synagogue in Greenwich Village, were prohibited from marching in the Jewish community's annual Salute to Israel parade.[61] After a letter from Orthodox Rabbi Aaron Soloveitchik urged that permission for the synagogue to march be rescinded, the temple's delegation was expelled from the planned parade. It eventually won the right to march with the Association of Reform Zionists of America behind a banner that would include the congregation's name without identifying it as gay and lesbian. That compromise was rejected after the synagogue's rabbi, Sharon Kleinbaum, was falsely accused of violating an agreement not to comment publicly on the issue; yet such a gag order never existed. Many liberal and reform groups, as well as the governor, the mayor, the Israeli consul-general, and three dozen rabbis, withdrew from the parade in protest and attended an alternative event at a prominent midtown synagogue. To Kleinbaum, it was an "amazing victory."[62]

The dispute brought this thirty-three-year-old spiritual leader, an overtly and proudly feminist lesbian, to public prominence. Kleinbaum's ascendancy to the pulpit of Congregation Beth Simchat Torah the year before had in fact been a sign of the increasing visibility of Jewish lesbian feminism within Jewish religious life; equally important, it symbolized the truly revolutionary path that Jewish women had trod over the course of a century of activism. One hundred years earlier, Kleinbaum might have given the invocation at the

Jewish Women's Congress at the Chicago World's Fair, where Ray Frank, the falsely labeled "first woman rabbi," pronounced the opening prayer. More likely, however, she would have been out organizing factory workers with Rose Pastor Stokes, or shared a prison cell with Emma Goldman for protesting militarism and economic injustice. For Kleinbaum, a passionate pacifist and activist deeply committed to the goals of social justice, had come to the rabbinate as a self-described "radical social activist."[63] What differentiates her from Jewish activists of the past is not only her open lesbianism but her deep spiritual commitment to traditional Judaism and the fact that she feels no need to choose between religion and activism. Over the course of a century, and in large part owing to the feminist revolution, Judaism had changed enough to offer her—as an activist, a feminist, and a lesbian—a place of comfort, indeed, of authority. But Kleinbaum has chosen to share the pulpit with members of her congregation, embodying in her practice the new openness of many more traditional women rabbis.

Kleinbaum grew up in suburban Bergen County, N.J., the youngest of four children. Her father, Max, directed a Jewish social service agency, while her mother, Josephine, worked for the United Jewish Appeal and other nonprofit organizations; she was also interested in women's reproductive issues. Kleinbaum's grandmother, a 1921 Phi Beta Kappa graduate of Tufts University and an active suffragist, was another early role model.[64]

Though Max Kleinbaum, a Yiddishist and secularist raised in the Sholom Aleichem Houses in the Bronx, had never attended synagogue until he married, the family was moderately observant and the four Kleinbaum children were sent to Hebrew School at a Conservative temple. By the time of her bat mitzvah, Kleinbaum had grown dissatisfied with the limited Jewish knowledge she had gained and even more with what she calls the sentimentalization of the "two crutches" of American Judaism at the time—the Holocaust and the State of Israel. With the approval of her parents, who by that time were seeking an alternative to the public schools, she enrolled in a new Orthodox yeshiva nearby, graduating in its first class. She credits a number of teachers at the yeshiva with opening her eyes to the passion and beauty of Hebrew texts, and allowing her to ask "meaning" questions about religion. Also influential was the system of *havruta* (study partners), which she later employed at Beth Simchat Torah. But most of all, she remembers the excitement of one of her teachers when she asked probing questions about the text that he could not answer. "He would go running to the principal, barely containing his enthusiasm, demanding that the principal hear the smart young girl's challenge." Admitting that he didn't know the answer, encouraging his students to question—this was Jewish learning at its best; Kleinbaum would also take this lesson to Beth Simchat Torah. She felt herself transformed at the yeshiva, becoming spiritually alive.

In her senior year, however, Kleinbaum discovered feminism, and became increasingly uncomfortable with the role of women in Orthodox Judaism. By the time she went off to Barnard College in the fall of 1977, she had rejected Judaism. Though she took courses in history and religion and some Yiddish, she chose political science as a major, because this was the field that asked the questions in which she was most interested, questions about moral responsibility and the meaning of a just society. She was deeply influenced by Dennis Dalton, who taught her about Gandhi and nonviolence, and by Paula Hyman, one of the original Ezrat Nashim members, who taught Jewish history at Columbia University. Hyman, who as a graduate student had organized a woman's caucus in the Columbia history department a decade before, was the co-author of the first history of Jewish women in the United States, *The Jewish Woman in America,* published in 1975.[65] Inspired by Hyman's classes, Kleinbaum began to find her way back to a Judaism seemingly without dogma. She imagined that her future might lie in the excitement of teaching and studying the history of Jewish culture, especially Jewish women's history.

In addition to her academic concerns, Kleinbaum became deeply engaged with feminist and pacifist groups at college. She participated in numerous demonstrations demanding Columbia's disinvestment in South Africa and an end to the nuclear arms race. Working with the War Resisters League and a feminist student group, she helped plan a rally at the Women's Pentagon Action, protesting the deployment of submarine missiles. When Columbia announced plans to house a military research laboratory, Kleinbaum was prominent in organizing protests against it. Columbia's student newspaper, *The Spectator,* referred to her as a "Communist" agitator. One of Kleinbaum's comrades in the antinuclear campaigns was Jewish writer and pacifist Grace Paley, who taught her the meaning of courage. "Once when the police knocked down an older woman, Grace leapt into action, rescuing the woman and ordering the federal marshals away. She never hesitated, and she never stopped. But the marshals stopped their beating."[66]

By the time she was twenty-one, Kleinbaum had been arrested several times for civil disobedience, spending a month in the federal prison for women in Virginia. Not long after her release, she helped organize the massive January 14, 1982, demonstration in Central Park against nuclear armaments. Soon afterwards, she went on a peace march from Copenhagen to Paris sponsored by the Scandinavian Peace Group. Struck by the absence of Jews and Jewish culture in several of the cities she visited, Kleinbaum began to realize how deeply she was connected to Judaism and to regret her lack of involvement. She also began to ponder an anomaly that she had noted during her years of working with women activists in peace work. While Catholic women in the peace movement seemed proud of their antiwar stance as Catholics, Jewish women seemed embarrassed by the fact that they were Jews, almost as if they were choosing social activism despite their Jewishness rather than because of it.

One day, hitchhiking in Amherst, Massachusetts, Kleinbaum found herself in a truck full of boxes of Yiddish books, including some by one of her favorite authors, Sholem Aleichem, whose works she had studied in Yiddish at Barnard. "What are these books doing in western Massachusetts?" she asked the young driver who had given her a ride. "And how is it," he replied, "that I've come across a hitchhiker who can read them?"[67] The driver, Aaron Lansky, on a self-assigned mission to save Yiddish culture from oblivion by rescuing discarded Yiddish books, was about to open a Yiddish book center in Amherst. Kleinbaum's chance meeting with Lansky led to her serving as assistant director of that organization, the National Yiddish Book Center, for three years.

At the center, Kleinbaum taught courses on Yiddish literature and was excited by the experience of conveying the richness of the daily culture of East European Jews and helping students make connections to their ancestors. But gradually she came to believe that in order to truly understand the world of Peretz, Aleichem, and other Yiddish authors, it was necessary to understand the spiritual significance of Shabbat, *kashruth,* and the other religious customs of the devout Eastern European Jewry about whom they wrote. She had begun to observe Shabbat herself; indeed, her house became a center of Sabbath celebrations in Amherst. Soon she had embarked on a spiritual quest that ultimately led her to enroll at the Reconstructionist Rabbinical College in Philadelphia. Again she would ask the "meaning questions" that she had probed at the yeshiva, but this time, she searched for explanations relevant to her concerns as a feminist and lesbian.

Kleinbaum came to Congregation Beth Simchat Torah after two years working at the Religious Action Center in Washington, D.C., the social action arm of the Reform movement. As one of fifty applicants for the job, she was advised by friends not to take the position if it were offered because identifying so closely with a gay synagogue would amount to "career suicide."[68] Kleinbaum obviously didn't agree. She has found the job complex and exhausting, but fascinating. Working with a thousand-member congregation, the majority of whom are gay or lesbian (approximately 15 percent are straight), with backgrounds in all branches of Judaism, poses unique challenges. Despite the religious diversity of the membership, Kleinbaum has been able to foster an unusual degree of unity in the congregation, encouraging the formation of smaller *minyanim* as well as larger, congregationwide services and events. Shabbat services draw several hundred people; for the High Holidays, the synagogue rents space to accommodate the more than 2,500 people who customarily attend. "We have an obligation to do this," Kleinbaum believes, "offering a place where homosexuals and their families can worship. Critics say that homosexuality destroys the family, but we reconstruct families that have been shattered."[69]

Kleinbaum sees herself as a "teacher and spiritual leader" but "not the only one who can do things." Although she feels that leading prayers is her greatest responsibility, she doesn't lead all the services herself, encouraging lay members to do so. And when a student in one of the many classes she teaches challenges her with a provocative question about the text, or about God, she becomes as excited as her former yeshiva teacher. Women, furthermore, are empowered in all religious roles. According to the congregation's brochure, all liturgies "have been supplemented to reflect the dignity of women, as well of men, the role of the matriarchs as well as the patriarchs, and a view of God not limited to masculine metaphors"; a monthly feminist *minyan* creates a special "safe place" for experimenting with liturgical innovations. "We want a Jewish community where people participate," Kleinbaum says, "one that truly welcomes all people, and different people, in our midst. The Torah tells us over and over . . . about the stranger in Egypt. . . . For us, exile is not a literary metaphor or convenient refrain. It has genuine meaning every day in our lives."[70]

Kleinbaum frequently uses the story of the Jewish experience in the wilderness as a model. Today, she notes, Jews are not in slavery, but neither have they arrived at the promised land. To truly come out of exile would mean the achievement of social justice—for all people, not just Jews—an effort that must be guided by faith and spiritual community. Here she differs with Jewish feminists who focus on a secular legacy as the means of connection to the Jewish heritage. Judaism makes clear, she says, that we cannot talk about the spiritual world while ignoring the word in which we live. "I think the world has to be startled a little bit," she confesses. "While being reverent about Jewish tradition, at the same time we have to be creative and bold." Gandhi remains her model for how social change rooted in spirituality can endure despite obstacles.

Since Kleinbaum has been with Beth Simchat Torah, there have been many setbacks. Over one hundred men and women (only four of them over the age of fifty) have died of AIDS, and Kleinbaum has had to bury many people around her own age. "We live in the epicenter of this tragedy," she comments. Yet despite the pain she grapples with every day, she finds hope in how her congregants "act Godly when the world is crumbling" and in the tremendous love and affection that they demonstrate. The AIDS crisis has pulled the congregation together. "A Jew's identity is rooted in community," Kleinbaum states; through communal prayer Jews can connect to each other, to their ancestors, and to God. Her aim continues to be to foster and strengthen religious community. Ironically, the publicity that Kleinbaum has received has caused many parents of homosexual Jews throughout the country, who are often unable to talk with their own clergy, to seek her out. The community she has created is not just a local one.

As more women with backgrounds in women's studies and feminist activism enter the rabbinate, we can expect significant changes in the style and substance of Judasim. Opening the synagogue to more diverse populations, creating sermons and texts that include women, and empowering congregants, women clergy are bringing a new openness and excitement to religious practice. These changes are in turn serving as a beacon to women who have been unaffiliated or estranged from Judaism. Seeing themselves reflected in the Jewish past and represented in ritual and liturgy has given Jewish women a more positive sense of Jewish identity as well as a role in shaping Judaism in the present and future.

Yet the path to a transformative feminist Judaism is not without pitfalls. When Jane Litman entered the Reconstructionist Rabbinical College in Philadelphia in the mid-1980s, her feminist God-language, including the term "Goddess" (which she claims she meant as a female representation of the Hebrew God), led the college to question her possibly "heretical theology." While the college ultimately ordained Litman, concluding she had been misquoted in a newspaper article, another article about the supposed heresy appeared in the Jewish journal *Midstream;* after Litman sued the magazine for libel, it retracted its statement, but Litman feels that her reputation was sullied by the incident.[71] Jewish feminists only sometimes find a comfortable place within Judaism, she believes. "We must always test the limits and be careful not to cross borders too hurriedly."[72]

As in the secular world, progress often carries a backlash in its wake; those who press hardest for change will inevitably feel its force. Judith Plaskow, who has been among the most vocal in calling for a radical transformation of Jewish theology, has also discovered that any mention of the Goddess is enough for many Jews to place her "outside the Jewish pale." "No one has ever asked me, when I speak on Jewish feminism," she notes, "whether I keep kosher or observe the Sabbath. But I have been asked again and again whether my understanding of God is really Jewish . . . how far I am willing to go in expanding the boundaries of Jewish belief."[73]

Feminist theologians and rabbis are not the only women on the front lines of change. In study and prayer groups, lay Jewish women are forming communities and creating new rituals and texts. In 1989, a Boston Rosh Hodesh group developed the ritual of Kos Miriam. Having learned from a book by Penina Adelman about the legend of Miriam's well—a well of fresh water that followed the children of Israel during their forty years in the desert, and that disappeared when Miriam died—the group created the ritual of drinking from the Cup of Miriam; it recalls the often neglected importance of Miriam to the survival of the Jewish people, and through the symbolism of water and well suggests redemption and renewal. In only a few years, the ritual has been incorporated into the Passover seder in many parts of the country.[74]

In the 1970s, Jewish women in a number of communities began to hold women's seders as a regular part of the Passover observance. In *The Telling* (1993), E.M. Broner has described one of the earliest women's seders, begun in New York in 1976 by a notable group of Jewish feminists including Gloria Steinem, Bella Abzug, Phyllis Chesler, and Letty Cottin Pogrebin. Daughter of a Christian mother and a Jewish father, Steinem had never been part of any Jewish or religious ceremony. With the women's seder as her first religious ritual, she began to see that "there was room in the women's movement for the spiritual." Along with Abzug, she became an inspiration—a "seder mother"— of the New York women's Passover gathering.[75]

Feminists unhappy about the invisibility of women in traditional Passover celebrations found new meanings in this women's seder. Its powerful effect was due in part to the *Women's Hagaddah* that Broner and Naomi Nimrod created in Israel in 1975. Structured around a council of elders and daughters asking and answering questions about their legacy as women, Broner and Nimrod's *Women's Hagaddah* was published by *Ms.* magazine two years later and found its way from one Jewish woman to another as stapled pages entitled "The Stolen Legacy."[76]

Over the next two decades, the experience of the New York seder group was repeated throughout the country in the development of new rituals and symbols (for example, placing an orange on the seder plate) and new feminist hagaddahs.[77] While the content of the hagaddahs varied, most linked women's presence to the Exodus tale by incorporating competent and heroic women in Jewish history into the story. In the 1990s, a new tradition of women's community seders has evolved; like other women's seders, these usually take place on a third night of Passover so as not to conflict with family gatherings. In Los Angeles, the American Jewish Congress has hosted a feminist seder since 1991. In 1995, the women's seder sponsored by Ma'yan, the Jewish Women's Project in New York, accommodated 900 women. Project Kesher, the Illinois-based group that has stimulated the revival of Judaism among women in the former Soviet Union, has developed global women's seders for women in the United States, the former Soviet Union, Israel, South Africa, Europe, New Zealand, and other areas around the world to celebrate Passover as a shared journey to freedom in which women are deeply involved.[78]

Women are empowering themselves not only by worshipping and celebrating together but also through scholarship. Although previous generations were unable to participate in close textual study because of their limited education, women of all denominations today are enthusiastically poring over Mishna, Talmud, and Torah at such Orthodox-sponsored institutes as Ma'yan in Boston, Drisha in New York, and Matan in Jerusalem. Their increasing mastery of complex Jewish texts will enable them to play a more authoritative role in communal discussions of such critical issues as religious divorce (*get*) and the problem of abandoned wives (*agunot*). In renewing traditional practices and revitalizing their own religious sensibilities and learning, they are contributing to the ongoing process of revitalizing Jewish faith.[79]

Rabbi Laura Geller comes back to the notion of exile. "Just as it took our people forty years of wandering in the desert to reach a rich and fertile promised land," she observes, "the journey toward the promised land of an egalitarian Judaism is far from over. But the years of wandering have provided a glimpse into the future, the opportunity to revolutionize old ways of thinking, and to begin to shift the paradigm from equality between men and women to the transformation of Judaism itself."[80]

Chapter 11

OUT OF EXILE

Toward Yavneh: Cynthia Ozick and Grace Paley

In the summer of 1970, in a provocative address at the Weizmann Institute in Rehovoth, Israel, writer Cynthia Ozick predicted the beginnings of an American Jewish cultural renewal based on a new literature that would be "centrally Jewish." To be written in English (the "new Yiddish"), this literature would become the instrument of Jewish preservation in the Diaspora.[1] Like ancient Yavneh, the small town where after the fall of Jerusalem a group of learned rabbis maintained the life of the Jewish community in exile, the renewal would focus not on universalist ideas or "pagan" art, which are anathema to Ozick, but on a specifically Jewish vision of history and community. Amid the seductions of an accommodating Gentile world, Jewish culture could maintain its uniqueness only by rooting itself in the moral urgency of the Jewish tradition.

In Ozick's view, it is the Hebrew Bible, especially the notion of covenant, that must ground this renewal. However, she acknowledges a problem:

> The relation of Torah to women calls Torah itself into question. Where is the missing Commandment that sits in judgment on the world? . . . Torah is silent, offers no principle of justice in relation to women. . . . The Covenant is silent about women; the Covenant consorts with the world at large. . . .[2]

For Ozick, the only solution is to "find, for this absent precept, a Yavneh"—only thus can the conditions be created whereby women will no longer be perceived "as lesser . . . and . . . dehumanized."[3]

The writings of Ozick and her contemporary Grace Paley, along with the contributions of a younger generation of authors, demonstrate that a vital and varied Jewish cultural renewal, prompted and shaped by feminism, is well under way. In addition to literature, the worlds of music, painting, performance art, drama, and film have been transformed by the bold new experiments of Jewish women.

How Strong They Were   Born in 1928 to Russian immigrant parents, Ozick grew up in an Orthodox home in the Bronx, where her father owned a pharmacy. She describes herself as a "third-generation American Jew (though the first to have been native-born) perfectly at home and yet perfectly insecure, perfectly acculturated and yet perfectly marginal."[4]

Perhaps more than any modern writer, Ozick has written consistently and imaginatively about Judaism as a religious heritage. Ignoring such popular American Jewish themes as assimilation, intrafamily conflict, and social class, Ozick focuses on the spiritual conflict between Jewish values and "pagan" influences—the idols of art, nature, human ambition, and greed—that tempt men and women away from God. *The Pagan Rabbi and Other Stories,* her first short story collection, published in 1971, treats this theme with linguistic inventiveness and a highly original display of fantasy and realism. Her three novels and other collections of short fiction also treat matters of Jewish faith and history.

Much of her fiction addresses issues that bear upon female lives and gender relations as well as Jewish values. Ozick's story "Virility" touches upon the unhappy consequences of abandoning the Jewish heritage and the gendered, double standard of artistic merit (in a later essay, she dubs this the "ovarian theory of literature").[5] The story tells of an immigrant male poet acclaimed for his masculine poetry ("controlled muscle," the critics call it), which he has published in a volume entitled *Virility;* in fact, the poems are those of his aunt Rivka. When, after her death, he no longer has any poetry to produce, he remorsefully publishes a volume of her most intellectual poems under her own name, entitled *Flowers from Liverpool;* critics deride the work as "secondary" and as "thin feminine art."[6] The gendered ironies of the story are compounded by the poet's failure to acknowledge his heritage, symbolized by his aunt (who has remained in the old country), and his own assimilation. After she starves to death, the failed poet, dead drunk, jumps off a bridge.[7]

In her next book of stories, *Levitation: Five Fictions,* Ozick introduces Ruth Puttermesser, a Yale Law School graduate who is an assistant corporation counsel for the New York City government. In "Puttermesser: Her Work History, Her Ancestry, Her Afterlife," the successful lawyer seeks a connection with her Jewish past, which her American-born, assimilated parents cannot give her. Claiming her great-uncle Zindel (who died before she was born) as "all her ancestry," she conjures up a scene in which Zindel teaches her Hebrew. In "Puttermesser and Xanthippe," the middle-aged Puttermesser is still working in municipal government but is now more tied to Judaism than in the earlier story. After she is demoted, she creates a "child" creature, Xanthippe (indeed, the first female golem), who makes her mayor of New York. When Xanthippe's insatiable appetites lead her to destroy Puttermesser's reforms and plunge the city back into chaos, Puttermesser renounces her powers and destroys her own creation. The story thus joins Ozick's deep concern about the blasphemous potentiality of art with Judaism's warnings against idolatry.

For Ozick, the deepest evil goes beyond the sins of ambition. Her story "The Shawl" tells of a magic shawl that helped Rosa, the main character, nurse her baby daughter, Magda, in a concentration camp. Through a startling immediacy of language and a combination of the supernatural and the realistic that allow the reader to comprehend the mother's love for her child and her helplessness inside the death camp, Ozick dramatically conveys the horror of the Holocaust. Her powerful sequel to this story, "Rosa," explores the traumatic effects on Rosa, many years later, of her daughter's murder.[8]

Although Ozick calls herself a "classical feminist" who believes that women need "equal access to the greater world," she argues that the separation of women as a class, with a distinct outlook and psychology, is deeply flawed. While she defines herself as a "Jewish writer," she considers the term "woman writer" to be sexist.[9] Despite this caveat, her fiction and essays reflect her continuing support for women's rights within both the secular and Jewish worlds.

Unlike Ozick, who denies the validity of a woman-centered artistic sensibility, Grace Paley affirms the significance of gender difference in art and politics. Born in the Bronx in 1922, she is the daughter of immigrants from czarist Russia, where her parents were active in the socialist movement.

Though her family was "extremely" antireligious—her father used to laugh when he passed a synagogue, and her mother refused to consider Paley's first marriage valid since she had been married by a rabbi—they took great pride in their Jewishness. Notwithstanding their secularism, they instilled in Paley a love of the Bible stories she heard throughout her childhood. She grew up "believ[ing] in the story . . . that the story is history."[10] As the author of three highly regarded collections of short stories, Paley is known for her personal, vigorous style, her experimentation with form, and the depth of feeling she brings to her unconventional plots and characters. Though her characters are highly varied, many of them are identifiably Jewish and, in their interactions, reveal the conflicts between the values of the immigrant generation and their contemporary descendants. Paley's precise imagery and masterful use of dialect enhance the verisimilitude of the changing Jewish milieus she depicts. Yet her comic sense and open-ended, inventive style take her stories beyond the limits of these conventional settings. While she does not probe the religious aspects of Judaism, her stories portray the moral dilemmas of contemporary urban Jews, and most poignantly, of women.[11]

Paley began writing after "that long period of very masculine writing which followed the Second World War." Though she admires the work of such writers as Saul Bellow and Philip Roth, she knew that "it wasn't written for me at all . . . there were no women in it."

The guys had a woman or there was an aunt that everybody loved or an aunt that everybody hated. Whatever. But the wives were terrible.[12]

The occasion for her first writing came after she heard someone read a story on Jewish themes. All of a sudden Paley felt that "somehow *I* was given permission to write," that she could write out of her experience. Her first story, "Goodbye and Good Luck," was "all about being Jewish and about the lives of women." Though Paley worried that perhaps her subject was "trivial," she became increasingly confident that the lives of the "bunch of women" who interested her—PTA women and the like—"were common and important." "As a woman," Paley says, "I'm trying to restore something to the scales, so that the woman can be seen"—not as she was before, as a sexual object or a victim—but in her full strength. "How strong they were" was what interested Paley in women's lives in the first place.[13]

It is through Paley's women characters that the link between individual daily life and the larger historical process is articulated.[14] Her leading protagonist, Faith Darwin, is a divorced wife and mother deeply involved in raising her children, devoted to her neighbors and friends, and urgently committed to her urban environment. Over the course of Paley's three collections, which span the 1950s to the 1980s, Faith moves out from the unliberated insecurity of her domestic role to become a committed social activist and aspiring writer. Her bonds to her family and friends are matched by a larger social and artistic vision rooted in the female world.

As Faith matures, she accepts the burden of social responsibility inherited from her Jewish ancestors, if not their darker visions. To be truly American, Faith learns, is not merely a matter of unflinching optimism but of commitment to others.[15] Indeed, Paley's characters are rarely defined separately from their communities; even as they assert their independence, they remain connected to others.

As several critics have observed, this attachment to community is an aspect not only of women's lives, but of Jewish ideology and behavior.[16] To be "in the hands of strangers," as one of Paley's characters admits, is a metaphor for the absence of community that Paley abhors—the marginalized outsider alienated to varying degrees from self and others. Through their friendships and their roles as mothers and social activists—their emphasis on "caring and responsibility"—Paley's characters avoid the isolating subjectivity that troubles many Jewish male protagonists. Her celebration of the women in her stories, the "little people" who though lacking in power and influence attempt to lead "morally aware and engaged lives," offers an alternative version of Jewish accommodation to the modern world.[17] In the view of critic Bonnie Lyons, Paley and Ozick differ not only in the nature of their feminism—Paley emphasizes sexual difference and Ozick androgyny—but in their uses of Jewish heritage. Ozick celebrates the great tradition of Jewish culture—its formal laws, texts, and traditions—while Paley honors the little tradition of *Yiddishkeit,* in particular, the code of *menshlekeit* that validates the worth of the common person—in Paley's case, the "ordinary, specifically female person."[18]

The Jewish Edge: Anne Roiphe, Kim Chernin, Marge Piercy, E.M. Broner, and Rebecca Goldstein

Ozick's and Paley's creative pathways into Jewish feminism mark the early terrain of Jewish cultural renewal in the modern period. In the 1980s and 1990s, they have been joined by younger Jewish women writers who have emerged as equally powerful voices in contemporary literature. Anne Roiphe, E.M. Broner, Marge Piercy, Kim Chernin, and Rebecca Goldstein are several of the many Jewish women writers born in the late 1930s, 1940s, and 1950s who are responsible for a growing body of novels, short stories, and poetry based on female and Jewish issues. The range of topics and invention these writers offer is astonishingly broad, encompassing multigenerational family sagas, political novels, spiritual searches, utopian fiction, and works relating to the Holocaust, World War II, and other historical events.

The theme of exile, search, and homecoming is dramatically explored in the work of Anne Roiphe and Kim Chernin. Like many of her leading characters, Roiphe began as a secular rationalist, a political feminist and assimilated Jew. However, even in her first novel, *Digging Out* (1967), the story of a young woman who like Roiphe rebels against the empty values of her wealthy, assimilated family, the protagonist recognizes the danger she faces standing "isolated from the tribe"—both from her family and from Jewish culture—and wonders how she can "find a place" in America.[19]

In her best-known book, *Up the Sandbox* (1970), Roiphe's alter ego is the submissive wife of a Columbia University professor who begins to question her apparent domestic contentment when she becomes pregnant with her third child. Through a series of wild fantasy adventures, she imagines a more liberated life, but ultimately resumes her nurturing role within the family. Although the character is not explicitly Jewish, the fact that Barbra Streisand played her in the 1972 film version of the book (the first film produced by Streisand's own company) indicates the story's relevance to Jewish women. A young mother at the time, Streisand has said that the film was her "statement about what it meant to be a woman."[20]

After *Up the Sandbox,* Roiphe's search to understand her place in the modern world became deeply entwined with her interrogation of her Jewish identity. In 1978, Roiphe wrote an op ed piece for the *New York Times* on being Jewish and having a Christmas tree. The essay provoked an enormous reaction, almost all of it hostile; Roiphe was lambasted for her apparent contempt for Judaism, her ignorance of Jewish history, and her advocacy of assimilation.[21] In her 1981 memoir, *Generation Without Memory: A Jewish Journey in Christian America,* and in later essays, Roiphe admits that she did not understand "the dark side" of assimilation—how it produced an identity that was "shallow, materialistic, uprooted and anxious."[22] Shortly after the fallout from her newspaper piece, she began a study of the Talmud and Jewish history under the guidance of rabbinical scholars. As her studies took her closer to Judaism, she felt that she could fully rejoin the Jewish community only if she found a synagogue to which she could take her daughters "without subjecting them to insults."[23]

Much of Roiphe's later fiction reflects the contradiction inherent in the impulse to return to a Judaism that she recognizes as "home" while remaining troubled about women's place within the tradition. In her best novel, *Lovingkindness* (1987), feminist scholar Annie Johnson, a self-described "secular humanist" much like Roiphe herself, confronts the rebellion of her twenty-two-year-old daughter Andrea (or Sarai, as she renames herself), who runs off to join an ultra-Orthodox sect in Jerusalem after a stormy adolescence full of drug abuse and sexual experimentation. Annie fears that her daughter has surrendered her free will to an oppressive, male-dominated religious system and is appalled at her plans for an arranged marriage. Ultimately, Annie begins to question her own secular feminism, acknowledging its lack of family and community connections, and is reconciled with her daughter; she learns to respect the religious community that Sarai has embraced as a source of love and security. There is no halfway position in this novel between ultra-Orthodox Judaism and total assimilation, no shadings or complexities on the spectrum of Jewish affiliation, no possibilities for a family-oriented Jewish feminism. Yet, in her own life, Roiphe was moving toward just such a position.[24]

Roiphe's next novel, *The Pursuit of Happiness* (1991), a sprawling epic spanning five generations of a Jewish immigrant family, is another chronicle of the failure of assimilation. The story of the Gruenbaums, Polish Jews who came to America in the 1880s, the novel depicts the rise and eventual fall of many members of the clan, an assimilated family much like Roiphe's own. The female characters are among the most robust and sympathetic of the dozens contained in the book; amidst the difficult circumstances of their lives, they struggle to survive with dignity and humor. The novel ends in Israel, where Namah, the young adult daughter of the narrator, Hedi Gruenbaum Aloni, has been shot working to bring about peace with the Arabs. As in *Lovingkindness,* Roiphe suggests that the Jewishness of assimilated Americans can be recovered in Israel; Namah and her mother, however, are more activist than Sarai, suggesting the possibility of a dynamic, vibrant, Jewish future redeemed by Jewish women.[25]

Kim Chernin has taken a similar journey through feminism to her Jewish identity. Born in 1940 (five years after Roiphe) to working-class Russian Jewish immigrants, she spent a childhood very different from Roiphe's upper-middle-class one. Both her parents were communists. Her mother, the more militant, left Chernin a legacy of "struggle: against the past, the limitations of shtetl existence, against the forces that oppress mothers and women and workers. And, of course, Jews."[26]

Chernin grew up in her mother's house, a girl who was "not supposed to become a Jewish woman."[27] She became a communist, and later, after rejecting Marxism, a feminist, therapist, and writer. Her first books on female self-image, *The Obsession: Reflections on the Tyranny of Slenderness* (1981) and *The Hungry Self: Women, Eating and Identity* (1985), became important components of a developing feminist psychology. With her third book, *Reinventing Eve: Modern Woman in Search of Herself* (1987), Chernin began to analyze Judeo-Christian myths as possible sources for a viable and authentic female voice. Drawing on the memoirs of Etty Hillesum, killed at Auschwitz, and other examples of female strength, Chernin imagines a less patriarchal story of Eve and advances the process begun in her earlier books to empower the female self.

In My Mother's House (1983), a compelling narrative of four generations of women in Chernin's family, preoccupied Chernin for seven years. Each time she finished telling her mother's story, she started again: "Something was missing; something had not yet been said." If she had gone on writing, Chernin believes she might eventually have told a different story—"the tale of the missing Jewish identity, the inheritance that should have been mine but was not handed down to me in my mother's house."[28] Though her mother told the stories of Passover (Moses was "a radical, a people's hero") and Chanukah (a "liberation struggle against a foreign imperialist ruling class"), Chernin had to approach Judaism "at a slant." She became "a patchwork Jew, stitched together from every sort of scrap."[29]

Chernin's subsequent writings attempt to make "whole cloth" out of her inheritance. In *The Flame-Bearers* (1986), she tells the story of Rae (Israel) Shadmi, the rebellious inheritor of leadership in a mystical Jewish women's sect who is expected to carry on the family's matriarchal tradition. Though some sect members rebel against women's exclusion from traditional Judaism, others accept Orthodox worship along with their own female-oriented texts; all consider themselves Jewish.

In *Crossing the Border: An Erotic Journey* (1994), a memoir of a life-changing trip to Israel when she was thirty-one, Chernin explores her emotional and sexual awakening among Jewish friends in Israel in a narrative told in the double voice of the Kim Chernin of the past and present. Looking back at the Chernin of twenty-five years ago, a young mother who leaves her child to find a temporary home on a kibbutz, the current Chernin sees that "Kim Chernin needed the love of a tribe, a collective of kindred-enough spirits; she needed to be stitched into them, woven into the dark web of their common identity, nothing else would have worked."[30]

Marge Piercy is another Jewish-identified writer who brings a radical feminist perspective to her many works of fiction and poetry. Born in 1936 to a Jewish mother and Welsh father in Detroit, Piercy was raised as a Jew. Her Yiddish-speaking grandmother, the daughter of a rabbi, was a wonderful storyteller; though poor, the family was "rich in legends," told by her grandmother and retold by her mother, whom she credits with sparking her curiosity about people and her love of language and reading. "My mother made me a poet," she says."[31]

An activist in the student movement of the 1960s and the early women's liberation movement, Piercy writes frequently about women in transition to a new feminist consciousness. *Small Changes* (1973) explores the effects of patriarchal oppression and women's liberation on a young working-class girl and a middle-class Jewish intellectual much like Piercy herself. *Woman on the Edge of Time* (1976) tells the story of a woman committed to a mental hospital and her travels into the future. *Braided Lives* (1982) deals with a young woman's coming of age in the 1950s and her unconventional desire to become a writer. *Vida* (1980), the story of a radical antiwar activist who must deal with personal tragedies as well as movement upheavals, and *Fly Away Home* (1984), the chronicle of a woman's growing awareness after divorce, also deal with themes of conflict and transformation in women's lives.

Though Jewish characters appear in many of Piercy's works, only in more recent novels like *Gone to Soldiers* (1987) and *He, She, and It* (1991) is their ethnicity essential to her themes. *Gone to Soldiers* tells the overlapping stories of ten characters during the Second World War; key to the narrative are Jacqueline Lévy-Monot, a Parisian Jew who becomes a resistance fighter and escapes to Palestine, and her sister who finds refuge in America.

Brave and independent women who are heroic combatants in war and against spiritual despair also appear in Piercy's *He, She and It*. Set in the twenty-first century in an ecologically devastated world dominated by high-tech corporations called "multis," the novel interweaves the story of Shira, a scientist who is a divorced, single mother, and her grandmother Malkah, the inventor of a cyborg that protects the community from hostile forces, with a Yiddish tale about a legendary sixteenth-century golem created by a rabbi to protect his Jewish village from outside enemies. Much of the novel takes place in Tikva, the Jewish community where Shira was raised, a protected city outside the polluted areas of the "Glop." Piercy's science fiction allegory is the first to use a specifically Jewish frame of reference. Within the gloomy portrait she paints of the prospects for human society are several hopeful forces: the passing down of the story of Jewish resistance by Malkah; Malkah's male cyborg who shares her feminist ideas; and a new strain of Amazon-like women who arise in the Middle East—"a joint community of the descendants of Israeli and Palestinian women who survived" without men.[32]

The fiction of E.M. Broner also deals with the theme of passing on Jewish tradition through matriarchal lines. Broner was born in Detroit to a father who was a Jewish historian and journalist and a mother who acted in the Yiddish theater in Poland. Her first book, *Summer Is a Foreign Land* (1966), is a verse drama concerning the death of the Baba, a Russian Jewish matriarch who possesses magical gifts inherited from her ancestors; as she lies dying, she is attended by her American grandchildren, who hope to receive her last gift. *Her Mothers* (1975), her first novel, is the story of a feminist journalist's search for strong female role models from the past to include in a book she is writing on "unafraid women." But she is unable to locate the "mothers" she seeks either in American history or in the stories of the Biblical matriarchs of the "Old Testicle," in which God typically punishes women by denying them fecundity.[33]

In her next novel, *A Weave of Women* (1978), Broner discontinues the search for models from the past, creating instead a new kind of feminist utopia in Jerusalem where fifteen Israeli and Diaspora women live together, producing their own myths and rituals. Like Chernin's *Flame-Bearers* and Piercy's *He, She and It,* Broner imagines a Jewish future where women can triumph over patriarchal oppression by inventing their own traditions in a woman-oriented society.

The works of Broner, Piercy, Chernin, and Roiphe, each born in the decade 1930 to 1940, have been augmented by those of younger Jewish women writers like Rebecca Goldstein, Leslea Newman, Daphne Merkin, Nessa Rapoport, Marci Hershman, Allegra Goodman, and Jyl Lynn Felman. Goldstein, Merkin, Rapoport, and Goodman write from a firm grounding in Orthdox Judaism; nevertheless, they join other contemporary Jewish women writers in the search for a viable identity that can join their feminism with inherited Jewish tradition.

Goldstein, who was born in 1950 into an Orthodox family in Westchester County, New York, and attended yeshiva briefly, writes the most consistently about the conflict between religious belief and feminist lifestyle. Her well-regarded first novel, *The Mind-Body Problem* (1983), is the story of a graduate student, Renee Feuer, who is married to a mathematical genius and struggles to come to terms with her "contradictory" identities. As an aspiring intellectual who is both beautiful and sensual, and as a Jew who has left the Orthodoxy of her youth but rejects the secularism of her "Jewish *goyim*" friends, Renee remains "alone in [her] own world." Although her friends expect her to return to "the hocus pocus she was raised on," Renee "despises the religiosity" of her past, including Judaism's treatment of women, although she cannot completely break from it. The novel leaves her in limbo, returning to her husband after several extramarital affairs brought on by his coldness and her own "soul sickness."[34]

Goldstein's latest novel, *Mazel,* is an ambitious recreation of Jewish women's lives across continents and generations—from the traditional but lively society of sisters growing up in the shtetl of Shluftchev in Poland, to the vibrant world of art and theater in Jewish Warsaw, to New York, where the leading character, Sorel (who later is called Sasha), immigrates in the late 1930s, and to the suburbs of New Jersey, where her granddaughter lives and works. The novel recreates the imaginative, emotional world of young women from the Yiddish past and the American present through an innovative, gendered, use of Jewish folklore, myth, and story. Sasha, star of the Warsaw Yiddish theater, retains her exuberance and theatricality as she becomes acculturated and increasingly removed from her history. Her daughter, Chloe, a classics professor at Columbia, is brought up without any connection to the family's past, as is Chloe's daughter Phoebe, a mathematician at Princeton. But Phoebe returns to Judaism by marrying her Orthodox New Jersey boyfriend; Goldstein implies that it is a matter of *mazel* (good fortune) that despite her grandmother's skepticism, she returns to her roots, and to a vibrant if stereotypically suburban Jewish community.

With their golems, cyborgs, matriarchs, and rebels, contemporary Jewish women writers render women's intellectual, emotional, and spiritual experiences vivid and significant in a variety of historical contexts. Although critics have long worried that the Jewish novel might have run its course now that alienation and marginality—the major themes of the classic works of Jewish American male fiction—are no longer relevant to the lives of most American Jews, several believe that the works of today's women writers mark the arrival of a more "cuturally confident" literary stage and stand as the best possibility for recapturing the increasingly frayed "Jewish edge" in fiction.[35] With these writers currently at work on projects that involve the retelling of traditional stories and the invention of new ones in diverse voices and styles, the next decade promises a rich imaginative literature created by Jewish female writers—a new Yavneh.

Musical Midrash: Elizabeth Swados

Boldly reimagining the biblical matriarchs as contemporary heroines, composer-lyricist Elizabeth Swados has created what one scholar respectfully calls a "musical Midrash" on fundamental issues concerning God's relationship with the Jewish people.[36] Born in Buffalo, N.Y., in 1951 to an upper-middle-class Jewish family, Swados went to Bennington College, becoming involved in radical politics and the "exotic" life of the sixties' flower children; she began her musical career as a self-designated "folk/protest" singer. Following her discovery by Ellen Stewart of New York's La Mama theater company, she worked professionally with André Serban and Peter Brooks, composing over twenty musicals on and off Broadway.[37]

Though her family attended Buffalo's Reform synagogue only on the High Holidays and Swados went to Sunday school only briefly (she was turned off by Bible stories told by "the Brotherhood and Fatherhood"), she considers herself strongly Jewish-identified. Jewishness, she feels, is not a matter of religious or ritual involvement, but of "being politically active, passionate, looking for the truth, fighting for people, not being afraid to be an outsider, trying to make things change."[38] Swados has been interested in Jewish music since childhood. "I would think mentally about rearranging the songs I heard at temple," she recalls. "I knew then I would have a music future."[39]

Swados began composing liturgically oriented music and music based on biblical stories in the early 1970s. To compensate for her lack of Jewish education when working on the scores for her musicals "Job" and "Jonah" and "The Haggadah" opera, she consulted numerous rabbis and scholars. The support and interest of a feminist community encouraged her to turn first to Ruth and Esther as sources. In 1994, she wrote *Bible Women,* a song cycle based on characters in the Hebrew Bible, each reflecting a different emotional and musical approach.[40] The cycle includes a choral piece based on the woman of valor from Proverbs; four songs about Purim heroine Esther; a folk opera about Ruth and her mother-in-law Naomi; a gospel-klezmer piece about Miriam; as well as songs about Sarah, Lilith, Eve, and Deborah.

While the cycle is rooted in Jewish storytelling, Swados's intent was to create a circle of women who had "a universality in their battles, sorrows, victories and contemplations," women who would be "secular as well as spiritual, feisty, lost, curious and intelligent." She also wanted to replace negative stereotypes of Jewish women as sexually deficient and materialistic with more positive images. Endowing her Biblical women with a sense of "irony, tragedy, and wisdom," Swados created a celebration of "what I hope I can become because I am a Jewish woman."[41]

Journey Through Darkness: Judy Chicago

Judy Chicago's controversial *Holocaust Project* presents in visual form the record of one artist's journey from the "darkness of the Holocaust"—slave labor, the extermination camps, the rape of women prisoners—to the "light" of the human spirit. For Chicago, the "journey" through the exhibit parallels her personal journey into the meaning of the Holocaust and her own Jewish identity. An assimilated Jew who identified herself primarily as a woman, Chicago astonished and dismayed many in the art world with her bold feminist art, especially *The Dinner Party,* her 1979 multimedia series of place settings depicting a symbolic history of women in the form of female genitalia, and her later *Birth Project,* a series of needlework images exploring the subject of birth and creation. Not until the *Holocaust Project,* however, did Chicago connect what she had learned about women's lives with her own experience as a Jew.[42]

Chicago (who uses the name of her city of birth rather than that of her father, Cohen, or those of her husbands) is descended from the Vilna Gaon through both her paternal grandparents. After twenty-three generations of rabbis, her father, chosen from his brothers to enter the rabbinate, exchanged the family calling for labor organizing and Marxism. Chicago grew up in a politically active household that eschewed any connections to Judaism, celebrating Christmas with a tree and presents. This distancing from the family's Jewish heritage was evident as well in its silence about the Holocaust.

While Chicago grew up feeling proud of her descent from the *kohanim* (rabbi class)—the aristocracy of Jewish culture—she did not know what being Jewish meant and did not believe in God ("especially a male God"). A real connection to Judaism began to be made only in 1985, when she embarked on a serious study of the Holocaust as a possible subject for artistic interpretation; from *The Dinner Party* and *The Birth Project* she had gone on to a show called *Powerplay,* which looked at how men viewed their world, and began to theorize about relationships between power and powerlessness and the global structure of dominance. The Nazis' extermination of the Jews seemed to fit the paradigm she had approached from the perspective of gender, although she had surprisingly little knowledge or understanding of fascism. With her third husband, Donald Woodman, a Jew who was even more assimilated than herself, Chicago undertook a two-year study, reading historical writings and survivor testimonies, visiting Holocaust memorials, and travelling throughout Europe to concentration camps and massacre sites. She also journeyed to Vilna; at the restored tomb of her ancestor, the Vilna Gaon, she realized that for Jews as well as women, "a people's identity and pride are largely determined by an understanding of their roots." At that moment, she made a connection between her understanding of herself as a woman and "what I was learning about being a Jew."[43]

Chicago framed the *Holocaust Project* in terms of the relationship between the Nazis' abuse of power and the powerlessness of their victims, connecting the experience of women to that of Jews by highlighting the sexual exploitation of women and homosexuals in the camps. The exhibit begins with a huge stained-glass logo consisting of a series of colored triangles, representing those that concentration camp inmates wore for identification; next comes a tapestry showing the link between anti-Semitism and antifeminism. Twelve works follow, organized into five groups—Bearing Witness: the Holocaust as Jewish Experience; Power and Powerlessness: The Holocaust as Prism; Echoes and Recurrences: The Holocaust as Lesson; Four Questions: The Moral and Ethical Issues Raised by the Holocaust; and Survival and Transformation. The final piece is the stained-glass "Rainbow Shabbat," which portrays a female-led multicultural Shabbat ceremony, promising optimism, hope, and peaceful connections between peoples.

The show has been attacked for trivializing the Holocaust by comparing it to other evils such as sexual exploitation, child abuse, black slavery, the annihilation of Native Americans, even the abuse of laboratory animals; Chicago's omnipresent authorial voice (she supplies a forty-five minute narration) has also been condemned.[44] But Chicago has supporters who praise her ability to heighten consciousness through her direct, though avowedly polemical, works. Holocaust survivors and art critics alike seem divided about the aesthetic merits of her most recent project.

Chicago's journey to the *Holocaust Project* suggests a surprising erasure of Jewish consciousness from this descendant of a family with deep connections to a religious past. "Had I always known I was Jewish?" Chicago asks herself at the outset of her Holocaust exploration; given her earliest autobiography, *Through the Flower,* the answer is unclear. The *Holocaust Project* thus represents a performance of identity, a public exhibit of Chicago's struggle to reclaim "who I was as a Jew" and link it to her other identities as a woman, an active feminist, and a renegade artist. Enacting her search for roots on the stage of public art and connecting her new-found consciousness of ethnic and spiritual heritage to her political activism as a feminist, she succeeds in visually representing the struggle for identity of many women of her time and in adding her voice to those of other Jewish women who have turned to Jewish subjects in their art.

From Rebbetzin to Rebel: Helene Aylon

The journey through feminism to an alternative consciousness of Judaism is exemplified in another visual project, the "Liberation of G–d," an installation by feminist performance artist Helene Aylon originally shown at New York's Jewish Museum. Challenging the fundamental structures of Jewish belief, the work consists of fifty-four copies of the Hebrew/English Pentateuch, each opened to a weekly portion of the Torah reading that the artist has covered with translucent film on which she highlights troublesome "patriarchal-macho" passages in pink; the marked passages concern issues of domination over women, the earth, and animals, as well as the omission of women. Aylon considers these passages as places where "G–d was spoken of by and for a patriarchy," and which emphasize attributes that are "manly and not Godly." By shining a highlighter on such portions, Aylon hoped to "rescue" God from "man-made projections" and allow more positive aspects of the text to be experienced.[45]

An avant-garde artist who identifies herself as an eco-feminist, sixty-five-year-old Aylon arrived at her "liberation" project after a long journey from

Orthodox Judaism to the peace and feminist movements and performance art. She was born and raised in Borough Park, Brooklyn, the daughter of a tie manufacturer and his wife, both of whom had emigrated from Eastern Europe. Her parents kept a traditional Orthodox home, and Aylon went to a yeshiva until she was thirteen. She credits her fifth grade teacher, Nechama (Morah) Cohen with encouraging her to make her own *midrashim* (study of the Holy Scriptures). Aylon dedicated the "Liberation of G–d" to Cohen and to the principal of the yeshiva, Judith Leiberman, both of whom "encouraged Jewish girls even then to ask questions."

At the age of eighteen, Aylon married a young Orthodox rabbi from Williamsburg. Though she found a "lot of beauty and meaning and associations" in her life as a *rebbetzin* (rabbi's wife), as an individual she was "almost erased. I never spoke before others because my husband was the family spokesman," she recalls.[46] Other than illustrate the synagogue bulletin, Aylon had little opportunity for the art work she had loved since childhood. But secretly, while her husband was in shul and her children in school, she painted still lifes in oils. "Around five o'clock I quickly put all the paints away. The house smelled from turpentine so I cooked something with garlic and opened the windows." Though she chose Sabbath candles or other ritual objects as her subject to make her work seem less of an "indulgence," painting still felt "like adultery" to her.[47]

When her youngest child was in kindergarten, Aylon enrolled at Brooklyn College; it would take her seven years, going part-time, to complete the degree. After her husband died, leaving her a widow at thirty-one with two young children, she began to pursue an art career. One of her first professional projects was a mural in the children's ward of Hadassah Hospital in Jerusalem in 1963. The children there took to calling her Doda Aylonna (Aunt Helene), and the following year, when a reporter asked her name, she instinctively felt that the time to declare her independence had arrived. "Helene Aylon," she replied, rejecting her husband's name and taking as her surname the Hebraicized version of her given name.

Soon afterwards, she had the idea of doing a piece for a synagogue then under construction at Kennedy Airport; this would serve to "mak[e] sense out of [her] former life" while cementing her new career as an artist and bridging the distance between the two. Her designs were accepted, and in 1966 she executed a mural on the library wall of the airport synagogue consisting of the three letters of the Hebrew word *ruach* painted over and over again in transparent layers. Meaning "spirit," "wind," and "breath," *ruach* symbolized for Aylon the feminine aspect of God. The mural pointed the way to the interrogation of traditional religious language that would produce the "Liberation of G–d" project thirty years later.

In the 1970s, Aylon became interested in paintings that changed as a result of light, absorption, or gravity. She created works in which linseed oil poured onto a canvas was allowed to coagulate into sacks; these broke when the paintings were lifted onto the wall, releasing a cascading liquid. The bursting, or "birthing," of these liquid sacks evolved into the peace and environmental performances of her later work. In 1981, for example, sand poured down from earth sacks that Aylon used for a ritual of healing at the border between Lebanon and Israel. That year, she designed a ceremony in which Arab and Is-raeli women collected stones to be placed inside peace sacks left in the arch-ways of a deserted Arab village.

In 1982, Aylon embarked on a journey to rescue sacks of "endangered" earth from nuclear weapons sites at twelve U.S. Armed Forces Strategic Air Command (SAC) bases across the country. The sacks were pillowcases on which Aylon had asked women to inscribe their dreams about nuclear war; they were picked up by a converted "Earth Ambulance" that Aylon drove across country, and delivered to a United Nations peace rally on old army stretchers. Emptied of their contents, the nearly one thousand pillowcases were hung on a clothesline across Dag Hammarskjöld Plaza. Other projects included a pillowcase exchange in the Soviet Union between Russian and American women, and a two-mile installation at the Seneca Women's Peace Encampment in upstate New York.

In 1985, Aylon floated two large sacks filled with seeds, pods, grains of rice, and other "resuscitative" ingredients down the Kamo River in Japan to the shores of Hiroshima and Nagasaki. Women who had survived the bomb-ings wrote their dreams on pillowcases in a related ceremony. In the early 1990s, she returned to studying Hebrew texts, encasing the pages of the Torah in translucent coverings, or "sacks," so that they could be changed by highlighting words and phrases that seemed to Aylon not to reflect God's real voice. She believes that this "sac-religion" is the final stop in her journey to "liberate" God and release the spirit of *ruach*.

Although Aylon works as a secular environmental artist, elements of her Jewish beliefs are contained in all of her projects. The women who dug up the earth at the SAC sites wore cloths representing *tallit* (prayer shawls); when the Earth Ambulance arrived at the U.N. after the cross-country trip, Aylon re-cited the *Shehechayanu,* the benediction used by Jews on many important oc-casions. And when she sent the sacks floating down the Kamo River, she read the section from the Torah describing Moses floating on the Nile in a basket as Miriam looks on from the bullrushes.

Aylon's ideas about art have been profoundly influenced by feminism as well as Judaism; she believes that the evolution of her work traces the history of the women's movement from private, individual concerns to a more global feminism. Its pervading spirit speaks to the possibility of transformation and renewal, which she sees at the core of Judaism as well. Although she hesitates to use the words "religious" or "spiritual" to describe her work, she speaks of a continuing "search" to heal the world. "Am I talking about faith or the women's movement?" she asks herself. "It is the same thing."[48]

Too Jewish?: Barbra Streisand

The impressive development of a body of cultural materials highlighting the multiplicity of American Jewish women's voices in literature, music, and the visual arts has not been accompanied by a similar renaissance in film and television. In fact, there is a marked absence of positive images of Jewish women in these media, with the notable exception of the films of writer-director Joan Micklin Silver and superstar Barbra Streisand.[49]

Streisand has appeared in a large number of movies with heroines who are explicitly or implicitly Jewish: *Funny Girl* (1968) and *Funny Lady* (1975), the story of Fanny Brice; *The Way We Were* (1973), about Katie Morosky, a politically ardent Jewish coed in the late 1930s; *Hello, Dolly!* (1969), about the widowed matchmaker Dolly Levi; *A Star Is Born* (1976), the story of a struggling singer named Esther Hoffman; *The Main Event* (1979), about a Beverly Hills business executive; *Yentl* (1983), the story of the passionate Yeshiva student; and *The Prince of Tides* (1991), in which Streisand plays a psychoanalyst, Dr. Susan Lowenstein. In these films, Jewishness is usually presented in a positive light and Streisand makes little attempt to disguise her own ethnicity. "I arrived [in Hollywood]," Streisand comments, "without having to have my nose fixed, my teeth capped or my name changed."[50] Her characters reflect the kind of person she is in real life: Fanny Brice the unconventional performance artist, Katie Morosky the political activist, and Yentl the passionate learner. Streisand recalls:

> I was always curious. I wanted to learn Japanese writing when I was sixteen. I read Zen Buddhism and Russian novels. I love knowledge. I was struck by the many similarities between myself and Yentl. And I would have done the same thing she does. I would have dressed up in my father's clothes and gone out as a boy to pursue my dream.[51]

Born in 1942 and raised in the Flatbush section of Brooklyn, Streisand is the granddaughter of a cantor who lived with her, her mother, and her sister after the death of her father. Until the family could no longer afford the tuition, Barbra was sent to a nearby yeshiva.

> I had very good marks, but my conduct was always poor. I was so impatient. I'd sit there holding up my hand and when the teacher ignored me, I'd talk anyway. We'd study the Bible and I had questions: why, why, why? It didn't go over well.[52]

Years later, when Streisand embarked on a program of Jewish study in preparation for filming *Yentl,* she had a chance to ask the questions that she had not been able to ask in her youth. Poring over the Torah, attending Bible study classes, Streisand became "more proud to be a Jew." What she learned that especially pleased her was a new understanding of the place of women in Judaism. "I don't believe God is a chauvinist," she insists.

> When you read the Bible there are two chapters of Genesis that have different interpretations of how woman was created. . . . I believe that woman was not created from a rib . . . but was created equally, like it says in one of the chapters: God created Adam and then split him in two so that each side has masculine and feminine qualities. They're different but equal.

"Where is it written that women have to be subservient?" she asks. "Men have interpreted the law to serve themselves and society's needs. In other words, it is *not* written!"[53]

While Streisand's films and performances are imbued with a generic, universalist liberalism rather than a Jewishness embedded in religion, for many Jews—especially women—she stands as a powerful symbol of ethnic identity.[54] In "Too Jewish?", a 1996 exhibit at New York's Jewish Museum, Streisand was the subject of several works: Deborah Kass's triptych of Streisand cross-dressed as Yentl follows an opening montage of three Barbie dolls under glass; in *Four Barbras* (subtitled the "Jewish Jackie Series"), Kass substitutes the repeated image of Streisand's multicolored profile for that of Jacqueline Kennedy in Andy Warhol's famous silkscreen; in Rhonda Lieberman's *Barbra Bush*, glossy photographs of Streisand in a famous pose from *Funny Girl* are inlaid on glittering Jewish stars adorning a white plastic Christmas tree. The ironic use of Streisand's image as a contrast to celebrated women of Gentile culture—Barbie, Jackie, and First Lady Barbara Bush—indicated that she has come to embody an alternative female identity—"unWASPy looks, a big nose, and a reputation for business shrewdness (read in the ethnic stereotype of 'pushy')."[55] Her physical presence challenges normative cultural standards of beauty and femininity, replacing them with a proudly assertive, kooky, "lovable, but ugly" Jewish body.[56]

Streisand's huge following extends far beyond her Jewish audience. She has become a veritable icon of popular culture; indeed, a Streisand museum—some call it shrine—opened in San Francisco in 1996.[57] But Jewish girls are among her most passionate admirers. As one such fan confesses, Streisand "validated my [different] looks. She made me feel sort of beautiful."[58]

Chronicles of a Generation: Wendy Wasserstein

Like Barbra Streisand, Brooklyn-born Wendy Wasserstein briefly attended yeshiva before switching to the Calhoun School, an exclusive Manhattan private school, when her family moved to the Upper East Side. The youngest of four children of a textile manufacturer and his wife, who was an avid fan of theater and dance, Wasserstein graduated from Mount Holyoke College. Her first play, *Uncommon Women and Others,* which she wrote as a master's thesis at the Yale School of Drama, draws on the incongruities of her experience at this all female, upper-crust WASP school. The play was produced off-Broadway in 1978 and won an Obie. It was followed by *Isn't It Romantic?* in 1981; *The Heidi Chronicles,* winner of a Pulitzer Prize, a Tony Award, and a host of other prizes, in 1988; and *The Sisters Rosensweig* in 1992.[59]

Famous for her snappy one-liners, Wasserstein is a comic writer first and foremost. But despite their humor (which is often compared to that of Neil Simon, whom she much admires), Wasserstein's plays deal with the serious issues that confront contemporary young women in the wake of the feminist movement—the high cost of autonomy, the forced choice between independence and family life, the possibility of intimacy. Although occasional Yiddishisms embellish the dialogue and several characters are Jewish, with the exception of *The Sisters Rosensweig,* the painful dilemmas of the modern women who are Wasserstein's subjects are neither ethnic nor religious in nature.

The Sisters Rosensweig tells the story of three sisters, who greatly resemble Wasserstein and her own two sisters, who spend a weekend in London to celebrate the birthday of the eldest. Sara, cool and self-controlled, an expatriate and atheist, is a high-powered international banker who has renounced all possibility of romance as she moves into her fifty-fourth year. "Funsy," clothes-conscious, garrulous Gorgeous, slightly younger, is a housewife, mother, and temple member from suburban Boston, where she is a talk-show personality. Pfeni, single and forty, is the "wandering Jew" of the family—an itinerant journalist who roams the world in search of causes and stories. By the time the play ends, the public identities of the sisters have evaporated, and they are revealed to the audience, and each other, in surprising ways. Intertwined with this unmasking is the drama of cultural assimilation and ethnic retrieval: Sara, in the company of her sisters, her daughter, and a very Jewish love interest, eventually acknowledges her roots. Says Wasserstein, "There's a reason why these three sisters are from Brooklyn and the play takes place in Queen Anne's Gate, London."[60]

The Rosensweigs join the pantheon of female characters who represent and help define the dilemmas of Wasserstein's postfeminist era. Chronicling their achievements, foibles, and fears with wry humor, she has helped put her generation—and contemporary women's lives—on the theatrical map.

The manifold achievements of Jewish women in contemporary culture represent a coming to Jewish voice that is unequalled in its breadth and diversity. Paralleling Jewish women's emergence in the worlds of feminist activism, scholarship, and religion, Jewish female writers, artists, musicians, and performers increasingly are choosing Jewish subjects relating to women's lives, boldly experimenting with form, content, and voice. They are rejecting "cultural amnesia," says poet Irena Klepfisz, the daughter of Holocaust survivors who has led a movement to restore the legacy of Yiddish women's culture as a route to a revitalized Jewish identity.[61]

As the twenty-first century approaches, the varieties of renewal and return that Jewish women have exemplified in recent years can serve as a touchstone of what is possible. Their capacity to assert and balance multiple loyalties, to remap boundaries and renegotiate connections in ways that enhance both their own identity and those of their communities, points to positive directions for Jewish life in the future. Jewish women's unprecedented involvement in prayer, liturgy, religious study, and ritual, their creation of new scholarship, fiction, music, art, and performance, their development of grassroots networks that are local, regional, national, and international, and their participation as Jews in multiple political arenas indicate the scope and depth of contemporary Jewish journeys. By modelling new forms of individual participation and collective activism, they can empower the next generation of Jews, both male and female.

Jewish women today constitute the most important resource for Jewish revival. Their complex and in many ways unique legacy deserves to be placed in the foreground of Jewish memory and identity so that it can help shape American Jewish life in the century to come.

WHEN DAUGHTERS ARE CHERISHED

Ruth Bader Ginsburg

Over the course of the twentieth century, Jewish women have made a re-markable journey. Lacking at the outset a sense of their place within Jewish tradition or the events of their own time, they were marginalized not only by their bifurcated identity as Jewish Americans and female Jews, but by their exclusion from history. Feminism, however, offered them a pathway out of the extended exile that many Jewish women experienced in America by au-thenticating new models of selfhood and creating alternative traditions and histories that acknowledge women's influence in all arenas of American and Jewish life.

The vibrant sense of Jewish female selfhood felt by many young women today was demonstrated in my own family several years ago when my daugh-ter Lauren, now a college student, surprised me with a casual remark. "There are two things I am proud of," she asserted. "One is being a woman; the other is being Jewish." I was startled not by the comment itself, which fit her life so perfectly, but because of the contrast it provided with my own younger self. My daughter had named the two aspects of my identity that have been pro-found and continuing sources of struggle in my own life.

Brought up with deeper connections to Judaism than I had, my daughter had several women in her life who served her as Jewish role models—family members, friends, and the associate rabbi of our temple, a dynamic young woman who had been a student in my women's studies classes and is a vivid female presence in our synagogue. My generation's questioning of female roles, passed on to my student, was transformed by her own pioneering gen-eration of women rabbis into a proud acknowledgment of women's contribu-tions to Judaism, which was in turn passed on to my daughters.

The passing on and transformation of heritage and tradition—and the cre-ation of ever new possibilities for women—are also exemplified in the life story of Ruth Bader Ginsburg, associate justice of the United States Supreme Court. When President Clinton announced the appointment of Ruth Bader Ginsburg to the Supreme Court in 1993, pending Senate approval, Ginsburg accepted the nomination by expressing gratitude to "the bravest and strongest person I have known," her mother, Celia Amster Bader, adding that she prayed that she might "be all that she would have been had she lived in an age when women could aspire and achieve and daughters are cherished as much as sons."[1] The fourth of seven children, Celia Bader was the first to be born in the United States, just four months after her mother arrived in New York. After graduating from high school at age fifteen, she worked in a garment factory to help support her family and enable an older brother to attend college. Though she never had an independent career, Bader impressed upon Ruth the importance of achievement and independence, and especially, the value of reading and aiding the poor and needy. "My mother would have been a wonderful lawyer," Ginsburg remarks. "She was a woman of great intelligence . . . a caring, resourceful individual."[2] Ginsburg credits what others have called her "Flatbush strategy"—"to love learning, to care about people, and to work hard for whatever I wanted or believed"—with helping her to surmount the barriers to women's professional achievement.[3]

Ruth Bader Ginsburg graduated from James Madison High School in Brooklyn (where she was born in 1933) just one day before her mother died of cervical cancer. At Cornell, which she entered on a scholarship in 1950, she was an eager student; although she denies an early interest in women's issues, Ginsburg participated in the Women's League for Self-Governance. While she had been confirmed at the East Midwood Jewish Center, she did not consider herself religious. Yet she was deeply troubled by the treatment of Jews at Cornell, including the segregation of Jewish women in one corner of her dormitory. She also believed that because she was Jewish she was not invited to join the sorority of some non-Jewish friends.[4]

Shortly after her graduation in 1954, Ginsburg married Martin D. Ginsburg, who had graduated from Cornell the previous year. Ginsburg's first encounter with sex discrimination came while working for the Social Security Office in Oklahoma, where Martin was serving in the military; after revealing her pregnancy to administrators, she was demoted. When she became pregnant again nine years later while teaching at Rutgers Law School, she hid it from colleagues.

Ginsburg applied to Harvard Law School, where Martin had re-enrolled after completing his service, not out of a desire to reform women's lives but because she believed she could do a lawyer's job better than any other. Facing skepticism on almost all sides, she was one of only nine women in a class of over five hundred. At a tea for the women, she remembers Dean Erwin Griswold asking each student in turn how she felt about taking a place earmarked for a man. Fearful of seeming too assertive and not yet a feminist, Ginsburg replied that her studies would help her to understand her husband's work and might lead to a part-time job. Ginsburg's mettle was proven during her second year, when Martin was diagnosed with a rare form of cancer; Ginsburg copied his notes and typed his papers while he underwent therapy. Martin recovered and graduated on time; Ruth made Law Review. Fellow students called her "scary smart."[5] When Ginsburg transferred to Columbia Law School in New York where Martin had taken a job, one classmate recalled that "we had heard that the smartest person on the East Coast was going to transfer and that we were all going to drop down one rank."[6]

But despite tying for first place in her class at Columbia and editing the Law Review (she was the first woman elected to Law Review at both Harvard and Columbia), Ginsburg received no job offers when she graduated in 1959. "In the Fifties," she noted, "the traditional law firms were just beginning to turn around on hiring Jews. But to be a woman, a Jew and a mother to boot—that combination was a bit too much." The reluctance to consider employing female attorneys extended even to the nation's highest court, and even to its Jewish justice. "Does she wear skirts?" Felix Frankfurter queried after he was asked to consider hiring Ginsburg, "I can't stand girls in pants."[7]

Ginsburg found a position as clerk to a federal district judge in Manhattan, then joined a Columbia Law School international project. She credits her awakening to feminist consciousness to several trips she took in the early 1960s to Sweden, where women had made great progress in the paid labor force, and to reading Simone de Beauvoir's *The Second Sex*. She took on a few cases of sex discrimination for the American Civil Liberties Union and "began to wonder: How have people [in the U.S.] been putting up with such arbitrary distinctions? How have I been putting up with them?"[8] In 1972, she began to teach at Columbia University Law School, as its first tenured female professor. At the same time, she became general counsel of the Women's Rights Project of the American Civil Liberties Union. In that position she invented a legal strategy which sought to persuade the nation's judicial system, and especially the Supreme Court, that protective legislation designed to benefit women could have harmful effects. In the years 1973 to 1976, she argued six women's rights cases before the Supreme Court and won five of them, pioneering the notion of gender discrimination as a legal category. Representing both male and female plaintiffs, Ginsburg argued that widowers should be entitled to the same benefits as widows to care for dependent children, that alimony should not favor women, that boys should be able to buy beer at the same age as girls, and that women should not be barred systematically from serving as executors of estates or on juries. In so doing, she shattered sexual stereotypes, forcing the Court to articulate a standard of gender discrimination that could be applied to both men and women.[9] Because of the influence of this strategy, she has been called "the Thurgood Marshall of gender equality law."[10]

Interestingly enough, Louis Brandeis, the first Jewish justice of the Court, came to prominence as a lawyer in *Muller v. Oregon,* a 1908 Supreme Court case in which Brandeis revolutionized jurisprudence by arguing on the basis of social experience, or what Brandeis called "reasoning from the facts"; his winning argument upheld the constitutionality of Oregon's law limiting working hours for women on the basis of their "special physical organiza- tion."[11] Amassing pages of statistical proofs showing that women were funda- mentally weaker than men in all matters of endurance, Brandeis changed the course of jurisprudence by establishing the legal significance of normative ideas about gender-based distinctions and roles. Sixty-five years later, in de- signing the strategy that recognized gender discrimination as a legal category, Ginsburg overturned her predecessor's famous victory. Not incidentally, her argument was one that addressed the core Jewish ideal of the *eyshet hayil,* which separates the duties of the sexes: while the wife is to manage her house- hold with competence and compassion, she is excluded from the "promi- nence" her husband attains for his public role as an "elder" (that is, a judge or scholar). Ginsburg's pioneering work as a feminist lawyer helped make it pos- sible for other Jewish women to become "elders" of their communities and nation.

As a judge on the U.S. Court of Appeals throughout the 1980s and early 1990s, Ginsburg wrote more than three hundred opinions on issues that in- cluded abortion rights, gay rights, and affirmative action. But she dismayed some feminists by stating, first in 1984 and then again in a speech to New York University Law School in 1993, that *Roe v. Wade* had "ventured too far" and "prolonged divisiveness." In Ginsburg's view, grounding the right to abortion in the Constitution's equal protection guarantee, and thus as a mat- ter of sex discrimination rather than a privacy issue, would have been a more productive strategy.[12]

In testimony before the Senate Judiciary Committee after her nomination to the Supreme Court, Ginsburg nevertheless held firm in her support both for the right of women to choose abortion and the Equal Rights Amendment. On the Court, she has taken a centrist, liberal position, participating in a unanimous decision making it easier for women to sue their employers for sexual harassment but agreeing that the 1991 Civil Rights Act protecting women and minorities should not be applied retroactively. In a bold and sweeping argument rejecting sexual stereotypes and the doctrine of "separate but equal," Ginsburg wrote the majority opinion in the historic 1996 ruling that the publicly funded Virginia Military Institute could not refuse to admit women. Ginsburg often cites the Grimké sisters (the nineteenth-century women's rights pioneers also important to Justine Wise Polier and Gerda Lerner) to explain her own stance: "I ask no favors for my sex. All I ask of our brethren is that they take their feet off our necks."[13]

Ginsburg has combined her feminist views with public identification as a

Jew. Although not religiously observant, she was "not just born Jewish," as one Jewish communal leader put it, but has affirmatively associated herself with Jewish interests as a lawyer and judge, serving on the board of the International Association of Jewish Lawyers and Jurists and participating in communal Jewish events. Jews have been divided about several of Ginsburg's judicial decisions concerning Jewish matters. She dissented from *Goldman v. Weinberger* (1984), a district court decision that upheld the Air Force's refusal to allow a Jewish airman to wear his *kippah* (skullcap); Ginsberg argued that the commander's decision against the airman reflected a "callous indifference" to his religious faith. Yet she rejected a motion by Jonathan Pollard to vacate his guilty plea for spying for Israel. Observant Jews were especially disturbed by the fact that Ginsburg participated in the panel that heard the Pollard motion on the second day of Rosh Hashanah, despite the Pollard family's plea for a postponement. Ginsburg was upset at the controversy this created, and insists that she remains firmly identified as a Jew.[14]

In an address to the American Jewish Committee, she pointed to the "age-old connection between Judaism and law" reflected in the primary cultural value that Jews attach to learning and their reliance on the law as a protector of "the oppressed, the poor, the loner." "I am a judge, born, raised, and proud of being a Jew," Ginsburg asserts; "the demand for justice runs through the entirety of the Jewish tradition." On her office wall hangs the biblical command—"Justice, justice shalt thou pursue"—that inspires her work, as she believes it also motivated her Jewish predecessors on the Court.[15] For Ginsburg as for many Jewish women professionals and activists before her, it is not the ancient ideal of the woman of valor but this gender-blind commandment to justice, and particularly to the achievement of a just society, that links her to Jewish tradition.

As much as she takes pride in her own accomplishments, Justice Ginsburg cherishes the achievements of her son, James, a producer of classical recordings, and her daughter Jane C. Ginsburg, a tenured professor at Columbia University Law School (the Ginsburgs are the first mother and daughter to have held tenured positions at the same law school). Jane recalls that although her mother worked when other mothers stayed home, "she always managed to be there for me." Far from receiving too little maternal attention, Jane received too much of it, although she admits that the kitchen was the only place where the justice was "an underachiever." Jane recalls with special fondness her mother's assiduous letter-writing when Jane was away at camp or on an exchange program, marveling now at "how much discipline, and affection it takes, on top of a job, a home, a spouse, and another child, to keep up that steady stream of correspondence."[16]

Ginsburg is one of a number of Jewish women who helped to change the rules of professional life and parenthood, making it more possible for mothers, as well as fathers, to become mentors to their offspring, and for daughters, as well as sons, to be fully cherished. A secular but identified Jew and feminist, she offers young Jewish women a powerful example of a committed, achieving, courageous modern professional woman connected to her ethnic roots as well as to the broad interests of American women as a class. When Ginsburg was nominated to the Supreme Court, she learned from a former classmate that her law school nickname had been "Bitch." Ginsburg's response was typical of the line of assertive Jewish women from which she had sprung: "Better bitch than mouse," she replied.[17]

The generational inheritance that Jewish women have embodied in their cultural, political, professional, and domestic pursuits, passed down from grandmothers and mothers (and sometimes fathers) to their daughters, inspired by Jewish traditions, values, models, and mentors, has been enriched and enlarged by the legacies of twentieth-century Jewish activists and innovators like Ginsburg and many of her contemporaries. Their daughters and granddaughters now stand poised on the stage of American Jewish life, ready to make their own contributions.

A GUIDE TO ARCHIVAL COLLECTIONS

Bella Abzug—Columbia University Rare Book and Manuscript Library
Sadie American—American Jewish Historical Society, Waltham, Mass.
Mary Antin—Gould Farm, Monterey, Mass.
Jennie Loitman Barron—Schlesinger Library, Radcliffe College, Cambridge, Mass.
Gertrude Berg—Syracuse University Special Collections
Wini Breines—Schlesinger Library, Radcliffe College, Cambridge, Mass.
Betty Friedan—Schlesinger Library, Radcliffe College, Cambridge, Mass.
Susan Brandeis Gilbert—Brandeis University Special Collections
Fanny Holtzmann—American Jewish Archives, Cincinnati, Ohio
Rose Jacobs—Brandeis University; Central Zionist Archives, Jerusalem
Gerda Lerner—Schlesinger Library, Radcliffe College, Cambridge, Mass.
Ray Frank Litman—American Jewish Historical Society, Waltham, Mass.
Alice Mencken—American Jewish Historical Society, Waltham, Mass.
Annie Nathan Meyer—American Jewish Archives, Cincinnati, Ohio
Martha Neumark Montor—American Jewish Archives, Cincinnati, Ohio
Fanny Nagel Brandeis—Hildegarde Nagel Papers, Schlesinger Library, Radcliffe College, Cambridge, Mass.
Maud Nathan—Schlesinger Library, Radcliffe College, Cambridge, Mass.
Pauline Newman—Schlesinger Library, Radcliffe College, Cambridge, Mass.
Molly Picon—American Jewish Historical Society, Waltham, Mass.
Rose Pesotta—New York Public Library Rare Books and Manuscript Division
Justine Wise Polier—Schlesinger Library, Radcliffe College, Cambridge, Mass.
Cecilia Razovsky—American Jewish Historical Society, Waltham, Mass.
Julia Richman—American Jewish Archives, Cincinnati, Ohio.
Muriel Rukeyser—Library of Congress Manuscript Division
Jessie Sampter—Central Zionist Archives, Jerusalem; Hadassah Archives, New York City
Rose Schneiderman—Tamiment Institute Library, New York University
Alice Selisberg—Central Zionist Archives, Jerusalem; Hadassah Archives, New York City
Clara Lemlich Shavelson—American Jewish Archives, Cincinnati, Ohio
Hannah Greenebaum Solomon—American Jewish Archives, Cincinnati, Ohio
Rosa Sonneschein—American Jewish Archives, Cincinnati, Ohio
Rose Pastor Stokes—Tamiment Institute Library, New York University
Henrietta Szold—Central Zionist Archives, Jerusalem; Hadassah Archives, New York City; Schlesinger Library, Radcliffe College, Cambridge, Mass.

Sophie Tucker—American Jewish Archives, Cincinnati, Ohio; Brandeis University Special Collections

Anzia Yezierska—Boston University Special Collections

Alumnae Papers (Estelle Frankfurter, Hetty Goldmark, Elizabeth Raushenbush)—Radcliffe College Archives, Radcliffe College, Cambridge, Mass.

American Jewish Committee Oral History Collection—New York Public Library

American Jewish Congress, Women's Division—American Jewish Historical Society, Waltham, Mass.

Emma Lazarus Federation of Jewish Women's Clubs—American Jewish Archives, Cincinnati, Ohio

Hadassah, The Women's Zionist Organization of America, Inc.—Hadassah Archives, New York City; Central Zionist Archives, Jerusalem

International Workers Organization—Tamiment Institute Library, New York University

National Council of Jewish Women—American Jewish Historical Society, Waltham, Mass.; Library of Congress

NOTES

Introduction

1. Marge Piercy, *Braided Lives* (New York: Summit Books, 1982).
2. Muriel Rukeyser, "Under Forty," from "Under Forty: A Symposium on American Literature and the Younger Generation of American Jews," in *Contemporary Jewish Record* 5, No. 7 (Feb. 1944); reprinted in *Bridges* 1, No. 1 (Spring 1990): 29.
3. Adrienne Rich, "Split at the Root," in Evelyn Torton Beck, ed., *Nice Jewish Girls: A Lesbian Anthology* (Boston: Beacon Press, 1982, 1989), 89.
4. Kim Chernin, *In My Mother's House: A Daughter's Story* (New York: Harper & Row, 1984), 296.
5. National Commission on American Jewish Women, *Voices for Change: Future Directions for American Jewish Women* (Waltham, Mass.: Brandeis University Press, 1995), 28.
6. Women are peripheral in such major histories of American Jewry as Irving Howe's *The World of Our Fathers* (New York: Harcourt, Brace, Jovanovich, 1969) and Arthur Hertzberg's *The Jews in America, Four Centuries of an Uneasy Encounter: A History* (New York: Simon & Schuster, 1989). They are much more visible in *The Jewish People in America,* a series sponsored by the American Jewish Historical Society and edited by Henry L. Feingold. Volume II of the series, Hasia Diner's *A Time for Gathering: The Second Migration, 1820–1880* (Baltimore: Johns Hopkns University Press, 1992), offers a model for integrating women's experiences into the main narrative of American Jewish history.
7. Charlotte Baum, Paula Hyman, and Sonya Michel, *The Jewish Woman in America* (New York: Dial Press, 1975), is the pioneering work in American Jewish women's history. Other helpful early surveys are Jacob R. Marcus, *The American Jewish Woman: A Documentary History* (New York: Ktav Publishing Co., 1981); Marcus, *The American Jewish Woman, 1765–1980* (New York: Ktav Publishing Co., 1981); and June Sochen, *Consecrate the Day: The Public Lives of Jewish American Women, 1880–1980* (Albany: State University of New York Press, 1981). Also see Sydney Stahl Weinberg, *The World of Our Mothers: The Lives of Jewish Immigrant Women* (Chapel Hill: University of North Carolina Press, 1989).
8. Cynthia Ozick, "Notes Toward Finding the Right Question," *Lilith*, No. 6 (1979): 21.
9. Joyce Antler, "Feminism as Life Process: The Life and Career of Lucy Sprague Mitchell," *Feminist Studies* 7, no. 1 (Spring 1981): 134–155.
10. James Clifford, *The Predicament of Culture: Twentieth-Century Ethnography* (Cambridge, Mass.: Harvard University Press, 1988), 341–42, 344.
11. Edna Ferber, *A Peculiar Treasure* (New York: Doubleday, Doran & Co., 1939), 129.

Prologue

1. Cited in Faith Rogow, *Gone to Another Meeting: The National Council of Jewish Women, 1893–1993* (Tuscaloosa: University of Alabama Press, 1993), 19.

2. Hannah Greenebaum Solomon, *Fabric of My Life: The Autobiography of Hannah Greenebaum Solomon* (New York: Bloch Publishing Co., National Council of Jewish Women, 1946), 80.

3. Cited in Rogow, *Gone to Another Meeting*, 17. On the National Council of Jewish Women, also see Linda Gordon Kuzmack, *Woman's Cause: The Jewish Woman's Movement in England and the United States, 1881–1933* (Columbus: Ohio State University Press, 1990), 32–33. On the 1893 Congress, see Deborah Grand Golomb, "The 1893 Congress of Jewish Women: Evolution or Revolution in American Jewish Women's History?" *American Jewish History* 70, No. 1 (1980); 52–67.

4. Rogow, *Gone to Another Meeting*, 19.

5. Sadie American, "Organization," *Papers of the Jewish Women's Congress, 1893* (Philadelphia: Jewish Publication Society, 1894), 249.

6. Diane Lichtenstein uses the term "Mother in Israel" to describe the model nineteenth-century Jewess, "the wife mother, daughter, who dedicated herself to the well-being of her family and, through the family, the Jewish nation." Lichtenstein, *Writing Their Nations: The Tradition of Nineteenth-Century American Jewish Women Writers* (Bloomington: Indiana University Press, 1992), 24. Also see Ellen M. Umansky, "Piety, Persuasion and Friendship: A History of Jewish Women's Spirituality," in Umansky and Dianne Ashton, eds., *Four Centuries of Jewish Women's Spirituality* (Boston: Beacon Press, 1994), 1–30.

7. *Ibid.*, 244, 247.

8. For a discussion of early Jewish women's societies, see William Toll, "A Quiet Revolution: Jewish Women's Clubs and the Widening Female Sphere, 1870–1920," *American Jewish Archives* 61 (Spring/Summer 1989): 7–26.

9. American, "Organization," 248.

10. *Ibid.*, 252.

11. Among the many studies of early Jewish life in the United States, see Eli Faber, *A Time for Planting: The First Migration, 1654–1820* (Baltimore: Johns Hopkins University Press, 1922), and Jacob R. Marcus, *The Colonial American Jew* (Detroit: Wayne State University Press, 1970).

12. For a comprehensive analysis of this migration, see Hasia R. Diner, *A Time for Gathering: The Second Migration, 1820–1880* (Baltimore: Johns Hopkins University Press, 1992).

13. See Karla Ann Goldman, "Beyond the Gallery: The Place of Women in the Development of American Judaism" (Ph.D. diss., Harvard University Press, 1993).

14. The NCJW refused to join the General Federation of Women's Clubs, the umbrella organization of women's associations, because it held that the Council was primarily a "religious" body. Solomon, *Fabric of My Life*, 108.

15. Alpheus Thomas Mason, *Brandeis, A Free Man's Life* (New York: Viking Press, 1946), 71; Karin Elisabeth Grundler, " 'Your Loving Sister Fannie': The Letters of Fannie Brandeis Nagel to Her Brother Louis Dembitz Brandeis" (M.A. thesis, Brandeis University, 1996).

16. See, for example, Fannie Nagel to Louis Brandeis, Sept. 1, 1883, and May 21, 1886, Hildegard Nagel Papers, Schlesinger Library, Radcliffe College, Cambridge, Mass.

17. Fannie Nagel to Louis Brandeis, Feb. 3, 1884, Hildegard Nagel Papers.

18. Fannie Nagel to Louis Brandeis, April 17, 1884, Hildegard Nagel Papers.

19. Louis Brandeis to Adolph Brandeis, Dec. 16, 1889, Hildegard Nagel Papers.

20. Fannie Nagel to Louis Brandeis, Oct. 21, n.d., Hildegard Nagel Papers. Among those

who believed that Fannie Nagel "committed suicide" is David C. Gross in *Justice for All People: Louis D. Brandeis* (New York: Lodestar Books/Penguin Books, 1987), 26. Also see Grundler, "Your Loving Sister Fannie," 11, 83.

21. See Jean Strouse, *Alice James: A Biography* (Boston: Houghton Mifflin Co., 1980).

22. Biographical information is taken from memoirs by Sonneschein's grandson, David Loth, at the American Jewish Archives, Cincinnati: "The American Jewess"; "Notes on the Marital Discord of Solomon and Rosa Sonneschein"; "Supplementary Memoir of the Sonnescheins." Also see Jack Nusan Porter, "Rose [*sic*] Sonneschein and 'The American Jewess': The First Independent English Language Jewish Women's Journal in the United States," *American Jewish History* 68 (1978): 57–63; Porter, "Rosa Sonneschein and 'The American Jewess' Revisited: New Historical Information on an Early American Zionist and Jewish Feminist," *American Jewish Archives* 32 (1980): 125–31; Karen Philipps, unpublished paper, Boston College, 1993.

23. Loth, "Notes on the Marital Discord of Solomon and Rosa Sonneschein."

24. Emily Toth, *Kate Chopin* (New York: Morrow, 1990), 246.

25. Loth, "Notes on the Marital Discord of Solomon and Rosa Sonneschein."

26. Rosa Sonneschein, "Salutatory," *The American Jewess* (April 1895): x.

27. Rosa Sonneschein, Editorial, April 1896, 381, October 1896, 94; "The American Jewess," *The American Jewess* (February 1898): 207–8.

28. Rosa Sonneschein, Editorial, *The American Jewess* (August 1899): 3.

29. Ray Frank to Rev. S.T. Willis, Dec. 15, 1896, Ray Frank Papers, American Jewish Historical Society, Waltham, Mass.

30. See C.A. Danziger, "Ray Frank," *The American Jewess* (1898): 19–21; "A Famous Jewess: Who Has Been Called 'A Female Messiah,' " *The* (Cincinnati) *Times Star,* Jan 11, 1893, and "Jewesses of Today—Ray Frank," clippings in Ray Frank Papers; Reva Clar and William M. Kramer, "The Girl Rabbi of the Golden West," Part 1, *Western States Jewish History* 18, No. 2 (January 1986): 109; Ray Frank to Charlotte Perkins Stetson, Sept. 14, 1894, Ray Frank Papers.

31. Ray Frank to Rev. S.T. Willis, Dec. 15, 1896, Ray Frank Papers.

32. See clippings, *San Francisco Examiner,* n.d., and *San Francisco Chronicle,* Oct. 19, 1883, Ray Frank Papers.

33. Ray Frank, *Papers of the Jewish Women's Congress,* 64–65.

34. Ray Frank to Charlotte Perkins Stetson, Sept. 14, 1894, Ray Frank Papers.

35. "Not Ready to Vote: Miss Ray Frank Is Conservative on the Suffrage Question," *Oakland Enquirer,* June 19, 1895; "A California Woman Who Opposes the Suffragists," *San Francisco Examiner,* n.d.; "Jewesses of Today: Ray Frank," Ray Frank Papers.

36. Clar and Kramer, "The Girl Rabbi of the Golden West," Part 2, *Western States Jewish History* 18, No. 3 (April 1986): 227–28.

37. Danziger, "Ray Frank"; "A California Woman Who Opposes the Suffragists."

38. See Simon Litman, *Ray Frank Litman: A Memoir* (New York: American Jewish Historical Society, 1957); Clar and Kramer, "The Girl Rabbi of the Golden West," Part 3, *Western States Jewish History* 18, No. 4 (July 1986): 336–51.

39. On Lazarus, see Morris U. Schappes, ed., *Emma Lazarus: Selections from Her Poetry and Prose* (New York: Emma Lazarus Federation of Jewish Women's Clubs, 1982); Schappes, ed., *Letters of Emma Lazarus* (New York: New York Public Library, 1949); Dan Vogel, *Emma Lazarus* (Boston: Twayne, 1980); and Lichtenstein, *Writing Their Nations,* ch. III.

40. Vogel, *Emma Lazarus,* 13.

41. *Ibid.,* 15; Lichtenstein, *Writing Their Nations,* 37.

42. Vogel, *Emma Lazarus,* p. 27.

43. *Ibid.,* 127; Schappes, ed., *Letters of Emma Lazarus,* 21.

44. *Ibid.*, 27.
45. Emma Lazarus, "An Epistle to the Hebrews," V, in Morris U. Schappes, ed., *An Epistle to the Hebrews* (New York: Jewish Historical Society of New York, 1987), 30.
46. "The Jewish Problem," *Century* (Feb. 1883): 608.
47. Lazarus, "An Epistle to the Hebrews," V, 30.
48. Emma Lazarus, "The New Year, Rosh-Hashanah, 5643 (1882)," in Schappes, ed., *Emma Lazarus: Selections from Her Poetry and Prose,* 38.
49. Emma Lazarus, "Echoes," in *ibid.*, 30.
50. Emma Lazarus, "The New Colossus," in *ibid.*, 48; see Lichtenstein's gendered interpretation of the poem in *Writing Their Nations,* 36–37.
51. Josephine Lazarus, "Emma Lazarus," in *The Poems of Emma Lazarus* (Boston: Houghton Mifflin, 1889), 1, 9; cited in Lichtenstein, *Writing Their Nations,* 42.
52. See *ibid.*, 41.

Chapter 1. The Paradox of Immigration

1. Mary Antin, *The Promised Land* (Princeton, N.J.: Princeton University Press, 1985), xix.
2. Among the commentaries on *The Promised Land* are Sarah Blacher Cohen, "Mary Antin's *The Promised Land:* A Breach of Promise," *Studies in American Jewish Literature* 3 (1977–78): 28–35; William A. Proefriedt, "The Education of Mary Antin," *Journal of Ethnic Studies* 17, No. 4 (1990): 81–100; Steven J. Rubin, "Style and Meaning in Mary Antin's *The Promised Land:* A Reevaluation," *Studies in American Jewish Literature* 5 (1986): 35–43; and Richard Tuerk, "The Youngest of America's Children in *The Promised Land," Studies in American Jewish Literature* 5 (1986): 29–34.
3. Sally Ann Drucker identifies fifteen such memoirs; see her " 'It Doesn't Say So in Mother's Prayerbook': Autobiographies in English by Immigrant Jewish Women," *American Jewish History* 79, No. 1 (August 1989): 70–71. For a cross-cultural comparison of immigrant women's autobiographies, see Emine Lale Demirturk, "The Female Identity in Cross-Cultural Perspective: Immigrant Women's Autobiographies" (Ph.D. diss., University of Iowa, 1986). On Yiddish women writers, see Norma Fain Pratt, "Culture and Radical Politics, 1890–1940," *American Jewish History* 70, No. 1 (Sept. 1980): 68–90.
4. On the relation of ethnic literature to identity, see Werner Sollors, ed., *The Invention of Ethnicity* (New York: Oxford University Press, 1989), and Sollors, *Beyond Ethnicity: Consent and Descent in American Culture* (New York: Oxford University Press, 1986). On women's autobiography, see Sheri Benstock, ed., *The Private Self: Theory and Practice of Women's Autobiographical Writings* (Chapel Hill: University of North Carolina Press, 1988); Margo Culley, ed., *American Women's Autobiography: Fea(s)ts of Memory* (Madison: University of Wisconsin Press, 1992); Shirley Neuman, ed., *Autobiography and Questions of Gender* (London: Frank Cass & Co., 1991); and Liz Stanley, *The Auto-Biographical I: The Theory and Practice of Feminist Auto/biography* (Manchester: Manchester University Press, 1992).
5. Several recent studies focus on this theme. See Gert Buelens, "The New Man and the Mediator: (Non)-Remembrance in Jewish American Immigrant Narrative," in Amritjit Singh, Joseph T. Skerrett, Jr., and Robert E. Hogan, eds., *Memory, Narrative and Identity* (Boston: Northeastern University Press, 1994), 89–113; and Magdalena J. Zabrowska, *How We Found America: Reading Gender through East European Immigrant Narratives* (Chapel Hill: University of North Carolina Press, 1995).
6. Howard M. Sachar, *The Course of Modern Jewish History* (New York: Vintage Books, 1990), 283–84.

7. Gerald Sorin, *A Time for Building: The Third Migration, 1880–1920* (Baltimore: Johns Hopkins University Press, 1992), 12, 39. Also see Roger Daniels, *Coming to America: A History of Immigration and Ethnicity in American Life* (New York: HarperCollins, 1990), 223–24.

8. Antin, *The Promised Land,* xx–xxi.

9. *Ibid.*, xxi, xxii.

10. *Ibid.*, 110; 41.

11. *Ibid.*, 40–41.

12. *Ibid.*, 40.

13. Mary Antin, "Malinke's Atonement," in Joyce Antler, ed., *America and I: Short Stories by American Jewish Women Writers* (Boston: Beacon Press, 1990), 32.

14. *Ibid.*, 34.

15. Antin, *The Promised Land,* 111.

16. *Ibid.*, 96.

17. *Ibid.*, 358.

18. *Ibid.*

19. Cited in Buelens, "The New Man and the Mediator," 95.

20. *Ibid.*, 92 (*The New York Times,* April 14, 1912).

21. Antin, *The Promised Land,* 223, 239, 242.

22. *Ibid.*, 270–71.

23. *Ibid.*, 249.

24. *Ibid.*, 248.

25. Zabrowska, *How We Found America,* 57–59.

26. Antin, *The Promised Land,* xxii.

27. *Ibid.*, xix–xxii, 364.

28. *Ibid.*, xxii.

29. *Ibid.*, 93.

30. Evelyn Salz, "The Letters of Mary Antin: A Life Divided," *American Jewish History* 84, No. 2 (June 1996), 72.

31. Mary Antin, *They Who Knock At Our Gates* (Boston: Houghton Mifflin, 1914).

32. See Mary Antin, "A Zionist's Confession of Faith," *The Maccabean,* Feb. 1917, 157.

33. Susan Koppelman, "Mary Antin," *Dictionary of Literary Biography Yearbook 1984* (Detroit: Gale, 1985), 231.

34. Mary Antin to Caroline Goodyear, March 18, 1930, Mary Antin Papers, Gould Farm, Monterey, Mass.

35. Mary Antin to Agnes Gould, Oct. 3, 1945, Mary Antin Papers; see also Antin to Gould, Feb. 19, 1930, Mary Antin Papers.

36. *Ibid.*

37. Stanley J. Kunitz and Howard Haycraft, *Twentieth Century Authors* (New York: H. W. Wilson, 1942), 34.

38. *Ibid.*

39. Mary Antin, "House of One Father," *Common Ground* (Spring 1941): 41.

40. *Ibid.*

41. *Ibid.*

42. *Ibid.*

43. Her sisters were Ida Perkins of Wollaston, Mass., who was married to a businessman and active in the Women's Auxiliary of the Boston Unitarian Church, and Clara and Rosemary Antin, both unmarried. Clara taught school for some years at the Little Red Schoolhouse, a progressive school in New York, and at a Jewish school in Brooklyn; Rosemary directed

a Jewish welfare project in Albany. Interviews with Roma Foreman and Harriet M. Phillips, at Gould Farm, Winter 1993.

44. M. Antin to C. Goodyear, March 18, 1930, and July 23, 1928, Mary Antin Papers.

45. See Carol B. Schoen's critical biography, *Anzia Yezierska* (Boston: Twayne, 1982); Louise Levitas Henriksen, *Anzia Yezierska: A Writer's Life* (New Brunswick, N.J.: Rutgers University Press, 1988); Alice Kessler-Harris's introductions to *The Bread Givers: A Novel* (New York: Persea Books, 1975) and *The Open Cage: An Anzia Yezierska Collection* (New York: Persea Books, 1979); and the following articles on Yezierska in *Studies in American Jewish Literature* 3 (1983): Rose Kamel, " 'Anzia Yezierska, Get Out of Your Own Way': Selfhood and Otherness in the Autobiographical Fiction of Anzia Yezierska," 40–50, Ellen Golub, "Eat Your Heart Out: The Fiction of Anzia Yezierska," 51–61, and Susan Hersch Sachs, "Anzia Yezierska: 'Her Words Dance with A Thousand Colors,' " 62–67. Also see Charlotte Goodman, "Anzia Yezierska," in *Dictionary of Literary Biography,* Vol. 28 (Detroit: Gale Research, 1984): 332–35, and "Anzia Yezierska," *Contemporary Literary Criticism,* Vol. 46 (Detroit: Gale Research, 1987): 44–49.

46. Goodman, "Anzia Yezierska," 333.

47. The collection has been republished as Anzia Yezierska, *Hungry Hearts & Other Stories* (New York: Persea Books, 1985).

48. Henriksen, *Anzia Yezierska,* 216.

49. *Ibid.,* 78–79

50. Anzia Yezierska, *All I Could Never Be,* 58, 60–61, cited in *ibid.,* 91. On the romance between Dewey and Yezierska, see Mary V. Dearborn, *Love in the Promised Land: The Story of Anzia Yezierska and John Dewey* (New York: Free Press, 1988), and Norma Rosen's novel, *John and Anzia: An American Romance* (New Brunswick, N.J.: Rutgers University Press, 1988).

51. Henriksen, *Anzia Yezierska,* 117.

52. Anzia Yezierska, *Red Ribbon on a White Horse* (New York: Persea Books, 1981), 45.

53. Mary V. Dearborn, "Anzia Yezierska and the Making of An American Ethnic Self," in Sollors, ed., *The Invention of Ethnicity,* 116.

54. Yezierska's unpublished stories from these years can be found in the Anzia Yezierska Papers, Boston University.

55. Yezierska, *The Bread Givers,* 9–10.

56. *Ibid.,* 137.

57. *Ibid.,* 204–5.

58. *Ibid.,* 297.

59. Yezierska, *Red Ribbon,* 216–17.

60. *Ibid.,* 217.

61. *Ibid.,* 219.

62. *Ibid.,* 72–74.

63. Anzia Yezierska, "Children of Loneliness," in *The Open Cage,* 160.

64. Henriksen, *Anzia Yezierska,* 237.

65. Yezierska, *Red Ribbon,* 212.

66. Yezierska, "America and I," in Antler, ed., *America and I,* 82.

67. Yezierska, *Red Ribbon,* 212.

68. Henriksen, *Anzia Yezierska,* 252, 227.

69. *Ibid.,* 254.

70. Louise Levitas Henriksen, Afterword to *The Open Cage,* 255, and interview with author, March 16, 1993.

71. See Mary Antin, "The Amulet," *Atlantic Monthly* 111 (1913): 177–90; and "Malinke's Atonement," in Antler, ed., *America and I,* 27–56.

72. Yezierska, *Red Ribbon,* 26–27, 31; Janet Handler Burstein, *Writing Mothers, Writing*

Daughters: Tracing the Maternal in Stories by American Jewish Women (Urbana: University of Illinois Press, 1996), 32.

73. Rose Gollup Cohen, *Out of the Shadow: A Russian Jewish Girlhood on the Lower East Side* (New York: Doran, 1918). The book was reprinted in 1995 by Cornell University Press with an introduction by Thomas Dublin. Also see Rose Gollup Cohen, "To the Friends of 'Out of the Shadow,' " *Bookman* 55 (March 1922): 36–40.

74. Cohen, *Out of the Shadow,* 294.

75. *Ibid.*, 231.

76. *Ibid.*, 266–68.

77. Antin, *The Promised Land,* 142.

78. Cohen, *Out of the Shadow,* 293–94.

79. The pattern is present in Elizabeth Stern's *I Am a Woman—And a Jew,* an autobiographical novel published in 1926 under the pseudonym Leah Morton. The novel, purportedly the true story of Stern, recounts the adventures of a Jewish daughter who painfully breaks from her punitive father and Jewish orthodoxy to become a social worker and eventually a writer. The character in the novel marries a Gentile social worker. In a privately published book, Stern's son reveals that his mother, though raised by Jewish foster parents, was not Jewish by birth; she was an "imaginary Jew." Ellen Umansky discusses the questions of memory and imagination in Stern's novel in "Representations of Jewish Women in the Works and Life of Elizabeth Stern," *Modern Judaism* 13 (1993): 165–76. Other scholars question the authenticity of the son's account; conversation with Barbara Sicherman, Dec. 1994.

80. On the "Pocahontas" theme of interracial, interethnic marriage, see Mary V. Dearborn, *Pocahontas's Daughters: Gender and Ethnicity in American Culture* (New York: Oxford University Press, 1986). Also see Joyce Antler, "The Problem of Gender in American-Jewish Literature," in Lynn Davidman and Shelly Tenenbaum, eds., *Feminist Perspectives on Jewish Studies* (New Haven: Yale University Press, 1994), 191–223.

81. Alvin H. Rosenfeld, "Inventing the Jew: Notes on Jewish Autobiography," *Midstream* 21, No. 4 (April 1975): 56–58.

82. Ruth Rosen and Sue Davidson, eds., *The Maimie Papers* (Bloomington: Indiana University Press, 1985), 160, 163, 166, 167.

83. Yezierska, *Red Ribbon,* 242.

84. Cited in David Mehegan, "Call It Writers' Block," *Boston Globe,* Feb. 1, 1992, 52.

85. See, for example, Mark Shechner's introduction to Isaac Rosenfeld, *Passage from Home* (New York: Markus Wiener Publishing, 1988), i–xx.

86. According to Sam Girgus, "the ideology of the independent self at the core of Yezierska's writings represents basic American attitudes toward freedom, success, and culture." *The New Covenant: Jewish Writers and the American Idea* (Chapel Hill: University of North Carolina Press, 1984), 111.

87. Antin, *Promised Land,* 364.

88. Yezierska, *Red Ribbon,* 220.

89. Yezierska, "America and I," in Antler, ed., *America and I,* 82.

90. Antin's great-granddaughter, recently married to an Israeli, has become interested in her Jewish roots. Interview with Evelyn Salz, December 1995; interview with Louise Levitas Henriksen, March 1993.

91. In *Gender and Assimilation in Modern Jewish History: The Roles and Representations of Women* (Seattle: University of Washington Press, 1995), Paula E. Hyman suggests that "assimilating Jewish women apparently retained more signs of Jewish identification than did the men in their families" (48–49).

92. Antin, "House of One Father," 41.

93. See Henriksen's Afterword to *The Open Cage,* 258.

Chapter 2.   "Uptown" Women and Social and Spiritual Reform

1. Rosalind Berry, "Rebekah Kohut Talks on Jewish Culture," *The Jewish Tribune,* April 3, 1925.
2. Rebekah Kohut, *My Portion: An Autobiography* (New York: Albert & Charles Boni, 1927), xii.
3. *Ibid.,* 9.
4. *Ibid.,* 52.
5. *Ibid.,* 61–62.
6. *Ibid.,* 63–64, 113.
7. *Ibid.,* 71.
8. *Ibid.,* 172.
9. *Ibid.,* 76.
10. *Ibid.,* 78.
11. *Ibid.,* 64.
12. *Ibid.,* 71.
13. Recounted in "Leaders in All Faiths Plan Jubilee for Rebecca [*sic*][Kohut," *New York Post,* Oct. 28, 1935.
14. Kohut, *My Portion,* 72.
15. *Ibid.,* 73.
16. *Ibid.,* 73–74.
17. *Ibid.,* 101, 99.
18. *Ibid.,* 102.
19. *Ibid.,* 118.
20. *Ibid.,* 119.
21. Cited in "Leaders in All Faiths Plan Jubilee for Rebecca Kohut."
22. Kohut, *My Portion,* 133.
23. *Ibid.,* 207.
24. *Ibid.,* 173.
25. *Ibid.* See Jenna Weissman Joselit, "The Special Sphere of the Middle-Class American Jewish Woman: The Synagogue Sisterhood, 1890–1940," in Jack Wertheimer, ed., *The American Synagogue: A Sanctuary Transformed* (New York: Cambridge University Press, 1987), 206–230.
26. Kohut, *My Portion,* 182.
27. *Ibid.,* 228.
28. *Ibid.,* 232.
29. Norma Fain Pratt, "Rebekah Kohut," in Barbara Sicherman and Carol Hurd Green, eds., *Notable American Women: The Modern Period* (Cambridge: Harvard University Press, 1980), 404.
30. Rebekah Kohut, "In the Matter of Employment," *American Hebrew,* Nov. 7, 1930, 740, 756, 765.
31. See Faith Rogow, *Gone to Another Meeting: The National Council of Jewish Women, 1893–1993* (Tuscaloosa: University of Alabama Press, 1993); Ellen Sue Levi Elwell, "The Founding and Early Programs of the National Council of Jewish Women: Study and Practice as Jewish Women's Religious Expression" (Ph.D. diss., Indiana University, 1982). On Jewish women and late-nineteenth-century philanthropy, see William Toll, "A Quiet Revolution: Jewish Women's Clubs and the Widening Female Sphere, 1870–1920," *American Jewish Archives* (Spring/Summer 1989): 7–26; Beth Wenger, "Jewish Women and Voluntarism: Beyond the Myth of Enablers," *American Jewish History* 79, No. 1 (1989): 16–36; and Wenger, "Jewish Women of the Club: The Changing Public Role of Atlanta's Jewish Women," *American Jewish History* 76, No. 3 (1987): 311 –33.

32. Elisabeth Israels Perry, *Belle Moskowitz: Feminine Politics and the Exercise of Power in the Age of Alfred E. Smith* (New York: Oxford University Press, 1987; paperback, Routledge, 1992).

33. *Ibid.*, 34.

34. Belle Lindner Israels, "Jewish Women as Settlement Workers," *The Hebrew Standard* 50, No. 11 (April 5, 1907): 9. Cited in Perry, *Belle Moskowitz*, 35. On maternalism and settlement house innovations, see Kathryn Kish Sklar, "Hull House in the 1890s: A Community of Women Reformers," *Signs* 10, No. 4 (Summer 1985): 658–77.

35. Rebekah Kohut, "Mission Work Among the Unenlightened Jews," *Papers of the Jewish Women's Congress, 1893* (Philadelphia: Jewish Publication Society, 1894), 188, 192.

36. New York Section of the NCJW, "Immigrant Aid and Americanization," *Yearbook 1919–1920,* NCJW Papers (American Jewish Historical Society, Waltham, Mass.), 74.

37. Kohut, "Mission Work," 193, 192.

38. Gerald Kane, interview with Mrs. Philip Angel of Charleston, W. Va. (Solomon's granddaughter), Hannah Greenbaum Solomon Papers, American Jewish Archives, Cincinnati, Ohio.

39. Kohut, "Mission Work," 194.

40. *Ibid.*

41. Cited in Rogow, *Gone to Another Meeting*, 151.

42. Anzia Yezierska, Letter to Chicago Woman's Aid, *Chicago Woman's Aid Bulletin* 7, No. 5 (Feb. 1924): 8.

43. Selma C. Berrol, *Julia Richman: A Notable Woman* (Philadelphia: Balch Institute Press, 1993), 17. Also see Berrol, "When Uptown Met Downtown: Julia Richman's Work in the Jewish Community of New York, 1880–1912," *American Jewish History* 70, No. 1 (1980); 35–51; and "Class or Ethnicity: The Americanized German Jewish Woman and Her Middle-Class Sisters in 1895," *Jewish Social Studies* 47, No. 1 (1985): 21–32. For an analysis of German Jewish acculturation and the impact of East European immigration, see Naomi W. Cohen, *Encounter with Emancipation: The German Jews in the United States, 1830–1914* (Philadelphia: Jewish Publication Society, 1984): 131–48; and Gerald Sorin, "Mutual Contempt: Mutual Benefit: The Strained Encounter Between German and Eastern European Jews in America, 1880–1920," *American Jewish History* 81, No. 1 (1993): 34–59.

44. Berrol, *Julia Richman*, 17.

45. "Miss Julia Richmond Dies in Paris," typescript, American Jewish Archives.

46. On Richman's life, see Berrol, *Julia Richman*.

47. "Lillian D. Wald, 1867–1940," The Hall of Fame for Great Americans on the campus of New York University, 1971, 14.

48. See Rivka Shpak Lissak, "Liberal Progressive and Immigration Restriction, 1896–1917," American Jewish Archives Brochure Series, Number XII (1991): 10, 24; Doris Groshen Daniels, *Always a Sister: The Feminism of Lillian D. Wald* (New York: Feminist Press, 1989), 116. On Wald, also see R.L. Duffus, *Lillian Wald: Neighbor and Crusader* (New York: Macmillan Company, 1938). On Jane Addams's Hull House and immigrant life, see Rivka Shpak Lissak, *Pluralism and Progressives: Hull House and the New Immigrants, 1890–1919* (Chicago: University of Chicago Press, 1989). The best history of the settlement movement is Allen Davis, *Spearheads for Reform: The Social Settlements and the Progressive Movement* (New York: Oxford University Press, 1967).

49. Alice Mencken Papers, American Jewish Historical Society, Waltham, Mass.

50. Rogow, *Gone to Another Meeting*, 61.

51. Cited in *ibid.*, 127.

52. On women's role in religion as seen by the sisterhoods, see Mrs. Abraham Simon, "Women and the Synagog," *The Reform Advocate*, May 2, 1914, 435–441.

53. Mrs. Solomon Schechter, "Aims and Ideals of the Women's League," *American Hebrew*, June 7, 1918, 101–2.

54. Linda Gordon Kuzmack, *Woman's Cause: The Jewish Woman's Movement in England and the United States* (Columbus: Ohio State University Press, 1990), 173–77.

55. "Women and the Synagogue: A Symposium," *American Hebrew*, April 14, 1916, 655.

56. Simon, "Women and the Synagog," 439, 441.

57. Gerald Kane, interview with Mrs. Philip Angel of Charleston, W. Va.

58. "Women and the Synagogue: A Symposium," 655–56.

59. *Ibid.*, 656.

60. Kuzmack, *Woman's Cause*, 181.

61. Maud Nathan, speeches on "The Heart of Judaism," *American Hebrew*, Dec. 31, 1897, and Baltimore Sun, [Feb. 5,] 1899, clippings in Maud Nathan Papers, Schlesinger Library, Radcliffe College, Cambridge, Mass.

62. Annie Nathan Meyer, *It's Been Fun: An Autobiography* (New York: Henry Schuman, 1951), 11.

63. Maud Nathan, *Once Upon a Time and Today* (New York: Arno Press, 1974), 20.

64. *Ibid.*, 33–34.

65. *Ibid.*, 30–31.

66. *Ibid.*, 41.

67. *Ibid.*, 44.

68. See Maud Nathan, *The Story of An Epoch-Making Movement* (New York: Doubleday, 1926), for an account of the Consumers' League.

69. Nathan, *Once Upon a Time*, 107.

70. *Ibid.*, 107; 22.

71. *Ibid.*, 305.

72. *Ibid.*, 179.

73. *Ibid.*, 183; Worcester (Mass.) *Telegram*, May 27, 1915, Maud Nathan Papers.

74. *Boston Traveler and Evening Herald*, June 2, 1915; Nathan, *Once Upon a Time*, 187.

75. *Ibid.*, 189; *New York Times*, Oct. 7, 1915.

76. See, for example, "The Jewish Woman and the Suffrage Movement," *American Hebrew*, Feb. 5, 1915, 378, and Abram Lipsky, "The Foreign Vote on Suffrage," *American Hebrew*, Nov. 26, 1915, 20. Also see Elinor Lerner, "Jewish Involvement in the New York City Woman Suffrage Movement," *American Jewish History* 70, No. 4 (June 1981): 442–61.

77. "Jews Besiege Theater to Hear Suffrage Plea," *Philadelphia Record*, Nov. [1], 1915, Maud Nathan Papers.

78. Article in *The American Jewish Chronicle*, circa Oct. 20, 1917, Maud Nathan Papers.

79. Letter to rabbis, April 23, 1917, Maud Nathan Papers.

80. "Jews Besiege Theater to Hear Suffrage Plea."

81. Maud Nathan, "Bible Ethics versus Business Ethics," *The Review* 11, No. 4 (March 1907): 1–9. Also see "American Jewesses in England," *American Hebrew*, July 7, 1899, 283.

82. Nathan, *Once Upon a Time*, 31.

83. "American Jewesses in England," 283.

84. Nathan, *Once Upon a Time*, 102–03.

85. *Ibid.*, 307.

86. *Ibid.*, 307, 305.

87. *Ibid.*, 311–312.

88. *Ibid.*, 127.

89. Herbert Shapiro and David L. Sterling, eds., *"I Belong to the Working Class": The Unfinished Autobiography of Rose Pastor Stokes* (Athens: University of Georgia Press, 1992).

90. Nathan, *Once Upon a Time*, 310.

91. *Ibid.*, 91.
92. National Council of Jewish Women, *Proceedings of the First Convention, Nov. 15–19, 1896* (Philadelphia: Jewish Publication Society, 1897), 28.
93. Wenger, "Jewish Women and Voluntarism," 33. Wenger cites Rabbi David Marx of Atlanta's Hebrew Benevolent Congregation, himself a supporter of Jewish women's groups, who nevertheless warned that women who sought "happiness and honor out in the busy world" were seeking the impossible "as much as if they were searching for a pot of gold at the end of the rainbow" (34).
94. Letter to Ruth Weill, cited in Lynn Gordon, "Annie Nathan Meyer and Barnard College: Mission and Identity in Women's Higher Education, 1889–1950," *History of Education Quarterly* 26, No. 4 (Winter 1986): 516–17.
95. Linda K. Kerber, "Annie Nathan Meyer," in Sicherman and Green, eds., *Notable American Women,* 473.
96. Meyer, *It's Been Fun,* 157, 159.
97. Kerber, "Annie Nathan Meyer," 473.
98. Annie Nathan Meyer to Virginia Gildersleeve, Feb. 12, 1944, Annie Nathan Meyer Papers, American Jewish Archives, Cincinnati, Ohio.
99. Gordon, "Annie Nathan Meyer and Barnard College," 508–09; Annie Nathan Meyer to Virginia Gildersleeve, Feb. 12 and Sept. 14, 1944, Annie Nathan Meyer Papers.
100. See Gordon, "Annie Nathan Meyer and Barnard College," 518, and Virginia Gildersleeve to Annie Nathan Meyer, Dec. 12, 1933, and April 4, 1934, Annie Nathan Meyer Papers.
101. See Annie Nathan Meyer, *Barnard Beginnings* (Boston: Houghton Mifflin, 1935); Annie Nathan Meyer to Virginia Gildersleeve, Feb. 4, 1927; Virginia Gildersleeve to Annie Nathan Meyer, March 30, 1933, and Feb. 4, Feb. 12, Sept. 14, 1944, Annie Nathan Meyer Papers; Gordon, "Annie Nathan Meyer and Barnard College," 516–17; Kerber, "Annie Nathan Meyer," 473.
102. Cited in Gordon, "Annie Nathan Meyer and Barnard College," 511.
103. Nathan, *Once Upon a Time,* 178.
104. Meyer, *It's Been Fun,* 20, 120, 50–51.
105. See *The New Republic,* Sept. 2 and Sept. 30, 1916, and the *New York Times,* Nov. 9, 1917.
106. Annie Nathan Meyer, "Spreadhenism," undated MSS., Annie Nathan Meyer Papers.
107. "Annie Nathan Meyer, Wife and Mother, Opposes Woman Suffrage," *American Hebrew,* June 12, 1914, 180.
108. Comments by Annie Nathan Meyer in "Forum on Suffrage," *American Hebrew,* Sept. 10, 1915.
109. Meyer, *It's Been Fun,* 205; Annie Nathan Meyer, letter to the *New York Times,* Nov. 9, 1917, Maud Nathan Papers; "Annie Nathan Meyer, Wife and Mother," 180.
110. Annie Nathan Meyer, *The Dominant Sex,* cited in Myrna Goldenberg, "Declaring a Self: Annie Nathan Meyer's Epistolary Presence" (Paper presented at the "Across Boundaries" Conference, University of Maryland, College Park, Oct. 31–Nov. 1, 1993).
111. "Spreadhenism" and "Annie Nathan Meyer, Wife and Mother," 180.
112. Kerber, "Annie Nathan Meyer," 474.
113. M. Carolyn Dellenbach, "An Inventory to the Annie Nathan Meyer Papers, 1858–1950," American Jewish Archives.
114. Annie Nathan Meyer, "Spreadhenism."
115. *Ibid.*
116. Annie Nathan Meyer, "Prejudice: A Challenge and a Discipline," unpublished MSS., Annie Nathan Meyer Papers.

117. See Josephine Lazarus, *The Spirit of Judaism* (New York: Dodd, Mead and Co., 1895).

118. Unpublished letter, n.d.; draft of untitled speech, "This is my maiden speech on the air"; "Prejudice: A Challenge and a Discipline," Annie Nathan Meyer Papers.

119. On anti-Semitism and Jewish self-hatred, see Leonard Dinnerstein, *Anti-Semitism in America* (New York: Oxford University Press, 1994); David A. Gerber, ed., *Anti-Semitism in American History* (Urbana: University of Illinois Press, 1987); and Sander Gilman, *The Jew's Body* (New York: Routledge, 1991).

120. For an example, see Virginia Gildersleeve to Annie Nathan Meyer, June 2, 1934, Annie Nathan Meyer Papers.

121. Goldenberg, "Declaring a Self"; Hendrick's articles were published as *Jews in America* (New York: Doubleday, Page & Co., 1923). For a discussion of Hendrick's anti-Semitism, see Dinnerstein, *Anti-Semitism in America*, 61–63, 94–96. For an example of Meyer's letters on anti-Semitism, see Annie Nathan Meyer, "A Little Hitler in the Zoo: A Communication," *Opinion: A Journal of Jewish Life and Letters* (May 1935), 27, 34.

122. Cited in Goldenberg, "Declaring a Self."

123. Annie Nathan Meyer, "Prejudice: A Challenge and a Discipline."

124. See "Dissent from the Zionist Stand," a letter Meyer wrote to the *New York Times*, Aug. 6, 1964, Annie Nathan Meyer Papers. Neither Maud Nathan nor most of her Council colleagues had originally been Zionists. Nathan and Kohut's views changed over time; Kohut had come to know Theodor Herzl, who converted her to the cause, while Nathan's several visits to Palestine sharpened her Zionist sympathies. Hannah Solomon, however, remained an anti-Zionist until her death in 1942.

125. See, for example, Goldenberg, "Declaring a Self."

126. Advertisement for "Black Souls," Annie Nathan Meyer Papers; Kerber, "Annie Nathan Meyer," 473.

127. Lillian Wald, *House on Henry Street* (New York: Henry Holt & Co., 1915), 254–55.

128. Marjorie N. Feld, "The 'Mutuality' of Society: The Life and Work of Lillian D. Wald, 1893–1919" (Seminar paper, Brandeis University, 1995).

129. Lillian Wald to Mrs. Rockefeller, July 11, 1934, Lillian Wald Papers, New York Public Library. Cited in Marjorie Feld, "Religion in the Life and Work of Lillian Wald" (Master's thesis, State University of New York at Binghamton, 1993).

130. See Kuzmack, *Woman's Cause*, 38–40.

131. Mary Garrett Hay, "When Jews and Christian Women Meet," *American Hebrew*, Sept. 22, 1922, 448.

132. Elinor Lerner, "American Feminism and the Jewish Question," in Gerber, ed., *Anti-Semitism in American History*, 311.

133. Annie Nathan Meyer, "Prejudice: A Challenge and a Discipline."

Chapter 3. Radical Politics and Labor Organizing

1. Emma Goldman, *Living My Life,* Vol. 1 (New York: Dover Publications, 1970), 11–12.

2. Cited by Susan A. Glenn, *Daughters of the Shtetl: Life and Labor in the Immigrant Generation* (Ithaca, N.Y.: Cornell University Press, 1990), 191.

3. Glenn, *Daughters of the Shtetl,* 240–41; Paula E. Hyman, "Immigrant Women and Consumer Protest: The New York City Kosher Meat Boycott of 1902," *American Jewish History* 70 (Sept. 1980): 91–105.

4. Cited in Alice Wexler, *Emma Goldman in Exile* (Boston: Beacon Press, 1989), 245.

5. *Ibid.,* 99, 253.

6. On Goldman's life, see Alice Wexler, *Emma Goldman in America* (Boston: Beacon Press, 1984), and Wexler, *Emma Goldman in Exile*; Candace Serena Falk, *Love, Anarchy and Emma Goldman: A Biography* (New Brunswick, N.J.: Rutgers University Press, 1990); and

Richard Drinnon, *Rebel in Paradise* (Chicago: University of Chicago, 1961). Also of in-terest are Marian J. Morton, *Emma Goldman and the American Left* (New York: Twayne Publishers, 1992), and Martha Solomon, *Emma Goldman* (Boston: Twayne Publishers, 1987).

7. Goldman, *Living My Life,* Vol. I, 16.
8. Emma Goldman, "Was My Life Worth Living?" in Alix Kates Shulman, ed., *Red Emma Speaks: An Emma Goldman Anthology* (New York: Schocken Books, 1983), 432.
9. Goldman, *Living My Life,* Vol. I, 370.
10. *Ibid.,* 12.
11. *Ibid.,* 11.
12. *Ibid.,* 25.
13. *Ibid.*
14. Visiting Rochester five years after she had left for New York, she saw her father weak and ill, a victim of the harassment of anti-Semitic co-workers. His suffering led her to view him as "one of the mass of the exploited and enslaved for whom I was living and work-ing," and while still estranged from him, she felt less hostile (*Living My Life,* Vol. I, 209).
15. *Ibid.,* 10.
16. *Ibid.*
17. *Ibid.*
18. Wexler, *Emma Goldman in America,* 53.
19. On Goldman's views on violence, see Drinnon, *Rebel in Paradise,* 81–83.
20. See Arthur Zipser and Pearl Zipser, *Fire and Grace: The Life of Rose Pastor Stokes* (Athens: University of Georgia Press, 1989), 55, 84. Other biographical information is provided in Herbert Shapiro and David L. Sterling, *"I Belong to the Working Class": The Unfinished Au-tobiography of Rose Pastor Stokes* (Athens: University of Georgia Press, 1992), and the Rose Pastor Stokes Papers at the Tamiment Library, New York University.
21. Zipser and Zipser, *Fire and Grace,* 183.
22. *Ibid.,* 192.
23. *Ibid.,* 217.
24. *Ibid.*
25. Shapiro and Sterling, *"I Belong to the Working Class,"* 3.
26. *Ibid.,* 23.
27. *Ibid.*
28. *Ibid.,* 55.
29. Clipping, *Cleveland Plain Dealer,* n.d., Rose Pastor Stokes Papers.
30. Shapiro and Sterling, Introduction to *"I Belong to the Working Class,"* xv.
31. Zipser and Zipser, *Fire and Grace,* 9–10.
32. *Ibid.,* 33, 36, 44.
33. *Ibid.,* 43, 66.
34. *Ibid.,* 40.
35. Cited in Harriet Marla Sigerman, "Daughters of the Book: A Study of Gender and Eth-nicity in the Lives of Three American Jewish Women" (Ph.D. diss., University of Massa-chusetts, 1992).
36. Shapiro and Sterling, *"I Belong to the Working Class,"* 148–49.
37. Sigerman, "Daughters of the Book," 350.
38. Wexler, *Emma Goldman in America,* 45.
39. *Ibid.,* 484.
40. *Ibid.,* 92.
41. Cited in *ibid.,* 97.
42. Goldman, *Living My Life,* Vol. I, 148.

43. Annette Rubenstein, interview with author, April 27, 1993.
44. Sanford Gifford, "The American Reception of Psychoanalysis," in Adele Heller and Lois Rudnick, eds., *1919, The Cultural Moment: The New Politics, The New Woman, the New Psychology, the New Art, and the New Theater in America* (New Brunswick: Rutgers University Press, 1991), 133.
45. Cited in *ibid.*
46. Wexler, *Emma Goldman in America,* 94.
47. *Ibid.*, 209.
48. *Ibid.*, 145, 159, 225.
49. Ernest May, *The End of American Innocence: A Study of the First Years of Our Own Time, 1912–1917* (Chicago: Quadrangle Paperbacks, 1964), 307–8.
50. Goldman, *Living My Life,* Vol. I, 452.
51. Wexler, *Emma Goldman in America,* 206–7.
52. Goldman, *Living My Life,* Vol. I, 155, 181.
53. Charles [Raper] to ISS, n.d., and unsigned letter to Alice Boehme, Dec. 14, 1916, Rose Pastor Stokes Papers.
54. *New York Morning Telegraph,* n.d., Rose Pastor Stokes Papers.
55. *Cincinnati Times Star,* n.d., Rose Pastor Stokes Papers.
56. See Judith Schwarz, *Radical Feminists of Heterodoxy: Greenwich Village, 1912–1940* (Norwich, Vt.; New Victoria Publishers, 1986).
57. Rose Pastor Stokes to Maxim Lieber, April 17, 1933, Rose Pastor Stokes Papers.
58. Zipser and Zipser, *Fire and Grace,* 98–99.
59. Rose Pastor Stokes to Lester Margon, n.d., Rose Pastor Stokes Papers.
60. Zipser and Zipser, *Fire and Grace,* 137.
61. *New York Times,* May 6, 1916, Rose Pastor Stokes Papers.
62. *Ibid.*, 138; Stokes to Lieber, April 17, 1933.
63. Zipser and Zipser, *Fire and Grace,* 237.
64. See David A. Shannon, "Rose Pastor Stokes," in Edward T. James and Janet Wilson James, eds., *Notable American Women: A Biographical Dictionary* (Cambridge: Harvard University Press, 1971), 385.
65. Zipser and Zipser, *Fire and Grace,* 295.
66. Wexler, *Emma Goldman in America,* 231.
67. *Ibid.*, 232.
68. *Ibid.*, 244.
69. *Ibid.*, 253.
70. *Ibid.*, 254.
71. Cited in Richard Drinnon, "Emma Goldman," in James and James, eds., *Notable American Women,* 59.
72. Wexler, *Emma Goldman in America,* 269.
73. *Ibid.*, 273–74.
74. Wexler, *Emma Goldman in Exile,* 45, 25, 61.
75. *Ibid.*, 91.
76. *Ibid.*, 115.
77. *Ibid.*, 121, 120.
78. *Ibid.*, 128.
79. *Ibid.*, 157.
80. *Ibid.*, 163.
81. *Ibid.*, 112.
82. *Ibid.*, 232.
83. *Ibid.*, 238.

84. *Ibid.*, 236.
85. *Ibid.*, 237.
86. *Ibid.*
87. Emma Goldman, "The Philosophy of Atheism," in Shulman, *Red Emma Speaks,* 247.
88. David Waldstreicher, "Radicalism, Religion, Jewishness: The Case of Emma Goldman," *American Jewish History* 80, No. 1 (Autumn 1990): 87.
89. Cited in *ibid.*, 91.
90. Wexler, *Emma Goldman in America,* 92. Naomi Shepherd underscores radical Jewish women's break with religion in *A Price Below Rubies: Jewish Women as Rebels & Radicals* (Cambridge: Harvard University Press, 1993), 15.
91. Wexler, *Emma Goldman in Exile,* 241.
92. On Pesotta, see her autobiographies, *Bread Upon the Waters* (New York: Dodd, Mead, 1944), and *Days of Our Life* (Boston: Excelsior, 1958), and Elaine Leeder, *The Gentle General: Rose Pesotta, Anarchist and Labor Organizer* (New York: State University of New York Press, 1993).
93. Rose Pesotta, interview, May 1937, cited in the Rose Pesotta Papers, New York Public Library.
94. Rose Pesotta to Emma Goldman, April 15 and July 31, 1935, Rose Pesotta Papers.
95. Emma Goldman to Rose Pesotta, August 31, 1935, Rose Pesotta Papers.
96. Emma Goldman to Rose Pesotta, April 6, 1935, and Dec. [14], 1935, Rose Pesotta Papers.
97. Rose Pesotta, "Anarchism in the Labor Movement," typescript, Rose Pesotta Papers.
98. Leeder, *The Gentle General,* 155.
99. Nancy Schrom Dye, "Rose Schneiderman," in James and James, eds., *Notable American Women,* 632. Also see Dye, "The Women's Trade Union League of New York, 1903–1920" (Ph.D. diss., University of Wisconsin, 1974).
100. See Annelise Orleck, *Common Sense and a Little Fire: Women and Working-Class Politics in the United States, 1900–1965* (Chapel Hill: University of North Carolina Press, 1995), for a discussion of the relationship between labor reform and working-class activism in the careers of Newman, Schneiderman, Clara Lemlich Shavelson, and Fannia Cohn. Also see Alice Kessler-Harris, "Organizing the Unorganizable: Three Jewish Women and Their Union," *Labor History* 17, No. 1 (Winter 1976): 5–23.
101. Pauline Newman, "A Challenging Assignment," in National Women's Trade Union League, *Life and Labor Bulletin,* No. 107 (Dec. 1949): 5; typescript on trip to Israel, 1967, Pauline Newman Papers, Schlesinger Library, Radcliffe College, Cambridge, Mass.
102. Orleck, *Common Sense and a Little Fire,* 191, 172.

Chapter 4. The Dream of a Jewish Homeland

1. Rose Jacobs, "Beginnings of Hadassah," Hadassah Archives, New York.
2. Rabbi Szold and Henrietta admired the Russian Jews' authenticity and passion, qualities they missed in Szold's German Jewish congregants, who "had the souls of bookkeepers. The Russians had the souls of Jews." *Daughters of Zion: Henrietta Szold and American Womanhood,* exhibition catalogue, Jewish Historical Society of Maryland, 1995, 65.
3. Also see Joyce Antler, "Zion in [Our] Hearts: Henrietta Szold and the American Jewish Women's Movement," *Daughters of Zion* exhibition catalogue, 35–55.
4. Henrietta Szold to Alice Selisberg, Jan. 7, 1938, Henrietta Szold Papers, Central Zionist Archives, Jerusalem.
5. On the life of Henrietta Szold, see Joan Dash, *Summoned to Jerusalem: The Life of Henrietta Szold* (New York: Harper & Row, 1979); Irving Fineman, *Woman of Valor: The Life*

of Henrietta Szold, 1860–1945 (New York: Simon & Schuster, 1961); Alexandra Lee Levin, *The Szolds of Lombard Street: Baltimore Family, 1859–1909* (Philadelphia: Jewish Publication Society of America, 1960); and Marvin Lowenthal, *Henrietta Szold: Life and Letters* (New York: Viking Press, 1942).

6. M. Jastrow Levin and Eva Leah Milbower, children of Bertha Szold Levin, interview with author, Baltimore, Sept. 1995.

7. Marvin Lowenthal, interview with Henrietta Szold, Dec. 29, 1935, Hadassah Archives, New York: 19.

8. *Ibid.*, 47.

9. Fineman, *Woman of Valor,* 57–58.

10. *Daughters of Zion* exhibition catalogue, 68. On the JPS, see especially Jonathan D. Sarna, *JPS: The Americanization of Jewish Culture, 1888–1988* (Philadelphia: Jewish Publication Society of America, 1960).

11. Lowenthal, interview with Szold, 42–43.

12. *Daughters of Zion* exhibition catalogue, 66.

13. Cited in Fineman, *Woman of Valor,* 95.

14. Henrietta Szold, "The Education of the Jewish Girl," *The Maccabaean* (July 1903). Cited in *Daughters of Zion* exhibition catalogue, 70.

15. Fineman, *Woman of Valor,* 124–26; Dash, *Summoned to Jerusalem,* 52–53.

16. Lowenthal, *Henrietta Szold,* 54.

17. *Daughters of Zion,* exhibition catalogue, 71.

18. Fineman, *Woman of Valor,* 128.

19. April 10, 1910, Henrietta Szold Papers, Central Zionist Archives.

20. *Ibid.*

21. *Ibid.*

22. Fineman, *Woman of Valor,* 261.

23. Henrietta Szold to Alice Selisberg, Jan. 1, 1909, Henrietta Szold Papers, Central Zionist Archives.

24. Henrietta Szold to Alice Selisberg, July 23, 1909, Henrietta Szold Papers, Central Zionist Archives. Also see Szold to Selisberg, Dec. 21, 1937.

25. Lotta Levensohn, "Recollections Concerning the Origin and Activities of the Hadassah Women's Study Group of New York," Hadassah Archives.

26. Lowenthal, interview with Szold, Hadassah Archives: 8.

27. Henrietta Szold to Alice Selisberg, Dec. 12, 1909, Henrietta Szold Papers, Central Zionist Archives.

28. Lowenthal, interview with Szold, 9.

29. Invitation Sent for the Formation of Hadassah, Feb. 14, 1924, Hadassah Archives; Lowenthal, interview with Szold, 9. See Eric L. Goldstein, "The Practical as Spiritual: Henrietta Szold's American Zionist Ideology, 1878–1920," in *Daughters of Zion* exhibition catalogue, 17–33. Allon Gal suggests that the choice of "Hadassah" was an effort to affirm the idea of Zionist work rooted in America, since "Esther saved her people in the diaspora." See Gal, "The Motif of Historical Continuity in American Zionist Ideology, 1900–1950," *Studies in Zionism* 13 (1992): 6.

30. Lowenthal, interview with Szold, 11.

31. Kussy, "Hadassah—How It Came Into Being."

32. *Ibid.*, 3. Rebecca Schatz of the Henry Street settlement noted that many of the principles that Hadassah used in Palestine were those that had "secured success" at Henry Street. See Alice Selisberg, "Chronicles of Hadassah: 1912–1914, Part I," Hadassah Archives: 9.

33. Henrietta Szold, address delivered at Hotel Astor, New York, Nov. 26, 1923, Hadassah Archives.

34. Selisberg, "Chronicles of Hadassah," printed in *Hadassah Newsletter* (May 1927): 6, 39, 125.

35. Sarah Kussy, "Hadassah—How It Came Into Being."

36. Report of the Proceedings of the First Annual Convention of the Daughters of Zion of America, New York, June 29–30, 1914, Hadassah Archives; Selisberg, "Chronicles of Hadassah," 9.

37. *Ibid.* On the founding of Hadassah, see Carol Bosworth Kutscher, "The Early Years of Hadassah, 1912–1921" (Ph.D. diss., Brandeis University, 1976).

38. "Our Reason for Being" and "The Group and the Individual," *The Maccabaean* 30, No. 2 (Feb. 1917): 146.

39. Henrietta Szold at the laying of the cornerstone of Hadassah University Hospital on Mt. Scopus, Oct. 16, 1934, Central Zionist Archives; Henrietta Szold to Junior Hadassah, Sept. 20, 1932, Hadassah Archives; Henrietta Szold, "Zionism: A Progressive and Democratic Movement" (speech delivered at the People's Institute, Cooper Union, New York, Feb. 13, 1916), Henrietta Szold Papers, Schlesinger Library, Radcliffe College, Cambridge, Mass.; Henrietta Szold to Alice Selisberg, Oct. 10, 1913, in Lowenthal, *Henrietta Szold: Life and Letters,* 82; Henrietta Szold to Elvira Solis, Jan. 18, 1918, Henrietta Szold Papers, Schlesinger Library. Also see Szold's letter to the editor, "The Promised Land," *The Nation* (Aug. 13, 1914).

40. Henrietta Szold, notes on a talk at Wilkes-Barre, Dec. 11, 1917, Henrietta Szold Papers, Schlesinger Library. Also see Henrietta Szold, Letter to Hadassah, June 27, 1928, Hadassah Archives.

41. Jessie Sampter, "The Speaking Heart," unpublished MSS., Jessie Sampter Papers, Central Zionist Archives.

42. Henrietta Szold to Hadassah, June 27, 1928, Hadassah Archives.

43. Henrietta Szold to Sadie American, March 27, 1900, Henrietta Szold Papers, Schlesinger Library.

44. Szold, address at Hotel Astor.

45. "The Woman in Zionism," *The Maccabaean* 30, No. 2 (Feb. 1917): 148.

46. See, for example, Henrietta Szold, "The Future of Women's Work for Palestine," May 1930, Henrietta Szold Papers, Central Zionist Archives.

47. Henrietta Szold to Alice Selisberg, Jan. 7, 1920, Hadassah Archives.

48. Alice Selisberg, "Follow On," *Hadassah Newsletter* (Dec. 1935): 12.

49. *Ibid.*

50. Sampter, "The Speaking Heart."

51. Lowenthal, interview with Szold, 12.

52. Henrietta Szold to Hadassah, June 27, 1928; Dash, *Summoned to Jerusalem,* 129. Szold's sister, Adele Seltzer, wrote of "the hatred of the men for Hadassah"; see her Jan. 25, 1928, letter to Szold, Henrietta Szold Papers, Central Zionist Archives.

53. Judah L. Magnes, "The Symbol of Hope," *Hadassah Newsletter* (Feb. 1936): 2.

54. Henrietta Szold to Hadassah, June 27, 1928, Hadassah Archives.

55. Bertha Badt-Strauss, *White Fire: The Life and Works of Jessie Sampter* (New York: Reconstructionist Press, 1955), 5.

56. Sampter, "The Speaking Heart," 12.

57. Jessie Sampter, "A Confession," *The Reconstructionist* (April 16, 1937): 12.

58. *Ibid.*

59. Sampter, "The Speaking Heart," 12.

60. *Ibid.*, 33, 63.

61. *Ibid.*, 11, 29, 35a.

62. Badt-Strauss, *White Fire,* 13–14; Sampter, "The Speaking Heart," 18.

63. Sampter, "The Speaking Heart," 67.
64. *Ibid.*, 76.
65. *Ibid.*, 76, 91.
66. *Ibid.*, 91.
67. *Ibid.*, 154.
68. *Ibid.*, 105.
69. Jessie Sampter, "In the Beginning," unpublished MSS., Jessie Sampter Papers, Central Zionist Archives: 28–30; Sampter, "The Speaking Heart," 105–6.
70. Sampter, "In the Beginning," 30, 41; "The Speaking Heart," 151–53; "A Confession," 13.
71. Sampter, "The Speaking Heart," 160–62.
72. *Ibid.*, 166–67.
73. Sampter, "A Confession," 13.
74. Margaret Doniger, " 'B'reshith'—In the Beginning," Hadassah Archives.
75. Sampter, "The Speaking Heart," 178.
76. *Ibid.*, 198.
77. Sampter, "In the Beginning," 54–55.
78. Sampter, "The Speaking Heart," 178.
79. *Ibid.*, 183, 188, 197.
80. *Ibid.*, 225.
81. *Ibid.*, 232.
82. *Ibid.*, 164.
83. *Ibid.*, 168.
84. *Ibid.*, 185–86.
85. *Ibid.*, 206.
86. Jessie Sampter, *A Course in Zionism* (New York: Federation of American Zionists, 1915); the second edition was published as *A Guide to Zionism* (New York: Zionist Organization of America, 1920); the third as *Modern Palestine: A Symposium* (New York: Hadassah, 1933).
87. Sampter, "The Speaking Heart," 203.
88. *Ibid.*, 250.
89. *Ibid.*, 245.
90. *Ibid.*, 246.
91. *Ibid.*, 256.
92. *Ibid.*, 264–81.
93. Jessie Sampter to Elvie Wachenheim, July 16, 1919, Jessie Sampter Papers, Central Zionist Archives.
94. Sampter, "The Speaking Heart," 182.
95. Henrietta Szold to Alice Selisberg, Nov. 30, 1919, Henrietta Szold Papers, Central Zionist Archives.
96. Alice Selisberg to Henrietta Szold, Oct. 25, 1919, Henrietta Szold Papers, Central Zionist Archives.
97. Sampter, "The Speaking Heart," 341–42; Jessie Sampter to Elvie Wachenheim, Dec. 26, 1920, Jessie Sampter Papers, Central Zionist Archives.
98. Sampter, "The Speaking Heart," 357.
99. Diary fragment, Henrietta Szold Papers, Hadassah Archives.
100. Henrietta Szold, "Jewish Palestine in the Making," *The New Palestine* (May 4, 1923); clipping, cited in Rose G. Jacobs, "Henrietta Szold—A Tribute," *Hadassah Newsletter* (March–April 1945), 6.
101. Adele Szold Seltzer to Henrietta Szold, Oct. 13, 1921, Henrietta Szold Papers, Central Zionist Archives.

102. Henrietta Szold to Elvie Wachenheim, May 30, 1920, cited in Badt-Strauss, *White Fire,* 65.
103. Jessie Sampter to Elvie Wachenheim, July 9, 1921, cited in *ibid.,* 86.
104. Sampter, "The Speaking Heart," 356.
105. *Ibid.,* 388.
106. *Ibid.,* 399, 405.
107. *Ibid.,* 350, 362.
108. Sampter, "The Speaking Heart," 386.
109. *Ibid.,* 406.
110. *Ibid.,* 367.
111. Jessie Sampter to Elvie Wachenheim, August 21, 1921, cited in Badt-Strauss, *White Fire,* 84.
112. Henrietta Szold to Jessie Sampter, Feb. 25, 1922, Hadassah Archives.
113. Henrietta Szold to Jessie Sampter, June 13, 1924, Hadassah Archives.
114. Henrietta Szold to Jessie Sampter, August 24, 1924, Hadassah Archives.
115. Henrietta Szold to Jessie Sampter, May 7, 1925, Hadassah Archives.
116. *Ibid.*
117. Lowenthal, interview with Szold, 51–52. Also see Henrietta Szold to Alice Selisberg, Jan. 24–27, 1920, Henrietta Szold Papers, Central Zionist Archives.
118. Lowenthal interview.
119. *Ibid.*
120. Bertha Szold Levin, Adele Szold Seltzer, and Benjamin Hartogensis, MSS. Notes on the Early Life of Henrietta Szold, n.d., Hadassah Archives; Henrietta Szold to Rose Jacobs, July 28, 1937, Henrietta Szold Papers, Central Zionist Archives.
121. Emma Ehrlich, typescript, "Notes and Impressions," March 1941, Henrietta Szold Papers, Central Zionist Archives.
122. Henrietta Szold to Jessie Sampter, Dec. 14, 1925, Hadassah Archives.
123. Jessie Sampter to Elvie Wachenheim, Dec. 26, 1919, Jessie Sampter Papers, Central Zionist Archives.
124. Henrietta Szold to Nellie Mochenson, Oct. 3, 1927, Hadassah Archives.
125. Henrietta Szold to Jessie Sampter, Oct. 3, 1927, Hadassah Archives.
126. Henrietta Szold to Jessie Sampter, Nov. 1, 1927, Hadassah Archives.
127. Henrietta Szold to Alice Selisberg, May 16, 1928, Alice Selisberg Papers, Central Zionist Archives.
128. Henrietta Szold to Jessie Sampter, Feb. 20, 1928, Hadassah Archives.
129. Henrietta Szold to Alice Selisberg, June 1, 1934, Alice Selisberg Papers, Central Zionist Archives.
130. Henrietta Szold, address delivered on Women's Day, Tel Aviv, May 31, 1934, Henrietta Szold Papers, Central Zionist Archives.
131. *Ibid.*
132. Jessie Sampter and Dorothy Ruth Kahn, "Collective" MSS. on Givat Brenner, Jessie Sampter Papers, Central Zionist Archives.
133. *Ibid.,* 149–50.
134. Sampter, "In the Beginning."
135. Jessie Sampter, "Anti-Semitism Is War," *Opinion: A Journal of Jewish Life and Letters,* (May 1937): 16.
136. *Ibid.,* 152.
137. David Umansky, untitled typescript, Hadassah Archives.
138. Dash, *Summoned to Jerusalem,* 282; M. Jastrow Levin, interview with author, Sept. 17, 1995.
139. Dash, *Summoned to Jerusalem,* 303.

140. Henrietta Szold to Rose Jacobs, June 7, 1942, Henrietta Szold Papers, Central Zionist Archives.
141. Henrietta Szold, address to 1935 WIZO Convention, Henrietta Szold Papers, Central Zionist Archives.
142. Report of the Cultural Committee at the Mid-Winter Conference of Hadassah, Palestine, Dec. 28, 1927, Henrietta Szold Papers, Central Zionist Archives.
143. See Henrietta Szold to Rose Jacobs, July 28, 1937; Henrietta Szold to Mrs. Joshua Kohn, Jan. 30, 1939, Henrietta Szold Papers, Central Zionist Archives.
144. Levin, Seltzer, and Hartogensis, MSS. Notes on the Early Life of Henrietta Szold.
145. Henrietta Szold, personal letter No. 7, April 14, 1919, Henrietta Szold Papers, Central Zionist Archives.
146. Emma Ehrlich Papers, uncatalogued material, Henrietta Szold Papers, Central Zionist Archives.
147. Marie Syrkin, *Way of Valor: A Biography of Golda Meyerson* (New York: Sharon Books, 1955), 27.
148. *Ibid.*, 28.
149. Golda Meir, *My Life* (New York: Dell Publishing Co., 1975), 29–30.
150. *Ibid.*, 37.
151. *Ibid.*, 43.
152. *Ibid.*, 32.
153. *Ibid.*, 54.
154. *Ibid.*, 61.
155. *Ibid.*, 64–65.
156. *Ibid.*, 66.
157. *Ibid.*, 88.
158. *Ibid.*, 94.
159. Syrkin, *Way of Valor,* 71.
160. Reprinted in Meir, *My Life,* 110–11. On women in the early Zionist movement, see Shulamit Reinharz, "Toward a Model of Female Political Action: The Case of Manya Shohat, Founder of the First Kibbutz," *Women's Studies International Forum* 7, No. 4 (1984): 275–84; Deborah Bernstein, "The Plough Women Who Cried into the Pots: The Position of Women in the Labor Force in Pre-State Israeli Society," *Jewish Social Studies* 45, No. 1 (Winter 1983): 43–56; Dafna N. Izraeli, "The Zionist Women's Movement in Palestine, 1911–1927: A Sociological Analysis," *Signs* 7, No. 1 (1981): 87–114; and the essays in Deborah S. Bernstein, ed., *Pioneers and Homemakers: Jewish Women in Pre-State Israel* (Albany: State University of New York Press, 1992).
161. Syrkin, *Way of Valor,* 72.
162. Dvorah Rothbard, cited in Nick Mandelkern, "The Story of Pioneer Women," Part 2, *Pioneer Woman* (Nov. 1980): 7.
163. Ralph G. Martin, *Golda—Golda Meir, the Romantic Years* (New York: Charles Scribner's Sons, 1988), 176.
164. Mandelkern, "The Story of Pioneer Women," Part 2, 25.
165. Mandelkern, "The Story of Pioneer Women," Part 1 (Sept. 1980): 28.
166. Mandelkern, "The Story of Pioneer Women," Part 3 (Jan.–Feb. 1981): 14.
167. *Ibid.*
168. *Ibid.*
169. Mandelkern, "The Story of Pioneer Women," Part 2, 7.
170. Martin, *Golda,* 176.
171. *Ibid.*, 7–8.
172. Martin, *Golda,* 185.

173. *Ibid.,* 190, 192.
174. *Ibid.,* 188–89.
175. *Ibid.,* 189.
176. Mandelkern, "The Story of Pioneer Women," Part 2, 8.
177. *Ibid.,* 82.
178. Syrkin, *Way of Valor,* 83.
179. Communication with Mark Raider, Sept. 27, 1996.

Chapter 5. Jewish Women in Popular Culture

1. Edna Ferber, *A Peculiar Treasure* (New York: Doran, 1918), 129; 5–6.
2. This point is made by Robert W. Snyder, *The Voice of the City: Vaudeville and Popular Culture in New York* (New York: Oxford University Press, 1989), 63.
3. See Henry L. Feingold, *A Time for Searching: Entering the Mainstream, 1920–45* (Baltimore: Johns Hopkins University Press, 1992), 93–94.
4. "I am no pillar of wisdom," untitled address, Sophie Tucker Papers, American Jewish Archives, Cincinnati, Ohio. This account of Tucker's life is derived from Sophie Tucker, *Some of These Days: The Autobiography of Sophie Tucker* (New York: Doubleday, Doran, 1945) and biographical materials in the Sophie Tucker Papers, American Jewish Archives.
5. Tucker, *Some of These Days,* 8.
6. *Ibid.,* 123, 11.
7. *Ibid.,* 12, 11.
8. *Ibid.,* 44–45, 60.
9. *Ibid.,* 34–35, 40–41.
10. On the racial implications of coon singing, see Snyder, *The Voice of the City,* 120–21; Michael Rogin, *Blackface, White Noise: Jewish Immigrants in the Hollywood Melting Pot* (Berkeley: University of California Press, 1996), 68. Also see Ronald Sanders, "The American Popular Song," cited in Lewis A. Ehrenberg, *Stepping Out: New York Nightlife and the Transformation of American Culture, 1890–1930* (Chicago: University of Chicago Press, 1981), 195.
11. Ted Shapiro, "My 31 Years with Sophie Tucker," Sophie Tucker Papers, American Jewish Archives; Tucker, *Some of These Days,* 64–65.
12. Tucker, *Some of These Days,* 94–95; Ehrenberg, *Stepping Out,* 196–97.
13. See Lillian Schlissel, "My Yiddishe Momme: Sophie Tucker and the Hierarchy of Women," paper presented at the American Studies Association meeting, Boston, 1993.
14. Tucker, *Some of These Days,* 6–7.
15. June Sochen, "Fannie Brice and Sophie Tucker: Blending the Particular with the Universal," in Sarah Blacher Cohen, ed., *From Hester Street to Hollywood: The Jewish American Stage and Screen* (Bloomington: Indiana University Press, 1983; pbk, 1986), 52–53.
16. Tucker, *Some of These Days,* 126; Hartford speech, n.d., Sophie Tucker Papers.
17. Tucker, *Some of These Days,* 134; Schlissel, "My Yiddishe Momme." Schlissel suggests that Tucker and her mother were "implacable foes, disguised as loving and intimate friends."
18. Tucker, *Some of These Days,* 2.
19. *Ibid.,* 224.
20. *Ibid.,* 124–25, 224–25.
21. *Ibid.,* 226.
22. Mark Slobin, cited in Snyder, *The Voice of the City,* 118–20.
23. Members of the Circus and Carnival Employees Divisions did not vote or participate in the resolution of actors' problems but were eligible for the union's various benefits. *AFA Reporter* 6, No. 6 (June 1939): 2.
24. *New York Times,* June 21, 1939; "Sophie Tucker Refutes Charges Point-by-Point," *AFA Reporter* 6, No. 6 (June 1939): 1.

25. "Verbatim Report of Sophie's Talk," *AFA Reporter* 6, No. 6 (June 1939): 3; see accounts in the *New York Times,* July 13, 15, 17, 1939.
26. Letter to Sophie Tucker, Aug. 17, 1939, Sophie Tucker Papers, American Jewish Archives.
27. Edna Ferber to Sophie Tucker, Sept. 1, 1939, Sophie Tucker Papers, American Jewish Archives.
28. *New York Times,* Sept. 10, 1939, sec. 4, p. 2; Sept. 15, 1939, p. 1; Tucker, *Some of These Days,* 303–7.
29. Tucker, *Some of These Days,* 300–305.
30. Hartford speech, n.d., Sophie Tucker Papers, American Jewish Archives.
31. *Ibid.*, and address to Jewish women's group, 1960, Sophie Tucker Papers, American Jewish Archives.
32. Address at dinner in honor of the trustees of Israel, Feb. 7, 1965, Sophie Tucker Papers, American Jewish Archives.
33. Dedication at Sophie Tucker Youth Center, Bet Shemesh, Israel, July 6, 1961, Sophie Tucker Papers, American Jewish Archives.
34. Talk at Abuza Talmud Torah [1962], Hartford, Conn.
35. Address at seder, April 22, 1959, Sophie Tucker Papers, American Jewish Archives.
36. Address at 1954 Golden Jubilee Dinner.
37. Address at Sophie Tucker Playground, 1960.
38. Address at dinner in honor of the trustees of Israel, Feb. 7, 1965; address at Sophie Tucker Playground.
39. Address at Sophie Tucker Playground; "Denver Hospital" speech, n.d.; address at Hartford temple, n.d.
40. Address at Hartford temple.
41. See Molly Picon, *Molly! An Autobiography* (New York: Simon & Schuster, 1980); Nahma Sandrow, *Vagabond Stars: A World History of Yiddish Theater* (New York: Harper & Row, 1977).
42. Sochen, "Fanny Brice and Sophie Tucker," 46; Barbara W. Grossman, *Funny Woman: The Life and Times of Fanny Brice* (Bloomington: Indiana University Press, 1991), 27–29.
43. Grossman, *Funny Woman,* 32.
44. *Ibid.*, 99, 170–72, 201–2, 208.
45. *Ibid.*, 226.
46. See June Sochen, "Jewish Women Entertainers as Reformers," in Joyce Antler, ed., *Talking Back: Images of Jewish Women in American Popular Culture* (Hanover: University of New England Press, forthcoming), for an expansion of this point.
47. Sochen, "Fanny Brice and Sophie Tucker," 56.
48. Norman Katlov, *The Fabulous Fanny: The Story of Fanny Brice* (New York: Alfred A. Knopf, 1953), 205. Cited in Sochen, "Fanny Brice and Sophie Tucker," 49.
49. Grossman, *Funny Woman,* 24.
50. *Ibid.*, 148.
51. *Ibid.*, 149.
52. *Ibid.*, 150.
53. *Ibid.*, 169.
54. *Ibid.*, 235.
55. See Robert C. Toll, "Fanny Brice," in Barbara Sicherman and Carol Hurd Green, eds., *Notable American Women: The Modern Period* (Cambridge: Harvard University Press, 1980), 107. Also see Sochen, "Jewish Women Entertainers as Reformers" and "Fanny Brice and Sophie Tucker."
56. Grossman, *Funny Woman,* 109–10, 241.
57. Paul Ritterband, "Modern Times and Jewish Assimilation," in Robert M. Seltzer and Norman J. Cohen, *The Americanization of the Jews* (New York: New York University Press,

1995), p. 379; Neil Gabler, *An Empire of Their Own: How the Jew Invented Hollywood* (New York: Crown Publishers, 1988), 5–6. Also see Stephen J. Whitfield, "Movies in America as Paradigms of Accommodation," in Seltzer and Cohen, *The Americanization of the Jews,* 79–94.

58. In an interview, Hurst acknowledged the "coolness" of critics but pronounced herself "warmed" by her popular audience. See *New York Times Book Review,* Jan. 25, 1942. For critical comment on Fannie Hurst, see the contribution by Susan Currier in *Dictionary of Literary Biography,* Vol. 86 (Detroit: Gale Research, 1989): 151–58. Cited in Steven P. Horowitz and Miriam J. Landsman, "Edna Ferber," *Dictionary of Literary Biography,* Vol. 28 (Detroit: Gale Research, 1984): 64. For critical comment on Ferber, also see contributions on "Edna Ferber" by Paula Reed in *Dictionary of Literary Biography,,* Vol. 9 (Detroit: Gale Research, 1981): 306–13; and Ellen Serlen Uffen in *Dictionary of Literary Biography,* Vol. 86 (Detroit: Gale Research, 1989): 91–98.

59. Ferber, *A Peculiar Treasure,* 164.

60. *New York Times,* n.d., 1948, Fannie Hurst Papers, Brandeis University, Waltham, Mass.

61. Polan Banks, "Fannie Hurst," clipping in Fannie Hurst Papers. Julie Goldsmith Gilbert, *Ferber: A Biography* (Garden City, N.Y.: Doubleday & Co., 1978), 376.

62. Fannie Hurst, *Anatomy of Me: A Wonderer in Search of Herself* (Garden City, N.Y.: Doubleday & Company, 1958), 2.

63. Ferber, *A Peculiar Treasure,* 2.

64. On ethnic writing, see Diane Lichtenstein, *Writing Their Nations: The Tradition of Nineteenth-Century Jewish Women Writers* (Bloomington: Indiana University Press, 1992); Mary Dearborn, *Pocahontas's Daughters: Gender and Ethnicity in American Culture* (New York: Oxford University Press, 1986); and Werner Sollors, *Beyond Ethnicity: Consent and Descent in American Culture* (New York: Oxford University Press, 1986). Lichtenstein offers an insightful discussion of Ferber's "anxiety of displacement," which she suggests is "encoded" in her regional writing (129–41).

65. Susan Koppelman, "Writings, Life and Social Activism of Fannie Hurst," address at Brandeis University, November 1993.

66. Ferber, *A Peculiar Treasure,* 18.

67. *Ibid.*

68. *Ibid.,* 94.

69. Hurst, *Anatomy of Me,* 14, 33.

70. *Ibid.,* 16, 18–19, 21, 74, 168, 171, 351.

71. *Ibid.,* 3.

72. Hurst told an interviewer that her autobiography, which she was then in the process of completing, was "completely, absolutely, fearfully truthful." She explained that she was writing about the "vulgarities in my family—horrible but necessary to be truthful." She thought the autobiography might well be "far and away" her best book (*New York Times Book Review,* May 12, 1942).

73. Hurst, *Anatomy of Me,* 125, 234. For a provocative discussion of Hurst's autobiography as a clue to possible childhood abuse, see Kathleen de Grave, "Miracle or Masquerade? Images of Abuse in Hurst's "Anatomy of Me," unpublished MSS. I am grateful to Susan Koppelman for this reference.

74. Hurst, *Anatomy of Me,* 235.

75. *Ibid.,* 67.

76. *Ibid.,* 4–6, 11.

77. *Ibid.,* 11, 39, 5.

78. Gilbert, *Ferber,* 366.

79. Ferber, *A Peculiar Treasure,* 223.

80. Gilbert, *Ferber,* 408.

81. *Ibid.*, 233.

82. *Ibid.*, 199.

83. Ferber, *A Peculiar Treasure,* 165.

84. Gilbert, *Ferber,* 308.

85. *Ibid.*, 2–3, 112, 268–71.

86. Carolyn Heilbrun, "Edna Ferber," in Barbara Sicherman and Carol Hurd Green, eds., *Notable American Women: The Modern Period* (Cambridge: Harvard University Press, 1980), 228.

87. Janet Handler Burstein, *Writing Mothers, Writing Daughters: Tracing the Maternal in Stories by American Jewish Women* (Urbana: University of Illinois Press, 1996), 48–49, 53–55.

88. Hurst, *Anatomy of Me,* 89, 166.

89. *Ibid.*, 75, 163–66, 209.

90. *Ibid.*, 170.

91. Edna Ferber, *A Peculiar Treasure,* 100–101.

92. *Ibid.*, 101.

93. *Ibid.*, 129.

94. *Ibid.*, 149.

95. *Ibid.*, 166.

96. See Maria K. Mootry, Introduction to Edna Ferber, *So Big* (Urbana: University of Chicago Press, 1995), ix.

97. Burstein, *Writing Mothers, Writing Daughters,* 53–54.

98. *Ibid.*, 56.

99. Susan Koppelman, "The Educations of Fannie Hurst," *Women's Studies International Forum* 10, No. 5 (1987): 507.

100. Cynthia Ann Brandimarte, "Fannie Hurst and Her Fiction: Prescriptions for America's Working Women" (Ph.D. diss., University of Texas at Austin, 1980), ch. 2.

101. Brandimarte suggests that Hurst's novels fit the requirements of melodrama as suggested by John G. Cawelti in his book *Adventure, Mystery, and Romance* (Chicago: University of Chicago Press, 1976): the characters are stereotyped and the plots end with the triumph of good over evil (48–50).

102. Hurst's least formulaic novel, *Lummox,* concerns Bertha, a kind-hearted, self-sacrificing domestic laborer of Eastern European descent who is consistently mistreated by the wealthy philanthropists, intellectuals, and businessmen whom she serves.

103. See "Joanna Russ on Fannie Hurst's Short Stories," *The Fannie Hurst Newsletter* 2, No. 2 (Winter 1992): 3–7; also see Brandimarte, "Fannie Hurst and Her Fiction," *passim.*

104. Koppelman, "The Educations of Fannie Hurst," 516.

105. Peter Biskind, *Seeing Is Believing: How Hollywood Taught Us to Stop Worrying and Love the Fifties* (New York: Pantheon Books, 1983), 293.

106. See the readings of intermarriage and miscegenation in Dearborn, *Pocahontas's Daughters,* 128–30, 152.

107. Ferber commented on the gap between authorial intentions and popular reception in regard to her novel *Cimarron:* while "hundreds of thousands" of readers took the novel as a "colorful romantic western American novel," Ferber considered it a "malevolent picture of what is known as American womanhood and American sentimentality." She doubted whether "more than a dozen people" recognized its "satire" and "bitterness." Ferber, *A Peculiar Treasure,* 339.

108. Mootry, Introduction to Ferber, *So Big,* ix, xv. Also see Horowitz and Landsman, "Edna Ferber," 64.

109. Hurst, *Anatomy of Me,* 235, 350.

110. *Ibid.*, 16.

111. *Ibid.*, 17.

112. *Ibid.*, 18, 22.

113. *Ibid.*, 43, 90–91.

114. *Ibid.*, 96, 91.

115. *Ibid.*, 102, 18.

116. Louis Harap, *Creative Awakening: The Jewish Presence in Twentieth-Century American Literature, 1900s–1940s* (New York: Greenwood Press, 1987), comments briefly on Hurst's stories, p. 20. For further descriptions see Brandimarte, "Fannie Hurst and Her Fiction"; Susan Currier, "Fannie Hurst."

117. On Hurst's *Family!*, see Diane Lichtenstein, "Fannie Hurst and Her Nineteenth Century Predecessors, *Studies in American Jewish Literature* 7 (Spring 1988): 26–39.

118. Cited in Gilbert, *Ferber,* 109.

119. Ferber, *A Peculiar Treasure,* 9.

120. Gilbert, *Ferber,* 430–33.

121. Ferber, *A Peculiar Treasure,* 31, 41–43.

122. *Ibid.*, 9.

123. *Ibid.*, 44.

124. *Ibid.*, 73.

125. On this point, see the discussion in Steven P. Horowitz and Miriam J. Landsman, "The Americanization of Edna: A Study of Ms. Ferber's Jewish American Identity," *Studies in American Jewish Literature* 2 (1982): 69–80.

126. Ferber, *A Peculiar Treasure,* 10.

127. *Ibid.*, 61.

128. Cited in Gilbert, *Ferber,* 291.

129. *Ibid.*, 291–92.

130. Ferber, *A Peculiar Treasure,* 187.

131. Margaret Culkin Banning, "Edna Ferber's America," *The Saturday Review of Literature* 19 (Feb. 4, 1939): 6. Cited in Horowitz and Landsman, "Edna Ferber," 78.

132. Ferber, *A Peculiar Treasure,* 181–82.

133. *Ibid.*, 4.

134. Ferber commented that in writing *Show Boat,* "I was a little Jewish slave girl on the Nile." *Ibid.*, 289.

135. *Ibid.*, 10.

136. Edna Ferber, *A Kind of Magic* (New York: Doubleday, 1963), 308.

137. Horowitz and Landsman, "Edna Ferber," 63.

138. Lichtenstein, *Writing Their Nations,* 132–33; Edna Ferber, "The Girl Who Went Right," in Joyce Antler, ed., *America and I: Short Stories by American Jewish Women Writers* (Boston: Beacon Press, 1990), 57–71.

139. Ferber, *A Kind of Magic,* 286.

140. Koppelman, "The Educations of Fannie Hurst," 505.

141. Hurst, *Anatomy of Me,* 278; Fannie Hurst, "St. Louis to Me," *Junior Bazaar,* November 1947, Fannie Hurst Papers.

142. "Fannie Hurst Tells of Her Career," *St. Louis Republic,* Jan. 10, 1915, Fannie Hurst Papers.

143. Gilbert, *Ferber,* 231, 275.

144. Fannie Hurst, "How Did I GET Where I Am?" cited in Brandimarte, "Fannie Hurst and Her Fiction," 63.

145. *Ibid.*, 90.

146. Hurst, *Anatomy of Me,* 242; Antoinette Frederick, "Fannie Hurst," in Sicherman and Green, eds., *Notable American Women: The Modern Period,* 360; Brandimarte, "Fannie Hurst and Her Fiction," 3.

147. Hurst, *Anatomy of Me,* 225.

148. Brandimarte, "Fannie Hurst and Her Fiction," 66.

149. *Ibid.*

150. See, for example, Rose C. Feld, "Eight Years After a Novel Marriage," *New York Times Sunday Magazine* (Dec. 9, 1923): 1, 14.

151. Hurst, *Anatomy of Me,* 296, 255, 250.

152. St. Louis *Post-Dispatch,* April 10, 1959, Fannie Hurst Papers.

153. Gilbert, *Ferber,* 223.

154. *Ibid.,* 376; the veracity of this remark, attributed to Ferber, is not established.

155. *Ibid.,* 376.

156. Hurst, *Anatomy of Me,* 225–26.

157. "Hallelujah, Another Hurst," *Newsweek* (Jan. 17, 1977): 88. Cited in Cynthia Ann Brandimarte, "Fannie Hurst: A Missouri Girl Makes Good," *Missouri Historical Review* 81 (April 1987): 295.

158. Fannie Hurst, draft on Eleanor Roosevelt, Fannie Hurst Papers.

159. See biographical materials, Fannie Hurst Papers; also see *New York Times,* Oct. 29, 1925; Nov. 18, 1925; April 23, 1926; April 10, 1940; May 6, 1940; June 26, 1940; Feb. 28, 1941; May 12, 1942, for accounts of Hurst's public speaking on behalf of Jewish charities and refugee relief. She received several awards from Jewish groups.

160. Gilbert, *Ferber,* 112.

161. Mootry, Introduction to Ferber, *So Big,* ix, xvi.

162. *Ibid.,* xv. Also see Uffen, "Edna Ferber," 96.

163. Cited in Gilbert, *Ferber,* 82.

164. Ferber, *A Kind of Magic,* 283. By the 1940s, Hurst had become disappointed in American women's failure to become politically active and politically literate. See, for example, an account of her address before the College of Pharmacy and Allied Sciences, *Providence Evening Bulletin,* March 8, 1948; "Fanny [*sic*] Hurst Says Idea of Women for President Premature," in the *Baltimore American,* June 8, 1947, in a widely syndicated column; and "Women Shirk Duty," *St. Louis Post-Dispatch,* June 8, 1947, Fannie Hurst Papers.

165. Frederick J. Hoffman, "Gertrude Stein," in Leonard Unger, ed., *American Writers: A Collection of Literary Biographies* (New York: Charles Scribner's Sons, 1974), 26.

166. Douglas Day, "Gertrude Stein," in Sicherman and Green, eds., *Notable American Women: The Modern Period,* 356.

167. *Ibid.*

168. Hoffman, "Gertrude Stein," 26.

169. Linda Wagner-Martin, *"Favored Strangers": Gertrude Stein and Her Family* (New Brunswick, N.J.: Rutgers University Press, 1995), 49.

170. *Ibid.*

171. Day, "Gertrude Stein," 358.

172. Hoffman, 41.

173. *Ibid.,* 40.

174. Maria Damon, "Gertrude Stein's Jewishness, Jewish Social Scientists, and the 'Jewish Question'," *Modern Fiction Studies* 42, No. 3 (Fall 1996): 492, 495, 499–500.

175. Brenda Wineapple, *Sister Brother: Gertrude and Leo Stein* (New York: G. P. Putnam's Sons, 1996), 56–57.

176. Wagner-Martin, *"Favored Strangers,"* 186.

177. *Ibid.,* 185.

178. *Ibid.,* 186.

179. *Ibid.,* 49.

180. The claim was recently made in a posthumous article by Wanda Van Dusen, "Portrait of

a National Fetish: Gertrude Stein's 'Introduction to the Speeches of Maréchal Pétain' (1942)" in *Modernism/Modernity* 3, No. 1 (1992). On the discovery of Stein's introduction, see Scott Heller, "A Study Shows that Gertrude Stein Backed the Vichy Government During World War II," *Chronicle of Higher Education* (Oct. 18, 1996): A14, 16.

181. Damon, "Gertrude Stein's Jewishness," 499; also see remarks of Brenda Wineapple cited in Heller, "Study Shows that Gertrude Stein Backed the Vichy Government," A16.

182. Van Dusen, "Portrait of a National Fetish," 73, 70.

183. Michael Davidson, in Van Dusen, "Portrait of a National Fetish," 87.

184. See, for example, Day, "Gertrude Stein," 358.

Chapter 6. Pioneers in the Professions

1. Oral Histories of Justine Wise Polier, 1982, clipping, n.d., Justine Wise Polier Papers, Schlesinger Library, Radcliffe College, Cambridge, Mass.; and Oral History of Justine Wise Polier, American Jewish Committee Oral History Collection, New York Public Library.

2. Ruth Jacknow Markowitz, *My Daughter, the Teacher: Jewish Teachers in New York City Schools* (New Brunswick, N.J.: Rutgers University Press, 1993), 2.

3. See Lewis J. Paper, *Brandeis* (Secaucus, N.J.: Citadel Press, 1983), 84, 291–93.

4. Elizabeth Brandeis Raushenbush file, Radcliffe College Archives; Susan Brandeis Gilbert Papers, Brandeis University, Waltham, Mass.; also see Paper, *Brandeis,* 94, 291–93, and Philippa Strum, *Louis D. Brandeis: Justice for the People* (New York: Schocken Books, 1984), 13–31.

5. Biographical material on Ruth Mack, Estelle Frankfurter, and Hetty Goldman, Radcliffe College Archives. Also see Nitza Rosovsky, *The Jewish Experience at Harvard and Radcliffe.* An Introduction to the Exhibition Presented by the Harvard Semitic Museum on the Occasion of Harvard's 350th Anniversary, 1986. Distributed by Harvard University Press.

6. George N. Shuster, *The Ground I Walked On: Reflections by the Former President of Hunter College* (New York: Farrar, Straus and Cudahy, 1961), 104. Cited in Katherina Kroo Grunfeld, "Purpose and Ambiguity: The Feminine World of Hunter College" (Ph.D. diss., Teachers College, Columbia University): 203.

7. Leola Cahn Newman, "Once It Was Normal," *The Hunter Magazine* (Sept. 1983): 8–9. Cited in Grunfeld, "Purpose and Ambiguity," 226.

8. Grunfeld, "Purpose and Ambiguity," 235.

9. *Ibid.*, 236–37.

10. *Ibid.*, 226. Kate Simon, *A Wider World* (New York: Harper, 1986), 111, 116, 156–57.

11. Grunfeld, "Purpose and Ambiguity"; Rosalyn Yalow Oral History, American Jewish Committee Collection.

12. See Bel Kaufman, "Mihi Cura Futuri," *The Hunter Magazine* (April 1984): 4–9.

13. Bel Kaufman, interview with author, Aug. 1994.

14. Markowitz, *My Daughter, the Teacher,* 79.

15. Bel Kaufman, interview, Aug. 1994.

16. *Ibid.*

17. The story on which it was based, Bel Kaufman's "From a Teacher's Wastebasket," appeared in *Saturday Review* (Nov. 17, 1962): 58–61.

18. *Time* (March 18, 1966), 74.

19. Kaufman, "From a Teacher's Wastebasket."

20. See, for example, Bel Kaufman, "Papa Sholom Aleichem," unpublished MSS., and "The Man Who Made Laughter," *GoodLife* (Dec. 1984): 34–36; and Rhonda Hoffman, "Author Bel Kaufman Follows Grandfather's Footsteps," *The Jewish Times,* Nov. 30, 1989.

21. Alexander Lesser, "Jewish Oratorio Staged in Moscow," *Forward,* Oct. 9, 1992; Virginia

M. Citrano, "Women Teach *bizness* to Aid Russian Sisters," *Crain's New York Business,* Aug. 9, 1993; Bel Kaufman, "What's Holding Russia Together? *Babushka,*" *New Choices* (May 26, 1993): 26–29; interview with Bel Kaufman, Aug. 1994.

22. Markowitz, *My Daughter, the Teacher,* 153.

23. *Ibid.,* 161.

24. *Ibid.,* 169.

25. *Ibid.,* 162.

26. "Professional Tendencies Among Jewish Students in Colleges, Universities and Professional Schools," *American Jewish Yearbook,* Vol. 22 (Sept. 1920–Oct. 2, 1921): 383–93.

27. Beatrice Doerschuk, *Women in the Law: Analysis of Training, Practice and Salaried Positions* (New York: Bureau of Vocational Information, 1920), 30; Michael Grossberg, "Institutionalizing Masculinity: The Law as a Masculine Profession," in Mark Carnes and Clyde Griffin, eds., *Meaning for Manhood: Constructions of Masculinity in Victorian America* (Chicago: Chicago University Press, 1990), 149.

28. Doerschuk, *Women in the Law,* 19–20.

29. Susan Brandeis, "The Woman Lawyer in the United States," Washington, D.C., 1929, Susan Brandeis Gilbert Papers, Brandeis University.

30. For a discussion of male Jewish lawyers and liberal reform interests, see Jerold S. Auerbach, "From Rags to Robes: The Legal Profession, Social Mobility and the American Jewish Experience," *American Jewish Historical Quarterly* 65, No. 2 (Dec. 1976): 249–84.

31. Jennie Loitman Barron Papers, Schlesinger Library.

32. Brandeis, "The Woman Lawyer in the United States."

33. Louis D. Brandeis to Alice Brandeis, July 9, 1917. Cited in Paper, *Brandeis,* 278.

34. Susan Brandeis claimed that losing this case was a "good start" that demonstrated her father's colleagues' fairness; she would win later cases she argued before the Court. Associate Press release by Albert W. Wilson, n.d., Susan Brandeis Gilbert Papers.

35. On Louise Waterman Wise, see Arthur Hertzberg, "Louise Waterman Wise," in Edward T. James, *Notable American Women 1607–1950* (Cambridge: Harvard University Press, 1971), 634–36, and James Waterman Wise, *The Legend of Louise: The Life Story of Mrs. Stephen S. Wise* (New York: Jewish Opinion Publishing Corp, 1949).

36. Oral Histories of Justine Wise Polier, Justine Wise Polier Papers, 3; "Reminiscences of Justine Wise Polier," Columbia University Oral History (by Kitty Gellhorn, 1982): 41; on Wise's career and the founding of the Free Synagogue, see Melvin I. Urofsky, *A Voice that Spoke for Justice: The Life and Times of Stephen S. Wise* (Albany: State University of New York Press, 1982), chs. 9 and 10. On the Reform movement in the United States, see Michael A. Meyer, *Response to Modernity* (New York: Oxford University Press, 1988), and Marc Lee Raphael, *Profiles in American Judaism: The Reform, Conservative, Orthodox, and Reconstructionist Traditions in Historical Perspective* (San Francisco: Harper & Row, 1985).

37. Trudy Festinger, granddaughter of Louise Waterman Wise, interview with author, July 1994.

38. *Ibid.*

39. Carl Herman Voss, *Rabbi and Minister: The Friendship of Stephen S. Wise and John Haynes Holmes* (Cleveland: World Publishing Co., 1964), 84.

40. Oral Histories of Justine Wise Polier, Justine Wise Polier Papers, 6, 12.

41. Justine Wise Polier and James Waterman Wise, *The Personal Letters of Stephen Wise* (Boston: Beacon Press, 1956), 229.

42. Obituary of Henry Holtzmann, *New York Times,* Dec. 17, 1940; Edward O. Berkman, *The Lady and the Law: The Remarkable Story of Fanny Holtzmann* (Boston: Little, Brown & Co., 1972). Roosevelt visited the Holtzmanns when he came to Brooklyn; he particularly admired their large family. When, on one occasion, Fanny's father showed him the

"horrendous firetraps" where immigrants lived, TR pronounced himself shocked. Oral History of Fanny Holtzmann, 1977–1978, by Stephen Chodorov, American Jewish Committee Oral History Collection, New York Public Library.

43. *New York Times,* obituary, Dec. 17, 1940.

44. Oral History of Fanny Holtzmann.

45. Berkman, *The Lady and the Law,* 21.

46. *Ibid.,* 22; Oral History of Fanny Holtzmann, American Jewish Committee Collection.

47. Berkman, *The Lady and the Laws,* 26; "Counsel to Celebrities: Fanny Ellen Holtzmann," *New York Times,* n.d., Fanny Holtzmann Papers, American Jewish Archives, Cincinnati, Ohio.

48. Berkman, *The Lady and the Law,* 27; Oral History of Fanny Holtzmann, American Jewish Committee Collection.

49. "A Conversation with Ted Berkman," *The Eternal Light,* program presented by the Jewish Theological Seminary of America, NBC Radio, June 27, 1976, Fanny Holtzmann Papers, American Jewish Archives.

50. Justine Wise Polier, Commencement Address at Bryn Mawr College, May 14, 1973, Justine Wise Polier Papers.

51. *Ibid.*

52. *New York Times,* Jan. 19, 1934, Justine Wise Polier Papers.

53. Justine Wise, "In Darkest Un-Democracy," *The New Student* (Oct. 18, 1924), 5; and "Testing Untried Ideals," *The World Tomorrow: A Journal Looking Toward a Social Order Based on the Principles of Jesus* 7, No. 5 (May 1924): 135–36.

54. Oral Histories of Justine Wise Polier, Justine Wise Polier Papers, 3; "Reminiscences," 97.

55. Deposition of Justine Wise, City of New Haven, April 24, 1926, Justine Wise Polier Papers.

56. Justine Waterman Wise, "World Peace and Industrial Peace," *The Jewish Woman* V, Nos. 3 and 4 (Oct. 1925): 1–3.

57. "Reminiscences of Justine Wise Polier," 102; and "Woman Lawyer in the Depression: An Oral History," *The Guild Practitioner,* 39, No. 4 (Fall 1982), 121–28; transcript of an internal by Ann Fagan Ginger, Justine Wise Polier Papers.

58. *Ibid.*

59. Stephen Wise to Justine Wise, Jan. 28 and March 3, 1926, cited in Urofsky, *A Voice that Spoke for Justice,* 232.

60. Stephen Wise to Justine Wise, Jan. 27, 1926, Justine Wise Polier Papers.

61. *Daily News, Evening Post,* and *Journal,* March 2, 1926, Justine Wise Polier Papers.

62. Stephen Wise to Justine Wise, May 18, 19, and June 5, 1926; Louise Wise to Justine Wise, April 12, 1926; Susan Brandeis to Justine Wise, April 27, 1926, Justine Wise Polier Papers. Also see Stephen Wise to Susan Brandeis, May 3, 1926, Susan Brandeis Gilbert Papers.

63. For a brief account of the strike, see Urofsky, *A Voice that Spoke for Justice,* 232–33.

64. "Woman Lawyer in the Depression."

65. *Ibid.*

66. Doerschuk, *Women in the Law,* 26, 38.

67. Oral Histories of Justine Wise Polier, Justine Wise Polier Papers, 185.

68. "Woman Lawyer in the Depression," p. 124.

69. *New Republic* (April 17, 1935): 272, Justine Wise Polier Papers; on Polier's early career, see *New York Times,* April 10, 1935, *New York Evening Post,* Jan. 4, 1934. Oral Histories of Justine Wise Polier, Schlesinger Library, and American Jewish Committee Collection.

70. Viola Bernard, interview with author, August 1994.

71. *Barnard College Alumnae* (Oct. 1935): 9, Justine Wise Polier Papers.

72. Oral Histories of Justine Wise Polier, Justine Wise Polier Papers, 10.

73. Interview, n.d., Justine Wise Polier Papers.

74. See, for example, articles on Polier in the *New York Times,* Jan. 19, 1934; *New York Post,*

Jan. 4, 1934; *Washington Post,* Dec. 7, 1941; *New York Daily Post,* April 19, 1945. On the occasion of her appointment, the *New York Evening Journal* noted that Justine Tulin "dimpled charmingly" at the mayor's compliments (July 8, 1935). She was "quietly feminine" in her dress, columnist Dorothy Kilgallen reported in the *New York Evening Journal,* with a "finely modulated voice."

75. Dorothy Kilgallen, "No Hero," *New York Evening Journal,* July 9, 1935; *Brooklyn Times Union,* August 7, 1935. Also see "Mrs. Tulin Sits as Judge; Bars 'Lady Justice' Title," *Brooklyn Times Union,* Aug. 5, 1935.

76. *New York Times,* Nov. 12, 1935; *New York Tribune,* July 2, 1935.

77. Oral Histories of Justine Wise Polier, Justine Wise Polier Papers, 2.

78. *New York Post, New York Evening Journal,* Aug. 28, 1935; *New York World Telegram,* Sept. 10, 1935; *New York Times,* Aug. 26, Sept. 15, 1935; Oral Histories of Justine Wise Polier, Justine Wise Polier Papers, 11.

79. See, for example, Al Black to the Honorable Robert F. Wagner, Sept. 23, 1959, Justine Wise Polier Papers. On the campaign to make Justine Polier presiding judge, see the correspondence between Shad Polier, Viola Bernard, Marion Kenworthy, and other supporters, 1959, Justine Wise Polier Papers.

80. *The Amsterdam News,* Dec. 12 and 19, 1959.

81. *Chicago Sun,* Jan. 31, 1948.

82. Robert Bremner, foreword to Justine Wise Polier, *Juvenile Justice in Double Jeopardy: The Distanced Community and Vengeful Retribution* (Hillsdale, N.J.: Lawrence Erlbaum Associates, 1989), x. 4.

83. Polier, *Juvenile Justice in Double Jeopardy,* 128–29, 131, 133.

84. Oral Histories of Justine Wise Polier, Justine Wise Polier Papers, 15.

85. Polier, *Juvenile Justice in Double Jeopardy,* 139; also see Shad Polier to Rabbi Harold Gordon, April 8, 1959, Justine Wise Polier Papers.

86. In addition to *Juvenile Justice in Double Jeopardy,* Polier's books include *Everyone's Children, Nobody's Child: A Judge Looks at Underprivileged Children in the United States* (New York: Charles Scribner's Sons, 1941) and *The Rule of Law and the Role of Psychiatry* (Baltimore: Johns Hopkins University Press, 1968).

87. See, for example, *New York Times,* Jan. 26 and 27, 1944, *Chicago Tribune,* Jan. 31, 1948; *New York Times,* Feb. 17, 1950, Justine Wise Polier Papers.

88. Elizabeth Wickenden, "Justine Wise Polier: In Memoriam," talk at Stephen Wise Synagogue, Nov. 11, 1987. After she retired from the bench, Polier served as director of the juvenile justice division of the Children's Defense Fund.

89. Maurice W. Russell, "Justine Wise Polier: In Memoriam," 26 or 27. Polier's combination of tenderness and toughness was cited by her close friends Viola Bernard and Naomi Levine in interviews, August 1994.

90. Teacher's College student after field trip to Polier's court, 1943, Oral Histories of Justine Wise Polier.

91. Oral Histories of Justine Wise Polier, 4.

92. Berkman, *The Lady and the Law,* 42–45, 52; Oral History of Fanny Holtzmann, American Jewish Committee Collection.

93. Jacob L. (Jack) Holtzmann was a member of the state Board of Regents from 1949 to 1958 (replacing Susan Brandeis, a Democrat). As chairman of the State Electoral College, Holtzmann officially notified President Eisenhower and Vice-President Nixon of their election in 1957. *New York Times,* obituary, July 12, 1963; also see Fanny Holtzmann to George Bush, August 12, 1974, Fanny Holtzmann Papers, American Jewish Archives.

94. Oral History of Fanny Holtzmann, American Jewish Committee Collection.

95. Berkman, *The Lady and the Law,* 57.

96. *Ibid.,* 58.

97. *Ibid.*
98. *Ibid.*, 79. Also see Idwal Broughton, "Noel Coward's Little Fanny," n.d., Fanny Holtzmann Papers.
99. Stephen Watts, "Why Not a British Film Ambassador?" interview with Fanny Holtzmann, *Film Weekly,* August 10, 1932; Fanny Holtzmann Papers.
100. Berkman, *The Lady and the Law,* 156–60; "A Conversation with Ted Berkman," transcript, Fanny Holtzmann Papers.
101. Clipping in *New York Times,* n.d., Fanny Holtzmann Papers.
102. Edward Berkman, "Eulogy," Fanny Holtzmann Papers. See also "Counsel to Celebrities," *New York Times,* n.d., in *ibid.*
103. Justine Wise Polier, "Prophetic Judaism: Fossil or Living Legacy?" address at Brandeis University, 1959, Justine Wise Polier Papers.
104. Justine Wise Polier, "This I Believe" (1953); "The Future of World Jewry" (1957); "The Jewish Commitment" (1958); and "Prophetic Judaism," Justine Wise Polier Papers.
105. Justine Wise Polier to Naomi Levine, April 5, 1973, Justine Wise Polier Papers.
106. Maurice V. Russell, "Justine Wise Polier: In Memoriam," 27.
107. Justine Wise Polier to Howard M. Squadron, April 10, 1978, Justine Wise Polier Papers.
108. Interview with Trudy Festinger; Polier, "Basic Elements of Friendly Frontiers," address at Christ Church, Oct. 14, 1952, Justine Wise Polier Papers.
109. Berkman, *The Lady and the Law,* x.
110. Holtzmann donated her fee from the Chinese government to Soochow University to establish a women's dormitory; *ibid.*, 256.
111. *Ibid.*, 279.
112. Rabbi Abba Hillel Silver noted her "prominent part in the accomplishment of an historic task," cited in "A Conversation with Ted Berkman," Fanny Holtzmann Papers.
113. Oral History of Fanny Holtzmann, 194.
114. *Ibid.*, 138, 161.
115. *Ibid.*, 130.
116. *Ibid.,* 49.
117. *Ibid.,* 72.
118. *Ibid.*, 107.
119. Her painting of a Central Park skating scene was made into a popular Hallmark card; Hallmark called her one of the fifty greatest artists of all time. *Ibid.*, 116, 113, 112.
120. "A Conversation with Ted Berkman," Fanny Holtzmann Papers.
121. Auerbach, "From Rags to Robes," 283.
122. "In Defense of Human Rights," Commencement Address, Bryn Mawr College, May 14, 1973, Justine Wise Polier Papers.
123. See Martha Neumark, "The Woman Rabbi: An Autobiographical Sketch of the First Woman Rabbinical Candidate," *Jewish Tribune and Hebrew Standard,* April 10, 1925, and Neumark, "Judgeship for Daughter of Dr. Wise as Reward [for] Civic Service," clipping, n.d., *Emanu-el and the Jewish Journal;* biographical material, Martha Neumark Montor Papers, American Jewish Archives.

Chapter 7. Entering the Theatres of the World

1. Muriel Rukeyser, *Breaking Open,* cited in Louise Kertesz, *The Poetic Vision of Muriel Rukeyser* (Baton Rouge: Louisiana State University Press, 1980), 329.
2. For views about American Jews' response to the Holocaust, see David D. Wyman, *The Abandonment of the Jews: America and the Holocaust, 1941–1945* (New York: Pantheon, 1984); Henry L. Feingold, *The Politics of Rescue: The Roosevelt Administration and the Holocaust, 1938–1945* (New York: Holocaust Library, 1980); Richard Breitman and Alan

M. Kraut, *American Refugee Policy and European Jewry, 1933–1945* (Bloomington: Indiana University Press, 1987); Haskel Lookstein, *Were We Our Brothers' Keepers? The Public Response of American Jews to the Holocaust, 1938–1945* (New York: Hartmore, 1986); and Seymour M. Finger, ed., *American Jewry During the Holocaust* (New York: Holmes and Meier, 1984).

3. Muriel Rukeyser, "Journey Changes," from *Waterlily Fire,* in Kate Daniels, ed., *Muriel Rukeyser: Out of Silence, Selected Poems* (Evanston, Ill.: Tri-Quarterly Books, Northwestern University Press, 1994), 120.

4. Unless otherwise noted, all biographical material about and quotations from Rose Jacobs are from drafts and notes of Jacobs's unpublished MSS. of Hadassah Story, Rose Jacobs Papers, Brandeis University, Waltham, Mass.

5. Rose Jacobs Papers.

6. *Ibid.*

7. Alice Selisberg to Rose Jacobs, Oct, 19, 1938, Central Zionist Archives, Jerusalem.

8. Alice Selisberg to Rose Jacobs, n.d. 1940, Central Zionist Archives.

9. Rose Jacobs Papers.

10. Tree was the founder of the Organic School in Alabama. An obscure progressive school at the time, it was discovered by John Dewey and made famous in his 1915 book, *Schools of Tomorrow.*

11. Rose Jacobs Papers.

12. *Ibid.*

13. *Ibid.*

14. According to Jacobs, many WIZO women were wives of men who led the fight for the Keren Hayesod (Foundation Fund) principle, which Hadassah rejected.

15. Rose Jacobs to Mrs. Joseph E. Friend, New Orleans, March 5, 1932, Rose Jacobs Papers.

16. Jeannette Steinberg to Board of Directors, Detroit Section, National Council of Jewish Women [n.d.], Rose Jacobs Papers.

17. See Henrietta Szold to Jeannette Steinberg, Aug. 18, 1932; Feb. 1, 1933, Rose Jacobs Papers.

18. Rose G. Jacobs, "Looking Ahead," *Hadassah Newsletter,* Hadassah Joint Convention, Nov. 28–Dec. 1, 193[5], Rose Jacobs Papers.

19. Rose Jacobs Papers.

20. *Ibid.*

21. Hadassah did not account for 100 percent of the funds raised for Youth Aliyah, since other agencies—Pioneer Women, Mizrachi Women, the Women's League for Palestine, and the Jewish Agency—also contributed. Although Hadassah did not enforce its "exclusive agency" arrangement, it was the largest single contributor to the program, with the exception of the Jewish Agency.

22. Melvin Urofsky, *American Zionism from Herzl to the Holocaust* (Lincoln: University of Nebraska Press, 1996), 397; "Youth Aliyah in Step with the Times," Jewish Agency for Israel, 1993, Hadassah Archives, New York City.

23. Rose Jacobs Papers, 71; also see Rose Jacobs to Henrietta Szold, Nov. 25, 1942, Rose Jacobs Papers.

24. Rose Jacobs to Alice Selisberg, March 6, 1938, Central Zionist Archives.

25. Rose Jacobs Papers.

26. *Ibid.*

27. Rose Jacobs, "On Louis D. Brandeis," Midwinter Conference of Hadassah, Jan. 15, 1957, Rose Jacobs Papers.

28. See the AJCOMM resolution, Dec. 6, 1942, Rose Jacobs Papers.

29. Declaration of the Association "Union" (IHUD); also see Judah Magnes to As-Barat Newspaper Agency, Rose Jacobs Papers.

30. Rose Jacobs to Henrietta Szold, Nov. 25, 1942, Rose Jacobs Papers.

31. Rose Jacobs to Henrietta Szold, Jan. 7, 1943, Rose Jacobs Papers.

32. Rose Jacobs Papers.

33. Autobiographical typescript, n.d., Cecilia Razovsky Papers, American Jewish Historical Society, Waltham, Mass.

34. Henry L. Feingold, *A Time for Searching: Entering the Mainstream, 1920–1945* (Baltimore: Johns Hopkins University Press, 1992), 29.

35. *The Immigrant,* Vol. 2, No. 2 (May 1923): 1–5.

36. Cecilia Razovsky, "Adult Immigrant Education in the Jewish Center," typescript, Cecilia Razovsky Papers.

37. Florine Lasker, "A Reply to Willa Cather," *The Immigrant,* Vol. 4, No. 7 (March 1925): 1–4.

38. Cecilia Razovsky, "Changing Standards in Social Service," *The Immigrant,* Vol. 5, No. 3 (Nov. 1925): 9, 12.

39. See Candace Dawn Bredbenner, "Toward Independent Citizenship: Married Women's Nationality Rights in the United States, 1855–1937" (Ph.D. diss., University of Virginia, 1990).

40. "Our First Regional Conference on Naturalization," *The Immigrant,* Vol. 4, No. 9 (May 1925); Rose Schneiderman, "The Right to Citizenship," *The Immigrant,* Vol. 5, No. 7 (May 1926): 6.

41. Razovsky, "Changing Standards in Social Service," 7.

42. "What Is the Cable Act?" *The Immigrant,* Vol. 2, No. 4 (Oct. 1922): 2.

43. "World Congress of Jewish Women," *The Immigrant,* Vol. 3, No. 1 (Sept. 1923): 7.

44. "Annual Report of Chairman of Department of Immigrant Aid, 1923–1924," Vol. 4, No. 4 (Dec. 1924): 15–16.

45. Lyman Crowell White, *300,000 New Americans: The Epic of a Modern Immigrant-Aid Service* (New York: Harper, 1957), 35–37.

46. *Ibid.*

47. Faith Rogow, *Gone to Another Meeting: The National Council of Jewish Women, 1893–1993* (Tuscaloosa: University of Alabama Press, 1993), 174.

48. Cecilia Razovsky, "Refuge or Refugees—Where?" notes on a talk given at the All-Day Institute on Immigration and Naturalization of the NCJW, Chicago Section, April 26, 1936, Cecilia Razovsky Papers. Also see Zosa Szajkowski, "The Attitude of American Jews to Refugees from Germany in the 1930s," *American Jewish Historical Quarterly* 61 (Dec. 1971): 101–43.

49. White, *300,000 New Americans,* 23.

50. *Ibid.,* 24.

51. Report of the Director of the Council of Service for Foreign Born, Nov. 13–16, 1939, Papers of the National Council of Jewish Women, Library of Congress, Washington, D.C.

52. White, *300,000 New Americans,* 8, 258–59, 261.

53. See *St. Louis* file, Cecilia Razovsky Papers; White, *300,000 New Americans,* 61; Feingold, *Politics of Rescue,* 66.

54. From a Norfolk newspaper, cited in White, *300,000 New Americans,* 62.

55. *Ibid.,* 61–63.

56. See George L. Warren to Cecilia Razovsky, April 11, 1940, and memo from Warren, April 12, 1940; also see William Haber to James Rosenberg, April 3, 1940, and memos on Dominican Republic Settlement Association, n.d., Cecilia Razovsky Papers.

57. On the initial enthusiasm for the project, see Frieda Kirchwey, "Caribbean Refuge," *Nation* (April 13, 1940): 466–68. Also see Feingold, *Politics of Rescue,* 111–13; and Joseph B. Schectmann, "Failure of the Dominican Scheme," *Congress Weekly* (Jan. 15, 1943): 8–9, and *Refugee Settlement in the Dominican Republic: A Survey Conducted Under the Auspices of the Brookings Institute,* 1942, cited in Feingold, *Politics of Rescue,* 325.

58. See Cecilia Razovsky to Albert Abrahamson, April 15, 1943; Cecilia Razovsky to Charles

A. Riegelman, May 12, 1943; and Joseph E. Beck to Cecilia Razovsky, May 4, 1943, Cecilia Razovsky Papers.

59. The agreement specified that the NRS would be the agency responsible for service and funds for the relief, transportation, internal migration, and resettlement of aliens out of port cities to other communities; the NCJW would continue with Americanization and naturalization. Report of the Director of the Council of Services for the Foreign Born, Nov. 13–16, 1939, Papers of the National Council of Jewish Women, Library of Congress, Washington, D.C. Also see Rogow, *Gone to Another Meeting,* 175.

60. Miscellaneous biographical material, Cecilia Razovsky Papers.

61. Cecilia Razovsky, "Paying Our Rent," typescript, n.d., Cecilia Razovsky Papers.

62. See biographical material, Cecilia Razovsky Papers.

63. See, for example, Michele S. Ware, "Opening 'The Gates': Muriel Rukeyser and the Poetry of Witness," *Women's Studies* 22, No. 3 (1993): 297–308, and Kertesz, *The Poetic Vision of Muriel Rukeyser,* 43, 80, 205.

64. Muriel Rukeyser, "Under Forty," *Bridges* I, No. 1 (Spring 1990): 27. Rukeyser's original essay appeared in "Under Forty: A Symposium on American Literature and the Younger Generation of American Jews," *The Contemporary Jewish Record,* Feb. 1944, published by the American Jewish Committee; Ruth Gruber, *Ahead of Time: My Early Years as a Foreign Correspondent* (New York: Wynwood Press, 1991), 16.

65. Rukeyser, "Under Forty," 27–29.

66. Ware, "Opening 'The Gates'," 298.

67. Kertesz, *The Poetic Vision of Muriel Rukeyser,* 21–22.

68. Adrienne Rich, Introduction, Jan Heller Levi, ed., *A Muriel Rukeyser Reader* (New York: W.W. Norton & Co., 1994), xii.

69. See Kertesz, *The Poetic Vision of Muriel Rukeyser,* 98–113, and Levi, ed., *A Muriel Rukeyser Reader,* 30.

70. *Ibid.,* 122.

71. Oscar Williams, ed., *The War Poets* (1945), cited in Kertesz, *The Poetic Vision of Muriel Rukeyser,* 175.

72. Gruber, *Ahead of Time,* 30–31, 33, 118.

73. *Ibid.,* 131, 136.

74. Ruth Gruber, *I Went to the Soviet Arctic* (New York: Simon & Schuster, 1939).

75. *Ibid.,* 223–27.

76. *Ibid.,* 171.

77. Ruth Gruber, *Haven: The Unknown Story of 1,000 World War II Refugees* (New York: Coward-McCann, Inc., 1983), 263.

78. *Ibid.,* 82.

79. *Ibid.,* 133.

80. *Ibid.* (Gruber elaborated on this revelation at a speech to the Annual Convention of Na'amat Women, Boston, July 17, 1995).

81. *Ibid.,* 194.

82. *Ibid.,* 195.

83. *Ibid.,* 264.

84. On the Oswego shelter and Truman's directive, also see Sharon L. Lowenstein, *Token Refuge: The Story of the Jewish Refugee Shelter at Oswego, 1944–1946* (Bloomington: Indiana University Press, 1986).

85. Gruber, *Haven,* 197.

86. *Ibid.*

87. Kertesz, *The Poetic Vision of Muriel Rukeyser,* 173–76.

88. *Ibid.,* 178.

89. *Ibid.*, 178–81. The unsigned attack on Rukeyser appeared in *Partisan Review,* Sept.–Oct. 1943.

90. *Ibid.*, 181. Rukeyser believed the vituperation of these comments came from the fact that she had refused the *Review's* offer to be poetry editor (180 n. 13).

91. *Ibid.*, 42.

92. From "Letter to the Front" in Muriel Rukeyser, *Beast in View* (1944), cited in Jan Heller Levi, ed., *A Muriel Rukeyser Reader* (New York: W.W. Norton, 1994), 103–4.

93. From "Käthe Kollwitz," in Muriel Rukeyser, *The Speed of Darkness* (1968), cited in Levi, above, 217.

94. From "Searching/Not Searching," in Muriel Rukeyser, *Breaking Open* (1973), cited in Kertesz, *The Poetic Vision of Muriel Rukeyser,* 387.

95. *Ibid.*, 324.

96. From Muriel Rukeyser, "July 4, 1972," Muriel Rukeyser Papers, Library of Congress, Washington, D.C.

97. The quote is from Rachel B. Du Plessis, "The Critique of Consciousness and Myth in Levertov, Rich and Rukeyser," *Writing Beyond the Ending: Narrative Strategies of 20th Century Women Writers,* p. 129, cited in Ware, "Opening 'The Gates,' " 303.

98. Rukeyser, "Under Forty," 28–29.

Chapter 8. Imagining Jewish Mothers

1. Naomi W. Cohen, *Jews in Christian America: The Pursuit of Religious Equality* (New York: Oxford University Press, 1992), 123.

2. See, for example, Leonard Dinnerstein, *Anti-Semitism in America* (New York: Oxford University Press, 1994).

3. For an extended discussion of Molly Goldberg in relation to Ethel Rosenberg, see my "A Bond of Sisterhood: Ethel Rosenberg, Molly Goldberg, and Radical Jewish Women of the 1950s," in Marjorie Garber and Rebecca L. Walkowitz, eds., *Secret Agents: The Rosenberg Case, McCarthyism, and Fifties America* (New York: Routledge, 1995), 197–214.

4. On the politicization of culture during the 1950s, see Stephen J. Whitfield, *The Culture of the Cold War* (Baltimore: Johns Hopkins University Press, 1991). On women's roles, see Elaine Tyler May, *Homeward Bound: American Families in the Cold War Era* (New York: Basic Books, 1988); Wini Breines, *Young, White and Miserable: Growing Up Female in the Fifties* (Boston: Beacon, 1992); and Joanne Meyerowitz, ed., *Not June Cleaver: Women and Gender in Postwar America, 1945–1960* (Philadelphia: Temple University Press, 1994).

5. Herman Wouk, *Marjorie Morningstar* (Boston: Little Brown, 1955/1983), 172, 562.

6. Philip Roth, *Goodbye Columbus and Five Short Stories* (Boston: Houghton Mifflin, 1959/1989).

7. See, for example, B. G. Bienstock, "The Changing Image of the American Jewish Mother," in Virginia Tufte and Barbara Myerhoff, eds., *Changing Images of the Family* (New Haven: Yale University Press, 1979).

8. Charles Angoff, " 'The Goldbergs' and Jewish Humor," *Congress Weekly* 18 (March 5, 1951): 13; "The Goldbergs March On," *Life* (April 25, 1949): 59; "The Goldbergs," script, Oct. 3, 1949, Gertrude Berg Papers, Special Collections, Syracuse University, Syracuse, N.Y.

9. Angoff, " 'The Goldbergs,' " 12–13.

10. Gertrude Berg cited in Jack Long, "Her Family Is Her Fortune," *American,* n.d., 111, Gertrude Berg Papers.

11. Joan Jacobs Brumberg, "Gertrude Berg"; "Gertrude Berg," *American Hebrew,* Oct. 8,

1943: 14; Sulamith Ish-Kishor, "Interesting People: Gertrude Berg," *Jewish Tribune* (Oct. 10, 1930): 7.

12. See Louis Berg, "Entertainment Programs and Wartime Morale: Radio's Ten Best Morale-Building Programs" (Address at the Regional Conference of the Association for Education by Radio, Stephens College, Columbia, Mo., Nov. 5, 1942), Gertrude Berg Papers.

13. Morris Freedman, "The Real Molly Goldberg," *Commentary* 21 (April 1954): 364; also see Donald Weber's insightful reading, "Popular Culture and Middle-Class Imagination: The Figure of Gertrude Berg in Radio and Television, 1930–1962," unpublished paper.

14. Freedman, "The Real Molly Goldberg," 360.

15. Hal Himmelstein, *Television Myth and the American Mind* (New York: Praeger, 1984), 84–97; David Marc, *Comic Visions: Television Comedy and American Culture* (Boston: Unwin Hyman, 1989) 65; Darrell Y. Hamamoto, *Nervous Laughter: Television Situation Comedy and Liberal Democratic Ideology* (New York: Praeger, 1989), 25. For a discussion of television's role as mediator between changing consumer roles and family life, see George Lipsitz, *Time Passages: Collective Memory and American Popular Culture* (Minneapolis: University of Minnesota Press, 1990), 39–75.

16. Hamamoto, *Nervous Laughter,* 24.

17. Milton Berle, *Milton Berle: An Autobiography* (New York: Delacorte Press, 1974), 293–94, cited in Weber, "Popular Culture."

18. Cohen, *Jews in Christian America,* 123–24.

19. National Council of Jewish Women, "Cultural Democracy—Pattern for America" (mimeograph, Sept. 1947): 5, NCJW Papers, Library of Congress, Washington, D.C.

20. *Ibid.,* 4.

21. *Ibid.,* 11.

22. *Ibid.,* 9–10.

23. *Ibid.,* 19.

24. See, for example, National Council of Jewish Women, Committee on Education and Social Action, *Spotlight,* Vol. 5, No. 8 (May 1949); Vol. 6, No. 5 (Feb. 1950); Vol. 8, No. 3 (Dec. 1951); Vol. 8, No. 5 (Feb. 1952); Vol. 9, No. 6 (March 1953), and Vol. 9, No. 8 (May 1953), NCJW Papers.

25. National Council of Jewish Women, Committee on Education and Social Action, *Spotlight,* Vol. 8, No. 4 (Jan. 1952): 2; Vol. 8, No. 2 (Nov. 1951): 2, NCJW Papers.

26. *Spotlight,* Vol. 9, No. 2 (Nov. 1952), 3, NCJW Papers.

27. National Council of Jewish Women and YWCA National Board, News Release Dec. 1961, NCJW Papers.

28. National Council of Jewish Women and YWCA, Joint Statement, Dec. 6, 1961, NCJW Papers.

29. For biographical material on Ethel Rosenberg, see Ilene Philipson, *Ethel Rosenberg: Beyond the Myths* (New Brunswick, N.J.: Rutgers University Press, 1988). Also see Tema Nason, *Ethel: A Novel of Ethel Rosenberg* (New York: Delacorte Press, 1990), and Carol Hurd Green, "Ethel Rosenberg," in Barbara Sicherman and Carol Hurd Green, eds., *Notable American Women: The Modern Period* (Cambridge: Harvard University Press, 1980), 601–4.

30. Virginia Gardner, *The Rosenberg Story* (New York: Masses and Mainstream, 1954), 67, cited in Sheila M. Brennan, "Popular Images of American Women in the 1950s and Their Impact on Ethel Rosenberg's Trial and Conviction," *Women's Rights Law Reporter* 14, No. 1 (Winter 1992): 47.

31. Ethel Rosenberg to Emanuel Bloch, August 31, 1951–Sept. 6, 1951, in Robert Meeropol and Michael Meeropol, *We Are Your Sons: The Legacy of Ethel and Julius Rosenberg* (Boston: Houghton Mifflin, 1975), 101.

32. Philipson, *Ethel Rosenberg,* 28.

33. *Ibid.*, 258.

34. *Ibid.*, 345.

35. See, for example, Barbara Ehrenreich and Deirdre English, *For Her Own Good: 150 Years of the Experts' Advice to Women* (New York: Doubleday, 1978), ch. 7.

36. Ronald Radosh and Joyce Milton, *The Rosenberg File: A Search for the Truth* (New York: Holt, Rinehart and Winston, 1973), 417.

37. Brennan, "Popular Images of American Women," 56.

38. Ted Morgan, "The Rosenberg Jury," *Esquire* (May 1979): 127, cited in Brennan, "Popular Images of American Women," 58.

39. Morgan, "The Rosenberg Jury," 131, in Brennan, "Popular Images of American Women," 59.

40. Fuchs and May received fourteen- and ten-year terms, respectively.

41. Brennan, "Popular Images," 60; David Oshinsky calls the FBI report "preposterous." See Oshinsky, "The Rosenberg Case,"in Jack Fischel and Sanford Pinsker, eds., *Jewish-American History and Culture: An Encyclopedia* (New York: Garland Publishers, 1992), 553–54.

42. Brennan, "Popular Images of American Women," 60.

43. On images of women in the Cold War era, see May, *Homeward Bound: American Families in the Cold War Era,* and Meyerowitz, ed., *Not June Cleaver: Women and Gender in Postwar America, 1945–1960.*

44. On the reaction of Jews to the Rosenberg case, see Deborah Dash Moore, "Reconsidering the Rosenbergs: Symbol and Substance in Second Generation American Jewish Consciousness," *Journal of American Ethnic History* 8, No. 1 (Fall 1988): 21–37.

45. Cited by Donald Weber, "Situating Gertrude Berg: *The Goldbergs* and the Construction of Jewish American Identity, 1930–50," in Joyce Antler, ed., *Talking Back: Images of Jewish Women in American Popular Culture* (Hanover, N.H.: University of New England Press, forthcoming).

46. I have written at greater length about the Emma Lazarus Federation in "Between Culture and Politics: The Emma Lazarus Federation of Jewish Women's Clubs and the Promulgation of Women's History, 1944–1989," in Linda K. Kerber, Alice Kessler-Harris, and Kathryn Kish Sklar, eds., *U.S. History as Women's History* (Chapel Hill: University of North Carolina Press, 1994), 267–95. Some material here is adapted from that essay.

47. For information on Shavelson, see Clara Lemlich Shavelson, "Remembering the Waistmakers General Strike, 1909," *Jewish Currents* 36 (Nov. 1982): 11; Paula Scheier, "Clara Lemlich Shavelson: Fifty Years in Labor's Front Line," *Jewish Life* (Nov. 1954): 7–11; and Annalise Orleck, *Common Sense and A Little Fire: Women and Working-Class Politics in the United States, 1900–1965* (Chapel Hill: University of North Carolina Press, 1995), ch. 6.

48. On an earlier protest by Jewish housewives, see Paula Hyman, "Immigrant Women and Consumer Protest: The New York Kosher Meat Boycott of 1902," *American Jewish History* 70 (Sept. 1980): 91–105. On the housewives' movement in the Depression, see Annalise Orleck, " 'We Are That Mythical Thing Called the Public': Militant Housewives During the Great Depression," *Feminist Studies* 19, No. 1 (Spring 1993): 147–72. Also see Mark Naison, *Communists in Harlem During the Great Depression* (New York: Grove Press, 1983), 149–50, for an account of the 1935 meat boycott led by Shavelson and Raynes.

49. Tape of Memorial Meeting for Clara Lemlich Shavelson, Oct. 1982, American Jewish Archives, Cincinnati, Ohio.

50. See, for example, "Class Struggle in Fraternal Organizations," *Daily Worker,* July 18, 1930, IWO Papers, Tamiment Library, New York University.

51. Mark Naison, "Remaking America: Communists and Liberals in the Popular Front," in Michael E. Brown, Randy Martin, Frank Rosengarten and George Snedeker, eds., *New Studies in the Politics and Culture of U.S. Communism* (New York: Monthly Review Press,

1993), 58–59; Arthur Leibman, *Jews and the Left* (New York; John Wiley and Sons, 1978), 350–51, 427.

52. "Straight from the Shoulder Fraternalism," JPFO Bulletin, IWO Papers. On the IWO, see Arthur Sabin, *Red Scare in Court: New York versus the International Workers Order* (Philadelphia: University of Pennsylvania Press, 1993). Rose Raynes, Gertrude Decker, Morris U. Shappes, and Annette Rosenthal, interviews with author, February–March 1993. On Jews and American Communism, see Paul Buhle, "Jews and American Communism: The Cultural Question," *Radical History Review* 23 (Spring 1980): 9–33; Leibman, *Jews and the Left;* and David Leviatin, *Followers of the Trail: Jewish Working-Class Radicals in America* (New Haven: Yale University Press, 1969).

53. Morris U. Schappes, ed., *Emma Lazarus: Selections from Her Poetry and Prose* (New York: Cooperative Book League, Jewish-American Section, International Workers Order, 1944); the Emma Lazarus Federation of Jewish Women's Clubs sponsored new editions of the volume in 1978 and 1982. Schappes also wrote an Introduction and Notes to *An Epistle to the Hebrews by Emma Lazarus* (New York: Jewish Historical Society of New York, 1987).

54. Biographical material in the Papers of the Emma Lazarus Federation of Jewish Women Clubs (hereafter ELF Papers), American Jewish Archives.

55. Biographical material, ELF Papers, and interview with Rose Raynes, Feb. 1993.

56. Rose Raynes interview with Paul Buhle, March 21, 1979, Oral History Interviews of the Left, Tamiment Library, New York University.

57. Arthur J. Sabin describes the prosecution as being without parallel in American law and concludes that the IWO was destroyed for political reasons. Sabin, *Red Scare in Court: New York versus the International Workers Order* (Philadelphia: University of Pennsylvania Press, 1993), 10–23. For further information, see the IWO Papers, including "Report of the Officers," IWO, Feb. 3–4, 1951.

58. Sabin, *Red Scare in Court.*

59. Robert Meeropol, interview with author, June 1993.

60. "Resume of a discussion by the Executive Committee of the Emma Lazarus Federation on the Destruction of Jewish Culture and Unjust Execution of Jewish Cultural and Civic Leadership," July 10, 1956, typescript, n.d.; author interviews with Rose Raynes and Gertrude Decker. Also see discussion of the ELF and the Soviet Jewish question in *Israel Horizons and Labour Israel* 21 (Jan.-Feb. 1974): 2, 28–30.

61. *Proceedings of the Third Convention,* Feb. 6–8, 1959, Emma Lazarus Federation of Jewish Women's Clubs, ELF Papers.

62. On postwar Jewry see Deborah Dash Moore, *At Home in America: Second Generation New York Jews* (New York: Columbia University Press, 1981); Edward S. Shapiro, *A Time for Healing: American Jewry Since World War II* (Baltimore: Johns Hopkins University Press, 1992); and Marshall Sklare and J. Greenblum, *Jewish Identity on the Suburban Frontier* (New York: Basic Books, 1967).

63. See, for example, the 1975 keynote address by Rose Raynes to the Emma Lazarus Federation of Jewish Women's Clubs convention, ELF Papers.

64. The Jewish Clubs and Societies, like the Yiddish Kultur Farband, supported such institutions as the newspaper *Morgen Freiheit,* the magazine *Yiddishe Kultur,* and Camp Kinderland, and it worked on behalf of the publication of Yiddish books.

65. Study outline on Emma Lazarus, ELF Papers.

66. Constitution and By-Laws of the Emma Lazarus Federation of Jewish Women's Clubs, Jan. 1951, ELF Papers.

67. Yuri Suhl, *Ernestine L. Rose and the Battle for Human Rights* (New York: Reynal, 1959).

68. "Women, Heroines of the Warsaw Ghetto," study guide, 1951, ELF Papers; these "mothers" included Niuta Teitelbaum, Dora Goldkorn, Zofia Lubetkin, and Hannah Senesh.

69. *The Lamp* (May 1952): 10, ELF Papers.
70. In 1963, the ELF initiated a petition campaign in favor of U.S. ratification of the Genocide Convention, which had been adopted by the U.N. General Assembly in 1948 and subsequently signed by 75 nations. ELF presented the first 4,000 signatures on the petitions to U.N. Ambassador Adlai Stevenson in December 1963. Two years later, when the 20th session of the General Assembly ratified a new treaty to eliminate all forms of racism, it issued a new petition calling upon the U.S. to ratify both treaties. In 1966, the Federation delivered 7,000 signatures to Ambassador Arthur Goldberg; in 1969, it sent a delegation (including three black women) to present 60,000 signatures to Sen. J. William Fulbright of the Senate Foreign Relations Committee. The Senate finally ratified the Genocide Convention on Feb. 19, 1986.
71. *The Lamp* (May-June 1960), ELF Papers.
72. Rose Raynes and Gertrude Decker, interview with author.
73. Twenty-three years later, Congresswoman Bella Abzug addressed another large ELF-sponsored meeting honoring the achievement of women's suffrage.
74. "The states recognized the different role men and women play in family life," the NCJW social action newletter, *Spotlight,* commented in 1945—"the husband is the breadwinner, the wife the homemaker." Although both political parties had voted to support the Equal Rights Amendment, the Council pledged to be "even more vigorous" in working toward its defeat, preferring a state-by-state approach to reform rather than a national amendment. *Spotlight,* Vol. 1, No. 1 (Feb. 1945): 3.
75. According to Faith Rogow, the NCJW in the postwar period "was a civic group to which Jews belonged more than it was a Jewish group that did civic work"; Rogow, *Gone to Another Meeting: The National Council of Jewish Women, 1893–1993* (Tuscaloosa: University of Alabama Press, 1993), 184.
76. Address (unsigned) of Leah Nelson to the 1971 Emma Lazarus Federation of Jewish Women's Clubs convention, ELF Papers.
77. NCJW Award Speech, 1950, Gertrude Berg Papers.

Chapter 9. Feminist Liberations

1. Naomi Braun Rosenthal, "Consciousness Raising: From Revolution to Re-Evaluation," *Psychology of Women Quarterly* 8, No. 4 (Summer 1984): 318.
2. For an account of her speech at the march, see Betty Friedan, "Women and Jews: The Quest for Selfhood," *Congress Monthly* (Feb./March 1985): 7, and Francine Klagsbrun, "Marching in Front," *Hadassah Magazine* (Nov. 1993): 24.
3. Klagsbrun, "Marching in Front," 24; Friedan, "Women and Jews," 7.
4. Steinem's father, Leo, was Jewish. Her grandmother, Pauline, was a pioneer feminist who served as president of the Ohio Women's Suffrage Association. On Steinem's life, see Carolyn G. Heilbrun, *The Education of a Woman: The Life of Gloria Steinem* (New York: Dial Press, 1995).
5. "Jewish Roots: An Interview with Betty Friedan," *Tikkun* 3, No. 1 (Jan./Feb. 1988): 26. Remarks of Anne Roiphe in "Woman as Jew, Jew as Woman," *Congress Monthly* 52, No. 2 (Feb./March 1985): 13. Also see interview with Phyllis Chesler, *Lilith* 1, No. 2 (Winter 1976/1977).
6. Blanche Linden-Ward and Carol Hurd Green, *Changing the Future: American Women in the 1960s* (New York: Twayne Publishers, 1993), 29–30, 49; also see Vicki L. Crawford, Jacqueline Anne Rouse, and Barbara Woods, eds., *Women in the Civil Rights Movement: Trailblazers and Torchbearers, 1941–1965* (Bloomington: Indiana University Press, 1993), and Sara M. Evans, *Personal Politics: The Roots of Women's Liberation in the Civil Rights Movement and the New Left* (New York: Knopf, 1979).
7. Amy Swerdlow, *Women Strike for Peace: Traditional Motherhood and Radical Politics in the*

1960s (Chicago: University of Chicago Press, 1993), 230. Also see Harriet Hyman Alonso, *Peace as a Women's Issue: A History of the U.S. Movement for World Peace and Women's Rights* (Syracuse, N.Y.: Syracuse University Press, 1993).

8. Betty Friedan, *The Feminine Mystique* (New York: W.W. Norton & Co., 1963), 337, 281.

9. See "Women and Jews: The Quest for Selfhood"; "Jewish Roots"; and Friedan, *"It Changed My Life": Writings on the Women's Movement* (New York: W.W. Norton & Co., 1985), 6–19; Amy Stone, "Friedan at 55: From Feminism to Judaism," *Lilith* 1, No. 1 (1976): 11.

10. Friedan, *"It Changed My Life,"* 6.

11. *Ibid.*

12. Paul Wilkes, "Mother Superior to Women's Lib," *New York Times,* Nov. 29, 1970, cited in Stone, "Friedan at 55," 40.

13. Sondra Henry and Emily Taitz, *Betty Friedan: Fighter for Women's Rights* (Hillside, N.J.: Enslow Publishers, 1990), 14; Justine Blau, *Betty Friedan* (New York: Chelsea House, 1990), 22.

14. Betty Friedan Papers, Schlesinger Library, Radcliffe College.

15. Friedan, *"It Changed My Life,"* 5–6.

16. Stone, "Friedan at 55," 11.

17. Friedan, "Women and Jews," 8.

18. Betty Friedan, "The ERA—Does It Play in Peoria?" *New York Times Magazine,* Nov. 19, 1978, 39, 134.

19. "Jewish Roots," 25.

20. Milton Meltzer, *Betty Friedan: A Voice for Women's Rights* (New York: Viking Kestrel, 1985), 9; Blau, *Betty Friedan,* 24.

21. "The ERA—Does It Play in Peoria?" 39, 134; Henry and Taitz, *Betty Friedan,* 15.

22. Stone, "Friedan at 55," 11.

23. "Jewish Roots," 25.

24. Stone, "Friedan at 55," 12,

25. Bettye Goldstein, "The Scapegoat," Betty Friedan Papers, Schlesinger Library.

26. Stone, "Friedan at 55," 12.

27. Henry and Taitz, *Betty Friedan,* 26, 29; Blau, 26.

28. This suggestion is made by Daniel Horowitz in his reassessment of Friedan's feminism. See his "Rethinking Betty Friedan and *The Feminine Mystique:* Labor Union Radicalism and Feminism in Cold War America," *American Quarterly,* 48, No. 1 (March 1996): 1–42.

29. Henry and Taitz, *Betty Friedan,* 33–35.

30. Friedan, *"It Changed My Life,"* 11.

31. *Ibid.,* 9, 14.

32. *Ibid.,* 6–7.

33. *Ibid.,* 17–19.

34. Ronald Schatz, *The Electrical Workers: A History of Labor at General Electric and Westinghouse, 1923–60* (Urbana, Ill.: University of Chicago Press, 1983), xiii. Cited in Horowitz, "Rethinking Betty Friedan and *The Feminine Mystique,"* 1.

35. Betty Friedan, "The ERA—Does It Play in Peoria?" 133.

36. Friedan, *The Feminine Mystique,* 305.

37. Stone, "Friedan at 55," 40.

38. Friedan, "Women and Jews," 8.

39. *Ibid.,* 9.

40. Friedan, "Jewish Roots," 27; and "Women and Jews," 10.

41. Bella Abzug, "Bella on Bella," *Moment* 1, No. 7 (Feb. 1976): 26; Doris Faber, *Bella Abzug* (New York: Lothrop, Lee & Shepard Co., 1976), 17; Bella Abzug, *Bella! Ms. Abzug Goes to Washington* (New York: Saturday Review Press, 1972), 84.

42. Abzug, "Bella on Bella," 26.

43. *Ibid.*

44. Bella Abzug to Temple Shalom Senior Youth Group, March 13, 1974, Bella Abzug Papers, Columbia University, New York, N.Y.

45. *Ibid.*

46. Abzug, "Bella on Bella," 27; also see Oral History of Bella Abzug, American Jewish Committee Oral Histories Collection, New York Public Library.

47. *Ibid.*

48. Abzug, "Bella on Bella," 26; Abzug, *Bella!*, 84.

49. Bella Abzug, interview with author, March 1995; Abzug, "Bella on Bella," 28, 27.

50. Faber, *Bella Abzug,* 61.

51. *Ibid.*, 73.

52. Abzug, *Bella!,* 87.

53. News clipping, Oct. 20, 1970; article by Joe Klein, n.d., Bella Abzug Papers, Columbia University.

54. *Boston Globe,* May 25, 1976.

55. Cited in *Congressional Record,* 92nd Cong. 2d sess., Vol. 122, No. 150, Pt. III: 11; Judith Martin, "Bella's Appeal," *New Republic,* July 31, 1976, 9. "About Bella Abzug," Women's Environmental and Development Organization mimeo, March 1995.

56. Memo on Legislation Sponsored on Israel and Soviet Jews, n.d.; "Solidarity Sunday," press release, April 30, 1976, Bella Abzug Papers.

57. "Bella S. Abzug Calls on Soviets to End the Arrests and Harassment of Jews," Dec. 24, 1970, press release, Bella Abzug Papers.

58. Elaine W. Winik to Bella Abzug, n.d.; Abzug to Winik, July 9, 1975; Abzug to Kay Camp, Women's International League for Peace and Freedom, June 11, 1975, Bella Abzug Papers.

59. *Village Voice,* July 23, 1970.

60. Abzug was the first in Congress to speak out against the confirmation of General George Brown as chief of the joint chiefs of staff because of anti-Semitic remarks. She also lobbied the president of Hunter College, Jacqueline Wexler, to drop her "devilish" and "discriminatory" plan to abolish Hebrew instruction, which Abzug had been instrumental in introducing at her alma mater, in order to save money. Wexler capitulated. See Abzug to Jacqueline Wexler, Dec. 19, 1975; Jan. 16, 1975; Wexler to Abzug, Jan. 5, 1976; Robert J. Kibbee to Harold Jacobs, Jan. 18, 1976, Bella Abzug Papers.

61. Letty Cottin Pogrebin, *Deborah, Golda and Me* (New York: Crown Publishers, 1991), 154.

62. "Statement by Rep. Bella S. Abzug on the Declaration of Mexico," n.d., Abzug Papers.

63. See Pesach Schindler to Bella Abzug, July 21, 1975; Bea Lerner to Abzug, Oct. 31, 1975; Elenore Lester, "Feminist-Zionist Caucus formed as reaction to Mexico City Resolution," *Jewish Week* clipping; Bella Abzug to Editor, *Jewish Week,* Jan. 28, 1976, Bella Abzug Papers; Abzug, "Bella on Bella."

64. Remarks by Rep. Bella Abzug at International Women's Year Conference, Mexico City, July 2, 1975, in Bella Abzug Papers.

65. Pogrebin, *Deborah, Golda and Me,* 157.

66. "Statement by Rep. Bella S. Abzug on the Declaration of Mexico"; Bella Abzug to Editor, Jan. 28, 1976, *Jewish Week,* Bella Abzug Papers.

67. Pogrebin, *Deborah, Golda and Me,* 160.

68. Bella Abzug with Mim Kelber, *Gender Gap: Bella Abzug's Guide to Political Power for American Women* (Boston: Houghton Mifflin, 1984), 71–72.

69. See Edith Van Horn to Bella Abzug, July 24, 1972, Bella Abzug Papers; Marcia Cohen, *The Sisterhood: The Inside Story of the Women's Movement and the Leaders Who Made It Happen* (New York: Ballantine Books, 1988), 313, 317–18, 336, 350.

70. Abzug, "Bella on Bella;" Bella Abzug, interview with author, March 1995.
71. *Ibid.*
72. Pogrebin, *Deborah, Golda and Me,* 320.
73. Abzug, "Bella on Bella."
74. Vivian Gornick, "The Next Great Moment Is Theirs," in Gornick, *Essays in Feminism* (New York: Harper & Row, 1978), 23.
75. Debra L. Schultz, " 'We Didn't Think in Those Terms Then': Narratives of Jewish Women in the Southern Civil Rights Movement, 1960–1966" (Ph.D. diss., Union Institute, 1995).
76. For biographical information on Morgan, see Blanche Linden, "Robin Morgan," in Carol Hurd Green and Mary Grimley Mason, eds., *American Women Writers from Colonial Times to the Present* (New York: Continuum, 1994), 319–22; and Morgan's autobiographical writings, *Going Too Far: The Personal Chronicles of a Feminist* (New York: Vintage Books, 1977); and *The Demon Lover: On the Sexuality of Terrorism* (New York: W.W. Norton & Co., 1989).
77. Morgan, *Going Too Far,* 4.
78. Linden, "Robin Morgan," 319.
79. *New York Post,* Aug. 25, 1971, cited in Cohen, *The Sisterhood,* 318.
80. Morgan, *The Demon Lover,* 250, 269; *Going Too Far,* 3.
81. Meredith Tax, "What Good Is a Smart Girl?" in Faye Moskowitz, ed., *Her Face in the Mirror: Jewish Women on Mothers and Daughters* (Boston: Beacon Press, 1994), 178, 181.
82. Meredith Tax, interview with author, Oct. 1995.
83. Meredith Tax, "For the People Hear Us Singing, 'Bread and Roses! Bread and Roses!'," unpublished essay, Wini Breines Papers, Schlesinger Library, Radcliffe College.
84. Meredith Tax, "Woman and Her Mind: The Story of Daily Life," reprinted in *Notes from the Second Year* (Boston: Bread and Roses, 1970).
85. Meredith Tax, "Anais Nin: A Woman's Diary," in *The Old Mole,* No. 13, in Wini Breines Papers.
86. Tax, "Woman and Her Mind," 17.
87. Meredith Tax, interview with author.
88. Paula Doress, interview with author, Jan. 1996.
89. Aviva Cantor Zuckoff, "An Exclusive Interview with Dr. Phyllis Chesler," *Lilith* 1, No. 2 (Winter 1976/1977): 25.
90. Pogrebin, *Deborah, Golda and Me,* 149.
91. *Ibid.,* 149.
92. *Ibid.,* 215. Pogrebin's article, "Anti-Semitism in the Women's Movement," appeared in *Ms.,* June 1982.
93. Pogrebin, *Deborah, Golda and Me,* 231.
94. Susan Weidman Schneider, remarks at conference, "From Beijing to Tikkun Olam: The Jewish Woman's Role in Repairing the World," Brandeis University, May 1995.
95. Letty Cottin Pogrebin, remarks at conference, "From Beijing to Tikkun Olam," Brandeis University, May 1995.

Chapter 10. Coming Out as Jewish Women

1. Jane Litman, "Judaism and Feminism," in *The Jewish Radical,* Berkeley, Calif., Feb. 1978: 4, 11.
2. Gerda Lerner, *The Majority Finds Its Past* (New York: Oxford University Press, 1979), xiv, 159.
3. An earlier marriage ended in divorce. Materials on Lerner's life are drawn from the Gerda Lerner Papers, Schlesinger Library, Radcliffe College.

4. Gerda Lerner to author, Nov. 1993.

5. Gerda Lerner, "A Personal Journey: Jewish Otherness and Women's History," paper delivered at conference on "Developing Images: Representations of Jewish Women in American Culture," Brandeis University, March 1993. The essay appears in Gerda Lerner's *Why History Matters* (New York: Oxford University Press, 1997).

6. Lerner, "A Personal Journey."

7. *Ibid.*

8. Gerda Lerner, *A Death of One's Own* (New York: Simon & Schuster, 1978), 184.

9. Gerda Lerner, remarks at Berkshire Conference on Women's History, Vassar College, June 1993; interview with author, March 1993.

10. Lerner, *A Death of One's Own*, 191. "A Personal Journey." Also see "Gerda Lerner on the Future of Our Past," interview with Catharine R. Stimpson, *Ms.* 10, No. 3 (Sept. 1981): 52.

11. Lerner, *A Death of One's Own,* 163–64.

12. *Ibid.,* 163.

13. *Ibid.,* 229.

14. Stimpson, "Gerda Lerner on the Future of Our Past," 51.

15. Gerda Jensen, "The Prisoners," *The Clipper* 2, No. 7 (Sept. 1941):19–22. (Jensen was the name of Gerda Lerner's first husband.)

16. Gerda Jensen, "The Russian Campaign," *Story* 23, No. 103 (Sept.–Oct. 1943): 59–66.

17. Lerner, "A Personal Journey."

18. *Ibid.*

19. *Ibid.*

20. *Ibid.*

21. Carolyn Heilbrun, *Reinventing Womanhood* (New York: W.W. Norton & Co., 1979), 20.

22. One result of the Jewish Studies Women's Caucus is Judith R. Baskin and Shelly Tenenbaum, eds., *Gender & Jewish Studies: A Curriculum Guide* (New York: Biblio Press, 1994).

23. On the origins of the Jewish feminist movement, see Alan Silverstein, "The Evolution of Ezrat Nashim," *Conservative Judaism* (Fall 1975): 41–51; and Reena Sigman Friedman, "The Jewish Feminist Movement," in Michael N. Dobkowski, ed., *Jewish American Voluntary Organizations* (New York: Greenwood Press, 1986), 575–601. For an analysis of the broader impact of feminism on Jewish religious practice and communal organization, see Sylvia Barack Fishman, *A Breath of Life: Feminism in the American Jewish Community* (New York: Free Press, 1993).

24. Friedman, "The Jewish Feminist Movement," 581–82.

25. Blu Greenberg, *On Women and Judaism: A View from Tradition* (Philadelphia: Jewish Publication Society, 1981), 27, 31–32.

26. *Ibid.,* 33.

27. On Amy Eilberg, see Raye T. Katz, "Exploring the Link Between Womanhood and the Rabbinate: *Lilith* Interviews the First Woman Ordained in the Conservative Movement," *Lilith,* No. 14 (1985–86): 20–21.

28. Friedman, "The Jewish Feminist Movement," 584.

29. "Feminists and Faith: A Discussion with Judith Plaskow and Annette Daum," *Lilith,* No. 7 (1980): 16.

30. Judith Plaskow, "Anti-Semitism: The Unacknowledged Racism," in B.H. Andolsen, C.E. Gudorf, and M.D. Pellaner, eds., *Women's Consciousness, Women's Conscience* (Minneapolis, Minn.: Winston Press, 1985), 81. Also see Judith Plaskow, "Blaming Jews for the Birth of Patriarchy," *Lilith,* No. 7 (1980):11–13.

31. Plaskow, "Blaming Jews for the Birth of Patriarchy," 11; "Feminists and Faith," 16.

32. "Regina Schreiber," "Copenhagen: One Year Later," *Lilith,* No. 8 (1981): 35.

33. See Sue Elwell to Judith Arcana, Sept. 1, 1983, Judith Arcana to Evi Beck and Sue Elwell, Aug. 21, 1983, Jewish Women's Resource Center, NCJW, New York City.

34. Alice Shalvi, "The Geopolitics of Jewish Feminism," in T.M. Rudavsky, ed., *Gender and Judaism: The Transformation of Tradition* (New York: New York University Press, 1995), 238.

35. Rivka Haut, "The Presence of Women," in Susan Grossman and Rivka Haut, eds., *Daughters of the King: Women and the Synagogue* (Philadelphia: Jewish Publication Society, 1992), 274.

36. Norma Baumel Joseph, interview with author, Nov. 1996.

37. Alice Shalvi, interview with author, Nov., 1996.

38. Sally Jane Priesand, "Toward a Course of Study for Reform High School Youth Dealing with the Historic and Changing Role of the Jewish Woman" (Master's thesis, Hebrew Union College–Hebrew Institute of Religion, June 1972). Also see Sally Priesand, *Judaism and the New Woman* (New York: Behrman House, 1975).

39. For biographical material on Priesand, see Sally Friedman, "Reflections of a 'Woman Who Dared,' " *New York Times,* Sept. 19, 1993; Judy Petsonk, "The Person Is the Message," *Hadassah Magazine* (June/July 1993): 28–29; "Monmouth Rabbi hailed as 'pioneering woman' of Judaism," Newark (N.J.) *Star-Ledger,* March 18, 1992; biographical material, courtesy Sally Priesand. Also see Sally Priesand, "From Promise to Reality," *Keeping Posted* (April 1972): 17–19, "Not for Men Only," *National Council of Jewish Women* (Feb. 1974): 10–12, and Cheryl Jensen, "Rabbi Sally Priesand: Going Nowhere Fast," *Cleveland Plain Dealer,* March 8, 1981.

40. Priesand, "Not for Men Only," 10.

41. *Ibid.,* 11.

42. Cited in Janet Marder, "How Women Are Changing the Rabbinate," *Reform Judaism* (Summer 1991): 5–8, 41–42.

43. Friedman, "Reflections of a 'Woman Who Dared' "; "Monmouth Rabbi hailed as 'pioneering woman.' "

44. Marder, "How Women Are Changing the Rabbinate," 41–42.

45. *Ibid.*; Rabbi Arnold Sher, cited in Laura Geller, "From Equality to Transformation: The Challenge of Women's Rabbinic Leadership," in Rudavsky, ed., *Gender and Judaism,* 252.

46. *Ibid.,* 248, 250.

47. *Ibid.,* 251–252.

48. Arthur Green, interview with author, Jan. 1996.

49. Amy Eilberg, interview with author, Feb. 1996.

50. See Lynn Davidman, *Tradition in a Rootless World: Women Turn to Orthodox Judaism* (Berkeley: University of California Press, 1991); and Debra Renée Kaufman, *Rachel's Daughters: Newly Orthodox Jewish Women* (New Brunswick, N.J.: Rutgers University Press, 1991).

51. Andrea Gurwitt, "The Seduction of Certainty: Losing Feminist Daughters to Orthodoxy," *On the Issues* (Winter 1996): 38–40.

52. Davidman, *Tradition in a Rootless World,* 94.

53. National Commission on American Jewish Women, *Voices for Change: Future Directions for American Jewish Women* (Waltham, Mass.: Brandeis University Press, 1995), 29; Fishman, *A Breath of Life,* 62–63.

54. Christie Balka and Andy Rose, *Twice Blessed: On Being Lesbian, Gay, and Jewish* (Boston: Beacon Press, 1989), 5.

55. Evelyn Torton Beck, ed., *Nice Jewish Girls: A Lesbian Anthology* (Boston: Beacon Press, 1989), xx, xxxii.

56. Adrienne Rich, "Split at the Root," in Beck, ed., *Nice Jewish Girls,* 81–82.

57. *Ibid.*, 89.
58. See her poems "1948: Jews," in *An Atlas of the Different World: Poems 1985–1991* (New York: W.W. Norton & Co., 1991), and "Yom Kippur 1984," in *Your Native Land, Your Life: Poems* (New York: W.W. Norton & Co., 1986).
59. For a discussion of the origins of Jewish lesbian feminism, see Faith Rogow, "Why Is This Decade Different from All Other Decades?: A Look at the Rise of Jewish Lesbian Feminism," *Bridges* 1, No. 1 (Spring 1989): 67–71.
60. Jennifer Moses, "She's Changed Our Lives: A Profile of Betty Friedan," *Present Tense* 15, No. 4 (May–June 1988): 26–31. Cited in Fishman, *A Breath of Life,* 114.
61. On Congregation Beth Simchat Torah, see Moshe Shokeid, *A Gay Synagogue in New York* (New York: Columbia University Press, 1995).
62. See Alex Witchel, " 'Luckiest Rabbi in America' Holds Faith Amid the Hate," *New York Times,* May 5, 1993; "Soloveitchik Letter Urged Ban on Gays," *Jewish Daily Forward,* May 14, 1993.
63. Rabbi Sharon Kleinbaum, interview with author, Oct. 1995.
64. Biographical details from *ibid.*; address by Rabbi Sharon Kleinbaum at session on "Jewish Feminism, Yiddish Secularism, and Religious Identity," *Die Froyen?* Conference on Women and Yiddish, Jewish Theological Seminary, Oct. 28, 1995; and Witchel, " 'Luckiest Rabbi.' "
65. See Charlotte Baum, Paula Hyman, and Sonya Michel, *The Jewish Woman in America* (New York: New American Library, 1975).
66. Interview with Rabbi Sharon Kleinbaum, Oct. 1995.
67. Kleinbaum, address at *Die Froyen?*
68. Peter Freiberg, "The Rabbi's Unorthodox Style," *Washington Post,* Sept. 9, 1994.
69. Interview with Rabbi Sharon Kleinbaum.
70. Witchel, " 'Luckiest Rabbi.' "
71. Samuel H. Dresner, "The Return of Paganism?" *Midstream* 34, No. 5 (June/July 1988): 32–38.
72. Interviews with Jane Litman and with Arthur Green, Jan. 1996.
73. Judith Plaskow, "Jewish Theology in Feminist Perspective," in Lynn Davidman and Shelly Tenebaum, eds., *Feminist Perspectives on Jewish Studies* (New Haven: Yale University Press, 1994), 64–65.
74. See Penina Adelman, "A Drink from Miriam's Cup: Invention of Tradition Among Jewish Women," in Maurie Sacks, ed., *Active Voices: Women in Jewish Culture* (Urbana: University of Illinois Press, 1995), 109–24. For an extended discussion of the impact of feminism on changes in ritual, see Fishman, *A Breath of Life,* ch. 6.
75. E.M. Broner, *The Telling* (New York: HarperCollins, 1993), 165, 23.
76. Maida Solomon, "Claiming Our Questions: Feminism and Judaism in Women's Hagaddahs," in Joyce Antler, ed., *Talking Back: Images of Jewish Women in American Popular Culture* (Hanover, N.H.: University of New England Press, forthcoming).
77. The orange as a Passover symbol of women's place at the center of Jewish life and practice developed out of a lecture by Susannah Heschel on women as teachers and students of Torah and as rabbis. A man in the audience shouted, "A woman belongs on the *bimah* [pulpit] as much as bread belongs on the seder plate." Heschel responded, "The teachings of women do not violate the tradition but renew it. Women bring to the *bimah* what an orange would bring to the seder plate: transformation, not transgression." The story is cited in Solomon, "Claiming Our Questions."
78. Solomon, "Claiming Our Questions." Among the innovative new hagaddahs, see Ma'yan: The Jewish Women's Project, *Journey to Freedom—Nisan 5755,* April 1995; and Project Kesher, *Project Kesher Hagaddah—Global Women's Seder* (1995).

79. Interviews with Gail Twersky Reimer and with Judith Kates, Nov. 1996. Also see Laura Geller and Sue Levi Elwell, "On the Jewish feminist frontier, a report," in *Sh'ma* (Nov. 13, 1992): 1.

80. Laura Geller, "From Equality to Transformation," 251.

Chapter 11.   Out of Exile

1. Cynthia Ozick, "Toward a New Yiddish," in Ozick, *Art & Ardor* (New York: E.P. Dutton, 1984), 151–77.

2. Cynthia Ozick, "Notes Toward Finding the Right Question," *Lilith,* No. 6 (Spring/Summer 1979): 29. Also see Ozick, "Torah as a Matrix for Feminism," *Lilith,* No. 12/13 (Spring 1985): 47–48.

3. *Ibid.*

4. Ozick, "Toward a New Yiddish," 152. On Cynthia Ozick, also see Joyce Antler, Introduction to Antler, ed., *America and I: Short Stories by American Jewish Women Writers* (Boston: Beacon Press, 1990), 14–15.

5. See Cynthia Ozick, "The Hole/Birth Catalogue" and "Justice to Feminism," in *Art & Ardor,* 249–62, 263–90.

6. Cynthia Ozick, "Virility," in *The Pagan Rabbi and Other Stories* (New York: Schocken Books, 1976), 257, 266.

7. See Sarah Blacher Cohen, "The Jewish Literary Comediennes," in her *Comic Relief: Humor in Contemporary American Literature* (Urbana: University of Illinois Press, 1978), 172–86.

8. Cynthia Ozick, *The Shawl* (New York: Alfred A. Knopf, 1989).

9. In "Literature and the Politics of Sex: A Dissent," *Ms.* 6 (Dec. 1977): 79–80, Ozick identifies herself as a "classical feminist" rather than a "radical" one, that is, as a feminist whose goals concern humankind rather than a narrower "female sensibility." Also see Ozick, "Torah as a Matrix for Feminism," "Notes Toward Finding the Right Question." The Fall 1987 volume (6) of *Studies in American Jewish Literature* is devoted to "The World of Cynthia Ozick."

10. Grace Paley, "Women's Voice: Jewish Women Repairing the World," remarks at Woman's Voice, New Israel Fund, Boston, June 7, 1995.

11. Among the writings on Paley's work, see Dena Mandel, "Keeping Up with Faith: Grace Paley's Sturdy American Jewess," in *Studies in American Jewish Literature* 3 (1983): 85–98, and Minako Baba, "Faith Darwin as Writer-Heroine: A Study of Grace Paley's Short Stories, *Studies in American Jewish Literature* 7 (Spring 1988): 40–55. Also see Antler "Introduction" to *America and I,* 15–16.

12. Neil Isaacs, *Grace Paley: A Study of the Short Fiction* (Boston: Twayne Publishers, 1990), 113.

13. Judith Arcana, *Grace Paley's Life Stories: A Literary Biography* (Urbana: University of Illinois Press, 1993), 85; Isaacs, *Grace Paley,* 119–20, 136, 113.

14. Cited in Adam J. Sorkin, "Grace Paley," in Daniel Walden, ed., *Dictionary of Literary Biography,* Vol. 28 (Detroit: Gale Research, 1984), 227.

15. See, for example, Grace Paley, "The Long-Distance Runner" and "A Conversation with My Father," in *Enormous Charges at the Last Minute* (New York: Farrar Straus & Giroux, 1987).

16. See Mandel, "Keeping Up with Faith"; Baba, "Faith Darwin as Writer-Heroine"; Bonnie Lyons, "Grace Paley's Jewish Miniatures," *Studies in American Jewish Literature* 8 (1989): 26–33; and Victoria Aarons, "Talking Lives: Storytelling and Renewal in Grace Paley's Short Fiction," *Studies in American Jewish Literature* 9 (1990): 20–35.

17. Aarons, "Talking Lives," 24; Lyons, "Grace Paley's Jewish Miniatures," 32.

18. See Bonnie Lyons, "Faith and Puttermesser: Contrasting Images of Two Jewish Feminists," in Joyce Antler, ed., *Talking Back: Images of Jewish Women in American Popular Culture* (Hanover, N.H.: University of New England Press, forthcoming). Also see Lyons, "Grace Paley's Jewish Miniatures," and "American Jewish Fiction Since 1945," in Lewis Fried, ed., *Handbook of American Jewish Literature* (New York: Greenwood Press, 1988), 60–89.

19. See Anne Richardson (Roiphe), *Digging Out* (New York: McGraw Hill, 1966).

20. James Spada, *Streisand: Her Life* (New York: Crown, 1995), 288, 297.

21. See Anne Roiphe, "Taking Down the Christmas Tree," *Tikkun* 4, No. 6 (Nov./Dec. 1989): 58–60.

22. *Ibid.*, 59.

23. Anne Roiphe, *Generation Without Memory: A Jewish Journey in Christian America* (New York: Simon & Schuster, 1981), 203–4.

24. See Naomi Sokoloff, "Imagining Israel in American Jewish Fiction: Anne Roiphe's *Lovingkindness* and Philip Roth's *The Counterlife, Studies in American Jewish Fiction* 10, No. 1 (1991): 65–80.

25. Anne Roiphe, "The Jewish Family: A Feminist Perspective," *Tikkun* 1, No. 2 (1986): 70–75; and National Commission on American Jewish Women, *Voices for Change: Future Directions for American Jewish Women* (Waltham, Mass.: Brandeis University Press, 1995).

26. Kim Chernin, "In the House of the Flame Bearers," *Tikkun* 2, No. 3 (July/Aug. 1987): 55.

27. *Ibid.*, 56.

28. *Ibid.*

29. *Ibid.*, 57.

30. Kim Chernin, *Crossing the Border: An Erotic Journey* (New York: Fawcett Columbine, 1994), 123.

31. "Marge Piercy," *Contemporary Authors Autobiography Series,* Vol. 1 (Detroit: Gale Research, 1984), 267–68.

32. See Rochelle Furstenberg, "Robojew," *Jerusalem Report* (Feb. 20, 1992): 37.

33. E. M. Broner, *Her Mothers* (Bloomington: Indiana University Press, 1985), 168. On Broner, see Ann R. Shapiro, "The Novels of E. M. Broner: A Study in Secular Feminism and Feminist Judaism," *Studies in American Jewish Literature* 10, No. 1 (1991): 93–103.

34. Rebecca Goldstein, *The Mind-Body Problem: A Novel* (New York: Laurel, 1983), 276–77, 295.

35. Nessa Rapoport, Introduction, in Ted Solotaroff and Nessa Rapoport, eds., *Writing Our Way Home: Contemporary Stories by American Jewish Writers* (New York: Schocken Books, 1992), xix, xxix; Theodore Solotaroff, "American Jewish Writers: On Edge Once More," *New York Times,* Dec. 18, 1988.

36. Mark Brettler, remarks at "Hearing Biblical Women: Art and Academia in Concert" (symposium held at Brandeis University, March 19, 1995).

37. Elizabeth Swados, "Stretching Boundaries: The Merlin of La Mama," *New York Times,* Oct. 26, 1986. Swados received four Obies for her off-Broadway work and was nominated for five Tonys for her Broadway hit *Runaways*. In addition to her work as a composer, songwriter, director, choreographer, and playwright, she is the author of two novels, *Leah and Lazar* (1982) and *The Myth Man* (1994), and the memoir *The Four of Us: The Story of a Family* (1992), the story of her growing up in a dysfunctional family with an emotionally disturbed older brother, a successful but tyrannical father (the great "catch" of Buffalo's Jewish community), and an alcoholic mother who gave up her artistic aspirations after marriage and eventually committed suicide.

38. Douglas Century, "The Way I Do Miriam is Really for Rock and Roll, *The Forward,* June 2, 1995.

39. Elizabeth Swados, remarks at "Hearing Biblical Women."
40. Elizabeth Swados, interview with author, March 1995.
41. Swados, Remarks at "Hearing Biblical Women."
42. Judy Chicago, *Holocaust Project: From Darkness to Light* (New York: Penguin, 1993), 11.
43. *Ibid.*, 9.
44. See Sharon Kahn, "Judy Chicago's *Holocaust Project: From Darkness into Light,*" *Bridges* 5, No. 1 (Summer 1995): 100–103.
45. Helene Aylon, "The Liberation of G–d," n.d.; biographical information provided in interview with author, Dec. 1995.
46. "Helane [sic] Aylon, Painter," in Gloria Frym, *Second Stories: Conversations with Women Whose Artistic Careers Began After Thirty-Five* (San Francisco: Chronicle Books, 1979), 18.
47. Frym, *Second Stories,* 21; Helene Aylon, interview with author.
48. Interview with Helene Aylon.
49. Joan Micklin Silver's films *Yekl* (1975) and *Crossing Delancey* (1987).
50. David Castell, *The Films of Barbra Streisand* (St. Paul, Minn: Greenhaven Press, 1978), 9.
51. Spada, *Streisand,* 402.
52. *Ibid.*, 16.
53. *Ibid.*, 407.
54. Felicia Herman, "The Way She *Really* Is: Images of Jews and Women in the Films of Barbra Streisand," in Antler, ed., *Talking Back.*
55. Marjorie Garber, *Vested Interests: Cross-Dressing and Cultural Anxiety* (New York: Harper Perennial, 1993), 79. Cited in Norman L. Kleeblatt, *Too Jewish? Challenging Traditional Identities* (New Brunswick, N.J.: Rutgers University Press, 1996), 10.
56. Marcy Sheiner, "Maybe I could be—like Barbra—Gawjus!" *Lilith* (Spring 1996): 11.
57. Carey Goldberg, "Barbra, Gorgeous! You Have a Shrine," *New York Times,* May 21, 1996.
58. Sheiner, "Maybe I could be—like Barbra—Gawjus!" 12.
59. On Wasserstein, see Stephen J. Whitfield, "Wendy Wasserstein, and the Crisis of (Jewish) Identity," in Jay L. Halio and Ben Siegel, eds., *Women of Valor: Contemporary Jewish American Women Writers* (Newark, Del.: University of Delaware Press, 1997), 226–46.
60. Wendy Wasserstein, Introduction to *The Sisters Rosensweig* (New York: Harcourt Brace & Co., 1993), xi.
61. See Irena Klepfisz, "*Di Mames, Dos Loshn/The Mothers, the Language:* Feminism, *Yiddishkayt* and the Politics of Memory," *Bridges* 4, No. 1 (1994): 12–47; also see Klepfisz, *Dreams of an Insomniac: Jewish Feminist Essays, Speeches and Diatribes* (Portland Ore.: Eighth Mountain, 1990).

Epilogue. When Daughters Are Cherished

1. Transcript of President's announcement and Judge Ginsburg's remarks, *New York Times,* June 15, 1993.
2. Ruth Bader Ginsburg, remarks at the 200th Anniversary Celebration of the Hebrew Congregation of St. Thomas, Virgin Islands, Jan. 1996, courtesy Justice Ruth Bader Ginsburg.
3. Neil A. Lewis, "Ginsburg Promises Judicial Restraint If She Joins Court"; Excerpts from Senate Hearings on Ginsburg Nomination to the Supreme Court, *New York Times,* July 21, 1993.
4. Jay Mathews, "The Spouse of Ruth: Marty Ginsburg, the Pre-Feminism Feminist," *Washington Post* (June 19, 1993).
5. David Margolick, "Judge Ginsburg's Life a Trial by Adversity," *New York Times,* June 25, 1993.
6. *Ibid.*

7. *Ibid.*
8. *Ibid.*
9. Jeffrey Rosen, "The Book of Ruth," *New Republic,* Aug. 2, 1993, 20; William H. Freivogel, "Famous Spouses Breaking Down Sex Stereotypes," *St. Louis Post-Dispatch,* July 12, 1993.
10. Neil A. Lewis, "Rejected as Clerk, Now Headed for Bench: Ruth Bader Ginsburg," *New York Times,* June 15, 1993.
11. Philippa Strum, *Louis D. Brandeis: Justice for the People* (New York: Schocken Books, 1984), 122, 114.
12. See Neil A. Lewis, "Judge Ginsburg's Opinions at Center, Yet Hard to Label," *New York Times,* June 27, 1993; "Ruth Bader Ginsburg," *Current Biography Yearbook,* 1994: 215–16; (Cleveland) *Plain Dealer,* July 10, 1993.
13. Cited in *The Key Reporter,* Summer 1974, 2.
14. In a 2 to 1 decision against Pollard's motion in May 1992, Ginsburg was joined by Judge Laurence Silberburg, who is also Jewish. See *The Reporter,* July 6, 1993, and Samuel Rabinove, "Justice Ginsburg and the 'Jewish Agenda,' *Reform Judaism* (Spring 1994): 74–75.
15. Justice Ruth Bader Ginsburg, "What Being Jewish Means to Me," Address to the annual meeting of the American Jewish Committee, May 1955, reprinted in the American Jewish Committee series on "Being Jewish Today," Op Ed page, *New York Times,* Jan. 14, 1996. Also Ginsburg, remarks at the 200th Anniversary Celebration of the Hebrew Congregation of St. Thomas.
16. Jane C. Ginsburg, "Personal Introduction," May 14, 1996, courtesy Justice Ruth Bader Ginsburg.
17. Rosen, "The Book of Ruth," 19.

ACKNOWLEDGMENTS

When I began this journey quite a number of years ago, I had no idea of its ultimate destination or just how many paths I would travel before I reached the end. Intellectually, emotionally, and spiritually, it has been quite an adventure. I am deeply grateful to the friends, family, and colleagues who have nurtured and sustained me along the way. Although scholarly writing is in many ways a solitary endeavor, the support of various communities has made this project anything but lonely.

I owe a great debt to the many historians and biographers—known and unknown to me—whose work has helped me better understand my subjects. I am especially grateful to the young scholars working on the history of Jewish women and to those who have toiled even longer in this field; it is a source of pleasure to me that their numbers have been continually growing. Reference to their work in the Notes can only inadequately acknowledge my appreciation of their contributions.

The Schlesinger Library of Radcliffe College, which has provided a home for me on many previous projects, continued to offer vital support on this one; I am grateful in particular to Mary Maples Dunn, Marie-Hélène Gold, Barbara Haber, Jane Knowles, Eva Mosely, and Wendy Thomas. For assisting my search for primary sources, I also thank, especially, Dr. Charles Cutter of the Special Collections Department at the Brandeis University Library; Michael Feldberg, Ellen Smith, Michelle Feller-Kopman, and Dawne Bear at the American Jewish Historical Society; Abraham Peck, Kevin Proffitt, and Kathy Spray at the American Jewish Archives; Ira Daly and Susan Woodland of the Hadassah Archives; and Dr. Leonard Gold of the New York Public Library's Jewish Division. The librarians and archivists at the Central Zionist Archives in Jerusalem, Columbia University's Rare Book and Manuscript Library, New York University's Tamiment Library, the New York Public Library's Rare Books and Manuscripts Division, and the Special Collections departments of the Boston University and Syracuse University libraries were invariably supportive. Ann Abrams, librarian of Boston's Temple Israel, provided gracious help.

In addition to archival materials, I benefited enormously from conversations with many individuals who shared their own stories and memories of friends, family, and colleagues. For their generosity and their powers of recall, I am grateful to Bella Abzug, Helene Aylon, Viola Bernard, Paul Buhle, Gertrude Decker, Paula Doress-Worters, Amy Eilberg, Trude Festinger, Roma Forman, Sallie Gratch, Arthur Green, Ruth Gruber, Nancy Miriam Hawley, Louise Levitas Henriksen, Norma Baumel Joseph, Bel Kaufman, Sharon Kleinbaum, Gerda Lerner, M. Jastrow Levin, Naomi Levine, Jane Litman, Robert Meeropol, Leah Milbower, Harriet Phillips, the late Rose Nelson Raynes, Annette Rubenstein, Morris U. Schappes, Alice Shalvi, Elizabeth Swados, and Meredith Tax. For suggesting sources of information that I might never have found on my own, I thank, in addition, Justice Ruth Bader Ginsburg and Sally Priesand.

Many colleagues generously agreed to comment on drafts of the almost complete manuscript. For their detailed and discerning remarks, I thank Hasia Diner, Jenna Weissman Joselit, Deborah Dash Moore, and Steven J. Whitfield. Their critiques were thoughtful, provocative, and enormously useful. I am also indebted to Joan Jacobs Brumberg, Nancy Cott, Sylvia Barack Fishman, Daniel Horowitz, Regina Morantz-Sanchez, Mark Raider, Lois Rudnick, Jonathan Sarna, and Karen Tolchin for their insightful suggestions regarding individual chapters. Susan Ware not only read every word of every draft of the book, but also helped me establish a structure for combining social history with collective biography. Her suggestions have been invaluable.

In addition, I thank Susan Koppelman for her generosity in sharing sources; Gail Twersky Reimer, Amy Sales, Judith Kates, and Barbara Sicherman for providing helpful information; and Sylvia Fuks-Fried, Miriam Hoffman, and Susanne Shavelson for their counsel on matters of Yiddish usage. Joan Roth not only permitted me to use her remarkable photographs, but worked hard to find the best and most telling ones in her collection.

Lecture invitations to speak about Jewish women from, among others, Joan Jacobs Brumberg (Cornell), Ann J. Lane (University of Virginia), Riv-Ellen Prell (University of Minnesota), Ann Schoenberger (University of Maine), Gerald Sorin (State University of New York), and Ellen Schrecker (Stern College) provided me with opportunities to clarify my thinking at important stages of my writing. I am grateful as well to the Brandeis University National Women's Committee for providing many opportunities to speak to members about my research. My thanks also go to Linda Kerber, Alice Kessler-Harris, and Kathryn Kish Sklar, editors of *U.S. History as Women's History: New Feminist Essays,* and Marge Garber and Rebecca Walkowitz, editors of *Secret Agents: The Rosenberg Case, McCarthyism and Fifties America,* each of which included portions of Chapter 8. A portion of Chapter 4 appeared in *Daughters of Zion: Henrietta Szold and American Jewish Womanhood,* the catalogue of an exhibition at the Jewish Historical Society of Maryland.

At the moment that I launched this book, I had the good fortune to join a biography group that has provided continuous intellectual sustenance. I thank Fran Malino, Megan Marshall, Susan Quinn, Lois Rudnick, and Judith Tick for their friendship and astute advice. They have shared in every aspect of this developing work, and serve, in many ways, as its godmothers. For their nurturance, I also thank Rabbi Elaine Zecher and the members of our Temple Israel women's studies group.

I have also benefited from an unusually supportive academic environment at Brandeis University. I thank each member of the American Studies Department, as well as Shulamit Reinharz and the large Women's Studies community, for their continuing encouragement and collegiality. I owe a special debt to Angie Simeone for her cheerful and skillful assistance.

Excellent research help was provided by Marjorie Feld, Seth Korelitz, and in the last frantic stages of the manuscript preparation, Lauren Antler. The curiosity and initiative of many Brandeis undergraduate and graduate students studying Jewish women's history (including Aviva Ben-Ur, Tobin Belzer, Marjorie Feld, Karin Grundler, Felicia Herman, Seth Korelitz, Andrea Most, and Rona Sheramy) have stimulated my own work.

The Lucius N. Littauer Foundation provided initial financial support; a Loewenstein-Weiner Fellowship in American Jewish Studies enabled me to carry out my research at the American Jewish Archives in Cincinnati. A short but splendid residence at the Virginia Center for the Creative Arts enabled me to complete the first draft of the manuscript.

I am particularly grateful to Joyce Seltzer for her early encouragement of this project and to Joyce Hackett for her close reading of the text and her many insightful suggestions. At The Free Press, I thank my supportive editor, Adam Bellow, and Chad Conway and Edith Lewis for expertly shepherding the book through the production process.

For creative and sage counsel at every stage of imagining and producing this book, Sydelle Kramer and the Frances Goldin Literary Agency deserve special mention. Sydelle's superb criticisms and editorial and publishing suggestions have made this a better book in every way. Her support at difficult times made all the difference.

Finally, I wish to thank my family for their part in the creation of this book. This project would not have been undertaken at all without the prodding and support of my husband, Stephen. He read, criticized, and discussed every aspect of the manuscript and helped me to shape central ideas. In many respects, this journey has been a joint one.

My daughters, Lauren and Rachel, have endured my absorption in this project with remarkable patience and empathy; their affection, understanding, and irrepressible humor remain sources of true joy.

Through her wonderful stories, my aunt, Dina Schechter, helped me construct many connections between the larger history of Jewish women and my own family history. My sister, Phoebe Becker, offered crucial and timely support.

Though my mother, Sophie Kessler, did not live to see the book completed, her unfailing support of my work, and her unconditional love, touch every page.

INDEX

ABOUT THE AUTHOR

JOYCE ANTLER is the Samuel Lane Professor of American Jewish History and Culture and the chair of the Department of American Studies at Brandeis University. She is the author of, among other works, *Lucy Sprague Mitchell: The Making of a Modern Woman*, and is the editor of *America and I: Short Stories of American Jewish Women Writers* and *Talking Back: Images of Jewish Women in American Popular Culture*. She lives in Brookline, Massachusetts.

Also Available from

SCHOCKEN

THE MEMOIRS OF GLÜCKEL OF HAMELN
The Diary of a Seventeenth-Century German-Jewish Woman
Glückel
0-8052-0572-1

WOMEN'S DIARIES OF THE WESTWARD JOURNEY
Lillian Schlissel
0-8052-1004-0

ON BEING A JEWISH FEMINIST
edited by Susannah Heschel
0-8052-1036-9

LOVE'S WORK
A Reckoning with Life
Gillian Rose
0-8052-1078-4

WOMEN AND JEWISH LAW
The Essential Texts, Their History, and Their Relevance for Today
Rachel Biale
0-8052-1049-0

Available at your local bookstore, or call toll-free:
1-800-733-3000 (credit cards only).